Elements of Argument

SEVENTH EDITION

Elements of Argument

A Text and Reader

Annette T. Rottenberg

Bedford/St. Martin's
Boston ◆ New York

For Bedford/St. Martin's

Developmental Editor: John E. Sullivan III
Production Editor: Deborah Baker
Senior Production Supervisor: Catherine Hetmansky
Marketing Manager: Brian Wheel
Editorial Assistant: Carrie Thompson
Copyeditor: Rosemary Winfield
Text Design: Claire Seng-Niemoeller
Cover Design: Donna Lee Dennison
Cover Art: John Gibson, *Simple Spirals*. Courtesy of the artist.
Composition: Pine Tree Composition
Printing and Binding: Haddon Craftsmen, Inc., an R. R. Donnelley & Sons
   Company

President: Joan E. Feinberg
Editor in Chief: Karen S. Henry
Director of Marketing: Karen Melton
Director of Editing, Design, and Production: Marcia Cohen
Managing Editor: Elizabeth M. Schaaf

Library of Congress Control Number: 2002102563

Manufactured in the United States of America.

6   5   4   3   2   1
f   e   d   c   b   a

For information, write: Bedford/St. Martin's, 75 Arlington Street, Boston, MA 02116
(617-399-4000)

ISBN: 0–312–39777–1

Acknowledgments

Stephen J. Adler. "Love and Death in New Jersey." From *The Jury: Trial and Error in the American
   Courtroom* by Stephen J. Adler. Copyright © 1994 by Stephen J. Adler (Random House, New
   York). Reprinted by permission of the author.
Gordon Allport. "The Nature of Prejudice." From the 17th Claremont Reading Conference Year-
   book, 1952. Reprinted by permission.
Julia Álvarez. "A White Woman of Color." From *Half and Half* by Claudine Chiawei O'Hearn. Copy-
   right © 1998 by Claudine Chiawei O'Hearn. "A White Woman of Color," copyright © 1998 by
   Julia Álvarez. Reprinted by permission of Pantheon Books, a division of Random House, Inc.

*Acknowledgments and copyrights are continued at the back of the book on pages
741–45, which constitute an extension of the copyright page. It is a violation of the law
to reproduce these selections by any means whatsoever without the written permission of
the copyright holder.*

Preface for Instructors

PURPOSE

Argumentation as the basis of a composition course should need no defense, especially at a time of renewed pedagogical interest in critical thinking. A course in argumentation encourages practice in close analysis, use of supporting materials, and logical organization. It encompasses all the modes of development around which composition courses are often built. It teaches students to read and to listen with more than ordinary care. Not least, argument can engage the interest of students who have been indifferent or even hostile to required writing courses. Because the subject matter of argument can be found in every human activity, from the most trivial to the most elevated, both students and teachers can choose the materials that appeal to them.

Composition courses using the materials of argument are, of course, not new. But the traditional methods of teaching argument through mastery of the formal processes of reasoning cannot account for the complexity of arguments in practice. Even more relevant to our purposes as teachers of composition is the tenuous relationship between learning about induction and deduction, however helpful in analysis, and the actual process of student composition. The challenge has been to find a method of teaching argument that assists students in defending their claims as directly and efficiently as possible, a method that reflects the way people actually go about organizing and developing claims outside the classroom.

One such method, first adapted to classroom instruction by teachers of rhetoric and speech, uses a model of argument advanced by Stephen Toulmin in *The Uses of Argument*. Toulmin was interested in producing a description of the real process of argument. His model was the law. "Arguments," he said, "can be compared with lawsuits, and the claims we make and argue for in extra-legal contexts with claims made in the courts."[1] Toulmin's model of argument was based on three principal elements: claim, evidence, and warrant. These elements answered the questions, "What are you trying to prove?" "What have you got to go on?" "How did you get from evidence to claim?" Needless to say, Toulmin's model of argument does not guarantee a classroom of skilled arguers, but his questions about the parts of an argument and their relationship are precisely the ones that students must ask and answer in writing their own essays and analyzing those of others. They lead students naturally into the formulation and development of their claims.

[1] *The Uses of Argument* (Cambridge: Cambridge University Press, 1958), p. 7.

In this text I have adapted—and greatly simplified—some of Toulmin's concepts and terminology for first-year students. I have also introduced two elements of argument with which Toulmin is not directly concerned. Most rhetoricians consider them indispensable, however, to discussion of what actually happens in the defense or rejection of a claim. One is motivational appeals—warrants based on appeals to the needs and values of an audience, designed to evoke emotional responses. A distinction between logic and emotion may be useful as an analytical tool, but in producing or attacking arguments human beings find it difficult, if not impossible, to make such a separation. In this text, therefore, persuasion through appeals to needs and values is treated as a legitimate element in the argumentative process.

I have also stressed the significance of audience as a practical matter. In the rhetorical or audience-centered approach to argument, to which I subscribe in this text, success is defined as acceptance of the claim by an audience. Arguers in the real world recognize intuitively that their primary goal is not to demonstrate the purity of their logic, but to win the adherence of their audiences. To gain this adherence, students need to be reminded of the necessity for establishing themselves as credible sources for their readers.

I hope *Elements of Argument* will lead students to discover not only the practical and intellectual rewards of learning how to argue but the real excitement of engaging in civilized debate.

ORGANIZATION

In Part One, after two introductory chapters, a chapter each is devoted to the chief elements of argument—the claims that students make in their arguments, the definitions and support they must supply for their claims, the warrants that underlie their arguments, the language that they use. Popular fallacies, as well as induction and deduction, are treated in Chapter 8; because fallacies represent errors of reasoning, a knowledge of induction and deduction can make clear how and why fallacies occur. Each chapter ends with an advertisement illustrating the element of argument treated in that chapter.

I have provided examples, readings, discussion questions, and writing suggestions that are, I hope, both practical and stimulating. With the exception of several student dialogues, the examples are real, not invented; they have been taken from speeches, editorial opinions, letters to the editor, advertisements, interviews, and news reports. They reflect the liveliness and complexity that invented examples often suppress.

The forty selections, two Web pages, and ten advertisements in Part One support the discussions in several important ways. First, they illustrate the elements of argument; in each chapter, one or more essays have been analyzed to emphasize the chapter's principles of argument. Second, they are drawn from current publications and cover as many different subjects as possible to convince students that argument is a pervasive force in the world they read about and live in. Third, some of the essays are obviously flawed and thus enable students to identify the kinds of weaknesses they should avoid in their own essays.

Part Two takes up the process of writing, researching, and presenting arguments. Chapter 9 explains how to find a topic, define the issues that it embraces, organize the information, and draft and revise an argument. Chapter 10 introduces students to the business of finding sources and using these sources effectively in research papers. The chapter concludes with two annotated student research papers, one of which employs the Modern Language Association (MLA) documentation system, the other of which represents research in the social and natural sciences and uses a modified American Psychological Association (APA) documentation style. Chapter 11 provides guidelines for presenting an argument orally.

Part Three, Multiple Viewpoints, exhibits arguers in action, using informal and formal language, debating head-on. The subjects of its fifty-seven selections and seventeen cartoons capture headlines every day, and despite their immediacy, they are likely to arouse passions and remain controversial for a long time. Whether as matters of national policy or personal choice, they call for decisions based on familiarity with competing views.

Part Four, Classic Arguments, reprints eight selections that have stood the tests of both time and the classroom. They are among the arguments that teachers find invaluable in any composition course.

The instructor's manual, *Resources for Teaching* Elements of Argument, provides additional suggestions for using the book, as well as for finding and using the enormous variety of materials available in a course on argument.

A companion Web site at <www.bedfordstmartins.com/rottenberg> includes annotated links for students and instructors looking for further information on controversial topics, online debates, and rhetorical theory. It also includes sample syllabi and exercises.

A briefer edition, *The Structure of Argument*, Fourth Edition, is available for instructors who prefer a shorter text with fewer readings. It presents only Parts One and Two, an appendix of Classic Arguments, and the appendix, Arguing about Literature, from the longer edition.

NEW TO THIS EDITION

Revising a successful textbook—the publisher says that *Elements of Argument* is the best-selling book of its kind—presents both a challenge and an opportunity. The challenge is to avoid undoing features that have been well received in the earlier editions. The opportunity is to tap into the experiences of instructors and students who have used the earlier editions and to make use of their insights to improve what needs improvement. For instance, the sections on critical reading, evaluating electronic sources, note-taking, and summarizing have been revised, and a sample analysis of a Web site has been added.

The principles and concerns of the book have not changed. Rather, I have included a greater breadth of material to increase the book's usefulness as a teaching tool. Also, in response to instructor requests, we have redesigned the book with a second color for a more lively look to appeal to today's visually oriented students.

For the short debates, we have retained two popular topics from the sixth edition—the necessity of animal research and the question of human cloning—and have added four familiar and timely subjects: the possibility of extraterrestrial life, God as the creator of the universe, the ethics of the genetic enhancement of children, and whether national identification cards will help to combat terrorism. Updated annotated Web links accompany these debates, encouraging students to conduct further research online.

Part Three, Multiple Viewpoints, retains four popular topics from the sixth edition—Corporate Responsibility, Freedom of Speech, Privacy in the Information Age, and Sex and Violence in Popular Culture—with many new selections that reflect the changes in law and public opinion. The four new topics—Criminal Justice: Trial by Jury, the Family, Reparations for Slavery, and Responding to Terrorism—are not only among the most controversial and newsworthy subjects engaging American society today, but they are also subjects that interest and affect college students at school, at work, and at home. Each of the selections in the Multiple Viewpoints section is now preceded by a prereading question that provides direction for students and will help stimulate class discussion. Part Four, Classic Arguments, now includes a provocative essay by Rachel Carson on environmental pollution.

Sixty-one of the 111 selections in the seventh edition are new. Taken as a whole, the changes in this edition should enhance the versatility of the book, deepen students' awareness of how pervasive argument is, and increase their ability to think critically and communicate persuasively. The newly expanded online study guide at <www.bedfordstmartins. com/rottenberg> offers sample syllabi for instructors. It will help students to understand argument by offering them annotated research links and additional information and exercises on fallacies and warrants.

This book has profited by the critiques and suggestions of reviewers and instructors who responded to a questionnaire. I appreciate the thoughtful consideration given to previous editions by Nancy E. Adams, Timothy C. Alderman, Yvonne Alexander, John V. Andersen, Lucile G. Appert, William Arfin, Alison K. Armstrong, Karen Arnold, Angel M. Arzán, Mark Edward Askren, Michael Austin, David B. Axelrod, Jacquelyn A. Babush, Peter Banland, Carol A. Barnes, Tim Barnett, Marilyn Barry,

Marci Bartolotta, Bonnie C. Bedford, Frank Beesley, Don Beggs, Martine Bellen, Bruce Bennett, Maureen Dehler Bennett, Chester Benson, Robert H. Bentley, Scott Bentley, Arthur E. Bervin, Patricia Bizzell, Don Black, Kathleen Black, Stanley S. Blair, Laurel Boyd, Mary Virginia Brackett, Robert J. Branda, Dianne Brehmer, Alan Brown, Paul L. Brown, Bill Buck, W. K. Buckley, Alison A. Bulsterbaum, Clarence Bussinger, Deborah N. Byrd, Gary T. Cage, Ruth A. Cameron, Rita Carey, Barbara R. Carlson, Eric W. Cash, Donna R. Chaney, Gail Chapman, Linda D. Chinn, Roland Christian, Gina Claywell, John O. Clemonts, Tammy S. Cole, Thomas S. Costello, Martha J. Craig, David J. Cranmer, Edward Crothers, Sara Cutting, Jo Ann Dadisman, Sandra Dahlberg, Mimi Dane, Judy Davidson, Cynthia C. Davis, Philip E. Davis, Stephanie Demma, Loretta Denner, Cecile de Rocher, Julia Dietrich, Marcia B. Dinnech, Felicia A. Dixon, Jane T. Dodge, Ellen Donovan, L. Leon Duke, P. Dunsmore, Bernard Earley, Carolyn Embree, Carolyn L. Engdahl, Gwyn Enright, David Estes, Kristina Faber, Lester Faigley, Faridoun Farroth, B. R. Fein, Delia Fisher, Catherine Fitzgerald, Evelyn Flores, David D. Fong, Donald Forand, Mary A. Fortner, Alice R. France, Leslye Friedberg, Sondra Frisch, Richard Fulkerson, Maureen Furniss, Diane Gabbard, Donald J. Gadow, Eric Gardner, Frieda Gardner, Gail Garloch, Darcey Garretson, Victoria Gaydosik, E. R. Gelber-Beechler, Scott Giantralley, Michael Patrick Gillespie, Paula Gillespie, Wallace Gober, Sara Gogol, Stuart Goodman, Joseph Gredler, Lucie Greenberg, Mildred Buza Gronek, Marilyn Hagans, Linda L. Hagge, Lee T. Hamilton, Carolyn Han, Phillip J. Hanse, Pat Hardré, Susan Harland, A. Leslie Harris, Carolyn G. Hartz, Theresia A. Hartz, Fredrik Hausmann, Michael Havens, William Hayes, Ursula K. Heise, Anne Helms, Tena Lea Helton, Peter C. Herman, Diane Price Herndl, Heidi Hobbs, William S. Hochman, Sharon E. Hockensmith, Andrew J. Hoffman, Joyce Hooker, Richard S. Hootman, Clarence Hundley, Patrick Hunter, Richard Ice, Mary Griffith Jackson, Ann S. Jagoe, Katherine James, Ruth Jeffries, Owen Jenkins, Ruth Y. Jenkins, Iris Jennings, Linda Johnson, Janet Jubnke, E. C. Juckett, Catherine Kaikowska, George T. Karnezis, Richard Katula, Mary Jane Kearny, Joanne Keel, Patricia Kellogg-Dennis, N. Kesinger, Susan Kincaid, Joanne Kirkland, Judith Kirscht, Nancy Klug, John H. Knight, Paul D. Knoke, Frances Kritzer, George W. Kuntzman, Barbara Ladd, M. Beardsley Land, Marlene J. Lang, Lisa Lebduska, Sara R. Lee, William Levine, Mary Levitt, Diana M. Liddle, Jack Longmale, Cynthia Lowenthal, Marjorie Lynn, Marcia MacLennan, Nancy McGee, Patrick McGuire, Ray McKerrow, Michael McKoski, Pamela J. McLagen, Suzanne McLaughlin, Dennis McMillan, Donald McQuade, Christina M. McVay, D'Ann Madewell, Beth Madison, Susan Maloney, Dan M. Manolescu, Barbara A. Manrigue, Joyce Marks, Quentin E. Martin, Michael Matzinger, Charles May, Jean-Pierre Meterean, Ekra Miezan, Carolyn R. Miller, Lisa K. Miller, Logan D. Moon, Dennis D. Moore, Dan Morgan, Karen L. Morris, Curt Mortenson, Philip A. Mottola, Thomas Mullen, Charlotte A. Myers, Joan Naake,

Michael B. Naas, Joseph Nassar, Byron Nelson, Elizabeth A. Nist, Jody Noerdlinger, Paralee F. Norman, Dr. Mary Jean Northcutt, Thomas O'Brien, James F. O'Neil, Mary O'Riordan, Arlene Okerland, Renee Olander, Amy Olsen, Richard D. Olson, Steven Olson, Lori Jo Oswald, Sushil K. Oswald, Gary Pak, Linda J. Palumbo, Jo Patterson, Laurine Paule, Leland S. Person, Betty Peters, Nancy L. Peterson, Susan T. Peterson, Steve Phelan, Gail W. Pieper, Gloria Platzner, Mildred Postar, Ralph David Powell, Jr., Teresa Marie Purvis, Barbara E. Rees, Karen L. Regal, Pat Regel, Charles Reinhart, Thomas C. Renzi, Janice M. Reynolds, Douglas F. Rice, G. A. Richardson, Beverly A. Ricks, Katherine M. Rogers, Marilyn Mathias Root, Judith Klinger Rose, Cathy Rosenfeld, Robert A. Rubin, Norma L. Rudinsky, Lori Ruediger, Cheryl W. Ruggiero, Richard Ruppel, Victoria Anne Sager, Joseph L. Sanders, Suzette Schlapkohl, Sybil Schlesinger, Richard Schneider, Eileen Schwartz, Esther L. Schwartz, Eugene Senff, Jeffrey Seyall, Ron Severson, Lucy Sheehey, William E. Sheidley, Sallye J. Sheppeard, Sally Bishop Shigley, John Shout, Dr. Barbara L. Siek, Thomas Simmons, Michael Simms, Jacqueline Simon, Richard Singletary, Roger L. Slakey, Thomas S. Sloane, Beth Slusser, Denzell Smith, Rebecca Smith, Margaret Smolik, Katherine Sotol, Donald L. Soucy, Minoo Southgate, Linda Spain, Richard Spilman, Sarah J. Stafford, Jim Stegman, Martha L. Stephens, Arlo Stoltenberg, Elissa L. Stuchlik, Judy Szaho, Andrew Tadie, Fernanda G. Tate-Owens, R. Terhorst, Marguerite B. Thompson, Arline R. Thorn, Mary Ann Trevathan, Sandia Tuttle, Whitney G. Vanderwerff, Jennie VerSteeg, David L. Wagner, Jeanne Walker, James Wallace, Linda D. Warwick, Carol Adams Watson, Roger D. Watson, Karen Webb, Raymond E. Whelan, Betty E. White, Julia Whitsitt, Toby Widdicombe, Mary Louise Willey, Heywood Williams, Matthew C. Wolfe, Alfred Wong, Bonnie B. Zitz, and Laura Zlogar.

I would also like to thank those instructors who took the time to complete a questionnaire for the seventh edition: Megan Brown, Paul D. Cockeram, John Conway, Jennifer Cunningham, Stephen Ersinghaus, Philip L. Fishman, Andrew J. Hoffman, Laura Hope-Aleman, Missy James, Richard M. Johnson, Jocelyn Ladner, Jack Longmate, Chantelle MacPhee, Alan Merickel, Elizabeth Oldfield, Roy Kenneth Pace II, Edna Parker, Kelly S. Petersen, Rossana Pronesti, Mark Razor, James M. Ritter, Irene Schiller, Craig L. Shurtleff, James R. Sodon, and Les Wade.

The instructor's manual is the better for the contribution of Gail Stygall of the University of Washington. Fred Kemp of Texas Tech University drafted the section on responding online in Chapter 2, and Barbara Fister of Gustavus Adolphus College revised Chapter 10's discussion of information technologies; my thanks to them both. I would also like to thank Tim Barnett of Northeastern Illinois University for enlarging and updating the sections on critical reading, evaluating electronic sources, note-taking, and summarizing, and for drafting the sample analysis of a Web site.

I am grateful to the people at Bedford/St. Martin's whose efforts have made the progress of the seventh edition a pleasure as well as a business: Charles Christensen, Joan Feinberg, Elizabeth Schaaf, Steve Scipione, Sandy Schechter, Coleen O'Hanley, Caroline Thompson, Deborah Baker, and John Sullivan.

Brief Contents

Contents

PART TWO

Writing, Researching, and Presenting Arguments 323

9. Writing an Argumentative Paper 325

10. Researching an Argumentative Paper   346

PART THREE

Multiple Viewpoints 429

13. Criminal Justice: Trial by Jury 453

14. The Family   490

15. Freedom of Speech   513

PART FOUR

Classic Arguments 633

Appendix: Arguing about Literature 711

Elements of Argument

PART ONE
The Structure of Argument

1

Understanding Argument

A conversation overheard in the school cafeteria:

"Hey, how come you didn't order the meat loaf special? It's pretty good today."

"Well, I read this book about vegetarianism, and I've decided to give up meat. The book says meat's unhealthy and vegetarians live longer."

"Don't be silly. Americans eat lots of meat, and we're living longer and longer."

"Listen, this book tells how much healthier the Danes were during World War II because they couldn't get meat."

"I don't believe it. A lot of these health books are written by quacks. It's pretty dumb to change your diet after reading one book."

These people are having what most of us would call an argument, one that sounds dangerously close to a quarrel. There are, however, significant differences between the colloquial meaning of argument as a quarrel and its definition as a process of reasoning and advancing proof, although even the exchange reported above exhibits some of the characteristics of formal argument. The kinds of arguments we deal with in this text are not

3

quarrels. They often resemble ordinary discourse about controversial issues. You may, for example, overhear a conversation like this one:

> *"This morning while I was trying to eat breakfast I heard an announcer describing the execution of that guy in Texas who raped and murdered a teenaged couple. They gave him an injection, and it took him ten minutes to die. I almost lost my breakfast listening to it."*
>
> *"Well, he deserved it. He didn't show much pity for his victims, did he?"*
>
> *"Okay, but no matter what he did, capital punishment is really awful, barbaric. It's murder, even if the state does it."*
>
> *"No, I'd call it justice. I don't know what else we can do to show how we feel about a cruel, pointless murder of innocent people. The punishment ought to be as terrible as we can make it."*

Each speaker is defending a value judgment about an issue that tests ideas of good and evil, right and wrong, and that cannot be decided by facts.

In another kind of argument the speaker or writer proposes a solution for a specific problem. Two men, both under twenty, are engaged in a conversation.

> *"I'm going to be broke this week after I pay my car insurance. I don't think it's fair for males under twenty to pay such high rates. I'm a good driver, much better than my older sister. Why not consider driving experience instead of age or sex?"*
>
> *"But I always thought that guys our age had the most accidents. How do you know that driving experience is the right standard to apply?"*
>
> *"Well, I read a report by the Highway Commission that said it's really driving experience that counts. So I think it's unfair for us to be discriminated against. The law's behind the times. They ought to change the insurance laws."*

In this case someone advocates a policy that appears to fulfill a desirable goal—making it impossible to discriminate against drivers just because they are young and male. Objections arise that the arguer must attempt to answer.

In these three dialogues, as well as in all the other arguments you will read in this book, human beings are engaged in explaining and defending their own actions and beliefs and opposing those of others. They do this for at least two reasons: to justify what they do and think both to themselves and to their opponents and, in the process, to solve problems and make decisions, especially those dependent on a consensus between conflicting views.

Unlike the examples cited so far, the arguments you will read and write will not usually take the form of dialogues, but arguments are implicit dialogues. Even when our audience is unknown, we write to persuade the unconvinced, to acquaint them with good reasons for changing their minds. As one definition has it, "Argumentation is the art of influencing others, through the medium of reasoned discourse, to believe or act as we wish them to believe or act."[1] This process is inherently dramatic; a good argument can create the kinds of tensions generated at sporting events. Who will win? What are the factors that enable a winner to emerge? One of the most popular and enduring situations on television is the courtroom debate, in which two lawyers (one, the defense attorney, the hero, unusually knowledgeable and persuasive; the other, the prosecuting attorney, bumbling and corrupt) confront each other before an audience of judge and jury that must render a heart-stopping verdict. Tensions are high because a life is in the balance. In the classroom the stakes are neither so intimidating nor so melodramatic, but even here a well-conducted argument can throw off sparks.

Of course, not all arguments end in clear victories for one side or another. Nor should they. The French philosopher Joseph Joubert said, "It is better to debate a question without settling it than to settle a question without debating it." In a democratic society of competing interests and values, a compromise between two or more extreme points of view may be the only viable solution to a vexing problem. Although formal debates under the auspices of a debating society, such as take place on many college campuses, usually end in winners and losers, real-life problems, both public and private, are often resolved through negotiation. Courtroom battles may result in compromise, and the law itself allows for exemptions and extenuating circumstances. Elsewhere in this book we speak of the importance of tradeoffs in social and political transactions, giving up one thing in return for another.

Keep in mind, however, that some compromises will not be morally defensible. In searching for a middle ground, the thoughtful arguer must determine that the consequences of a negotiated solution will contribute to "the common good," not, in the words of one essayist, merely the good of "the sovereign self." (In Chapter 9 you will find a detailed guide for writing arguments in which you look for common ground.)

Most of the arguments in this book will deal with matters of public controversy, an area traditionally associated with the study of argument. As the word *public* suggests, these matters concern us as members of a community. "They are," according to one rhetorician, "the problems of war and peace, race and creed, poverty, wealth, and population, of democracy and communism. . . . Specific issues arise on which we must take decision from time to time. One day it is Suez, another Cuba. One week it is the Congo, another it is the plight of the American farmer or the railroads. . . . On these subjects the experts as well as the many take sides."[2] Today the issues are different from the issues that writers

---

[1] J. M. O'Neill, C. Laycock, and R. L. Scale, *Argumentation and Debate* (New York: Macmillan, 1925), p. 1.

[2] Karl R. Wallace, "Toward a Rationale for Teachers of Writing and Speaking," *English Journal*, September 1961, p. 386.

confronted more than twenty years ago. Today we are concerned about the death penalty, human cloning, corporate responsibility, privacy, and freedom vs. security to name only a few.

Clearly, if all of us agreed about everything, if harmony prevailed everywhere, the need for argument would disappear. But given what we know about the restless, seeking, contentious nature of human beings and their conflicting interests, we should not be surprised that many controversial questions, some of them as old as human civilization itself, will not be settled nor will they vanish despite the energy we devote to settling them. Unresolved, they are submerged for a while and then reappear, sometimes in another form, sometimes virtually unchanged. Capital punishment is one such stubborn problem; abortion is another. Nevertheless, we value the argumentative process because it is indispensable to the preservation of a free society. In *Areopagitica,* his great defense of free speech, John Milton, the seventeenth-century poet, wrote, "I cannot praise a fugitive and cloistered virtue, unexercised and unbreathed, that never sallies out and sees her adversary." How can we know the truth, he asked, unless there is a "free and open encounter" between all ideas? "Give me liberty to know, to utter, and to argue freely according to conscience, above all liberties."

WHY STUDY ARGUMENT?

Perhaps the question has already occurred to you: Why *study* argument? Since you've engaged in some form of the argumentative process all your life, is there anything to be learned that experience hasn't taught you? We think there is. If you've ever felt frustration in trying to decide what is wrong with an argument, either your own or someone else's, you might have wondered if there were rules to help in the analysis. If you've ever been dissatisfied with your attempt to prove a case, you might have wondered how good arguers, the ones who succeed in persuading people, construct their cases. Good arguers do, in fact, know and follow rules. Studying and practicing these rules can provide you with some of the same skills.

You will find yourself using these skills in a variety of situations, not only in arguing important public issues. You will use them, for example, in your academic career. Whatever your major field of study—the humanities, the social sciences, the physical sciences, business—you will be required to defend views about materials you have read and studied.

> HUMANITIES   Why have some of the greatest novels resisted translation into great films?

> SOCIAL SCIENCE   What is the evidence that upward social mobility continues to be a positive force in American life?

PHYSICAL SCIENCE   What will happen to the world climate as the amount of carbon dioxide in the atmosphere increases?

BUSINESS   Are the new tax laws beneficial or disadvantageous to the real estate investor?

For all these assignments, different as they may be, you would use the same kinds of analysis, research techniques, and evaluation. The conventions or rules for reporting results might differ from one field of study to another, but for the most part the rules for defining terms, evaluating evidence, and arriving at conclusions cross disciplinary lines. Many employers, not surprisingly, are aware of this. One sheriff in Arizona advertised for an assistant with a degree in philosophy. He had discovered, he said, that the methods used by philosophers to solve problems were remarkably similar to the methods used in law enforcement.

Whether or not you are interested in serving as sheriff's assistant, you will encounter situations in the workplace that call for the same analytical and argumentative skills employed by philosophers and law enforcement personnel. Almost everywhere—in the smallest businesses as well as the largest corporations—a worker who can articulate his or her views clearly and forcefully has an important advantage in gaining access to positions of greater interest and challenge. Even when they are primarily informative, the memorandums, reports, instructions, questions, and explanations that issue from offices and factories obey the rules of argumentative discourse.

You may not anticipate doing the kind of writing or speaking at your job that you will practice in your academic work. It is probably true that in some careers, writing constitutes a negligible part of a person's duties. But outside the office, the studio, and the salesroom, you will be called on to exhibit argumentative skills as a citizen, as a member of a community, and as a consumer of leisure. In these capacities you can contribute to decision making if you are knowledgeable and prepared. By writing or speaking to the appropriate authorities, you can argue for a change in the meal ticket plan at your school or the release of pornographic films at the neighborhood theater or against a change in automobile insurance rates. Most of us are painfully aware of opportunities we lost because we were uncertain of how to proceed, even in matters that affected us deeply.

A course in argumentation offers another invaluable dividend: It can help you to cope with the bewildering confusion of voices in the world around you. It can give you tools for distinguishing between what is true and what is false, what is valid and what is invalid, in the claims of politicians, promoters of causes, newscasters, advertisers, salespeople, teachers, parents and siblings, employers and employees, neighbors, friends, and lovers, any of whom may be engaged at some time in attempting to persuade you to accept a belief or adopt a course of action. It can even offer strategies for arguing with yourself about a personal dilemma.

So far we have treated argument as an essentially pragmatic activity that benefits the individual. But choosing argument over force or evasion has clear moral benefits for society as well. We can, in fact, defend the study of argumentation for the same reasons that we defend universal education despite its high cost and sometimes controversial results. In a democracy, widespread literacy ultimately benefits all members of society, not only those who are the immediate beneficiaries of education, because only an informed citizenry can make responsible choices. One distinguished writer explains that "democracy depends on a citizenry that can reason for themselves, on men who know whether a case has been proved, or at least made probable."[3]

It is not too much to say that argument is a civilizing influence, the very basis of democratic order. In repressive regimes, coercion, which may express itself in a number of reprehensible forms—censorship, imprisonment, exile, torture, or execution—is a favored means of removing opposition to establishment "truth." In free societies, argument and debate remain the preeminent means of arriving at consensus.

Of course, rational discourse in a democracy can and does break down. Confrontations with police at abortion clinics, shouting and heckling at a meeting to prevent a speaker from being heard, student protests against university policies—such actions have become common in recent years. The demands of the demonstrators are often passionately and sincerely held, and the protesters sometimes succeed through force or intimidation in influencing policy changes. When this happens, however, we cannot be sure that the changes are justified. History and experience teach us that reason, to a far greater degree than other methods of persuasion, ultimately determines the rightness or wrongness of our actions.

A piece of folk wisdom sums up the superiority of reasoned argument as a vehicle of persuasion: "A man convinced against his will is of the same opinion still." Those who accept a position after engaging in a dialogue offering good reasons on both sides will think and act with greater willingness and conviction than those who have been coerced or denied the privilege of participating in the decision.

WHY WRITE?

If we agree that studying argumentation provides important critical tools, one last question remains: Why *write*? Isn't it possible to learn the rules by reading and talking about the qualities of good and bad arguments? Not quite. All writers, both experienced and inexperienced, will probably con-

[3]Wayne C. Booth, "Boring from Within: The Art of the Freshman Essay," adapted from a speech delivered to the Illinois Council of College Teachers of English in May 1963.

fess that looking at what they have written, even after long thought, can produce a startled disclaimer: But that isn't what I meant to say! They know that more analysis and more hard thinking are in order. Writers are also aware that words on paper have an authority and a permanency that invite more than casual deliberation. It is one thing to make an assertion, to express an idea or a strong feeling in conversation, and perhaps even to deny it later; it is quite another to write out an extended defense of your own position or an attack on someone else's that will be read and perhaps criticized by people unsympathetic to your views.

Students are often told that they must become better thinkers if they are to become better writers. It works the other way, too. In the effort to produce a clear and convincing argument, a writer matures as a thinker and a critic. The very process of writing calls for skills that make us better thinkers. Writing argumentative essays tests and enlarges important mental skills—developing and organizing ideas, evaluating evidence, observing logical consistency, expressing ourselves clearly and economically—that we need to exercise all our lives in our various social roles, whether or not we continue to write after college.

THE TERMS OF ARGUMENT

One definition of argument, emphasizing audience, has been given earlier: "Argumentation is the art of influencing others, through the medium of reasoned discourse, to believe or act as we wish them to believe or act." A distinction is sometimes made between argument and persuasion. Argument, according to most authorities, gives primary importance to logical appeals. Persuasion introduces the element of ethical and emotional appeals. The difference is one of emphasis. In real-life arguments about social policy, the distinction is hard to measure. In this book we use the term *argument* to represent forms of discourse that attempt to persuade readers or listeners to accept a claim, whether acceptance is based on logical or on emotional appeals or, as is usually the case, on both. The following brief definition includes other elements: *An argument is a statement or statements offering support for a claim.*

An argument is composed of at least three parts: the claim, the support, and the warrant.[4]

■ The Claim

The claim (also called a *proposition*) answers the question "What are you trying to prove?" It may appear as the thesis statement of your essay,

[4]Some of the terms and analyses used in this text are adapted from Stephen Toulmin's *The Uses of Argument* (Cambridge: Cambridge University Press, 1958).

although in some arguments it may not be stated directly. There are three principal kinds of claim (discussed more fully in Chapter 3): claims of fact, of value, and of policy. (The three dialogues at the beginning of this chapter represent these three kinds of claim respectively.) *Claims of fact* assert that a condition has existed, exists, or will exist and are based on facts or data that the audience will accept as being objectively verifiable:

> The present cocaine epidemic is not unique. From 1885 to the 1920s, cocaine was as widely used as it is today.

> Horse racing is the most dangerous sport.

> California will experience colder, stormier weather for the next ten years.

All these claims must be supported by data. Although the last example is an inference or an educated guess about the future, a reader will probably find the prediction credible if the data seem authoritative.

Claims of value attempt to prove that some things are more or less desirable than others. They express approval or disapproval of standards of taste and morality. Advertisements and reviews of cultural events are one common source of value claims, but such claims emerge whenever people argue about what is good or bad, beautiful or ugly.

> The opera *Tannhäuser* provides a splendid viewing as well as listening experience.

> Football is one of the most dehumanizing experiences a person can face.   —Dave Meggyesy

> Ending a patient's life intentionally is absolutely forbidden on moral grounds.   —Presidential Commission on Medical Ethics, 1983

Claims of policy assert that specific policies should be instituted as solutions to problems. The expression *should, must,* or *ought to* usually appears in the statement.

> Prisons should be abolished because they are crime-manufacturing concerns.

> Our first step must be to immediately establish and advertise drastic policies designed to bring our own population under control.
>   —Paul Ehrlich, biologist

> The New York City Board of Education should make sure that qualified women appear on any new list of candidates for Chancellor of Education.

Policy claims call for analysis of both fact and value. (A full discussion of claims follows in Chapter 3.)

■ The Support

Support consists of the materials used by the arguer to convince an audience that his or her claim is sound. These materials include *evidence* and *motivational appeals.* The evidence or data consist of facts, statistics, and testimony from experts. The motivational appeals are the ones that the arguer makes to the values and attitudes of the audience to win support for the claim. The word *motivational* points out that these appeals are the reasons that move an audience to accept a belief or adopt a course of action. For example, in his argument advocating population control, Ehrlich first offered statistical evidence to prove the magnitude of the population explosion. But he also made a strong appeal to the generosity of his audience to persuade them to sacrifice their own immediate interests to those of future generations. (See Chapter 5 for detailed discussion of support.)

■ The Warrant

The warrant is an inference or an assumption, a belief or principle that is taken for granted. A warrant is a guarantee of reliability; in argument it guarantees the soundness of the relationship between the support and the claim. It allows the reader to make the connection between the support and the claim.

Warrants or assumptions underlie all the claims we make. They may be stated or unstated. If the arguer believes that the audience shares his assumption, he may feel it unnecessary to express it. But if he thinks that the audience is doubtful or hostile, he may decide to state the assumption to emphasize its importance or argue for its validity.

This is how the warrant works. In the dialogue beginning this chapter, one speaker made the claim that vegetarianism was more healthful than a diet containing meat. As support he offered the evidence that the authors of a book he had read recommended vegetarianism for greater health and longer life. He did not state his warrant—that the authors of the book were trustworthy guides to theories of healthful diet. In outline form the argument looks like this:

CLAIM: Adoption of a vegetarian diet leads to healthier and longer life.

SUPPORT: The authors of *Becoming a Vegetarian Family* say so.

WARRANT: The authors of *Becoming a Vegetarian Family* are reliable sources of information on diet.

A writer or speaker may also need to offer support for the warrant. In the case cited above, the second speaker is reluctant to accept the unstated warrant, suggesting that the authors may be quacks. The first speaker will need to provide support for the assumption that the authors are trustworthy, perhaps by introducing proof of their credentials in science and medicine. Notice that although the second speaker accepts the evidence, he cannot agree that the claim has been proved unless he also accepts the warrant. If he fails to accept the warrant—that is, if he refuses to believe that the authors are credible sources of information about diet—then the evidence cannot support the claim.

The following example demonstrates how a different kind of warrant, based on values, can also lead an audience to accept a claim.

CLAIM: Laws making marijuana illegal should be repealed.

SUPPORT: People should have the right to use any substance they wish.

WARRANT: No laws should prevent citizens from exercising their rights.

Support for repeal of the marijuana laws often consists of medical evidence that marijuana is harmless. Here, however, the arguer contends that an important ethical principle is at work: Nothing should prevent people from exercising their rights, including the right to use any substance, no matter how harmful. Let us suppose that the reader agrees with the supporting statement, that individuals should have the right to use any substance. But to accept the claim, the reader must also agree with the principle expressed in the warrant—that government should not interfere with the individual's right. He or she can then agree that laws making marijuana illegal should be repealed. Notice that this warrant, like all warrants, certifies that the relationship between the support and the claim is sound.

One more important characteristic of the warrant deserves mention. In many cases, the warrant is a more general statement of belief than the claim. It can, therefore, support many claims, not only the one in a particular argument. For example, the warrant you have just read—"No laws should prevent citizens from exercising their rights"—is a broad assumption or belief that we take for granted and that can underlie claims about many other practices in American society. (For more on warrants, see Chapter 6.)

■ Definition, Language, Logic

In addition to the claim, the support, and the warrant, several other elements of clear, persuasive prose are crucial to good argument. For this reason we have devoted separate chapters to each of them.

One of the most important is definition. In fact, many of the controversial questions you will read or write about are primarily arguments of definition. Such terms as *abortion, pornography, racism, poverty, addiction,* and *mental illness* must be defined before useful solutions to the problems they represent can be formulated. (Chapter 4 deals with definition.)

Another important resource is the careful use of language, not only to define terms and express personal style but also to reflect clarity of thought and avoid the clichés and outworn slogans that frequently substitute for fresh ideas. (See Chapter 7 for more on language.)

Last, we have included an examination of induction and deduction, the classic elements of logic. Understanding the way in which these reasoning processes work can help you to determine the truth and validity of your own and other arguments and to identify faulty reasoning. (Induction and deduction are covered in Chapter 8.)

THE AUDIENCE

All arguments are composed with an audience in mind. We have already pointed out that an argument is an implicit dialogue or exchange. Often the writer of an argument about a public issue is responding to another writer or speaker who has made a claim that needs to be supported or opposed. In writing your own arguments, you should assume that there is a reader who may not agree with you. Throughout this book, we will continue to refer to ways of reaching such a reader.

Speechmakers are usually better informed than writers about their audience. Some writers, however, are familiar with the specific persons or groups who will read their arguments; advertising copywriters are a conspicuous example. They discover their audiences through sophisticated polling and marketing techniques and direct their messages to a well-targeted group of prospective buyers. Other professionals may be required to submit reports to persuade a specific and clearly defined audience of certain beliefs or courses of action: An engineer may be asked by an environmental interest group to defend his plans for the building of a sewage treatment plant; or a town planner may be called on to tell the town council why she believes that rent control may not work; or a sales manager may find it necessary to explain to his superior why a new product should be launched in the Midwest rather than the South.

In such cases the writer asks some or all of the following questions about the audience:

Why has this audience requested this report? What do they want to get out of it?

How much do they already know about the subject?

Are they divided or agreed on the subject?

What is their emotional involvement with the issues?

■ Assessing Credibility

Providing abundant evidence and making logical connections between the parts of an argument may not be enough to win agreement from an audience. In fact, success in convincing an audience is almost always inseparable from the writer's credibility or the audience's belief in the writer's trustworthiness. Aristotle, the Greek philosopher who wrote a treatise on argument that has influenced its study and practice for more than two thousand years, considered credibility—what he called *ethos*—the most important element in the arguer's ability to persuade the audience to accept his or her claim.

Aristotle named "intelligence, character, and goodwill" as the attributes that produce credibility. Today we might describe these qualities somewhat differently, but the criteria for judging a writer's credibility remain essentially the same. First, the writer must convince the audience that he is knowledgeable, that he is as well informed as possible about the subject. Second, he must persuade his audience that he is not only truthful in the presentation of his evidence but also morally upright and dependable. Third, he must show that, as an arguer with good intentions, he has considered the interests and needs of others as well as his own.

As an example in which the credibility of the arguer is at stake, consider a wealthy Sierra Club member who lives on ten acres of a magnificent oceanside estate and who appears before a community planning board to argue against future development of the area. His claim is that more building will destroy the delicate ecological balance of the area. The board, acting in the interests of all the citizens of the community, will ask themselves: Has the arguer proved that his information about environmental impact is complete and accurate? Has he demonstrated that he sincerely desires to preserve the wilderness, not merely his own privacy and space? And has he also made clear that he has considered the needs and desires of those who might want to live in a housing development by the ocean? If the answers to all these questions are yes, then the board will hear the arguer with respect, and the arguer will have begun to establish his credibility.

A reputation for intelligence, character, and goodwill is not often won overnight. And it can be lost more quickly than it is won. Once a writer or speaker has betrayed an audience's belief in her character or judgment, she may find it difficult to persuade an audience to accept subsequent claims, no matter how sound her data and reasoning are. "We give no credit to a liar," said Roman statesman Cicero, "even when he speaks the truth."

Political life is full of examples of lost and squandered credibility. After it was discovered that President Lyndon Johnson had deceived the American public about U.S. conduct in the Vietnam War, he could not regain his popularity. After President Gerald Ford pardoned former President Richard Nixon for his complicity in the cover up of the bugging and burglary of the Democratic National Committee headquarters at the Watergate office complex, Ford was no longer a serious candidate for re-election. After proof that President Clinton had lied to a grand jury and the public about his sexual relationship with a young White House intern, public approval of his political record remained high, but approval of his moral character declined and threatened to diminish his influence.

We can see the practical consequences when an audience realizes that an arguer has been guilty of a deception—misusing facts and authority, suppressing evidence, distorting statistics, violating the rules of logic. But suppose the arguer is successful in concealing his or her manipulation of the data and can persuade an uninformed audience to take the action or adopt the idea that he or she recommends. Even supposing that the argument promotes a "good" cause, is the arguer justified in using evasive or misleading tactics?

The answer is no. To encourage another person to make a decision on the basis of incomplete or dishonestly used data is profoundly unethical. It indicates lack of respect for the rights of others—their right to know at least as much as you do about the subject, to be allowed to judge and compare, to disagree with you if they challenge your own interests. If the moral implications are still not clear, try to imagine yourself not as the perpetrator of the lie but as the victim.

There is also a danger in measuring success wholly by the degree to which audiences accept our arguments. Both as writers and readers, we must be able to respect the claim, or proposition, and what it tries to demonstrate. The English philosopher Stephen Toulmin has said: "To conclude that a proposition is true, it is not enough to know that this [person] or that finds it 'credible': the proposition itself must be *worthy* of credence."[5]

■ Acquiring Credibility

You may wonder how you can acquire credibility. You are not yet an expert in many of the subjects you will deal with in assignments, although you are knowledgeable about many other things, including your cultural and social activities. But there are several ways in which you can create confidence by your treatment of topics derived from academic disciplines, such as political science, psychology, economics, sociology, and art, on which most assignments will be based.

First, you can submit evidence of careful research, demonstrating that you have been conscientious in finding the best authorities, giving credit, and attempting to arrive at the truth. Second, you can adopt a thoughtful and judicious tone that reflects a desire to be fair in your conclusion. Tone expresses the attitude of the writer toward his or her subject. When the writer feels strongly about the subject and adopts a belligerent or complaining tone, for example, he or she forgets that readers who feel differently may find the tone disagreeable and

---

[5] *An Examination of the Place of Reason in Ethics* (Cambridge: Cambridge University Press, 1964), p. 71.

unconvincing. In the following excerpt a student expresses his feelings about standard grading—that is, grading by letter or number on a scale that applies to a whole group.

> You go to school to learn, not to earn grades. To be educated, that's what they tell you. "He's educated, he graduated magna cum laude." What makes a magna cum laude man so much better than a man that graduates with a C? They are both still educated, aren't they? No one has a right to call someone less educated because they got a C instead of an A. Let's take both men and put them in front of a car. Each car has something wrong with it. Each man must fix his broken car. Our C man goes right to work while our magna cum laude man hasn't got the slightest idea where to begin. Who's more educated now?

Probably a reader who disagreed with the claim—that standard grading should not be used—would find the tone, if not the evidence itself, unpersuasive. The writer sounds as if he is defending his own ability to do something that an honors graduate can't do, while ignoring the acknowledged purposes of standard grading in academic subjects. He sounds, moreover, as if he's angry because someone has done him an injury. Compare the preceding passage to the following one, written by a student on the same subject.

> Grades are the play money in a university Monopoly game. As long as the tokens are offered, the temptation will be largely irresistible to play for them. Students are so busy taking notes, doing tests, and getting tokens that they have forgotten to ask: Of what worth is all this? Or perhaps they ask and the grade is their answer.
>
> One certainly learns something in the passive lecture-note-read-note-test process: how to do it all more efficiently next time (in the hope of eventually owning Boardwalk and Park Place). As Marshall McLuhan has said, we learn what we do. In this process most students come to view learning as studying and remembering what other people have learned. They assume that knowledge is logically and for practical reasons divided up into discrete pieces called "disciplines" and that the highest knowledge is achieved by specializing in a discipline. By getting good grades in a lot of disciplines they conclude they have learned a lot. They have indeed, and it is too bad.[6]

Most readers would consider this writer more credible than the first, in part because he has adopted a tone that seems moderate and impersonal. That is, he does not convey the impression that he is interested only in defending his own grades. Notice also that the language of this passage suggests a higher level of learning and research.

Sometimes, of course, an expression of anger or even outrage is appropriate and morally justified. But if readers do not share your sense of outrage, you must try to reach them through a more moderate approach.

---

[6] Roy E. Terry in "Does Standard Grading Encourage Excessive Competitiveness?" *Change*, September 1974, p. 45.

In his autobiography, Benjamin Franklin recounted his attempts to acquire the habit of temperate language in argument:

> Retaining . . . the habit of expressing myself in terms of modest diffidence, never using when I advance anything that may possibly be disputed, the words *certainly, undoubtedly,* or any others that give the air of positiveness to an opinion; but rather say, *I conceive,* or *I apprehend* a thing to be so or so; *it appears to me,* or *I should think it so or so for such and such reasons,* or *I imagine* it to be so, or *it is so if I am not mistaken.* — This habit I believe has been of great advantage to me, when I have had occasion to inculcate my opinions and persuade men into measures that I have been from time to time engaged in promoting.[7]

This is not to say that the writer must hedge his or her opinions or confess uncertainty at every point. Franklin suggests that the writer must recognize that other opinions may also have validity and that, although the writer may disagree, he or she respects the other opinions. Such an attitude will also dispose the reader to be more generous in evaluating the writer's argument.

A final method of establishing credibility is to produce a clean, literate, well-organized paper, with evidence of care in writing and proofreading. Such a paper will help persuade the reader to take your efforts seriously.

Now let us turn to one of the most famous arguments in American history and examine its elements.

SAMPLE ANALYSIS

The Declaration of Independence

THOMAS JEFFERSON

When in the course of human events, it becomes necessary for one people to dissolve the political bands which have connected them with another, and to assume among the Powers of the earth, the separate and equal station to which the Laws of Nature and Nature's God entitle them, a decent respect to the opinions of mankind requires that they should declare the causes which impel them to the separation.

We hold these truths to be self-evident, that all men are created equal, that they are endowed by their Creator with certain unalienable Rights, that among these are Life, Liberty and the pursuit of Happiness.

That to secure these rights, Governments are instituted among Men, deriving their just powers from the consent of the governed.

---

[7] *The Autobiography of Benjamin Franklin,* ed. Louis P. Masur (Boston: Bedford Books, 1993), pp. 39–40. Italics are Franklin's.

That whenever any Form of Government becomes destructive of these ends, it is the Right of the People to alter or to abolish it, and to institute a new Government laying its foundation on such principles and organizing its powers in such form, as to them shall seem most likely to effect their Safety and Happiness. Prudence, indeed, will dictate that Governments long established should not be changed for light and transient causes; and accordingly all experience hath shown that mankind are more disposed to suffer, while evils are sufferable, than to right themselves by abolishing the forms to which they are accustomed. But when a long train of abuses and usurpations pursuing invariably the same Object evinces a design to reduce them under absolute Despotism, it is their right, it is their duty, to throw off such government, and to provide new Guards for their future security.

Such has been the patient sufferance of these Colonies; and such is 5 now the necessity which constrains them to alter their former Systems of Government. The history of the present King of Great Britain is a history of repeated injuries and usurpations, all having in direct object the establishment of an absolute Tyranny over these States. To prove this, let Facts be submitted to a candid world.

He has refused his Assent to Laws, the most wholesome and necessary for the public good.

He has forbidden his Governors to pass Laws of immediate and pressing importance, unless suspended in their operation till his Assent should be obtained; and when so suspended, he has utterly neglected to attend to them.

He has refused to pass other Laws for the accommodation of large districts of people, unless those people would relinquish the right of Representation in the Legislature, a right inestimable to them and formidable to tyrants only.

He has called together legislative bodies at places unusual, uncomfortable, and distant from the depository of their Public Records, for the sole purpose of fatiguing them into compliance with his measures.

He has dissolved Representative Houses repeatedly, for opposing 10 with manly firmness his invasions on the rights of the people.

He has refused for a long time, after such dissolutions, to cause others to be elected; whereby the Legislative Powers, incapable of Annihilation, have returned to the People at large for their exercise; the State remaining in the mean time exposed to all the danger of invasion from without, and convulsions within.

He has endeavored to prevent the population of these States; for that purpose obstructing the Laws of Naturalization of Foreigners; refusing to pass others to encourage their migration hither, and raising the conditions of new Appropriations of Lands.

He has obstructed the Administration of Justice, by refusing his Assent to Laws for establishing Judiciary Powers.

He has made Judges dependent on his Will alone, for the tenure of their offices, and the amount and payment of their salaries.

He has erected a multitude of New Offices, and sent hither swarms of 15 Officers to harass our People, and eat out their substance.

He has kept among us, in time of peace, Standing Armies without the consent of our Legislature.

He has affected to render the Military independent of and superior to the Civil Power.

He has combined with others to subject us to jurisdictions foreign to our constitution, and unacknowledged by our laws; giving his Assent to their acts of pretended Legislation:

For quartering large bodies of armed troops among us:

For protecting them, by a mock Trial, from Punishment for any Mur- 20 ders which they should commit on the Inhabitants of these States:

For cutting off our Trade with all parts of the world:

For imposing Taxes on us without our Consent:

For depriving us in many cases, of the benefits of Trial by Jury:

For transporting us beyond Seas to be tried for pretended offenses:

For abolishing the free System of English Laws in a Neighbouring 25 Province, establishing therein an Arbitrary government, and enlarging its boundaries so as to render it at once an example and fit instrument for introducing the same absolute rule into these Colonies:

For taking away our Charters, abolishing our most valuable Laws, and altering fundamentally the Forms of our Governments:

For suspending our own legislatures, and declaring themselves in-vested with Power to legislate for us in all cases whatsoever.

He has abdicated Government here, by declaring us out of his Protec-tion and waging War against us.

He has plundered our seas, ravaged our Coasts, burnt our towns and destroyed the Lives of our people.

He is at this time transporting large Armies of foreign Mercenaries to 30 compleat the works of death, desolation and tyranny, already begun with circumstances of Cruelty & perfidy scarcely paralleled in the most barbarous ages, and totally unworthy the Head of a civilized nation.

He has constrained our fellow Citizens taken Captive on the high Seas to bear Arms against their Country, to become the executioners of their friends and Brethren, or to fall themselves by their Hands.

He has excited domestic insurrections amongst us, and has endeav-ored to bring on the inhabitants of our frontiers, the merciless Indian Savages, whose known rule of warfare is an undistinguished destruction of all ages, sexes, and conditions.

In every stage of these Oppressions We Have Petitioned for Redress in the most humble terms. Our repeated petitions have been answered only by repeated injury. A Prince, whose character is thus marked by every act which may define a Tyrant, is unfit to be the ruler of a free People.

Not have We been wanting in attention to our British brethren. We have warned them from time to time of attempts by their legislature to extend an unwarrantable jurisdiction over us. We have reminded them of the circumstances of our emigration and settlement here. We have appealed to their native justice and magnanimity and we have conjured them by the ties of our common kindred to disavow these usurpations, which would inevitably interrupt our connections and correspondence. They too have been deaf to the voice of justice and of consanguinity. We must, therefore, acquiesce in the necessity, which denounces our Separation, and hold them, as we hold the rest of mankind, Enemies in War, in Peace Friends.

We, therefore, the Representatives of the United States of America, in   35
General Congress, Assembled, appealing to the Supreme Judge of the world for the rectitude of our intentions, do, in the Name, and by Authority of the good People of these Colonies, solemnly publish and declare, That these United Colonies are, and of Right ought to be, Free and Independent States; that they are Absolved from all Allegiance to the British Crown, and that all political connection between them and the State of Great Britain, is and ought to be totally dissolved; and that as Free and Independent States, they have full power to levy War, conclude Peace, contract Alliances, establish Commerce, and to do all other Acts and Things which Independent States may of right do. And for the support of this Declaration, with a firm reliance on the protection of Divine Providence, we mutually pledge to each other our lives, our Fortunes and our sacred Honor.

■ Analysis

Claim: What is Jefferson trying to prove? *The American colonies are justified in declaring their independence from British rule.* Jefferson and his fellow signers might have issued a simple statement such as appears in the last paragraph, announcing the freedom and independence of these United Colonies. Instead, however, they chose to justify their right to do so.

Support: What does Jefferson have to go on? The Declaration of Independence bases its claim on two kinds of support: *factual evidence* and *motivational appeals* or appeals to the values of the audience.

FACTUAL EVIDENCE: Jefferson presents a long list of specific acts of tyranny by George III, beginning with "He has refused his Assent to Laws, the most wholesome and necessary for the public good." This list constitutes more than half the text. Notice how Jefferson introduces these grievances: "The history of the present King of Great Britain is a history of repeated injuries and usurpations, all having in direct object the establishment of an absolute Tyranny over these States. *To prove this, let Facts be submitted to a candid world*" (italics for emphasis added). Jefferson hopes that a recital of these specific acts will convince an honest audience that the United Colonies have indeed been the victims of an intolerable tyranny.

APPEAL TO VALUES: Jefferson also invokes the moral values underlying the formation of a democratic state. These values are referred to throughout. In the second and third paragraphs he speaks of equality, "Life, Liberty and the pursuit of Happiness," "just powers," "consent of the governed," and in the fourth paragraph, safety. In the last paragraph he refers to freedom and independence. Jefferson believes that the people who read his appeal will, or should, share these fundamental values. Audience acceptance of these values constitutes the most important part of the support. Some historians have called the specific acts of oppression cited by Jefferson trivial, inconsequential, or distorted. Clearly, however, Jefferson felt that the list of specific grievances was vital to definition of the abstract terms in which values are always expressed.

Warrant: How does Jefferson get from support to claim? *People have a right to revolution to free themselves from oppression.* This warrant is explicit: "But when a long train of abuses and usurpations pursuing invariably the same Object evinces a design to reduce them under absolute Despotism, it is their right, it is their duty, to throw off such government, and to provide new Guards for their future security." Some members of Jefferson's audience, especially those whom he accuses of oppressive acts, will reject the principle that any subject people have earned the right to revolt. But Jefferson believes that the decent opinion of mankind will accept this assumption. Many of his readers will also be aware that the warrant is supported by seventeenth-century political philosophy, which defines government as a social compact between the government and the governed.

If Jefferson's readers do, in fact, accept the warrant and if they also believe in the accuracy of the factual evidence and share his moral values, then they will conclude that his claim has been proved—that Jefferson has justified the right of the colonies to separate themselves from Great Britain.

Audience: The Declaration of Independence is addressed to several audiences: to the American colonists; to the British people; to the British Parliament; to the British king, George III; and to humanity or a universal audience.

Not all the American colonists were convinced by Jefferson's argument. Large numbers remained loyal to the king and for various reasons opposed an independent nation. In the next-to-the-last paragraph, Jefferson refers to previous addresses to the British people. Not surprisingly, most of the British citizenry as well as the king also rejected the claims of the Declaration. But the universal audience, the decent opinion of humanity, found Jefferson's argument overwhelmingly persuasive. Many of the liberal reform movements of the eighteenth and nineteenth centuries were inspired by the Declaration. In basing his claim on universal principles of justice and equality, Jefferson was certainly aware that he was addressing future generations.

Definition: Several significant terms are not defined. Modern readers will ask for further definition of "all men are created equal," "Life, Liberty and the pursuit of Happiness," "Laws of Nature and Nature's God," among others. We must assume that the failure to explain these terms more strictly was deliberate, in part because Jefferson thought that his readers would understand the references—for example, to the eighteenth-century belief in freedom as the birthright of all human beings—and in part because he wished the terms to be understood as universal principles of justice, applicable in all struggles, not merely those of the colonies against the king of England. But a failure to narrow the terms of argument can have unpredictable consequences. In later years the Declaration of Independence would be used to justify other rebellions, including the secession of the South from the Union in 1861.

Language: Although some stylistic conventions of eighteenth-century writing would not be observed today, Jefferson's clear, elegant, formal prose—"a surprising mixture of simplicity and majesty," in the words of one writer—remains a masterpiece of English prose and persuades us that we are reading an important document. Several devices are worth noting:

1. *Parallelism,* or balance of sentence construction, gives both emphasis and rhythm to the statements in the introduction (first four paragraphs) and the list of grievances.

2. *Diction* (choice of words) supports and underlines the meaning: nouns that have positive connotations—*safety, happiness, prudence, right, duty, Supreme Judge, justice;* verbs and verbals that suggest negative actions (taken by the king)—*refused, forbidden, dissolved, obstructed, plundered, depriving, abolishing.*

3. The *tone* suggests reason and patience on the part of the author or authors (especially paras. 5, 33, and 34).

Logic: As a logical pattern of argument, the Declaration of Independence is largely *deductive.* Deduction usually consists of certain broad general statements which we know or believe to be true and which lead us to other statements that follow from the ones already laid down. The Declaration begins with such general statements, summarizing a philosophy of government based on the equality of men, the inalienable rights derived from the Creator, and the powers of the governed. These statements are held to be "self-evident"—that is, not needing proof—and if we accept them, then it follows that a revolution is necessary to remove the oppressors and secure the safety and happiness to which the governed are entitled. The particular grievances against the king are proof that the king has oppressed the colonies, but they are not the basis for revolution.

The fact that Jefferson emphasized the universal principles underlying the right of revolution meant that the Declaration of Independence could appeal to all people everywhere, whether or not they had suffered the particular grievances in Jefferson's list.

EXERCISES

1. From the following list of claims, select the ones you consider most controversial. Tell why they are difficult to resolve. Are the underlying assumptions controversial? Is support hard to find or disputed? Can you think of circumstances under which some of these claims might be resolved?

   a. Congress should endorse the right-to-life amendment.

   b. Solar power can supply 20 percent of the energy needs now satisfied by fossil and nuclear power.

   c. Homosexuals should have the same job rights as heterosexuals.

   d. Rapists should be treated as mentally ill rather than depraved.

   e. Whale hunting should be banned by international law.

   f. Violence on television produces violent behavior in children who watch more than four hours a day.

   g. Both creationism and evolutionary theory should be taught in the public schools.

   h. Mentally defective men and women should be sterilized or otherwise prevented from producing children.

   i. History will pronounce Reggie Jackson a greater all-around baseball player than Joe DiMaggio.

   j. Bilingual instruction should not be permitted in the public schools.

   k. Some forms of cancer are caused by a virus.

   l. Dogs are smarter than horses.

   m. Curfews for teenagers will reduce the abuse of alcohol and drugs.

   n. The federal government should impose a drinking age of twenty-one.

   o. The United States should proceed with unilateral disarmament.

   p. Security precautions at airports are out of proportion to the dangers of terrorism.

   q. Bodybuilding cannot be defined as a sport; it is a form of exhibitionism.

2. Report on an argument you have heard recently. Identify the parts of that argument—claim, support, warrant—as they are defined in this chapter. What were the strengths and weaknesses in the argument you heard?

3. Choose one of the more controversial claims in the previous list and explain the reasons it is controversial. Is support lacking or in doubt? Are the warrants unacceptable to many people? Try to go as deeply as you

can, exploring, if possible, systems of belief, traditions, societal customs. You may confine your discussion to personal experience with the problem in your community or group. If there has been a change over the years in the public attitude toward the claim, offer what you think may be an explanation for the change.

4. Write your own argument for or against the value of standard grading in college.

5. Discuss an occasion when a controversy arose that the opponents could not settle. Describe the problem, and tell why you think the disagreement was not settled.

2

Responding to Argument

Most of us learn how to read, to listen, and to write arguments by attending critically to the arguments of those who have already mastered the important elements as well as those who have not. As we acquire skill in reading, we learn to uncover the clues that reveal meaning and to become sensitive to the kinds of organization, support, and language that experienced writers use in persuading their audiences. Listening, too, is a skill often underrated but increasingly important in an era when the spoken voice can be transmitted worldwide with astonishing speed. In becoming more expert listeners, we can engage in discussions with a wide and varied audience and gain proficiency in distinguishing between responsible and irresponsible speech.

A full response to any argument means more than understanding the message. It also means evaluating, deciding whether the message is successful and then determining *how* it succeeds or fails in persuading us. In making these judgments about the written and spoken arguments of others, we learn how to deliver our own. We try to avoid what we perceive to be flaws in another's arguments, and we adapt the strategies that produce clear, honest, forceful arguments.

RESPONDING AS A CRITICAL READER

Critical reading is essential for mastery of most college subjects, but its importance for reading and writing about argument, where meaning is often complex and multilayered, cannot be overestimated. Reading arguments critically requires you to at least temporarily suspend notions of absolute "right" and "wrong" and to intellectually inhabit grey areas that do not allow for simple "yes" and "no" answers. Of course, even in these areas, significant decisions about such things as ethics, values, politics, and the law must be made, and in studying argument you shouldn't fall into the trap of simple relativism: the idea that all answers to a given problem are equally correct at all times. We must make decisions about arguments with the understanding that reasonable people can disagree on the validity of ideas. Read or listen to others' arguments carefully and consider how their ideas can contribute to or complicate your own. Also recognize that what appears to be a final solution will always be open to further negotiation as new participants, new historical circumstances, and new ideologies become involved in the debate.

The ability to read arguments critically is essential to advanced academic work—even in science and math—since it requires the debate of multifaceted issues rather than the memorization of facts. Just as important, learning to read arguments critically helps you develop the ability to *write* effective arguments, a process valued at the university, in the professional world, and in public life.

■ Comprehending Arguments

The first step in the critical reading process is comprehension—understanding what an author is trying to prove. Comprehending academic arguments can be difficult, because they are often complex and challenge accepted notions of common sense. Academic writing also sometimes assumes that readers already have a great deal of knowledge about a subject, and can require further research for comprehension.

In addition, readers sometimes fail to comprehend an argument they disagree with or that is new to them, especially in dealing with essays or books making controversial, value-laden arguments. Some research even shows that readers will sometimes remember only those parts of texts that match their points of view.[1] The study of argument does not require you to accept points of view you find morally or otherwise reprehensible, but to engage with these views, no matter how strange or repugnant they might seem, on your own terms.

---

[1] See, for example, Slattery, Patrick J. "The Argumentative, Multiple-Source Paper: College Students Reading, Thinking, and Writing about Multiple Points of View." *Journal of Teaching Writing* 10 (Fall/Winter 1991): 181–99.

Reading an argument on its own terms means reading rhetorically. Imagine the initial context the author was writing in, the problem the author was trying to deal with, the reason the author might give for the language and the methods of persuasion being used, the warrants—or assumptions—underlying the author's point of view. In particular, imagine the author's ideal audience: Who would respond most favorably to the author's words and why? What values and ideals are shared by the author and the audience most likely to agree with the argument? How do these values and ideals help make sense of the argument?

To comprehend difficult texts you should understand that reading and writing are linked processes, and use writing to help your reading. This can mean writing comments in the margins of the book or essay itself or in a separate notebook; highlighting passages in the text that seem particularly important; or freewriting about the author's essential ideas after you finish reading. For complex arguments, write down the methods the author uses to make the argument: Did the text make use of historical evidence or rely on the voice of experts? Were emotional appeals made to try to convince readers or did the text rely on scientific or logical forms of evidence? Did the author use analogies or comparisons to help readers understand the argument? Was some combination of these or other strategies used? Writing down the author's methods for argumentation can make even the most complex arguments understandable, and once you grasp an argument on its own terms, you are ready to evaluate it.

■ Evaluating Arguments

The second step in the critical reading of arguments involves evaluation—careful judgment of the extent to which the author has succeeded in making a point—which can be difficult because some readers who do not thoroughly engage with an author's point of view may immediately label an argument they disagree with as "wrong," and some readers believe they are incapable of evaluating the work of a published, "expert" author, because they do not feel expert enough to make such judgments.

Evaluating arguments means moving beyond comprehending the context the author was writing within and starting to question it. One way to do this is to envision audiences the text was probably *not* written for, by considering, for example, whether an essay written for an academic audience takes into account the world outside the university. In addition, why is the problem significant to the author? For whom would it not be significant, and why?

When you evaluate an argument, imagine at least two kinds of audience for the text. Decide whose views would conflict most with the author's, and why. What ideology or values underlie the point of view most diametrically opposed to the author's argument? Then imagine yourself as a friend of the writer who simply wants him or her to succeed in clarifying and developing the argument. You could ask what additional methods should the author use to make the argument more effective or how could the writer more fully address opposing points of view. Are there any significant questions or issues the author has left unaddressed? How could he or she build on the strengths of the argument and downplay the weaknesses?

At this point consider how you personally respond to the argument presented in the text, and your own response in light of the questions you've asked. Critically evaluating an argument means not simply reading a text and agreeing or disagreeing with it, but doing serious analytical work that addresses multiple viewpoints before deciding on the effectiveness of an argument.

■ Critical Reading Strategies

Since comprehension and evaluation depend on each other so greatly, it is vital for you to take both steps seriously, and reading complex or important materials more than once and maybe several times. Of course, this is not possible for every assigned reading, and it is essential that you come to understand which texts require multiple readings.

Below are some general strategies for reading critically as well as more specific ones for comprehending and evaluating academic arguments, all of which should help your reading become more meaningful and productive. Since reading for comprehension and evaluation does not always require using completely different strategies, and sometimes simply requires using similar strategies in different ways, there is overlap between the two lists.

■ General Reading Strategies

Whether reading to comprehend or to evaluate an argument, do the following:

1. Take prereading activities seriously. Clearly, the more information you have about an author and subject, the easier and more productive your reading will be. However, you should learn to read in a way that allows you to discover not just meaning in the text itself but information about the author's point of view and background, the audience the author is writing for, and the author's motives and ideology. Such understanding comes from close analysis of texts, background reading on the author or the subject (a task made significantly easier by the Internet), and discussion with your classmates and instructors on the material.

2. Read as a writer. Since you will be asked to produce your own written arguments, it is important for you to read from a writer's point

of view. What engages your attention about what you are reading, and what surprises you? How would you classify the author's style of writing or rhetorical strategies? Most important, could you use similar writing strategies to organize and present your own ideas?

3. Work hard to understand the kind of text you are reading. Was it published recently? Was it written for a specific or a general audience? Is it a textbook and therefore likely to cover the basic points of an issue but not to take a strong stance on anything? Does it come from a journal that publishes primarily conservative or liberal writers?

4. When reading an Internet site, carefully read the Web address or URL. This can provide clues about the author of the site (is it an individual or an organization?) and about the purpose of the Web site (for example, the domain suffix *.com* represents a business site, while *.edu* represents academic institutions). In addition, most Web material is not checked for factual accuracy, so you must learn to distinguish between Web writing that represents a free-for-all of ideas and Web writing that has certain standards of reliability, especially when dealing with new information (see the sections on Sample Analysis of a Web Site (p. 49) and Evaluating Web Sources (p. 359) for more information).

■ Strategies for Comprehending Arguments

1. As you consider an essay or book for the first time, skim it for the main idea and overall structure. At this stage, avoid concentrating on details. As part of your prereading activities, try some or all of the following:

   a. Pay attention to the title, as it may state the purpose of the argument in specific terms, as in "Single-Sex Education Benefits Men Too" (p. 177). The title of the article that follows, "The Pursuit of Whining" (p. 32), brings to mind the famous "pursuit of Happiness" phrase from the Declaration of Independence. The subtitle clinches the connection: "Affirmative Action circa 1776." Titles can also express the author's attitude toward the subject, and in the case of "The Pursuit of Whining," we realize that "whining," because it has negative connotations, will probably be attacked as a means of achieving happiness.

   b. Make a skeleton outline of the text in your mind or on paper. From this outline and the text itself, consider the relationship between the beginning, middle, and end of the argument. How has the author divided these sections? Are there subheadings in the body of the text? If you are reading a book, how are the chapters broken up? What appears to be the logic of the author's organization?

   c. From your overview, what is the central claim or argument of the essay? What is the main argument against the author's central claim and how would the author respond to it?

2. For your first reading of the text, remember that the central argument—also known as the thesis statement or claim—is usually in one of the first two or three paragraphs (if it is an essay) or in the first chapter (if it is a book). The beginning of an argument can have other purposes, however; it may describe the position that the author will oppose, or provide background for the whole argument.

3. Pay attention to topic sentences. The topic sentence is usually but not always the first sentence of a paragraph. It is the general statement that controls the details and examples in the paragraph.

4. Don't overlook language signposts, especially transitional words and phrases that tell you whether the writer will change direction or offer support for a previous point—words and phrases like *but, however, nevertheless, yet, moreover, for example, at first glance, more important, the first reason,* and so on.

5. When it comes to vocabulary, you can either guess the meaning of an unfamiliar word from the context and go on, or look it up immediately. The first method makes for more rapid reading and is sometimes recommended by teachers, but guessing can be risky. Keep a good dictionary handy. If a word you don't understand seems crucial to meaning, look it up before going on.

6. If you use a colored marker to highlight main points, use it sparingly. Marking passages in color is meant to direct you to the major ideas and reduce the necessity for rereading the whole passage when you review. Look over the marked passages after reading and do a five-minute freewrite to sum up the central parts of the argument.

7. Once you are done reading, think again about the original context the text was written in: Why did the author write it and for whom? Why might an editor have published it in a book or journal and why did your instructor assign it for you to read?

■ Strategies for Evaluating Arguments

1. As you read the argument, don't be timid about asking questions of the text. No author is infallible, and some are not always clear. Disagree with the author if you feel confident of the support for your view, but first read the whole argument to see if your questions have been answered. If not, this may be a signal to read the article again. Be cautious about concluding that the author hasn't proved his or her point.

2. Reading an assigned work is usually a solitary activity, but what follows a reading should be shared. Talk about the material with classmates or others who have read it, especially those who have responded to the text differently than yourself. Consider their points of view. You probably know that discussion of a book or a movie strengthens both your memory of details and your understanding of the whole. And defending or modifying your evaluation will mean going back to the text and finding clues that you may have overlooked. Not least, it can be fun to discuss even something you didn't enjoy.

3. Consider the strengths of the argument, and examine the useful methods of argumentation, the points that are successfully made, (and those which help the reader to better understand the argument), and what makes sense about the author's argument.

4. Consider the weaknesses of the argument, and locate instances of faulty reasoning, unsupported statements, and the limitations of the author's assumptions about the world (the warrants that underlie the argument).

5. Consider how effective the title of the reading is, and whether it accurately sums up a critical point of the essay. Come up with an alternative title that would suit the reading better, and be prepared to defend this alternative title.

6. Evaluate the organizational structure of the essay. The author should lead you from idea to idea in a logical progression, and each section should relate to the ones before and after it and to the central argument in significant ways. Determine whether the writer has organized things more clearly, logically, or efficiently.

7. Look at how the author follows through on the main claim, or thesis, of the argument. The author should stick with this thesis, and not waver throughout the text. If the thesis does waver, there could be a reason for the shift in the argument or perhaps the author is being inconsistent. The conclusion should drive home the central argument.

8. Evaluate the vocabulary and style the author uses. Is it too simple or too complicated? The vocabulary and sentence structure the author uses could relate to the audience the author was initially writing for.

The following essay is annotated by a student as he reads. He is already familiar, as you are, with the Declaration of Independence. After reading and commenting on the essay, he adds a brief summary for his own review.

SAMPLE ANNOTATED ARGUMENT

The Pursuit of Whining:
Affirmative Action circa 1776

JOHN PATRICK DIGGINS

[margin annotation: Anything to do with "the pursuit of happiness"? Who's doing the whining in 1776?]

All politics, we are now told, will not be local but universal, a struggle over values. In these "culture wars," a candidate who can touch the core nerve of American values will be sure to be elected. How will affirmative action stand up to such a contest?

[margin annotation: Is this about affirmative action or the Revolution? Or both?]

At first glance, affirmative action appears to be consistent with America's commitment to egalitarianism, which derives from the Declaration of Independence and its ringing pronouncement that "all men are created equal" and are "endowed by their creator with certain unalienable rights."

[margin annotation: Usually means that a second glance will show the opposite]

[margin annotation: Means it's not what it seems]

Actually affirmative action, as carried out, has little to do with equality and is so dependent on biology, ancestry, and history that it subverts the individualist spirit of the Declaration.

[margin annotation: So he's against aff. action because it violates the D of I?]

But the second part of the Declaration, which no one remembers, may affirm affirmative action as the politics of group opportunity.

[margin annotation: Seems to be his thesis; is group opportunity bad?]

The Declaration held rights to be equal and unalienable because in the state of nature, before social conventions had been formed, "Nature and Nature's God" (Jefferson's phrase) gave no person or class the authority to dominate over others. Aristocracy became such a class, and the idea of equality was not so much an accurate description of the human species as it was a protest against artificial privilege and hereditary right.

[margin annotation: Reason for the Revolution]

[margin annotation: Interesting point — today's affirmative action is like yesterday's aristocracy (both claim privileges of birth).]

Today we have a new identity politics of entitle- 5 ment, and who one is depends on ethnic categories and descriptions based on either ancestry or sex. This return to a pseudo-aristocratic politics of privilege based on inherited rights by reason of

John Patrick Diggins teaches history at the Graduate Center of the City University of New York. This column appeared in the *New York Times* on September 25, 1995.

The founding fathers were against inherited privileges.

So far, he's proved that first part of D of I argues against affirmative action.

But the second part, listing grievances, is consistent with it.

Thinks the colonists are crybabies!

Strong language

Even Jefferson gets a few lumps!

Help! I can't find it in the D of I! (Look it up?)

birth means that equality has been replaced by diversity as the criteri[on] of governmental decisions.

Jefferson loved diversity, but he and Thomas Paine trusted the many and suspected the few who saw themselves entitled to preferential treatment as an accident of birth. Paine was unsparing in his critique of aristocracy as a parasitic "no-ability." Speaking for the colonists, many of whom had worked their way out of conditions of indentured servitude, he insisted that hereditary privilege was "as absurd as an hereditary mathematician, or an hereditary wise man; and as ridiculous as an hereditary poet-laureate."

But if America's egalitarian critique of aristocratic privilege could be in conflict with affirmative action, the second part of the Declaration may be perfectly consistent with it. Here begins the art of protest as the Declaration turns to the colonists' grievances, and we are asked to listen to a long tale of woe. Instead of admitting that they simply had no desire to cough up taxes, even to pay for a war that drove the French out of North America and thus made possible a situation where settlers were now secure enough to demand self-government, the colonists blamed King George for every outrage conceivable.

"He has erected . . . swarms of offices to harass our people and eat out their substance." Because the King, in response to the colonists' refusal to pay for the cost of protection, withdrew such protection, he is charged with abdicating "his allegiance and protection: he has plundered our seas, ravaged our coasts, burnt our towns, destroyed the lives of our people." Even Edmund Burke, the British parliamentarian and orator who supported the colonists, saw them as almost paranoid, "protestants" who protest so much that they would "snuff the approach of tyranny in every tainted breeze."

The ultimate hypocrisy comes when Jefferson accuses the King of once tolerating the slave trade, only "he is now exciting those very people to rise up in arms among us, and to purchase their liberty of which he has deprived them, by murdering the people upon whom he has obtruded them." The notion that slavery was forced upon

Wow!

the innocent colonists, who in turn only sought to be free of "tyranny," suggests the extent to which the sentiment of the Revolution grumbles with spurious charges.

Were any of their complaints justified?

"Paranoia" seems a bit much.

He's talking about blacks and women. Is he saying, "no justification for complaints against whites and males?" No way!

The Declaration voiced America's first procla- 10 mation of victimology. Whatever the theoretical complexities embedded in the doctrine of equality, the Declaration demonstrated that any politics that has its own interests uppermost is best put forward in the language of victimization and paranoia.

The very vocabulary of the document ("harass," "oppress," and so on) is consistent with affirmative action, where white racists and male chauvinists have replaced King George as the specter of complaint.

Explain a bit further.

Seeing themselves as sufferers to whom awful things happen, the colonists blamed their alleged oppressors and never acknowledged that they had any responsibility for the situation in which they found themselves.

Our choices

An ending that's all questions. I like it. But they're fake questions. He knows the answers and wants us to agree with him.

What then is America's core value? Is it equality and civic virtue? Or is it the struggle for power that legitimizes itself in the more successful, and least demanding, shameless politics of whining?

Summary: Is affirmative action consistent with the Declaration of Independence? On that subject the two parts of the Declaration contradict each other. The first part says that equality and individual rights are the principles of the American Revolution. Because the founding fathers opposed privileges awarded on account of ancestry and history, they would be against affirmative action. But in the second part of the Declaration, the grievances of the colonists sound like the complaints of groups today that claim they are victims of oppression and want special privileges because of their ancestry and history. Today America must choose between equality and privileges for special groups. Note: From The Declaration of Independence, a book by Carl Becker, I found out that the excerpts in paragraph 9 come from an earlier draft of the Declaration. This argument about slavery was omitted from the final draft because Jefferson thought that it was weaker than the others. So was it fair to include it here?

RESPONDING AS A WRITER

The following essay is a claim of value in which an author argues that a belief or a form of behavior is either desirable or undesirable. Here, as the title suggests, the author claims that competitive sports are destructive. In arguments about values, the author may or may not suggest a solution to the problem caused by the belief or behavior. If so, the solution will be implicit—that is, unexpressed, or undeveloped—as is the case here, and the emphasis will remain on support for the claim.

Keep in mind that an essay of this length can never do justice to a complicated and highly debatable subject. It will probably lack sufficient evidence, as this one does, to answer all the questions and objections of readers who enjoy and approve of competitive games. What it can do is provoke thought and initiate an intelligent discussion.

SAMPLE ANNOTATED ANALYSIS

No-Win Situations

ALFIE KOHN

Intro: personal
experience

I learned my first game at a birthday party. You remember it: X players scramble for X-minus-one chairs each time the music stops. In every round a child is eliminated until at the end only one is left triumphantly seated while everyone else is standing on the sidelines, excluded from play, unhappy . . . losers.

This is how we learn to have a good time in America.

Competition

Warrant

Several years ago I wrote a book called *No Contest*, which, based on the findings of several hundred studies, argued that competition undermines self-esteem, poisons relationships, and holds us back from doing our best. I was mostly interested in the win/lose arrangement

---

This article by Alfie Kohn, author of *No Contest: The Case against Competition* (1986) and *The Case against Standardized Testing* (2000), appeared in *Women's Sports and Fitness Magazine* (July–August 1990).

that defines our workplaces and classrooms, but I found myself nagged by the following question: If competition is so destructive and counterproductive during the week, why do we take for granted that it suddenly becomes benign and even desirable on the weekend?

This is a particularly unsettling line of inquiry for athletes or parents. Most of us, after all, assume that competitive sports teach all sorts of useful lessons and, indeed, that games by definition must produce a winner and a loser. But I've come to believe that recreation at its best does not require people to try to triumph over others. Quite to the contrary.

Terry Orlick, a sports psychologist at the University of Ottawa, took a look at musical chairs and proposed that we keep the basic format of removing chairs but change the goal; the point becomes to fit everyone on a diminishing number of seats. At the end, a group of giggling children tries to figure out how to squish onto a single chair. Everybody plays to the end; everybody has a good time.

Orlick and others have devised or collected hundreds of such games for children and adults alike. The underlying theory is simple: All games involve achieving a goal despite the presence of an obstacle, but nowhere is it written that the obstacle has to be someone else. The idea can be for each person on the field to make a specified contribution to the goal, or for all the players to reach a certain score, or for everyone to work with her partners against a time limit.

Note the significance of an "opponent" becoming a "partner." The entire dynamic of the game shifts, and one's attitude toward the other players changes with it. Even the friendliest game of tennis can't help but be affected by the game's inherent structure, which demands that each person try to hit the ball where the other can't get to it. You may not be a malicious person, but to play tennis means that you try to make the other person fail.

I've become convinced that not a single one of the advantages attributed to sports actually requires competition. Running, climbing, biking,

Claim or *thesis* statement

Support: expert opinion, alternatives to competitive games

Refuting the opposing view

No advantages in competition

swimming, aerobics—all offer a fine workout without any need to try to outdo someone else.

1) Some people point to the <u>camaraderie</u> that results from teamwork, but that's precisely the benefit of cooperative activity, whose very essence is that *everyone* on the field is working together for a common goal. By contrast, the distinguishing feature of team competition is that a given player works with and is encouraged to feel warmly toward only half of those present. Worse, a we-versus-they dynamic is set up, which George Orwell once called "war minus the shooting."

2) The dependence on sports to provide <u>a sense of accomplishment</u> or to test one's wits is similarly misplaced. One can aim instead at an objective standard (How far did I throw? How many miles did we cover?) or attempt to do better than last week. Such individual and group striving—like cooperative games—provides satisfaction and challenge without competition.

If large numbers of people insist that we can't 10 do without win/lose activities, the first question to ask is whether they've ever tasted the alternative. When Orlick taught a group of children non-competitive games, two-thirds of the boys and all of the girls preferred them to the kind that require opponents. If our culture's idea of fun requires beating someone else, it may just be because we don't know any other way.

It may also be because we overlook the
3) <u>psychological costs of competition</u>. Most people lose in most competitive encounters, and it's obvious why that causes self-doubt. But even winning doesn't build character. It just lets us gloat temporarily. Studies have shown that feelings of self-worth become dependent on external sources of evaluation as a result of competition. Your value is defined by what you've done and who you've beaten. The whole affair soon becomes a vicious circle: The more you compete, the more you *need* to compete to feel good about yourself. It's like drinking salt water when you're thirsty. This process is bad enough for us; it's a disaster for our children.

While this is going on, competition is having
4) an equally <u>toxic effect on our relationships</u>. By

definition, not everyone can win a contest. That means that each child inevitably comes to regard others as obstacles to his or her own success. Competition leads children to envy winners, to dismiss losers (there's no nastier epithet in our language than "loser!"), and to be suspicious of just about everyone. Competition makes it difficult to regard others as potential friends or collaborators; even if you're not my rival today, you could be tomorrow.

This is not to say that competitors will always detest one another. But trying to outdo someone is not conducive to trust—indeed it would be irrational to trust a person who gains from your failure. At best, competition leads one to look at others through narrowed eyes; at worst, it invites outright aggression.

Changing the Structure of Sports

Conclusion

But no matter how many bad feelings erupt during competition, we have a marvelous talent for <u>blaming the individuals rather than focusing on the structure of the game itself, a structure that makes my success depend on your failure</u>. Cheating may just represent the logical conclusion of this arrangement rather than an aberration. And sportsmanship is nothing more than an artificial way to try to limit the damage of competition. If we weren't set against each other on the court or the track, we wouldn't need to keep urging people to be good sports; they might well be working *with* each other in the first place.

New idea that confirms his claim

As radical or surprising as it may sound, the   15 problem isn't just that we compete the wrong way or that we push winning on our children too early. <u>The problem is competition itself</u>. What we need to be teaching our daughters and sons is that it's possible to have a good time—a better time— without turning the playing field into a battlefield.

■ Organization

While there are numerous conventional patterns of organization (see Chapter 9), it is worth pointing out that most essays of more than 750 words are rarely perfect examples of such patterns. Authors mix structures wherever it seems necessary to make a stronger case. The pattern of organization in this essay is primarily a *defense of the main idea*—that competitive sports are psychologically unhealthy. But because the claim is highly controversial, the author must also try to *refute the opposing view*—that competition is rewarding and enjoyable.

The *claim,* expressed as the *thesis statement* of the essay, appears at the end of paragraph 4: "recreation at its best does not require people to try to triumph over others. Quite to the contrary." The three-paragraph introduction recounts a relevant personal experience as well as the reasons that prompted Kohn to write his essay. Because we are all interested in stories, the recital of a personal experience is a popular device for introducing almost any subject (see "The Childswap Society," p. 258).

The rest of the essay, until the last two paragraphs, is devoted to summarizing the benefits of cooperative play and the disadvantages of competitive sport. The emphasis is overwhelmingly on the disadvantages as stated in the third paragraph: "competition undermines self-esteem, poisons relationships, and holds us back from doing our best." This is the *warrant,* the assumption that underlies the claim. In fact, Kohn is here referring to a larger study that he wrote about competition in workplaces and classrooms. We must accept this broad generalization, which applies to many human activities, before we can agree that the claim about competition in sports is valid.

The last two paragraphs sum up his argument that "The problem is competition itself" (para. 15)—the structure of the game, rather than the people who play. Notice that this summary does not merely repeat the main idea. Like many thoughtful summaries, it also offers *a new idea* about good sportsmanship that confirms his conclusion.

■ Support

Because the author knows that competitive sports are hugely popular not only in the United States but in many other parts of the world, he must give most of his argument to refuting the specific claims of those who value the spirit of competition. Kohn relies for support on examples from common experience and on the work of Terry Orlick, a sports psychologist. The examples from experience are ones that most of us will recognize. Here we are in a position to judge for ourselves, without the mediation of an expert, whether the influence of competition in sports is as hurtful as Kohn insists. Orlick's research suggests a solution—adaptations of familiar games that will provide enjoyment but avoid competition.

On the other hand, the results from studies by one psychologist whose work we aren't able to verify and the mention of "studies" in paragraph 3 without further attribution are probably not enough to answer all the arguments in favor of competition. Critics may also ask if Kohn has offered support for one of his contentions—that competition "holds us back from doing our best" (para. 3). (Support for this may appear in one of Kohn's books.)

In addition, Kohn fails to make clear distinctions between competitive sports for children, who may find it difficult to accept defeat, and for adults, who understand the consequences of any competitive game and are psychologically equipped to deal with them. Readers may therefore share Kohn's misgivings about competition for children but doubt that his criteria apply equally to adults.

■ Style

The language is clear and direct. Kohn's article, which appeared in a women's sports magazine, is meant for the educated general reader, not the expert. This is also the audience for whom most student papers are written. But the written essay need not be unduly formal. Kohn uses contractions and the personal pronouns "I" and "you" to establish a conversational context. One of the particular strengths of his style is the skillful use of transitional expressions, words like "this" and "also" and clauses like "This is not to say that" and "Note the significance of" to make connections between paragraphs and new ideas.

The tone is temperate despite the author's strong feelings about the subject. Other authors, supporting the same argument, have used language that borders on the abusive about coaches and trainers of children's games. But a less inflammatory voice is far more effective with an audience that may be neutral or antagonistic.

You will find it helpful to look back over the essay to see how the examples we've cited and others work to fulfill the writer's purpose.

RESPONDING AS A CRITICAL LISTENER

Of course, not all public arguments are written. Oral arguments on radio and television now enjoy widespread popularity and influence. In fact, their proliferation means that we listen far more than we talk, read, or write. Today the art of listening has become an indispensable tool for learning about the world we live in. One informed critic predicts that the dissemination of information and opinions through the electronic media will "enable more and more Americans to participate directly in making the laws and policies by which they are governed."[2]

Because we are interested primarily in arguments about public issues — those that involve democratic decision making — we will not be

---

[2]Lawrence K. Grossman, *The Electronic Republic: Reshaping Democracy in the Information Age* (New York: Viking, 1995).

concerned with the afternoon television talk shows that are largely devoted to personal problems. (Occasionally, however, *Oprah* introduces topics of broad social significance.) More relevant to the kinds of written arguments you will read and write about in this course are the television and radio shows that also examine social and political problems. The most intelligent and responsible programs usually consist of a panel of experts—politicians, journalists, scholars—led by a neutral moderator (or one who, at least, allows guests to express their views). Some of these programs are decades old; others are more recent—*Meet the Press, Face the Nation, Firing Line, The McLaughlin Group, The NewsHour with Jim Lehrer*. An outstanding radio show, *Talk of the Nation* on National Public Radio, invites listeners, who are generally informed and articulate, to call in and ask questions of, or comment on remarks made by, experts on the topic of the day.

Several enormously popular radio talk shows are hosted by people with strong, sometimes extreme ideological positions. They may use offensive language and insult their listeners in a crude form of theater. Among the most influential shows are those of Don Imus and Howard Stern. In addition, elections and political crises bring speeches and debates on radio and television by representatives of a variety of views. Some are long and formal, written texts that are simply read aloud, but others are short and impromptu.

Whatever the merits or shortcomings of individual programs, significant general differences exist between arguments on radio and television and arguments in the print media. These differences include the degree of organization and development and the risk of personal attacks.

First (excluding for the moment the long, prepared speeches), contributions to a panel discussion must be delivered in fragments, usually no longer than a single paragraph, weakened by time constraints, interruptions, overlapping speech, memory gaps, and real or feigned displays of derision, impatience, and disbelief by critical panelists. Even on the best programs, the result is a lack of both coherence—or connections between ideas—and solid evidence that requires development. Too often we are treated to conclusions with little indication of how they were arrived at.

The following brief passage appeared in a newspaper review of "Resolved: The flat tax is better than the income tax," a debate on *Firing Line* by an impressive array of experts. It illustrates some of the difficulties that accompany programs attempting to capture the truth of a complicated issue on television or radio.

> "It is absolutely true," says a proponent. "It is factually untrue," counters an opponent. "It's factually correct," responds a proponent. "I did my math right," says a proponent. "You didn't do your math right," says an opponent. At one point in a discussion of interest income, one of the experts says, "Oh, excuse me, I think I got it backward."

No wonder the television critic called the exchange "disjointed and at times perplexing."[3]

In the sensational talk shows the participants rely on personal experience and vivid anecdotes, which may not be sufficiently typical to prove anything.

Second, listeners and viewers of all spoken arguments are in danger of evaluating them according to criteria that are largely absent from evaluation of written texts. It is true that writers may adopt a persona or a literary disguise, which the tone of the essay will reflect. But many readers will not be able to identify it or recognize their own response to it. Listeners and viewers, however, can hardly avoid being affected by characteristics that are clearly definable: a speaker's voice, delivery, bodily mannerisms, dress, and physical appearance. In addition, listeners may be adversely influenced by clumsy speech containing more slang, colloquialisms, and grammar and usage errors than written texts that have had the benefit of revision.

But if listeners allow consideration of physical attributes to influence their judgment of what the speaker is trying to prove, they are guilty of an ad hominem fallacy — that is, an evaluation of the speaker rather than the argument. This is true whether the evaluation is favorable or unfavorable. (See pp. 295–96 for a discussion of this fallacy.)

Talk shows may indeed be disjointed and perplexing, but millions of us find them both instructive and entertaining. Over time we are exposed to an astonishing variety of opinions from every corner of American life, and we also acquire information from experts who might not otherwise be available to us. Then there is the appeal of hearing the voices, seeing the faces of people engaged in earnest, sometimes passionate, discourse — a short, unrehearsed drama in which we also play a part as active listeners in a far-flung audience.

■ Guidelines to Critical Listening

Listening is hearing with attention, a natural and immensely important human activity, which, unfortunately, many people don't do very well. The good news is that listening is a skill that can be learned and, unlike some other skills, practiced every day without big investments of money and effort.

Here are some of the characteristics of critical listening most appropriate to understanding arguments.

1. Above all, listening to arguments requires concentration. If you are distracted, you cannot go back as you do with the written word to clarify a point or recover a connection. Devices such as flow sheets and

---

[3]Walter Goodman, "The Joys of the Flat Tax, Excluding the Equations," *New York Times*, December 21, 1995, sec. C, p. 14.

outlines can be useful aids to concentration. In following a debate, for example, judges and other listeners often use flow sheets—distant cousins of baseball scorecards—to record the major points on each side and their rebuttals. For roundtable discussions or debates you can make your own simple flow chart to fill out as you listen, with columns for claims, different kinds of support, and warrants. Leave spaces in the margin for your questions and comments about the soundness of the proof. An outline is more useful for longer presentations, such as lectures. As you listen, try to avoid being distracted by facts alone. Look for the overall pattern of the speech.

2. Listeners often concentrate on the wrong things in the spoken argument. We have already noted the distractions of appearance and delivery. Research shows that listeners are likely to give greater attention to the dramatic elements of speeches than to the logical ones. But you can enjoy the sound, the appearance, and the drama of a spoken argument without allowing these elements to overwhelm what is essential to the development of a claim.

3. Good listeners try not to allow their prejudices to prevent careful evaluation of the argument. This doesn't mean accepting everything or even most of what you hear. It means trying to avoid premature judgments about what is actually said. This precaution is especially relevant when the speakers and their views are well known and the listener has already formed an opinion about them, favorable or unfavorable.

RESPONDING TO A VISUAL ARGUMENT

Man has been communicating by pictures longer than he has been using words. With the development of photography in this century we are using pictures as a means of communication to such an extent that in some areas they overshadow verbal language.[4]

You've probably seen some of the powerful images in photographic journalism to which the author refers: soldiers in battle, destruction by weather disasters, beautiful natural landscapes, inhuman living conditions, the great mushroom cloud of early atomic explosions. These photographs and thousands of others encapsulate arguments of fact, value, and policy. We don't need to read their captions to understand what they tell us: *The tornado devastated the town. The Grand Canyon is our most stupendous national monument. We must not allow human beings to live like this.* The pictures stay with us long after we have forgotten the words that accompanied them.

---

[4] Paul Wendt, "The Language of Pictures," in S. I. Hayakawa, ed., *The Use and Misuse of Language* (Greenwich, Conn.: Fawcett, 1962), p. 175.

Photographs, of course, function everywhere as instruments of persuasion. Animal-rights groups show pictures of brutally mistreated dogs and cats; children's rights advocates publish pictures of sick and starving children in desolate refugee camps. On a very different scale, alluring photographs from advertisers—travel agencies, restaurants, sporting goods manufacturers, clothiers, jewelers, movie studios—promise to fulfill our dreams of pleasure.

But photographs are not the only visual images we respond to. We are also susceptible to other kinds of illustrations and to signs and symbols which over the years have acquired connotations, or suggestive significance. The flag or bald eagle, the shamrock, the crown, the cross, the hammer and sickle, and the swastika can all rouse strong feelings for or against the ideas they represent. These symbols may be defined as abbreviated claims of value. They summarize the moral, religious, and political principles by which groups of people live and often die. In commercial advertisements we recognize symbols that aren't likely to enlist our deepest loyalties but, nevertheless, have impact on our daily lives: the apple with a bite in it, the golden arches, the Prudential rock, the Nike swoosh, and a thousand others.

In fact, a closer look at commercial and political advertising, which is heavily dependent on visual argument and is something we are all familiar with, provides a useful introduction to this complex subject. We know that advertisements, with or without pictures, are short arguments, often lacking fully developed support, whose claims of policy urge us to take an action: Buy this product or service; vote for this candidate or issue. The claim may not be directly expressed, but it will be clearly implicit. In print, on television, or on the Internet, the visual representation of objects, carefully chosen to appeal to a particular audience, can be as important as, if not more important than, any verbal text.

In a political advertisement, for example, we often see a picture of the candidate surrounded by a smiling family. The visual image is by now a cliché, suggesting traditional values—love and security, the importance of home and children. Even if we know little or nothing about his or her platform, we are expected to make a sympathetic connection with the candidate.

In a commercial advertisement the image may be a picture of a real or fictitious person to whom we will react favorably. Consider the picture on a jar of spaghetti sauce. As a famous designer remarked, "When you think about it, sauce is mostly sauce. It's the label that makes the difference."[5] And what, according to the designer, does the cheerful face of Paul Newman on jars of his spaghetti sauce suggest to the prospective buyer? "Paul Newman. Paul Newman. Paul Newman. Blue eyes. All the

[5] Tibor Kalman, "Message: Sweet-Talking Spaghetti Sauce," *New York Times Magazine,* December 13, 1998, p. 81.

money goes to charity. It's humanitarian, funny, and sexy. Selling this is like falling off a log." Not a word about the quality of the sauce.

Even colleges, which are also selling a product, must think of appropriate images to attract their prospective customers—students. Today the fact that more women than men are enrolled in college has caused some schools to rethink their images. One college official explained:

> We're having our recruiting literature redesigned, and we've been thinking about what's a feminine look and what's a masculine look. We have a picture of a library with a lot of stained glass, and people said that was kind of a feminine cover. Now we're using a picture of the quadrangle.[6]

In addition to the emblem itself, the designer pays careful attention to a number of other elements in the ad: colors, light and shadow, foreground and background, relative sizes of pictures and text, and placement of objects on the page or screen. Each of these contributes to the total effect, although we may be unaware of how the effect has been achieved. (In the ad that follows, you will be able to examine some of the psychological and aesthetic devices at work.)

When there is no verbal text, visual images are less subject to analysis and interpretation. For one thing, if we are familiar with the objects in the picture, we see the whole image at once, and it registers immediately. The verbal message is linear and takes far longer to be absorbed. Pictures, therefore, appear to need less translation. Advertisers and other arguers depend on this characteristic to provide quick and friendly acceptance of their claims, although the image may, in fact, be deceptive.

This expectation of easy understanding poses a danger with another visual ally of the arguer—the graph or chart. Graphics give us factual information at a glance. In addition to the relative ease with which they can be read, they are "at their best . . . instruments for reasoning about quantitative information. . . . Of all methods for analyzing and communicating statistical information, well-designed data graphics are usually the simplest and at the same time the most powerful."[7]

Nevertheless, they may mislead the quick reader. Graphics can lie. "The lies are told about the major issues of public policy—the government budget, medical care, prices, and fuel economy standards, for example. The lies are systematic and quite predictable, nearly always exaggerating the rate of recent change."[8]

Visual images, then, for all their apparent immediacy and directness, need to be read with at least the same attention we give to the verbal message if we are to understand the arguments they represent.

[6]*New York Times,* December 6, 1998, p. 38.

[7]Edward R. Tufte, *The Visual Display of Quantitative Information* (Cheshire, Conn.: Graphics Press, 1983), introduction.

[8]Tufte, *The Visual Display,* p. 76.

QUESTIONS FOR ANALYSIS

1. What does the arguer want me to do or believe? How important is the visual image in persuading me to comply?

2. Has the visual image been accompanied by sufficient text to answer questions I may have about the claim?

3. Are the visual elements more prominent than the text? If so, why?

4. Is the visual image representative of a large group, or is it an exception that cannot support the claim?

5. Does the arrangement of elements in the message tell me what the arguer considers most important? If so, what is the significance of this choice?

6. Can the validity of this chart or graph be verified?

7. Does the visual image lead me to entertain unrealistic expectations? (Can using this shampoo make hair look like that shining cascade on the television screen? Does the picture of the candidate for governor, shown answering questions in a classroom of eager, smiling youngsters, mean that he has a viable plan for educational reform?)

SAMPLE ANALYSIS OF AN ADVERTISEMENT

We have pointed out that a commercial advertisement is a short argument that makes an obvious policy claim, which may or may not be explicit: *You should buy this product.* Depending on the medium—television, print, radio, or Internet—an ad may convey its message through language, picture, or sound.

Here is how one analyst of advertising sums up the goals of the advertiser: (1) attract attention, (2) arouse interest, (3) stimulate desire, (4) create conviction, and (5) get action.[9] Needless to say, not every ad successfully fulfills all these objectives. If you examine the ad reproduced on page 48, you can see how the advertiser brings language and visual image together in an attempt to support the claim.

First of all, you must imagine the principal objects of the ad in color—white bread on one side, red ravioli on the other. Of course, the advertiser, Chef Boyardee, expects the reader to find the ravioli more attractive. Like most pictures of food, these are designed to attract attention and arouse interest. Whether they stimulate desire depends on a number of things that the advertiser cannot control—who the reader is, how much the reader likes such food, how hungry he or she is at the time of the reading, and so on.

Notice the word *simple,* which is printed in bright red in the headline. This word emphasizes both the visual image (the clear, uncluttered

[9]J. V. Lund, *Newspaper Advertising* (New York: Prentice-Hall, 1947), p. 83.

arrangement of the pictures, lots of white space, the neat lineup of the comparative data) and the content message as well (that is, that the claim is unambiguous and uncontroversial). Simplicity is not always a positive attribute, but to advertisers the word *simple* is a magic wand that dispels the buyer's fear of whatever might be complicated or obscure.

You may not be immediately aware that the word *simple* makes a connection with the word *goodness,* also in bright red, in the lower right corner. One analyst points to this arrangement as "an extremely important dimension" because "when we read, the eye moves from the upper left corner of the page to the lower right corner."[10] The ravioli, too, appear on the preferred side, the right, where the eye will pause or encounter the end of the message. It is the emphatic position.

Support for the claim that Chef Boyardee Beef Ravioli should be your choice appears in the data under the pictures. The data here are limited to numbers, as the headline predicts: "An after-school lesson in simple mathematics." Again, even the visual arrangement of the numbers suggests openness and clarity. The numbers themselves are meant to create conviction. The advertiser, however, omits any authority for them, and critics have noted that such numbers on containers are sometimes inaccurate. Not surprisingly, the advertiser concentrates on fat content because in this respect, perhaps *only* in this respect, is the ravioli superior. (Arguers about social issues also engage in this strategy of calculated omission.)

Additional support appears in the paragraph below. Here, too, the spacing is open, generous, and easy to read, and we learn about other healthful qualities of the beef ravioli. The advertiser *seems* to allege that its product is distinctive in regard to these good things. But, in fact, they are true for almost all pasta and meat sold in the United States, and all preservatives, contrary to the advertiser's implication, are not harmful. Other producers have made equally ambiguous claims. Schlitz Beer boasted in its ads that its bottles were steam-sterilized, without revealing that bottles of all other beer companies were also steam-sterilized.[11]

The warrant that underlies the claim becomes clear in the last one-sentence paragraph. We've been aware all along that the appeal is not to children, the chief consumers of peanut-butter and jelly sandwiches. The phrase "your kids" tells us that the appeal is directed to parents. We now understand the unexpressed warrant: Parents can be counted on to provide what is most healthful for their children.

It's worth noting, too, that the paragraph of text probably doesn't play a significant role in the argument. The emphasis rests on the picture and the chart, and the advertiser counts on them to make an impression

[10]Torben Vestergaard and Kim Schroder, *The Language of Advertising* (Oxford: Oxford University Press, 1986), p. 44.

[11]Daniel J. Boorstin, *The Image; or, What Happened to the American Dream?* (New York: Atheneum, 1962), p. 214.

An after-school lesson
in simple mathematics.

Peanut Butter & Jelly Sandwich
(2 Tbsp PB, 1Tbsp Jelly, 2 Slices Bread)

Calories 360
Calories from Fat 150
Fat 18g

Chef Boyardee® Beef Ravioli
(1 cup serving)

Calories 230
Calories from Fat 45
Fat 5g

An after-school meal doesn't have to be a fat fest. Consider a hot

bowl of Chef Boyardee® Beef Ravioli. One serving has fewer calories and

less than 1/3 the fat of a PB&J. Chef Boyardee Beef Ravioli is made with

enriched pasta, sun-ripened tomatoes and 100% USDA-

inspected beef. With no preservatives.

So when your kids come home starving

after school, give them something you both like.

Thank goodness
for Chef Boyardee

See product label for information on sodium and other nutrients.

©International Home Foods, Inc.

that will persuade the reader to buy its product even if he or she doesn't read the text. Their place in the upper half of the ad is like a headline and the first paragraph of a news story, which is all that many people read.

Is the ad successful in getting action? The advertiser has tried to establish itself, in both the visual and the verbal content of its message, as a friend of the reader, open, truthful, committed to the health of children. It has assumed that the fat content of food is of high importance to the parents who read the ad. And perhaps it is, but despite the apparent validity of the warrant, the success of the ad is unpredictable. The plump red ravioli may appeal to the parent, but many children will prefer the sandwich, and for reasons that advertisers can't control, the parent may choose what the children *want.* Advertisers who show pictures of expensive toys on children's television programs have already learned this lesson.

SAMPLE ANALYSIS OF A WEB SITE

The Internet provides an important forum for individuals and organizations to make arguments. Through the Internet, anyone with access to a networked computer can potentially publish his or her ideas. While this ease of publication is exciting, it also means writers hoping to obtain reliable information from the Web need to read Web sites critically (see Critical Reading Strategies on page 28 for further insight into this issue).

With new genres being created daily, some researchers[12] have noted five major types of Web pages:

1. *Advocacy Web Pages:* Advocacy pages are typically created by not-for-profit organizations wishing to influence public opinion, and the URL for the site is likely to contain the domain suffix *.org* (organization).

2. *Business/Marketing Web Pages:* The majority of businesses in the United States have a Web presence today, and most business pages are either advertising or provide online opportunities to purchase goods and services. The addresses for such sites typically contain the domain suffix *.com* (for commercial).

3. *News Web Pages:* News pages provide current information on local, national, and international events. The addresses for news sites also contain the abbreviation *.com* reflecting the fact that the news industry is also a business.

4. *Informational Web Pages:* Informational pages provide data such as that found in dictionaries or atlases. The addresses for these sites sometimes include *.edu* (university), *.k12* (primary or secondary school), or *.gov* (government) because they are often sponsored by academic institutions or government agencies.

5. *Personal Web Pages:* Personal pages are created by individuals, and can be intimate, entertaining, informative, bizarre, or some combination of these things. While the addresses for personal sites can end in *.com, .edu, .k12, .org,* or *.gov,* the presence of a tilde (~) in the address suggests that the page represents an individual.

[12]See, for example, the Widener University Wolfgram Memorial Library Web site at http://www2.widener.edu/Wolfgram-Memorial-Library/webevaluation/webeval.htm.

On the facing page is a copy of the home page for *The Hunger Site* (a home page introduces and often provides a guide or table of contents for an entire site, which can consist of many pages). At first glance, *The Hunger Site* appears to be a combination informational page (because it contains facts about world hunger) and business/marketing page (because it advertises a variety of products). It is in fact both these things as well as a site for philanthropy (since advertisers' money pays for the food).

The significance of charitable giving to the site's mission is suggested by several things. Maybe most directly, a viewer's eye is immediately drawn to a gold icon reading "GIVE FREE FOOD: Click Here." This icon appears at the bottom of the home page and draws the eye immediately with its color and placement. It also presents an appealing prospect to readers: that they can be generous by supporting a significant cause and do so without spending money (the food is "free"). When you click on the icon, *The Hunger Site* donates two cups of food (or the financial equivalent) to the hungry.

The emphasis on giving is furthered by a link on the right side of the page that reads "Register Today & Give Up to 8 Extra Cups." As this suggests, readers can register as a member of *The Hunger Site* and donate additional food to hungry people. Directly underneath this is the announcement reading "More Ways To Help: Each purchase made gives up to 50 cups of food." Clicking here offers more opportunities to provide food for others, opportunities linked to purchases made from sponsoring companies.

It is this connection that links *The Hunger Site* to business interests, interests highlighted by the *.com* in the site's URL. Though donations can be given without spending money, the site also links consumer needs and desires to philanthropy by providing visitors the opportunity to support the hungry by purchasing a wide variety of goods—from clothing to flowers to seasonal gifts and decorations. Consumer givers, then, can feel good that the money they are spending is contributing to a valuable cause. In return, site sponsors, companies such as L.L. Bean who help subsidize the donations made to the hungry, receive advertising and gain new customers. In this way, viewers feel inspired to shop more, meaning that *The Hunger Site* has the potential to bind together corporate interests, consumer interests, and international benevolence.

In many ways, then, *The Hunger Site* reads like a traditional advertisement. It appeals to customers because it represents an easy way to do something socially responsible. To develop customer loyalty, businesses and organizations strive for "brand recognition," and *The Hunger Site* is no exception. It uses a golden strand of wheat as its logo. Gold, symbolizing both wheat and true value, is the color of the central icon that allows browsers to contribute food with a single click.

However, while *The Hunger Site* incorporates many traditional methods in appealing to its readers, it also makes use of Web technology. Directly above the "GIVE FREE FOOD" icon is a map that reflects deaths from hunger under the headline "24,000 die daily. Please click every

The Hunger Site Home Page

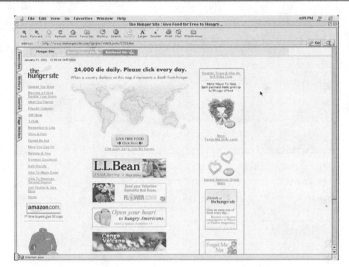

day," and every few seconds a different country on the map darkens to represent a death from hunger. The print statistic that "24,000 die daily" is supplemented by this graphic reminder, of what it means for so many thousands to die every day. Viewers cannot help noticing the slow and steady stream of blackening countries, which make an abstract number more real.

Interactivity is further displayed in the way the site acknowledges its readers' influence and importance. For example, the menu on the left-hand side of the home page begins with four links that directly involve visitor participation. The first, which reads "Spread the Word," opens onto a page that gives viewers the opportunity to e-mail friends an electronic form letter with prewritten statistics and information provided by *The Hunger Site*. However, viewers are also encouraged to personalize the e-mail with their own thoughts and ideas about the significance of *The Hunger Site*. In this way, viewers become coauthors of a letter with the authors of the site. Other icons acknowledge and celebrate "friends" of *The Hunger Site*. Becoming a friend of the site can be accomplished virtually instantaneously, and friends are then able to enter the "Friends' Gateway," which offers unique opportunities for both purchasing and giving. The value of this option is also made more real because it involves an actual locking out of those who have not attained the status of friends.

The emphasis on the immediacy of this interaction between reader and text can also be seen in the features that allow readers of the site to keep track of their giving by clicking on the link that reads "See your giving history at the bottom of our Thank You page." This displays up-to-the-minute statistics regarding the number of clicks the viewer has made, making the visitor feel like carefully accounted for participants in the

The Hunger Site Thank You Page

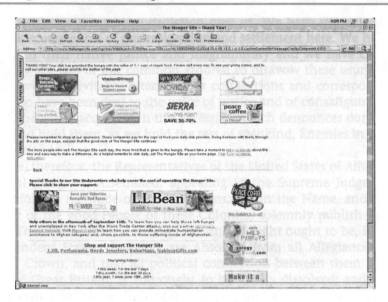

fight against hunger. In addition, the "Remember to Click" and "Forget Me Not" features bind viewers to the site. If viewers sign up for the "Remember to Click" option, an e-mail reminder regularly reminds them to visit the site and click to give food. The "Forget Me Not" option reminds the computer user whenever he or she begins to shop online to shop through *The Hunger Site.* Visitors can choose these options, and they can always be dismantled once they are chosen, giving individuals control over how they are marketed to and a connection to the Web site.

Distinguishing *The Hunger Site* from traditional print text is its embeddedness in a "web" of other pages. *The Hunger Site* links directly to pages that provide additional information about the site as well as sales and charitable giving opportunities. Some pages are official parts of *The Hunger Site,* others such as *Second Harvest,* which receives donations from *The Hunger Site,* are separate sites.

One aim of a comprehensive Web site is to provide answers to questions about the site. Unlike a print advertisement, *The Hunger Site* has enough space to provide, for example, information about the site owners and answers to frequently asked questions (FAQ) about the site. Readers interested in more information on *The Hunger Site* can do a general search of the Web to determine the legitimacy of the site.

Although it consists of multiple pages, *The Hunger Site* is also different from printed articles and books because it does not follow any traditional sense of order. Readers typically start on the site's home page, but from there they can go in multiple directions, each one equally logical.

The authors of *The Hunger Site* have not determined a set path for readers to follow: Viewers can find information about world hunger, about hunger in the United States, about the owners of the site, about ways of providing food to the hungry, and about bargains at L.L. Bean or Patagonia. The reader is in control of the direction to be taken in the text, and the possible directions are numerous and cater to multiple needs.

RESPONDING ONLINE

You have learned that writers need the responses of readers and other writers to improve their writing. As the influence of computers permeates our society and more people rely on the Internet to send e-mail, it has become ever easier for writers to distribute their writing and for readers to respond to it. Only a decade ago, if you wanted feedback for your writing, you had to either read it aloud to others or copy and distribute it by hand or postal mail. Both methods were cumbersome and time-consuming, even expensive. Electronic networks now allow your writing to be distributed almost instantaneously to dozens or even thousands of readers with virtually no copying or mailing costs. Readers can respond to you just as quickly and cheaply. Even though there can be pitfalls and problems with communicating online, the overall ease of use encourages writers to seek, and readers to provide, editorial feedback.

■ Guidelines for Responding Online

You know that in face-to-face conversation the words themselves constitute only a part of your message. Much of what you say is communicated through your body language and tone of voice. Written words provide a much narrower channel of communication, which is why you must be more careful when you write to someone than when you speak directly to them. Electronic writing, however, especially through e-mail, fosters a casualness and immediacy that often fools writers into assuming they are talking privately rather than writing publicly. Online you may find yourself writing quickly, carelessly, and intimately; without the help of your tone and body language, you may end up being seriously misunderstood. Words written hastily are often read much differently than intended; this is especially true when the writer attempts an ironic or sarcastic tone. For example, if a classmate walks up to you with a critical comment about one of your sentences and you respond by saying "I didn't realize you were so smart," the words, if unaccompanied by a placating smile and a pleasant, jocular tone, may come across as sarcastic or hostile. In e-writing, the same words appear without the mitigating body language and may be perceived as harsh, possibly insulting. You must keep this danger in mind as you respond online or risk alienating your reader.

Keep in mind, too, that e-mail may be read not only by your addressee but also by anyone with whom the addressee chooses to share your message. An intemperate or indiscreet message may be forwarded to other classmates or your instructor, or, depending on the limits of the system, to many other readers whom you do not know.

Experienced online communicators advocate a set of network etiquette guidelines called *Netiquette*. Here are some generally accepted Netiquette rules:

- Keep your sentences short and uncomplicated.

- Separate blocks of text — which should be no more than four or five lines long — by blank lines. For those rare occasions when a comment requires more than ten or fifteen consecutive lines of text, use subheadings on separate lines to guide your reader.

- Refer specifically to the text to which you are responding. You may want to quote directly from it, cutting and pasting phrases or sentences from the document to help show exactly what you are responding to.

- Greet the person(s) to whom you are writing politely and by name.

- Be wary about attempting to be funny. Humor, as just explained, often requires a context, tone of voice, and body language to emphasize that it is not to be taken seriously. Writing witty comments that are sure to be taken humorously calls for skill and care, and e-mail messages usually are written too quickly for either.

- Avoid profanity or invective, and be wary of brusque or abrupt statements. Consider how you would feel if someone wrote to you that way.

- Avoid discussion of politics or religion unless that is the specific topic of your message.

- Do not ridicule public figures. Your reader may not share your opinions of, say, Senator Edward Kennedy or radio talk show host Rush Limbaugh.

- Frame all comments in a helpful, not critical, tone. For instance, rather than beginning a critique with "I found a number of problems in your text," you may want to start out more like this: "You have some good ideas in this paper, and with a few changes I think it will do well."

EXERCISES

PREREADING

1. If you haven't read "Kids in the Mall: Growing Up Controlled" (p. 71), do the following. Take note of the title of the book in which this excerpt

appears. Now, write down briefly what you guess the attitude of the author will be toward his subject. Tell which words in the titles of the excerpt and the book suggest his approach. Next, read the quotation that heads the essay and the first paragraph. If you think there are further clues here, explain briefly how you interpreted them. (For example, did your own experience with malls enter into your thinking as you read?)

Keep your notes. Refer to them after you have read the whole article (and perhaps discussed it in class). How well did your preparation help you to find the main point and understand the examples that supported it? Are there other things you might do to improve your prereading?

ANNOTATING

2. Choose an editorial of at least two paragraphs in a newspaper or your school paper on a controversial subject that interests you. The title will probably reveal the subject. Annotate the editorial as you read, questioning, agreeing, objecting, offering additional ideas. (The annotation of the "The Pursuit of Whining," p. 32, will suggest ways of doing this, although your personal responses are what make the annotation useful.) Then read the editorial again. You should discover that annotating the article caused you to read more carefully, more critically, with greater comprehension and a more focused response.

EVALUATING

3. Summarize the claim of the editorial in one sentence. Omit the supporting data and concentrate on the thesis. Then explain briefly your reaction to it. Has the author proved his or her point? Your annotation will show you where you expressed doubt or approval. If you already know a good deal about the subject, perhaps you will be reasonably confident of your judgment. If not, you may find that your response is tentative and that you need to read further for more information about the subject and to consult guidelines for making evaluations about the elements of argument.

LISTENING

4. People sometimes object to lectures as an educational tool. Think about some of the specific lectures you have listened to recently, and analyze the reasons that you liked or disliked them (or liked some aspects and disliked others). Do you think that you learned everything that the lecturer intended you to learn? If the results were doubtful, how much did your listening skills, good or bad, contribute to the result? Should the lecturer have done something differently to improve your response?

5. Watch (and *listen* to) one of the afternoon talk shows like *Oprah Winfrey* in which audiences discuss a controversial social problem. (The *TV Guide* and daily newspapers often list the subject. Past topics on *Oprah* include when parents abduct their children and when children kill children.) Write a critical review of the discussion, mentioning as completely as you can the major claims, the most important evidence, and the

declared or hidden warrants. (Unspoken warrants or assumptions may be easier to identify in arguments on talk shows where visual and auditory clues can reveal what participants try to hide.) How much did the oral format contribute to success or failure of the argument(s)?

6. Listen to one of the television talk shows that feature invited experts. Write a review, telling how much you learned about the subject(s) of discussion. Be specific about the elements of the show that were either helpful or unhelpful to your understanding.

7. Listen with a friend or friends to a talk show discussion. Take notes as you listen. Then compare notes to discover if you agree on the outstanding points, the degree to which claims have been supported, and the part that seeing or hearing the discussion played in your evaluation. If there is disagreement about any of the elements, how do you account for it?

ONLINE

8. With three or four of your classmates select an argumentative essay in this book that all of you agree to read. Each of you should draft a response to the essay, either agreeing or disagreeing with the author's position, citing evidence to support your position. Then each of you prepare a letter soliciting a response to your draft from the members of your group. For example, you may want to state what your objective was, suggest what you think are the strengths and weaknesses of the draft, and ask what sort of revisions seem appropriate. E-mail the letter and the draft to each of your peer responders. Based on their comments, which should either be e-mailed to you or handwritten on a printed copy of your draft, revise your draft.

3

Claims

Claims, or propositions, represent answers to the question: "What are you trying to prove?" Although they are the conclusions of your arguments, they often appear as thesis statements. Claims can be classified as *claims of fact, claims of value,* and *claims of policy.*

CLAIMS OF FACT

Claims of fact assert that a condition has existed, exists, or will exist and that their support consists of factual information—information such as statistics, examples, and testimony that most responsible observers assume can be verified.

Many facts are not matters for argument: Our own senses can confirm them, and other observers will agree about them. We can agree that a certain number of students were in the classroom at a particular time, that lions make a louder sound than kittens, and that apples are sweeter than potatoes.

We can also agree about information that most of us can rarely confirm for ourselves—information in reference books, such as atlases, almanacs, and telephone directories; data from scientific resources about the physical world; and happenings reported in the media. We can agree on the reliability of such information because we trust the observers who report it.

However, the factual map is constantly being redrawn by new data in such fields as history and science that cause us to reevaluate our conclusions. For example, the discovery of the Dead Sea Scrolls in 1947 revealed that some books of the Bible—Isaiah, for one—were far older than we had thought. Researchers at New York Hospital–Cornell Medical Center say that many symptoms previously thought inevitable in the aging process are now believed to be treatable and reversible symptoms of depression.[1]

In your conversations with other students you probably generate claims of fact every day, some of which can be verified without much effort, others of which are more difficult to substantiate.

CLAIM: Most of the students in this class come from towns within fifty miles of Boston.

To prove this the arguer would need only to ask the students in the class where they come from.

CLAIM: Students who take their courses pass/fail make lower grades than those who take them for specific grades.

In this case the arguer would need to have access to student records showing the specific grades given by instructors. (In most schools the instructor awards a letter grade, which is then recorded as a pass or a fail if the student has elected this option.)

CLAIM: The Red Sox will win the pennant this year.

This claim is different from the others because it is an opinion about what will happen in the future. But it can be verified (in the future) and is therefore classified as a claim of fact.

More complex factual claims about political and scientific matters remain controversial because proof on which all or most observers will agree is difficult or impossible to obtain.

CLAIM: Bilingual programs are less effective than English-only programs in preparing students for higher education.

CLAIM: The only life in the universe exists on this planet.

Not all claims are so neatly stated or make such unambiguous assertions. Because we recognize that there are exceptions to most generalizations, we often qualify our claims with words such as *generally, usually, probably,* and *as a rule.* It would not be true to state flatly, for example, "College graduates earn more than high school graduates." This state-

[1] *New York Times,* February 20, 1983, sec. 22, p. 4.

ment is generally true, but we know that some high school graduates who are electricians or city bus drivers or sanitation workers earn more than college graduates who are schoolteachers or nurses or social workers. In making such a claim, therefore, the writer should qualify it with a word that limits the claim.

To support a claim of fact, the writer needs to produce sufficient and appropriate data—that is, examples, statistics, and testimony from reliable sources. Provided this requirement is met, the task of establishing a factual claim would seem to be relatively straightforward. But as you have probably already discovered in ordinary conversation, finding convincing support for factual claims can pose a number of problems. Whenever you try to establish a claim of fact, you will need to ask at least three questions about the material you plan to use: *What are sufficient and appropriate data? Who are the reliable authorities?* and *Have I made clear whether my statements are facts or inferences?*

■ Sufficient and Appropriate Data

The amount and kind of data for a particular argument depend on the importance and complexity of the subject. The more controversial the subject, the more facts and testimony you will need to supply. Consider the claim "The murder rate in New York City is lower this year than last year." If you want to prove the truth of this claim, obviously you will have to provide a larger quantity of data than for a claim that says, "By following three steps, you can train your dog to sit and heel in fifteen minutes." In examining your facts and opinions, an alert reader will want to know if they are accurate, current, and typical of other facts and opinions that you have not mentioned.

The reader will also look for testimony from more than one authority, although there may be cases where only one or two experts who have achieved a unique breakthrough in their field will be sufficient. These cases would probably occur most frequently in the physical sciences. The Nobel Prize winners James Watson and Francis Crick, who first discovered the structure of the DNA molecule, are an example of such experts. However, in the case of the so-called Hitler diaries that surfaced in 1983, at least a dozen experts—journalists, historians, bibliographers who could verify the age of the paper and the ink—were needed to establish that they were forgeries.

■ Reliable Authorities

Not all those who pronounce themselves experts are trustworthy. Your own experience has probably taught you that you cannot always believe the reports of an event by a single witness. The witness may be poorly trained to make accurate observations—about the size of a crowd, the speed of a vehicle, his distance from an object. Or his own physical conditions—illness, intoxication, disability—may prevent him from seeing or hearing or smelling accurately. The circumstances under which he observes the event—darkness, confusion, noise—may also impair his observation. In addition, the witness may be biased for or against the outcome of the event, as in a hotly contested baseball game, where the observer sees the play that he wants to see. You will find the problems associated with the biases of witnesses to be relevant to your work as a reader and writer of argumentative essays.

You will undoubtedly want to quote authors in some of your arguments. In most cases you will not be familiar with the authors. But there are guidelines for determining their reliability: the rank or title of the experts, the acceptance of their publications by other experts, their association with reputable universities, research centers, or think tanks. For example, for a paper on euthanasia, you might decide to quote from an article by Paul R. McHugh, the Henry Phipps Professor of Psychiatry at the Johns Hopkins University School of Medicine and psychiatrist in chief at the Johns Hopkins Hospital in Baltimore. For a paper on crime by youth groups, you might want to use material supplied by Elizabeth Glazer, chief of Crime Control Strategies in the U.S. Attorney's office for the Southern District of New York, where she previously served as chief of both the Organized Crime Unit and Violent Gang Unit. Most readers of your arguments would agree that these authors have impressive credentials in their fields.

What if several respectable sources are in conflict? What if the experts disagree? After a preliminary investigation of a controversial subject, you may decide that you have sufficient material to support your claim. But if you read further, you may discover that other material presented by equally qualified experts contradicts your original claim. In such circumstances you will find it impossible to make a definitive claim. (On pp. 157–70, in the treatment of support of a claim by evidence, you will find a more elaborate discussion of this vexing problem.)

■ Facts or Inferences

We have defined a fact as a statement that can be verified. An inference is "a statement about the unknown on the basis of the known."[2] The difference between facts and inferences is important to you as the writer of an argument because an inference is an *interpretation*, or an opinion reached after informed evaluation of evidence. As you and your classmates wait in your classroom on the first day of the semester, a middle-aged woman wearing a tweed jacket and a corduroy skirt appears and stands in the front of the room. You don't know who this woman is. However, based on what you do know about the appearance of many

---

[2]S. I. Hayakawa, *Language in Thought and Action* (New York: Harcourt, Brace, Jovanovich, 1978), p. 35.

college teachers and the fact that teachers usually stand in front of the classroom, you may *infer* that this woman is your teacher. You will probably be right. But you cannot be certain until you have more information. Perhaps you will find out that this woman has come from the department office to tell you that your teacher is sick and cannot meet the class today.

You have probably come across a statement such as the following in a newspaper or magazine: "Excessive television viewing has caused the steady decline in the reading ability of children and teenagers." Presented this way, the statement is clearly intended to be read as a factual claim that has been or can be proved. But it is an inference. The facts, which can be and have been verified, are (1) the reading ability of children and teenagers has declined and (2) the average child views television for six or more hours a day. (Whether this amount of time is "excessive" is also an opinion.) The cause-and-effect relation between the two facts is an interpretation of the investigator, who has examined both the reading scores and the amount of time spent in front of the television set and *inferred* that one is the cause of the other. The causes of the decline in reading scores are probably more complex than the original statement indicates. Since we can seldom or never create laboratory conditions for testing the influence of television separate from other influences in the family and the community, any statement about the connection between reading scores and television viewing can only be a guess.

By definition, no inference can ever do more than suggest probabilities. Of course, some inferences are much more reliable than others and afford a high degree of probability. Almost all claims in science are based on inferences, interpretations of data on which most scientists agree. Paleontologists find a few ancient bones from which they make inferences about an animal that might have been alive millions of years ago. We can never be absolutely certain that the reconstruction of the dinosaur in the museum is an exact copy of the animal it is supposed to represent, but the probability is fairly high because no other interpretation works so well to explain all the observable data—the existence of the bones in a particular place, their age, their relation to other fossils, and their resemblance to the bones of existing animals with which the paleontologist is familiar.

Inferences are profoundly important, and most arguments could not proceed very far without them. But an inference is not a fact. The writer of an argument must make it clear when he or she offers an inference, an interpretation, or an opinion that it is not a fact.

DEFENDING A CLAIM OF FACT

Here are some guidelines that should help you to defend a factual claim. (We'll say more about support of factual claims in Chapter 5.)

1. Be sure that the claim — what you are trying to prove — is clearly stated, preferably at the beginning of your paper.

2. Define terms that may be controversial or ambiguous. For example, in trying to prove that "radicals" had captured the student government, you would have to define "radicals," distinguishing them from "liberals" or members of other ideological groups, so that your readers would understand exactly what you meant.

3. As far as possible, make sure that your evidence — facts and opinions, or interpretations of the facts — fulfills the appropriate criteria. The data should be sufficient, accurate, recent, typical; the authorities should be reliable.

4. Make clear when conclusions about the data are inferences or interpretations, not facts. For example, you might write, "The series of lectures titled Modern Architecture, sponsored by our fraternity, was poorly attended because the students at this college aren't interested in discussions of art." What proof could you offer that this *was* the reason and that your statement was a *fact*? Perhaps there were other reasons that you hadn't considered.

5. Emphasize your most important evidence by placing it at the beginning or the end of your paper (the most emphatic positions in an essay) and devoting more space to it.

SAMPLE ANNOTATED ANALYSIS: CLAIM OF FACT

A Reassuring Scorecard for Affirmative Action
MICHAEL M. WEINSTEIN

Introduction:
a) Review of the attack
on affirmative action

Affirmative action—preferential treatment toward women and minority applicants as practiced by employers, university admissions officers, and government contractors—remains under attack thirty-two years after President Johnson ordered federal contractors to seek female and minority employees. Two states have voted to wipe out the use of race- and gender-

Michael M. Weinstein, Ph.D., is a senior fellow on the Council on Foreign Relations. He was on the editorial board of the *New York Times* when he wrote this October 17, 2000, article.

based preferences by state agencies. Parents have challenged the race-based admissions policies of public schools. Even Joseph Lieberman, the Democratic candidate for vice president, once opposed policies "based on group preference instead of individual merit."

b) Specific criticism

Some of affirmative action's critics contend that preferential hiring and admissions are always wrong in principle no matter how attractive the consequences. But other critics focus on affirmative action's alleged failings. According to this argument, the policy creates divisive workplaces, breeds cynicism and corruption, and hurts many of the individuals it is supposed to help. That debate should turn on the facts. Instead it has been fueled almost entirely by anecdotes—until now.

Refutation: authoritative source of new data

In the most recent issue of the *Journal of Economic Literature*, a publication of the American Economic Association, two respected economists provide an eighty-five page review of over two hundred serious scientific studies of affirmative action. Harry Holzer of Georgetown University and David Neumark of Michigan State University ferret out every statistic from the studies to measure the effects of affirmative action. Harsh critics of affirmative action will not find much comfort.

Claim: general benefits for women and minorities under affirmative action

The authors concede the evidence is sometimes murky. Yet they find that affirmative action produces tangible benefits for women, for minority entrepreneurs, students, and workers, and for the overall economy. Employers adopting the policy increase the relative number of women and minority employees by an average of between 10 and 15 percent. Affirmative action has helped boost the percentage of blacks attending college by a factor of three and the percentage of blacks enrolled in medical school by a factor of four since the early 1960s. Between 1982 and 1991 the number of federal contracts going to black-owned businesses rose by 125 percent, even though the total number of federal contracts rose by less than 25 percent during the period.

Support:
a) Data about employment, education, business

To no one's surprise, the two economists rivet on economic performance. Here, the survey is 5

b) Data about credentials

c) Data about worker performance

d) Data about student performance

e) Data about social benefits

interesting for what it does *not* find. There is, the authors say, little credible evidence that affirmative action appointees perform badly or diminish the overall performance of the economy.

Women hired under affirmative action, they say, largely match their male counterparts in credentials and performance. Blacks and Hispanics hired under affirmative action generally lag behind on credentials, such as education, but usually perform about as well as nonminority employees.

In a separate study, Mr. Holzer and Mr. Neumark interviewed thousands of supervisors and showed that they ranked most affirmative action hires roughly the same as ordinary hires. The authors find that companies undertaking affirmative action use extensive recruitment and training to bring workers who fall a notch below average on credentials up to the performance level of other workers.

Critics have often pointed to the wide gap between SAT scores of black and white students admitted to selective universities as proof that they are lowering standards for minority students and putting them in settings they cannot handle. But the use of a test gap as a measure of reverse discrimination is misleading. Much of the gap would exist even if admissions were race-blind. Colleges pull applicants from a population that includes many more high-scoring whites than blacks.

A discrimination-free procedure would start by tapping the pool, largely white, of high scorers and then turn to the pool of lower-scoring whites and blacks. The average test scores for whites admitted to the college would thus exceed that of the blacks admitted.

To be sure, some selective universities add to   10 the test gap by giving preference to minority applicants. But, the data shows, black students at elite colleges graduate at greater rates than blacks at less demanding colleges, disproving claims that affirmative action disserves minority students.

The Holzer-Neumark survey shows that affirmative action in admissions has produced significant social benefits. For example, black doctors choose more often than their white medical school classmates to serve indigent or minority patients in inner cities and rural areas.

Conclusion: Contrary to criticism, evidence justifies affirmative action.

Though favorable, these findings hardly end the debate on affirmative action. The critics who refuse to accept government-sanctioned racial or gender preferences no matter what the benefit will continue to object. Affirmative action can be misused, as when whites running a company create a fiction of black ownership to qualify for credits in seeking government contracts. But the evidence marshaled by the authors largely vindicates affirmative action and should provide the ammunition for rebutting those critics who refuse to take facts into account.

■ Analysis

This article offers evidence that affirmative action provides benefits to women and minorities. A claim of fact often responds to some widely held belief that the author considers to be wrong—in this case, the failure of affirmative action. We need to ask three questions about a claim of fact: Are the data sufficient and appropriate? Are the authorities reliable? Are the distinctions between facts and inferences clear? Within its brief compass, this argument comes close to satisfying these criteria. In addition, its organization is straightforward, with clearly defined introduction, body, and conclusion.

The first three paragraphs constitute the introduction. First, the author reviews some of the claims of the opposition. At the end of the second paragraph, he makes clear his own emphasis: "That debate should turn on the facts." He then cites his source for the facts—a report in a respected professional journal by two university economists, who have examined the data on affirmative action in over two hundred serious scientific studies. This information reassures the reader that the first two criteria for judging a claim of fact will be met.

The body of the essay contains support for the claim, first in a short summary, then in substantial detail. Much of the data is statistical, a specific form of information that most readers find convincing and relatively easy to assimilate. (Of course, readers must regard the source as trustworthy.) The author has offered some interpretations—in paragraph 8, for example—to clarify what he considers a misunderstanding. Notice also the use of "To be sure," an expression that usually indicates that the writer recognizes an exception to his view. But the argument stands firmly on the facts. The ending is one often used by debaters—a modest challenge to the opposing side.

A NOTE ON CAUSAL ARGUMENT

Causal argument attempts to establish a relationship between two events or conditions by speculating about cause and effect. Suppose you read a report that states that more women than men are enrolled in colleges and universities. You may wonder what has caused this development or what are and will be the consequences for society of a population in which women are better educated than men. Your essay could answer one of these questions by examining one event or condition for either its causes or its effects. In a long paper you could answer both questions.

Several of the essays in this book use cause-and-effect development to support their claims. "A New Look, an Old Battle" (p. 184) describes the positive effects on health of stem-cell research. "Happiness Is a Warm Planet" (p. 83) suggests that a cause, global warming, will produce beneficial effects for human beings. "Kids in the Mall: Growing Up Controlled" (p. 71) begins with an effect—many American teens spend a lot of time at the mall—and provides probable causes for this behavior.

Such arguments—although we engage in them every day, both formally and informally—are more complicated than they seem and often highly controversial. For one thing, the cause of even the most ordinary event involving human behavior is not always easy to identify. Events usually have more than one cause and often have a chain of causes that began well before the immediate cause. We can often find evidence of this complexity when we ask the question "Why?" about events in our own lives. In literature, too, we see the search for meaning in a chain of events. Macbeth does not murder King Duncan only because Lady Macbeth urges him to do so. He has already heard a prophecy that he will be king; in addition, he has tasted power in his recent elevation to Thane of Cawdor. Even after we have learned about these provocations, we look for other causes in his character and his history.

Second, we cannot perform the kinds of controlled experiments in human behavior that verify causes in the physical sciences. We are told, for example, that married men live longer than unmarried men. It would be interesting and useful to know why, but the answer will probably not be found in the laboratory. For the present the causes, certainly more than one and rooted in psychology, can only be guessed.

Lastly, when two things occur in close proximity, we may leap to the conclusion that one thing is the cause of the other. Superstitions are the most familiar examples of such thinking. One book sums up the difficulty this way:

> Scientists are keenly aware of how easy it is to uncover associations and how hard it is to determine whether these links are actually cause-and-effect relationships. If you select a group of people and compile data about their health, lifestyle, and environment, you could uncover hundreds of associations. You may find direct associations between shirt size

Writer's Guide to the Causal Paper
Writing an Essay of Cause and Effect

1. You can begin your argument by describing the situation and by stating both your claim and your reasons for addressing this question. We often undertake the examination of causes and effects to explain or solve a problem.

2. Make an outline or notes of the main ideas that will support your claim. In a paper of fewer than 700 words, you probably cannot follow a long chain of causes. In fact, you may discover that only one important cause or effect deserves development in a short paper. In "Divorce and Our National Values" (p. 285), the author provides extended proof for one significant cause of divorce — our commitment to self-fulfillment.

3. Since causes are often hard to identify, you should use as many examples, studies by experts, graphs, etc. as you can accommodate to prove that there is a pattern, that the cause of some condition is not an anomaly or irregularity.

4. If your evidence shows that some causes in your outline seem stronger than others, emphasize the strong causes, and omit those for which the evidence is weak.

5. Be cautious in predicting that certain effects follow or will follow a particular cause or causes, and qualify your predictions. This means avoiding words like *always* and *never*. The past may not be a reliable guide to the future, and experts make predictions that sometimes are proved wrong.

6. When no solid evidence can be found, an educated guess can sometimes serve as a modest substitute. Educated guesses are reasonable inferences that are based on experience and common sense and are capable of proof. Analogies and comparisons to similar situations can be helpful, but remember that analogies are not proof.

7. Anticipate objections to your own explanations and predictions. If the objections are widely held, acknowledge them and try to point out their weaknesses.

8. Your essay may also rebut statements about cause and effect with which you disagree. Ideas that you oppose — for good reasons, of course — will inspire some of your most stimulating and insightful essays. In other college courses you may have acquired data that contradict conclusions about situations you are familiar with.

and blood pressure, or body weight and ownership of Ford pickup trucks. . . . But few of these links would be causal. . . . The physical height of children increases as their lifetime total of hours spent watching television increases. Does television watching promote physical growth?[3]

[3]Theodore Schick Jr. and Lewis Vaughan, *How to Think about Weird Things* (Mountain View, Calif.: Mayfield, 1995), p. 179.

Despite the problems associated with isolating the causes of things both ordinary and mysterious, the importance of sound cause-and-effect reasoning can hardly be overestimated. Think how few advances medical science made before researchers could prove that certain organisms cause disease. In the social sciences causes are much harder to find, but solutions for crime, poverty, poor education, bigotry, and dozens of other problems depend in large part on uncovering those causes.

Elsewhere in this book you will find other references to cause-and-effect argument: causal connection (p. 160), doubtful-cause fallacy (p. 293), and cause credibility (p. 342).

CLAIMS OF VALUE

Unlike claims of fact, which attempt to prove that something is true and which can be validated by reference to the data, claims of value make a judgment. They express approval or disapproval. They attempt to prove that some action, belief, or condition is right or wrong, good or bad, beautiful or ugly, worthwhile or undesirable.

CLAIM: Democracy is superior to any other form of government.

CLAIM: Killing animals for sport is wrong.

CLAIM: The Sam Rayburn Building in Washington is an aesthetic failure.

Some claims of value are simply expressions of tastes, likes and dislikes, or preferences and prejudices. The Latin proverb "De gustibus non est disputandum" states that we cannot dispute about tastes. Suppose you express a preference for chocolate over vanilla. If your listener should ask why you prefer this flavor, you cannot refer to an outside authority or produce data or appeal to her moral sense to convince her that your preference is justified.

Many claims of value, however, can be defended or attacked on the basis of standards that measure the worth of an action, a belief, or an object. As far as possible, our personal likes and dislikes should be supported by reference to these standards. Value judgments occur in any area of human experience, but whatever the area, the analysis will be the same. We ask the arguer who is defending a claim of value: *What are the standards or criteria for deciding that this action, this belief, or this object is good or bad, beautiful or ugly, desirable or undesirable? Does the thing you are defending fulfill these criteria?*

There are two general areas in which people often disagree about matters of value: aesthetics and morality. They are also the areas that offer the greatest challenge to the writer. What follows is a discussion of some of the elements of analysis that you should consider in defending a claim of value in these areas.

Aesthetics is the study of beauty and the fine arts. Controversies over works of art—the aesthetic value of books, paintings, sculpture, architecture, dance, drama, and movies—rage fiercely among experts and laypeople alike. They may disagree on the standards for judging or, even if they agree about standards, may disagree about how successfully the art object under discussion has met these standards.

Consider a discussion about popular music. Hearing someone praise the singing of Manu Chao, a hugely popular European singer now playing to American crowds, you might ask why he is highly regarded. You expect Chao's fans to say more than "I like him" or "He's great." You expect them to give reasons to support their claims. They might show you a short review from a respected newspaper that says, "Mr. Chao's gift is simplicity. His music owes a considerable amount to Bob Marley . . . but Mr. Chao has a nasal, regular-guy voice, and instead of the Wailers' brooding, bass-heavy undertow, Mr. Chao's band delivers a lighter bounce. His tunes have the singing directness of nursery rhymes."[4] Chao's fans accept these criteria for judging a singer's appeal.

You may not agree that simplicity, directness, and a regular-guy voice are the most important qualities in a popular singer. But the establishment of standards itself offers material for a discussion or an argument. You may argue about the relevance of the criteria, or you may agree with the criteria but argue about the success of the singer in meeting them. Perhaps you prefer complexity to simplicity. Or even if you choose simplicity, you may not think that Chao has exhibited this quality to good effect.

It is probably not surprising then, that, despite wide differences in taste, professional critics more often than not agree on criteria and whether an art object has met the criteria. For example, almost all movie critics agree that *Citizen Kane* and *Gone with the Wind* are superior films. They also agree that *Plan 9 from Outer Space,* a horror film, is terrible.

Value claims about morality express judgments about the rightness or wrongness of conduct or belief. Here disagreements are as wide and deep as in the arts. The first two examples on page 68 reveal how controversial such claims can be. Although you and your reader may share many values—among them a belief in democracy, a respect for learning, and a desire for peace—you may also disagree, even profoundly, about other values. The subject of divorce, for example, despite its prevalence in our society, can produce a conflict between people who have differing moral standards. Some people may insist on adherence to absolute standards, arguing that the values they hold are based on immutable religious precepts derived from God and biblical scripture. Since marriage is sacred, divorce is always wrong, they say, whether or not the conditions of society change. Other people may argue that values are relative, based on the changing needs of societies in different places and at different times. Since marriage is an institution created by human beings at a

---

[4]Jon Pareles, *New York Times,* July 10, 2001, p. B1.

Writer's Guide to the Evaluation Paper
Defending a Claim of Value

The following suggestions are a preliminary guide to the defense of a value claim. (We discuss value claims further in Chapter 5.)

1. Try to make clear that the values or principles you are defending are important and relatively more significant than other values. Keep in mind that you and your readers may differ about their relative importance. For example, although your readers may agree with you that brilliant photography is important in a film, they may think that a well-written script is even more crucial to its success. And although they may agree that freedom of the press is a mainstay of democracy, they may regard the right to privacy as even more fundamental.

2. Suggest that adherence to the values you are defending will bring about good results in some specific situation or bad results if respect for the values is ignored. You might argue, for example, that a belief in freedom of the press will make citizens better informed and the country stronger while a failure to protect this freedom will strengthen the forces of authoritarianism.

3. Since value terms are abstract, use examples and illustrations to clarify meanings and make distinctions. Comparisons and contrasts are especially helpful. If you use the term *heroism*, can you provide examples to differentiate between *heroism* and *foolhardiness* or *exhibitionism*?

4. Use testimony of others to prove that knowledgeable or highly regarded people share your values.

particular time in history to serve particular social needs, they may say, it can also be dissolved when other social needs arise. The same conflicts between moral values might occur in discussions of abortion or suicide.

As a writer you cannot always know what system of values your reader holds. Yet it might be possible to find a rule on which almost all readers agree. One such rule was expressed by the eighteenth-century German philosopher Immanuel Kant: "Man and, in general, every rational being exists as an end in itself and not merely as a means to be arbitrarily used by this or that will." Kant's prescription urges us not to subject any creature to a condition that it has not freely chosen. In other words, we cannot use other creatures, as in slavery, for our own purposes. (Some philosophers would extend this rule to the treatment of animals by human beings.) This standard of judgment has, in fact, been invoked in recent years against medical experimentation on human beings in prisons and hospitals without their consent and against the sterilization of poor or mentally retarded women without their consent.

Nevertheless, even where people agree about standards for measuring behavior, a majority preference is not enough to confer moral value. If in a certain neighborhood a majority of heterosexual men decide to harass a few gay men and lesbians, that consensus does not make their action right. In formulating value claims, you should be prepared to ask and answer questions about the way in which your value claims and those of others have been arrived at. Lionel Ruby, an American philosopher, sums it up in these words: "The law of rationality tells us that we ought to justify our beliefs by evidence and reasons, instead of asserting them dogmatically."[5]

Of course, you will not always be able to persuade those with whom you argue that your values are superior to theirs and that they should therefore change their attitudes. Nor, on the other hand, would you want to compromise your values or pretend that they were different to win an argument. What you can and should do, however, as Lionel Ruby advises, is give *good reasons* that you think one thing is better than another. If as a child you asked why it was wrong to take your brother's toys, you might have been told by an exasperated parent, "Because I say so." Some adults still give such answers in defending their judgments, but such answers are not arguments and do nothing to win the agreement of others.

SAMPLE ANNOTATED ANALYSIS: CLAIM OF VALUE

Kids in the Mall: Growing Up Controlled

WILLIAM SEVERINI KOWINSKI

> Butch heaved himself up and loomed over the group. "Like it was different for me," he piped. "My folks used to drop me off at the shopping mall every morning and leave me all day. It was like a big free baby-sitter, you know? One night they never came back for me. Maybe they moved away. Maybe there's some kind of a Bureau of Missing Parents I could check with."
>
> —Richard Peck,
> *Secrets of the Shopping Mall,*
> a novel for teenagers

[5] *The Art of Making Sense* (New York: Lippincott, 1968), p. 271.

William Severini Kowinski is a freelance writer who has been the book review editor and managing arts editor of the *Boston Phoenix*. This excerpt is from his book *The Malling of America: An Inside Look at the Great Consumer Paradise* (1985).

Introduction:
interesting personal
anecdote

From his sister at Swarthmore, I'd heard about a kid in Florida whose mother picked him up after school every day, drove him straight to the mall, and left him there until it closed—all at his insistence. I'd heard about a boy in Washington who, when his family moved from one suburb to another, pedaled his bicycle five miles every day to get back to his old mall, where he once belonged.

Additional examples of
mall experience

These stories aren't unusual. The mall is a common experience for the majority of American youth; they have probably been going there all their lives. Some ran within their first large open space, saw their first fountain, bought their first toy, and read their first book in a mall. They may have smoked their first cigarette or first joint, or turned them down, had their first kiss or lost their virginity in the mall parking lot. Teenagers in America now spend more time in the mall than anywhere else but home and school. Mostly it is their choice, but some of that mall time is put in as the result of two-paycheck and single-parent households, and the lack of other viable alternatives. But are these kids being harmed by the mall?

Reasons for the
author's interest

I wondered first of all what difference it makes for adolescents to experience so many important moments in the mall. They are, after all, at play in the fields of its little world and they learn its ways; they adapt to it and make it adapt to them. It's here that these kids get their street sense, only it's mall sense. They are learning the ways of a large-scale, artificial environment; its subtleties and flexibilities, its particular pleasures and resonances, and the attitudes it fosters.

The presence of so many teenagers for so much time was not something mall developers planned on. In fact, it came as a big surprise. But kids became a fact of mall life very easily, and the International Council of Shopping Centers found it necessary to commission a study, which they published along with a guide to mall managers on how to handle the teenage incursion.

Expert opinion

The study found that "teenagers in suburban 5 centers are bored and come to the shopping centers mainly as a place to go. Teenagers in suburban centers spent more time fighting, drinking, littering and walking than did their urban counterparts, but presented fewer overall problems." The report observed that "adolescents congregated in groups of two to four and predominantly at locations selected by them rather than management." This probably had something to do with the decision to install game arcades, which allow management to channel these restless adolescents into naturally contained areas away from major traffic points of adult shoppers.

Why the malls encourage adolescent presence

The guide concluded that mall management should tolerate and even encourage the teenage presence because, in the words of the report, "The vast majority support the same set of values as does shopping center management." *The same set of values* means simply that mall kids are already preprogrammed to be consumers and that the mall can put the finishing touches to them as hard-core, lifelong shoppers just like everybody else. That, after all, is what the mall is about. So it shouldn't be surprising that in spending a lot of time there, adolescents find little that challenges the assumption that the goal of life is to make money and buy products, or that just about everything else in life is to be used to serve those ends.

Disadvantages:
a) Exposure to high-consumption society

Growing up in a high-consumption society already adds inestimable pressure to kids' lives. Clothes consciousness has invaded the grade schools, and popularity is linked with having the best, newest clothes in the currently acceptable styles. Even what they read has been affected. "Miss [Nancy] Drew wasn't obsessed with her wardrobe," noted the *Wall Street Journal*. "But today the mystery in teen fiction for girls is what outfit the heroine will wear next." Shopping has become a survival skill and there is certainly no better place to learn it than the mall, where its importance is powerfully reinforced and certainly never questioned.

b) Social pressures to buy

The mall as a university of suburban materialism, where Valley Girls and Boys from coast to coast are educated in consumption, has its other lessons in this era of change in family life and sexual mores and their economic and social ramifications. The plethora of products in the mall, plus the pressure on teens to buy them, may contribute to the phenomenon that psychologist David Elkind calls "the hurried child": kids who are exposed to too much of the adult world too quickly and must respond with a sophistication that belies their still-tender emotional development. Certainly the adult products marketed for children—form-fitting designer jeans, sexy tops for preteen girls—add to the social pressure to look like an adult, along with the home-grown need to understand adult finances (why mothers must work) and adult emotions (when parents divorce).

c) Mall as babysitter

Kids spend so much time at the mall partly because their parents allow it and even encourage it. The mall is safe, doesn't seem to harbor any unsavory activities, and there is adult supervision; it is, after all, a controlled environment. So the temptation, especially for working parents, is to let the mall be their baby-sitter. At least the kids aren't watching TV. But the mall's role as a surrogate mother may be more extensive and more profound.

Karen Lansky, a writer living in Los Angeles, 10 has looked into the subject, and she told me some of her conclusions about the effects on its

d) Mall as substitute for home

teenaged denizens of the mall's controlled and controlling environment. "Structure is the dominant idea, since true 'mall rats' lack just that in their home lives," she said, "and adolescents about to make the big leap into growing up crave more structure than our modern society cares to acknowledge." Karen pointed out some of the elements malls supply that kids used to get from their families, like warmth (Strawberry Shortcake dolls and similar cute and cuddly merchandise), old-fashioned mothering ("We do it all for you," the fast-food slogan), and even home cooking (the "homemade" treats at the food court).

e) Encouragement of passivity

The problem in all this, as Karen Lansky sees it, is that while families nurture children by encouraging growth through the assumption of responsibility and then by letting them rest in the bosom of the family from the rigors of growing up, the mall as a structural mother encourages passivity and consumption, as long as the kid doesn't make trouble. Therefore all they learn about becoming adults is how to act and how to consume.

f) Undemanding jobs

Kids are in the mall not only in the passive role of shoppers—they also work there, especially as fast-food outlets infiltrate the mall's enclosure. There they learn how to hold a job and take responsibility, but still within the same value context. When *CBS Reports* went to Oak Park Mall in suburban Kansas City, Kansas, to tape part of their hour-long consideration of malls, "After the Dream Comes True," they interviewed a teenaged girl who worked in a fast-food outlet there. In a sequence that didn't make the final program, she described the major goal of her present life, which was to perfect the curl on top of the ice-cream cones that were her store's specialty. If she could do that, she would be moved from the lowly soft-drink dispenser to the more prestigious ice-cream division, the curl on top of the status ladder at her restaurant. These are the achievements that are important at the mall.

Example

Details

Other benefits of such jobs may also be over-rated, according to Laurence D. Steinberg of the University of California at Irvine's social ecology department, who did a study on teenage employment. Their jobs, he found, are generally simple, mindlessly repetitive and boring. They don't really learn anything, and the jobs don't lead anywhere. Teenagers also work primarily with other teenagers; even their supervisors are often just a little older than they are. "Kids need to spend time with adults," Steinberg told me. "Although they get benefits from peer relationships, without parents and other adults it's one-side socialization. They hang out with each other, have age-segregated jobs, and watch TV."

Advantages:
a) Time with other
adolescents

Perhaps much of this is not so terrible or even so terribly different. Now that they have so much more to contend with in their lives, adolescents probably need more time to spend with other adolescents without adult impositions, just to sort things out. Though it is more concentrated in the mall (and therefore perhaps a clearer target), the value system there is really the dominant one of the whole society. Attitudes about curiosity, initiative, self-expression, empathy, and disinterested learning aren't necessarily made in the mall; they are mirrored there, perhaps a bit more intensely—as through a glass brightly.

b) Educational opportunities

Besides, the mall is not without its educational opportunities. There are bookstores, where there is at least a short shelf of classics at great prices, and other books from which it is possible to learn more than how to do sit-ups. There are tools, from hammers to VCRs, and products, from clothes to records, that can help the young find and express themselves. There are older people with stories, and places to be alone or to talk one-on-one with a kindred spirit. And there is always the passing show. 15

The mall itself may very well be an education about the future. I was struck with the realization, as early as my first forays into Greengate, that the mall is only one of a number of enclosed and controlled environments that are part of the lives of today's young. The mall is just an extension, say, of those large suburban schools—only there's Karmelkorn instead of chem lab, the ice rink instead of the gym: It's high school without the impertinence of classes.

Conclusion and <u>claim</u> of value: mall as a controlled environment that teaches a few valuable lessons

Growing up, moving from home to school to the mall—from enclosure to enclosure, transported in cars—is a curiously continuous process, without much in the way of contrast or contact with unenclosed reality. Places must tend to blur into one another. But whatever differences and dangers there are in this, the skills these adolescents are learning may turn out to be useful in their later lives. For we seem to be moving inexorably into an age of preplanned and regulated environments, and this is the world they will inherit.

Still, it might be better if they had more of a choice. One teenaged girl confessed to *CBS Reports* that she sometimes felt she was missing something by hanging out at the mall so much. "But I'm here," she said, "and this is what I have."

■ Analysis

Kowinski has chosen to evaluate one aspect of an extraordinarily success-ful economic and cultural phenomenon—the commercial mall. He asks whether the influence of the mall on adolescents is good or bad. The answer seems to be a little of both. The good values may be described as exposure to a variety of experiences, a protective structure for adolescents who often live in unstable environments, and immersion in a world that may well serve as an introduction to adulthood. But the bad values, which Kowinski thinks are more influential (as the title suggests) are those of the shoppers' paradise, a society that believes in acquisition and consumption of goods as ultimate goals, and too much control over the choices available to adolescents. The tone of the judgment, however, is moderate and reflects a balanced, even scholarly, attitude. More than other arguments, the treatment of values requires such a voice, one which respects differences of opinion among readers. But serious doesn't mean heavy. His style is formal but highly readable, brightened by interesting examples and precise details. The opening paragraph is a strikingly effective lead.

Some of his observations are personal, but others are derived from studies by professional researchers, from *CBS Reports* to a well-known writer on childhood. These studies give weight and authority to his conclusions. Here and there we detect an appealing sympathy for adolescents who spend time in their controlled mall environments.

Like any thoughtful social commentator, Kowinski casts a wide net. He sees the mall not only as a hangout for teens but as a good deal more, an institution that offers insights into family life and work, the changing urban culture, the nature of contemporary entertainment, even glimpses of a somewhat forbidding future.

CLAIMS OF POLICY

Claims of policy argue that certain conditions should exist. As the name suggests, they advocate adoption of policies or courses of action because problems have arisen that call for solution. Almost always *should* or *ought to* or *must* is expressed or implied in the claim.

CLAIM: Voluntary prayer should be permitted in public schools.

CLAIM: A dress code should be introduced for all public high schools.

CLAIM: A law should permit sixteen-year-olds and parents to "divorce" each other in cases of extreme incompatibility.

CLAIM: Mandatory jail terms should be imposed for drunk driving violations.

In defending such claims of policy you may find that you must first convince your audience that a problem exists. This will require that, as part of your longer argument, you make a factual claim, offering data to prove that present conditions are unsatisfactory. You may also find it necessary to refer to the values that support your claim. Then you will be ready to introduce your policy, to persuade your audience that the solution you propose will solve the problem.

We will examine a policy claim in which all these parts are at work. The claim can be stated as follows: "The time required for an undergraduate degree should be extended to five years." Immediate agreement with this policy among student readers would certainly not be universal. Some students would not recognize a problem. They would say, "The college curriculum we have now is fine. There's no need for a change. Besides, we don't want to spend more time in school." First, then, the arguer would have to persuade a skeptical audience that there is a problem—that four years of college are no longer enough because the stock of knowledge in almost all fields of study continues to increase. The arguer would provide data to show that students today have many more choices in history, literature, and science than students had in those fields a generation ago. She would also emphasize the value of greater

Writer's Guide to the Proposal Paper
Defending a Claim of Policy

The following steps will help you organize arguments for a claim of policy.

1. Make your proposal clear. The terms in the proposal should be precisely defined.

2. If necessary, establish that there is a need for a change. When changes have been resisted, present reasons that explain this resistance. (It is often wrongly assumed that people cling to cultural practices long after their significance and necessity have eroded. But rational human beings observe practices that serve a purpose. The fact that you and I may see no value or purpose in the activities of another is irrelevant.)

3. Consider the opposing arguments. You may want to state the opposing arguments in a brief paragraph before answering them in the body of your argument.

4. Devote the major part of your essay to proving that your proposal is an answer to the opposing arguments and enumerating its distinct benefits for your readers.

5. Support your proposal with solid data, but don't neglect the moral considerations and the commonsense reasons, which may be even more persuasive.

knowledge and more schooling compared to the value of other goods the audience cherishes, such as earlier independence. Finally, the arguer would offer a plan for implementing her policy. Her plan would have to consider initial psychological resistance, revision of the curriculum, costs of more instruction, and costs of lost production in the workforce. Most important, she would point out the benefits for both individuals and society if this policy were adopted.

In this example, we assumed that the reader would disagree that a problem existed. In many cases, however, the reader may agree that there is a problem but disagree with the arguer about the way to solve it. Most of us, no doubt, agree that we want to reduce or eliminate the following problems: misbehavior and vandalism in schools, drunk driving, crime on the streets, child abuse, pornography, pollution. But how should we go about solving those problems? What public policy will give us well-behaved, diligent students who never destroy school property? Safe streets where no one is ever robbed or assaulted? Loving homes where no child is ever mistreated? Some members of society would choose to introduce rules or laws that punish infractions so severely that wrongdoers would be unwilling or unable to repeat their offenses. Other members of society would prefer policies that attempt to rehabilitate or reeducate offenders through training, therapy, counseling, and new opportunities.

SAMPLE ANNOTATED ANALYSIS: CLAIM OF POLICY

Dependency or Death?
Oregonians Make a Chilling Choice

WESLEY J. SMITH

Introduction: misinterpretation of information in a new study of assisted suicide

Assisted suicide in Oregon has operated in a shroud of secrecy since the procedure was legalized by a 1997 referendum. But a new study, published in the *New England Journal of Medicine*, purports to shed light on the law's actual workings. Advocates of assisted suicide

Wesley J. Smith is an attorney and author or coauthor of eight books, including *Culture of Death: The Assault on Medical Ethics in America* (2001). Smith's writing and opinion columns on medical ethics, legal ethics, and public affairs have appeared in publications throughout the country, including *Newsweek*, the *New York Times*, and the *Wall Street Journal*, the source of this February 2, 1999, piece.

Refutation:
a) Real reason for suicide

b) Statement of the problem

Support:
a) Fears of the disabled and the elderly

Expression of values

b) Hasty decisions of doctors

claim the report proves all is well. But a close reading reveals that many of the worries of assisted-suicide opponents are entirely justified.

Fifteen people in Oregon, we are told, legally committed suicide with the assistance of their doctors in 1998. According to the report, not one of them was forced into the act by intractable pain or suffering. Rather, those who died had strong personal beliefs in individual autonomy and chose suicide based primarily on fears of future dependence.

That isn't how assisted suicide was supposed to work. For many years, we have been told repeatedly by advocates that assisted suicide is to be a "last resort," applied only when nothing else can be done to alleviate "unrelenting and intolerable suffering." Yet pain wasn't a factor in a single one of the Oregon suicides. Thus, rather than being a limited procedure performed out of extreme medical urgency, legalization in Oregon has actually widened the category of conditions for which physician-hastened death is seen as legitimate.

Disability-rights advocates point out that allowing assisted suicide based upon fear of needing help going to the toilet, bathing, and performing other daily life activities will involve far more disabled and elderly people than terminally ill ones. They also note that dependency is an issue primarily for people who are not actually dependent and that like other difficulties in life dependency is a circumstance to which people adjust with time. To accept the notion that worry about the potential need for living assistance is a legitimate reason for doctors to write lethal prescriptions is to put disabled and elderly people at lethal risk. The dehumanizing message is that society regards such lives as undignified and not worth living. That is why nine national disability-rights organizations have come out strongly against legalizing assisted suicide and none support it.

The study also reports that the people who 5 committed assisted suicide had "shorter" relationships with the doctors who prescribed lethally than did a control group of patients who

Example

died naturally. The exact time difference is not given, but we do know from earlier media reports that it may be quite short. The first woman to commit assisted suicide in Oregon had a two-and-a-half-week relationship with the doctor who wrote her lethal prescription. Her own doctor had refused to assist her suicide, as had a second doctor who diagnosed her with depression. So she went to an advocacy group, which referred her to a doctor willing to do the deed. Hers was not a unique case. The report states that six of the fifteen people sought lethal prescriptions from two or more doctors.

Assisted suicide proponents told us this wouldn't happen either. They promised that assisted suicide would only occur after a deep exploration of values between patients and doctors who had long-term relationships. Thanks to the study, we now know that death decisions are being made by doctors the patients barely know. This isn't careful medical practice; it is rampant Kevorkianism.

c) Omission of data from the study

The study is as notable for what it omits as for what it includes. Information about the people who committed assisted suicide came from death-prescribing doctors. Treating doctors who did not participate in their patients' deaths — professionals who could have provided invaluable information about the health of the people who died — were not interviewed. Nor were the doctors who refused to write lethal prescriptions. Family members were not contacted either. Significantly, the investigators made no attempt to learn whether the prescribing doctors were affiliated with assisted-suicide advocacy groups, a matter of some importance if we are to judge whether the decisions to prescribe lethally were based on medicine or ideology. Moreover, none of the patients were autopsied to determine whether they were actually terminally ill.

Examples

d) Data from the Netherlands of unauthorized euthanasia

Near the end of the report, investigators admit that they do not know whether any unreported assisted suicides occurred. If history is any example, such deaths probably did happen. A recent *Journal of Medical Ethics* study about euthanasia in the Netherlands reveals that the

Dutch policy is "beyond effective control" since 59 percent of doctors do not report euthanasia or assisted suicide to authorities as required by law. (In Oregon, there is no punishment for failing to report an assisted suicide.)

Examples

Moreover, killing by doctors in the Netherlands has expanded far beyond the rare case originally contemplated when euthanasia was first permitted in that country more than twenty years ago. Patients who are not terminally ill are routinely assisted in suicide. Depressed people can also be killed upon request even if they have no underlying organic disease. The lives of children born with birth defects are terminated by doctors based primarily on "qualify of life" considerations. Most chilling, in one out of five euthanasia cases—nearly 1,000 per year—the patient has not asked to be killed.

Claim of policy: indictment of the present state of affairs, implying that it should be changed

The *New England Journal of Medicine* study is a warning that Oregon has started down the same destructive path. Rather than alleviating concerns, the study reveals that assisted suicide is bad medicine and even worse public policy.   10

■ Analysis

In this claim of policy, the course of action is suggested in the last paragraph: Assisted suicide must be eliminated because it is "bad medicine and even worse public policy." That is, the law in Oregon that permits assisted suicide must be repealed. In the body of his argument, the author supports this claim with an array of facts and an appeal to deeply felt human values.

He begins, as many arguers do, with a brief reference to the situation he will attack. (It is summarized in the last section of the third paragraph.) The facts he provides come largely from a study in a distinguished professional journal that claims to establish the success of the Oregon law. But Smith interprets the facts of the study—and its omissions—to mean that the program is *not* fulfilling its humanitarian objective. Another study that is cited, from a journal of medical ethics, discusses the state of euthanasia in the Netherlands, where it is legal. This report appears at the end of Smith's article. Its position here emphasizes a disturbing conclusion—the dangerous future that the Oregon law may introduce. (In the Netherlands, says the report, "in one out of five euthanasia cases . . . the patient has not asked to be killed.")

An interesting and effective strategy in this argument is the author's reference to information which has been omitted from the debate on euthanasia. This lack of information is clearly spelled out in two paragraphs of the essay. In any debate, an accusation that the opposite side has failed to supply important data suggests that the data will prove damaging to the opponent's argument.

The most important element of this argument, however, is its appeal, both direct and implied, to the values of compassion and the natural desire to protect the helpless. All the examples are designed to heighten our sensitivity to the plight of those who have been victimized by death-prescribing doctors. But there is also an appeal to fear for readers who can imagine possible threats to their own welfare under such a law.

We don't, of course, expect neutrality from a lawyer for an anti-euthanasia organization. Nevertheless, one of the strengths of this argument is its use of sober language, despite the emotionally charged subject matter. There are no vivid descriptions of suffering or maltreatment, and the author does not personalize his account. The absence of the pronoun *I*, in fact, lends his argument the formality of a legal brief. Undecided readers often find such restraint more persuasive than a passionate assault on the opposition.

READINGS FOR ANALYSIS

Happiness Is a Warm Planet

THOMAS GALE MOORE

President Clinton convened a conference on global warming yesterday, as the White House agonizes over its posture at the forthcoming talks in Kyoto, Japan, on a worldwide global warming treaty. Mr. Clinton is eager to please his environmentalist supporters, but industry, labor and members of the Senate have told the administration that this treaty would wreck the economy, cost millions of jobs and provoke a flight of investment to more hospitable climes.

A crucial point gets lost in the debate: Global warming, if it were to occur, would probably *benefit* most Americans.

If mankind had to choose between a warmer or a cooler climate, we would certainly choose the former: Humans, nearly all other animals and most plants would be better off with higher temperatures. The climate models suggest, and so far the record confirms, that under global

Thomas Gale Moore is a senior fellow at the Hoover Institution. His book *A Politically Incorrect View of Global Warming: Foreign Aid Masquerading as Climate Policy* was published in 1998 by the Cato Institute. This article appeared in the *Wall Street Journal* on October 7, 1997.

warming nighttime winter temperatures would rise the most, and daytime summer temperatures the least. Most Americans prefer a warmer climate to a colder one—and that preference is justified. More people die of the cold than of the heat; more die in the winter than the summer. Statistical evidence suggests that the climate predicted for the end of the next century might reduce U.S. deaths by about 40,000 annually.

In addition, less snow and ice would reduce transportation delays and accidents. A warmer winter would cut heating costs, more than offsetting any increase in air conditioning expenses in the summer. Manufacturing, mining and most services would be unaffected. Longer growing seasons, more rainfall and higher concentrations of carbon dioxide would benefit plant growth. Already there is evidence that trees and other plants are growing more vigorously. Although some locales may become too dry, too wet or too warm, on the whole mankind should benefit from an upward tick in the thermometer.

What about the economic effects? In the pessimistic view of the Intergovernmental Panel on Climate Change, the costs of global warming might be as high as 1.5 percent of the U.S. gross domestic product by the end of the next century. The cost of reducing carbon dioxide emissions, however, would be much higher. William Cline of the Institute for International Economics has calculated that the cost of cutting emissions by one-third from current levels by 2040 would be 3.5 percent of worldwide GDP. The IPCC also reviewed various estimates of losses from stabilizing emissions at 1990 levels, a more modest objective, and concluded that the cost to the U.S. economy would be at least 1.5 percent of GDP by 2050, with the burden continuing to increase thereafter.

The forecast cost of warming is for the end of the next century, not the middle. Adjusting for the time difference, the cost to the U.S. from a warmer climate at midcentury, according to the IPCC, would be at most 0.75 percent of GDP, meaning that the costs of holding carbon dioxide to 1990 levels would be twice the gain from preventing any climate change. But the benefit-cost calculus is even worse. The administration is planning to exempt Third World nations, such as China, India and Brazil, from the requirements of the treaty. Under such a scheme, Americans would pay a huge price for virtually no benefit.

And even if the developing countries agreed to return emissions to 1990 levels, greenhouse gas concentrations would not be stabilized. Since for many decades more carbon dioxide would be added to the atmosphere than removed through natural processes, the buildup would only slow; consequently temperatures would continue to go up. Instead of saving the full 0.75 percent of GDP by keeping emissions at 1990 levels, we would be saving much less.

It is true that whatever dangers global warming may pose, they will be most pronounced in the developing world. It is much easier for rich countries to adapt to any long-term shift in weather than it is for poor countries, which tend to be much more dependent on agriculture.

Poor countries lack the resources to aid their flora and fauna in adapting, and many of their farmers earn too little to survive a shift to new conditions. But the best insurance for these poor countries is an increase in their wealth, which would diminish their dependence on agriculture and make it easier for them to adjust to changes in weather, including increases in precipitation and possible flooding or higher sea level. Subjecting Americans to high taxes and onerous regulations will help neither them — we could buy less from them — nor us.

The optimal way to deal with potential climate change is not to embark on a futile attempt to prevent it, but to promote growth and prosperity so that people will have the resources to deal with the normal set of natural disasters. Based on the evidence, including historical records, global warming is likely to be good for most of mankind. The additional carbon, rain and warmth should promote the plant growth necessary to sustain an expanding world population. Global change is inevitable; warmer is better; richer is healthier.

READING AND DISCUSSION QUESTIONS

1. This article is a claim of value in which the author tries to prove that something is good or bad — in this case, that a warmer climate would be better than a cold one. How many different reasons does he give to support his claim?

2. Moore offers a solution for the problems of a warm planet. Does this solution have shortcomings? If so, what are they?

3. Moore, an economist, spends the greater part of his argument on the economic consequences of global warming. Do you think he should have tried to develop other effects? Give examples of data that seem insufficient.

4. How much of the author's evidence comes from experts? If more testimony is needed, what kind should it be?

WRITING SUGGESTIONS

5. To ascertain whether Moore is right about the consequences of global warming, you will have to consult experts who disagree with him. They will not be hard to find. Most of those who have studied climatic changes think we are in trouble. Based on the testimony of other experts, write a paper that refutes some of Moore's claims.

6. Moore says that most of mankind would choose to live in a warm climate (para. 3). If you could choose, would you live in a tropical climate? A subtropical climate? In your answer, try to go beyond the most superficial reasons, like being tan all year long. Provide sufficient detail and personal background to bring to life the various reasons that would govern your choice.

A White Woman of Color

JULIA ÁLVAREZ

Growing up in the Dominican Republic, I experienced racism within my own family—though I didn't think of it as racism. But there was definitely a hierarchy of beauty, which was the main currency in our daughters-only family. It was not until years later, from the vantage point of this country and this education, that I realized that this hierarchy of beauty was dictated by our coloring. We were a progression of whitening, as if my mother were slowly bleaching the color out of her children.

The oldest sister had the darkest coloring, with very curly hair and "coarse" features. She looked the most like Papi's side of the family and was considered the least pretty. I came next, with "good hair," and skin that back then was a deep olive, for I was a tomboy—another dark mark against me—who would not stay out of the sun. The sister right after me had my skin color, but she was a good girl who stayed indoors, so she was much paler, her hair a golden brown. But the pride and joy of the family was the baby. She was the one who made heads turn and strangers approach asking to feel her silken hair. She was white white, an adjective that was repeated in describing her color as if to deepen the shade of white. Her eyes were brown, but her hair was an unaccountable towheaded blond. Because of her coloring, my father was teased that there must have been a German milkman in our neighborhood. How could *she* be *his* daughter? It was clear that this youngest child resembled Mami's side of the family.

It was Mami's family who were *really* white. They were white in terms of race, and white also in terms of class. From them came the fine features, the pale skin, the lank hair. Her brothers and uncles went to schools abroad and had important businesses in the country. They also emulated the manners and habits of North Americans. Growing up, I remember arguments at the supper table on whether or not it was proper to tie one's napkin around one's neck, on how much of one's arm one could properly lay on the table, on whether spaghetti could be eaten with the help of a spoon. My mother, of course, insisted on all the protocol of knives and forks and on eating a little portion of everything

Novelist and poet Julia Álvarez was born in the Dominican Republic and emigrated to the United States at age ten with her parents. Her work includes the novels *How the García Girls Lost Their Accents* (1991), *In the Time of the Butterflies* (1994), *¡Yo!* (1997), and *In the Name of Salomé* (2000); two books of poems, *Homecoming: New and Collected Poems* (1996) and *The Other Side* (1995); and a collection of nonfiction essays, *Something to Declare* (1998). She teaches literature and creative writing at Middlebury College. This essay appeared in *Half and Half: Writers on Growing Up Biracial and Bicultural,* edited by Claudine C. O'Hearn (1998).

served; my father, on the other hand, defended our eating whatever we wanted, with our hands if need be, so we could "have fun" with our food. My mother would snap back that we looked like *jibaritas* who should be living out in the country. Of course, that was precisely where my father's family came from.

Not that Papi's family weren't smart and enterprising, all twenty-five brothers and sisters. (The size of the family in and of itself was considered very country by some members of Mami's family.) Many of Papi's brothers had gone to the university and become professionals. But their education was totally island—no fancy degrees from Andover and Cornell and Yale, no summer camps or school songs in another language. Papi's family still lived in the interior versus the capital, in old-fashioned houses without air conditioning, decorated in ways my mother's family would have considered, well, tasteless. I remember antimacassars on the backs of rocking chairs (which were the living-room set), garish paintings of flamboyant trees, ceramic planters with plastic flowers in bloom. They were *criollos*—creoles—rather than cosmopolitans, expansive, proud, colorful. (Some members had a sixth finger on their right—or was it their left hand?) Their features were less aquiline than Mother's family's, the skin darker, the hair coarse and curly. Their money still had the smell of the earth on it and was kept in a wad in their back pockets, whereas my mother's family had money in the Chase Manhattan Bank, most of it with George Washington's picture on it, not Juan Pablo Duarte's.

It was clear to us growing up then that lighter was better, but there 5 was no question of discriminating against someone because he or she was dark-skinned. Everyone's family, even an elite one like Mami's, had darker-skinned members. All Dominicans, as the saying goes, have a little black behind the ears. So, to separate oneself from those who were darker would have been to divide *una familia*, a sacrosanct entity in our culture. Neither was white blood necessarily a sign of moral or intellectual or political superiority. All one has to do is page through a Dominican history book and look at the number of dark-skinned presidents, dictators, generals, and entrepreneurs to see that power has not resided exclusively or even primarily among the whites on the island. The leadership of our country has been historically "colored."

But being black was something else. A black Dominican was referred to as a "dark Indian" (*indio oscuro*)—unless you wanted to come to blows with him, that is. The real blacks were the Haitians who lived next door and who occupied the Dominican Republic for twenty years, from 1822 to 1844, a fact that can still so inflame the Dominican populace you'd think it had happened last year. The denial of the Afro-Dominican part of our culture reached its climax during the dictatorship of Trujillo, whose own maternal grandmother was Haitian. In 1937, to protect Dominican race purity, Trujillo ordered the overnight genocide of thousands (figures range from 4,000 to 20,000) of Haitians by his military, who committed this atrocity using only machetes and knives in order to make this planned extermination look like a "spontaneous" border skirmish. He also had the Dominican Republic declared a white nation despite the evidence of the mulatto senators who were forced to pass this ridiculous measure.

So, black was not so good, kinky hair was not so good, thick lips not so good. But even if you were *indio oscuro con pelo malo y una bemba de aquí a Baní,* you could still sit in the front of the bus and order at the lunch counter—or the equivalent thereof. There was no segregation of races in the halls of power. But in the aesthetic arena—the one to which we girls were relegated as females—lighter was better. Lank hair and pale skin and small, fine features were better. All I had to do was stay out of the sun and behave myself and I could pass as a pretty white girl.

Another aspect of my growing up also greatly influenced my thinking on race. Although I was raised in the heart of a large family, my day-to-day caretakers were the maids. Most of these women were dark-skinned, some of Haitian background. One of them, Misiá, had been spared the machetes of the 1937 massacre when she was taken in and hidden from the prowling *guardias* by the family. We children spent most of the day with these women. They tended to us, nursed us when we were sick, cradled us when we fell down and scraped an elbow or knee (as a tomboy, there was a lot of this scraping for me), and most important, they told us stories of *los santos* and *el barón del cementerio,* of *el cuco* and *las ciguapas,* beautiful dark-skinned creatures who escaped capture because their feet were turned backwards so they left behind a false set of footprints. These women spread the wings of our imaginations and connected us deeply to the land we came from. They were the ones with the stories that had power over us.

We arrived in Nueva York in 1960, before the large waves of Caribbean immigrants created little Habanas, little Santo Domingos, and little San Juans in the boroughs of the city. Here we encountered a whole new kettle of wax—as my malapropping Mami might have said. People of color were treated as if they were inferior, prone to violence, uneducated, untrustworthy, lazy—all the "bad" adjectives we were learning in our new language. Our dark-skinned aunt, Tía Ana, who had lived in New York for several decades and so was the authority in these matters, recounted stories of discrimination on buses and subways. These Americans were so blind! One drop of black and you were black. Everyone back home would have known that Tía Ana was not black: she had "good hair" and her skin color was a light *indio.* All week, she worked in a *factoría* in the Bronx, and when she came to visit us on Saturdays to sew our school clothes, she had to take three trains to our nice neighborhood where the darkest face on the street was usually her own.

We were lucky we were white Dominicans or we would have had a 10 much harder time of it in this country. We would have encountered a lot more prejudice than we already did, for white as we were, we found that our Latino-ness, our accents, our habits and smells, added "color" to our complexion. Had we been darker, we certainly could not have bought our mock Tudor house in Jamaica Estates. In fact, the African American family who moved in across the street several years later needed police protection because of threats. Even so, at the local school, we endured the bullying of classmates. "Go back to where you came from!" they yelled at my sisters and me in the playground. When some of them started throwing stones, my mother made up her mind that we were not safe and began applying to boarding schools where privilege transformed prejudice into patronage.

"So where are you from?" my classmates would ask.

"Jamaica Estates," I'd say, an edge of belligerence to my voice. It was obvious from my accent, if not my looks, that I was not *from* there in the way they meant being from somewhere.

"I mean *originally.*"

And then it would come out, the color, the accent, the cousins with six fingers, the smell of garlic.

By the time I went off to college, a great explosion of American cul- 15 ture was taking place on campuses across the country. The civil rights movement, the Vietnam War and subsequent peace movement, the women's movement, were transforming traditional definitions of American identity. Ethnicity was in: my classmates wore long braids like Native Americans and peasant blouses from Mexico and long, diaphanous skirts and dangly earrings from India. Suddenly, my foreignness was being celebrated. This reversal felt affirming but also disturbing. As huipils, serapes, and embroidered dresses proliferated about me, I had the feeling that my ethnicity had become a commodity. I resented it.

When I began looking for a job after college, I discovered that being a white Latina made me a nonthreatening minority in the eyes of these employers. My color was a question *only* of culture, and if I kept my cultural color to myself, I was "no problem." Each time I was hired for one of my countless "visiting appointments"—they were never permanent "invitations," mind you—the inevitable questionnaire would accompany my contract in which I was to check off my RACE: CAUCASIAN, BLACK, NATIVE AMERICAN, ASIAN, HISPANIC, OTHER. How could a Dominican divide herself in this way? Or was I really a Dominican anymore? And what was a Hispanic? A census creation—there is no such culture—how could it define who I was at all? Given this set of options, the truest answer might have been to check off other.

For that was the way I had begun to think of myself. Adrift from any Latino community in this country, my culture had become an internal homeland, periodically replenished by trips "back home." But as a professional woman on my own, I felt less and less at home on the island. My values, the loss of my Catholic faith, my lifestyle, my wardrobe, my hippy ways, and my feminist ideas separated me from my native culture. I did not subscribe to many of the mores and constraints that seemed to be an intrinsic part of that culture. And since my culture had always been my "color," by rejecting these mores I had become not only Americanized but whiter.

If I could have been a part of a Latino community in the United States, the struggle might have been, if not easier, less private and therefore less isolating. These issues of acculturation and ethnicity would have been struggles to share with others like me. But all my North American life I had lived in shifting academic communities—going to boarding schools, then college, and later teaching wherever I could get those yearly appointments—and these communities reflected the dearth of Latinos in the profession. Except for friends in Spanish departments, who tended to have come from their countries of origin to teach rather than being raised in this country as I was, I had very little daily contact with Latinos.

Where I looked for company was where I had always looked for company since coming to this country: in books. At first the texts that I read and taught were the ones prescribed to me, the canonical works which formed the content of the bread-and-butter courses that as a "visiting instructor" I was hired to teach. These texts were mostly written by white male writers from Britain and the United States, with a few women thrown in and no Latinos. Thank goodness for the occasional creative writing workshop where I could bring in the multicultural authors I wanted. But since I had been formed in this very academy, I was clueless where to start. I began to educate myself by reading, and that is when I discovered that there were others out there like me, hybrids who came in a variety of colors and whose ethnicity and race were an evolving process, not a rigid paradigm or a list of boxes, one of which you checked off.

This discovery of my ethnicity on paper was like a rebirth. I had been 20 going through a pretty bad writer's block: the white page seemed impossible to fill with whatever it was I had in me to say. But listening to authors like Maxine Hong Kingston, Toni Morrison, Gwendolyn Brooks, Langston Hughes, Maya Angelou, June Jordan, and to Lorna Dee Cervantes, Piri Thomas, Rudolfo Anaya, Edward Rivera, Ernesto Galarza (that first wave of Latino writers), I began to hear the language "in color." I began to see that literature could reflect the otherness I was feeling, that the choices in fiction and poetry did not have to be bleached out of their color or simplified into either/or. A story could allow for the competing claims of different parts of ourselves and where we came from.

Ironically, it was through my own stories and poems that I finally made contact with Latino communities in this country. As I published more, I was invited to read at community centers and bilingual programs. Latino students, who began attending colleges in larger numbers in the late seventies and eighties, sought me out as a writer and teacher "of color." After the publication of *How the García Girls Lost Their Accents,* I found that I had become a sort of spokesperson for Dominicans in this country, a role

I had neither sought nor accepted. Of course, some Dominicans refused to grant me any status as a "real" Dominican because I was "white." With the color word there was also a suggestion of class. My family had not been among the waves of economic immigrants that left the island in the seventies, a generally darker-skinned, working-class group, who might have been the maids and workers in my mother's family house. We had come in 1960, political refugees, with no money but with "prospects": Papi had a friend who was the doctor at the Waldorf Astoria and who helped him get a job; Mami's family had money in the Chase Manhattan Bank they could lend us. We had changed class in America—from Mami's elite family to middle-class spics—but our background and education and most especially our pale skin had made mobility easier for us here. We had not undergone the same kind of race struggles as other Dominicans; therefore, we could not be "real" Dominicans.

What I came to understand and accept and ultimately fight for with my writing is the reality that ethnicity and race are not fixed constructs or measurable quantities. What constitutes our ethnicity and our race— once there is literally no common ground beneath us to define it— evolves as we seek to define and redefine ourselves in new contexts. My Latino-ness is not something someone can take away from me or leave me out of with a definition. It is in my blood: it comes from that mixture of biology, culture, native language, and experience that makes me a different American from one whose family comes from Ireland or Poland or Italy. My Latino-ness is also a political choice. I am choosing to hold on to my ethnicity and native language even if I can "pass." I am choosing to color my Americanness with my Dominicanness even if it came in a light shade of skin color.

I hope that as Latinos, coming from so many different countries and continents, we can achieve solidarity in this country as the mix that we are. I hope we won't shoot ourselves in the foot in order to maintain some sort of false "purity" as the glue that holds us together. Such an enterprise is bound to fail. We need each other. We can't afford to reject the darker or lighter varieties, and to do so is to have absorbed a definition of ourselves as exclusively one thing or the other. And haven't we learned to fear that word "exclusive"? This reductiveness is absurd when we are talking about a group whose very definition is that of a mestizo race, a mixture of European, indigenous, African, and much more. Within this vast circle, shades will lighten and darken into overlapping categories. If we cut them off, we diminish our richness and we plant a seed of ethnic cleansing that is the root of the bloodshed we have seen in Bosnia and the West Bank and Rwanda and even our own Los Angeles and Dominican Republic.

As we Latinos redefine ourselves in America, making ourselves up and making ourselves over, we have to be careful, in taking up the promises of America, not to adopt its limiting racial paradigms. Many of us have shed customs and prejudices that oppressed our gender, race, or class on our native islands and in our native countries. We should not re-place these with modes of thinking that are divisive and oppressive of our rich diversity. Maybe as a group that embraces many races and differ-ences, we Latinos can provide a positive multicultural, multiracial model to a divided America.

READING AND DISCUSSION QUESTIONS

1. What is the meaning of the title of this essay? Is it an oxymoron?

2. Explain Álvarez's "hierarchy of beauty" (para. 1) in the Dominican Re-public. What does she mean by "white in terms of race, and white also in terms of class" (para. 3)?

3. Does such a hierarchy of beauty have parallels in the United States? If it is not skin color, are other physical attributes rated as good or bad? How do you think such preferences arose?

4. Why did Álvarez think of herself as "adrift" (para. 17)? How does Álvarez explain the "discovery of my ethnicity" (para. 20)?

5. Álvarez ends her essay by summarizing what she has learned from her experience as a white woman "of color" (para. 21). How do the last three paragraphs differ in tone and content from the narrative that precedes it? Do you think they are effective? Would the essay have been stronger or weaker if she had ended it before the last three paragraphs?

WRITING SUGGESTIONS

6. Álvarez mentions a number of authors who inspired her with their views of otherness (para. 20). Perhaps you are familiar with their works or the works of other writers who explore ethnicity in America, such as *The Joy Luck Club, I Know Why the Caged Bird Sings, Native Son,* and *Reservation Blues.* Write a review of a book in which the author describes the experi-ence of being different in the United States.

7. If you know any immigrants—in your own family or perhaps on cam-pus—describe their attempts at acculturation. What aspects of American life have been most challenging for them? What aspects have been easi-est to understand and accept?

College Life versus My Moral Code

ELISHA DOV HACK

Many people envy my status as a freshman at Yale College. My class-mates and I made it through some fierce competition, and we are excited to have been accepted to one of the best academic and extracur-ricular programs in American higher education. I have an older brother who attended Yale, and I've heard from him what life at Yale is like.

He spent all his college years living at home because our parents are New Haven residents, and Yale's rules then did not require him to live in the dorms. But Yale's new regulations demand that I spend my freshman and sophomore years living in the college dormitories.

I, two other freshmen, and two sophomores have refused to do this because life in the dorms, even on the floors Yale calls "single sex," is contrary to the fundamental principles we have been taught as long as we can remember—the principles of Judaism lived according to the Torah and 3,000-year-old rabbinic teachings. Unless Yale waives its resi-dence requirement, we may have no choice but to sue the university to protect our religious way of life.

Bingham Hall, on the Yale quadrangle known as the Old Campus, is one of the dorms for incoming students. When I entered it two weeks ago during an orientation tour, I literally saw the handwriting on the wall. A sign titled "Safe Sex" told me where to pick up condoms on cam-pus. Another sign touted 100 ways to make love without having sex, like "take a nap together" and "take a steamy shower together."

That, I am told, is real life in the dorms. The "freshperson" issue of 5 the *Yale Daily News* sent to entering students contained a "Yale lexicon" defining *sexile* as "banishment from your dorm room because your room-mate is having more fun than you." If you live in the dorms, you're ex-pected to be part of the crowd, to accept these standards as the framework for your life.

Can we stand up to classmates whose sexual morality differs from ours? We've had years of rigorous religious teaching, and we've watched and learned from our parents. We can hold our own in the intellectual debate that flows naturally from exchanges during and after class. But I'm upset and hurt by this requirement that I live in the dorms. Why is Yale—an institution that professes to be so tolerant and open-minded—making it particularly hard for students like us to maintain our moral standards through difficult college years?

We are not trying to impose our moral standards on our classmates or on Yale. Our parents tell us that things were very different in college

Elisha Dov Hack was a member of the Yale College class of 2001. This article appeared on September 9, 1997, in the *New York Times*.

dormitories in their day and that in most colleges in the 1950s students who allowed guests of the opposite sex into their dorm rooms were subject to expulsion. We acknowledge that today's morality is not that of the 50s. We are asking only that Yale give us the same permission to live off campus that it gives any lower classman who is married or at least twenty-one years old.

Yale is proud of the fact that it has no "parietal rules" and that sexual morality is a student's own business. Maybe this is what Dean Richard H. Brodhead meant when he said that "Yale's residential colleges carry . . . a moral meaning." That moral meaning is, basically, "Anything goes." This morality is Yale's own residential religion, which it is proselytizing by force of its regulations.

We cannot, in good conscience, live in a place where women are permitted to stay overnight in men's rooms, and where visiting men can traipse through the common halls on the women's floors—in various stages of undress—in the middle of the night. The dormitories on Yale's Old Campus have floors designated by gender, but there is easy access through open stairwells from one floor to the next.

The moral message Yale's residences convey today is not one that 10 our religion accepts. Nor is it a moral environment in which the five of us can spend our nights, or a moral surrounding that we can call home.

Yale sent me a glossy brochure when it welcomed me as an entering student. It said, "Yale retains a deep respect for its early history and for the continuity that its history provides—a continuity based on constant reflection and reappraisal." Yale ought to reflect on and reappraise a policy that compels us to compromise our religious principles.

READING AND DISCUSSION QUESTIONS

1. Summarize Hack's "moral code" in a sentence or two. What examples of conduct does he give to make his definition clear?

2. What solution to his problem does the author propose? Why does Yale refuse to accept the solution? Are Yale's rules justified?

3. Hack says that religious students "may have no choice but to sue the university to protect our religious way of life" (para. 3). What support could he offer in a court of law for his claim that these students should be allowed to live off campus? If you can, ask a legal expert for ideas.

4. Many arguments, like this one between religious students and a university, arise out of a conflict not between good and evil but between two goods. Can you propose a compromise that would satisfy both sides in this case?

WRITING SUGGESTIONS

5. How do you think Yale could defend the sexual freedom that prevails on its campus? Write an argument setting out the philosophical principles and cultural values that justify tolerance for the practices Hack rejects.

6. Members of some minority groups on college campuses often insist on living together in separate dorms, taking their meals together, engaging in separate activities, etc. In light of today's emphasis on the multicultural experience, should the university allow such segregation?

The Right to Bear Arms

WARREN E. BURGER

Our metropolitan centers, and some suburban communities of America, are setting new records for homicides by handguns. Many of our large centers have up to ten times the murder rate of all of Western Europe. In 1988, there were 9,000 handgun murders in America. Last year, Washington, D.C., alone had more than 400 homicides — setting a new record for our capital.

The Constitution of the United States, in its Second Amendment, guarantees a "right of the people to keep and bear arms." However, the meaning of this clause cannot be understood except by looking to the purpose, the setting, and the objectives of the draftsmen. The first ten amendments — the Bill of Rights — were not drafted at Philadelphia in 1787; that document came two years later than the Constitution. Most of the states already had bills of rights, but the Constitution might not have been ratified in 1788 if the states had not had assurances that a national Bill of Rights would soon be added.

People of that day were apprehensive about the new "monster" national government presented to them, and this helps explain the language and purpose of the Second Amendment. A few lines after the First Amendment's guarantees — against "establishment of religion," "free exercise" of religion, free speech and free press — came a guarantee that grew out of the deep-seated fear of a "national" or "standing" army. The same First Congress that approved the right to keep and bear arms also limited the national army to 840 men; Congress in the Second Amendment then provided:

> A well regulated Militia, being necessary to the security of a free State, the right of the people to keep and bear Arms, shall not be infringed.

In the 1789 debate in Congress on James Madison's proposed Bill of Rights, Elbridge Gerry argued that a state militia was necessary:

> to prevent the establishment of a standing army, the bane of liberty. . . . Whenever governments mean to invade the rights and liberties of the

Warren E. Burger (1907–1995) was chief justice of the United States from 1969 to 1986. This article is from the January 14, 1990, issue of *Parade* magazine.

people, they always attempt to destroy the militia in order to raise an army upon their ruins.

We see that the need for a state militia was the predicate of the "right" guaranteed; in short, it was declared "necessary" in order to have a state military force to protect the security of the state. That Second Amendment clause must be read as though the word "because" was the opening word of the guarantee. Today, of course, the "state militia" serves a very different purpose. A huge national defense establishment has taken over the role of the militia of 200 years ago.

Some have exploited these ancient concerns, blurring sporting guns—rifles, shotguns, and even machine pistols—with all firearms, including what are now called "Saturday night specials." There is, of course, a great difference between sporting guns and handguns. Some regulation of handguns has long been accepted as imperative; laws relating to "concealed weapons" are common. That we may be "overregulated" in some areas of life has never held us back from more regulation of automobiles, airplanes, motorboats, and "concealed weapons."

Let's look at the history.

First, many of the 3.5 million people living in the thirteen original Colonies depended on wild game for food, and a good many of them required firearms for their defense from marauding Indians—and later from the French and English. Underlying all these needs was an important concept that each able-bodied man in each of the thirteen independent states had to help or defend his state.

The early opposition to the idea of national or standing armies was maintained under the Articles of Confederation; that confederation had no standing army and wanted none. The state militia—essentially a part-time citizen army, as in Switzerland today—was the only kind of "army" they wanted. From the time of the Declaration of Independence through the victory at Yorktown in 1781, George Washington, as the commander in chief of these volunteer-militia armies, had to depend upon the states to send those volunteers.

When a company of New Jersey militia volunteers reported for duty to Washington at Valley Forge, the men initially declined to take an oath to "the United States," maintaining, "Our country is New Jersey." Massachusetts Bay men, Virginians, and others felt the same way. To the American of the eighteenth century, his state was his country, and his freedom was defended by his militia.

The victory at Yorktown—and the ratification of the Bill of Rights a decade later—did not change people's attitudes about a national army. They had lived for years under the notion that each state would maintain its own military establishment, and the seaboard states had their own navies as well. These people, and their fathers and grandfathers before them, remembered how monarchs had used standing armies to oppress their ancestors in Europe. Americans wanted no part of this. A state militia, like a rifle and powder horn, was as much a part of life as the automobile is today; pistols were largely for officers, aristocrats—and dueling.

Against this background, it was not surprising that the provision concerning firearms emerged in very simple terms with the significant predicate—basing the right on the *necessity* for a "well regulated militia," a state army.

In the two centuries since then—with two world wars and some lesser ones—it has become clear, sadly, that we have no choice but to maintain a standing national army while still maintaining a "militia" by way of the National Guard, which can be swiftly integrated into the national defense forces.

Americans also have a right to defend their homes, and we need not challenge that. Nor does anyone seriously question that the Constitution protects the right of hunters to own and keep sporting guns for hunting game any more than anyone would challenge the right to own and keep fishing rods and other equipment for fishing—or to own automobiles. To "keep and bear arms" for hunting today is essentially a recreational activity and not an imperative of survival, as it was 200 years ago; "Saturday night specials" and machine guns are not recreational weapons and surely are as much in need of regulation as motor vehicles.

Americans should ask themselves a few questions. The Constitution 15 does not mention automobiles or motorboats, but the right to keep and own an automobile is beyond question; equally beyond question is the power of the state to regulate the purchase or the transfer of such vehicle and the right to license the vehicle and the driver with reasonable standards. In some places, even a bicycle must be registered, as must some household dogs.

If we are to stop this mindless homicidal carnage, is it unreasonable:

1. to provide that, to acquire a firearm, an application be made reciting age, residence, employment, and any prior criminal convictions?

2. to require that this application lie on the table for ten days (absent a showing for urgent need) before the license would be issued?

3. that the transfer of a firearm be made essentially as that of a motor vehicle?

4. to have a "ballistic fingerprint" of the firearm made by the manufacturer and filed with the license record so that, if a bullet is found in a victim's body, law enforcement might be helped in finding the culprit?

These are the kinds of questions the American people must answer if we are to preserve the "domestic tranquility" promised in the Constitution.

READING AND DISCUSSION QUESTIONS

1. This essay can be divided into three or four parts. Provide headings for these parts.

2. Which part of the essay is most fully developed? What explains the author's emphasis?

3. Why does Burger recount the history of the Second Amendment so fully? Explain his reason for arguing that the Second Amendment does not guarantee the right of individuals to "bear arms."

4. Burger also uses history to argue that there is a difference between legislation against sporting guns and legislation against handguns. Summarize his argument.

5. How effective is his analogy between licensing vehicles and licensing handguns?

WRITING SUGGESTIONS

6. Other people interpret "the right to bear arms" differently. Look at some of their arguments, and write an essay summarizing their interpretations and defending them.

7. Burger outlines a policy for registration of handguns that would prevent criminal use. But at least one sociologist has pointed out that most guns used by criminals are obtained illegally. Examine and evaluate some of the arguments claiming that registration is generally ineffective.

8. Analyze arguments of the National Rifle Association, the nation's largest gun lobby. You may want to consult their Web site, <http://www.nra.org>. Do they answer Burger's claims?

The "MCAS" Teens Give Each Other

JEFF JACOBY

More states are requiring high school students to pass a standardized test before they can collect a diploma, and the protests are growing louder. The objections in Massachusetts are especially noisy. In part that is because Bay Staters are a querulous bunch; in part it's because the Massachusetts Comprehensive Assessment System—the MCAS—is regarded as one of the nation's tougher high school tests.

The complaints about the MCAS are many, but the key ones seem to be that (1) it requires students to master an arbitrary collection of facts, while (2) giving short shrift to all the other kinds of knowledge they have acquired.

Jeff Jacoby is a nationally syndicated columnist for the *Boston Globe*, where this article appeared on December 4, 2000.

"The MCAS test," growls SCAM, the Student Coalition for Alternatives to MCAS, "includes an enormous amount of information, much of which is irrelevant or so specialized that many adults do not know it." It also "devalues technical, linguistic, musical, athletic, and vocational skills . . . that cannot be assessed on a standardized test."

The state's largest teachers union is spending $600,000 on an anti-MCAS ad campaign. "Learning," mourns the narrator in a TV spot, "used to be about a lot of things—imagination, creativity, discovery, and dreams. But now the state says it's about one thing—a flawed and unfair test, the one-size-fits-all, high-stakes, do-or-die MCAS."

Last spring, Dara Byer of Cambridge was one of hundreds of students 5 who boycotted the test. "That a child's future should be determined by knowing or not knowing certain dates or formulas," she argued in an essay excerpted in the *Globe*, "is ridiculous and unfair."

Maybe so. But if the argument is that teenagers cannot meet rigorous standards of knowledge or memorize all kinds of "irrelevant" details, it is easily refuted. Just ask the nearest teenager.

Talk to the boy who thought he couldn't hang with the popular guys in his high school without first committing to memory the thousand and one sports details they expect each other to be conversant with— the names of the home team's starting lineup, their stats and history, the score in last night's game, the details of that awesome play in the third quarter, and the latest rumor about the coach's imminent firing. When our young man takes the MCAS, he'll face only questions whose answers are fixed—why Henri IV issued the Edict of Nantes, say, or the value of x in a given quadratic equation. Meeting his classmates' expectations when it comes to sports knowledge, by contrast, means staying abreast of information that changes daily. A "ridiculous and unfair" challenge? Perhaps. But millions of boys meet it.

"Kids set truly high performance learning standards for each other," says Will Fitzhugh, who publishes *The Concord Review*—a quarterly journal of essays on history by secondary school students—and has done more to promote top-shelf research and writing at the high school level than any five teachers I know. "If students don't know the details of the latest clothing fashions or the hot computer games or the to-die-for movie stars, they're liable to be mocked, shunned, and generally 'flunked' by others their age. That's why so many spend hours each day absorbing the facts and names of popular culture."

You think the MCAS and tests like it are too difficult? You find it crazy that so much should ride on a teen's ability to spit back dates and figures he'll never use again? You object that preparing for these exams eats up too many hours that could be spent more meaningfully? What then do you make of the "MCAS" to which teenagers routinely subject their peers? For example, consider some questions from the "Current Music" category—mandatory for tenth-graders who wish to graduate to the "in" crowd:

1. Fred Durst is the lead singer of

   (a) papa roach

   (b) Orgy

   (c) Limp Bizkit

   (d) Deftones

2. Eminem's mentor was

   (a) Ice Cube

   (b) Dr. Dre

   (c) Method Man

   (d) ODB

3. Essay topic: Who is Carson Daly, what is his relationship to *TRL*, and why are they important to the music video industry?

4. Essay topic: Your younger sister and her friends are enamored of 'N Sync, Backstreet Boys, and 98 Degrees. Your friends find them unbearable. Explain the contrast.

Perhaps even SCAM would agree that the knowledge needed to an- 10 swer such questions is "irrelevant or so specialized that many adults do not know it." Yet countless teens consider that knowledge essential— and make it their business to learn it, along with vast amounts of material in other "essential" categories.

Standardized exams surely have their faults. But pressuring kids to master reams of facts isn't one of them. We already know they can do it. The question on the table is whether the subjects to be memorized will include English, math, science, and history—or whether the only mandatory subjects will be music, television, movies, and fashion.

READING AND DISCUSSION QUESTIONS

1. This article is a claim of fact—that students are capable of mastering the information in the Massachusetts Comprehensive Assessment System (MCAS). In your view, what is the strongest evidence in support of this claim? Evaluate the argument made by the student coalition that attacks the test (para. 3).

2. What specific expressions do you recognize that indicate the author's attitude toward the MCAS? Do you think such language is persuasive? Explain why or why not.

3. Does the author explain why students do not do as well in formal tests as they do in the tests they give each other? What is your explanation? Do you agree with the critics of the MCAS that it is irrelevant?

4. The ninth paragraph consists of questions. Is this an effective rhetorical device?

5. One of the strengths of this article is the use of specific examples and details. Point out some that are especially successful in advancing the claim.

WRITING SUGGESTIONS

6. After twelve years in school, you probably have ideas of your own about testing. How do you feel about relying on statewide tests in English and mathematics to determine whether a student graduates from high school? What would be the advantages and disadvantages of such a requirement for a high school diploma?

7. Perhaps you have had experience with individually tailored projects, called *portfolios,* which sometimes are accepted in place of standardized tests for meeting graduation requirements. Write an evaluation of such a project, either one you have prepared yourself or one by which you would have liked to be judged. Be as specific as possible about the goal of the project and the way in which it was implemented.

8. Write about your own experiences with a particular test in school, in a job, or elsewhere. With hindsight, decide whether it was useful or irrelevant. If it was irrelevant, can you suggest a better test for that particular assessment?

DISCUSSION QUESTIONS

1. Notice the headline. The advertiser has supplied lots of numbers. What claim are these numbers meant to support?

2. Did you find the ad interesting to read? Do you think the advertiser was correct in thinking that people would read seven paragraphs about numbers? Explain your answer.

3. What specific aspects of the language might induce people to continue reading even if they find numbers tedious?

The initials of a friend

You will find these letters on many tools by which electricity works. They are on great generators used by electric light and power companies; and on lamps that light millions of homes.

They are on big motors that pull railway trains; and on tiny motors that make hard housework easy.

By such tools electricity dispels the dark and lifts heavy burdens from human shoulders. Hence the letters G-E are more than a trademark. They are an emblem of service—the initials of a friend.

GENERAL ELECTRIC

This advertisement first appeared in 1923. Today, you'll find our initials on many more things — from appliances, plastics, motors and lighting to financial services and medical equipment. Wherever you see our initials, we want them to mean the same thing to you — the initials of a friend.

We bring good things to life.

DISCUSSION QUESTIONS

1. To what need does the ad make an appeal?
2. What devices in the ad—both objects and the choice of objects to discuss—contribute to the effectiveness of the message?
3. How does the company's present-day slogan compare?

DISCUSSION QUESTIONS

1. Would this claim of policy be just as successful if the note were excluded? Would additional facts about guns contribute to its effectiveness?

2. Why is the gun so much larger than the printed message?

3. What is the basis of the emotional appeal? Is there more than one? Does the note go too far in exploiting our emotions?

Get Set to Say Hi to the Neighbors

JOHN NOBLE WILFORD

If there is life here on Earth, why not elsewhere?

The question has long inspired wonder and some fear, doomed a few to the heretic's stake, and invigorated recent investigations of other planets in the solar system and of the stars beyond. If life is indeed the inevitable outcome of cosmic evolution, a "cosmic imperative," in the words of the Nobel Prize–winning chemist Christian de Duve, the first clear evidence of extraterrestrial life will most likely be discovered in the first century of this new millennium.

One reason for the optimism is as old as speculations by the ancient Greeks and Romans impressed by the vastness of the heavens. "Space contains such a huge supply of atoms that all eternity would not be enough time to count them and the force which drives the atoms into various places just as they have been driven together in this world," wrote the Roman philosopher Lucretius in the first century B.C. "So we must realize that there are other worlds in other parts of the universe, with races of different men and different animals."

The modern variation of this reasoning stems from astronomy's recent estimates of upward of 100 billion galaxies, each with tens of billions of stars. So many opportunities for life to have emerged, as it did on one planet of one star, the sun. And everything scientists learn shows that the physical forces nearby apply everywhere; there is no reason to think that the solar system or its Milky Way galaxy are unique.

Biological studies on earth suggest that, if anything, scientists have 5 been underestimating the potential for life and its resilience in seemingly adverse environments. Drilling deep into Earth's crust, geochemists have encountered bacteria living there, without sunlight and probably on a diet of chemicals. Similarly, oceanographers have been surprised to find undersea vents disgorging mineral-rich hot water that supports a teeming community of exotic life, also existing without sunlight.

"The question may not be the probability of the origin of life," Dr. Norman R. Pace, a University of California biologist, has said, "but rather the probability that life, having arisen, survives and comes to dominate a planet."

John Noble Wilford is the winner of two Pulitzer Prizes and has written for the *Wall Street Journal*, *Time* magazine, and the *New York Times*, where this article originally appeared. He has also written or edited five books, including *We Reach the Moon* (1969) and *Mars Beckons* (1990).

Seekers of extraterrestrial life, at least in its humblest forms, were encouraged by discoveries in the 1990s. The Galileo spacecraft found strong evidence of a global ocean of water, where simple life just may exist, under the ice of Europa, a moon of Jupiter; Europa will be a target of life-seeking exploration in coming years. A report that a meteorite from Mars contained circumstantial evidence for microbial life created a stir; though the findings were suspect, they galvanized a renewed drive to explore Mars for fossil or extant life.

Of surpassing significance, the recent discovery of planets around other stars is fixing for scientists the places to look for extraterrestrial life. Knowing where to search, the National Aeronautics and Space Administration is developing instruments for spacecraft to be launched over the next two decades. These instruments will be capable of finding Earth-sized planets and detecting there the chemical signatures associated with life: oxygen, water, and carbon dioxide. The absolute clincher, scientists say, would be to find oxygen and methane together.

Current efforts to detect radio signals from other intelligent beings, begun in the 1960s, are a long shot. But for the first time in human history the technology exists to search other planetary systems for worlds harboring life in some form. The results could be the most reverberating scientific discovery of the new century.

Left the Light on, but Nobody Came

MALCOLM W. BROWNE

In 1939, the physicist Enrico Fermi posed his famous paradox: If life is common in our galaxy, why have we never seen extraterrestrial visitors on Earth?

Since then, and particularly since 1960, scientists have searched the cosmic radio spectrum for signals of intelligence, landed robotic laboratories on Mars to look for hints of biological activity, probed meteorite fragments for chemical or geological evidence of life, and tried to invent chemical pathways analogous to those from which life arises.

So far, all efforts have failed to show the existence of life anywhere except on Earth.

To find out just one extraterrestrial microorganism (or better, a bug-eyed Martian humanoid) would be sensational. But I think the human race must reconcile itself to the strong possibility that it is alone in the

Malcolm W. Browne, who began his journalism career in the U.S. Army, won the Pulitzer Prize in 1964 for his reporting from Vietnam. He joined the *New York Times* in 1968 as a foreign correspondent and in 1977 became a science reporter.

galaxy—perhaps even in the universe. I would bet that the twenty-first century will pass without anyone finding conclusive evidence of extraterrestrial life, intelligent or not.

There have been many false alarms in the past, like the discovery of   5
"canals" on Mars, which proved to be illusions imagined by the American astronomer Percival Lowell. There will be many more. And many investigators will take comfort from the Copernican Principle, the assumption that no particular place or time is likely to be special and that inhabited planets like Earth must therefore be common.

But one of the faults of statistical estimates of extraterrestrial life is that it is impossible to extrapolate anything from a single data point. And that's all we have: Earth.

The environmental conditions favoring the creation of life may not be nearly as common as was postulated in 1961 by Frank Drake, one of the main instigators of SETI, the search for extraterrestrial intelligence. The Drake Equation, as it came to be known, incorporated estimates of the rate at which stars are born in the galaxy, the fraction of stars with planets, the fraction of those planets on which life originates, and so forth. By that calculation, there should be about 10,000 civilizations in our galaxy capable of interstellar communication.

But in the thirty-nine years since radio telescopes began searching, nothing has turned up.

Certainly, sending signals across tens, hundreds or thousands of light years poses staggering difficulties. But a more fundamental reason for our failure to find extraterrestrial life could be that we are, indeed, alone.

Many astronomers have suggested that the conditions for life can   10
exist only on a rocky planet with lots of liquid water and other possibly rare assets like a reliable sun producing steady radiation over a long period; a Jupiter-size planet in the outer solar system to sweep up asteroids and other objects that would otherwise continuously bombard an Earth-like planet; and an exceptionally large moon like ours, to cushion the disruptive gravitational influences of other planets. These and other conditions may be so unlikely as to rule out all life except that inhabiting a unique fluke—Earth.

We have already searched for signals from nearby stars like Alpha Centauri and found nothing.

Lots of reasons can be adduced to explain these failures, but the simplest explanation—and so the one favored by Occam's razor—is that there is nothing out there to find. In any case, I'm not holding my breath.

DISCUSSION QUESTIONS

1. What parts of Wilford's argument are based on facts? What parts on analogy? On inference? Which of his claims is most convincing?

2. How does Wilford assure the reader that he is informed about the subject?

3. When Wilford speaks of extraterrestrial life, what kind of life is he referring to? Is this different from what sky-watchers refer to as extraterrestrials?

4. How does Browne use history and logic to support his skeptical view?

5. Does Browne's description of the necessary conditions for life convince you of his claim? Why or why not?

6. Are there any issues in this debate on which the two writers agree? What is the strongest point of difference between them? Did either argument convince you to change your mind?

TAKING THE DEBATE ONLINE

For these and additional research URLs, see www.bedfordstmartins.com/rottenberg.

- *Astrobiology Central: The Quest for Extraterrestrial Life*
  http://www.angelfire.com/on2/daviddarling

  This frequently updated collection of links lists sources on the Internet concerning life on other planets.

- *Life on Other Planets in the Solar System*
  http://www.resa.net/nasa

  This site examines the scientific issues concerning the search for extraterrestrial life, with links to articles and other sources on the Internet.

- *The Search for Extraterrestrial Life*
  http://www.sciam.com/explorations/010697sagan/010697sagan3.html

  This *Scientific American* article, written by Carl Sagan, examines evidence of organic life on other planets.

- *The Shape of Extraterrestrial Life*
  http://science.nasa.gov/newhome/headlines/ast19may99_8.htm

  This article describes the use of mathematical computations to identify and classify the tiniest life forms found on Earth and in samples from Mars.

- *SETI Institute*
  http://www.seti-inst.edu

  The mission of the SETI Institute is to explore, understand, and explain the origin, nature, prevalence, and distribution of life in the universe.

- *SETI@home*
  http://setiathome.ssl.Berkeley.edu

  SETI@home is a scientific experiment that uses Internet-connected computers in the Search for Extraterrestrial Intelligence (SETI). You can participate by running a free program that downloads and analyzes radio telescope data.

For further information, try entering the terms *extraterrestrial life* or *alien life* on a search engine such as *Google, Metacrawler,* or *Hotbot.*

EXERCISES

1. Look for personal advertisements (in which men and women advertise for various kinds of companionship) in a local or national paper or magazine. (The *Village Voice,* a New York paper, is an outstanding source.) What inferences can you draw about the people who place these ads? About the facts they choose to provide? How did you come to these conclusions? You might also try to infer the reasons that more women than men place ads and why this change has occurred.

2. "I Like Colonel Sanders" is the title of an article that praises ugly architecture, shopping malls, laundromats, and other symbols of "plastic" America. The author claims that these aspects of the American scene have unique and positive values. Defend or refute his claim by pointing out some of the values of these things and giving reasons for your own assessments.

3. A psychiatrist says that in pro football personality traits determine the positions of the players. Write an essay developing this idea and providing adequate evidence for your claim. Or make inferences about the relationship between the personalities of the players and another sport that you know well.

4. At least one city in the world—Reykjavik, the capital of Iceland—bans dogs from the city. Defend or attack this policy by using both facts and values to support your claim.

5. Write a review of a movie, play, television program, concert, restaurant, or book. Make clear your criteria for judgment and their order of importance.

6. The controversy concerning seat belts and air bags in automobiles has generated a variety of proposals, one of which is mandatory use of seat belts in all the states. Make your own policy claim regarding laws about safety devices (the wearing of motorcycle helmets is another thorny subject), and defend it by using both facts and values—facts about safety, values concerning individual freedom and responsibility.

7. Select a familiar ritual, and argue for or against the value it represents. *Examples:* the high school prom, Christmas gift-giving, a fraternity initiation, a wedding, a confirmation or bar mitzvah, a funeral ceremony, a Fourth of July celebration.

8. Choose a recommended policy—from the school newspaper or elsewhere—and argue that it will or will not work to produce beneficial changes. *Examples:* expansion of core curriculum requirements, comprehensive tests as a graduation requirement, reinstitution of a

physical education requirement, removal of junk food from vending machines.

CRITICAL LISTENING

9. Have you ever been a member of a group which tried but failed to solve a problem through discussion? Communication theorists talk about *interference*, defined by one writer as "anything that hinders or lessens the efficiency of communication."[6] Some of the elements of interference in the delivery of oral messages are fatigue, anger, inattention, vague language, personality conflict, and political bias. You will probably be able to think of others. Did any of these elements prevent the group from arriving at an agreement? Describe the situation and the kinds of interference that you noticed.

[6]Richard E. Crable, *One to Another* (New York: Harper and Row, 1981), p. 18.

4

Definition

THE PURPOSES OF DEFINITION

Before we examine the other elements of argument, we need to consider definition, a component you may have to deal with early in writing an essay. Definition may be used in two ways: to clarify the meanings of vague or ambiguous terms or as a method of development for the whole essay. In some arguments your claims will contain words that need explanation before you can proceed with any discussion. But you may also want to devote an entire essay to the elaboration of a broad concept or experience that cannot be adequately defined in a shorter space.

The Roman statesman Cicero said, "Every rational discussion of anything whatsoever should begin with a definition in order to make clear what is the subject of dispute." You have probably already discovered the importance of definition in argument. If you have ever had a disagreement with your parents about using the car or drinking or dyeing your hair or going away for a weekend or staying out till three in the morning, you know that you were really arguing about the meaning of the term *adolescent freedom*.

Arguments often revolve around definitions of crucial terms. For example, how does one define *democracy*? Does a democracy guarantee freedom of the press, freedom of worship, freedom of assembly, and freedom of movement? In the United States, we would argue that such freedoms are essential to any definition of *democracy*. But countries in which these freedoms are nonexistent also represent themselves as democracies or governments of the people. In the words of Senator Daniel P. Moynihan, "For years now the most brutal totalitarian regimes have called themselves 'people's' or 'democratic' republics." Rulers in such governments are aware that defining their regimes as democratic may win the approval of people who would otherwise condemn them. In his formidable attack on totalitarianism, *Nineteen Eighty-Four,* George Orwell coined the slogans "War Is Peace" and "Slavery Is Freedom," phrases that represent the corrupt use of definition to distort reality.

But even where there is no intention to deceive, the snares of definition are difficult to avoid. How do you define *abortion*? Is it "termination of pregnancy"? Or is it "murder of an unborn child"? During a celebrated trial in 1975 of a physician who performed an abortion and was accused of manslaughter, the prosecution often used the word *baby* to refer to the fetus, but the defense referred to "the products of conception." These definitions of *fetus* reflected the differing judgments of those on opposite sides. Not only do judgments create definitions; definitions influence judgments. In the abortion trial, the definitions of *fetus* used by both sides were meant to promote either approval or disapproval of the doctor's action.

Definitions can indeed change the nature of an event or a "fact." How many farms are there in the state of New York? The answer to the question depends on the definition of *farm*. In 1979 the *New York Times* reported:

> Because of a change in the official definition of the word "farm," New York lost 20 percent of its farms on January 1, with numbers dropping from 56,000 to 45,000. . . .
>
> Before the change, a farm was defined as "any place from which $250 or more of agricultural products is sold" yearly or "any place of 10 acres or more from which $50 or more of agricultural products is sold" yearly. Now a farm is "any place from which $1,000 or more of agricultural products is sold" in a year.[1]

A change in the definition of *poverty* can have similar results. An article in the *New York Times,* whose headline reads, "A Revised Definition of Poverty May Raise Number of U.S. Poor," makes this clear.

> The official definition of *poverty* used by the Federal Government for three decades is based simply on cash income before taxes. But in a report to be issued on Wednesday, a panel of experts convened by the [National] Academy of Sciences three years ago at the behest of Congress says the Government should move toward a concept of poverty

---

[1] *New York Times,* March 4, 1979, sec. 1, p. 40.

based on disposable income, the amount left after a family pays taxes and essential expenses.[2]

The differences are wholly a matter of definition. But such differences can have serious consequences for those being defined, most of all in the disposition of billions of federal dollars in aid of various kinds. In 1992 the Census Bureau classified 14.5 percent of Americans as poor. Under the new guidelines, at least 15 or 16 percent would be poor, and, under some measures recommended by a government panel, 18 percent would be so defined.

In fact, local and federal courts almost every day redefine traditional concepts that can have a direct impact on our everyday lives. The definition of *family,* for example, has undergone significant changes that acknowledge the existence of new relationships. In January 1990 the New Jersey Supreme Court ruled that a family may be defined as "one or more persons occupying a dwelling unit as a single nonprofit housekeeping unit, who are living together as a stable and permanent living unit, being a traditional family unit or the *functional equivalent* thereof" (italics for emphasis added). This meant that ten Glassboro State College students, unrelated by blood, could continue to occupy a single-family house despite the objection of the borough of Glassboro.[3] Even the legal definition of maternity has shifted. Who is the mother — the woman who contributes the egg or the woman (the surrogate) who bears the child? Several states, acknowledging the changes brought by medical technology, now recognize a difference between the birth mother and the legal mother.

DEFINING THE TERMS IN YOUR ARGUMENT

In some of your arguments you will introduce terms that require definition. We've pointed out that a definition of *poverty* is crucial to any debate on the existence of poverty in the United States. The same may be true in a debate about the legality of euthanasia, or mercy killing. Are the arguers referring to passive euthanasia (the withdrawal of life-support systems) or to active euthanasia (the direct administration of drugs to hasten death)?

It is not uncommon, in fact, for arguments about controversial questions to turn into arguments about the definition of terms. If, for example, you wanted to argue in favor of the regulation of religious cults, you would first have to define *cult.* In so doing, you might discover that it is not easy to distinguish clearly between conventional religions and cults. Then you would have to define *regulation,* spelling out the legal restrictions you favored so as to make them apply only to cults, not to

[2] *New York Times,* April 10, 1995, sec. A, p. 1.
[3] *New York Times,* February 1, 1990, sec. B, p. 5.

established religions. An argument on the subject might end almost before it began if writer and reader could not agree on definitions of these terms. While clear definitions do not guarantee agreement, they do ensure that all parties understand the nature of the argument.

■ Defining Vague and Ambiguous Terms

You will need to define other terms in addition to those in your claim. If you use words and phrases that have two or more meanings, they may appear vague and ambiguous to your reader. In arguments of value and policy abstract terms such as *freedom, justice, patriotism,* and *equality* require clarification. Despite their vagueness, however, they are among the most important in the language because they represent the ideals that shape our laws. When conflicts arise, the courts must define these terms to establish the legality of certain practices. Is the Ku Klux Klan permitted to make disparaging public statements about ethnic and racial groups? That depends on the court's definition of *free speech.* Can execution for some crimes be considered cruel and unusual punishment? That, too, depends on the court's definition of *cruel and unusual punishment.* In addition, such terms as *happiness, mental health, success,* and *creativity* often defy precise definition because they reflect the differing values within a society or a culture.

The definition of *success,* for example, varies not only among social groups but also among individuals within the group. One scientist has postulated five signs by which to measure success: wealth (including health), security (confidence in retaining the wealth), reputation, performance, and contentment.[4] Consider whether all of these are necessary to your own definition of *success.* If not, which may be omitted? Do you think others should be added? Notice that one of the signs—reputation—is defined by the community; another—contentment—can be measured only by the individual. The assessment of performance probably owes something to both the group and the individual.

Christopher Atkins, an actor, gave an interviewer an example of an externalized definition of success—that is, a definition based on the standards imposed by other people:

> Success to me is judged through the eyes of others. I mean, if you're walking around saying, "I own a green Porsche," you might meet somebody who says, "Hey, that's no big deal I own a green Porsche and a house." So all of a sudden, you don't feel so successful. Really, it's in the eyes of others.[5]

---

[4] Gwynn Nettler, *Social Concerns* (New York: McGraw-Hill, 1976), pp. 196–197.
[5] *New York Times,* August 6, 1982, sec. 3, p. 8.

So difficult is the formulation of a universally accepted measure for success that some scholars regard the concept as meaningless. Nevertheless, we continue to use the word as if it represented a definable concept because the idea of success, however defined, is important for the identity and development of the individual and the group. It is clear, however, that when crossing subcultural boundaries, even within a small group, we need to be aware of differences in the use of the word. If contentment—that is, the satisfaction of achieving a small personal goal—is enough, then a person lying under a palm tree subsisting on handouts from picnickers may be a success. But you should not expect all your readers to agree that these criteria are enough to define *success*.

In arguing about aesthetic matters, whose vocabulary is almost always abstract, the criteria for judgment must be revealed, either directly or indirectly, and then the abstract terms that represent the criteria must be defined. If you want to say that a film is distinguished by great acting, have you made clear what you mean by *great*? That we do not always understand or agree on the definition of *great* is apparent, say, on the morning after the Oscar winners have been announced.

Even subjects that you feel sure you can identify may offer surprising insights when you rethink them for an extended definition. One critic, defining *rock music*, argued that the distinguishing characteristic of rock music was noise—not beat, not harmonies, not lyrics, not vocal style, but noise, "nasty, discordant, irritating noise—or, to its practitioners, unfettered, liberating, expressive noise."[6] In producing this definition, the author had to give a number of examples to prove that he was justified in rejecting the most familiar criteria.

Consider the definition of *race*, around which so much of American history has revolved, often with tragic consequences. Until recently, the only categories listed in the census were white, black, Asian-Pacific, and Native American, "with the Hispanic population straddling them all." But rapidly increasing intermarriage and ethnic identity caused a number of political and ethnic groups to demand changes in the classifications of the Census Bureau. Some Arab Americans, for example, prefer to be counted as "Middle Eastern" rather than white. Children of black-white unions are defined as black 60 percent of the time, while children of Asian-white unions are described as Asian 42 percent of the time. Research is now being conducted to discover how people feel about the terms being used to define them. As one anthropologist pointed out, "Socially and politically assigned attributes have a lot to do with access to economic resources."[7]

[6]Jon Pareles, "Noise Evokes Modern Chaos for a Band," *New York Times*, March 9, 1986, sec. H, p. 26.

[7]*Wall Street Journal*, September 9, 1995, sec. B, p. 1.

METHODS FOR DEFINING TERMS

The following strategies for defining terms in an argument are by no means mutually exclusive. You may use all of them in a single argumentative essay.

■ Dictionary Definition

Giving a dictionary definition is the simplest and most obvious way to define a term. An unabridged dictionary is the best source because it usually gives examples of the way a word can be used in a sentence; that is, it furnishes the proper context.

In many cases, the dictionary definition alone is not sufficient. It may be too broad or too narrow for your purpose. Suppose, in an argument about pornography, you wanted to define the word *obscene*. *Webster's New International Dictionary* (third edition, unabridged) gives the definition of *obscene* as "offensive to taste; foul; loathsome; disgusting." But these synonyms do not tell you what qualities make an object or an event or an action "foul," "loathsome," and "disgusting." In 1973 the Supreme Court, attempting to narrow the definition of *obscenity*, ruled that obscenity was to be determined by the community in accordance with local standards. One person's obscenity, as numerous cases have demonstrated, may be another person's art. The celebrated trials in the early twentieth century about the distribution of novels regarded as pornographic—D. H. Lawrence's *Lady Chatterley's Lover* and James Joyce's *Ulysses*—emphasized the problems of defining obscenity.

Another dictionary definition may strike you as too narrow. *Patriotism,* for example, is defined in one dictionary as "love and loyal or zealous support of one's country, especially in all matters involving other countries." Some readers may want to include an unwillingness to support government policies they consider wrong.

■ Stipulation

In stipulating the meaning of a term, the writer asks the reader to accept a definition that may be different from the conventional one. He or she does this to limit or control the argument. Someone has said, "Part of the task of keeping definitions in our civilization clear and pure is to keep a firm democratic rein on those with the power, or craving the power, to stipulate meaning." Perhaps this writer was thinking of a term like *national security,* which can be defined by a nation's leaders in such a way as to sanction persecution of citizens and reckless military adventures. Likewise, a term such as *liberation* can be appropriated by terrorist groups whose activities often lead to oppression rather than liberation.

Religion is usually defined as a belief in a supernatural power to be obeyed and worshiped. But in an article entitled "Civil Religion in America," a sociologist offers a different meaning.

> While some have argued that Christianity is the national faith, and others that church and synagogue celebrate only the generalized religion of "the American way of life," few have realized that there actually exists alongside of and rather clearly differentiated from the churches an elaborate and well-institutionalized civil religion in America. This article argues not only that there is such a thing, but also that this religion . . . has its own seriousness and integrity and requires the same care in understanding that any other religion does.[8]

When the author adds, "This religion—there seems no other word for it—was neither sectarian nor in any specific sense Christian," he emphasizes that he is distinguishing his definition of religion from definitions that associate religion and church.

Even the word *violence,* which the dictionary defines as "physical force used so as to injure or damage" and whose meaning seems so clear and uncompromising, can be manipulated to produce a definition different from the one normally understood by most people. Some pacifists refer to conditions in which "people are deprived of choices in a systematic way" as "institutionalized quiet violence." Even where no physical force is employed, this lack of choice in schools, in the workplace, in the black ghettos is defined as violence.[9]

In *Through the Looking-Glass* Alice asked Humpty Dumpty "whether you can make words mean so many different things."

> "When *I* use a word," Humpty Dumpty said scornfully, "it means just what I choose it to mean—neither more nor less."[10]

A writer, however, is not free to invent definitions that no one will recognize or that create rather than solve problems between writer and reader.

■ Negation

To avoid confusion it is sometimes helpful to tell the reader what a term is *not.* In discussing euthanasia, a writer might say, "By euthanasia I do not mean active intervention to hasten the death of the patient."

A negative definition may be more extensive, depending on the complexity of the term and the writer's ingenuity. The critic of rock music quoted earlier in this chapter arrived at his definition of *noise* by rejecting

[8] Robert N. Bellah, "Civil Religion in America," *Daedalus,* Winter 1967, p. 1.

[9] Newton Garver, "What Violence Is," in James Rachels, ed., *Moral Choices* (New York: Harper and Row, 1971), pp. 248–249.

[10] Lewis Carroll, *Alice in Wonderland and Through the Looking-Glass* (New York: Grosset and Dunlap, 1948), p. 238.

attributes that seemed misleading. The former Communist party member Whittaker Chambers, in a foreword to a book on the spy trial of Alger Hiss, defined *communism* this way:

> First, let me try to say what Communism is not. It is not simply a vicious plot hatched by wicked men in a subcellar. It is not just the writings of Marx and Lenin, dialectical materialism, the Politburo, the labor theory of value, the theory of the general strike, the Red Army secret police, labor camps, underground conspiracy, the dictatorship of the proletariat, the technique of the coup d'état. It is not even those chanting, bannered millions that stream periodically, like disorganized armies, through the heart of the world's capitals: Moscow, New York, Tokyo, Paris, Rome. These are expressions, but they are not what Communism is about.[11]

This, of course, is only part of the definition. Any writer beginning a definition in the negative must go on to define what the term *is*.

■ Examples

One of the most effective ways of defining terms in an argument is to use examples. Both real and hypothetical examples can bring life to abstract and ambiguous terms. The writer in the following passage defines *preferred categories* (classes of people who are meant to benefit from affirmative action policies) by invoking specific cases:

> The absence of definitions points up one of the problems with preferred categories. . . . These preferred categories take no account of family wealth or educational advantages. A black whose father is a judge or physician deserves preferential treatment over any nonminority applicant. The latter might have fought his way out of the grinding poverty of Appalachia, or might be the first member of an Italian American or a Polish American family to complete high school. But no matter.[12]

Insanity is a word that has been used and misused to describe a variety of conditions. Even psychiatrists are in dispute about its meaning. In the following anecdote, examples narrow and refine the definition.

> Dr. Zilboorg says that present-day psychiatry does not possess any satisfactory definition of mental illness or neurosis. To illustrate, he told a story: A psychiatrist was recently asked for a definition of a "well-adjusted person" (not even slightly peculiar). The definition: "A person who feels in harmony with himself and who is not in conflict with his environment." It sounded fine, but up popped a heckler. "Would you

[11] *Witness* (New York: Random House, 1952), p. 8.
[12] Anthony Lombardo, "Quotas Work Both Ways," *U.S. Catholic*, February 1974, p. 39.

then consider an anti-Nazi working in the underground against Hitler a maladjusted person?" "Well," the psychiatrist hemmed, "I withdraw the latter part of my definition." Dr. Zilboorg withdrew the first half for him. Many persons in perfect harmony with themselves, he pointed out, are in "distinctly pathological states."[13]

■ Extended Definition

When we speak of an extended definition, we usually refer not only to length but also to the variety of methods for developing the definition. Let's take the word *materialism*. A dictionary entry offers the following sentence fragments as definitions: "1. the doctrine that comfort, pleasure, and wealth are the only or highest goals or values. 2. the tendency to be more concerned with material than the spiritual goals or values." But the term *materialism* has acquired so many additional meanings, especially emotional ones, that an extended definition serves a useful purpose in clarifying the many different ideas surrounding our understanding of the term.

Below is a much longer definition of *materialism*, which appears at the beginning of an essay entitled "People and Things: Reflections on Materialism."[14]

> There are two contemporary usages of the term *materialism*, and it is important to distinguish between them. On the one hand we can talk about *instrumental materialism*, or the use of material objects to make life longer, safer, more enjoyable. By instrumental, we mean that objects act as essential means for discovering and furthering personal values and goals of life, so that the objects are instruments used to realize and further those goals. There is little negative connotation attached to this meaning of the word, since one would think that it is perfectly sensible to use things for such purposes. While it is true that the United States is the epitome of materialism in this sense, it is also true that most people in every society aspire to reach our level of instrumental materialism.
>
> On the other hand the term has a more negative connotation, which might be conveyed by the phrase *terminal materialism*. This is the sense critics use when they apply the term to Americans. What they mean is that we not only use our material resources as instruments to make life more manageable, but that we reduce our ultimate goals to the possession of things. They believe that we don't just use our cars to get from place to place, but that we consider the ownership of expensive cars one of the central values in life. Terminal materialism means that the object is valued only because it indicates an end in itself, a possession.

---

[13] Quoted in *The Art of Making Sense*, p. 48.
[14] Mihaly Csikszentmihalyi and Eugene Rochberg-Halton, "People and Things: Reflections on Materialism," *University of Chicago Magazine*, Spring 1978, pp. 7–8.

In instrumental materialism there is a sense of directionality, in which a person's goals may be furthered through the interactions with the object. A book, for example, can reveal new possibilities or widen a person's view of the world, or an old photograph can be cherished because it embodies a relationship. But in terminal materialism, there is no sense of reciprocal interaction in the relation between the object and the end. The end is valued as final, not as itself a means to further ends. And quite often it is only the status label or image associated with the object that is valued, rather than the actual object.

In the essay from which this passage is taken, the authors distinguish between two kinds of materialism and provide an extended explanation, using contrast and examples as methods of development. They are aware that the common perception of materialism—the love of things for their own sake—is a negative one. But this view, according to the authors, doesn't fully account for the attitudes of many Americans toward the things they own. There is, in fact, another more positive meaning that the authors call *instrumental materialism.* You will recognize that the authors are *stipulating* a meaning with which their readers might not be familiar. In their essay they distinguish between *terminal materialism,* in which "the object is valued only because it indicates an end in itself," and *instrumental materialism,* "the use of material objects to make life longer, safer, more enjoyable." Since *instrumental materialism* is the less familiar definition, the essay provides a great number of examples that show how people of three different generations value photographs, furniture, musical instruments, plants, and other objects for their memories and personal associations rather than as proof of the owners' ability to acquire the objects or win the approval of others.

THE DEFINITION ESSAY

The argumentative essay can take the form of an extended definition. An example of such an essay is the one from which we've just quoted, as well as the five essays at the end of this chapter. The definition essay is appropriate when the idea under consideration is so controversial or so heavy with historical connotations that even a paragraph or two cannot make clear exactly what the arguer wants his or her readers to understand. For example, if you were preparing a definition of *patriotism,* you would want to answer some or all of the following questions. You would probably use a number of methods to develop your definition: personal narrative, examples, stipulation, comparison and contrast, and cause-and-effect analysis.

DEFINITION

Dictionary definition   Is the dictionary definition the one I will elaborate on? Do I need to stipulate other meanings?

Personal history   Where did I first acquire my notions of patriotism? What was taught? How and by whom was it taught?

Cultural context   Has my patriotic feeling changed in the last few years? Why or why not? Does my own patriotism reflect the mood of the country or the group to which I belong?

Values   What is the value of patriotism? Does it make me more humane, more civilized? Is patriotism consistent with tolerance of other systems and cultures? Is patriotism the highest duty of a citizen? Can other values take precedence? What did President Kennedy's injunction mean: "Ask not what your country can do for you; ask what you can do for your country"?

Behavior   How do I express my patriotism (or lack of it)? Can it be expressed through dissent? What sacrifice, if any, would I make for my country?

Writer's Guide to the Definition Paper
Writing a Paper That Defines Terms

The following important steps should be taken when you write an essay of definition.

1. Choose a term that needs definition because it is controversial or ambiguous, or because you want to offer a personal definition that differs from the accepted interpretation. Explain why an extended definition is necessary. Or choose an experience that lends itself to treatment in an extended definition. One student defined *culture shock* as she had experienced it while studying abroad in Hawaii among students of a different ethnic background.

2. Decide on the thesis — the point of view you wish to develop about the term you are defining. If you want to define *heroism,* for example, you may choose to develop the idea that this quality depends on motivation and awareness of danger rather than on the specific act performed by the hero.

3. Begin by consulting the dictionary for the conventional definition. Make clear whether you want to elaborate on the dictionary definition or take issue with it because you think it is misleading or inadequate.

4. Distinguish wherever possible between the term you are defining and other terms with which it might be confused. If you are defining *love,* can you make a clear distinction between the different kinds of emotional attachments contained in the word?

5. Try to think of several methods of developing the definition — using examples, comparison and contrast, analogy, cause-and-effect analysis.

However, you may discover that one method alone — say, use of examples — will suffice to narrow and refine your definition. See the sample essay "The Nature of Prejudice" on page 138 for an example of such a development.

6. Arrange your supporting material in an order that gives emphasis to the most important ideas.

A NOTE ON COMPARISON AND CONTRAST

One writing assignment in this chapter calls for using comparison or contrast to clarify a term (page 153). But defining terms is not the only use for this argumentative strategy. We can use it to defend or refute all kinds of claims. Comparison is an obvious device for claims of value, in which we argue that one thing is better or worse than another. Advertisers, in their claims of policy, routinely contrast their own products with those of others.

Although we use two words—*compare* and *contrast*—to describe this form of development, the two processes are not really different. In fact, dictionaries list *contrast* as a synonym for *compare* because both words share this meaning: "to set side by side in order to show differences and likenesses." When we make a distinction, a comparison emphasizes likenesses, and a contrast emphasizes differences. But we would not undertake to compare things unless we suspected some contrasts. That is, you might compare headache remedies, but only if you thought there were differences among them.

A comparison-and-contrast essay observes two basic rules. First, it compares two things belonging to the same general class, as in the following questions: How does the 2001 movie *Ocean's Eleven* compare with the 1960 version starring Frank Sinatra? How do computer games compare with board games such as chess and checkers? How does bilingual education compare with English-only instruction? A popular admonition says, "You can't compare apples and oranges." But you *can* compare them because, like the subjects mentioned above, they share several significant characteristics. You can't compare apples and monkeys because they do not. Notice that in the article "Addiction Is Not a Disease" (p. 124) the author finds a common element in the condition of disease; this allows him to stress the differences between "real" and "addictive" diseases. In "Single-Sex Education Benefits Men Too" (p. 177), the shared element is the advantages for both men and women of education in single-sex colleges. The author argues the unfairness of insisting that men's colleges admit women.

Second, the things you compare or contrast must be roughly of the same magnitude. Although Michael Jordan and the kid who shoots baskets in the driveway both play basketball, contrasting them would serve

Writer's Guide to the Comparison Paper
Writing an Essay of Comparison or Contrast

1. Choose subjects worth reading about. Ask yourself: Is there some contro- versy or misunderstanding about the subject that needs to be clarified? Or some new information that might prove useful? It ought to be clear that you are comparing or contrasting to make an important point.

2. Make sure that the two or more subjects you choose are close enough in essential characteristics to lend themselves to this treatment.

3. Organize your essay in one of two ways. For relatively simple arguments, use the *block method,* in which you first assemble all the support material for one side and then assemble all the material for the other. For example, in a long essay arguing for gun control, one writer has chosen to contrast Seattle in the United States with Vancouver in Canada.[15] In a short essay she might begin with this thesis statement: "The twin cities of Seattle and Vancouver resemble each other in many ways, but there is a life and death difference because guns are reasonably restricted in Vancouver but out of control in Seattle." This would be followed by several paragraphs about crime and gun control in Seattle and then by several paragraphs about the same conditions in Vancouver. Her conclusion would offer an interpreta- tion of her data. In a comparison-and-contrast essay with many points, your argument will probably be easier to follow if you use another kind of organization — the *alternating* or *point-by-point method.* With this form of development, relevant points of interest are presented, and each city's re- lationship to these topics is discussed. They might include crime rates, ac- quisitions of guns, gun injuries and deaths, and penalties for infractions. Which approach you choose depends on the subject and the length of your paper.

4. Use transitional expressions where necessary for coherence. For com- parison, use words and phrases like *moreover, in addition, likewise,* and *also.* For contrast, use *but, unlike, however,* and *on the other hand.*

little purpose. Similarly, to compare crime in the United States with crime in a small tribal society in the rain forest would not be effective.

All successful essays of comparison and contrast do more than sim- ply list the distinguishing characteristics of the subjects. Good essays pro- vide evidence to support their claim that the similarities or differences are meaningful. (No writer wants the reader to say, "So what?") The com- parison or contrast should give readers new and useful information, an- swer a challenging question, lead them to a consideration of some larger issue or even guide them to a solution of a problem.

[15]Claire Safran, "A Tale of Two Cities—and the Differences Guns Make," *Good Housekeeping,* November 1993.

For example, a recent television newsmagazine report contrasted the upbringing of girls and boys in the United States. We learned that girls are allowed, even encouraged, to express and share their emotions. Boys, on the other hand, are discouraged from expressing them, especially if the emotions are fear or sadness. This was interesting information, but the reporter wanted to establish a reason for emphasizing the contrast. He went on to evaluate the consequences of these patterns for the well-being of boys. In other words, the contrast supported the conclusion that the upbringing of boys was creating serious problems for them that persisted into adulthood.

Another example of the use of contrast to support a controversial claim appears in the short debate at the end of Chapter 5. In arguing for the health benefits derived from the use of animals for research, Heloisa Sabin contrasts the years of the early fifties, when polio was epidemic, to the years after a vaccine was developed as a result of such research.

SAMPLE ANNOTATED ANALYSIS

Addiction Is Not a Disease

STANTON PEELE

Why Addiction Is Not a Disease

Medical schools are finally teaching about alcoholism; Johns Hopkins will require basic training for all students and clinicians. . . . Alcoholism, as a chronic disease, offers "a fantastic vehicle to teach other concepts," says Jean Kinney [of Dartmouth's Cork Institute]. . . . William Osler, Kinney remarks, coined the aphorism that "to know syphilis is to know medicine." . . . Now, she says, the same can be said of alcoholism.

— "The Neglected Disease in Medical Education," *Science*[16]

OCD (obsessive-compulsive disorder) is apparently rare in the general population.

—American Psychiatric Association, 1980[17]

[16]C. Holden, "The Neglected Disease in Medical Education," *Science* 229 (1985), pp. 741–742.

[17]*Diagnostic and Statistical Manual of Mental Disorders,* 3rd ed. (Washington, D.C.: American Psychiatric Association, 1980).

Stanton Peele, who received his Ph.D. in social psychology from the University of Michigan, is a fellow at the Lindsmith Center, a drug policy think tank in New York City. He is also the coauthor of the best-selling *Love and Addiction* (1975). This excerpt is from *Diseasing of America* (Boston: Houghton Mifflin, 1989).

The evidence is strong OCD is a common mental disorder that, like other stigmatized and hidden disorders in the past, may be ready for discovery and demands for treatment on a large scale.

—National Institute of Mental Health, 1988[18]

Statement of the
problem: definition of
addiction as a disease

Exaggeration of the
problem

Real problems of drug
users in the ghetto

In America today, we are bombarded with news about drug and alcohol problems. We may ask ourselves, "How did we get here?" Alternatively, we may wonder if these problems are really worse now than they were five or ten years ago, or fifty or one hundred. Actually, in many cases the answer is no. Estimates of the number of alcoholics requiring treatment are wildly overblown, and reputable epidemiological researchers find that as little as 1 percent of the population fits the clinical definition of alcoholism—as opposed to the 10 percent figure regularly used by the alcoholism industry. Meanwhile, cocaine use is down. All indicators are that very few young people who try drugs ever become regular users, and fewer still get "hooked."

Of course, we have real problems. The nightly news carries story after story of inner-city violence between crack gangs and of totally desolate urban environments where drugs reign supreme. The cocaine problem has resolved itself—not exclusively, but very largely—into a ghetto problem, like many that face America. A *New York Times* front-page story based on an eight-year study of young drug users showed that those who abuse drugs have a number of serious background problems, and *that these problems don't disappear from their lives when they stop using drugs.*[19] In other words, the sources—and solutions—for what is going on in our ghettos are only very secondarily a matter of drug availability and use.

America is a society broken into two worlds. The reality of the crack epidemic and of inner cities and poor environments sometimes explodes

[18]M. Karno et al., "The Epidemiology of Obsessive-Compulsive Disorder in Five U.S. Communities," *Archives of General Psychiatry* 45 (1988), pp. 1094–1099.

[19]S. Blakeslee, "Eight-Year Study Finds Two Sides to Teen-Age Drug Use," *New York Times,* July 21, 1988, p. 1.

Broadening of the
definition of <u>addiction</u>

and impinges unpleasantly on our consciousness. For the most part, however, our reality is that of the middle class, which fills our magazines with health stories and warnings about family problems and the strivings of young professionals to find satisfaction. And for some time now, this other world has also focused on addiction. But this new addiction marketplace is only sometimes linked to alcohol and drugs. Even when it is, we have to redefine alcoholism as the new Betty Ford kind, which is marked by a general dull malaise, a sense that one is drinking too much, and—for many, like Betty Ford and Kitty Dukakis—relying on prescribed drugs to make life bearable.

However we define loss-of-control drinking, Betty Ford didn't experience it. But treating problems like hers and those of so many media stars is far more rewarding and profitable than trying to deal with street derelicts or ghetto addicts. At the same time, *everything can be an addiction*. This remarkable truth—which I first described in *Love and Addiction* in 1975—has so overwhelmed us as a society that we have gone haywire. We want to pass laws to excuse compulsive gamblers when they embezzle money to gamble and to force insurance companies to pay to treat them. We want to treat people who can't find love and who instead (when they are women) go after dopey, superficial men or (when they are men) pursue endless sexual liaisons without finding true happiness. And we want to call all these things—and many, many more—addictions.

Examples of the
extremes

Since I was part of the movement to label non-drug-related behaviors as addictions, what am I complaining about? My entire purpose in writing *Love and Addiction* was to explain addictions as part of a larger description of people's lives. Addiction is an experience that people can get caught up in but that still expresses their values, skills at living, and personal resolve—or lack of it. The label *addiction* does not obviate either the meaning of the addictive involvement within people's lives, or their responsibility for their misbehavior or for their choices in continuing the addiction. Forty million Americans

Claim: addiction as an
expression of values

have quit smoking. What, then, are we to think about the people who do not quit but who sue a tobacco company for addicting them to cigarettes after they learn they are going to die from a smoking-related ailment?

This discrepancy between understanding addiction within the larger context of a person's life and regarding it as an *explanation* of that life underlies my opposition to the "disease theory" of addiction, which I contest throughout this book. My view of addiction explicitly refutes this theory's contentions that (1) the addiction exists *independently* of the rest of a person's life and *drives* all of his or her choices; (2) it is progressive and irreversible, so that the addiction *inevitably worsens* unless the person seeks medical treatment or joins an AA-type support group; (3) addiction means the person is incapable of controlling his or her behavior, either in relation to the addictive object itself or — when the person is intoxicated or in pursuit of the addiction — in relation to the person's dealings with the rest of the world. Everything I oppose in the disease view is represented in the passive, *1984*-ish phrase, *alcohol abuse victim,* to replace *alcohol abuser.* On the contrary, this book maintains that people are *active agents* in — not passive victims of — their addictions.

While I do believe that a host of human habits and compulsions can be understood as addictions, I think the disease version of addiction does *at least* as much harm as good. An addiction does not mean that God in heaven decided which people are alcoholics and addicts. There is no biological urge to form addictions, one that we will someday find under a microscope and that will finally make sense of all these different cravings and idiocies (such as exercising to the point of injury or having sex with people who are bad for you). No medical treatment will ever be created to excise addictions from people's lives, and support groups that convince people that they are helpless and will forever be incapable of controlling an activity are better examples of self-fulfilling prophecies than of therapy.

The opposing view that addiction is a disease

Harmfulness of this view

Growth of an addiction
industry

What is this new addiction industry meant to accomplish? More and more addictions are being discovered, and new addicts are being identified, until all of us will be locked into our own little addictive worlds with other addicts like ourselves, defined by the special interests of our neuroses. What a repugnant world to imagine, as well as a hopeless one. Meanwhile, *all of the addictions we define are increasing.* In the first place, we tell people they can never get better from their "diseases." In the second, we constantly find new addicts, looking for them in all sorts of new areas of behavior and labeling them at earlier ages on the basis of more casual or typical behaviors, such as getting drunk at holiday celebrations ("chemical-dependency disease") or checking to see whether they locked their car door ("obsessive-compulsive disorder").

Refutation of the
opposing view: dangers
in absolving people of
responsibility

We must oppose this nonsense by understanding its sources and contradicting disease ideology. . . . Our society is going wrong in excusing crime, compelling people to undergo treatment, and wildly mixing up moral responsibility with disease diagnoses. Indeed, understanding the confusion and self-defeating behavior we display in this regard is perhaps the best way to analyze the failure of many of our contemporary social policies. . . . [We must] confront the actual social, psychological, and moral issues that we face as individuals and as a society—the ones we are constantly repressing and mislabeling through widening our disease nets. It is as though we were creating distorted microscopes that actually muddy our vision and that make our problems harder to resolve into components we can reasonably hope to deal with.

Definition of real
disease

What are real diseases? If we are to distin- 10 guish between addiction and other diseases, then we first need to understand what have been called diseases historically and how these differ from what are being called diseases today. To do so, let us review three generations of diseases— physical ailments, mental disorders, and addictions.

a) Bodily symptoms

The *first* generation of diseases consists of disorders known through their physical manifestations, like malaria, tuberculosis, cancer, and AIDS. The era of medical understanding that these diseases ushered in began with the discovery of specific microbes that cause particular diseases and for which preventive inoculations— and eventually antibodies—were developed. These maladies are the ones we can unreservedly call diseases without clouding the issue. This first generation of diseases differs fundamentally from what were later called diseases in that the former are *defined by their measurable physical effects.* They are clearly connected to the functioning of the body, and our concern is with the damage the disease does to the body.

b) Behavioral symptoms

The *second* generation of diseases are the so-called mental illnesses (now referred to as emotional disorders). They are not defined in the same way as the first generation. Emotional disorders are apparent to us not because of what we measure in people's bodies but because of the feelings, thoughts, and behaviors that they produce in people, which we can only know from what the sufferers say and do. We do not diagnose emotional disorders from a brain scan; if a person cannot tell reality from fantasy, we call the person mentally ill, no matter what the person's EEG says.

Addiction as a different kind of disease — goal-directed

The *third* generation of diseases—addictions— strays still farther from the model of physical disorder to which the name *disease* was first applied by modern medicine. That is, unlike a mental illness such as schizophrenia, which is indicated by disordered thinking, addictive disorders *are known by the goal-directed behaviors they describe.* We call a person a drug addict who consumes drugs compulsively or excessively and whose life is devoted to seeking out these substances. If an addicted smoker gives up smoking or if a habituated coffee drinker decides to drink coffee only after Sunday dinner, then each ceases to be addicted. We cannot tell whether a person is addicted or will be addicted in the absence of the ongoing behavior—the person with a hypothetical alcoholic predisposition (say, one who has an alcoholic parent or whose face flushes when drinking) but who drinks occasionally and moderately is not an alcoholic.

Clarification of differences between real diseases and addiction

In order to clarify the differences between third-generation and first-generation diseases, we often have to overcome shifting definitions that have been changed solely for the purpose of obscuring crucial differences between problems like cancer and addiction. After a time, we seem not to recognize how our views have been manipulated by such gerrymandered disease criteria. For example, by claiming that alcoholics are alcoholics even if they haven't drunk for fifteen years, alcoholism is made to seem less tied to drinking behavior and more like cancer. Sometimes it seems necessary to remind ourselves of the obvious: that a person does not get over cancer by stopping a single behavior or even by changing a whole life-style, but the sole and essential indicator for successful remission of alcoholism is that the person ceases to drink.

Addictions involve appetites and behaviors. While a connection can be traced between individual and cultural beliefs and first- and second-generation diseases, this connection is most pronounced for addictions. Behaviors and appetites are addictions only in particular cultural contexts—obviously, obesity matters only where people have enough to eat and think it is important to be thin. Symptoms like loss-of-control drinking depend *completely* on cultural and personal meanings, and cultural groups that don't understand how people can lose control of their drinking are almost immune to alcoholism. What is most important, however, is not how cultural beliefs affect addictions but how our defining of addictions as diseases affects our views of ourselves as individuals and as a society. . . .

Influence of culture on addiction

What Is Addiction, and How Do People Get It?

Definition of addiction: distinction between real diseases and addiction

While individual practitioners and recovering addicts—and the whole addiction movement—may believe they are helping people, they succeed principally at expanding their industry by finding more addicts and new types of addictions to treat. I too have argued—in books from *Love and Addiction* to *The Meaning of Addiction*—that addiction *can* take place with any human activity. Addiction is *not*, however, something people are born with. Nor is it a biological imperative, one that means the addicted individual is not able to consider or choose alternatives. The disease view of addiction is equally untrue when applied to gambling, compulsive sex, and everything else that it has been used to explain. Indeed, the fact that people become addicted to all these things *proves* that addiction is not *caused* by chemical or biological forces and that it is not a special disease state.

The nature of addiction: fulfillment of a need

The nature of addiction. People seek specific, essential human experiences from their addictive involvement, no matter whether it is drinking, eating, smoking, loving, shopping, or gambling. People can come to depend on such an involvement for these experiences until—in the extreme—the involvement is totally consuming and potentially destructive. Addiction can occasionally veer into total abandonment, as well as periodic excesses and loss of control. Nonetheless, even in cases where addicts die from their excesses, an addiction must be understood as a human response that is motivated by the addict's desires and principles. All addictions *accomplish something for the addict.* They are ways of coping with feelings and situations with which addicts cannot otherwise cope. What is wrong with disease theories as science is that they are *tautologies;* they avoid the work of understanding *why* people drink or smoke in favor of simply declaring these activities to be addictions, as in the statement "He drinks so much because he's an alcoholic."

Addicts seek experiences that satisfy needs they cannot otherwise fulfill. Any addiction involves three components—the person, the situation or environment, and the addictive involvement or experience (see Table 1). In addition to the individual, the situation, and the

Table 1

THE PERSON	THE SITUATION	THE ADDICTIVE EXPERIENCE
Unable to fulfill essential needs	Barren and deprived: disadvantaged social groups, war zones	Creates powerful and immediate sensations; focuses and absorbs attention
Values that support or do not counteract addiction: e.g., lack of achievement motivation	Antisocial peer groups	Provides artificial or temporary sense of self-worth, power, control, security, intimacy, accomplishment
Lack of restraint and inhibition	Absence of supportive social groups; disturbed family structure	
Lack of self-efficacy; sense of powerlessness vis-à-vis the addiction	Life situations: adolescence, temporary isolation, deprivation, or stress	Eliminates pain, uncertainty, and other negative sensations

experience, we also need to consider the overall cultural and social factors that affect addiction in our society.

Social and cultural differences among addicts: comparison/contrast

The social and cultural milieu. We must also consider the enormous social-class differences in addiction rates. That is, the farther down the social and economic scale a person is, the more likely the person is to become addicted to alcohol, drugs, or cigarettes, to be obese, or to be a victim or perpetrator of family or sexual abuse. How does it come to be that addiction is a "disease" rooted in certain social experiences, and why in particular are drug addiction and alcoholism associated primarily with certain groups? A smaller range of addiction and behavioral problems are associated with the middle and upper social classes. These associations must also be explained. Some addictions, like shopping, are obviously connected with the middle class. Bulimia and exercise addiction are also primarily middle-class addictions.

Finally, we must explore why addictions of 20 one kind or another appear on our social landscape all of a sudden, almost as though floodgates were released. For example, alcoholism was unknown to most colonial Americans and to most

Examples

Americans earlier in this century; now it dominates public attention. This is not due to greater consumption, since we are actually drinking *less* alcohol than the colonists did. Bulimia, PMS, shopping addiction, and exercise addiction are wholly new inventions. Not that it isn't possible to go back in time to find examples of things that appear to conform to these new diseases. Yet their widespread—almost commonplace—presence in today's society must be explained, especially when the disease—like alcoholism—is supposedly biologically inbred. . . .

Are addicts disease victims? The development of an addictive life-style is an accumulation of patterns in people's lives of which drug use is neither a result nor a cause but another example. Sid Vicious was the consummate drug addict, an exception even among heroin users. Nonetheless, we need to understand the extremes to gain a sense of the shape of the entire phenomenon of addiction. Vicious, rather than being a passive victim of drugs, seemed intent on being and remaining addicted. He avoided opportunities to escape and turned every aspect of his life toward his addictions—booze, Nancy, drugs—while sacrificing anything that might have rescued him—music, business interests, family, friendships, survival instincts. Vicious was pathetic; in a sense, he was a victim of his own life. But his addiction, like his life, was more an active expression of his pathos than a passive victimization.

Addiction theories have been created because it stuns us that people would hurt—perhaps destroy—themselves through drugs, drinking, sex, gambling, and so on. While people get caught up in an addictive dynamic over which they do not have full control, it is at least as accurate to say that people consciously select an addiction as it is to say an addiction has a person under its control. And this is why addiction is so hard to ferret out of the person's life—because it fits the person. The bulimic woman who has found that self-induced vomiting helps her to control her weight and who feels more attractive after

(margin notes)

Addiction as an active expression of life choices

Support: examples

More examples

throwing up is a hard person to persuade to give up her habit voluntarily. Consider the homeless man who refused to go to one of Mayor Koch's New York City shelters because he couldn't easily drink there and who said, "I don't want to give up drinking; it's the only thing I've got."

Support: expert opinion

The researcher who has done the most to explore the personalities of alcoholics and drug addicts is psychologist Craig MacAndrew. MacAndrew developed the MAC scale, selected from items on the MMPI (a personality scale) that distinguish clinical alcoholics and drug abusers from normal subjects and from other psychiatric patients. This scale identifies antisocial impulsiveness and acting out: "an assertive, aggressive, pleasure-seeking character," in terms of which alcoholics and drug abusers closely "resemble criminals and delinquents."[20] These characteristics are not the *results* of substance abuse. Several studies have measured these traits in young men *prior* to [their] becoming alcoholics and in young drug and alcohol abusers.[21] This same kind of antisocial thrill-seeking characterizes most women who become alcoholic. Such women more often have disciplinary problems at school, react to boredom by "stirring up some kind of excitement," engage in more disapproved sexual practices, and have more trouble with the law.[22]

The typical alcoholic, then, fulfills antisocial drives and pursues immediate, sensual, and aggressive rewards while having underdeveloped inhibitions. MacAndrew also found that another, smaller group comprising both men and women alcoholics—but more often women—

Support: results of a survey

[20]C. MacAndrew, "What the MAC Scale Tells Us about Men Alcoholics," *Journal of Studies on Alcohol* 42 (1981), p. 617.

[21]H. Hoffman, R. G. Loper, and M. L. Kammeier, "Identifying Future Alcoholics with MMPI Alcoholism Scores," *Quarterly Journal of Studies on Alcohol* 35 (1974), pp. 490–498; M. C. Jones, "Personality Correlates and Antecedents of Drinking Patterns in Adult Males," *Journal of Consulting and Clinical Psychology* 32 (1968), pp. 2–12; R. G. Loper, M. L. Kammeier, and H. Hoffman, "MMPI Characteristics of College Freshman Males Who Later Become Alcoholics," *Journal of Abnormal Psychology* 82 (1973), pp. 159–162; C. MacAndrew, "Toward the Psychometric Detection of Substance Misuse in Young Men," *Journal of Studies on Alcohol* 47 (1986), pp. 161–166.

[22]C. MacAndrew, "Similarities in the Self-Depictions of Female Alcoholics and Psychiatric Outpatients," *Journal of Studies on Alcohol* 47 (1986), pp. 478–484.

drank to alleviate internal conflicts and feelings like depression. This group of alcoholics viewed the world, in MacAndrew's words, "primarily in terms of its potentially punishing character." For them, "alcohol functions as a palliation for a chronically fearful, distressful internal state of affairs." While these drinkers also sought specific rewards in drinking, these rewards were defined more by internal states than by external behaviors. Nonetheless, we can see that this group too did not consider normal social strictures in pursuing feelings they desperately desired.

MacAndrew's approach in this research was to identify particular personality types identified by the experiences they looked to alcohol to provide. But even for alcoholics or addicts without such distinct personalities, the purposeful dynamic is at play. For example, in *The Lives of John Lennon,* Albert Goldman describes how Lennon — who was addicted over his career to a host of drugs — would get drunk when he went out to dinner with Yoko Ono so that he could spill out his resentments of her. In many families, drinking allows alcoholics to express emotions that they are otherwise unable to express. The entire panoply of feelings and behaviors that alcohol may bring about for individual drinkers thus can be motivations for chronic intoxication. While some desire power from drinking, others seek to escape in alcohol; for some drinking is the route to excitement, while others welcome its calming effects.

25

Examples of purposeful drinking

Emotional needs that are satisfied by addiction

Alcoholics or addicts may have more emotional problems or more deprived backgrounds than others, but probably they are best characterized as feeling powerless to bring about the feelings they want or to accomplish their goals without drugs, alcohol, or some other involvement. Their sense of powerlessness then translates into the belief that the drug or alcohol is extremely powerful. They see in the substance the ability to accomplish what they need or want but can't do on their own. The double edge to this sword is that the person is easily convinced that he or she cannot function without the substance or addiction, that he or she requires it to survive. This sense of personal powerlessness, on the one hand, and of the extreme power of an involvement or substance, on the other, readily translates into addiction.[23]

Conclusion: addiction, unlike a real disease, as a means of coping with problems

People don't manage to become alcoholics over years of drinking simply because their bodies are playing tricks on them—say, by allowing them to imbibe more than is good for them without realizing it until they become dependent on booze. Alcoholics' long drinking careers are motivated by their search for essential experiences they cannot gain in other ways. The odd thing is that—despite a constant parade of newspaper and magazine articles and TV programs trying to convince us otherwise—most people recognize that alcoholics drink for specific purposes. Even alcoholics, however much they spout the party line, know this about themselves. Consider, for example, . . . Monica Wright, the head of a New York City treatment center, [who] describes how she drank over the twenty years of her alcoholic marriage to cope with her insecurity and with her inability to deal with her husband and children. It is impossible to find an alcoholic who does not express similar reasons for his or her drinking, once the disease dogma is peeled away. . . .

■ Analysis

Peele is not the only writer to take issue with the popular practice of defining all kinds of mental and social problems as addictions. (A recent satirical newspaper article is entitled, "It's Not Me That's Guilty. My Addiction Just Took Over.") Peele's definition probably can be disputed by many doctors, psychologists, and a powerful industry of self-appointed healers. But definitions that attack popular opinions are often the liveliest and most interesting both to read and to write. In addition, they may serve a useful purpose, even if they are misguided, in encouraging new thinking about apparently intractable problems.

In defense of a controversial definition, an author must do at least two things: (1) make clear why a new definition is needed—that is, why

[23]G. A. Marlatt, "Alcohol, the Magic Elixir," in *Stress and Addiction*, ed. E. Gottheil et al. (New York: Brunner/Mazel, 1987); D. J. Rohsenow, "Alcoholics' Perceptions of Control," in *Identifying and Measuring Alcoholic Personality Characteristics*, ed. W. M. Cox (San Francisco: Jossey-Bass, 1983).

the old definition does not work to explain certain conditions—and (2) argue that the new definition offers a better explanation and may even lead to more effective solutions of a problem.

The first part of Peele's argument is definition by negation. (Notice the title of this section.) Peele insists that the number of drug and alcohol addicts among both the poor and the well-to-do is not nearly so large as practitioners would have it. Next, he points out that addiction is not an explanation of a person's life, as some have insisted, and does not mean that the addict is a victim to be absolved of responsibility for the consequences of his actions. Last, he provides the reasons that addiction is not a disease, basing his argument on the historic definition of disease as a bodily ailment whose physical effects are measurable. Defining mental illness and addiction as diseases is, Peele thinks, an evasion of the truth.

Some readers will question the narrowness of Peele's stipulation. Since the term *disease* has come to signify almost everywhere (including the dictionary) a disorder that need not be biological in origin, these readers may feel that Peele is attacking a nonexistent problem. But in the next section—"What Is Addiction?"—he elaborates on his major point: Addicts are not passive victims. Addiction is a choice, derived from the addict's desires and principles. Because this is the heart of the controversy, Peele devotes the rest of his essay to its development. In "The Nature of Addiction" he gives an overview of the motives that lead addicts to alcohol or drugs. Later, in "Are Addicts Disease Victims?" he enlarges on the descriptions of their behavior and identifies specific reasons for their actions. One of the strengths of his argument is the breadth of the analysis. In a few pages he touches on all the relevant causes of the addict's choices: the individual, the situation, the addictive experience, the social and cultural milieu.

The support for his claim is not exhaustive, but it offers a variety of evidence: examples of familiar individuals and types (Sid Vicious, John Lennon, the bulimic, the homeless man, the head of a treatment center), clear explanations of different kinds of addictive behavior, and a detailed summary of expert opinion.

All this evidence, if it is to work, must make an appeal to the common sense and experience of the reader. As Peele says, "The odd thing is that—despite a constant parade of newspaper and magazine articles and TV programs trying to convince us otherwise—most people recognize that alcoholics drink for specific purposes" (para. 27). Most readers, of course, will not be experts, but if they find the evidence consistent with their knowledge of and experience with addiction, they will find Peele's definition deserving of additional study.

The Nature of Prejudice

GORDON ALLPORT

Before I attempt to define *prejudice*, let us have in mind four instances that I think we all would agree are prejudice.

The first is the case of the Cambridge University student who said, "I despise all Americans. But," he added, a bit puzzled, "I've never met one that I didn't like."

The second is the case of another Englishman, who said to an American, "I think you're awfully unfair in your treatment to Negroes. How *do* Americans feel about Negroes?" The American replied, "Well, I suppose some Americans feel about Negroes just the way you feel about the Irish." The Englishman said, "Oh, come now. The Negroes are human beings."

Then there's the incident that occasionally takes place in various parts of the world (in the West Indies, for example, I'm told). When an American walks down the street the natives conspicuously hold their noses till the American goes by. The case of odor is always interesting. Odor gets mixed up with prejudice because odor has great associative power. We know that some Chinese deplore the odor of Americans. Some white people think Negroes have a distinctive smell and vice versa. An intrepid psychologist recently did an experiment; it went as follows. He brought to a gymnasium an equal number of white and colored students and had them take shower baths. When they were nice and clean he had them exercise vigorously for fifteen minutes. Then he brought his judges in, and each went to the sheeted figures and sniffed. They were to say "white" or "black," guessing at the identity of the subject. The experiment seemed to prove that when we are sweaty we all smell the same way. It's good to have experimental demonstration of the fact.

The fourth example I'd like to bring before you is a piece of writing that I quote. Please ask yourselves who, in your judgment, wrote it. It's a passage about the Jews.

> The synagogue is worse than a brothel. It's a den of scoundrels. It's a criminal assembly of Jews, a place of meeting for the assassins of Christ, a den of thieves, a house of ill fame, a dwelling of iniquity. Whatever

Gordon Allport (1897–1967) was a psychologist who taught at Harvard University from 1924 until his death. He was the author of numerous books, among them *Personality: A Psychological Interpretation* (1937). Allport delivered "The Nature of Prejudice" at the Seventeenth Claremont Reading Conference in 1952. The speech was published as a paper in 1952 in the Seventeenth Claremont Reading Conference Yearbook.

name more horrible to be found, it could never be worse than the syna-
gogue deserves.

I would say the same things about their souls. Debauchery and
drunkenness have brought them to the level of lusty goat and pig.
They know only one thing: to satisfy their stomachs and get drunk,
kill, and beat each other up. Why should we salute them? We should
not even have the slightest converse with them. They are lustful,
rapacious, greedy, perfidious robbers.

Now who wrote that? Perhaps you say Hitler, or Goebbels, or one of
our local anti-Semites? No, it was written by Saint John Chrysostom, in
the fourth century A.D. Saint John Chrysostom, as you know, gave us the
first liturgy in the Christian church, still used in the Orthodox churches
today. From it all services of the Holy Communion derive. Episcopalians
will recognize him also as the author of that exalted prayer that closes
the offices of both matins and evensong in the *Book of Common Prayer*. I
include this incident to show how complex the problem is. Religious
people are by no means necessarily free from prejudice. In this regard be
patient even with our saints.

What do these four instances have in common? You notice that all
of them indicate that somebody is "down" on somebody else—a feeling
of rejection, or hostility. But also, in all these four instances, there is indication that the person is not "up" on his subject—not really informed
about Americans, Irish, Jews, or bodily odors.

So I would offer, first a slang definition of prejudice: *Prejudice is being
down on somebody you're not up on.* If you dislike slang, let me offer the
same thought in the style of St. Thomas Aquinas. Thomists have defined
prejudice as *thinking ill of others without sufficient warrant.*

You notice that both definitions, as well as the examples I gave, specify
two ingredients of prejudice. First there is some sort of faulty generalization
in thinking about a group. I'll call this the process of *categorization*. Then
there is the negative, rejective, or hostile ingredient, a *feeling* tone. "Being
down on something" is the hostile ingredient; "that you're not up on" is the
categorization ingredient; "thinking ill of others" is the hostile ingredient;
"without sufficient warrant" is the faulty categorization.

Parenthetically I should say that of course there is such a thing as *posi-* 10
tive prejudice. We can be just as prejudiced *in favor of* as we are *against*. We
can be biased in favor of our children, our neighborhood, or our college.
Spinoza makes the distinction neatly. He says that *love prejudice* is "thinking well of others, through love, more than is right." *Hate prejudice,* he says,
is "thinking ill of others, through hate, more than is right."

READING AND DISCUSSION QUESTIONS

1. This was a speech, obviously not delivered extemporaneously but read to
   the audience. What characteristics suggest an oral presentation? If you were
   to revise this essay into a paper, what changes would you make? Why?

2. Allport has arranged his anecdotes carefully. What principle of organization has he used?

3. Allport says that "'thinking ill of others' is the hostile ingredient; 'without sufficient warrant' is the faulty categorization" (para. 9). How would you define the word *warrant* in this part of Allport's definition? How is it related to the definition given on page 11?

4. This essay was written in 1952. Are there any references or examples that seem dated? Why or why not?

WRITING SUGGESTIONS

5. Some media critics claim that negative prejudice exists in the treatment of certain groups in movies and television. If you agree, select a group that seems to you to be the object of prejudice in these media, and offer evidence of the prejudice and the probable reasons for it. Or disagree with the media critics, and provide evidence that certain groups are *not* the object of prejudice.

6. Can you think of examples of what Allport calls *positive prejudice*? Perhaps you can find instances that are less obvious than the ones Allport mentions. Explain in what way these prejudices represent a love that is "more than is right" (para. 10).

The Hard Questions: Beyond Consent

JEAN BETHKE ELSHTAIN

The concept of consent seems to have acquired magical cleansing properties, like a brand of detergent with its own built-in stain remover. Consent is invoked incessantly in current discussions of the president's[24] behavior and the public's insouciance concerning that behavior. Why does the public not care? Because it isn't clear anyone was harmed, we are told. And, besides, with the possible exception of Kathleen Willey—and why should we believe an obviously hysterical woman?—all the many alleged, documented, and narrated sexual encounters of a small army of women with the president, before or during his presidency, took place via the magic of consent. One might consider the alleged Lewinsky sexual contact a bit vulgar. But she consented, after

[24] Bill Clinton.

Jean Bethke Elshtain has a Ph.D. in politics from Brandeis University and teaches at the University of Chicago. She has published more than two hundred articles and several books on topics encompassing feminist theory, theology, international relations, war, the family, and political theory. This article is from *The New Republic*, May 4, 1998.

all, and, we are reminded, she was above the age of consent when her involvement with the president began. So what's the problem?

There is, of course, great force in the use of the term *consent* in a culture as rights-based, as legalistic, and as committed to the view that individuals are free-standing and self-sovereign as our own. Consent carries with it the presupposition that an individual is capable of making up his or her own mind and of being responsible for his or her behavior. If we stumble, we must pick ourselves up; if we are caught committing an infraction, we must pay the socially dictated price. Historically, political struggles raged around who was capable of consent and who was in a situation of permanent nonage. At one point women were perpetual children, as were slaves, together with all the hapless souls usually called "Idiots, Cretins, and Madmen." Criminals were shoved into the nonconsenting category as well, as long as their criminal status was socially enjoined. But the folks in these various categories fought their way out of political and legal infantilization. The category of consent has been extended so far that "functioning" persons with mental retardation are now incorporated within the legal definition of consenting adults for the purpose of the franchise, marriage — even contracts.

Children continue as nonconsenters, of course, although there are dissenters even here. I recall a bizarre episode in the late 1960s (when else?) when I found myself in a group of self-declared anarchists who were railing against various tyrannies, including the fact that children were not permitted to vote. "How far down would you go?" I queried. And the guru of the group, a senior anarchist of rather authoritarian ways, proclaimed that he would extend the vote to four-year-olds. I opined that when a four-year-old raises her hand it usually means "I have to go to the bathroom." But this quip didn't impress the assorted radicals.

What this would mean in practice, of course, is that very young children could "consent" to sex with much older adults. But isn't such a relationship bound to be exploitative? As a society, we have made this determination, and that is why the age of consent for sex is most often, for most purposes, sixteen. Surely, however, consent does not and should not exhaust what we have to say about sex between sixteen-year-olds and, say, fifty-year-olds. There is something that strikes us as inappropriate, sordid, unethical, and likely exploitative about such a relationship, and for good reason. A fifty-year-old, whether male or female, has years of experience and seasoning behind him or her. We expect — or used to expect — greater maturity in judgment from a "real" adult; a sixteen-year-old is still a kid. That a particular action or relationship is or was narrowly legal or consensual does not mean we find it good or decent or fair or reasonable.

Take this one step further. Consider how impoverished our moral 5 universe would be if the only thing we could say about the sexual abuse of an underage child by an adult was that the relationship was not consensual. Consent doesn't come close to covering what is wrong about an adult preying on children. I fear, however, that we have entered a cultural moment in which the exhaustion of our ethical and civic repertoire is a real danger. We think we have everything covered if a legalistic and contractual language is intact. But this is not true.

It is worth reminding ourselves that there are all sorts of things we do not permit people to consent to. We do not allow people to consent to sell themselves into slavery. We do not permit people to get other people to consent to kill them. (Although we're getting closer to crossing that particular line all the time.) We do not permit two drivers to consent to a high-speed road chase. We do not allow a cabal of consenting students to cheat on an examination. No one can "consent" to violate an oath.

Consent is a narrow legal term that confers a certain sort of standing. It is a concept that a rights-based liberal society cannot do without. But it is also a concept that such a society can do altogether too much with. When we make consent do all the work for us, our political and ethical vocabulary languishes. To say, then, that a sexual relationship was presumably consensual ought to be the beginning, not the end, of the discussion if the issue is the wisdom, decency, discretion, fairness, maturity, and judgment of a president or a colleague or the next-door neighbor. Consent can do many things. But it isn't a magical conceptual detergent.

READING AND DISCUSSION QUESTIONS

1. The dictionary defines *consent* as "permission" or "agreement." Based on her discussion and her examples, what might Elshtain add to that definition?

2. On what grounds does Elshtain criticize a consensual relationship between a sixteen-year-old and a fifty-year-old? Do you agree with her judgment?

3. In her last paragraph the author refers to the "judgment of a president" (that is, President Clinton). Why is she critical of some consensual relationships?

4. Elshtain twice uses an unusual adjective for consent: "magical" (paras. 1 and 7). Explain the term in the context of her essay.

WRITING SUGGESTIONS

5. Having passed your sixteenth birthday by at least a couple of years, perhaps you remember how you felt when your parents refused to give consent to certain activities. Were they right or wrong to impose boundaries? Or, if they did not impose boundaries, how do you now regard their decisions?

6. Elshtain points out that the law does not permit people to consent to certain things, including marrying, driving, voting, and drinking below a certain age. Can you defend the right of young teenagers to engage in these activities? Develop an argument for or against the need for consent from the state.

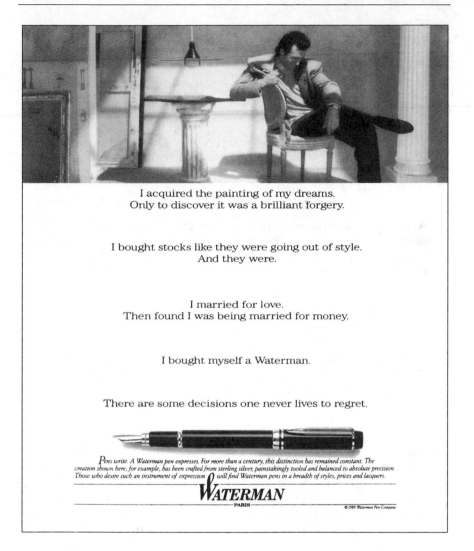

I acquired the painting of my dreams.
Only to discover it was a brilliant forgery.

I bought stocks like they were going out of style.
And they were.

I married for love.
Then found I was being married for money.

I bought myself a Waterman.

There are some decisions one never lives to regret.

Pens write. A Waterman pen expresses. For more than a century, this distinction has remained constant. The creation shown here, for example, has been crafted from sterling silver, painstakingly tooled and balanced to absolute precision. Those who desire such an instrument of expression will find Waterman pens in a breadth of styles, prices and lacquers.

WATERMAN
PARIS

© 1989 Waterman Pen Company

DISCUSSION QUESTIONS

1. This ad is divided into two parts. The part in small print extols the distinctive attributes of the Waterman pen. Why does the advertiser relegate the description of his pen to the small print?

2. How does the advertiser define a superior "instrument of expression"? Does calling a pen an "instrument of expression" add something to the definition?

3. What contrast is the reader invited to examine in the humorous first part of the ad?

God May Be the Creator

ROBERT JASTROW

> There was too much logic, too much purpose—it was just too beautiful to have happened by accident. It doesn't matter how you choose to worship God, or by whatever name you call him, but he has to exist to have created what I was privileged to see.
> —Eugene Cernan, astronaut, quoted in *St. Paul Pioneer Press*, April 9, 1985

> As biochemists discover more and more about the awesome complexity of life, it is apparent that the chances of it originating by accident are so minute that they can be completely ruled out. Life cannot have arisen by chance. —Fred Hoyle, *The Intelligent Universe*, 1983

When an astronomer writes about God, his colleagues assume he is either over the hill or going bonkers. In my case it should be understood from the start that I am an agnostic in religious matters. However, I am fascinated by some strange developments going on in astronomy—partly because of their religious implications and partly because of the peculiar reactions of my colleagues.

In the Beginning

The essence of the strange developments is that the universe had, in some sense, a beginning—that it began at a certain moment in time, and under circumstances that seem to make it impossible—not just now, but *ever*—to find out what force or forces brought the world into being at that moment. Was it, as the Bible says, that "Thou, Lord, in the beginning hast laid the foundations of the earth, and the heavens are the work of thine hands"?

No scientist can answer that question; we can never tell whether the prime mover willed the world into being, or the creative agent was one of the familiar forces of physics; for the astronomical evidence proves that the universe was created twenty billion years ago in a fiery explosion, and in the searing heat of that first moment, all the evidence needed for a scientific study of the cause of the great explosion was melted down and destroyed.

This is the crux of the new story of Genesis. It has been familiar for years, as the "big bang" theory, and has shared the limelight with other

---

Robert Jastrow is the founder and director of NASA's Goddard Institute and the author of *God and the Astronomers* (1978), from which this excerpt is taken.

theories, especially the steady-state cosmology; but adverse evidence has led to the abandonment of the steady state theory by nearly everyone, leaving the big bang theory exposed as the only adequate explanation of the facts.

An Expanding Universe

The general scientific picture that leads to the big bang theory is well 5 known. We have been aware for fifty years that we live in an expanding universe, in which all the galaxies around us are moving apart from us and one another at enormous speeds. The universe is blowing up before our eyes, as if we are witnessing the aftermath of a gigantic explosion. If we retrace the motions of the outward-moving galaxies backward in time, we find that they all come together, so to speak, fifteen or twenty billion years ago.

At that time all the matter in the universe was packed into a dense mass, at temperatures of many trillions of degrees. The dazzling brilliance of the radiation in this dense, hot universe must have been beyond description. The picture suggests the explosion of a cosmic hydrogen bomb. The instant in which the cosmic bomb exploded marked the birth of the universe.

Now we see how the astronomical evidence leads to a biblical view of the origin of the world. The details differ, but the essential elements in the astronomical and biblical accounts of Genesis are the same: the chain of events leading to man commenced suddenly and sharply at a definite moment in time, in a flash of light and energy.

Penzias and Wilson

Some scientists are unhappy with the idea that the world began in this way. Until recently many of my colleagues preferred the steady-state theory, which holds that the universe had no beginning and is eternal. Evidence makes it almost certain that the big bang really did occur many millions of years ago. In 1965 Arno Penzias and Robert Wilson of the Bell Laboratories discovered that the earth is bathed in a faint glow of radiation coming from every direction in the heavens. The measurements showed that the earth itself could not be the origin of this radiation, nor could the radiation come from the direction of the moon, the sun, or any other particular object in the sky. The entire universe seemed to be the source.

The two physicists were puzzled by their discovery. They were not thinking about the origin of the universe, and they did not realize they had stumbled upon the answer to one of the cosmic mysteries. Scientists who believed in the theory of the big bang had long asserted that the universe must have resembled a white-hot fireball in the very first moments after the big bang occurred. Gradually, as the universe expanded and cooled, the fireball would have become less brilliant, but its radiation would have never disappeared entirely. It was the diffuse glow of this ancient radiation, dating back to the birth of the universe, that Penzias and Wilson apparently discovered.

A Puzzling Conflict

No explanation other than the big bang has been found for the fireball 10 radiation. The clincher, which has convinced almost the last doubting Thomas, is that the radiation discovered by Penzias and Wilson has exactly the pattern of wavelengths expected for the light and heat produced in a great explosion. Supporters of the steady-state theory have tried desperately to find an alternative explanation, but they have failed. At the present time, the big bang theory has no competitors.

Theologians generally are delighted with the proof that the universe had a beginning, but astronomers are curiously upset. Their reactions provide an interesting demonstration of the response of the scientific mind—supposedly a very objective mind—when evidence uncovered by science itself leads to a conflict with the articles of faith in our profession. It turns out that the scientist behaves the way the rest of us do when our beliefs are in conflict with the evidence. We become irritated, we pretend the conflict does not exist, or we paper it over with meaningless phrases. . . .

Violation of Scientific Faith

Scientists cannot bear the thought of a natural phenomenon which cannot be explained, even with unlimited time and money. There is a kind of religion in science; it is the religion of a person who believes there is order and harmony in the universe, and every event can be explained in a rational way as the product of some previous event; every effect must have its cause; there is no first cause. Einstein wrote, "The scientist is possessed by the sense of universal causation." This religious faith of the scientist is violated by the discovery that the world had a beginning under conditions in which the known laws of physics are not valid, and as a product of forces or circumstances we cannot discover. When that happens, the scientist has lost control. If he really examined the implications, he would be traumatized. As usual when faced with trauma, the mind reacts by ignoring the implications—in science this is known as "refusing to speculate"—or trivializing the origin of the world by calling it the big bang, as if the universe were a firecracker.

An Unanswerable Question

Consider the enormity of the problem. Science has proven that the universe exploded into being at a certain moment. It asks, What cause produced this effect? Who or what put the matter and energy into the universe? Was the universe created out of nothing, or was it gathered together out of preexisting materials? And science cannot answer these questions, because, according to the astronomers, in the first moments of its existence the universe was compressed to an extraordinary degree, and consumed by the heat of a fire beyond human imagination. The shock of that instant must have destroyed every particle of evidence that could have yielded a clue to the cause of the great explosion. An entire world, rich in structure and history, may have existed before our universe appeared, but if it did, science cannot tell what kind of world it was. A sound explanation may exist for the explosive birth of our universe; but if it does, science cannot find out what the explanation is. The scientist's pursuit of the past ends in the moment of creation.

This is an exceedingly strange development, unexpected by all but the theologians. They have always accepted the word of the Bible: In the beginning God created heaven and earth. To which St. Augustine added, "Who can understand this mystery or explain it to others?" It is unexpected because science has had such extraordinary success in tracing the chain of cause and effect backward in time. We have been able to connect the appearance of man on this planet to the crossing of the threshold of life, the manufacture of the chemical ingredients of life within stars that have long since expired, the formation of those stars out of the primal mists, and the expansion and cooling of the parent cloud of gases out of the cosmic fireball.

Now we would like to pursue that inquiry farther back in time, but the barrier to further progress seems insurmountable. It is not a matter of another year, another decade of work, another measurement, or another theory; at this moment it seems as though science will never be able to raise the curtain on the mystery of creation. For the scientist who has lived by his faith in the power of reason, the story ends like a bad dream. He has scaled the mountains of ignorance; he is about to conquer the highest peak; as he pulls himself over the final rock, he is greeted by a band of theologians who have been sitting there for centuries.

God Is Not the Creator

ISAAC ASIMOV

> Genesis is not a book of science. It is accidental if some things agree in detail. I believe the heavens declare the glory of God only to people who've made a religious commitment.
> —Owen Gingerich, historian-astronomer, Harvard University

The speculation concerning the beginning of the universe has been right at the top of the list of things for man to understand for as long as there

An extraordinarily prolific writer (with over 300 books to his credit) as well as a professor of biochemistry, Isaac Asimov wrote a number of prize-winning science fiction novels and short stories. This essay, entitled "Do Scientists Believe in God?", appeared in the June 1979 *Gallery* magazine.

has been recorded history. It is not hard for me to imagine that the same
was true long before recorded history as well. . . .

It stands to reason that whatever was "before" must have been the
same as "now." It may have been total energy, or it may have been very
dense matter, or it may have been just as it is now.

The only thing of which I feel certain: god didn't do it.

—Thomas W. Gurley, *American Atheist,* October 1980

Some scientists are making their peace with theology. If we listen to
them, they will tell us that science has only managed to find out,
with a great deal of pain, suffering, storm, and strife, exactly what theologians knew all along.

A case in point is Robert Jastrow, an authentic professor of astronomy who has written a book called *God and the Astronomers.* In it he explains that astronomers have discovered that the universe began very
suddenly and catastrophically in what is called a big bang and that
they're upset about it.

The theologians, however, Jastrow says, are happy about it, because
the Bible says that the universe began very suddenly when god said, *Let
there be light!*

Or, to put it in Jastrow's very own words: "For the scientist who has
lived by his faith in the power of reason, the story ends like a bad dream.
He has scaled the mountains of ignorance; he is about to conquer the
highest peak; as he pulls himself over the final rock, he is greeted by a
band of theologians who have been sitting there for centuries."

If I can read the English language, Jastrow is saying that astronomers 5
were sure, to begin with, that the Bible was all wrong; that if the Bible
said the universe had a beginning, astronomers were sure the universe
had *no* beginning; that when they began to discover that the universe *did*
have a beginning, they were so unhappy at the Bible being right that
they grew all downcast about their own discoveries.

Nothing in Common

Furthermore, if I can continue to read the English language, Jastrow is
implying that since the Bible has all the answers—after all, the theologians have been sitting on the mountain peak for centuries—it has been
a waste of time, money, and effort for astronomers to have been peering
through their little spyglasses all this time.

Perhaps Jastrow, abandoning his "faith in the power of reason" (assuming he ever had it), will now abandon his science and pore over the
Bible until he finds out what a quasar is, and whether the universe is open
or closed, and where black holes might exist—questions astronomers are
working with now. Why should he waste his time in observatories?

But I don't think Jastrow will, because I don't really think he believes
that all the answers are in the Bible—or that he takes his own book very
seriously.

In the first place, any real comparison between what the Bible says and what the astronomer thinks shows us instantly that the two have virtually nothing in common. And here are some real comparisons:

1. The Bible says that the Earth was created at the same time as the universe was (*In the beginning god created the heavens and the earth*), with the whole process taking six days. In fact, whereas the Earth was created at the very beginning of creation, the sun, moon, and stars were not created until the fourth day.

The astronomer, on the other hand, thinks the universe was created 15 billion years ago and the Earth (together with the sun and the moon) was not created until a little less than five billion years ago. In other words, for ten billion years the universe existed, full of stars, but without the Earth (or the sun or the moon).

The Age of the Universe

2. The Bible says that in the six days of creation, the whole job was finished. (*Thus the heavens and the earth were finished, and all the host of them. And on the seventh day god ended his work which he had made.*)

The astronomer, on the other hand, thinks stars were being formed all through the 15 billion years since the universe was created. In fact, stars are still being formed now, and planets and satellites along with them; and stars will continue being formed for billions of years to come.

3. The Bible says that human beings were created on the sixth day of creation, so that the Earth was empty of human intelligence for five days only.

The biologist, on the other hand, thinks (and the astronomer does not disagree) the earliest beings that were even vaguely human didn't appear on the Earth until well over 4½ billion years after its creation.

4. The Bible doesn't say when the creation took place, but the most popular view among the theologians on that mountain peak is that creation took place in 4004 B.C.

As I've said, the astronomer thinks creation took place 15 billion years ago.

5. The Bible says the universe was created through the word of god.

The astronomer, on the other hand, thinks the universe was created through the operation of the blind, unchanging laws of nature—the same laws that are in operation today.

(Notice, by the way, that in these comparisons I say, "The Bible says. . ." but "The astronomer thinks. . . ." That is because theologians are always certain in their conclusions and scientists are always tentative in theirs. That, too, is an important distinction.)

Theologians on Their Backs

There are enormous differences, and it would be a very unusual astronomer who could imagine finding any theologians on *his* mountain peak. Where are the theologians who said that creation took place

15 billion years ago? That the Earth was formed ten billion years later? That human beings appeared 4½ billion years later still?

Some theologians may be willing to believe this *now,* but that would only be because scientists showed them the mountain peak and carried them up there.

So what the devil is Jastrow talking about? Where is the similarity between the book of Genesis and astronomical conclusions?

One thing. One thing only.

The Bible says the universe had a beginning. The astronomer thinks 25 the universe had a beginning.

That's all.

But even this similarity is not significant, because it represents a *conclusion,* and conclusions are cheap. *Anyone* can reach a conclusion—the theologian, the astronomer, the shoeshine boy down the street.

Anyone can reach a conclusion in any way—by guessing it, by experiencing a gut feeling about it, by dreaming it, by copying it, by tossing a coin over it.

And no matter who reaches a conclusion, and no matter how he manages to do it, he may be right, provided there are a sharply limited number of possible conclusions. If eight horses are running a race, you might bet on a particular horse because the jockey is wearing your favorite colors or because the horse looks like your aunt Hortense—and you may win just the same.

If two men are boxing for the championship and you toss a coin to 30 pick your bet, you have one chance in two of being right—even if the fight is rigged.

Three Choices

How does this apply to the astronomical and theological view of the universe? Well, we're dealing with something in which there are a sharply limited number of conclusions—more than a two-man prizefight, but fewer than an eight-animal horserace. There are, after all, just three things that might be happening to the universe in the long run:

A. The universe may be unchanging, on the whole, and therefore have neither a beginning nor an end—like a fountain, which, although individual water drops rise and fall, maintains its overall shape indefinitely.

B. The universe may be changing progressively; that is, in one direction only, and may therefore have a distinct beginning and a different end—like a person, who is born, grows older (never younger), and eventually dies.

C. The universe may be changing cyclicly, back and forth, and therefore have an end that is at the beginning, so that the process starts over endlessly—like the seasons, which progress from spring, through summer, fall, and winter, but then return to spring again, so that the process starts over. . . .

Questions No Theologian Can Answer

What counts is *not* that astronomers are currently of the opinion that   35
there was once a big bang, in which an enormously concentrated "cosmic egg" that contained all the matter there is exploded with unimagin-
ably catastrophic intensity to form the universe. What counts is the long
chain of investigation that led to the observation of the isotropic radio
wave background (short-wave radio waves that reach Earth faintly, and
equally, from all directions) that supports that opinion.

So when the astronomer climbs the mountain, it is irrelevant
whether theologians are sitting at the peak or not, if they have not
climbed the mountain.

As a matter of fact, the mountain *peak* is no mountain peak; it is
merely another crossroad. The astronomer will continue to climb.
Jastrow seems to think the search has come to an end and there is nothing more for astronomers to find. There occasionally have been scientists
who thought the search was all over. They are frequently quoted today,
because scientists like a good laugh.

What was the cosmic egg and how did it come to explode at a particular moment in time? How did it form? Was there something before the
big bang? Will the results of the explosion make themselves felt forever,
or will the exploding fragments at some time begin to come together
again? Will the cosmic egg form again and will there be another big
bang? Is it alternative C that is the true explanation of the universe? —
these are only some of the infinite number of questions that those astronomers who are not convinced it is all over are interested in. In their
search they may eventually reach new and better conclusions, find new
and higher mountain peaks, and no doubt, find on each peak guessers
and dreamers who have been sitting there for ages and will continue to
sit there. And the scientists will pass by on a road that, it seems possible,
will never reach an end, but will provide such interesting scenery *en route*
that this, by itself, gives meaning to life and mind and thought.

DISCUSSION QUESTIONS

1. Explain how the big bang theory supports Jastrow's claims about God.
   What does he mean by the last sentence of his argument?

2. What is the basis of his criticism of other scientists? Do you think he is
   being fair?

3. How would you characterize Asimov's language? Find specific examples
   that prove your description.

4. What rhetorical strategy does Asimov use to demolish Jastrow's argument? How do you think Jastrow would reply to certain specific charges?

5. What does Asimov mean when he says that the theologians "have not
   climbed the mountain" (para. 36)?

6. Does either of these writers think he has discovered a final answer?

TAKING THE DEBATE ONLINE

For these and additional research URLs, see www.bedfordstmartins.com/rottenberg.

- *Arguments for and against the Existence of God*
  http://pespmc1.vub.ac.be/GODEXIST.html

  Philosophers have tried to provide rational proofs of God's existence that go beyond dogmatic assertion or appeal to ancient scripture. The major proofs, with their corresponding objections, are examined on this page.

- *The Existence of God and the Beginning of the Universe*
  http://www.leaderu.com/truth/3truth01.html

  William Craig, who earned a doctorate in philosophy at the University of Birmingham, England, argues in this essay that it is "rational to believe that God exists."

- *Scientific Evidence for the Existence of God*
  http://www.leaderu.com/real/ri9403/evidence.html

  This essay, written by Walter Bradley, a professor in the department of mechanical engineering at Texas A&M University, concludes that "It is abundantly clear evidence abounds for the existence of an intelligent creator."

- *On the Proofs for the Existence of God*
  http://www.aquinasonline.com/Topics/5ways.html

  This page contains analyses of the five proofs of God's existence that Saint Thomas Aquinas developed, along with criticisms of those proofs.

- *Agnosticism: Being Uncertain about the Existence of God*
  http://www.religioustolerance.org/agnostic.htm

  This page contains a list of famous agnostics and a list of Internet resources for agnostics.

- *Arguments for Atheism*
  http://www.infidels.org/library/modern/nontheism/atheism/arguments.html

  This page contains "arguments *for* atheism" meaning "arguments for the nonexistence of God."

- *God Does Not Exist*
  http://www.inform.umd.edu/News/Diamondback/00-03-14/op-ed3.html

  This brief essay argues against the existence of God. The author, Katrina Martinez, is a philosophy major at the University of Maryland, College Park.

EXERCISES

1. Choose one of the following statements, and define the italicized term. Make the context as specific as possible (for example, by referring to the Declaration of Independence or your own experience).

   a. All men are created *equal.*

   b. I believe in *God.*

   c. This school doesn't offer a *liberal education.*

   d. The marine corps needs *good men.*

   e. *Friends* is a *better* television show than *Just Shoot Me.*

2. Many recent controversial movements and causes are identified by terms that have come to mean different things to different people. Choose one of the following and define it, explaining both the favorable and unfavorable connotations of the term. Use examples to clarify the meaning.

   a. comparative worth

   b. Palestinian homeland

   c. affirmative action

   d. codependency

   e. nationalism

3. Choose two words that are sometimes confused, and define them to make their differences clear. *Examples:* authoritarianism and totalitarianism, envy and jealousy, sympathy and pity, cult and established church, justice and equality, liberal and radical, agnostic and atheist.

4. Define *good parent, good teacher,* or *good husband* or *wife.* Try to uncover the assumptions on which your definition is based. (For example, in defining a good teacher, students sometimes mention the ability of the teacher to maintain order. Does this mean that the teacher alone is responsible for classroom order?)

5. Define any popular form of entertainment, such as *soap opera, western, detective story,* or *science fiction story* or *film.* Support your definition with references to specific shows or books. *Or* define an idealized type from fiction, film, the stage, advertising, or television, describing the chief attributes of that type and the principal reasons for its popularity.

6. From your own experience write an essay describing a serious misunderstanding that arose because two people had different meanings for a term they were using.

7. Write about an important or widely used term whose meaning has changed since you first learned it. Such terms often come from the slang of particular groups: drug users, rock music fans, musicians, athletes, computer programmers, or software developers.

8. Define the differences between *necessities, comforts,* and *luxuries.* Consider how they have changed over time.

CRITICAL LISTENING

9. Listen for several nights to the local or national news on television or radio. Keep a record of the *kinds* of news items that are repeated. How do you think *news* is defined by the broadcasters? Is it relevant that radio, television, and film have been characterized as the "dramatic media"? Is the definition of *broadcast news* different from *print news*? If so, how do you account for it?

10. You and your friends have probably often argued about subjects that required definition—for example, a good teacher, a good parent, a good popular singer or band, a good movie or television show. Think of a specific discussion. Were you able to reach agreement? How did the acts of listening and talking affect the outcome?

5

Support

All the claims you make—whether of fact, of value, or of policy—must be supported. Support for a claim represents the answer to the question, "What have you got to go on?"[1] There are two basic kinds of support in an argument: evidence and appeals to needs and values.

Evidence, as one dictionary defines it, is "something that tends to prove; ground for belief." When you provide evidence, you use facts, including statistics, and opinions, or interpretations of facts—both your own and those of experts. In the following conversation, the first speaker offers facts and the opinion of an expert to convince the second speaker that robots are exceptional machines.

> "You know, robots do a lot more than work on assembly lines in factories."
> "Like what?"
> "They shear sheep, pick citrus fruit, and even assist in neurosurgery. And by the end of the century, every house will have a robot slave."

[1] Stephen Toulmin, *The Uses of Argument* (Cambridge: Cambridge University Press, 1958), p. 98.

155

"No kidding. Who says so?"
"An engineer who's the head of the world's largest manufacturer of industrial robots."

A writer often appeals to readers' needs (that is, requirements for physical and psychological survival and well-being) and values (or standards for right and wrong, good and bad). In the following conversation, the first speaker makes an appeal to the universal need for self-esteem and to the principle of helping others, a value the second speaker probably shares.

"I think you ought to come help us at the nursing home. We need an extra hand."
"I'd like to, but I really don't have the time."
"You could give us an hour a week, couldn't you? Think how good you'd feel about helping out, and the old people would be so grateful. Some of them are very lonely."

Although they use the same kinds of support, conversations are less rigorous than arguments addressed to larger audiences in academic or public situations. In the debates on public policy that appear in the media and in the courts, the quality of support can be crucial in settling urgent matters. The following summary of a well-known court case demonstrates the critical use of both evidence and value appeals in the support of opposing claims.

On March 30, 1981, President Ronald Reagan and three other men were shot by John W. Hinckley Jr., a young drifter from a wealthy Colorado family. Hinckley was arrested at the scene of the shooting. In his trial the factual evidence was presented first: Dozens of reliable witnesses had seen the shooting at close range. Hinckley's diaries, letters, and poems revealed that he had planned the shooting to impress actress Jodie Foster. Opinions, consisting of testimony by experts, were introduced by both the defense and the prosecution. This evidence was contradictory. Defense attorneys produced several psychiatrists who defined Hinckley as insane. If this interpretation of his conduct convinced the jury, then Hinckley would be confined to a mental hospital rather than a prison. The prosecution introduced psychiatrists who interpreted Hinckley's motives and actions as those of a man who knew what he was doing and knew it was wrong. They claimed he was *not* insane by legal definition. The fact that experts can make differing conclusions about the meaning of the same information indicates that interpretations are less reliable than other kinds of support.

Finally, the defense made an appeal to the moral values of the jury. Under the law, criminals judged to be insane are not to be punished as harshly as criminals judged to be sane. The laws assume that criminals who cannot be held responsible for their actions are entitled to more compassionate treatment, confinement to a mental hospital rather than prison. The jury accepted the interpretive evidence supporting the claim of the defense, and Hinckley was pronounced not guilty by reason of insanity. Clearly the moral concern for the rights of the insane proved to be decisive.

In your arguments you will advance your claims, not unlike a lawyer, with these same kinds of support. But before you begin, you should ask two questions: Which kind of support should I use in convincing an audience to accept my claim? and How do I decide that each item of support is valid and worthy of acceptance? This chapter presents the different types of evidence and appeals you can use to support your claim and examines the criteria by which you can evaluate the soundness of that support.

EVIDENCE

■ Factual Evidence

In Chapter 3, we defined facts as statements possessing a high degree of public acceptance. In theory, facts can be verified by experience alone. Eating too much will make us sick; we can get from Hopkinton to Boston in a half hour by car; in the Northern Hemisphere it is colder in December than in July. The experience of any individual is limited in both time and space, so we must accept as fact thousands of assertions about the world that we ourselves can never verify. Thus we accept the report that human beings landed on the moon in 1969 because we trust those who can verify it. (Country people in Morocco, however, received the news with disbelief because they had no reason to trust the reporters of the event. They insisted on trusting their senses instead. One man said, "I can see the moon very clearly. If a man were walking around up there, wouldn't I be able to see him?")

Factual evidence appears most frequently as examples and statistics, which are a numerical form of examples.

Examples

Examples are the most familiar kind of factual evidence. In addition to providing support for the truth of a generalization, examples can enliven otherwise dense or monotonous prose.

In the following paragraph the writer supports the claim in the topic sentence by offering a series of specific examples.

> Americans expect the next century to bring some striking political and social changes, but people are discerning. Two-thirds believe gay marriages probably will be legal and over half think that fathers will spend as much time and energy with their kids as mothers. Half of the public

also predicts that Social Security will probably die; that view is particularly prevalent among younger Americans. But a majority doubts that cigarette smoking will be illegal or that all racial and gender discrimination will disappear.[2]

Hypothetical examples, which create imaginary situations for the audience and encourage them to visualize what might happen under certain circumstances, can also be effective. The following paragraph illustrates the use of hypothetical examples. (The author is describing megaschools, high schools with more than 2000 students.)

> And in schools that big there is inevitably a critical mass of kids who are neither jocks nor artists nor even nerds, kids who are nothing at all, nonentities in their own lives. . . . The creditable ballplayer who might have made the team in a smaller school is edged out by better athletes. The artist who might have had work hung in a smaller school is supplanted by abler talents. And the disaffected and depressed boy who might have found a niche, or a friend, or a teacher who noticed, falls between the cracks. Sometimes he quietly drops out. Sometimes he quietly passes through. And sometimes he comes to school with a gun.[3]

All claims about vague or abstract terms would be boring or unintelligible without examples to illuminate them. For example, if you claim that a movie contains "unusual sound effects," you will certainly have to describe some of the effects to convince the reader that your generalization can be trusted.

Statistics

Statistics express information in numbers. In the following example statistics have been used to express raw data in numerical form.

> Surveys have shown that almost half of all male high school seniors— and nearly 20 percent of all ninth grade boys—can be called "problem drinkers." . . . Over 5,000 teenagers are killed yearly in auto accidents due to drunken driving.[4]

These grim numbers probably have meaning for you, partly because you already know that alcoholism exists even among young teenagers and partly because your own experience enables you to evaluate the numbers. But if you are unfamiliar with the subject, such numbers may be difficult or impossible to understand. Statistics, therefore, are more effective in comparisons that indicate whether a quantity is relatively large or

[2] Elizabeth Crowley, "Putting Faith in Technology for Year 3000." *The Wall Street Journal,* September 15, 2000, A10.

[3] Anna Quindlen, "The Problem of the Megaschool," *Newsweek,* March 26, 2001, p. 68.

[4] "The Kinds of Drugs Kids Are Getting Into" (Spring House, Pa.: McNeil Pharmaceutical, n.d.).

small and sometimes even whether a reader should interpret the result as gratifying or disappointing. For example, if a novice gambler were told that for every dollar wagered in a state lottery, 50 percent goes back to the players as prizes, would the gambler be able to conclude that the percentage is high or low? Would he be able to choose between playing the state lottery and playing a casino game? Unless he had more information, probably not. But if he were informed that in casino games, the return to the players is over 90 percent and in slot machines and racetracks the return is around 80 percent, the comparison would enable him to evaluate the meaning of the 50 percent return in the state lottery and even to make a decision about where to gamble his money.[5]

Comparative statistics are also useful for measurements over time. A national survey by The Institute for Social Research of the University of Michigan, in which 17,000 of the nation's 2.7 million high school seniors were questioned about their use of drugs, revealed a continuing downward trend.

> 50.9 percent of those questioned in 1989 reported that they had at least tried an illicit drug like marijuana or cocaine, as against 53.9 percent in 1988 and 56.6 percent in 1987.[6]

Diagrams, tables, charts, and graphs can make clear the relations among many sets of numbers. Such charts and diagrams allow readers to grasp the information more easily than if it were presented in paragraph form. The bar graph[7] that is shown on page 160 summarizes the information produced by a poll on gambling habits. A pie chart[8] such as the one on page 161 can also clarify lists of data.

■ Opinions: Interpretations of the Facts

We have seen how opinions of experts influenced the verdict in the trial of John Hinckley. Facts alone were not enough to substantiate the claim that Hinckley was guilty of attempted assassination. Both the defense and the prosecution relied on experts—psychiatrists—to interpret the facts. Opinions or interpretations about the facts are the inferences discussed in Chapter 3. They are an indispensable source of support for your claims.

Suppose a nightclub for teenagers has opened in your town. That is a fact. What is the significance of it? Is the club's existence good or bad? What consequences will it have for the community? Some parents oppose the idea of a nightclub, fearing that it may allow teenagers to escape from parental control and engage in dangerous activities. Other parents approve of a club, hoping that it will serve as a substitute for unsuper-

---

[5] Curt Suphee, "Lotto Baloney," *Harper's*, July 1983, p. 201.
[6] *New York Times*, February 14, 1990, sec. A, p. 16.
[7] *New York Times*, May 28, 1989, p. 24.
[8] *Wall Street Journal*, February 2, 1990, sec. B, p. 1.

Bar graph

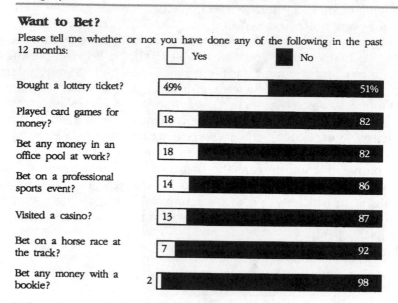

Want to Bet?

Please tell me whether or not you have done any of the following in the past 12 months:

☐ Yes   ■ No

	Yes	No
Bought a lottery ticket?	49%	51%
Played card games for money?	18	82
Bet any money in an office pool at work?	18	82
Bet on a professional sports event?	14	86
Visited a casino?	13	87
Bet on a horse race at the track?	7	92
Bet any money with a bookie?	2	98

Based on a phone survey of 1,412 people nationwide conducted April 13–16, 1989.

vised congregation in the streets. The importance of these interpretations is that they, not the fact itself, help people decide what actions they should take. If the community accepts the interpretation that the club is a source of delinquency, they may decide to revoke the owner's license and close it. As one writer puts it, "The interpretation of data becomes a struggle over power."

Opinions or interpretations of facts generally take four forms: (1) They may suggest the cause for a condition or a causal connection between two sets of data; (2) they may offer predictions about the future; (3) they may suggest solutions to a problem; (4) they may refer to the opinion of experts.

Causal Connection

Anorexia is a serious, sometimes fatal, disease characterized by self-starvation. It is found largely among young women. Physicians, psychologists, and social scientists have speculated about the causes, which remain unclear. A leading researcher in the field, Hilde Bruch, believes that food refusal expresses a desire to postpone sexual development. Another authority, Joan Blumberg, believes that one cause may be biological, a nervous dysfunction of the hypothalamus. Still others infer that the causes are cultural, a response to the admiration of the thin female body.[9]

[9] Phyllis Rose, "Hunger Artists," *Harper's,* July 1988, p. 82.

Pie chart

Plastic That Goes to Waste

Components of municipal solid waste, by volume

Types of plastic in municipal solid waste, by weight

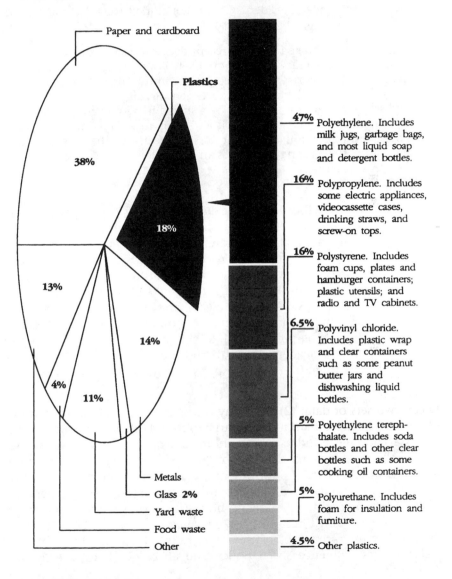

Paper and cardboard

Plastics

38%

18%

13%

14%

4%

11%

Metals

Glass **2%**

Yard waste

Food waste

Other

47% Polyethylene. Includes milk jugs, garbage bags, and most liquid soap and detergent bottles.

16% Polypropylene. Includes some electric appliances, videocassette cases, drinking straws, and screw-on tops.

16% Polystyrene. Includes foam cups, plates and hamburger containers; plastic utensils; and radio and TV cabinets.

6.5% Polyvinyl chloride. Includes plastic wrap and clear containers such as some peanut butter jars and dishwashing liquid bottles.

5% Polyethylene tereph-thalate. Includes soda bottles and other clear bottles such as some cooking oil containers.

5% Polyurethane. Includes foam for insulation and furniture.

4.5% Other plastics.

Source: Franklin Associates Ltd.

Predictions about the Future

In the fall and winter of 1989 to 1990 extraordinary events shook Eastern Europe, toppling Communist regimes and raising more popular forms of government. Politicians and scholars offered predictions about future changes in the region. One expert, Zbigniew Brzezinski, former national security adviser under President Carter, concluded that the changes for the Soviet Union might be destructive.

> It would be a mistake to see the recent decisions as marking a breakthrough for democracy. Much more likely is a prolonged period of democratizing chaos. One will see the rise in the Soviet Union of increasingly irreconcilable conflicts between varying national political and social aspirations, all united by a shared hatred for the existing Communist nomenklatura. One is also likely to see a flashback of a nationalist type among the Great Russians, fearful of the prospective breakup of the existing Great Russian Empire.[10]

Solutions to Problems

How shall we solve the problems caused by young people in our cities "who commit crimes and create the staggering statistics in teenage pregnancies and the high abortion rate"? The minister emeritus of the Abyssinian Baptist Church in New York City proposes establishment of a national youth academy with fifty campuses on inactive military bases. "It is a 'parenting' institution. . . . It is not a penal institution, not a prep school, not a Job Corps Center, not a Civilian Conservation Camp, but it borrows from them." Although such an institution has not been tried before, the author of the proposal thinks that it would represent an effort "to provide for the academic, moral, and social development of young people, to cause them to become responsible and productive citizens."[11]

Expert Opinion

For many of the subjects you discuss and write about, you will find it necessary to accept and use the opinions of experts. Based on their reading of the facts, experts express opinions on a variety of controversial subjects: whether capital punishment is a deterrent to crime; whether legalization of marijuana will lead to an increase in its use; whether children, if left untaught, will grow up honest and cooperative; whether sex education courses will result in less sexual activity and fewer illegitimate births. The interpretations of the data are often profoundly important because they influence social policy and affect our lives directly and indirectly.

[10] *New York Times,* February 9, 1990, sec. A, p. 13.
[11] Samuel D. Proctor, "To the Rescue: A National Youth Academy," *New York Times,* September 16, 1989, sec. A, p. 27.

For the problems mentioned above, the opinions of people recognized as authorities are more reliable than those of people who have neither thought about nor done research on the subject. But opinions may also be offered by student writers in areas in which they are knowledgeable. If you were asked, for example, to defend or refute the statement that work has advantages for teenagers, you could call on your own experience and that of your friends to support your claim. You can also draw on your experience to write convincingly about your special interests.

One opinion, however, is not as good as another. The value of any opinion depends on the quality of the evidence and the trustworthiness of the person offering it.

EVALUATION OF EVIDENCE

Before you begin to write, you must determine whether the facts and opinions you have chosen to support your claim are sound. Can they convince your readers? A distinction between the evaluation of facts and the evaluation of opinions is somewhat artificial because many facts are verified by expert opinion, but for our analysis we discuss them separately.

■ Evaluation of Factual Evidence

As you evaluate factual evidence, you should keep in mind the following questions:

1. Is the evidence up to date? The importance of up-to-date information depends on the subject. If you are defending the claim that suicide is immoral, you will not need to examine new data. For many of the subjects you write about, recent research and scholarship will be important, even decisive, in proving the soundness of your data. "New" does not always mean "best," but in fields where research is ongoing—education, psychology, technology, medicine, and all the natural and physical sciences—you should be sensitive to the dates of the research.

In writing a paper a few years ago warning about the health hazards of air pollution, you would have used data referring only to outdoor pollution produced by automobile and factory emissions. But writing about air pollution today, you would have to take into account new data about indoor pollution, which has become a serious problem as a result of attempts to conserve energy. Because research studies in indoor pollution are continually being updated, recent evidence will probably be more accurate than past research.

2. Is the evidence sufficient? The amount of evidence you need depends on the complexity of the subject and the length of your paper. Given the relative brevity of most of your assignments, you will need to be selective. For the claim that indoor pollution is a serious problem, one example would obviously not be enough. For a 750- to 1,000-word paper, three or four examples would probably be sufficient. The choice of examples should reflect different aspects of the problem: in this case, different sources of indoor pollution—gas stoves, fireplaces, kerosene heaters, insulation—and the consequences for health.

Indoor pollution is a fairly limited subject for which the evidence is clear. But more complex problems require more evidence. A common fault in argument is generalization based on insufficient evidence. In a 1,000-word paper you could not adequately treat the causes of conflict in the Middle East; you could not develop workable proposals for health-care reform; you could not predict the development of education in the next century. In choosing a subject for a brief paper, determine whether you can produce sufficient evidence to convince a reader who may not agree with you. If not, the subject may be too large for a brief paper.

3. Is the evidence relevant? All the evidence should, of course, contribute to the development of your argument. Sometimes the arguer loses sight of the subject and introduces examples that are wide of the claim. In defending a national health-care plan, one student offered examples of the success of health maintenance organizations, but such organizations, although subsidized by the federal government, were not the structure favored by sponsors of a national health-care plan. The examples were interesting but irrelevant.

Also keep in mind that not all readers will agree on what is relevant. Is the unsavory private life of a politician relevant to his or her performance in office? If you want to prove that a politician is unfit to serve because of his or her private activities, you may first have to convince some members of the audience that private activities are relevant to public service.

4. Are the examples representative? This question emphasizes your responsibility to choose examples that are typical of all the examples you do not use. Suppose you offered Vermont's experience to support your claim that passage of a bottle bill would reduce litter. Is the experience of Vermont typical of what is happening or may happen in other states? Or is Vermont, a small, mostly rural New England state, different enough from other states to make the example unrepresentative?

5. Are the examples consistent with the experience of the audience? The members of your audience use their own experiences to judge the soundness of your evidence. If your examples are unfamiliar or extreme, they will probably reject your conclusion. Consider the following hypothetical description, which is meant to represent the thinking of your generation.

> Imagine coming to a beach at the end of a long summer of wild goings-on. The beach crowd is exhausted, the sand shopworn, hot, and full of

debris—no place for walking barefoot. You step on a bottle, and some cop yells at you for littering. The sun is directly overhead and leaves no patch of shade that hasn't already been taken. You feel the glare beating down on a barren landscape devoid of secrets or innocence. You look around at the disapproving faces and can't help but sense, somehow, that the entire universe is gearing up to punish you.

This is how today's young people feel, as members of the thirteenth generation (born 1961–1981).[12]

If most members of the audience find that such a description doesn't reflect their own expectations or those of their friends, they will probably question the validity of the claim.

■ Evaluation of Statistics

The questions you must ask about examples also apply to statistics. Are they recent? Are they sufficient? Are they relevant? Are they typical? Are they consistent with the experience of the audience? But there are additional questions directed specifically to evaluation of statistics.

1. Do the statistics come from trustworthy sources? Perhaps you have read newspaper accounts of very old people, some reported to be as old as 135, living in the Caucasus or the Andes, nourished by yogurt and hard work. But these statistics are hearsay; no birth records or other official documents exist to verify them. Now two anthropologists have concluded that the numbers were part of a rural mythology and that the ages of the people were actually within the normal range for human populations elsewhere.[13]

Hearsay statistics should be treated with the same skepticism accorded to gossip or rumor. Sampling a population to gather statistical information is a sophisticated science; you should ask whether the reporter of the statistics is qualified and likely to be free of bias. Among the generally reliable sources are polling organizations such as Gallup, Roper, and Louis Harris and agencies of the U.S. government such as the Census Bureau and the Bureau of Labor Statistics. Other qualified sources are well-known research foundations, university centers, and insurance companies that prepare actuarial tables. Statistics from underdeveloped countries are less reliable for obvious reasons: lack of funds, lack of trained statisticians, lack of communication and transportation facilities to carry out accurate censuses.

2. Are the terms clearly defined? In an example in Chapter 4, the reference to poverty (p. 112) made clear that any statistics would be meaningless

---

[12]Neil Howe and Bill Strauss, *Thirteenth GEN: Abort, Retry, Ignore, Fail?* (New York: Vintage Books, 1993), p. 13.

[13]Richard B. Mazess and Sylvia H. Forman, "Longevity and Age Exaggeration in Vilcabamba, Ecuador," *Journal of Gerontology* (1979), pp. 94–98.

unless we knew exactly how *poverty* was defined by the user. *Unemployment* is another term for which statistics will be difficult to read if the definition varies from one user to another. For example, are seasonal workers employed or unemployed during the off-season? Are part-time workers employed? (In Russia they are unemployed.) Are workers on government projects employed? (During the 1930s they were considered employed by the Germans and unemployed by the Americans.) The more abstract or controversial the term, the greater the necessity for clear definition.

3. Are the comparisons between comparable things? Folk wisdom warns us that we cannot compare apples and oranges. Population statistics for the world's largest city, for example, should indicate the units being compared. Greater London is defined in one way, greater New York in another, and greater Tokyo in still another. The population numbers will mean little unless you can be sure that the same geographical units are being compared.

4. Has any significant information been omitted? *The Plain Truth*, a magazine published by the World-Wide Church of God, advertises itself as follows:

> *The Plain Truth* has now topped 5,000,000 copies per issue. It is now the fastest-growing magazine in the world and one of the widest circulated mass-circulation magazines on earth. Our circulation is now greater than *Newsweek*. New subscribers are coming in at the rate of around 40,000 per week.

What the magazine neglects to mention is that it is *free*. There is no subscription fee, and the magazine is widely distributed in drugstores, supermarkets, and airports. *Newsweek* is sold on newsstands and by subscription. The comparison therefore omits significant information.

■ Evaluation of Opinions

When you evaluate the reliability of opinions in subjects with which you are not familiar, you will be dealing almost exclusively with opinions of experts. Most of the following questions are directed to an evaluation of authoritative sources. But you can also ask these questions of students or of others with opinions based on their own experience and research. Keep them in mind when doing research on the Web.

1. Is the source of the opinion qualified to give an opinion on the subject? The discussion on credibility in Chapter 1 (pp. 13–15) pointed out that certain achievements by the interpreter of the data—publications, acceptance by colleagues—can tell us something about his or her competence. Although these standards are by no means foolproof (people of outstanding reputations have been known to falsify their data), nevertheless they offer assurance that the source is generally trustworthy. The answers to questions you must ask are not hard to find: Is the source qualified by education? Is the source associated with a reputable institution—a university or a research organization? Is the source credited with having made contributions to the field—books, articles, research studies? Suppose that in writing a paper on organ transplants you came across an article by Peter Medawar. He is identified as follows:

> Sir Peter Medawar, British zoologist, winner of the 1960 Nobel Prize in Physiology or Medicine, for proving that the rejection by the body of foreign organs can be overcome; president of the Royal Society; head of the National Institute for Medical Research in London; a world leader in immunology.

These credentials would suggest to almost any reader that Medawar was a reliable source for information about organ transplants.

If the source is not so clearly identified, you should treat the data with caution. Such advice is especially relevant when you are dealing with popular works about such subjects as miracle diets, formulas for instant wealth, and sightings of monsters and UFOs. Do not use such data until you can verify them from other, more authoritative sources.

In addition, you should question the identity of any source listed as "spokesperson" or "reliable source" or "an unidentified authority." The mass media are especially fond of this type of attribution. Sometimes the sources are people in public life who plant stories anonymously or off the record for purposes they prefer to keep hidden.

Even when the identification is clear and genuine, you should ask if the credentials are relevant to the field in which the authority claims expertise. So specialized are areas of scientific study today that scientists in one field may not be competent to make judgments in another. William Shockley is a distinguished engineer, a Nobel Prize winner for his contribution to the invention of the electronic transistor. But when he made the claim, based on his own research, that blacks are genetically inferior to whites, geneticists accused Shockley of venturing into a field where he was unqualified to make judgments. Similarly, advertisers invite stars from the entertainment world to express opinions about products with which they are probably less familiar than members of their audience. All citizens have the right to express their views, but this does not mean that all views are equally credible or worthy of attention.

2. Is the source biased for or against his or her interpretation? Even authorities who satisfy the criteria for expertise may be guilty of bias. Bias arises as a result of economic reward, religious affiliation, political loyalty, and other interests. The expert may not be aware of the bias; even an expert can fall into the trap of ignoring evidence that contradicts his or her own intellectual preferences. A British psychologist has said:

The search for meaning in data is bound to involve all of us in distortion to greater or lesser degree. . . . Transgression consists not so much in a clear break with professional ethics, as in an unusually high-handed, extreme or self-deceptive attempt to promote one particular view of reality at the expense of all others.[14]

Before accepting the interpretation of an expert, you should ask: Is there some reason why I should suspect the motives of this particular source?

Consider, for example, an advertisement claiming that sweetened breakfast cereals are nutritious. The advertisement, placed by the manufacturer of the cereal, provides impeccable references from scientific sources to support its claims. But since you are aware of the economic interest of the company in promoting sales, you may wonder if they have reproduced only facts that favor their claims. Are there other facts that might prove the opposite? As a careful researcher you would certainly want to look further for data about the advantages and disadvantages of sugar in our diets.

It is harder to determine bias in the research done by scientists and university members even when the research is funded by companies interested in a favorable review of their products. If you discover that a respected biologist who advocates the use of sugar in baby food receives a consultant's fee from a sugar company, should you conclude that the research is slanted and that the scientist has ignored contrary evidence? Not necessarily. The truth may be that the scientist arrived at conclusions about the use of sugar legitimately through experiments that no other scientist would question. But it would probably occur to you that a critical reader might ask about the connection between the results of the research and the payment by a company that profits from the research. In this case you would be wise to read further to find confirmation or rejection of the claim by other scientists.

The most difficult evaluations concern ideological bias. Early in our lives we learn to discount the special interest that makes a small child brag, "My mother (or father) is the greatest!" Later we become aware that the claims of people who are avowed Democrats or Republicans or supply-side economists or Yankee fans or zealous San Franciscans or joggers must be examined somewhat more carefully than those of people who have no special commitment to a cause or a place or an activity. This is not to say that all partisan claims lack support. They may, in fact, be based on the best available support. But whenever special interest is apparent, there is always the danger that an argument will reflect this bias.

3. Has the source bolstered the claim with sufficient and appropriate evidence? In an article attacking pornography, one author wrote, "Statistics

---

[14]Liam Hudson, *The Cult of the Fact* (New York: Harper and Row, 1972), p. 125.

prove that the recent proliferation of porno is directly related to the increasing number of rapes and assaults on women."[15] But the author gave no further information—neither statistics nor proof that a cause-effect relation exists between pornography and violence against women. The critical reader will ask, "What are the numbers? Who compiled them?"

Even those who are reputed to be experts in the subjects they discuss must do more than simply allege that a claim is valid or that the data exist. They must provide facts to support their interpretations.

■ When Experts Disagree

Authoritative sources can disagree. Such disagreement is probably most common in the social sciences. They are called the "soft" sciences precisely because a consensus about conclusions in these areas is more difficult to arrive at than in the natural and physical sciences. Consider the controversy over what determines the best interests of the child where both biological and foster parents are engaged in trying to secure custody. Experts are deeply divided on this issue. Dr. Daniel J. Cohen, a child psychologist and director of the Yale Child Study Center, argues that the psychological needs of the child should take precedence. If the child has a stable and loving relationship with foster parents, that is where he should stay. But Bruce Bozer and Bernadine Dohrn of the Children and Family Justice Center at Northwestern University Law School insist that "such a solution may be overly simplistic." The child may suffer in later life when he learns that he has been prevented from returning to biological parents "who fought to get him back."[16]

But even in the natural and physical sciences, where the results of observation and experiment are more conclusive, we encounter heated differences of opinion. A popular argument concerns the extinction of the dinosaurs. Was it the effect of an asteroid striking the earth? Or widespread volcanic activity? Or a cooling of the planet? All these theories have their champions among the experts.

Environmental concerns also produce lively disagreements. Scientists have lined up on both sides of a debate about the importance of protecting the tropical rain forest as a source of biological, especially mammalian, diversity. Dr. Edward O. Wilson, a Harvard biologist, whose books have made us familiar with the term *biodiversity*, says, "The great majority of organisms appears to reach maximum diversity in the rain forest. There is no question that the rain forests are the world's headquarters of diversity." But in the journal *Science* another biologist, Dr. Michael Mares, a professor of zoology at the University of Oklahoma, argues that "if one could choose only a single South American habitat in which to

[15] Charlotte Allen, "Exploitation for Profit," *Daily Collegian* [University of Massachusetts], October 5, 1976, p. 2.
[16] *New York Times*, September 4, 1994, sec. E, p. 3.

preserve the greatest mammalian diversity, it would be the dry lands. . . . The dry lands are very likely far more highly threatened than the largely inaccessible rain forests."[17] A debate of more immediate relevance concerns possible dangers in genetically modified foods, as distinguished from foods modified by traditional breeding practices. Dr. Louis Pribyl, a U.S. Food and Drug Administration microbiologist, has accused the agency of claiming "that there are no unintended effects that raise the FDA's level of concern. But . . . there are no data to back up this contention." On the other hand, Dr. James Marjanski, the FDA's biotechnology coordinator, maintains that "as long as developers of these foods follow agency guidelines, genetically engineered foods are as safe as any on the market."[18]

How can you choose between authorities who disagree? If you have applied the tests discussed so far and discovered that one source is less qualified by training and experience or makes claims with little support or appears to be biased in favor of one interpretation, you will have no difficulty in rejecting that person's opinion. If conflicting sources prove to be equally reliable in all respects, then continue reading other authorities to determine whether a greater number of experts support one opinion rather than another. Although numbers alone, even of experts, don't guarantee the truth, nonexperts have little choice but to accept the authority of the greater number until evidence to the contrary is forthcoming. Finally, if you are unable to decide between competing sources of evidence, you may conclude that the argument must remain unsettled. Such an admission is not a failure; after all, such questions are considered controversial because even the experts cannot agree, and such questions are often the most interesting to consider and argue about.

APPEALS TO NEEDS AND VALUES

Good factual evidence is usually enough to convince an audience that your factual claim is sound. Using examples, statistics, and expert opinion, you can prove, for example, that women do not earn as much as men for the same work. But even good evidence may not be enough to convince your audience that unequal pay is wrong or that something should be done about it. In making value and policy claims, an appeal to the needs and values of your audience is absolutely essential to the success of your argument. If you want to persuade the audience to change their minds or adopt a course of action—in this case, to demand legalization of equal pay for equal work—you will have to show that assent to your claim will bring about what they want and care deeply about.

[17] *New York Times*, April 7, 1992, sec. C, p. 4.
[18] *New York Times*, December 1, 1999, A15.

As a writer, you cannot always know who your audience is; it's impossible, for example, to predict exactly who will read a letter you write to a newspaper. Even in the classroom, you have only partial knowledge of your readers. You may not always know or be able to infer what the goals and principles of your audience are. You may not know how they feel about big government, the draft, private school education, feminism, environmental protection, homosexuality, religion, or any of the other subjects you might write about. If the audience concludes that the things you care about are very different from what they care about, if they cannot identify with your goals and principles, they may treat your argument with indifference, even hostility, and finally reject it. But you can hope that decent and reasonable people will share many of the needs and values that underlie your claims.

■ Appeals to Needs

Suppose that you are trying to persuade Joan Doakes, a friend who is still undecided, to attend college. In your reading you have come across a report about the benefits of a college education written by Howard Bowen, a former professor of economics at Claremont (California) Graduate School, former president of Grinnell College, and a specialist in the economics of higher education. Armed with his testimony, you write to Joan. As support for your claim that she should attend college, you offer evidence that (1) college graduates earn more throughout their lifetime than high school graduates; (2) college graduates are more active and exert greater influence in their communities than high school graduates; and (3) college graduates achieve greater success as partners in marriage and as thoughtful and caring parents.[19]

Joan writes back that she is impressed with the evidence you've provided—the statistics, the testimony of economists and psychologists—and announces that she will probably enroll in college instead of accepting a job offer.

How did you succeed with Joan Doakes? If you know your friend pretty well, the answer is not difficult. Joan has needs that can be satisfied by material success; more money will enable her to enjoy the comforts and luxuries that are important to her. She also needs the esteem of her peers and the sense of achievement that political activity and service to others will give her. Finally, she needs the rootedness to be found in close and lasting family connections.

Encouraged by your success with Joan Doakes, you write the same letter to another friend, Fred Fox, who has also declined to apply for admission to college. This time, however, your argument fails. Fred, too, is

---

[19] "The Residue of Academic Learning," *Chronicle of Higher Education*, November 14, 1977, p. 13.

impressed with your research and evidence. But college is not for him, and he repeats that he has decided not to become a student.

Why such a different response? The reason, it turns out, is that you don't know what Fred really wants. Fred Fox dreams of going to Alaska to live alone in the wilderness. Money means little to him, influence in the community is irrelevant to his goals, and at present he feels no desire to become a member of a loving family.

Perhaps if you had known Fred better, you would have offered different evidence to show that you recognized what he needed and wanted. You could have told him that Bowen's study also points out that "college-educated persons are healthier than are others," that "they also have better ability to adjust to changing times and vocations," that "going to college enhances self-discovery" and enlarges mental resources, which encourage college graduates to go on learning for the rest of their lives. This information might have persuaded Fred that college would also satisfy some of his needs.

As this example demonstrates, you have a better chance of persuading your reader to accept your claim if you know what he or she wants and what importance he or she assigns to the needs that we all share. Your reader must, in other words, see some connection between your evidence and his or her needs.

The needs to which you appealed in your letters to Joan and Fred are the requirements for physiological or psychological well-being. The most familiar classification of needs was developed by the psychologist Abraham H. Maslow in 1954.[20] These needs, said Maslow, motivate human thought and action. In satisfying our needs, we attain both long- and short-term goals. Because Maslow believed that some needs are more important than others, he arranged them in hierarchical order from the most urgent biological needs to the psychological needs that are related to our roles as members of a society.

Physiological needs   Basic bodily requirements: food and drink; health; sex

Safety needs   Security; freedom from harm; order and stability

Belongingness and love needs   Love within a family and among friends; roots within a group or a community

Esteem needs   Material success; achievement; power, status, and recognition by others

Self-actualization needs   Fulfillment in realizing one's potential

For most of your arguments you won't have to address the audience's basic physiological needs for nourishment or shelter. The desire for health, however, now receives extraordinary attention. Appeals to

---

[20]*Motivation and Personality* (New York: Harper and Row, 1954), pp. 80–92.

buy health foods, vitamin supplements, drugs, exercise and diet courses, and health books are all around us. Many of the claims are supported by little or no evidence, but readers are so eager to satisfy the need for good health that they often overlook the lack of facts or authoritative opinion. The desire for physical well-being, however, is not so simple as it seems; it is strongly related to our need for self-esteem and love.

Appeals to our needs to feel safe from harm, to be assured of order and stability in our lives are also common. Insurance companies, politicians who promise to rid our streets of crime, and companies that offer security services all appeal to this profound and nearly universal need. (We say "nearly" because some people are apparently attracted to risk and danger.) At this writing those who monitor global warming are attempting both to arouse fear for our safety and to suggest ways of reducing the dangers that make us fearful.

The last three needs in Maslow's hierarchy are the ones you will find most challenging to appeal to in your arguments. It is clear that these needs arise out of human relationships and participation in society. Advertisers make much use of appeals to these needs.

BELONGINGNESS AND LOVE NEEDS

"Whether you are young or old, the need for companionship is universal." (ad for dating service)

"Share the Fun of High School with Your Little Girl!" (ad for a Barbie Doll)

ESTEEM NEEDS

"Enrich your home with the distinction of an Oxford library."

"Apply your expertise to more challenges and more opportunities. Here are outstanding opportunities for challenge, achievement, and growth." (Perkin-Elmer Co.)

SELF-ACTUALIZATION NEEDS

"Be all that you can be." (former U.S. Army slogan)

"Are you demanding enough? Somewhere beyond the cortex is a small voice whose mere whisper can silence an army of arguments. It goes by many names: integrity, excellence, standards. And it stands alone in final judgment as to whether we have demanded enough of ourselves and, by that example, have inspired the best in those around us." (*New York Times*)

Of course, it is not only advertisers who use these appeals. We hear them from family and friends, from teachers, from employers, from editorials and letters to the editor, from people in public life.

■ Appeals to Values

Needs give rise to values. If we feel the need to belong to a group, we learn to value commitment, sacrifice, and sharing. And we then respond to arguments that promise to protect our values. It is hardly surprising that values, the principles by which we judge what is good or bad, beautiful or ugly, worthwhile or undesirable, should exercise a profound influence on our behavior. Virtually all claims, even those that seem to be purely factual, contain expressed or unexpressed judgments. When Michael M. Weinstein in Chapter 3 (pp. 62–65) quotes evidence that affirmative action does not promote unqualified candidates, he does so not because he is doing research for academic reasons but because he hopes to persuade people that affirmative action is good social policy.

For our study of argument, we will speak of groups or systems of values because any single value is usually related to others. People and institutions are often defined by such systems of values. We can distinguish, for example, between those who think of themselves as traditional and those who think of themselves as modern by listing their differing values. One writer contrasts such values in this way:

> Among the values of traditionalism are merit, accomplishment, competition, and success; self-restraint, self-discipline, and the postponement of gratification; the stability of the family; and a belief in certain moral universals. The modernist ethos scorns the pursuit of success; is egalitarian and redistributionist in emphasis; tolerates or encourages sensual gratification; values self-expression as against self-restraint; accepts alternative or deviant forms of the family; and emphasizes ethical relativism.[21]

Systems of values are neither so rigid nor so distinct from one another as this list suggests. Some people who are traditional in their advocacy of competition and success may also accept the modernist values of self-expression and alternative family structures. Values, like needs, are arranged in a hierarchy; that is, some are clearly more important than others to the people who hold them. Moreover, the arrangement may shift over time or as a result of new experiences. In 1962, for example, two speech teachers prepared a list of what they called "Relatively Unchanging Values Shared by Most Americans."[22] Included were "puritan and pioneer standards of morality" and "perennial optimism about the future." More than thirty years later, an appeal to these values might fall on a number of deaf ears.

---

[21]Joseph Adelson, "What Happened to the Schools," *Commentary*, March 1981, p. 37.

[22]Edward Steele and W. Charles Redding, "The American Value System: Premises for Persuasion," *Western Speech*, 26 (Spring 1962), pp. 83–91.

You should also be aware of not only changes over time but also different or competing value systems that reflect a multitude of subcultures in our country. Differences in age, sex, race, ethnic background, social environment, religion, even in the personalities and characters of its members define the groups we belong to. Such terms as *honor, loyalty, justice, patriotism, duty, responsibility, equality, freedom,* and *courage* will be interpreted very differently by different groups.

All of us belong to more than one group, and the values of the several groups may be in conflict. If one group to which you belong—say, peers of your own age and class—is generally uninterested in and even scornful of religion, you may nevertheless hold to the values of your family and continue to place a high value on religious belief.

How can a knowledge of your readers' values enable you to make a more effective appeal? Suppose you want to argue in favor of a sex education program in the junior high school you attended. The program you support would not only give students information about contraception and venereal disease but also teach them about the pleasures of sex, the importance of small families, and alternatives to heterosexuality. If the readers of your argument are your classmates or your peers, you can be fairly sure that their agreement will be easier to obtain than that of their parents, especially if their parents think of themselves as conservative. Your peers are more likely to value experimentation, tolerance of alternative sexual practices, freedom, and novelty. Their parents are more likely to value restraint, conformity to conventional sexual practices, obedience to family rules, and foresight in planning for the future.

Knowing that your peers share your values and your goals will mean that you need not spell out the values supporting your claim; they are understood by your readers. Convincing their parents, however, who think that freedom, tolerance, and experimentation have been abused by their children, will be a far more challenging task. In one written piece you have little chance of changing their values, a result that might be achieved only over a longer period of time. So you might first attempt to reduce their hostility by suggesting that, even if a community-wide program were adopted, students would need parental permission to enroll. This might convince some parents that you share their values regarding parental authority and primacy of the family. Second, you might look for other values to which the parents subscribe and to which you can make an appeal. Do they prize maturity, self-reliance, responsibility in their children? If so, you could attempt to prove, with authoritative evidence, that the sex education program would promote these qualities in students who took the course.

But familiarity with the value systems of prospective readers may also lead you to conclude that winning assent to your argument will be impossible. It would probably be fruitless to attempt to persuade a group of lifelong pacifists to endorse the use of nuclear weapons. The beliefs, attitudes, and habits that support their value systems are too fundamental to yield to one or two attempts at persuasion.

EVALUATION OF APPEALS TO NEEDS AND VALUES

If your argument is based on an appeal to the needs and values of your audience, the following questions will help you evaluate the soundness of your appeal.

1. Have the values been clearly defined? If you are appealing to the patriotism of your readers, can you be sure that they agree with your definition? Does patriotism mean "Our country, right or wrong!" or does it mean dissent, even violent dissent, if you think your country is wrong? Because value terms are abstractions, you must make their meaning explicit by placing them in context and providing examples.

2. Are the needs and values to which you appeal prominent in the reader's hierarchy at the time you are writing? An affluent community, fearful of further erosion of quiet and open countryside, might resist an appeal to allow establishment of a high-technology firm, even though the firm would bring increased prosperity to the area.

3. Is the evidence in your argument clearly related to the needs and values to which you appeal? Remember that the reader must see some connection between your evidence and his or her goals. Suppose you were writing an argument to persuade a group of people to vote in an upcoming election. You could provide evidence to prove that only 20 percent of the town voted in the last election. But this evidence would not motivate your audience to vote unless you could provide other evidence to show that their needs were not being served by such a low turnout.

SAMPLE ANNOTATED ANALYSIS

Single-Sex Education Benefits Men Too

CLAUDIUS E. WATTS III

Introduction: background of the problem

The values that the author will defend

Claim of policy: to preserve single-sex education for men

Support: benefits of single-sex education for men

Last week Virginia Military Institute, an all-male state college, got the good news from a federal judge that it can continue its single-sex program if it opens a leadership program at Mary Baldwin College, a nearby private women's school. But it is likely that the government will appeal the decision. Meanwhile, the Citadel, another such institution in Charleston, S.C., remains under attack. Unwittingly, so are some fundamental beliefs prevalent in our society: namely, the value of single-sex education, the need for diversity in education, and the freedom of choice in associating with, and not associating with, whomever one chooses.

When Shannon Faulkner received a preliminary injunction to attend day classes with the Citadel's Corps of Cadets, she was depicted as a nineteen-year-old woman fighting for her constitutional rights, while the Citadel was painted as an outdated and chauvinistic Southern school that had to be dragged into the twentieth century.

But the Citadel is not fighting to keep women out of the Corps of Cadets because there is a grandiose level of nineteenth-century machismo to protect. Rather, we at the Citadel are trying to preserve an educational environment that molds young men into grown men of good character, honor, and integrity. It is part of a single-sex educational system that has proven itself successful throughout history.

The benefits of single-sex education for men are clear: Says Harvard sociologist David Riesman, not only is single-sex education an optimal means of character development, but it

Lieutenant General Claudius E. Watts III, retired from the U.S. Air Force, is a former president of the Citadel in South Carolina. This selection is from the May 3, 1995, edition of the *Wall Street Journal*.

also removes the distractions of the "mating-dating" game so prevalent in society and enables institutions to focus students on values and academics.

In short, the value of separate education is, 5 simply, the fact it is separate.

In October 1992, a federal appeals court ruled that "single-sex education is pedagogically justifiable." Indeed, a cursory glance at some notable statistics bears that out. For instance, the Citadel

a) Retention

has the highest retention rate for minority students of any public college in South Carolina: 67 percent of black students graduate in four years, which is more than 2½ times the national average. Additionally, the Citadel's four-year graduation rate for all students is 70 percent, which compares with 48 percent nationally for all

b) Opportunity

other public institutions and 67 percent nationally for private institutions. Moreover, many of the students come from modest backgrounds. Clearly, the Citadel is not the bastion of male privilege that the U.S. Justice Department, in briefs filed by that agency, would have us all believe.

While the Justice Department continues to reject the court's ruling affirming the values of single-sex education, others continue to argue that because the federal military academies are coeducational, so should the Citadel be. However, it is not the Citadel's primary mission to train officers for the U.S. armed forces. We currently commission approximately 30 percent of our graduates, but only 18 percent actually pursue military careers. At the Citadel, the military model is a means to an end, not the end itself.

Today there are eighty-four women's colleges scattered throughout the United States, includ-

Support: benefits of single-sex education for women

ing two that are public. These colleges defend their programs as necessary to help women overcome intangible barriers in male-dominated professions. This argument has merit; women's colleges produce only 4.5 percent of all female college graduates but have produced one-fourth of all women board members of Fortune 500 companies and one-half of the women in Congress. However, the educational benefits of men's colleges are equally clear; and to allow women alone to benefit from single-sex education seems to perpetuate the very stereotypes that women—including Ms. Faulkner—are trying to correct.

If young women want and need to study and learn in single-sex schools, why is it automatically wrong for young men to want and need the same? Where is the fairness in this assumption?

"At what point does the insistence that one 10 individual not be deprived of choice spill over into depriving countless individuals of choice?" asks Emory University's Elizabeth Fox Genovese in an article by Jeffrey Rosen published in the February 14 *New Republic.*

Yet so it is at the Citadel. While one student maintains that she is protecting her freedom to associate, we mustn't forget that the Citadel's cadets also have a freedom—the freedom not to associate. While we have read about one female student's rights, what hasn't been addressed are the rights of the 1,900 cadets who chose the Citadel—and the accompanying discipline and drill—because it offered them the single-sex educational experience they wanted. Why do one student's rights supersede all theirs?

One might be easily tempted to argue on the grounds that Ms. Faulkner is a taxpayer and the Citadel is a tax-supported institution. But if the taxpayer argument holds, the next step is to forbid all public support for institutions that enroll students of only one sex. A draconian measure such as this would surely mean the end of private—as well as public—single-gender colleges.

Most private colleges—Columbia and Converse, the two all-female schools in South Carolina, included—could not survive without federal financial aid, tax exemptions, and state tax support in the form of tuition grants. In fact, nearly 900 of Columbia and Converse's female students receive state-funded tuition grants, a student population that is almost half the size of the Corps of Cadets. In essence, South Carolina's two private women's colleges may stand or fall with the Citadel.

Warrant: men should enjoy the same freedom of choice

Backing for warrant: tax-supported education should be equal for men and women

> Carried to its logical conclusion, then, the effort to coeducate the Citadel might mean the end of all single-sex education—for women as well as men, in private as well as public schools.

■ Analysis: Support

In 1993 Shannon Faulkner, a woman, was rejected for admission to the Citadel, an all-male state-supported military academy in South Carolina. In 1995, after a long court battle, she was admitted but resigned after a week of physical and emotional stress. The Court was asked to decide if an education equal to that of the Citadel could be provided for women at a nearby school.

Claudius Watts III tackles a subject that is no longer controversial in regard to women's colleges: the virtues of single-sex education. But in this essay he argues that colleges for men only deserve the same right as women's colleges to exclude the opposite sex.

The author has taken care in the limited space available to cover all the arguments that have emerged in the case of Shannon Faulkner. At the end of the opening paragraph he lays out the three ideas he will develop—the value of single-sex education, the need for diversity in education, and freedom of choice. In paragraphs 3 through 6 he supports his case for the benefits of separate education by first quoting a prominent sociologist and then offering statistics to prove that the Citadel population is both diverse and successful. In paragraph 7 he refutes a popular analogy—that since the service academies, like West Point and the Naval Academy, admit women, so should the Citadel. The goals of the Citadel, he says, are broader than those of the service academies. But he does more. In paragraph 8 he provides data that women's colleges produce successful graduates. This reinforces his claim that separate education has advantages over coed schooling. Perhaps it also helps to make friends of opponents who might otherwise be hostile to arguments favoring male privileges.

Notice the transition in paragraph 10. This leads the author to the defense of his last point, the far more elusive concept of freedom of choice and the rights of individuals, ideas whose validity cannot be measured in numbers. He introduces this part of his argument by quoting the words of a supporter of single-sex education, a woman professor at Emory University. He makes a strong appeal to the reader's sense of fairness and belief in the rights of the majority, represented here by the male students at the Citadel. There is also an obvious appeal to fear, an implied threat of the danger to women's colleges, in the next-to-last sentence of the essay. Finally, he invokes logic. If single-sex education cannot be defended for males, neither can it be defended for females. He assumes that against logic there can be no real defense.

Some leading advocates for women's rights have, in fact, agreed with General Watts's arguments for that reason. But those who support both Shannon Faulkner's admission to the Citadel and the sanctity of women's colleges will claim that women, as a disadvantaged group, deserve special consideration, while men do not. (One writer even insisted that the Citadel *needed* women as a civilizing influence.) General Watts's argument, however, should go some distance toward reopening the dialogue.

READINGS FOR ANALYSIS

Race by the Numbers

ORLANDO PATTERSON

In recent weeks, reporting and commentary that misinterpret early census results have been persistently misinforming the nation about its ethnic and racial composition. The misinformation is dangerous, since it fuels fears of decline and displacement among some whites, anxieties that are not only divisive but groundless. The Center for Immigration Studies, for example, a think tank in Washington, recently warned that by the middle of the century non-Hispanic whites will cease to be a majority and that "each group in the new minority-majority country has longstanding grievances against whites."

Many articles have echoed the view that whites are fast becoming a minority in many areas of the country, largely because of the growth of the Hispanic population. The *New York Times* reported that seventy-one of the top 100 cities had lost white residents and made clear only in the third paragraph of the article that it is really "non-Hispanic whites" who are now a minority in these cities. Similarly, the *Miami Herald* reported that 20 cities and unincorporated communities in Miami-Dade county "went from majority to minority white, non-Hispanic." Left without commentary was the fact that the total white population—including Hispanic whites—of Miami, for example, is actually a shade under 70 percent.

These articles and too many others have failed to take account of the fact that nearly half of the Hispanic population is white in every social sense of this term; 48 percent of so-called Hispanics classified themselves as solely white, giving only one race to the census taker. Although all reports routinely note that "Hispanics can be of any race," they almost

---

Orlando Patterson is a professor of sociology at Harvard and the author of *Rituals of Blood,* the second volume of a trilogy on race relations.

always go on to neglect this critical fact, treating Hispanics as if they were, in fact, a sociological race comparable to "whites" and "blacks."

In any case, the suggestion that the white population of America is fast on the way to becoming a minority is a gross distortion. Even if we view only the non-Hispanic white population, whites remain a robust 69.1 percent of the total population of the nation. If we include Hispanic whites, as we should, whites constitute 75.14 percent of the total population, down by only 5 percent from the 1990 census. And this does not take account of the 6.8 million people who identified in the census with "two or more races," 80 percent of whom listed white as one of these races.

Even with the most liberal of assumptions, there is no possibility 5 that whites will become a minority in this nation in this century. The most recent census projections indicate that whites will constitute 74.8 percent of the total population in 2050, and that non-Hispanic whites will still be 52.8 percent of the total. And when we make certain realistic sociological assumptions about which groups the future progeny of Hispanic whites, mixed couples, and descendants of people now acknowledging two or more races are likely to identify with, there is every reason to believe that the non-Hispanic white population will remain a substantial majority—and possibly even grow as a portion of the population.

Recent studies indicate that second-generation Hispanic whites are intermarrying and assimilating mainstream language and cultural patterns at a faster rate than second-generation European migrants of the late nineteenth and early twentieth centuries.

The misleading reports of white proportional decline are likely not only to sustain the racist fears of white supremacist groups but also to affect the views of ordinary white, nonextremist Americans. A false assumption that whites are becoming a minority in the nation their ancestors conquered and developed may be adding to the deep resentment of poor or struggling whites toward affirmative action and other policies aimed at righting the wrongs of discrimination.

How do we account for this persistent pattern of misinformation? Apart from the intellectually lazy journalistic tendency to overemphasize race, two influences are playing into the discussion.

One is the policy of the Census Bureau itself. Though on the one hand, the census has taken the progressive step of allowing citizens to classify themselves in as many racial ways as they wish, breaking up the traditional notion of races as immutable categories, on the other hand it is up to its age-old mischief of making and unmaking racial groups. As it makes a new social category out of the sociologically meaningless collection of peoples from Latin America and Spain, it is quietly abetting the process of demoting and removing white Hispanics from the "true" white race—native-born non-Hispanic whites.

There is a long history of such reclassification by federal agencies. In 10 the early decades of the twentieth century, the Irish, Italians, and Jews were classified as separate races by the federal immigration office, and the practice was discontinued only after long and vehement protests from Jewish leaders. In 1930 Mexicans were classified as a separate race by the Census Bureau—which reclassified them as white in 1940, after protests. Between then and the 1960s, people from Latin America were routinely classified as whites; then, when vast numbers of poor immigrants began coming from Latin America, the Hispanic category emerged.

The first stage of racial classification, now nearly successfully completed for Hispanics, is naming and nailing them all together while disingenuously admitting that they can be "of any race." Next, the repeated naming and sociological classification of different groups under a single category inevitably leads to the gradual perception and reconstruction of the group as another race. Much the same process of racialization is taking place with that other enormous sociological nongroup, Asian Americans.

The other influence on perceptions of who is "white" originates among the so-called Hispanics. For political and economic reasons, including the benefits of affirmative action programs, the leadership of many Hispanic groups pursues a liberal, coalition-based agenda with African Americans and presses hard for a separate, unified Latino classification. This strategy is highly influential even though nearly half of Hispanics consider themselves white.

For African Americans, the nation's major disadvantaged minority, these tendencies are problematic, although African American leaders are too shortsighted to notice. Latino coalition strategies, by vastly increasing the number of people entitled to affirmative action, have been a major factor in the loss of political support for it. And any fear of a "white" group that it might lose status tends to reinforce stigmatization of those Americans who will never be "white."

In this volatile transitional situation, where the best and worst are equally possible in our racial relations and attitudes, the very worst thing that journalists, analysts and commentators can do is to misinform the white majority that it is losing its majority status—something that recent surveys indicate it is already all too inclined to believe. We should stop obsessing on race in interpreting the census results. But if we must compulsively racialize the data, let's at least keep the facts straight and the interpretations honest.

READING AND DISCUSSION QUESTIONS

1. Where does Patterson state his claim?
2. What subtitles can you provide for the different parts of his argument? The topic sentences in several paragraphs offer clues to the organization.
3. According to Patterson, what is the danger in releasing inaccurate statistics about race?

4. Patterson's claim is strongly supported by statistics, history, and political analysis. Do you think these different kinds of support are equally persuasive? Which one is most susceptible to challenge? Why?

5. What is Patterson's objection to the definitions of *Hispanic* and *non-Hispanic* that are published by the Census Bureau and other agencies?

WRITING SUGGESTIONS

6. Find a subject that might be defended or opposed with the use of statistics but modest enough to be argued successfully in a 750- to 1,000-word paper. Sports, both professional and amateur, for example, offer topics for research: the decline of attendance at big-league baseball games, the rising salaries of professional players, injuries and deaths suffered by high school athletes. Your essay should provide proof for a claim. (Patterson uses numbers to prove that whites need not fear that their numbers are declining.) Other subjects that depend on statistical support—such as corporate responsibility, the family, and reparations for slavery—can be found throughout this book.

7. In November 2002, California voters may be asked to approve an initiative that would prohibit the state government from classifying people by race, color, ethnicity, or national origin. This proposal has generated controversy. (A question about race in the U.S. Census of 2000 also created opposition.) Try to determine whether adoption of this proposal would be beneficial or pernicious for the individual and for society. In other words, what is good or bad about classifying people?

A New Look, an Old Battle

ANNA QUINDLEN

Public personification has always been the struggle on both sides of the abortion battle lines. That is why the people outside clinics on Saturday mornings carry signs with photographs of infants rather than of zygotes, why they wear lapel pins fashioned in the image of tiny feet and shout, "Don't kill your baby," rather than, more accurately, "Don't destroy your embryo." Those who support the legal right to an abortion have always been somewhat at a loss in the face of all this. From time to time women have come forward to speak about their decision to have an abortion, but when they are prominent, it seems a bit like grandstanding, and when they are not, it seems a terrible invasion of privacy when privacy is the point in the first place. Easier to marshal the act of pre-

Anna Quindlen is a Pulitzer Prize–winning journalist and best-selling novelist. This piece appeared in the April 9, 2001, issue of *Newsweek* magazine.

sumptive ventriloquism practiced by the opponents, pretending to speak for those unborn unknown to them by circumstance or story.

But the battle of personification will assume a different and more sympathetic visage in the years to come. Perhaps the change in the weather was best illustrated when conservative Sen. Strom Thurmond invoked his own daughter to explain a position opposed by the anti-abortion forces. The senator's daughter has diabetes. The actor Michael J. Fox has Parkinson's disease. Christopher Reeve is in a wheelchair because of a spinal-cord injury, Ronald Reagan locked in his own devolving mind by Alzheimer's. In the faces of the publicly and personally beloved lies enormous danger for the life-begins-at-conception lobby.

The catalytic issue is research on stem cells. These are versatile building blocks that may be coaxed into becoming any other cell type; they could therefore hold the key to endless mysteries of human biology, as well as someday help provide a cure for ailments as diverse as diabetes, Parkinson's, spinal-cord degeneration, and Alzheimer's. By some estimates, more than 100 million Americans have diseases that scientists suspect could be affected by research on stem cells. Scientists hope that the astonishing potential of this research will persuade the federal government to help fund it and allow the National Institutes of Health to help oversee it. This is not political, researchers insist. It is about science, not abortion.

And they are correct. Stem-cell research is typically done by using frozen embryos left over from in vitro fertilization. If these embryos were placed in the womb, they might eventually implant, become a fetus, then a child. Unused, they are the earliest undifferentiated collection of cells made by the joining of the egg and sperm, no larger than the period at the end of this sentence. One of the oft-used slogans of the anti-abortion movement is "abortion stops a beating heart." There is no heart in this preimplantation embryo, but there are stem cells that, in the hands of scientists, might lead to extraordinary work affecting everything from cancer to heart disease.

All of which leaves the anti-abortion movement trying desperately to 5 hold its hard line, and failing. Judie Brown of the American Life League can refer to these embryos as "the tiniest person," and the National Right to Life organization can publish papers that refer to stem-cell research as the "destruction of life." But ordinary people with family members losing their mobility or their grasp on reality will be able to be more thoughtful and reasonable about the issues involved.

The anti-abortion activists know this, because they have already seen the defections. Some senators have abandoned them to support fetal-tissue research, less promising than stem-cell work but still with significant potential for treating various ailments. Elected officials who had voted against abortion rights found themselves able to support procedures that used tissue from aborted fetuses; perhaps they were men who had fathers with heart disease, who had mothers with arthritis and

whose hearts resonated with the possibilities for alleviating pain and pro-
longing life. Senator Thurmond was one, Senator McCain another. Former senator Connie Mack of Florida recently sent a letter to the
president, who must decide the future role of the federal government in
this area, describing himself "as a conservative pro-life now former member" of Congress, and adding that there "were those of us identified as
such who supported embryonic stem-cell research."

When a recent test of fetal tissue in patients with Parkinson's had
disastrous side effects, the National Right to Life Web site ran an almost
gloating report: "horrific," "rips to shreds," "media cheerleaders," "defy
description." The tone is a reflection of fear. It's the fear that the use of
fetal tissue to produce cures for debilitating ailments might somehow
launder the process of terminating a pregnancy, a positive result from
what many people still see as a negative act. And it's the fear that thinking—really thinking—about the use of the earliest embryo for lifesaving
research might bring a certain long-overdue relativism to discussions of
abortion across the board.

The majority of Americans have always been able to apply that relativism to these issues. They are more likely to accept early abortions than
later ones. They are more tolerant of a single abortion under exigent circumstances than multiple abortions. Some who disapprove of abortion
in theory have discovered that they can accept it in fact if a daughter or a
girlfriend is pregnant.

And some who believe that life begins at conception may look into
the vacant eyes of an adored parent with Alzheimer's or picture a para-
lyzed child walking again, and take a closer look at what an embryo really is, at what stem-cell research really does, and then consider the true
cost of a cure. That is what Senator Thurmond obviously did when he
looked at his daughter and broke ranks with the true believers. It may be
an oversimplification to say that real live loved ones trump the imagined
unborn, that a cluster of undifferentiated cells due to be discarded anyway is a small price to pay for the health and welfare of millions. Or perhaps it is only a simple commonsensical truth.

READING AND DISCUSSION QUESTIONS

1. Understanding Quindlen's argument requires understanding of the
   terms she uses. In her introductory paragraph, she refers to "public personification," "grandstanding," and "presumptive ventriloquism." Explain these terms in the context of her argument.

2. Why are anti-abortion activists opposed to the use of stem-cell research?
   How does Quindlen defend her own position?

3. What does Quindlen mean when she says that stem-cell research "might
   bring a certain long-overdue relativism to discussions of abortion"
   (para. 7)? (The meaning of *relativism* is the key.)

4. Although this essay clearly suggests a policy, it is primarily a claim of value: Stem-cell research is vital because it will contribute to the life and health of our loved ones. Point out places in the essay where Quindlen makes an emotional appeal to our compassion.

WRITING SUGGESTIONS

5. The debate about stem-cell research in the Congress, the media, and the medical and scientific professions, expanded after a speech by President Bush on August 9, 2001, in which he agreed to permit limited research on stem cells. Look up some of the news stories, editorials, and letters to the editors that followed his speech, and summarize the opposition to the president's proposal.

6. Quindlen explores the possible influence of stem-cell research on increased acceptance of abortion. Write an essay that argues for or against the right of a woman to an abortion. If you have reservations, make clear what circumstances would govern your judgment.

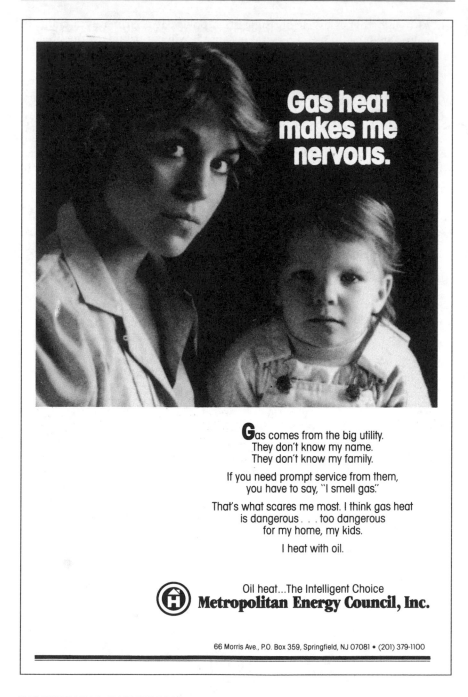

DISCUSSION QUESTIONS

1. What strong emotional appeal does the ad make? Is it justified?
2. How would you verify the validity of the appeal?

Animal Research Saves Human Lives

HELOISA SABIN

That scene in *Forrest Gump* in which young Forrest runs from his school-mate tormentors so fast that his leg braces fly apart and his strong legs carry him to safety may be the only image of the polio epidemic of the 1950s etched in the minds of those too young to remember the actual devastation the disease caused. Hollywood created a scene of triumph far removed from the reality of the disease.

Some who have benefited directly from polio research, including that of my late husband, Albert, think winning the real war against polio was just as simple. They have embraced a movement that denounces the very process that enables them to look forward to continued good health and promising futures. This "animal rights" ideology—espoused by groups such as People for the Ethical Treatment of Animals, the Humane Society of the United States and the Fund for Animals—rejects the use of laboratory animals in medical research and denies the role such research played in the victory over polio.

The leaders of this movement seem to have forgotten that year after year in the early fifties, the very words *infantile paralysis* and *poliomyelitis* struck great fear in young parents that the disease would snatch their children as they slept. Each summer public beaches, playgrounds, and movie theaters were places to be avoided. Polio epidemics condemned millions of children and young adults to lives in which debilitated lungs could no longer breathe on their own and young limbs were left forever wilted and frail. The disease drafted tiny armies of children on crutches and in wheelchairs who were unable to walk, run, or jump. In the United States, polio struck down nearly 58,000 children in 1952 alone.

Unlike the braces on Forrest Gump's legs, real ones would be replaced only as the children's misshapen legs grew. Other children and young adults were entombed in iron lungs. The only view of the world these patients had was through mirrors over their heads. These memories, however, are no longer part of our collective cultural memory.

Albert was on the front line of polio research. In 1961, thirty years 5 after he began studying polio, his oral vaccine was introduced in the United States and distributed widely. In the nearly forty years since, polio has been eradicated in the Western Hemisphere, the World Health Organization reports, adding that, with a full-scale effort, polio could be eliminated from the rest of the world by the year 2000.

Without animal research, polio would still be claiming thousands of lives each year. "There could have been no oral polio vaccine without the

Heloisa Sabin is honorary director of Americans for Medical Progress in Alexandria, Virginia. This essay appeared in the *Wall Street Journal* on October 18, 1995.

use of innumerable animals, a very large number of animals," Albert told a reporter shortly before his death in 1993. Animals are still needed to test every new batch of vaccine that is produced for today's children.

Animal activists claim that vaccines really didn't end the epidemic — that, with improvements in social hygiene, polio was dying out anyway, before the vaccines were developed. This is untrue. In fact, advanced sanitation was responsible in part for the dramatic *rise* in the number of paralytic polio cases in the fifties. Improvements in sanitation practices reduced the rate of infection, and the average age of those infected by the polio virus went up. Older children and young adults were more likely than infants to develop paralysis from their exposure to the polio virus.

Every child who has tasted the sweet sugar cube or received the drops containing the Sabin vaccine over the past four decades knows polio only as a word, or an obscure reference in a popular film. Thank heavens it's not part of their reality.

These polio-free generations have grown up to be doctors, teachers, business leaders, government officials, and parents. They have their own concerns and struggles. Cancer, heart disease, strokes, and AIDS are far more lethal realities to them now than polio. Yet, those who support an "animal rights" agenda that would cripple research and halt medical science in its tracks are slamming the door on the possibilities of new treatments and cures.

My husband was a kind man, but he was impatient with those who 10 refused to acknowledge reality or to seek reasoned answers to the questions of life.

The pioneers of polio research included not only the scientists but also the laboratory animals that played a critical role in bringing about the end of polio and a host of other diseases for which we now have vaccines and cures. Animals will continue to be as vital as the scientists who study them in the battle to eliminate pain, suffering, and disease from our lives.

That is the reality of medical progress.

Why We Don't Need Animal Experimentation

PEGGY CARLSON

The issue of animal experimentation has become so polarized that rational thinking seems to have taken a back seat. Heloisa Sabin's October 18 editorial-page article "Animal Research Saves Lives" serves only to further misinform and polarize. She does a great disservice to science to incorrectly portray the debate about animal experimentation as occur-

Peggy Carlson, M.D., was the research director of the Physicians Committee for Responsible Medicine in Washington, D.C. at the time her letter appeared in the *Wall Street Journal* on November 7, 1995.

ring between "animal rights activists" and scientists. The truth is, the value of animal experimentation is being questioned by many scientists.

Mrs. Sabin uses the example of the polio vaccine developed by her husband to justify animal experimentation. However, in the case of the polio vaccine, misleading animal experiments detoured scientists away from reliable clinical studies thereby, according to Dr. Sabin himself, delaying the initial work on polio prevention. It was also unfortunate that the original polio vaccine was produced using monkey cells instead of available human cells as can be done today. The use of monkey cells resulted in viruses with the potential to cause serious disease being transferred to humans when the polio vaccine was administered.

The polio vaccine example cannot logically be used to justify the current level of animal experimentation—several billion dollars and about 30 million animals yearly. Although most people would prefer to believe that the death and suffering of all these animals is justified, the facts do not support that conclusion.

Nearly everything that medicine has learned about what substances cause human cancer and birth defects has come from human clinical and epidemiological studies because animal experiments do not accurately predict what occurs in humans. Dr. Bross, the former Director of Biostatistics at the Roswell Institute for Cancer Research states, "While conflicting animal results have often delayed and hampered advances in the war on cancer, they have never produced a single substantial advance either in the prevention or treatment of cancer." A 1990 editorial in *Stroke* notes that none of the twenty-five compounds "proven" efficacious for treating stroke in animal experiments over the preceding ten years had been effective for use in humans. From human studies alone we have learned how to lessen the risk of heart attacks. Warnings to the public that smoking cigarettes leads to an increased risk of cancer were delayed as researchers sought, unsuccessfully, to confirm the risk by using animals.

Animal tests for drug safety, cancer-causing potential, and toxicity 5 are unreliable, and science is leading us to more accurate methods that will offer greater protection. But if we refuse to acknowledge the inadequacies of animal tests we put a stranglehold on the very progress that will help us. Billions of precious health-care dollars have been spent to fund animal experiments that are repetitious or that have no human relevance.

An uncritical acceptance of the value of animal experiments leads to its overfunding, which, in turn, leads to the underfunding of other more beneficial areas.

DISCUSSION QUESTIONS

1. Sabin uses the vaccine against polio as the principal example in her support of animal research. Does this limit her argument? Should she have been more specific in her references to other diseases?
2. What is the significance of Sabin's repeated references to "reality"?

3. Mention all the kinds of support that Carlson provides. Which of the supporting materials is most persuasive?

4. Does Carlson refute all the arguments in Sabin's article? Be specific.

5. Sabin makes strong emotional appeals. Describe them, and decide how large a part such appeals play in her argument. Does Carlson appeal to the emotions of her readers?

TAKING THE DEBATE ONLINE

For these and additional research URLs, see www.bedfordstmartins.com/rottenberg.

- *University of Colorado at Boulder: Frequently Asked Questions*
  http://www.colorado.edu/Research/animal_resources/faqs.html

  This multilayered site examines animal resources at the university and explores many ethical questions on animal research.

- *University of Delaware: Animal Testing—Pro or Con?*
  http://www.ash.udel.edu/incoming/rcap/index.html

  This reference tool contains numerous links addressing the pros and cons of animal testing, as well as statistical evidence to back up or condemn the validity of animal research.

- *National Institutes of Health*
  http://www.nih.gov/

  This institute investigates America's premier medical research facilities for their treatment of animals.

- *People for the Ethical Treatment of Animals Online*
  http://www.peta.org

  This association unequivocally condemns animal research.

- *Scientific American*
  http://www.sciam.com/

  This site contains links to featured stories about animal experimentation in the February 1997 issue of the magazine.

- *Fund for the Replacement of Animals in Medical Experiments*
  http://www.frame.org.uk/

  This association promotes the researching of alternatives to animal testing.

EXERCISES

1. What kind of evidence would you offer to prove to a skeptic that the moon landings—or any other space ventures—have actually occurred? What objections would you anticipate?

2. A group of heterosexual people in a middle-class community who define themselves as devout Christians have organized to keep a group of ho-

mosexuals from joining their church. What kind of support would you offer for your claim that the homosexuals should be welcomed into the church? Address your argument to the heterosexuals unwilling to admit the group of homosexuals.

3. In the summer of 1983, after an alarming rise in the juvenile crime rate, the mayor of Detroit instituted a curfew for young people under the age of eighteen. What kind of support can you provide for or against such a curfew?

4. "Racism [or sexism] is [not] a major problem on this campus [or home town or neighborhood]." Produce evidence to support your claim.

5. Write a full-page advertisement to solicit support for a project or cause that you believe in.

6. How do you account for the large and growing interest in science fiction films and books? In addition to their entertainment value, are there other less obvious reasons for their popularity?

7. According to some researchers soap operas are influential in transmitting values, lifestyles, and sexual information to youthful viewers. Do you agree? If so, what values and information are being transmitted? Be specific.

8. Choose one of the following stereotypical ideas and argue that it is true or false or partly both. Discuss the reasons for the existence of the stereotype.

   a. Jocks are stupid.

   b. The country is better than the city for bringing up children.

   c. Television is justly called "the boob tube."

   d. A dog is man's best friend.

   e. Beauty contests are degrading to women.

9. Defend or refute the view that organized sports build character.

10. The philosopher Bertrand Russell said, "Most of the work that most people have to do is not in itself interesting, but even such work has certain advantages." Defend or refute this assertion. Use your own experience as support.

CRITICAL LISTENING

11. Choose a product advertised on television by many different makers. (Cars, pain relievers, fast food, cereals, and soft drinks are some of the most popular products.) What kinds of support do the advertisers offer? Why do they choose these particular appeals? Would the support be significantly different in print?

12. From time to time advocates of causes speak on campus. The causes may be broadly based—minority rights, welfare cuts, abortion, foreign aid—or they may be local issues, having to do with harassment policy, course requirements, or tuition increases. Attend a meeting or a rally at which a speaker argues his or her cause. Write an evaluation of the speech, paying particular attention to the kinds of support. Did the speaker provide sufficient and relevant evidence? Did he or she make emotional appeals? What signs, if any, reflected the speaker's awareness of the kinds of audience he or she was addressing?

6

Warrants

We now come to the third element in the structure of the argument—the warrant. In the first chapter we defined the warrant as an *assumption*, a belief we take for granted, or a general principle. Claim and support, the other major elements we have discussed, are more familiar in ordinary discourse, but there is nothing mysterious or unusual about the warrant. All our claims, both formal and informal, are grounded in warrants or assumptions that the audience must share with us if our claims are to prove acceptable.

These warrants reflect our observations, our personal experience, and our participation in a culture. But because these observations, experiences, and cultural associations will vary, the audience may not always agree with the warrants or assumptions of the writer. The British philosopher Stephen Toulmin, who developed the concept of warrants, dismissed more traditional forms of logical reasoning in favor of a more audience-based, courtroom-derived approach to argumentation. He refers to warrants as "general, hypothetical statements, which can act as bridges" and "entitle one to draw conclusions or make claims."[1] The word *bridges* to denote the action of the warrant is crucial. One dictionary defines warrant as a "guar-

---

[1] Stephen Toulmin, *The Uses of Argument* (Cambridge: Cambridge University Press, 1958), p. 98.

antee or justification." We use the word *warrant* to emphasize that in an argument it guarantees a connecting link—a bridge—between the claim and the support. This means that even if a reader agrees that the support is sound, the support cannot prove the validity of the claim unless the reader also agrees with the underlying warrant. Recall the sample argument outlined in Chapter 1 (p. 3):

CLAIM: Adoption of a vegetarian diet leads to healthier and longer life.

SUPPORT: The authors of *Becoming a Vegetarian Family* say so.

WARRANT: The authors of *Becoming a Vegetarian Family* are reliable sources of information on diet.

Notice that the reader must agree with the assumption that the testimony of experts is trustworthy before he or she arrives at the conclusion that a vegetarian diet is healthy. Simply providing evidence that the authors say so is not enough to prove the claim.

The following dialogue offers another example of the relationship between the warrant and the other elements of the argument.

"I don't think that Larry can do the job. He's pretty dumb."
"Really? I thought he was smart. What makes you say he's dumb?"
"Did you know that he's illiterate—can't read above third-grade level? In my book that makes him dumb."

If we put this into outline form, the warrant or assumption in the argument becomes clear.

CLAIM: Larry is pretty dumb.

EVIDENCE: He can't read above third-grade level.

WARRANT: Anybody who can't read above third-grade level must be dumb.

We can also represent the argument in diagram form, which shows the warrant as a bridge between the claim and the support.

Support ⎯⎯⎯⎯⎯⎯⎯⎯⎯⎯⎯⎯⎯⎯➤ *Claim*

Warrant
(Expressed or Unexpressed)

The argument above can then be written like this:

Support ⎯⎯⎯⎯⎯⎯⎯⎯⎯⎯⎯➤ *Claim*
Larry can't read above   He's pretty dumb.
third-grade level.

Warrant
Anybody who can't read above third-grade
level must be pretty dumb.

Is this warrant valid? We cannot answer this question until we consider the *backing*. Every warrant or assumption rests on something else that gives it authority; this is what we call backing. Backing or authority for the warrant in this example would consist of research data that prove a relationship between stupidity and low reading ability. This particular warrant, we would discover, lacks backing because we know that the failure to learn to read well may be due to a number of things unrelated to intelligence. So if the warrant is unprovable, the claim—that Larry is dumb—is also unprovable, even if the evidence is true. In this case, then, the evidence does not guarantee the soundness of the claim.

Now consider this example of a somewhat more complicated warrant: The beautiful and unspoiled Eastern Shore of Maryland is being discovered by thousands of tourists, vacationers, and developers who will, according to the residents, change the landscape and the way of life, which is now based largely on fishing and farming. In a few years the Eastern Shore may become a noisy, crowded string of resorts. Mrs. Walkup, the Kent County commissioner, says,

> Catering to the wealthy puts property back on the tax rolls, but it's going to make the Eastern Shore look like the rest of the country. Everything that made our way of life so special is being eroded. We are a fragile area. The Eastern Shore is still special, but it is feeling pressure from all directions. Lots of people don't seem to appreciate the fact that God made us to need a little peace and quiet now and then.[2]

In simplified form the argument of those opposed to development would be outlined this way:

CLAIM: Development will bring undesirable changes to the present way of life on the Eastern Shore, a life of farming and fishing, peace and quiet.

SUPPORT: Developers will build express highways, condominiums, casinos, and nightclubs.

WARRANT: A pastoral life of fishing and farming is superior to the way of life brought by expensive, fast-paced modern development.

Notice that the warrant is a broad generalization that can apply to a number of different situations, while the claim is about a specific place and time. It should be added that in other arguments the warrant may not be stated in such general terms. However, even in arguments in which the warrant makes a more specific reference to the claim, the reader can infer an extension of the warrant to other similar arguments. In the vegetarian diet example (p. 3, outlined on p. 11), the warrant mentions a specific book. But it is clear that such warrants can be gener-

---

[2]Michael Wright, "The Changing Chesapeake," *New York Times Magazine*, July 10, 1983, p. 27.

alized to apply to other arguments in which we accept a claim based on the credibility of the sources.

To be convinced of the validity of Mrs. Walkup's claim, you must first find that the support is true, that the developers plan to introduce drastic changes that will destroy the pastoral life of the Eastern Shore. You may, however, believe that the support is not entirely sound, that the development will be much more modest than residents fear, and that the Eastern Shore will not be seriously altered. Next, you may want to see more justification for the warrant. Is pastoral life superior to the life that will result from large-scale development? Perhaps you have always thought that a life of fishing and farming means poverty and limited opportunities for the majority of the residents. Although the superiority of a way of life is largely a matter of taste and therefore difficult to prove, Mrs. Walkup may need to produce backing for her belief that the present way of life is more desirable than one based on developing the area for new residents and summer visitors. If you find either the support or the warrant unconvincing, you cannot accept the claim.

Remember that a claim is often modified by one or more qualifiers, which limit the claim. Mrs. Walkup might have said, "Development will *probably* destroy *some aspects of* the present way of life on the Eastern Shore." Warrants can also be modified or limited by *reservations,* which remind the reader that there are conditions under which the warrants will not be relevant. Mrs. Walkup might have added, "unless increased prosperity and exposure to the outside world brought by development improve some aspects of our lives."

A diagram of Mrs. Walkup's argument shows the additional elements:

Support ⎯⎯⎯⎯⎯⎯⎯⎯⎯▶ *Claim*

The developers will build highways, condos, casinos, nightclubs.

Development will bring undesirable changes to life on the Eastern Shore.

Warrant

A way of life devoted to farming and fishing is superior to a way of life brought by development.

Qualifier

Development will *most likely* bring undesirable changes.

Backing

We have experienced crowds, traffic, noise, rich strangers, and high-rises, and they destroy peace and quiet.

Reservation

But increased development might improve some aspects of our lives.

Claim and support (or lack of support) are relatively easy to uncover in most arguments. One thing that makes the warrant different is that it is often unexpressed and therefore unexamined by both writer and reader because they take it for granted. In the argument about Larry's intelligence, the warrant was stated. But in the argument about development on the Eastern Shore, Mrs. Walkup did not state her warrant directly, although her meaning is perfectly clear. She probably felt that it was not necessary to be more explicit because her readers would understand and supply the warrant.

We can make the discovery of warrants even clearer by examining another argument, in this case a policy claim. We've looked at a factual claim (that Larry is dumb) and a value claim (that Eastern Shore development is undesirable). Now we examine a policy claim that rests on one expressed and one unexpressed warrant. Policy claims are usually more complicated than other claims because the statement of policy is preceded by an array of facts and values. In addition, such claims may represent chains of reasoning in which one argument is dependent on another. These complicated arguments may be difficult or impossible to summarize in a simple diagram, but careful reading, asking the same kinds of questions that the author may have asked about his claim, can help you to find the warrant or chain of warrants that must be accepted before evidence and claim can be linked.

In a familiar argument that appeared a few years ago,[3] the author argues for a radical reform in college sports—the elimination of subprofessional intermural team sports, as practiced above all in football and basketball. The claim is clear, and evidence for the professional character of college sports not hard to find: the large salaries paid to coaches, the generous perquisites offered to players, the recruitment policies that ignore academic standing, the virtually full-time commitment of the players, the lucrative television contracts. But can this evidence support the author's claim that such sports do not belong on college campuses? Advocates of these sports may ask, Why not? In the conclusion of the article the author states one warrant or assumption underlying his claim.

> Even if the money to pay college athletes could be found, though, a larger question must be answered—namely, why should a system of professional athletics be affiliated with universities at all? For the truth is that the requirements of athletics and academics operate at cross purposes, and the attempt to play both games at once serves only to reduce the level of performance of each.

In other words, the author assumes that the goals of an academic education on the one hand and the goals of big-time college sports on the other hand are incompatible. In the article he develops the ways in which each enterprise harms the other.

[3]D. G. Myers, "Why College Sports?" *Commentary*, December 1990, pp. 49–51.

But the argument clearly rests on another warrant that is not expressed because the author takes for granted that his readers will supply it: The academic goals of the university are primary and should take precedence over all other collegiate activities. This is an argument based on an authority warrant, the authority of those who define the goals of the university—scholars, public officials, university administrators, and others. (Types of warrants are discussed in the following section.)

This warrant makes clear that the evidence of the professional nature of college sports cited above supports the claim that they should be eliminated. If quasiprofessional college sports are harmful to the primary educational function of the college or university, then they must go. In the author's words, "The two are separate enterprises, to be judged by separate criteria. . . . For college sports, the university is not an educational institution at all; it is merely a locus, a means of coordinating the different aspects of the sporting enterprise."

This argument may be summarized in outline form as follows:

CLAIM: Intermural college team sports should be abolished.

SUPPORT: College sports have become subprofessional.

WARRANT: The goals of an academic education and big-time college sports are incompatible.

BACKING FOR   Academic education is the primary goal of the
THE WARRANT: college and must take precedence over athletic activity.

Arguers will often neglect to state their warrants for one of two reasons: First, like Mrs. Walkup, they may believe that the warrant is obvious and need not be expressed; second, they may want to conceal the warrant in the hope that the reader will overlook its weakness.

What kinds of warrants are so obvious that they need not be expressed? Here are a few that will probably sound familiar:

Mothers love their children.

The more expensive the product, the more satisfactory it will be.

A good harvest will result in lower prices for produce.

First come, first served.

These statements seem to embody beliefs that most of us would share and that might be unnecessary to make explicit in an argument. The last statement, for example, is taken as axiomatic, an article of faith that we seldom question in ordinary circumstances. Suppose you hear someone make the claim, "I deserve to get the last ticket to the concert." If you ask why he is entitled to a ticket that you also would like to have, he may answer in support of his claim, "Because I was here first." No doubt you accept his claim without further argument because you understand and agree with the warrant that is not expressed: "If you arrive first, you deserve to be served before those who come later." Your acceptance of the warrant probably also takes into account the unexpressed backing that is based on a belief in justice: "It is only fair that those who sacrifice time and comfort to be first in line should be rewarded for their trouble."

In this case it may not be necessary to expose the warrant and examine it. Indeed, as Stephen Toulmin tells us, "If we demanded the credentials of all warrants at sight and never let one pass unchallenged, argument could scarcely begin."[4]

But even those warrants that seem to express universal truths invite analysis if we can think of claims for which these warrants might not, after all, be relevant. "First in line," for example, may justify the claim of a person who wants a concert ticket, but it cannot in itself justify the claim of someone who wants a vital medication that is in short supply. Moreover, offering a rebuttal to a long-held but unexamined warrant can often produce an interesting and original argument. If someone exclaims, "All this buying of gifts! I think people have forgotten that Christmas celebrates the birth of Christ," she need not express the assumption—that the buying of gifts violates what ought to be a religious celebration. It goes unstated by the speaker because it has been uttered so often that she knows the hearer will supply it. But one writer, in an essay titled "God's Gift: A Commercial Christmas," argued that, contrary to popular belief, the purchase of gifts, which means the expenditure of time, money, and thought on others rather than oneself, is not a violation but an affirmation of the Christmas spirit.[5]

The second reason for refusal to state the warrant lies in the arguer's intention to disarm or deceive the reader, although the arguer may not be aware of this. For instance, failure to state the warrant is common in advertising and politics, where the desire to sell a product or an idea may outweigh the responsibility to argue explicitly. The following advertisement is famous not only for what it says but for what it does not say:

> In 1918 Leona Currie scandalized a New Jersey beach with a bathing suit cut above her knees. And to irk the establishment even more, she smoked a cigarette. Leona Currie was promptly arrested.
> Oh, how Leona would smile if she could see you today.
> You've come a long way, baby. *Virginia Slims*. The taste for today's woman.

What is the unstated warrant? The manufacturer of Virginia Slims hopes we will agree that being permitted to smoke cigarettes is a significant sign of female liberation. But many readers would insist that proving "You've come a long way, baby" requires more evidence than women's freedom to smoke (or wear short bathing suits). The shaky warrant weakens the claim.

---

[4] *The Uses of Argument* (Cambridge: Cambridge University Press, 1958), p. 106.
[5] Robert A. Sirico, *Wall Street Journal*, December 21, 1993, sec. A, p. 12.

Politicians, too, conceal warrants that may not survive close scrutiny. In the 1983 mayoral election in Chicago, one candidate revealed that his opponent had undergone psychiatric treatment. He did not have to state the warrant supporting his claim. He knew that many in his audience would assume that anyone who had undergone psychiatric treatment was unfit to hold public office. This same assumption contributed to the withdrawal of a vice-presidential candidate from the 1972 campaign.

TYPES OF WARRANTS

Arguments may be classified according to the types of warrants offered as proof. Because warrants represent the reasoning process by which we establish the relationship between support and claim, analysis of the major types of warrants enables us to see the whole argument as a sum of its parts.

Warrants may be organized into three categories: *"authoritative, substantive,* and *motivational."*[6] We have already given examples of these types of warrants in this chapter and in Chapter 1. The *authoritative warrant* (see p. 11) is based on the credibility or trustworthiness of the source. If we assume that the source of the data is authoritative, then we find that the support justifies the claim. A *substantive warrant* is based on beliefs about reliability of factual evidence. In the example on page 195 the speaker assumes, although mistakenly, that the relationship between low reading level and stupidity is a verifiable datum, one that can be proved by objective research. A *motivational warrant,* on the other hand, is based on the needs and values of the audience. For example, the warrant on page 11 reflects a preference for individual freedom, a value that would cause a reader who held it to agree that laws against marijuana should be repealed.

Each type of warrant requires a different set of questions for testing its soundness. The following list of questions will help you to decide whether a particular warrant is valid and can justify a particular claim.

1. *Authoritative* (based on the credibility of the sources)
   Is the authority sufficiently respected to make a credible claim?
   Do other equally reputable authorities agree with the authority
      cited?
   Are there equally reputable authorities who disagree?

2. *Substantive* (based on beliefs about the reliability of factual evidence)
   Are sufficient examples given to convince us that a general state-
      ment is justified? That is, are the examples given representative
      of the whole community?

[6] D. Ehninger and W. Brockriede, *Decision by Debate* (New York: Dodd, Mead, 1953).

If you have argued that one event or condition can bring about another (a cause-and-effect argument), does the cause given seem to
account entirely for the effect? Are other possible causes equally
important as explanations for the effect?

If you have used comparisons, are the similarities between the two
situations greater than the differences?

If you have used analogies, does the analogy explain or merely describe? Are there sufficient similarities between the two elements
to make the analogy appropriate?

3. *Motivational* (based on the values of the arguer and the audience)
Are the values ones that the audience will regard as important?
Are the values relevant to the claim?

SAMPLE ANNOTATED ANALYSIS

The Case for Torture

MICHAEL LEVIN

Introduction: statement
of opposing view

I t is generally assumed that torture is impermissible, a throwback to a more brutal age. Enlightened societies reject it outright, and regimes
suspected of using it risk the wrath of the United
States.

Claim of policy:
rebuttal of opposing
view

I believe this attitude is unwise. There are situations in which torture is not merely permissible but morally mandatory. Moreover, these
situations are moving from the realm of imagination to fact.

Support: hypothetical
example to test the
reader's belief

Suppose a terrorist has hidden an atomic
bomb on Manhattan Island which will detonate
at noon on July 4 unless . . . (here follow the
usual demands for money and release of his
friends from jail). Suppose, further, that he is
caught at 10 A.M. of the fateful day, but — preferring death to failure — won't disclose where the
bomb is. What do we do? If we follow due
process — wait for his lawyer, arraign him — millions of people will die. If the only way to save

Michael Levin is a professor of philosophy at the City College of New York. This essay
is reprinted from the June 7, 1982, issue of *Newsweek*.

those lives is to subject the terrorist to the most excruciating possible pain, what grounds can there be for not doing so? I suggest there are none. In any case, I ask you to face the question with an open mind.

Torturing the terrorist is unconstitutional? Probably. But millions of lives surely outweigh constitutionality. Torture is barbaric? Mass murder is far more barbaric. Indeed, letting millions of innocents die in deference to one who flaunts his guilt is moral cowardice, an unwillingness to dirty one's hands. If *you* caught the terrorist, could you sleep nights knowing that millions died because you couldn't bring yourself to apply the electrodes?

Once you concede that torture is justified in extreme cases, you have admitted that the decision to use torture is a matter of balancing innocent lives against the means needed to save them. You must now face more realistic cases involving more modest numbers. Someone plants a bomb on a jumbo jet. He alone can disarm it, and his demands cannot be met (or if they can, we refuse to set a precedent by yielding to his threats). Surely we can, we must, do anything to the extortionist to save the passengers. How can we tell 300, or 100, or 10 people who never asked to be put in danger, "I'm sorry, you'll have to die in agony, we just couldn't bring ourselves to . . ."

Here are the results of an informal poll about a third, hypothetical, case. Suppose a terrorist group kidnapped a newborn baby from a hospital. I asked four mothers if they would approve of torturing kidnappers if that were necessary to get their own newborns back. All said yes, the most "liberal" adding that she would administer it herself.

I am not advocating torture as punishment. Punishment is addressed to deeds irrevocably past. Rather, I am advocating torture as an acceptable measure for preventing future evils. So understood, it is far less objectionable than many extant punishments. Opponents of the death penalty, for example, are forever insisting that executing a murderer will not bring back his victim (as if the purpose of capital

Marginal annotations:

Support: hypothetical example

Support: informal poll

Defense of the claim
a) Not punishment but protection of the innocent

Marginal note: 5

punishment were supposed to be resurrection, not deterrence or retribution). But torture, in the cases described, is intended not to bring anyone back but to keep innocents from being dispatched. The most powerful argument against using torture as a punishment or to secure confessions is that such practices disregard the rights of the individual. Well, if the individual is all that important—and he is—it is correspondingly important to protect the rights of individuals threatened by terrorists. If life is so valuable that it must never be taken, the lives of the innocents must be saved even at the price of hurting the one who endangers them.

Hypothetical examples:

b) Analogies with World War II

Better precedents for torture are assassination and preemptive attack. No Allied leader would have flinched at assassinating Hitler, had that been possible. (The Allies did assassinate Heydrich.) Americans would be angered to learn that Roosevelt could have had Hitler killed in 1943—thereby shortening the war and saving millions of lives—but refused on moral grounds. Similarly, if nation A learns that nation B is about to launch an unprovoked attack, A has a right to save itself by destroying B's military capability first. In the same way, if the police can by torture save those who would otherwise die at the hands of kidnappers or terrorists, they must.

c) Denial that terrorists have rights

There is an important difference between terrorists and their victims that should mute talk of the terrorists' "rights." The terrorist's victims are at risk unintentionally, not having asked to be endangered. But the terrorist knowingly initiated his actions. Unlike his victims, he volunteered for the risks of his deed. By threatening to kill for profit or idealism, he renounces civilized standards, and he can have no complaint if civilization tries to thwart him by whatever means necessary.

Just as torture is justified only to save lives 10 (not extort confessions or recantations), it is justifiably administered only to those *known* to hold innocent lives in their hands. Ah, but how can the authorities ever be sure they have the right malefactor? Isn't there a danger of error and abuse? Won't We turn into Them?

d) Easy identification
of terrorists

Questions like these are disingenuous in a world in which terrorists proclaim themselves and perform for television. The name of their game is public recognition. After all, you can't very well intimidate a government into releasing your freedom fighters unless you announce that it is your group that has seized its embassy. "Clear guilt" is difficult to define, but when 40 million people see a group of masked gunmen seize an airplane on the evening news, there is not much question about who the perpetrators are. There will be hard cases where the situation is murkier. Nonetheless, a line demarcating the legitimate use of torture can be drawn. Torture only the obviously guilty, and only for the sake of saving innocents, and the line between Us and Them will remain clear.

Conclusion warrant:
"Paralysis in the face
of evil is the greater
danger."

There is little danger that the Western democracies will lose their way if they choose to inflict pain as one way of preserving order. Paralysis in the face of evil is the greater danger. Some day soon a terrorist will threaten tens of thousands of lives, and torture will be the only way to save them. We had better start thinking about this.

■ Analysis

Levin's controversial essay attacks a popular assumption that most people have never thought to question—that torture is impermissible under any circumstances. Levin argues that in extreme cases torture is morally justified to bring about a greater good than the rights of the individual who is tortured.

Against the initial resistance that most readers may feel, Levin makes a strong case. Its strength lies in the backing he provides for the warrant that torture is sometimes necessary. This backing consists in the use of two effective argumentative strategies. One is the anticipation of objections. Unprecedented? No. Unconstitutional? No. Barbaric? No. Second, and more important, are the hypothetical examples that compel readers to rethink their positions and possibly arrive at agreement with the author. Levin chooses extreme examples—kidnapping of a newborn child, planting a bomb on a jumbo jet, detonating an atomic bomb in Manhattan—that draw a line between clear and murky cases and make agreement easier. And he bolsters his moral position by insisting that torture is not to be used as punishment or revenge but only to save innocent lives.

To support such an unpopular assumption the writer must convey the impression that he is a reasonable man, and this Levin attempts to do by a searching definition of terms, the careful organization and development of his argument, including references to the opinions of other people, and the expression of compassion for innocent lives.

Another strength of the article is its readability — the use of contractions, informal questions, conversational locutions. This easy, familiar style is disarming; the reader doesn't feel threatened by heavy admonitions from a writer who affects a superior, moral attitude.

READINGS FOR ANALYSIS

A Proposal to Abolish Grading

PAUL GOODMAN

Let half a dozen of the prestigious universities — Chicago, Stanford, the Ivy League — abolish grading, and use testing only and entirely for pedagogic purposes as teachers see fit.

Anyone who knows the frantic temper of the present schools will understand the transvaluation of values that would be effected by this modest innovation. For most of the students, the competitive grade has come to be the essence. The naive teacher points to the beauty of the subject and the ingenuity of the research; the shrewd student asks if he is responsible for that on the final exam.

Let me at once dispose of an objection whose unanimity is quite fascinating. I think that the great majority of professors agree that grading hinders teaching and creates a bad spirit, going as far as cheating and plagiarizing. I have before me the collection of essays, *Examining in Harvard College,* and this is the consensus. It is uniformly asserted, however, that the grading is inevitable; for how else will the graduate schools, the foundations, the corporations *know* whom to accept, reward, hire? How will the talent scouts know whom to tap?

By testing the applicants, of course, according to the specific task-requirements of the inducting institution, just as applicants for the Civil Service or for licenses in medicine, law, and architecture are tested. Why should Harvard professors do the testing *for* corporations and graduate schools?

The objection is ludicrous. Dean Whitla, of the Harvard Office of 5 Tests, points out that the scholastic-aptitude and achievement tests used

Paul Goodman (1911–1972) was a college professor and writer whose outspoken views were popular with students during the 1960s. This essay is from *Compulsory Miseducation* (1964).

for *admission* to Harvard are a superexcellent index for all-around Harvard performance, better than high-school grades or particular Harvard course-grades. Presumably, these college-entrance tests are tailored for what Harvard and similar institutions want. By the same logic, would not an employer do far better to apply his own job-aptitude test rather than to rely on the vagaries of Harvard section-men? Indeed, I doubt that many employers bother to look at such grades; they are more likely to be interested merely in the fact of a Harvard diploma, whatever that connotes to them. The grades have most of their weight with the graduate schools—here, as elsewhere, the system runs mainly for its own sake.

It is really necessary to remind our academics of the ancient history of Examination. In the medieval university, the whole point of the grueling trial of the candidate was whether or not to accept him as a peer. His disputation and lecture for the Master's was just that, a masterpiece to enter the guild. It was not to make comparative evaluations. It was not to weed out and select for an extramural licensor or employer. It was certainly not to pit one young fellow against another in an ugly competition. My philosophic impression is that the medievals thought they knew what a good job of work was and that we are competitive because we do not know. But the more status is achieved by largely irrelevant competitive evaluation, the less will we ever know.

(Of course, our American examinations never did have this purely guild orientation, just as our faculties have rarely had absolute autonomy; the examining was to satisfy Overseers, Elders, distant Regents—and they as paternal superiors have always doted on giving grades, rather than accepting peers. But I submit that this set-up itself makes it impossible for the student to *become* a master, to *have* grown up, and to commence on his own. He will always be making A or B for some overseer. And in the present atmosphere, he will always be climbing on his friend's neck.)

Perhaps the chief objectors to abolishing grading would be the students and their parents. The parents should be simply disregarded; their anxiety has done enough damage already. For the students, it seems to me that a primary duty of the university is to deprive them of their props, their dependence on extrinsic valuation and motivation, and to force them to confront the difficult enterprise itself and finally lose themselves in it.

A miserable effect of grading is to nullify the various uses of testing. Testing, for both student and teacher, is a means of structuring, and also of finding out what is blank or wrong and what has been assimilated and can be taken for granted. Review—including high-pressure review—is a means of bringing together the fragments, so that there are flashes of synoptic insight.

There are several good reasons for testing, and kinds of test. But if the 10
aim is to discover weakness, what is the point of down-grading and punishing it, and thereby inviting the student to conceal his weakness, by
faking and bulling, if not cheating? The natural conclusion of synthesis
is the insight itself, not a grade for having had it. For the important purpose of placement, if one can establish in the student the belief that one
is testing *not* to grade and make invidious comparisons but for his own
advantage, the student should normally seek his own level, where he is
challenged and yet capable, rather than trying to get by. If the student
dares to accept himself as he is, a teacher's grade is a crude instrument
compared with a student's self-awareness. But it is rare in our universities
that students are encouraged to notice objectively their vast confusion.
Unlike Socrates, our teachers rely on power-drives rather than shame and
ingenuous idealism.

Many students are lazy, so teachers try to goad or threaten them by
grading. In the long run this must do more harm than good. Laziness is a
character-defense. It may be a way of avoiding learning, in order to protect the conceit that one is already perfect (deeper, the despair that one
never can be). It may be a way of avoiding just the risk of failing and
being down-graded. Sometimes it is a way of politely saying, "I won't."
But since it is the authoritarian grown-up demands that have created
such attitudes in the first place, why repeat the trauma? There comes a
time when we must treat people as adult, laziness and all. It is one thing
courageously to fire a do-nothing out of your class; it is quite another
thing to evaluate him with a lordly F.

Most important of all, it is often obvious that balking in doing the
work, especially among bright young people who get to great universities,
means exactly what it says: The work does not suit me, not this subject, or
not at this time, or not in this school, or not in school altogether. The student might not be bookish; he might be school-tired; perhaps his development ought now to take another direction. Yet unfortunately, if such a
student is intelligent and is not sure of himself, he *can* be bullied into passing, and this obscures everything. My hunch is that I am describing a
common situation. What a grim waste of young life and teacherly effort!
Such a student will retain nothing of what he has "passed" in. Sometimes
he must get mononucleosis to tell his story and be believed.

And ironically, the converse is also probably commonly true. A student flunks and is mechanically weeded out, who is really ready and
eager to learn in a scholastic setting, but he has not quite caught on. A
good teacher can recognize the situation, but the computer wreaks its
will.

READING AND DISCUSSION QUESTIONS

1. Goodman divides his argument into several parts, each of which develops a different idea. How would you subtitle these parts?

2. Are some parts of the argument stronger than others? Does Goodman indicate what points he wants to emphasize?

3. Why do you think Goodman calls on "half a dozen of the prestigious universities" (para. 1) instead of all universities to abolish grading?

4. Where does the author reveal the purposes of his proposal?

5. Most professors, Goodman argues, think that grading hinders teaching. Why, then, do they continue to give grades? How does Goodman reply to their objections?

6. What does Goodman think the real purpose of testing should be? How does grading "nullify the various uses of testing" (para. 9)?

WRITING SUGGESTIONS

7. Do you agree that grading prevents you from learning? If so, write an essay in which you support Goodman's thesis by reporting what your own experience has been.

8. If you disagree with Goodman, write an essay that outlines the benefits of grading.

9. Is there a better way than grading to evaluate the work of students — a way that would achieve the goals of education Goodman values? Suggest a method, and explain why it would be superior to grading.

An Unjust Sacrifice

ROBERT A. SIRICO

An appeals court in London has made a Solomonic ruling, deciding that eight-week-old twins joined at the pelvis must be separated. In effect, one twin, known as Mary, is to be sacrificed to save the other, known as Jodie, in an operation the babies' parents oppose.

The judges invoked a utilitarian rationale, justified on the basis of medical testimony. The specialists agreed that there is an 80 to 90 percent chance that the strong and alert Jodie could not survive more than a few months if she continued to support the weak heart and lungs of Mary, whose brain is underdeveloped.

This is a heartbreaking case, and the decision of the court was not arrived at lightly. But even the best of intentions, on the part of the state or the parents, is no substitute for sound moral reasoning. Utilitarian considerations like Mary's quality of life are not the issue. Nor should doctors' expert testimony, which is subject to error, be considered decisive.

Robert A. Sirico, a Roman Catholic priest, is president of the Acton Institute for the Study of Religion and Liberty in Grand Rapids, Michigan. This article appeared in the September 28, 2000, *New York Times*.

Here, as in the case of abortion, one simple principle applies: There is no justification for deliberately destroying innocent life. In this case, the court has turned its back on a tenet that the West has stood by: Life, no matter how limited, should be protected.

While this case is so far unique, there are guidelines that must be fol- 5
lowed. No human being, for instance, can be coerced into donating an organ—even if the individual donating the organ is unlikely to be harmed and the individual receiving the organ could be saved. In principle, no person should ever be forced to volunteer his own body to save another's life, even if that individual is a newborn baby.

To understand the gravity of the court's error, consider the parents' point of view. They are from Gozo, an island in Malta. After being told of their daughters' condition, while the twins were in utero, they went to Manchester, England, seeking out the best possible medical care. Yet, after the birth on August 8, the parents were told that they needed to separate the twins, which would be fatal for Mary.

They protested, telling the court: "We cannot begin to accept or contemplate that one of our children should die to enable the other one to survive. That is not God's will. Everyone has a right to life, so why should we kill one of our daughters to enable the other one to survive?"

And yet, a court in a country in which they sought refuge has overruled their wishes. This is a clear evil: coercion against the parents and coercion against their child, justified in the name of a speculative medical calculus.

The parents' phrase "God's will" is easily caricatured, as if they believed divine revelation were guiding them to ignore science. In fact, they believe in the merit of science, or they would not have gone to Britain for help in the first place.

But utilitarian rationality has overtaken their case. The lawyer ap- 10
pointed by the court to represent Jodie insisted that Mary's was "a futile life." That is a dangerous statement—sending us down a slippery slope where lives can be measured for their supposed value and discarded if deemed not useful enough.

Some might argue that in thinking about the twins, we should apply the philosophical principle known as "double effect," which, in some circumstances, permits the loss of a life when it is an unintended consequence of saving another. But in this case, ending Mary's life would be a deliberate decision, not an unintended effect.

Can we ever take one life in favor of another? No, not even in this case, however fateful the consequences.

READING AND DISCUSSION QUESTIONS

1. Underlying the author's claim that the parents of the twins should not separate them is the warrant—a broad assumption about life, in this case. What sentences express that warrant?

2. If you do not agree with Sirico's argument, point out what you think are flaws in his reasoning, based on your own understanding of moral principles.

3. In the fifth paragraph, Sirico cites another kind of medical dilemma as an analogy to that of the twins. How effective is it in supporting his claim?

4. The author condemns "utilitarianism" (para. 2). This ethical doctrine holds, as one dictionary defines it, "that conduct should be directed toward the greatest happiness of the greatest number of persons." Find statements in this essay that might explain why this philosophy is unacceptable to Sirico.

WRITING SUGGESTIONS

5. The author's conclusion is expressed as an absolute—a rule of behavior for which there are no exceptions. Can you think of any rules of human conduct which ought to be obeyed without exception? Reviewing the Ten Commandments might be a place to start. If so, define the rule, and tell why it must be so observed. If not, explain why some rules of behavior are subject to exception.

6. Peter Singer, a philosopher at Princeton University who subscribes to the utilitarian doctrine, has said that if the parents of a handicapped infant decide to kill him before he is two months old because his death would increase their happiness and decrease the infant's suffering, they have a right to do so. In another case he has argued that instead of spending money to reduce the suffering of a family member, a person should "send the same sum to ease the suffering of ten Sudanese."[7] Write an argument for or against the practice of utilitarianism in one of these cases or any other in which the sacrifice of life is an issue.

Computers and the Pursuit of Happiness
DAVID GELERNTER

In recent years we have been notified almost continuously that we are living in an "information age." Mankind (it is suggested) has completed a sort of phase shift: the solid agricultural age was replaced two centuries ago by the liquid industrial age, which has now given way to the gaseous (so to speak) age of information. Everyone says so, but is it true? *Has* an

---

[7] George F. Will, "Life and Death at Princeton," *Newsweek,* September 13, 1999, p. 82. This article is critical of Singer's philosophy.

David Gelernter is a professor of computer science at Yale. In addition to the books on computer technology mentioned in this essay, he is the author of the memoir *Drawing Life* and the novel *1939.* This essay appeared in the January, 2001 issue of *Commentary.*

old age ended, and are we, thanks to computers and the Internet, living in a new one? A related question: computers have been around for roughly a half-century; have they been good or bad for mankind? And finally: are they likely to do good or bad over the next half-century?

1

We are *not* in an information age, and computers and the Internet are not a revolutionary development in human history.

In the old industrial age (people say) coal, steel, and concrete mattered; in the new age, information counts. Yet it is obvious that coal, steel, and concrete still count just as much as they ever did. We have always needed food, clothing, shelter, possessions, and above all each other. We always *will* need those things, and the "information revolution" will never lessen our needs by half a hair's breadth. So whom are we kidding? What nouveau cyber-billionaire ever used his billions to buy *information?* Who ever worried about poverty because he would be unable to keep his family well-informed?

Not long ago I saw a rented U-Haul trailer with the inevitable web address in big letters on the side, "uhaul.com"—the information age in nine easy characters. Yes, it is convenient to check a Web site for information about trailers for rent; but the Internet will never (*can* never) change our need for physical stuff, or for trailers to haul it around in. Fifty years from now, it may be possible to download artistically designed experiences and beam them via trick signals into your brain. (To many people this will sound like a junior grade of hell, but some technologists think of it as a Coming Attraction.) The interesting fact remains: virtual gourmet food will make you feel full but will not keep you from starving. Virtual heat will make you feel warm but will not keep you from freezing. Virtual sex will make you feel satisfied in the sense that a pig feels satisfied.

About computers in particular, believers in a new information age 5 make three arguments. They say it is a new age because we now have sophisticated machines to create, store, and deliver information; because computer networks can overcome geography; and because machines (in their own special areas) can act intelligently. All three claims are wrong. Computers have done marvelous deeds—but in each case, their great deeds are in keeping with the long-established patterns of the industrial age. Computation today is a dusting of snow that makes everything look different—on the surface.

Fancy machines to create, move, and store information were a main preoccupation of the whole twentieth century, not just the computerized part of it. Movies, phonographs, color photography and color printing, the electronic transmission of photos, the invention of radio and radio networks and international radio hookups, newsreels, television, transistorized electronics, long-distance phone networks, communication satellites, fax machines, photocopiers, audio and video tapes, compact disks, cell phones, cable TV—and then, with the emergence of PC's and the Internet, suddenly we are in an information age? The twentieth century was one information-gusher after another; information pouring into people's lives through more and more stuck-open faucets.

The defeat of geography? In *Cyberspace and the American Dream* (1994), distributed electronically by the Progress and Freedom Foundation, a distinguished group of authors argued that "we constitute the final generation of an old civilization and, at the very same time, the first generation of a new one." Their claim centered on the idea that, thanks to computer networks, geography had (in effect) been overcome; henceforth, shared interests and not physical proximity would shape community and society.

But using technology to defeat distance has been another goal of the industrial revolution from the start, from railroads through the Panama Canal and onward. Rail networks, telegraph networks, air and phone and highway and radio and TV networks—the Internet is the latest in a long line.

The twentieth century teemed with smart machines, too, long before the computer showed up—simple ones like the thermostat or a car's electrical system (with automatic spark-advance); complex, sophisticated ones like automatic transmissions or the Norden bombsight in World War II. Granted, computers are a huge advance over the machines that came before, but huge advances are the stuff of the industrial age. The Web is a big deal, but flying machines were a pretty big deal, too. Radio and TV changed the nature of American democracy. The electric-power industry turned society inside out.

The cost of not knowing history is not ignorance so much as arro- 10 gance. A popular book about the Internet and the Web begins with this "personal note" from the author:

> The Internet is, by far, the greatest and most significant achievement in the history of mankind. What? Am I saying that the Internet is more impressive than the pyramids? More beautiful than Michelangelo's *David?* More important to mankind than the wondrous inventions of the industrial revolution? Yes, yes, and yes.

That sort of statement suggests that technologists are fundamentally unserious. By the way: a useful and interesting book. But the author protests too much. It is hard to picture comparable statements greeting the airplane's or the electric-power industry's emergence; they were too big and too obviously important to need this sort of cheerleading. What the author is really announcing is not a new age of information but a new age of hype, a new age of new ages.

Computers and the Internet *have* made a revolution in science and engineering. Studying computational models of reality can be cheaper and better than studying reality. Sometimes reality is impossible to measure or too steep to scale, and computational models are the only way to get any purchase on it. Those are the *actual* computer revolutions; the others are mostly potential and not real, locked up in awe-inspiring icebergs that just float around eliciting admiration and making trouble. The computer revolution is still frozen, latent, waiting to happen.

As for the information age, it must have begun at least a hundred years ago if it exists at all. *Are* we better informed than we used to be? I doubt it. Is anyone prepared to assert that the U.S. electorate is better informed today than it was at the time of (say) the 1960 presidential election? That our fifth graders are better informed about reading, writing, history, or arithmetic? That our fifth-grade *teachers* are better informed? (Recently my fifth-grade son learned from his English teacher that "incredible" and "incredulous" are synonyms. That's the information age for you.)

2

Have computers been good or bad for mankind since they were invented roughly fifty years ago?

Other things being equal, information is good. Wealth is good. Computers have supplied lots of information, and generated much wealth.

But we are marvelously adaptable. We can take miserable conditions 15 in stride and triumph over them; we can take wonderful conditions in stride and triumph over *them*. Humanity in any given age has a wealth threshold and an information threshold. If you are below either one, living in poverty or ignorance, you need more wealth or information. But once you are over the threshold, only the rate of change matters. Acquire more wealth or information, and presumably you will be happier; then you stabilize at your new, higher level, and chances are you are no happier than before. It is not exactly a deep or novel observation that money doesn't buy happiness. Neither does information.

In this country, the majority—obviously not everyone, but most of us—have been over-threshold in wealth and information for several generations, roughly since the end of World War II. That is a remarkable achievement; it ought to make us proud and thankful. But it follows that increasing our level of wealth or information is unlikely to count terribly much in the larger scheme of things. The increase itself will feel good, but the substance of our new wealth or information won't matter much.

Here is a small case in point. My two boys, who are ten and thirteen, love playing with computers, like most children nowadays. The computer is their favorite toy, and unquestionably it makes them happy. Computer play as it is practiced in real life, at least at our house, is a mindless activity; like many families, we have to limit the time our boys are allowed at it or they would spend all day wrecking pretend Porsches and blowing up enemy airplanes. But mindless activities are fine in reasonable doses. It's good for children to have fun, and I'm glad ours have so much fun with computers.

When my wife and I were children, we didn't have computers to play with. We lacked these wonderful, happiness-generating devices. But—so what? Other things made us happy. We never felt deprived on account of our lack of computer power. It would be crazy to deny that computers are great toys, but it would be equally crazy to argue that they have made children any happier, on the whole, than children used to be. Fifty years from now, the computer-based toys will make today's look pathetic, and children will love all their snazzy new stuff—just as much, probably, as children loved their bats and balls and blocks and trains and jump-ropes and dollhouses in 1900.

What we ordinarily fail to take into account when we are adding up the score is the nature of technological change. Technology is a tool for building social structures. Granted, each new technology is better than the one it replaces. But new technologies engender new social structures, and the important question is not whether the new technology is better but whether the new structure is better. Except in the case of medical technologies, the answer will nearly always be debatable; nearly always *must* be debatable. We can easily show that, with each passing generation, paints have improved. It is much harder to show that art has improved.

Human nature does not change; human needs and wants remain ba- 20 sically the same. Human ingenuity dreams up a new technology, and we put it to use—doing in a new way something we have always done in some other way. In years past, many towns had shared public wells. They were communal gathering places: you met neighbors, heard the news, checked out strangers, sized up the competition, made deals, dates, matches. Plumbing was a great leap forward, which few of us (certainly not me) would be willing to trade in. The old system was a nuisance, especially if *you* were the one carrying the water; but it was neighborly. The new, plumbing-induced social structure was far more convenient, not to say healthier. It was also lonelier. The old and new structures excelled in different ways and cannot be directly compared.

The Web is an improvement much like plumbing, without the health benefits. Fifty years ago, most shopping was face to face. In the Internet age, face-to-face stores will not survive long, any more than communal wells survived the advent of plumbing. To our great-grandchildren, shopping will mean "online," as it meant "face to face" to our great-grandparents. Future generations will look back wistfully but probably not unhappily. On the whole, their happiness and their ancestors' will probably be about the same. To the extent future generations *are* happier or unhappier than we—and "national happiness" does change, it's hard to doubt that America in 1950 was a happier country than America today—we can be fairly sure of one thing. The net change will have nothing to do with technology.

A major new technology remakes society—picks up the shoebox, shakes it hard, puts back. The new social structures we build almost always incorporate less human labor than the old ones. The old structures (in other words) have a larger "human ingredient," the new ones a larger "machine ingredient." It is nearly always impossible to compare the two directly. And in the meantime the old ones have disappeared. Where technology is concerned, we demolish the past and live in a permanent present.

In the lush technology future, we will be kids in a candy store. The old zero-sum economics of Malthus and his modern disciples has long since been discredited; we will swagger into that Candy Store of the Future with more money all the time, and find more and fancier candy in there every day. Our inventiveness, productivity, and potential wealth are all unlimited. Only our appetite for candy is not.

3

If mankind were somehow prevented from continuing to develop computers and software—that would be a tragedy, and the world would suffer. Nothing comes more naturally to us than building and playing with machines. Inventing technology is the intellectual equivalent of breathing.

Is breathing helpful? Yes. Will it conduce to a better world in 2050?   25
Right again! But only in a certain sense.

In 1991 I published a book called *Mirror Worlds;* in a way, it was a celebration of computing technology (although it was ambivalent about computers in the end). It predicted the emergence of software versions of real-world institutions that you would "tune in" by means of a global network. It claimed that this would be a good development: you would be able to tour the world "without changing out of your pajamas." These mirror worlds would be "the new public square," would "monopolize the energy and attention of thousands . . . , broadcast an aesthetic and a world-view to millions, mold behavior and epitomize the age."

Talk about modest claims—although in looking back at the Web boom that began in 1994 they seem, if anything, too modest. In predicting that "the software revolution hasn't begun yet, but it will soon," I was basically right. The industrial age ushered in new categories and possibilities, and computers and software are creating new possibilities, too: new types of structures that are just as unprecedented as the Eiffel Tower.

Consider an online school. Such a school might offer guided naturewalks through teeming, chattering, blossoming rain forests of the intellect where your guide knows exactly what you are capable of, can make the path expand or shrink to suit you, can point out the biggest vistas or the tiniest orchid—and the whole structure can be moored in cyberspace, where anyone who likes can climb aboard. Instead of merely reteaching the same class year after year, we could make the path better every year. As a student follows a trail, we could turn that trail into his personal diary, for review or revisiting whenever he likes; he could keep his whole school career in his back pocket. We could plant pictures or maps at the center of lessons if they belonged there, instead of pasting them in as afterthoughts.

And these new software structures could be world-spanning switch-boards, connecting the right student to the right teacher. If Mrs. Feinstein is the English teacher for little Kate Smith, then wherever Mrs. Feinstein lives (Auckland, Nome, Passaic), whatever hours she keeps, whatever her formal qualifications, we could patch her into the system.

I would rather put Kate in an actual school where actual teachers 30 could look her in the face when they are trying to teach her something. But American education is in desperate trouble—and under the circumstances, software-based teaching is probably our best hope. In the future we will compare our ubiquitous software schools to the face-to-face education of the pre-1970s the way we compare online shopping to long-ago Main Streets: we will be wistful, as usual, but not wistful enough to do anything about it. On the whole we will be content.

Of course, we are talking about new software *structures*—not mere computers, not mere information. And we are talking about something that *could* happen, but hasn't yet.

Human beings are mainly interested in human beings. If computers do good in the next fifty years, the good they are most likely to do lies in helping mankind know itself better.

A large part of cognitive science is built on a famous analogy, the analogy that did so much for the functionalist school of philosophy in the 1950s and 60s and that many researchers still believe today: mind is to brain as software is to computer. This analogy is fundamentally wrong.

Just the fact that software is portable (it can be moved from one computer to another) and minds are not (they cannot be moved from one brain to another) should have told us at the very start that the analogy was fishy. There is no reason to believe that you will ever be able to offload Joe Schwartz's mind and run it on Melissa Clark's brain. It is not even clear what this would mean in principle, because *part* of Schwartz's mind is the fact that it belongs to Schwartz. "Porting a mind" is not only impossible, but in principle meaningless.

In *The Muse in the Machine* (1994) I argued that you cannot under- 35 stand human thought unless you understand the "cognitive spectrum" that exists in every mind. That spectrum ranges from highly focused, highly aware-of-the-environment "analytic" thought all the way down to "low-focus," oblivious-of-the-environment thought—all the way down, in other words, to the kind of hallucinatory thought that happens routinely when we are asleep and dreaming. We will never get a computer to think until we have figured out how to make one hallucinate. To reproduce thought on a computer, we will need to reproduce the whole cognitive spectrum and not just one narrow slice of it.

For many years, the biggest challenge in cognitive science and philosophy has been to understand how we discover analogies, where we get our amazing capacity to notice that two things—objects, situations, events—that *seem* completely unrelated in fact have deep, hidden similarities. This capacity to draw analogies underlies human creativity and our useful knack of discovering and inventing new things. How does it work?

The evidence suggests, it seems to me, that analogy is driven by emotion. The remarkable thing about human emotion is that two wholly different-*seeming* scenes or memories or circumstances can make us *feel* exactly the same way. Emotion lets us make spectacularly nonobvious connections; in so doing, it lets us discover new analogies, lets us create.

Now, human emotions obviously depend not only on the mind but on the body. You don't think them, you feel them. So we cannot hope to simulate thought on a computer unless we can simulate the discovery of analogies. We cannot hope to do *that* unless we can simulate emotions on a machine. And we cannot hope to do *that* unless we can simulate not merely abstract mental processes but the complex, nuanced physical reality of the human body.

Eventually, this will be done. Certainly not soon (and certainly not by me)—but it will be done. But even at the end of this enormously difficult, complex task, when humanity has achieved the technological marvel of a machine that can accurately fake human emotions and (therefore) can realistically fake human thought, where exactly will we be?

The human body and its brain have the "emergent property"—or "ensemble property"—of consciousness. When you put exactly the right pieces together in exactly the right way . . . consciousness emerges. 40

There is no reason, in principle, why computers and software could not have this property as well, and thus lead us to a deeper appreciation of what consciousness means and what it represents. It could be that we will wind up with a "thinking machine" that does not merely talk about daffodils, identify them, draw pictures of them; we might in principle end up with a machine that actually knows what a daffodil *is*. That actually experiences fragrance as we do, color as we do, form as we do—or at least experiences fragrance, color, and form in *some* way; or at least experiences *something* in some way. In other words, that is actually conscious.

All this *could* be. But we have no good reason to think it ever will be. It could be that consciousness will emerge from exactly the right combination of electronics and software; it could be that consciousness will emerge from exactly the right combination of mozzarella and tomato sauce, or bricks and mortar, or cardboard and rubber cement. None of these things is (in principle) impossible, but none of them is terribly likely, either.

Machines can move faster than we do; so it cannot be that the important thing (the distinguishing thing) about humans is how fast we are. Cannot be how strong we are. Cannot be how well we do arithmetic. It might easily be that in fifty years, machines will be smarter than we are, too. . . .

But I do not think we will conclude that to be human is no big deal after all. I have heard one of technology's most honored, distinguished men tell a large audience how he wished human beings would stop thinking that they are somehow different from animals; it pained him to hear the old canard about man's "uniqueness." He is offering us an easy out: it is simple to be an animal and complicated (Lord knows) to be a man. Should we stop trying, call it a day, and relocate to the barnyard?

Not yet. Most of us are not quite ready to toss out the scraps of morality and sanctity we have pieced together over the long, hard centuries; they may look shabby but they are the best clothes we own. They might even be as important as the Internet. I think we will decide not that we are merely animals after all but that our uniqueness lies beyond strength speed *and* intellect. 45

People have said so for a long time, of course. Jews and Christians have long believed it. Chances are that, fifty years from now—thanks to computers—many more people will believe it. Chances are that, fifty years from now, we will be grateful to computer technology for showing us what marvelously powerful machines we can build—and how little they mean after all.

READING AND DISCUSSION QUESTIONS

1. State the warrant underlying the author's claim that computers cannot guarantee happiness. Look for it in the last part of the essay, although it is not stated directly.

2. Summarize Gelernter's responses to the three questions asked in the first paragraph. Do you find all of his arguments equally persuasive? Explain your answer.

3. Gelernter uses history, psychology, and personal experiences to support his claim. Point out some specific examples of these forms of support. Did any of his evidence surprise you? Does your own experience with computers confirm his insights?

4. The use of language in this essay is worth noting. The author has a highly readable style that encompasses both the formal and the informal. Find places where he speaks directly to the reader, using conversational language—colloquial in both grammar and vocabulary—to reach his audience.

5. The ending of this essay resembles one in a short story (and, in fact, Gelernter writes fiction, too). There is no explicit summing up. The meaning of the ending is indirect: It must be inferred from all that has been said before. (Contrast, for example, the closing statements of "An Unjust Sacrifice.") Why does Gelernter say that computers will not mean much, after all? What is the significance of the reference to Jews and Christians? Do you find the ending inspiring, as the author clearly intends? Or too elusive?

WRITING SUGGESTIONS

6. Write an essay elaborating on some of the ways in which the use of the computer has changed your life, for better or worse. You might want to refute or confirm one or more of the issues raised by Gelernter.

7. A few years ago a student took first prize in an essay contest in which she argued the superiority of printed books over books on the computer. The writer ended her essay this way: "It all boils down to which definition of communication you prefer: interpersonal or technological. A library of empty bookshelves would be a travesty." What is the difference between "interpersonal" and "technological"? Write a response to the student's comment, spelling out some advantages of the electronic book.

PERHAPS THE MOST BEAUTIFUL THING ABOUT USING ENERGY
MORE EFFICIENTLY ISN'T THE FUEL IT CAN SAVE.

Use natural gas and you'll help protect the environment two ways. First, natural gas is much
cleaner than other fossil fuels. You can also take advantage of our programs to reduce natural gas use up to
30% in your home or business. And that's something that's good for the environment, too.
To find out more, call 1-800-427-3089. You'll be surprised how much you can save.

Boston gas
FOR THESE TIMES, IT'S A NATURAL.

BOS/5

DISCUSSION QUESTIONS

1. What advantages of natural gas does this ad stress? Are butterflies superior to plants or other animals as persuasive elements?

2. What warrants or assumptions about the user underlie the advertiser's approach?

3. Contrast this ad with the ad on page 188. Which argument is stronger? Notice that one is negative, the other positive. Does that influence your choice?

DEBATE: Should We Fear the Cloning of Human Beings?

Cloning Misperceptions

LEE M. SILVER

Why do four out of five Americans think that human cloning is "against God's will" or "morally wrong"? Why are people so frightened by this technology? One important reason is that many people have a muddled sense of what cloning is. They confuse the popular meaning of the word *clone* and the specific meaning it takes on in the context of biology.

In its popular usage, *clone* refers to something that is a duplicate, or cheaper imitation, of a brand-name person, place, or thing. The British politician Tony Blair has been called a clone of Bill Clinton, and an IBM PC clone is not only built like an IBM PC, it *behaves* like an IBM PC. It is this popular meaning of the word that caused many people to believe that human cloning would copy not just a person's body but a person's consciousness as well. This concept of cloning was at the center of the movie *Multiplicity,* which was released just months before the Dolly announcement. In it, a geneticist makes a clone of the star character played by Michael Keaton and explains that the clone will have "all of his feelings, all of his quirks, all of his memories, right up to the moment of cloning." The clone himself says to the original character, "You are me, I am you." It is this image that Jeremy Rifkin probably had in mind when he criticized the possible application of the sheep cloning technology to humans by saying, "It's a horrendous crime to make a Xerox (copy) of someone."

But this popular image bears absolutely no resemblance to actual cloning technology, in either process or outcome. Scientists cannot make full-grown adult copies of any animal, let alone humans. All they can do is start the process of development over again, using genetic material obtained from an adult. Real biological cloning can only take place at the level of the cell—life *in the general sense.* It is only long after the cloning event is completed that a unique—and independent—life *in the special sense* could emerge in the developing fetus. Once again, it is the inability of many people to appreciate the difference between the two meanings of "life" that is the cause of confusion.

A second reason people fear cloning is based on the notion that a clone is an imperfect imitation of the real thing. This causes some people to think that—far from having the same soul as someone else—a clone

---

Lee M. Silver is a professor of molecular biology at Princeton University. This essay is from *Remaking Eden: Cloning and Beyond in a Brave New World* (1997).

would have no soul at all. Among the earliest popular movies to explore this idea was *Blade Runner,* in which synthetic people were produced that were just like humans in all respects but one—they had no empathy. (Coincidentally, *Blade Runner* was based on a 1968 book by Philip K. Dick entitled *Do Androids Dream of Electric Sheep?*) And the same general idea of imperfection is explored in *Multiplicity* when a clone of the Michael Keaton character has himself cloned. The clone of the clone is a dimwitted clown because, as the original clone says, "Sometimes you make a copy of a copy and it's not as sharp as the original."

The Irvine, California, rabbi Bernard King was seriously frightened by 5 this idea when he asked, "Can the cloning create a soul? Can scientists create the soul that would make a being ethical, moral, caring, loving, all the things we attribute humanity to?" The Catholic priest Father Saunders suggested that "cloning would only produce humanoids or androids—soulless replicas of human beings that could be used as slaves." And Brent Staples, a member of the *New York Times* editorial board, warned that "synthetic humans would be easy prey for humanity's worst instincts."

Yet there is nothing synthetic about the cells used in cloning. They are alive before the cloning process, and they are alive after fusion has taken place. The newly created embryo can only develop inside the womb of a woman in the same way that all embryos and fetuses develop. Cloned children will be full-fledged human beings, indistinguishable in biological terms from all other members of the species. Thus, the notion of a soulless clone has no basis in reality.

When the misperceptions are tossed aside, it becomes clear what a cloned child will be. She, or he, will simply be a later-born identical twin—nothing more and nothing less. And while she may go through life looking similar to the way her progenitor-parent looked at a past point in time, she will be a unique human being, with a completely unique consciousness and a unique set of memories that she will build from scratch.

To many people, the mere word *clone* seems ominous, conjuring up images from movies like *The Boys from Brazil* with evil Nazis intent on ruling the world. How likely is it that governments or organized groups will use cloning as a tool to build future societies with citizens bred to fulfill a particular need?

The *Brave New World* Scenario

"Bokanovsky's Process," repeated the Director. . . . One egg, one embryo, one adult—normality. But a bokanovskified egg will bud, will proliferate, will divide. From eight to ninety-six buds, and every bud will grow into a perfectly formed embryo, and every embryo into a full-sized adult. Making ninety-six human beings grow where only one grew before. Progress. . . . Identical twins—but not in piddling twos and threes as in the old viviparous days, when an egg would sometimes accidentally divide; actually by dozens, by scores at a time. . . . "But, alas," the Director shook his head, "we can't bokanovskify indefinitely." Ninety-six seemed to be the limit; seventy-two a good average.

Thus did Aldous Huxley present one of the technological underpinnings of his brave new world where cloning would be used "as one of the major instruments of social stability." With cloning, it was possible to obtain "standard men and women; in uniform batches. The whole of a factory staffed with the products of a single bokanovskified egg."

Brave New World evoked powerful feelings within people not only because they could see inklings of the rigid conformity of the brave new world society within their own, but because the science was presented in a hyperrealistic manner. Even the most minor technical details were carefully described. 10

Huxley, for one, was convinced that political forces would evolve in the direction he described. In the foreword to the 1946 edition, he wrote: "It is probable that all the world's governments will be more or less completely totalitarian even before the harnessing of atomic energy; that they will be totalitarian during and after the harnessing seems almost certain." It was the *science* that he was less certain of.

Yet, like so many other twentieth-century intellectuals, Huxley underestimated the power of technology to turn yesterday's fantasy into today's reality. Only sixty-four years after he speculated on the possibility of human cloning, it is on the verge of happening. But now that one aspect of science has caught up to *Brave New World,* what can we say about the politics? Will there be governments that choose to clone?

Definitely not in a democratic society for a very simple reason. Cloned children cannot appear out of the air. Each one will have to develop within the womb of a woman (for the time being). And in a free society, the state cannot control women's bodies and minds in a way that would be necessary to build an army of clones.

But what about a totalitarian government that wanted to produce clones to serve its own social needs: "Standard men and women; in uniform batches. The whole of a factory staffed with the products of a single bokanovskified egg."

This scenario is highly improbable. First, only an extremely controlling totalitarian state would have the ability to enslave women *en masse* to act as surrogate mothers for babies that would be forcibly removed and raised by the state. Ruling governments this extreme are rare at the end of the twentieth century. But even if one did emerge, it is hard to imagine why it would want to clone people. 15

Would it be to produce an army of powerful soldiers? Any government that could clone would certainly get more fighting power out of high-tech weapons of destruction than even the most muscular and obedient soldier clones.

Would it be to produce docile factory workers? Cloning is not necessary for this objective, which has already been reached throughout many societies. And mind control could be achieved much more effectively with New Age drugs targeted at particular behaviors and emotions (another prediction made by Huxley).

Would it be to produce people with great minds? It is not clear how a government would choose a progenitor for such clones, or what it would do during the twenty years or so that it took for clones to mature into adults. After all that time, a new set of leaders might decide that the wrong characteristics had been chosen for cloning. A better approach would be to simply build a superior system of public education that allowed the brightest children to rise to the top, no matter where on society's ladder they began their lives.

In the end, one is hard-pressed to come up with a single strategic advantage that any government might get from breeding clones rather than allowing a population to regenerate itself naturally. Thus, the Huxleyan use of cloning as a means for building a stable society seems very unlikely. But there is an obvious exception—one that could occur in a state or society controlled by a single egomaniacal dictator with substantial financial and scientific resources.

The example that comes to mind is that of the Japanese cult leader 20 Shoko Asahara. Asahara's group, Aum Shinrikyo, included well-educated chemists who produced nerve gas for the purpose of holding the Japanese government hostage. The group was exposed, and their leader was arrested and put on trial after a lethal gas attack on the Tokyo subway system in March 1995. Based on what we have learned about the group, it is possible that it might have had both the financial and technical resources required to put together the facility and equipment needed for cloning, as well as the power of persuasion required to convince skilled personnel to carry it out. And the aura that Asahara projected was such that he might well have succeeded in convincing women to become pregnant with his clones. Finally, Asahara himself seems to have been exactly the kind of egomaniac who would have preferred child clones over naturally conceived sons.

I doubt that we could stop people like Shoko Asahara from cloning themselves. But would it make any difference? Let us imagine that Asahara had cloned himself into a dozen children. It seems extremely unlikely that these children would have any greater effect on society, twenty years down the road, than sons conceived the old-fashioned way. It's not only that they wouldn't grow up in the same adverse environment that played an important role in turning Asahara into the cult leader that he became. It's also that they would grow up among different people who would be unlikely to respond to them in exactly the same way that people responded to Asahara. The same could be said for modern-day clones of Adolf Hitler. In both cases, the original men were catapulted into positions of leadership through chance personal or historical events that will never repeat themselves. An adult alive today with Adolf Hitler's mind, personality, and behavior would be more likely to find himself barricaded in a militia outpost or in jail than in the White House or the German Bundesrat.

While Hitler's Third Reich and Asahara's Aum Shinrikyo were both short-lived phenomena, there are still examples of royal families—albeit with little real power today—that have handed down the crown from parent to child over hundreds of years. If after ascending to the throne, Prince Charles of Great Britain decided to place his clone—rather than his eldest son—next in line, would that upset the world order? On the contrary, I doubt if anyone would care.

The Risks of Human Cloning Outweigh the Benefits

NATIONAL BIOETHICS ADVISORY COMMISSION

There is one basis of opposition to somatic cell nuclear transfer cloning on which almost everyone can agree. (A somatic cell is any cell of the embryo, fetus, child, or adult which contains a full complement of two sets of chromosomes; in contrast with a germ cell—that is, an egg or a sperm, which contains only one set of chromosomes. During somatic cell nuclear transfer cloning, the nucleus—which contains a full set of chromosomes—is removed from the somatic cell and transferred to an egg cell which has had its nucleus removed.) There is virtually universal concern regarding the current safety of attempting to use this technique in human beings. Even if there were a compelling case in favor of creating a child in this manner, it would have to yield to one fundamental principle of both medical ethics and political philosophy—the injunction, as it is stated in the Hippocratic canon, to "first, do no harm." In addition, the avoidance of physical and psychological harm was established as a standard for research in the Nuremberg Code, 1946–49. At this time, the significant risks to the fetus and physical well-being of a child created by somatic cell nuclear transplantation cloning outweigh arguably beneficial uses of the technique.

It is important to recognize that the technique that produced Dolly the sheep was successful in only 1 of 277 attempts. If attempted in humans, it would pose the risk of hormonal manipulation in the egg donor;

This article is from *Cloning Human Beings: Reports and Recommendations of the National Bioethics Advisory Commission* (June 1997).

multiple miscarriages in the birth mother; and possibly severe developmental abnormalities in any resulting child. Clearly the burden of proof to justify such an experimental and potentially dangerous technique falls on those who would carry out the experiment. Standard practice in biomedical science and clinical care would never allow the use of a medical drug or device on a human being on the basis of such a preliminary study and without much additional animal research. Moreover, when risks are taken with an innovative therapy, the justification lies in the prospect of treating an illness in a patient, whereas, here no patient is at risk until the innovation is employed. Thus, no conscientious physician or Institutional Review Board should approve attempts to use somatic cell nuclear transfer to create a child at this time. For these reasons, prohibitions are warranted on all attempts to produce children through nuclear transfer from a somatic cell at this time.

A Difference of Opinion

Even on this point, however, NBAC (National Bioethics Advisory Committee) has noted some difference of opinion. Some argue, for example, that prospective parents are already allowed to conceive, or to carry a conception to term, when there is a significant risk—or even certainty—that the child will suffer from a serious genetic disease. Even when others think such conduct is morally wrong, the parents' right to reproductive freedom takes precedence. Since many of the risks believed to be associated with somatic cell nuclear transfer may be no greater than those associated with genetic disorders, some contend that such cloning should be subject to no more restriction than other forms of reproduction.

And, as in any new and experimental clinical procedure, harms cannot be accurately determined until trials are conducted in humans. Law professor John Robertson noted before NBAC on March 13, 1997 that:

> [The] first transfer [into a uterus] of a human [embryo] clone [will occur] before we know whether it will succeed. . . . [Some have argued therefore] that the first transfers are somehow unethical . . . experimentation on the resulting child, because one does not know what is going to happen, and one is . . . possibly leading to a child who could be disabled and have developmental difficulties. . . . [But the] child who would result would not have existed but for the procedure at issue, and [if] the intent there is actually to benefit that child by bringing it into being . . . [this] should be classified as experimentation for [the child's] benefit and thus it would fall within recognized exceptions. . . . We have a very different set of rules for experimentation intended to benefit [the experimental subject].

But the argument that somatic cell nuclear transfer cloning experiments are "beneficial" to the resulting child rest on the notion that it is a "benefit" to be brought into the world as compared to being left unconceived and unborn. This metaphysical argument, in which one is forced 5 to compare existence with non-existence, is problematic. Not only does it require us to compare something unknowable—non-existence—to something else, it also can lead to absurd conclusions if taken to its logical extreme. For example, it would support the argument that there is no degree of pain and suffering that cannot be inflicted on a child, provided that the alternative is never to have been conceived. Even the originator of this line of analysis rejects this conclusion.

In addition, it is true that the actual risks of physical harm to the child born through somatic cell nuclear transfer cannot be known with certainty unless and until research is conducted on human beings. It is likewise true that if we insisted on absolute guarantees of no risk before we permitted any new medical intervention to be attempted in humans, this would severely hamper if not halt completely the introduction of new therapeutic interventions, including new methods of responding to infertility. The assertion that we should regard attempts at human cloning as "experimentation for [the child's] benefit" is not persuasive. . . .

Cloning and Individuality

The concept of creating a genetic twin, although separated in time, is one aspect of somatic cell nuclear transfer cloning that most find both troubling and fascinating. The phenomenon of identical twins has intrigued human cultures across the globe, and throughout history. It is easy to understand why identical twins hold such fascination. Common experience demonstrates how distinctly different twins are, both in personality and in personhood. At the same time, observers cannot help but imbue identical bodies with some expectation that identical persons occupy those bodies, since body and personality remain intertwined in human intuition. With the prospect of somatic cell nuclear transfer cloning comes a scientifically inaccurate but nonetheless instinctive fear of multitudes of identical bodies, each housing personalities that are somehow less than distinct, less unique, and less autonomous than usual.

Is there a moral or human right to a unique identity, and if so would it be violated by this manner of human cloning? For such somatic cell nuclear transfer cloning to violate a right to a unique identity, the relevant sense of identity would have to be genetic identity, that is a right to a unique unrepeated genome. Even with the same genes, two individuals—for example homozygous twins—are distinct and not identical, so what is intended must be the various properties and characteristics that make each individual qualitatively unique and different than others. Does having the same genome as another person undermine that unique qualitative identity?

Ignorance and Knowledge

Along these lines of inquiry some question whether reproduction using somatic cell nuclear transfer would violate what philosopher Hans Jonas called a right to ignorance, or what philosopher Joel Feinberg called a right to an open future, or what Martha Nussbaum called the quality of "separateness." Jonas argued that human cloning, in which there is a substantial time gap between the beginning of the lives of the earlier and later twin, is fundamentally different from the simultaneous beginning of the lives of homozygous twins that occur in nature. Although contemporaneous twins begin their lives with the same genetic inheritance, they also begin their lives or biographies at the same time, in ignorance of what the twin who shares the same genome will by his or her choices make of his or her life. To whatever extent one's genome determines one's future, each life begins ignorant of what that determination will be, and so remains as free to choose a future as are individuals who do not have a twin. In this line of reasoning, ignorance of the effect of one's genome on one's future is necessary for the spontaneous, free, and authentic construction of a life and self.

A later twin created by cloning, Jonas argues, knows, or at least be- 10
lieves he or she knows, too much about him or herself. For there is already in the world another person, one's earlier twin, who from the same genetic starting point has made the life choices that are still in the later twin's future. It will seem that one's life has already been lived and played out by another, that one's fate is already determined, and so the later twin will lose the spontaneity of authentically creating and becoming his or her own self. One will lose the sense of human possibility in freely creating one's own future. It is tyrannical, Jonas claims, for the earlier twin to try to determine another's fate in this way.

And even if it is a mistake to believe such crude genetic determinism according to which one's genes determine one's fate, what is important for one's experience of freedom and ability to create a life for oneself is whether one thinks one's future is open and undetermined, and so still to be largely determined by one's own choices. One might try to interpret Jonas' objection so as not to assume either genetic determinism, or a belief in it. A later twin might grant that he or she is not destined to follow in his or her earlier twin's footsteps, but that nevertheless the earlier twin's life would always haunt the later twin, standing as an undue influence on the latter's life, and shaping it in ways to which others' lives are not vulnerable. . . .

Potential Harms to Important Social Values

Those with grave reservations about somatic cell nuclear transfer cloning ask us to imagine a world in which cloning human beings via somatic cell nuclear transfer were permitted and widely practiced. What kind of people, parents, and children would we become in such a world? Opponents fear that such cloning to create children may disrupt the interconnected web of social values, practices, and institutions that support the healthy growth of children. The use of such cloning techniques might encourage the undesirable attitude that children are to be valued according to how closely they meet parental expectations, rather than loved for their own sake. In this way of looking at families and parenting, certain values are at the heart of those relationships, values such as love, nurturing, loyalty, and steadfastness. In contrast, a world in which such cloning were widely practiced would give, the critics claim, implicit approval to vanity, narcissism, and avarice. To these critics, changes that undermine those deeply prized values should be avoided if possible. At a minimum, such undesirable changes should not be fostered by public policies. . . .

Treating People as Objects

Some opponents of somatic cell nuclear cloning fear that the resulting children will be treated as objects rather than as persons. This concern often underlies discussions of whether such cloning amounts to "making" rather than "begetting" children, or whether the child who is created in this manner will be viewed as less than a fully independent moral agent. In sum, will being cloned from the somatic cell of an existing person result in the child being regarded as less of a person whose humanity and dignity would not be fully respected?

One reason this discussion can be hard to capture and to articulate is that certain terms, such as "person," are used differently by different people. What is common to these various views, however, is a shared understanding that being a "person" is different from being the manipulated "object" of other people's desires and expectations. Writes legal scholar Margaret Radin,

> The person is a subject, a moral agent, autonomous and self-governing. An object is a non-person, not treated as a self-governing moral agent. . . . [By] "objectification of persons," we mean, roughly, "what Kant would not want us to do."

That is, to objectify a person is to act towards the person without regard for his or her own desires or well-being, as a thing to be valued according to externally imposed standards, and to control the person rather than to engage her or him in a mutually respectful relationship. Objectification, quite simply, is treating the child as an object—a creature less deserving of respect for his or her moral agency. Commodification is sometimes distinguished from objectification and concerns treating persons as commodities, including treating them as a thing that can be exchanged, bought or sold in the marketplace. To those who view the intentional choice by another of one's genetic makeup as a form of manipulation by others, somatic cell nuclear transfer cloning represents a form of objectification or commodification of the child.

Some may deny that objectification is any more a danger in somatic cell nuclear transfer cloning than in current practices such as genetic screening or, in the future perhaps, gene therapy. These procedures aim either to avoid having a child with a particular condition, or to compensate for a genetic abnormality. But to the extent that the technology is used to benefit the child by, for example, allowing early preventive measures with phenylketonuria, no objectification of the child takes place.

When such cloning is undertaken not for any purported benefit of the child himself or herself, but rather to satisfy the vanity of the nucleus donor, or even to serve the need of someone else, such as a dying child in need of a bone marrow donor, then some would argue that it goes yet another step toward diminishing the personhood of the child created in this fashion. The final insult, opponents argue, would come if the child created through somatic cell nuclear transfer is regarded as somehow less than fully equal to the other human beings, due to his or her diminished physical uniqueness and the diminished mystery surrounding some aspects of his or her future physical development.

Eugenic Concerns

The desire to improve on nature is as old as humankind. It has been played out in agriculture through the breeding of special strains of domesticated animals and plants. With the development of the field of genetics over the past 100 years came the hope that the selection of advantageous inherited characteristics—called eugenics, from the Greek eugenes meaning wellborn or noble in heredity—could be as beneficial to humankind as selective breeding in agriculture.

The transfer of directed breeding practices from plants and animals to human beings is inherently problematic, however. To begin, eugenic proposals require that several dubious and offensive assumptions be made. First, that most, if not all people would mold their reproductive behavior to the eugenic plan; in a country that values reproductive freedom, this outcome would be unlikely absent compulsion. Second, that means exist for deciding which human traits and characteristics would be favored, an enterprise that rests on notions of selective human superiority that have long been linked with racist ideology.

Equally important, the whole enterprise of "improving" humankind 20 by eugenic programs oversimplifies the role of genes in determining human traits and characteristics. Little is known about the correlation between genes and the sorts of complex, behavioral characteristics that are associated with successful and rewarding human lives; moreover, what little is known indicates that most such characteristics result from complicated interactions among a number of genes and the environment. While cows can be bred to produce more milk and sheep to have softer fleece, the idea of breeding humans to be superior would belong in the realm of science fiction even if one could conceive how to establish the metric of superiority, something that turns not only on the values and prejudices of those who construct the metric but also on the sort of a world they predict these specially bred persons would face.

Nonetheless, at the beginning of this century eugenic ideas were championed by scientific and political leaders and were very popular with the American public. It was not until they were practiced in such a grotesque fashion in Nazi Germany that their danger became apparent. Despite this sordid history and the very real limitations in what genetic selection could be expected to yield, the lure of "improvement" remains very real in the minds of some people. In some ways, creating people through somatic cell nuclear transfer offers eugenicists a much more powerful tool than any before. In selective breeding programs, such as the "germinal choice" method urged by the geneticist H. J. Muller a generation ago, the outcome depended on the usual "genetic lottery" that occurs each time a sperm fertilizes an egg, fusing their individual genetic heritages into a new individual. Cloning, by contrast, would allow the selection of a desired genetic prototype which would be replicated in each of the "offspring," at least on the level of the genetic material in the cell nucleus.

Objections to a Eugenics Program

It might be enough to object to the institution of a program of human eugenic cloning—even a voluntary program—that it would rest on false scientific premises and hence be wasteful and misguided. But that argument might not be sufficient to deter those people who want to push the genetic traits of a population in a particular direction. While acknowledging that a particular set of genes can be expressed in a variety of ways and therefore that cloning (or any other form of eugenic selection) does not guarantee a particular phenotypic manifestation of the genes, they might still argue that certain genes provide a better starting point for the next generation than other genes.

The answer to any who would propose to exploit the science of cloning in this way is that the moral problems with a program of human eugenics go far beyond practical objections of infeasibility. Some objections are those that have already been discussed in connection with the possible desire of individuals to use somatic cell nuclear transfer that the creation of a child under such circumstances could result in the child being objectified, could seriously undermine the value that ought to attach to each individual as an end in themselves, and could foster inappropriate efforts to control the course of the child's life according to expectations based on the life of the person who was cloned.

In addition to such objections are those that arise specifically because what is at issue in eugenics is more than just an individual act, it is a collective program. Individual acts may be undertaken for singular and often unknown or even unknowable reasons, whereas a eugenics program would propagate dogma about the sorts of people who are desirable and those who are dispensable. That is a path that humanity has tread before, to its everlasting shame. And it is a path to whose return the science of cloning should never be allowed to give even the slightest support. . . .

Cloning Is Unethical

In summary, the Commission reached several conclusions in considering 25 the appropriateness of public policies regarding the creation of children through somatic cell nuclear transfer. First and foremost, creating children in this manner is unethical at this time because available scientific evidence indicates that such techniques are not safe at this time. Even if concerns about safety are resolved, however, significant concerns remain about the negative impact of the use of such a technology on both individuals and society. Public opinion on this issue may remain divided. Some people believe that cloning through somatic cell nuclear transfer will always be unethical because it . . . will always risk causing psychological or other harms to the resulting child. In addition, although the Commission acknowledged that there are cases for which the use of such cloning might be considered desirable by some people, overall these cases were insufficiently compelling to justify proceeding with the use of such techniques. . . .

Finally, many scenarios of creating children through somatic cell nuclear transfer are based on the serious misconception that selecting a child's genetic makeup is equivalent to selecting the child's traits or accomplishments. A benefit of more widespread discussion of such cloning would be a clearer recognition that a person's traits and achievements depend heavily on education, training, and the social environment, as well as on genes. Should this type of cloning proceed, however, any children born as a result of this technique should be treated as having the same rights and moral status as any other human being.

DISCUSSION QUESTIONS

1. What distinction does Silver make between the popular and the scientific meanings of *clone*? What two definitions of *life* does he emphasize to make his meaning clear?

2. One form of support in Silver's argument depends on references to movies and literature, as well as direct quotations from critics. Look back over the article, and decide if these references make the development stronger. How effective are they if the reader is unfamiliar with the movies or the novel?

3. How does Silver refute the view that totalitarian governments will "produce clones to serve its own social needs" (para. 14)? Is his argument persuasive? Explain your answer.

4. According to the National Bioethics Advisory Commission, why would a conscientious physician decline to perform the cloning procedure?

5. How does the Commission respond to Robertson's defense of cloning? Which argument seems more convincing?

6. Summarize the objections of the Commission to human cloning. The headings as well as the last paragraph are a guide to the issues.

7. Both articles use definitions to defend their arguments. Point out the issues in which definition is important. Do these definitions make it harder or easier to reach a conclusion about this debate? Explain why.

TAKING THE DEBATE ONLINE

For these and additional research URLs, see www.bedfordstmartins.com/rottenberg.

- ***The Ethics and Religious Liberty Commission***
  http://www.erlc.com/Biomed/1997/65Comsn.htm

  This site reflects the unfavorable views on human cloning held by the Ethics and Religious Liberty Commission. It also provides links to other articles relating to cloning and biomedical ethics.

- ***Genetic Encores: The Ethics of Human Cloning***
  http://www.puaf.umd.edu/IPPP/Fall97Report/cloning.htm

  This report, from the Institute for Philosophy and Public Policy, examines the ethical issues surrounding human cloning.

- ***Science and Technology in Congress: President's Commission Issues Cloning Recommendations***
  http://www.aaas.org/spp/dspp/cstc/bulletin/articles/7-97/
  CLONING.HTM

  This site of the American Association for the Advancement of Science presents an overview of cloning from the perspective of the U.S. Congress.

- ***New Scientist: Cloning—A Special Report***
  http://www.nsplus.com/hottopics/cloning

  This multilayered site explores issues relating to cloning and addresses the implications such scientific advancement has for humans.

- ***The Human Cloning Foundation***
  http://www.humancloning.org/

  This association is wholly in support of human cloning.

EXERCISES

1. What are some of the assumptions underlying the preference for *natural* foods and medicines? Can *natural* be clearly defined? Is this preference part of a broader philosophy? Try to evaluate the validity of the assumption.

2. Is plagiarism wrong? What assumptions about education are relevant to the issue of plagiarism? (Some students defend it. What kinds of arguments do they provide?)

3. Choose an advertisement, and examine the warrants on which the advertiser's claim is based.

4. "Religious beliefs are (or are not) necessary to a satisfactory life." Explain the warrants underlying your claim. Define any ambiguous terms.

5. Should students be given a direct voice in the hiring of faculty members? On what warrants about education do you base your answer?

6. Discuss the validity of the warrant in this statement from *The Watch Tower* (a publication of the Jehovah's Witnesses) about genital herpes: "The sexually loose are indeed 'receiving in themselves the full recompense, which was due for their error' (Romans 1:27)."

7. Read the following passage about suicide by the Greek philosopher Aristotle (adapted from his *Ethics*). Then defend or attack his argument, being careful to make clear both Aristotle's and your own warrants.

> Just as a murderer does not have the right to take a mother from her family or a child from her parents and simultaneously to deny society the use of a productive citizen, so the suicide, even though he or she freely chooses to be his or her own victim, does not possess the right to thus diminish the welfare of so many others.

8. In view of increasing interest in health in general, and nutrition and exercise in particular, do you think that universities and colleges should impose physical education requirements? If so, what form should they take? If not, why not? Defend your reasons.

9. Both state and federal governments have been embroiled in controversies concerning the rights of citizens to engage in harmful practices. In Massachusetts, for example, a mandatory seat-belt law was repealed by rebellious voters who considered the law an infringement of their freedom. What principles do you think ought to guide government regulation of dangerous practices?

10. The author of the following passage, Katherine Butler Hathaway, became a hunchback as a result of a childhood illness. Here she writes about the relationship between love and beauty from the point of view of someone who is deformed. Discuss the warrants on which the author bases her conclusion.

> I could secretly pretend that I had a lover . . . but I could never risk showing that I thought such a thing was possible for me . . . with any man. Because of my repeated encounters with the mirror and my irrepressible tendency to forget what I had seen, I had begun to force myself to believe and to remember, and especially to remember, that I would never be chosen for what I imagined to be the supreme and most intimate of all experience. I thought of sexual love as an honor that was too great and too beautiful for the body in which I was doomed to live.

CRITICAL LISTENING

11. People often complain that they aren't listened to. Children complain about parents, patients about doctors, wives about husbands, citizens

about government. Are the complaints to be taken literally? Or are they based on unexpressed warrants or assumptions about communication? Choose a specific familiar situation, and explain the meaning of the complaint.

12. Barbara Ehrenreich, in a *Time* essay, defends "talk shows of the *Sally Jessy Raphael* variety" as highly moralistic. Listen to a couple of these shows— *Ricki Lake, Jerry Springer*—and determine what moral assumptions about personal relationships and behavior underlie the advice given to the participants by the host and the audience. Do you think Ehrenreich is correct?

7

Language and Thought

THE POWER OF WORDS

Words play such a critical role in argument that they deserve special treatment. Elsewhere we have referred directly and indirectly to language: Chapter 4 discusses definitions, and Part Two discusses style—the choice and arrangement of words and sentences—and shows how successful writers express arguments in language that is clear, vivid, and thoughtful. An important part of these writers' equipment is a large and active vocabulary, but no single chapter in a book can give this to you; only reading and study can widen your range of word choices. Even in a brief chapter, however, we can point out how words influence the feelings and attitudes of an audience, both favorably and unfavorably.

One kind of language responsible for shaping attitudes and feelings is *emotive language,* language that expresses and arouses emotions. Understanding it and using it effectively are indispensable to the arguer who wants to move an audience to accept a point of view or undertake an action.

Long before you thought about writing your first argument, you learned that words had the power to affect you. Endearments and affectionate and flattering nicknames evoked good feelings about the speaker and yourself. Insulting nicknames and slurs produced dislike for the speaker and bad feelings about yourself. Perhaps you were told, "Sticks and stones may break your bones, but words will never hurt you." But even to a small child it is clear that ugly words are as painful as sticks and stones and that the injuries are sometimes more lasting.

Nowhere is the power of words more obvious and more familiar than in advertising, where the success of a product may depend on the feelings that certain words produce in the prospective buyer. Even the names of products may have emotive significance. In recent years a new industry, composed of consultants who supply names for products, has emerged. Although most manufacturers agree that a good name won't save a poor product, they also recognize that the right name can catch the attention of the public and persuade people to buy a product at least once. According to an article in the *Wall Street Journal,* a product name not only should be memorable but also should "remind people of emotional or physical experiences." One consultant created the name Magnum for a malt liquor from Miller Brewing Company: "The product is aimed at students, minorities, and lower-income customers." The president of the consulting firm says that Magnum "implies strength, masculinity, and more bang for your buck."[1] This naming of products has been called the "Rumpelstiltskin effect," a phrase coined by a linguist. "The whole point," he said, "is that when you have the right name for a thing, you have control over it."[2]

Even scientists recognize the power of words to attract the attention of other scientists and the public to discoveries and theories that might otherwise remain obscure. A good name can even enable the scientist to visualize a new concept. One scientist says that "a good name," such as "quark," "black hole," "big bang," "chaos," or "great attractor," "helps in communicating a theory and can have substantial impact on financing."

It is not hard to see the connection between the use of words in conversation and advertising and the use of emotive language in the more formal arguments you will be writing. Emotive language reveals your approval or disapproval, assigns praise or blame—in other words, makes a judgment about the subject. Keep in mind that unless you are writing purely factual statements, such as scientists write, you will find it hard to avoid expressing judgments. Neutrality does not come easily, even where it may be desirable, as in news stories or reports of historical events. For this reason you need to attend carefully to the statements in your argument, making sure that you have not disguised judgments as statements of fact. Of course, in attempting to prove a claim, you will not be neutral. You will be revealing your judgment about the subject, first in the selection of facts and opinions and the emphasis you give to them and second in the selection of words.

[1] *Wall Street Journal,* August 5, 1982, p. 19.
[2] *Harvard Magazine,* July–August 1995, p. 18.

Like the choice of facts and opinions, the choice of words can be effective or ineffective in advancing your argument, moral or immoral in the honesty with which you exercise it. The following discussions offer some insights into recognizing and evaluating the use of emotive language in the arguments you read, as well as into using such language in your own arguments where it is appropriate and avoiding it where it is not.

CONNOTATION

The connotations of a word are the meanings we attach to it apart from its explicit definition. Because these added meanings derive from our feelings, connotations are one form of emotive language. For example, the word *rat* denotes or points to a kind of rodent, but the attached meanings of "selfish person," "evil-doer," "betrayer," and "traitor" reflect the feelings that have accumulated around the word.

In Chapter 4 we observed that definitions of controversial terms, such as *poverty* and *unemployment,* may vary so widely that writer and reader cannot always be sure that they are thinking of the same thing. A similar problem arises when a writer assumes that the reader shares his or her emotional response to a word. Emotive meanings originate partly in personal experience. The word *home,* defined merely as "a family's place of residence," may suggest love, warmth, and security to one person; it may suggest friction, violence, and alienation to another. The values of the groups to which we belong also influence meaning. Writers and speakers count on cultural associations when they refer to our country, our flag, and heroes and enemies we have never seen. The arguer must also be aware that some apparently neutral words trigger different responses from different groups—words such as *cult, revolution, police, beauty contest,* and *corporation.*

Various reform movements have recognized that words with unfavorable connotations have the power not only to reflect but also to shape our perceptions of things. The words *Negro* and *colored* were rejected by the civil rights movement in the 1960s because they bore painful associations with slavery and discrimination. Instead, the word *black,* which was free from such associations, became the accepted designation; more recently, the Reverend Jesse Jackson suggested another term, *African American,* to reflect ethnic origins. People of "Spanish/Hispanic/Latino" origin (as they are designated on the 2000 census) are now engaged in a debate about the appropriate term for a diverse population of more than 22 million American residents from Mexico, Puerto Rico, Cuba, and more than a dozen Central and South American countries. To some, the word *Hispanic* is unacceptable because it is an anglicization and recalls the colonization of America by Spain and Portugal.

The women's liberation movement also insisted on changes that would bring about improved attitudes toward women. The movement condemned the use of *girl* for a female over the age of eighteen and the use in news stories of descriptive adjectives that emphasized the physical appearance of women. And the homosexual community succeeded in reintroducing the word *gay,* a word current centuries ago, as a substitute for words they considered offensive. Now *queer,* a word long regarded as offensive, has been adopted as a substitute for *gay* by a new generation of gays and lesbians, although it is still considered unacceptable by many members of the homosexual community.

Members of certain occupations have invented terms to confer greater respectability on their work. The work does not change, but the workers hope that public perceptions will change if janitors are called custodians, if garbage collectors are called sanitation engineers, if undertakers are called morticians, if people who sell makeup are called cosmetologists. Events considered unpleasant or unmentionable are sometimes disguised by polite terms, called *euphemisms.* During the 1992 to 1993 recession new terms emerged that disguised, or tried to, the grim fact that thousands of people were being dismissed from their jobs: *skill-mix adjustment, workforce-imbalance correction, redundancy elimination, downsizing, indefinite idling,* even a daring *career-change opportunity.* Many people refuse to use the word *died* and choose *passed away* instead. Some psychologists and physicians use the phrase *negative patient care outcome* for what most of us would call *death.* Even when referring to their pets, some people cannot bring themselves to say *put to death* but substitute *put to sleep* or *put down.* In place of a term to describe an act of sexual intercourse, some people use *slept together* or *went to bed together* or *had an affair.*

Polite words are not always so harmless. If a euphemism disguises a shameful event or condition, it is morally irresponsible to use it to mislead the reader into believing that the shameful condition does not exist. In his powerful essay "Politics and the English Language" George Orwell pointed out that politicians and reporters have sometimes used terms like "pacification" or "rectification of frontiers" to conceal acts that result in torture and death for millions of people. An example of such usage was cited by a member of Amnesty International, a group monitoring human rights violations throughout the world. He objected to a news report describing camps in which the Chinese were promoting "reeducation through labor." This term, he wrote, "makes these institutions seem like a cross between Police Athletic League and Civilian Conservation Corps camps." On the contrary, he went on, the reality of "reeducation through labor" was that the victims were confined to "rather unpleasant prison camps." The details he offered about the conditions under which people lived and worked gave substance to his claim.[3] More recently, when news organizations referred to the expulsion of Romanian gypsies

[3]Letter to the *New York Times,* August 30, 1982, p. 25.

from Germany as part of a "deportation treaty," an official of Germany's press agency objected to the use of the word *deportation*. "You must know that by using words such as *deportation* you are causing great sadness. . . . We prefer that you use the term *readmission* or *retransfer*."[4]

Some of the most interesting changes in language usage occur in modern Bible translations. The vocabulary and syntax of earlier versions have been greatly simplified to make the Bible more accessible to that half of the American public who cannot read above eighth-grade level. Another change responds to arguments by feminists, environmentalists, and multiculturalists for more "inclusive language." God is no longer the *Father,* human beings no longer have *dominion* over creation, and even the word *blindness* as a metaphor for sin or evil has been replaced by other metaphors.

Perhaps the most striking examples of the way that connotations influence our perceptions of reality occur when people are asked to respond to questions of poll-takers. Sociologists and students of poll-taking know that the phrasing of a question, or the choice of words, can affect the answers and even undermine the validity of the poll. In one case poll-takers first asked a selected group of people if they favored continuing the welfare system. The majority answered no. But when the poll-takers asked if they favored government aid to the poor, the majority answered yes. Although the terms *welfare* and *government aid to the poor* refer to essentially the same forms of government assistance, *welfare* has acquired for many people negative connotations of corruption and shiftless recipients.

In a *New York Times*/CBS poll conducted in January 1998, "a representative sample of Americans were asked which statement came nearer to their opinion: 'Is abortion the same thing as murdering a child, or is abortion not murder because the fetus really isn't a child?'" Thirty-eight percent chose "the fetus really isn't a child." But 58 percent, including a third of those who chose "abortion is the same thing as murdering a child," agreed that abortion "was sometimes the best course in a bad situation." The author of the report suggests an explanation of the fact that a majority of those polled seemed to have chosen "murder" as an acceptable solution to an unwanted pregnancy:

> These replies reveal, at least, a considerable moral confusion.
> Or maybe only verbal confusion? Should the question have asked whether abortion came closer, in the respondent's view, to "killing" rather than "murdering" a child? That would leave room for the explanation that Americans, while valuing life, are ultimately not pacifists: killing, they hold, may be justified in certain circumstances (self-defense, warfare, capital punishment).

[4] *International Herald Tribune,* November 5, 1992.

So one can challenge the wording of the question. Indeed, one can almost always challenge the wording of poll questions. . . . Poll takers themselves acknowledge the difficulty of wording questions and warn against relying too much on any single finding.[5]

This is also true in polls concerning rape, another highly charged subject. Dr. Neil Malamuth, a psychologist at the University of California at Los Angeles, says, "When men are asked if there is any likelihood they would force a woman to have sex against her will if they could get away with it, about half say they would. But if you ask them if they would rape a woman if they knew they could get away with it, only about 15 percent say they would." The men who change their answers aren't aware that "the only difference is in the words used to describe the same act."[6]

The wording of an argument is crucial. Because readers may interpret the words you use on the basis of feelings different from your own, you must support your word choices with definitions and with evidence that allows readers to determine how and why you made them.

SLANTING

Slanting, says one dictionary, is "interpreting or presenting in line with a special interest." The term is almost always used in a negative sense. It means that the arguer has selected facts and words with favorable or unfavorable connotations to create the impression that no alternative view exists or can be defended. For some questions it is true that no alternative view is worthy of presentation, and emotionally charged language to defend or attack a position that is clearly right or wrong would be entirely appropriate. We aren't neutral, nor should we be, about the tragic abuse of human rights anywhere in the world or even about less serious infractions of the law, such as drunk driving or vandalism, and we should use strong language to express our disapproval of these practices.

Most of your arguments, however, will concern controversial questions about which people of goodwill can argue on both sides. In such cases, your own judgments should be restrained. Slanting will suggest a prejudice—that is, a judgment made without regard to all the facts. Unfortunately, you may not always be aware of your bias or special interest; you may believe that your position is the only correct one. You may also feel the need to communicate a passionate belief about a serious problem. But if you are interested in persuading a reader to accept your belief and to act on it, you must also ask: If the reader is not sympathetic, how will he or she respond? Will he or she perceive my words as "loaded"—one-sided and prejudicial—and my view as slanted?

---

[5]Peter Steinfels, "Beliefs," *New York Times,* January 24, 1998, sec. A, p. 15.
[6]*New York Times,* August 29, 1989, sec. C, p. 1.

R. D. Laing, a Scottish psychiatrist, defined *prayer* in this way: "Someone is gibbering away on his knees, talking to someone who is not there."[7] This description probably reflects a sincerely held belief. Laing also clearly intended it for an audience that already agreed with him. But the phrases "gibbering away" and "someone who is not there" would be offensive to people for whom prayer is sacred.

The following remarks by one writer attacking another appeared in *Salon,* an online magazine:

> Urging the hyperbolic *Salon* columnist David Horowitz to calm down and cite facts instead of spewing insults seems as pointless as asking a dog not to defecate on the sidewalk. In either instance, the result is always and predictably the same: Somebody has to clean up a stinking pile.[8]

An audience, whether friendly or unfriendly, interested in a discussion of the issues, would probably be both embarrassed and repelled by this use of language in a serious argument.

In the mid-1980s an English environmental group, London Greenpeace, began to distribute leaflets accusing the McDonald's restaurants of a wide assortment of crimes. The leaflets said in part:

> McDollars, McGreedy, McCancer, McMurder, McDisease, McProfits, McDeadly, McHunger, McRipoff, McTorture, McWasteful, McGarbage.
>
> This leaflet is asking you to think for a moment about what lies behind McDonald's clean, bright image. It's got a lot to hide. . . .
>
> McDonald's and Burger King are two of the many U.S. corporations using lethal poisons to destroy vast areas of Central American rain forest to create grazing pastures for cattle to be sent back to the States as burgers and pet food. . . .
>
> What they don't make clear is that a diet high in fat, sugar, animal products and salt . . . and low in fiber, vitamins and minerals—which describes an average McDonald's meal—is linked with cancers of the breast and bowel, and heart disease. . . .[9]

Even readers who share the belief that McDonald's is not a reliable source of good nutrition might feel that London Greenpeace has gone too far, and that the name-calling, loaded words, and exaggeration have damaged the credibility of the attackers more than the reputation of McDonald's.

---

[7]"The Obvious," in David Cooper, ed. *The Dialectics of Liberation* (Penguin Books, 1968), p. 17.

[8]July 6, 2000.

[9]*New York Times,* August 6, 1995, sec. E, p. 7. In 1990 McDonald's sued the group for libel. In June 1997, after the longest libel trial in British history, the judge ruled in favor of the plaintiff, awarding McDonald's £60,000. In March 1999 an appeal partially overturned the verdict, and reduced the damages awarded to McDonald's by approximately one-third.

We find slanting everywhere, not only in advertising and propaganda, where we expect to find it, but in news stories, which should be strictly neutral in their recounting of events, and in textbooks. In the field of history, for example, it is often difficult for scholars to remain impartial about significant events. Like the rest of us, they may approve or disapprove, and their choice of words will reflect their judgments.

The following passage by a distinguished Catholic historian describes the events surrounding the momentous decision by Henry VIII, king of England, to break with the Roman Catholic Church in 1534, in part because of the Pope's refusal to grant him a divorce from the Catholic princess Catherine of Aragon so that he could marry Anne Boleyn.

> The *protracted* delay in receiving an annulment was very *irritating* to the *impulsive* English king. . . . Gradually Henry's former *effusive* loyalty to Rome gave way to a settled conviction of the tyranny of the papal power, and there *rushed* to his mind the recollections of efforts of earlier English rulers to restrict that power. A few *salutary* enactments against the Church might *compel* a favorable decision from the Pope.
>
> Henry seriously opened his campaign against the Roman Church in 1531, when he *frightened* the clergy into paying a fine of over half a million dollars for violating an *obsolete* statute . . . and in the same year he *forced* the clergy to recognize himself as supreme head of the Church. . . .
>
> His *subservient* Parliament then empowered him to stop the payments of annates to the Pope and to appoint bishops in England without recourse to the papacy. *Without waiting longer* for the decision from Rome, he had Cranmer, *one of his own creatures,* whom he had just named Archbishop of Canterbury, declare his marriage null and void. . . .
>
> Yet Henry VIII encountered considerable *opposition* from the *higher clergy,* from the monks, and from many *intellectual leaders.* . . . A *popular uprising*—the Pilgrimage of Grace—was *sternly* suppressed, and such men as the *brilliant* Sir Thomas More and John Fisher, the *aged* and *saintly* bishop of Rochester, were beheaded because they retained their former belief in papal supremacy.[10] [Italics added]

In the first paragraph the italicized words help make the following points: that Henry was rash, impulsive, and insincere and that he was intent on punishing the church (the word *salutary* means healthful or beneficial and is used sarcastically). In the second paragraph the choice of words stresses Henry's use of force and the cowardly submission of his followers. In the third paragraph the adjectives describing the opposition to Henry's campaign and those who were executed emphasize Henry's cruelty and despotism. Within the limits of this brief passage the author has offered support for his strong indictment of Henry VIII's actions, both in defining the statute as obsolete and in describing the popular opposition. In a longer exposition you would expect to find a more elab-

---

[10] Carlton J. H. Hayes, *A Political and Cultural History of Modern Europe,* vol. 1 (New York: Macmillan, 1933), pp. 172–173.

orate justification with facts and authoritative opinion from other sources.

The advocate of a position in an argument, unlike the reporter or the historian, must express a judgment, but the preceding examples demonstrate how the arguer should use language to avoid or minimize slanting and to persuade readers that he or she has come to a conclusion after careful analysis. The careful arguer must not conceal his or her judgments by presenting them as if they were statements of fact, but must offer convincing support for his or her choice of words and respect the audience's feelings and attitudes by using temperate language.

Depending on the circumstances, *exaggeration* can be defined, in the words of one writer, as "a form of lying." An essay in *Time* magazine, "Watching Out for Loaded Words," points to the danger for the arguer in relying on exaggerated language as an essential part of the argument.

> The trouble with loaded words is they tend to short-circuit thought. While they may describe something, they simultaneously try to seduce the mind into accepting a prefabricated opinion about the something described.[11]

PICTURESQUE LANGUAGE

Picturesque language consists of words that produce images in the mind of the reader. Students sometimes assume that vivid picture-making language is the exclusive instrument of novelists and poets, but writers of arguments can also avail themselves of such devices to heighten the impact of their messages.

Picturesque language can do more than render a scene. It shares with other kinds of emotive language the power to express and arouse deep feelings. Like a fine painting or photograph, it can draw readers into the picture where they partake of the writer's experience as if they were also present. Such power may be used to delight, to instruct, or to horrify. In 1741 the Puritan preacher Jonathan Edwards delivered his sermon "Sinners in the Hands of an Angry God," in which people were likened to repulsive spiders hanging over the flames of Hell to be dropped into the fire whenever a wrathful God was pleased to release them. The congregation's reaction to Edwards's picture of the everlasting horrors to be suffered in the netherworld included panic, fainting, hysteria, and convulsions. Subsequently Edwards lost his pulpit in Massachusetts, in part as a consequence of his success at provoking such uncontrollable terror among his congregation.

[11] *Time*, May 24, 1982, p. 86.

Language as intense and vivid as Edwards's emerges from very strong emotion about a deeply felt cause. In an argument against abortion, a surgeon recounts a horrifying experience as if it were a scene in a movie.

> You walk toward the bus stop. . . . It is all so familiar. All at once you step on something soft. You feel it with your foot. Even through your shoe you may have the sense of something unusual, something marked by a special "give." It is a foreignness upon the pavement. Instinct pulls your foot away in an awkward little movement. You look down, and you see . . . a tiny naked body, its arms and legs flung apart, its head thrown back, its mouth agape, its face serious. A bird, you think, fallen from the nest. But there is no nest here on 73rd Street, no bird so big. It is rubber, then. A model, a . . . a joke. And you bend to see. Because you must. And it is no joke. Such a gray softness can be but one thing. It is a baby, and dead. You cover your mouth, your eyes. You are fixed. Horror has found its chink and crawled in, and you will never be the same as you were. Years later you will step from a sidewalk to a lawn, and you will start at its softness and think of that upon which you have just trod.[12]

Here the use of the pronoun *you* serves to draw readers into the scene and intensify their experience.

The rules governing the use of picturesque language are the same as those governing other kinds of emotive language. Is the language appropriate? Is it too strong, too colorful for the purpose of the message? Does it result in slanting or distortion? What will its impact be on a hostile or indifferent audience? Will they be angered, repelled? Will they cease to read or listen if the imagery is too disturbing?

We expect strong language in arguments about life and death. For subjects about which your feelings are not so passionate, your choice of words will be more moderate. The excerpt below, from an article arguing against repeal of Sunday closing laws, creates a sympathetic picture of a market-free Sunday. Most readers, even those who oppose Sunday closing laws, would enjoy the picture and perhaps react more favorably to the argument.

> Think of waking in the city on Sunday. Although most people no longer worship in the morning, the city itself has a reverential air. It comes to life slowly, even reluctantly, as traffic lights blink their orders to empty streets. Next, joggers venture forth, people out to get the paper, families going to church or grandma's. Soon the city is its Sunday self: People cavort with their children, discuss, make repairs, go to museums, gambol. Few people go to work, and any shopping is incidental. The city on Sunday is a place outside the market. Play dominates, not the economy.[13]

[12] Richard Selzer, *Mortal Lessons: Notes on the Art of Surgery* (New York: Simon and Schuster, 1974), pp. 153–154.
[13] Robert K. Manoff, "New York City, It Is Argued, Faces 'Sunday Imperialism,'" *New York Times,* January 2, 1977, sec. 4, p. 13.

CONCRETE AND ABSTRACT LANGUAGE

Writers of argument need to be aware of another use of language—the distinction between concrete and abstract. Concrete words point to real objects and real experiences. Abstract words express qualities apart from particular things and events. *Beautiful roses* is concrete; we can see, touch, and smell them. *Beauty* in the eye of the beholder is abstract; we can speak of the quality of beauty without reference to a particular object or event. *Returning money found in the street to the owner, although no one has seen the discovery* is concrete. *Honesty* is abstract. In abstracting we separate a quality shared by a number of objects or events, however different from each other the individual objects or events may be.

Writing that describes or tells a story leans heavily on concrete language. Although arguments also rely on the vividness of concrete language, they use abstract terms far more extensively than other kinds of writing. Using abstractions effectively, especially in arguments of value and policy, is important for two reasons: (1) Abstractions represent the qualities, characteristics, and values that the writer is explaining, defending, or attacking; and (2) they enable the writer to make generalizations about his or her data. Equally important is knowing when to avoid abstractions that obscure the message.

In some textbook discussions of language, abstractions are treated as inferior to concrete and specific words, but such a distinction is misleading. Abstractions allow us to make sense of our experience, to come to conclusions about the meaning of the bewildering variety of emotions and events we confront throughout a lifetime. One writer summarized his early history as follows: "My elementary school had the effect of *destroying any intellectual motivation*, of *stifling* all *creativity*, of *inhibiting personal relationships* with either my teachers or my peers" (emphasis added). Writing in the humanities and in some social and physical sciences would be impossible without recourse to abstractions that express qualities, values, and conditions.

You should not, however, expect abstract terms alone to carry the emotional content of your message. The effect of even the most suggestive words can be enhanced by details, examples, and anecdotes. One mode of expression is not superior to the other; both abstractions and concrete detail work together to produce clear, persuasive argument. This is especially true when the meanings assigned to abstract terms vary from reader to reader.

In establishing claims based on the support of values, for example, you may use such abstract terms as *religion, duty, freedom, peace, progress, justice, equality, democracy,* and *pursuit of happiness.* You can assume that some of these words are associated with the same ideas and emotions for almost all readers; others require further explanation. Suppose you write, "We have made great progress in the last fifty years." One dictionary defines *progress* as "a gradual betterment," another abstraction. How will you define "gradual betterment" for your readers? Can you be sure that they have in mind the same references for progress that you do? If not, misunderstandings are inevitable. You may offer examples: supersonic planes, computers, shopping malls, nuclear energy. Many of your readers will react favorably to the mention of these innovations, which to them represent progress; others, for whom these inventions represent change but not progress, will react unfavorably. You may not be able to convince all of your readers that "we have made great progress," but all of them will now understand what you mean by "progress." And intelligent disagreement is preferable to misunderstanding.

Abstractions tell us what conclusions we have arrived at; details tell us how we got there. But there are dangers in either too many details or too many abstractions. For example, a writer may present only concrete data without telling readers what conclusions are to be drawn from them. Suppose you read the following:

> To Chinese road-users, traffic police are part of the grass . . . and neither they nor the rules they're supposed to enforce are paid the least attention. . . . Ignoring traffic-lights is only one peculiarity of Chinese traffic. It's normal for a pedestrian to walk straight out into a stream of cars without so much as lifting his head; and goodness knows how many Chinese cyclists I've almost killed as they have shot blindly in front of me across busy main roads.[14]

These details would constitute no more than interesting gossip until we read, "It's not so much a sign of ignorance or recklessness . . . but of fatalism." The details of specific behavior have now acquired a significance expressed in the abstraction *fatalism*.

A more common problem, however, in using abstractions is omission of details. Either the writer is not a skilled observer and cannot provide the details, or he or she feels that such details are too small and quiet compared to the grand sounds made by abstract terms. These grand sounds, unfortunately, cannot compensate for the lack of clarity and liveliness. Lacking detailed support, abstract words may be misinterpreted. They may also represent ideas that are so vague as to be meaningless. Sometimes they function illegitimately as short cuts (discussed on pp. 250–57), arousing emotions but unaccompanied by good reasons for their use. The following paragraph exhibits some of these common faults. How would you translate it into clear English?

> We respectively petition, request, and entreat that due and adequate provision be made, this day and the date hereinafter subscribed, for the satisfying of these petitioners' nutritional requirements and for the organizing of such methods of allocation and distribution as may be deemed necessary and proper to assure the reception by and for said

[14]Philip Short, "The Chinese and the Russians," *The Listener*, April 8, 1982, p. 6.

petitioners of such quantities of baked cereal products as shall, in the judgment of the aforesaid petitioners, constitute a sufficient supply thereof.[15]

If you had trouble decoding this, it was because there were almost no concrete references—the homely words *baked* and *cereal* leap out of the paragraph like English signposts in a foreign country—and too many long words or words of Latin origin when simple words would do: *requirements* instead of *needs, petition* instead of *ask.* An absence of concrete references and an excess of long Latinate words can have a depressing effect on both writer and reader. The writer may be in danger of losing the thread of the argument, the reader at a loss to discover the message.

The paragraph above, according to James B. Minor, a lawyer who teaches courses in legal drafting, is "how a federal regulation writer would probably write, 'Give us this day our daily bread.'" This brief sentence with its short, familiar words and its origin in the Lord's Prayer has a deep emotional effect. The paragraph composed by Minor deadens any emotional impact because of its preponderance of abstract terms and its lack of connection with the world of our senses.

That passage was invented to educate writers in the government bureaucracy to avoid inflated prose. But writing of this kind is not uncommon among professional writers, including academics. If the subject matter is unfamiliar and the writer an acknowledged expert, you may have to expend a special effort in penetrating the language. But you may also rightly wonder if the writer is making unreasonable demands on you.

> The human race is now entering upon a new phase of evolutionary consciousness and progress, a phase in which, impelled by the forces of evolution itself, it must converge upon itself and convert itself into one single human organism infused by a reconciliation of knowing and being in their inner unity and destined to make a qualitative leap into a higher form of consciousness as we know it, or otherwise destroy itself. For the entire universe is one vast field, potential for incarnation, and achieving incandescence here and there of reason and spirit. And in the whole world of *quality* with which by the nature of our minds we necessarily make contact, we here and there apprehend preeminent value. This can be achieved only if we recognize that we are unable to focus our attention on the particulars of the whole, without diminishing our comprehension of the whole, and of course, conversely, we can focus on the whole only by diminishing our comprehension of the particulars which constitute the whole.[16]

You probably found this paragraph even more baffling than the previous example. Although there is some glimmer of meaning here—that mankind must attain a higher level of consciousness, or perish—you

---

[15] *New York Times,* May 10, 1977, p. 35.
[16] Ruth Nanda Anshen, "Credo Perspectives," introduction to James Bryant Conant, *Two Modes of Thought* (New York: Simon and Schuster, 1964), p. x.

should ask whether the extraordinary overload of abstract terms is justified. In fact, most readers would be disinclined to sit still for an argument with so little reference to the real world. One critic of social science prose maintains that if preeminent thinkers like Bertrand Russell can make themselves clear but social scientists continue to be obscure, "then you can justifiably suspect that it might all be nonsense."[17]

Finally, there are the moral implications of using abstractions that conceal a disagreeable reality. George Orwell pointed them out more than forty years ago in "Politics and the English Language." Another essayist, Joseph Wood Krutch, in criticizing the attitude that cheating "doesn't really hurt anybody," observed, "'It really doesn't hurt anybody' means it doesn't do that abstraction called society any harm." The following news story reports a proposal with which Orwell and Krutch might have agreed. His intention, says the author, is to "slow the hand of any President who might be tempted to unleash a nuclear attack."

> It has long been feared that a President could be making his fateful decision while at a "psychological distance" from the victims of a nuclear barrage; that he would be in a clean, air-conditioned room, surrounded by well-scrubbed aides, all talking in abstract terms about appropriate military responses in an international crisis, and that he might well push to the back of his mind the realization that hundreds of millions of people would be exterminated.
>
> So Roger Fisher, professor of law at Harvard University, offers a simple suggestion to make the stakes more real. He would put the codes needed to fire nuclear weapons in a little capsule, and implant the capsule next to the heart of a volunteer, who would carry a big butcher knife as he accompanied the President everywhere. If the President ever wanted to fire nuclear weapons, he would first have to kill, with his own hands, that human being.
>
> He has to look at someone and realize what death is — what an innocent death is. "It's reality brought home," says Professor Fisher.[18]

The moral lesson is clear: It is much easier to do harm if we convince ourselves that the object of the injury is only an abstraction.

SHORT CUTS

Short cuts are arguments that depend on readers' responses to words. Short cuts, like other devices we have discussed so far, are a common use of emotive language but are often mistaken for valid argument.

Although they have power to move us, these abbreviated substitutes for argument avoid the hard work necessary to provide facts, expert

[17]Stanislav Andreski, *Social Sciences as Sorcery* (New York: St. Martin's Press, 1972), p. 86.
[18]*New York Times,* September 7, 1982, sec. C, p. 1.

opinion, and analysis of warrants. Even experts, however, can be guilty of using short cuts, and the writer who consults an authority should be alert to that authority's use of language. Two of the most common uses of short cuts are clichés and slogans.

■ Clichés

"I'm against sloppy, emotional thinking. I'm against fashionable thinking. I'm against the whole cliché of the moment."[19] This statement by the late Herman Kahn, the founder of the Hudson Institute, a famous think tank, serves as the text for this section. A cliché is an expression or idea grown stale through overuse. Clichés in language are tired expressions that have faded like old photographs; readers no longer see anything when clichés are placed before them. Clichés include phrases like "cradle of civilization," "few and far between," "rude awakening," "follow in the footsteps of," "fly in the ointment."

But more important to recognize and avoid are clichés of thought. A cliché of thought may be likened to a formula, which one dictionary defines as "any conventional rule or method for doing something, especially when used, applied, or repeated without thought." Clichés of thought represent ready-made answers to questions, stereotyped solutions to problems, "knee-jerk" reactions. Two writers who call these forms of expression "mass language" describe it this way: "Mass language is language which presents the reader with a response he is expected to make without giving him adequate reason for having this response."[20] These "clichés of the moment" are often expressed in single words or phrases. For example, the term "Generation Y" has been repeated so often that it has come to represent an undisputed truth about a huge age group from 12 to 18 who are supposed to share the same primitive tastes in entertainment. But, in fact, moviemakers attempting to capitalize on their alleged preferences for horror and teen romance have discovered that "There is no way to program them." One of the teenagers says, "Our generation is very diverse."[21]

Certain cultural attitudes encourage the use of clichés. The liberal American tradition has been governed by hopeful assumptions about our ability to solve problems. A professor of communications says that "we tell our students that for every problem there must be a solution."[22] But real solutions are hard to come by. In our haste to provide them, to

[19] *New York Times*, July 8, 1983, sec. B, p. 1.

[20] Richard E. Hughes and P. Albert Duhamel, *Rhetoric: Principles and Usage* (Englewood Cliffs, N.J.: Prentice-Hall, 1962), p. 161.

[21] Bruce Orwall, "It's Hollywood's Turn to Scream," *Wall Street Journal*, August 10, 2001, Bi.

[22] Malcolm O. Sillars, "The New Conservatism and the Teacher of Speech," *Southern Speech Journal* 21 (1956), p. 240.

prove that we can be decisive, we may be tempted to produce familiar responses that resemble solutions.

History teaches us that a solution to an old and serious problem is almost always accompanied by unexpected drawbacks. As the writer quoted in the previous paragraph warns us, "Life is not that simple. There is no one answer to a given problem. There are multiple solutions, all with advantages and disadvantages." By solving one problem, we often create another. Automobiles, advanced medical techniques, industrialization, and liberal divorce laws have all contributed to the solution of age-old problems: lack of mobility, disease, poverty, domestic unhappiness. We now see that these solutions bring with them new problems that we nevertheless elect to live with because the advantages seem greater than the disadvantages. A well-known economist puts it this way: "I don't look for solutions; I look for trade-offs. I think the person who asks, 'What is the solution to this problem?' has a fundamental misconception of the way the world works. We have trade-offs, and that's all we have."[23]

This means that we should be skeptical of solutions promising everything and ignoring limitations and criticism. Such solutions have probably gone around many times. Having heard them so often, we are inclined to believe that they have been tried and proven. Thus they escape serious analysis.

Some of these problems and their solutions represent the fashionable thinking to which Kahn objected. They confront us everywhere, like the public personalities who gaze at us week after week from the covers of magazines and tabloid newspapers at the checkout counter in the supermarket. Alarms about the failures of public education, about drug addiction or danger to the environment or teenage pregnancy are sounded throughout the media continuously. The same solutions are advocated again and again: "Back to basics"; "Impose harsher sentences"; "Offer sex education." Their popularity, however, should not prevent us from asking: Are the problems as urgent as their prominence in the media suggests? Are the solutions workable? Does sufficient evidence exist to justify their adoption?

Your arguments will not always propose solutions. They will sometimes provide interpretations of or reasons for social phenomena, especially for recurrent problems. Some explanations have acquired the status of folk wisdom, like proverbs, and careless arguers will offer them as if they needed no further support. One object of stereotyped responses is the problem of juvenile delinquency, which liberals attribute to poverty, lack of community services, meaningless education, and violence on television. Conservatives blame parental permissiveness, decline in religious influence, lack of individual responsibility, lenient courts. Notice

[23]Thomas Sowell, "Manhattan Report" (edited transcript of *Meet the Press*) (New York: International Center for Economic Policy Studies, 1981), p. 10.

that the interpretations of the causes of juvenile delinquency are related to an ideology, to a particular view of the world that may prevent the arguer from recognizing any other way of examining the problem. Other stereotyped explanations for a range of social problems include inequality, competition, self-indulgence, alienation, discrimination, technology, lack of patriotism, excessive governmental regulation, and lack of sufficient governmental regulation. All of these explanations are worthy of consideration, but they must be defined and supported if they are to be used in a thoughtful, well-constructed argument.

Although formulas change with the times, some are unexpectedly hardy and survive long after critics have revealed their weaknesses. Overpopulation is often cited as the cause of poverty, disease, and war. It can be found in the writing of the ancient Greeks 2,500 years ago. "That perspective," says the editor of *Food Monitor*, a journal published by World Hunger Year, Inc., "is so pervasive that most Americans have simply stopped thinking about population and resort to inane clucking of tongues."[24] If the writer offering overpopulation as an explanation for poverty were to look further, he or she would discover that the explanation rested on shaky data. Singapore, the most densely populated country in the world (11,574 persons per square mile) is also one of the richest ($16,500 per capita income per year). Chad, one of the most sparsely populated (11 persons per square mile) is also one of the poorest ($190 per capita income per year).[25] Strictly defined, overpopulation may serve to explain some instances of poverty; obviously it cannot serve as a blanket to cover all or even most instances. "By repeating stock phrases," one columnist reminds us, "we lose the ability, finally, to hear what we are saying."

■ Slogans

I have always been rather impressed by those people who wear badges stating where they stand on certain issues. The badges have to be small, and therefore the message has to be small, concise, and without elaboration. So it comes out as "I hate something" or "I love something," or ban this or ban that. There isn't space for argument, and I therefore envy the badge-wearer who is so clear-cut about his or her opinions.[26]

The word *slogan* has a picturesque origin. A slogan was the war cry or rallying cry of a Scottish or Irish clan. From that early use it has come to mean a "catchword or rallying motto distinctly associated with a political party or other group" as well as a "catch phrase used to advertise a product."

[24]Letter to the *New York Times*, October 4, 1982, sec. A, p. 18.
[25]*World Almanac and Book of Facts*, 1995 (New York: World Almanac, 1995), pp. 754, 818.
[26]Anthony Smith, "Nuclear Power—Why Not?" *The Listener*, October 22, 1981, p. 463.

Slogans, like clichés, are short, undeveloped arguments. They represent abbreviated responses to often complex questions. As a reader you need to be aware that slogans merely call attention to a problem; they cannot offer persuasive proof for a claim in a dozen words or less. As a writer you should avoid the use of slogans that evoke an emotional response "without giving [the reader] adequate reason for having this response."

Advertising slogans are the most familiar. Some of them are probably better known than nursery rhymes: "Got milk?" "L'Oréal, because I'm worth it," "Nike, just do it." Advertisements may, of course, rely for their effectiveness on more than slogans. They may also give us interesting and valuable information about products, but most advertisements give us slogans that ignore proof — short cuts substituting for argument.

The persuasive appeal of advertising slogans heavily depends on the connotations associated with products. In Chapter 5 (see p. 170, under "Appeals to Needs and Values"), we discussed the way in which advertisements promise to satisfy our needs and protect our values. Wherever evidence is scarce or nonexistent, the advertiser must persuade us through skillful choice of words and phrases (as well as pictures), especially those that produce pleasurable feelings. "Let it inspire you" is the slogan of a popular liqueur. It suggests a desirable state of being but remains suitably vague about the nature of the inspiration. Another familiar slogan — "Noxzema, clean makeup" — also emphasizes a quality that we approve of, but what is "clean" makeup? Since the advertisers are silent, we are left with warm feelings about the word and not much more.

Advertising slogans are persuasive because their witty phrasing and punchy rhythms produce an automatic yes response. We react to them as we might react to the lyrics of popular songs, and we treat them far less critically than we treat more straightforward and elaborate arguments. Still, the consequences of failing to analyze the slogans of advertisers are usually not serious. You may be tempted to buy a product because you were fascinated by a brilliant slogan, but if the product doesn't satisfy, you can abandon it without much loss. However, ignoring ideological slogans coined by political parties or special-interest groups may carry an enormous price, and the results are not so easily undone.

Ideological slogans, like advertising slogans, depend on the power of connotation, the emotional associations aroused by a word or phrase. In the 1960s and 1970s, a period of well-advertised social change, slogans flourished; they appeared by the hundreds of thousands on buttons, T-shirts, and bumper stickers. One of them read, "Student Power!" To some readers of the slogan, distrustful of young people and worried about student unrest on campuses and in the streets, the suggestion was frightening. To others, mostly students, the idea of power, however undefined, was intoxicating. Notice that "Student Power!" is not an argument; it is only a claim. (It might also represent a warrant.) As a claim, for example, it might take this form: Students at this school should have the power to select the faculty. Of course, the arguer would need to provide the kinds of proof that support his or her claim, something the slogan by itself cannot do. Many people, whether they accepted or rejected the claim, supplied the rest of the argument without knowing exactly what the issues were and how a developed argument would proceed. They were accepting or rejecting the slogan largely on the basis of emotional reaction to words.

American political history is, in fact, a repository of slogans. Leaf through a history of the United States and you will come across "Tippecanoe and Tyler, too," "manifest destiny," "fifty-four forty or fight," "make the world safe for democracy," "the silent majority," "the domino theory," "the missile gap," "the window of vulnerability." Each administration tries to capture the attention and allegiance of the public by coining catchy phrases. Roosevelt's New Deal in 1932 was followed by the Square Deal and the New Frontier. Today, slogans must be carefully selected to avoid offending groups that are sensitive to the ways in which words affect their interests. In 1983 Senator John Glenn, announcing his candidacy for president, talked about bringing "old values and new horizons" to the White House. "New horizons" apparently carried positive connotations. His staff, however, worried that "old values" might suggest racism and sexism to minorities and women.

A professor of politics and international affairs at Princeton University explains why public officials use slogans, despite their obvious shortcomings:

> Officials long have tried to capture complicated events and to dominate public discussion of foreign policy by using simple phrases and slogans. They engage in phrase-making in order to reach wide audiences. . . .
> Slogans and metaphors often express the tendencies of officials and academics who have a common wish to be at once sweeping, unequivocal, easily understood, and persuasive. The desire to capture complicated phenomena through slogans stems also from impatience with the particular and unwillingness or inability to master interrelationships.[27]

Over a period of time slogans, like clichés, can acquire a life of their own and, if they are repeated often enough, come to represent an unchanging truth we no longer need to examine. "Dangerously," says the writer quoted above, "policy makers become prisoners of the slogans they popularize."

Following are two examples. The first is part of the second inaugural address of George C. Wallace, governor of Alabama, in 1971. The second is taken from an article in the *Militia News,* the organ of a group that

[27]Henry Bienen, "Slogans Aren't the World," *New York Times,* January 16, 1983, sec. 4, p. 19.

believed the United States government was engaged in a "satanic conspiracy" to disarm the American people and then enslave them. Timothy McVeigh, who blew up the Oklahoma City federal building in 1995, was influenced by the group.

> The people of the South and those who think like the South, represent the majority viewpoint within our constitutional democracy, but they are not organized and do not speak with a loud voice. Until the day arrives when the voice of the people of the South and those who think like us is, within the law, thrust into the face of the bureaucrats, only then can the "people's power" express itself legally and ethically and get results. . . . Too long, oh, too long, has the voice of the people been silenced by their own disruptive government—by governmental bribery in quasi-governmental handouts such as H.E.W. and others that exist in America today! An aroused people can save this nation from those evil forces who seek our destruction. The choice is yours. The hour is growing late![28]

> Every gun owner who is the least bit informed knows that those who are behind this conspiracy—who now have their people well placed in political office, in the courts, in the media, and in the schools, are working for the total disarming of the American people and the surrender of our nation and our sovereignty. . . . The time is at hand when men and women must decide whether they are on the side of freedom and justice, the American republic, and Almighty God, or if they are on the side of tyranny and oppression, the New World Order, and Satan.[29]

Whatever power these recommendations might have if their proposals were more clearly formulated, as they stand they are collections of slogans and loaded words. (Even the language falters: Can the voice of the people be thrust into the face of the bureaucrats?) We can visualize some of the slogans as brightly colored banners: "Dislodge Big Money!" "Power to the People!" "Save This Nation from Evil Forces!" "The Choice Is Yours!" Do all the groups mentioned share identical interests? If so, what are they? Given the vagueness of the terms, it is not surprising that arguers on opposite sides of the political spectrum—loosely characterized as liberal and conservative—sometimes resort to the same clichés and slogans: the language of populism, or a belief in conspiracies against God-fearing people, in these examples.

Slogans have numerous shortcomings as substitutes for the development of an argument. First, their brevity presents serious disadvantages. Slogans necessarily ignore exceptions or negative instances that might qualify a claim. They usually speak in absolute terms without describing the circumstances in which a principle or idea might not work. Their

---

[28] Second Inaugural Address as governor of Alabama, January 18, 1971.
[29] Chip Berlet and Matthew N. Lyons, *Right-Wing Populism in America* (New York: Guildford Press, 2000), p. 301.

claims therefore seem shrill and exaggerated. In addition, brevity prevents the sloganeer from revealing how he or she arrived at conclusions.

Second, slogans may conceal unexamined warrants. When Japanese cars were beginning to compete with American cars, the slogan "Made in America by Americans" appeared on the bumpers of thousands of American-made cars. A thoughtful reader would have discovered in this slogan several implied warrants: American cars are better than Japanese cars; the American economy will improve if we buy American; patriotism can be expressed by buying American goods. If the reader were to ask a few probing questions, he or she might find these warrants unconvincing.

Silent warrants that express values hide in other popular and influential slogans. "Pro-life," the slogan of those who oppose abortion, assumes that the fetus is a living being entitled to the same rights as individuals already born. "Pro-choice," the slogan of those who favor abortion, suggests that the freedom of the pregnant woman to choose is the foremost or only consideration. The words *life* and *choice* have been carefully selected to reflect desirable qualities, but the words are only the beginning of the argument.

Third, although slogans may express admirable sentiments, they often fail to tell us how to achieve their objectives. They address us in the imperative mode, ordering us to take an action or refrain from it. But the means of achieving the objectives may be nonexistent or very costly. If the sloganeer cannot offer workable means for implementing his or her goals, he or she risks alienating the audience.

Sloganeering is one of the recognizable attributes of propaganda. Propaganda for both good and bad purposes is a form of slanting, of selecting language and facts to persuade an audience to take a certain action. Even a good cause may be weakened by an unsatisfactory slogan. The slogans of some organizations devoted to fundraising for people with physical handicaps have come under attack for depicting those with handicaps as helpless. According to one critic, the popular slogan "Jerry's kids" promotes the idea that Jerry Lewis is the sole support of children with muscular dystrophy. Perhaps increased sensitivity to the needs of people with disabilities will produce new words and new slogans. If you assume that your audience is sophisticated and alert, you will probably write your strongest arguments, devoid of clichés and slogans.

SAMPLE ANNOTATED ANALYSIS

The Childswap Society

SANDRA FELDMAN

Introduction: reference
to a sci-fi story that
suggests her subject

The subject: the
problem of child
neglect

Development: the plot
of the sci-fi story

Many years ago, when I was a teenager, I read a science fiction story that I've never been able to forget. It came back to me with special force this holiday season because I was thinking about this country's national shame—a child poverty rate of 25 percent—and about our lack of urgency in dealing with the problems this poverty creates.

The story described a society with a national child lottery which was held every four years. Every child's name was put into it—there were no exceptions—and children were randomly redistributed to new parents, who raised them for the next four years.

Babies were not part of this lottery. Parents got to keep their newborn children until the next lottery, but then they became part of the national childswap. The cycle was broken every third swap and kids were sent back to their original parents until the next lottery. So by the time you were considered an adult, at age twenty-six, the most time you could have spent with your birth parents was ten years. The other sixteen were simply a matter of chance.

The Luck of the Draw

Maybe one of your new parents would be the head of a gigantic multinational company and the most powerful person in the country or the president of a famous university. Or you might find yourself the child of a family living in a public housing project or migrant labor camp.

The whole idea sounded horrible to me, but 5 people in the childswap society took the lottery

Sandra Feldman is president of the American Federation of Teachers. This essay appeared in the *New York Times* on January 4, 1998, as part of an ongoing "Where We Stand" advertising campaign for the American Federation of Teachers.

for granted. They didn't try to hide their children or send them away to other countries; childswapping was simply part of their culture. And one thing the lottery did was to make the whole society very conscientious about how things were arranged for kids. After all, you never knew where your own child would end up after the next lottery, so in a very real sense everyone's child was—or could be—yours. As a result, children growing up under this system got everything they needed to thrive, both physically and intellectually, and the society itself was harmonious.

Virtues of the childswap society

What if someone wrote a story about what American society in the late twentieth century takes for granted in the arrangements for its children? We might not want to admit it, but don't we take for granted that some kids are going to have much better lives than others? Of course. We take for granted that some will get the best medical treatment and others will be able to get little or none. We take for granted that some kids will go to beautiful, well-cared-for schools with top-notch curriculums, excellent libraries, and computers for every child and others will go to schools where there are not enough desks and textbooks to go around—wretched places where even the toilets don't work.

Further development and support: contrast of the childswap society with American society

(implicit warrant: All children are entitled to decent lives.)

We take for granted that teachers in wealthy suburban schools will be better paid and better trained than those in poor inner-city or rural schools. We take for granted, in so many ways, that the children whom the lottery of birth has made the most needy will get the least. "After all," we say to ourselves, "it's up to each family to look after its own. If some parents can't give their children what they need to thrive, that's *their* problem."

What Would Happen?

transition to conclusion

Obviously I'm not suggesting that the United States adopt a childswap system. The idea makes me cringe, and, anyway, it's just a fable. But I like to imagine what would happen if we did.

Conclusion: claim of policy

We'd start with political figures and their children and grandchildren, with governors and

We should treat all children as if they were our own.

mayors and other leaders. What do you suppose would happen when they saw that their children would have the same chance as the sons and daughters of poor people—no more and no less? What would happen to our schools and health-care system—and our shameful national indifference to children who are not ours?

I bet we'd quickly find a way to set things straight and make sure *all* children had an equal chance to thrive. 10

■ Analysis

This essay concerns a serious educational challenge—equalizing opportunities for all children in this country, whatever their social or economic status. This subject might appear in a State of the Union address or another formal public-policy pronouncement before a large audience. In this essay the author has chosen to treat the subject as if she were engaged in a dialogue with the reader, speaking in familiar language that is neither technical, scholarly, nor literary. But despite its informality, it retains the patterns and grammar of written, not spoken, discourse.

Feldman begins with a kind of introduction that you've already encountered in other essays, an anecdote recounting a personal experience. Because this anecdote consumes a third of the essay, we know that the author considers it a crucial element in her appeal. Although no single personal experience unaccompanied by other evidence provides enough support to change public policy, it can gain our attention and arouse suspense. It can be effective in arguments about policies where personal feelings are relevant and where scientific research has little or no influence on the conclusion. And the use of the personal pronoun throughout ("I," "you," and "we")—even if the subject of the essay is not the author, as in this case—can often make a broad generalization seem more immediate.

Other stylistic devices contribute to the informality of the language. Feldman uses contractions such as "didn't," "can't," and "I've" to maintain the closeness to ordinary speech. In addition, she introduces expressions like "I bet" and the word "kids" for children and homely examples, like "even the toilets don't work." She also inserts rhetorical questions—to which she knows the answers—as a way of provoking thought about the issues. Even using "and" and "but" to begin sentences, a practice frowned on in technical and scientific papers, emphasizes the conversational style of the argument.

In a technical or scientific paper expression of the author's personality and feelings might divert attention from the objective research on which a sound conclusion rests. Feldman's language is appropriate for an article on the op-ed page of a newspaper or a column like "My Turn" in

Newsweek. In an essay on the future of children or, for that matter, on any subject about human welfare that stirs compassion, the language of personal concern can go far in persuading the reader to sympathize with the arguer and her claim.

READINGS FOR ANALYSIS

The Speech the Graduates Didn't Hear

JACOB NEUSNER

We the faculty take no pride in our educational achievements with you. We have prepared you for a world that does not exist, indeed, that cannot exist. You have spent four years supposing that failure leaves no record. You have learned at Brown that when your work goes poorly, the painless solution is to drop out. But starting now, in the world to which you go, failure marks you. Confronting difficulty by quitting leaves you changed. Outside Brown, quitters are no heroes.

With us you could argue about why your errors were not errors, why mediocre work really was excellent, why you could take pride in routine and slipshod presentation. Most of you, after all, can look back on honor grades for most of what you have done. So, here grades can have meant little in distinguishing the excellent from the ordinary. But tomorrow, in the world to which you go, you had best not defend errors but learn from them. You will be ill-advised to demand praise for what does not deserve it, and abuse those who do not give it.

For four years we created an altogether forgiving world, in which whatever slight effort you gave was all that was demanded. When you did not keep appointments, we made new ones. When your work came in beyond the deadline, we pretended not to care.

Worse still, when you were boring, we acted as if you were saying something important. When you were garrulous and talked to hear yourself talk, we listened as if it mattered. When you tossed on our desks writing upon which you had not labored, we read it and even responded, as though you earned a response. When you were dull, we pretended you were smart. When you were predictable, unimaginative, and routine, we listened as if to new and wonderful things. When you demanded free lunch, we served it. And all this why?

Jacob Neusner, formerly university professor at Brown University, is distinguished professor of religious studies at the University of South Florida in Tampa. His speech appeared in Brown's *Daily Herald* on June 12, 1983.

Despite your fantasies, it was not even that we wanted to be liked by 5
you. It was that we did not want to be bothered, and the easy way out
was pretense: smiles and easy Bs.

It is conventional to quote in addresses such as these. Let me quote
someone you've never heard of: Professor Carter A. Daniel, Rutgers University (*Chronicle of Higher Education,* May 7, 1979):

> College has spoiled you by reading papers that don't deserve to be read,
> listening to comments that don't deserve a hearing, paying attention
> even to the lazy, ill-informed, and rude. We had to do it, for the sake of
> education. But nobody will ever do it again. College has deprived you
> of adequate preparation for the last fifty years. It has failed you by being
> easy, free, forgiving, attentive, comfortable, interesting, unchallenging
> fun. Good luck tomorrow.

That is why, on this commencement day, we have nothing in which
to take much pride.

Oh, yes, there is one more thing. Try not to act toward your co-
workers and bosses as you have acted toward us. I mean, when they give
you what you want but have not earned, don't abuse them, insult them,
act out with them your parlous relationships with your parents. This too
we have tolerated. It was, as I said, not to be liked. Few professors actually care whether or not they are liked by peer-paralyzed adolescents,
fools so shallow as to imagine professors care not about education but
about popularity. It was, again, to be rid of you. So go, unlearn the lies
we taught you. To Life!

READING AND DISCUSSION QUESTIONS

1. Neusner condemns students for various shortcomings. But what is he
   saying, both directly and indirectly, about teachers? Find places where
   he reveals his attitude toward them, perhaps inadvertently.
2. Pick out some of the language devices—connectives, parallel structures,
   sentence variety—that the author uses effectively.
3. Pick out some of the words and phrases—especially adjectives and
   verbs—used by Neusner to characterize both students and teachers. Do
   you think these terms are loaded? Explain.
4. Has the author chosen "facts" to slant his article? If so, point out where
   slanting occurs. If not, point out where the article seems to be truthful.
5. As a student you will probably object to Neusner's accusations. How
   would you defend your behavior as a student in answer to his specific
   charges?

WRITING SUGGESTIONS

6. Rewrite Neusner's article with the same "facts"—or others from your experience—using temperate language and a tone of sadness rather than
   anger.

7. Write a letter to Neusner responding to his attack. Support or attack his argument by providing evidence from your own experience.

8. Write your own short commencement address. Do some things need to be said that commencement speakers seldom or never express?

9. Write an essay using the same kind of strong language as Neusner uses about some aspect of your education of which you disapprove. Or write a letter to a teacher using the same form as "The Speech the Graduates Didn't Hear."

Tightening the Nuts and Bolts of Death by Electric Chair

A. C. SOUD JR., WITH TOM KUNTZ

*N*o *one doubts that things went wrong at the execution of Pedro Medina in Florida last March: as thousands of volts of electricity coursed through the murderer's body, flames burst from his face mask, startling the assembled witnesses and prompting a public outcry. But does this unsettling episode mean that execution in Florida's electric chair is cruel and unusual punishment?*

No, a Florida circuit court judge ruled last month. In rejecting a death-row inmate's constitutional challenge, Judge A. C. Soud Jr. provided many details of the mechanics and procedures of electrocution in Florida, along with the reasoning behind his decision. Excerpts follow.

TOM KUNTZ

The judge upheld Florida's execution procedures, attributing the malfunction at the Medina execution to "unintentional human error" that caused a sponge used to conduct electricity to the inmate's head to ignite inside his headgear. A similar problem was blamed in the fiery execution of Jesse Tafero in 1990. The judge gave details of execution procedures since then:

Findings of Fact

1. . . . There were sixteen executions carried out between the execution of Tafero and the most recent execution of Pedro Medina. There were no changes made in the design to or the material used in the electric chair apparatus during that period of time. No malfunction of the electric chair occurred during the sixteen executions. . . .

2. The procedures used for testing the electric chair and its apparatus 5 have been consistently the same, through the Medina execution, for all

---

A. C. Soud Jr. is a circuit court judge in Jacksonville, Florida. Tom Kuntz writes for the *New York Times* where this article appeared on August 3, 1997.

seventeen executions since Tafero's execution. The testing procedures included the testing of the electrical equipment, the meters, the switches, the voltage output, and the amount of amperage created. Testing occurred three times before an execution: when the [death] warrant was signed, a week before the scheduled execution, and the day before an execution. . . .

The judge paid particular attention to the preparation of sponges:

3. The procedures for the preparation of the sponges used in an execution have been employed consistently since the Tafero execution. . . . The preparation consisted of soaking one large and two smaller natural sea sponges in a container of water having a 9 percent saline content [saltwater]. The sponges were placed in the saline solution the night before the day of a scheduled execution. The large wet sponge is placed around the inmate's shaved right leg and the leg electrode is then placed on the inmate's right calf. The leg electrode is three-and-a-half inches high and eight inches long shaped in a semicircular fashion. The leg electrode was made of lead. The head piece is principally made of leather. The inside crown of the head piece consists of a brass screen secured by a nut to a high voltage wire, which enters the head piece from the outside. The brass screen is round and measures four inches in diameter. A dry natural sea sponge was laced into the bottom of the brass screen electrode. This component served as the head electrode. The head piece is turned over and one of the two smaller wet sponges is placed on top of the dry sponge in the head piece. The head piece is then turned back to an upright position and placed on top of the inmate's head (the brass head electrode was, therefore, separated from the inmate's head by a dry sponge and a wet sponge, in that descending order). The second smaller soaked sponge is left in the soaking solution as a spare.

4. Preparation of inmate Medina was performed in all respects as was performed on the previous sixteen inmates who were executed since the execution of Tafero in 1990, and consisted of the shaving of Medina's head and the application of the normal amount of electroconductive gel to Medina's scalp. The gel is used to further reduce the normal amount of postmortem burning that occurs to the inmate's scalp during the electrocution process. . . .

5. Consistent with the previous sixteen executions, Medina was placed in the electric chair and straps were placed around Medina's chest, abdomen, arms, and legs. Medina's head was firmly secured to the back of the chair using a mouth and chin strap. A large wet (saline soaked) sponge was placed around Medina's right leg and the leg electrode was then strapped to his leg. The head piece, as previously described, was then placed over Medina's head.

6. Pursuant to the standard procedure used by the death chamber 10 team, death was brought on by activating the electrical system, which automatically—by a programmed controlled circuitry—administered

three cycles of electricity in the following amounts and durations without interruption:

First Cycle: High Voltage — 2,200 to 2,350 volts — for eight seconds;

Second Cycle: Low Voltage — 750 to 1,000 volts — for twenty-two seconds;

Third Cycle: High Voltage — 2,200 to 2,350 volts — for eight seconds.

As with the sixteen previous executions, and according to the normal procedures used, the third cycle was manually shut down four seconds into the third cycle.

The switch at the panel box was activated at 7:04 A.M. Electricity was administered to Medina at 7:04.50 A.M. and cut off at 7:05.25 A.M. Electricity was administered continually for 35 seconds. Medina was pronounced dead at 7:10 A.M.

The judge then turned to what went wrong:

7. When Pedro Medina was executed on March 25, 1997, the following events occurred. When the electrical current was activated, within seconds, a little smoke emanated from under the right side of Medina's head piece, followed by a four- to five-inch yellow-orange flame, which lasted four to five seconds and then disappeared. After the flame went out, more smoke emanated from under the head piece to the extent that the death chamber was filled with smoke — but the smoke was not dense enough to impair visibility. . . .

Although several witnesses to the execution tried to describe the odor of the smoke, only one witness, Florida State prison Superintendent Ronald McAndrews, described the odor as burnt sponge. Mr. McAndrews was the only witness who was subsequently in attendance on April 8, 1997, when two experts appointed by the Governor [Lawton Chiles] were conducting tests on the electric chair apparatus and similarly ignited a dry sponge, resulting in smoke. Mr. McAndrews described both odors as being the same. This court finds that the odor smelled was burnt sponge, not burnt flesh. . . .

There was a further unsettling moment when a physician examined Mr. Medina just after the current was turned off.

Medina's chest was seen to move two or three times in a two- to four-minute period. A couple of witnesses thought Medina was trying to breathe. . . . A neurologist testified that this movement could be caused by the last vestiges of survival in the brain stem after the brain itself has died. . . .

The malfunction was widely reported (journalists are always included among the witnesses in an observation room), and the state ordered an autopsy of Mr. Medina's body:

[The pathologists] concluded in their testimony that Medina's death was instantaneous due to massive depolarization of Medina's brain and brain stem when the initial surge of 2,200 to 2,350 volts of electricity entered Medina's head. [One doctor] described it as "like turning the lights off." . . . Cause of death was further exacerbated by a dramatic rise in the brain's temperature to between 138 degrees Fahrenheit to 148 degrees Fahrenheit. . . .

But other expert witnesses called to testify on behalf of the death-row in- 20 *mate seeking to avoid the chair theorized that Mr. Medina might have suffered an agonizing death. The appellant was Leo Alexander Jones, sentenced to death by Judge Soud for the 1981 slaying of a police officer. The judge rejected the alternate theories:*

He suffered no conscious pain. This can be said for all inmates who will be executed in Florida's electric chair hereafter. . . . The Florida electric chair — its apparatus, equipment, and electrical circuitry — is in excellent condition. Testimony in this regard is unrefuted. . . .

But the judge did recommend improvements:

1. The fire and smoke during the Medina execution was the result of the dry sponge laced onto the brass electrode in the head piece catching fire and burning almost completely due to a lack of saline solution in that sponge. The lack of saline solution in the dry sponge caused the dry sponge to act as a resistor. The resistance produced heat which ignited and consumed the dry sponge.

2. Any future executions should be performed using only one wet sponge in the head piece. . . . The sponge should be thoroughly soaked in a saturated saline solution and not a 9 percent saline solution . . . [to] further reduce any possibility of a reoccurrence of a burning sponge. . . .

[In addition,] although the lead leg electrode was not defective . . . it 25 should be changed from lead to brass, as brass is a better conductor of electricity than lead. . . .

READING AND DISCUSSION QUESTIONS

1. What is your reaction to this objective description of an electrocution? Notice that this description appeared in a ruling by a judge that electrocution was not a violation of the Eighth Amendment's prohibition of cruel and unusual punishment. Does the description's lack of emotional language make the act itself seem less terrible? Explain the reason for your response.

2. Find the places in the report where specific language has been used to depersonalize the act of electrocution and remove emotional connotations. Is this strategy successful in distancing the reader from the actual event?

3. Why do you think the newspaper published this report?

4. If you were revolted by this description, do you think it would make any difference to know the details of the crime(s) that the murderer has committed? Theodore Kaczinski, the Unabomber, wrote in his diary about a secretary who opened a package containing a bomb he had mailed to her boss: "The bomb drove fragments of wood into her flesh. But no indication that she was permanently disabled. Frustrating that I can't seem to make a lethal bomb." Does such a specific reference make you more inclined to favor a death sentence for the bomber, or not?

WRITING SUGGESTIONS

5. Look up "A Hanging" by George Orwell (from *Shooting an Elephant and Other Essays*), a powerful description of an execution Orwell witnessed as an officer in the Indian Imperial Police in Burma. Compare Orwell's treatment of an execution with Soud's treatment in the report you have just read. Choose a claim that establishes the main difference between the two descriptions, and develop two or three points of difference in the language as support for your claim.

6. Write an essay about some incident in your life that taught you an important lesson. You might begin with a statement that summarizes what you learned. Use the language of description and emotion—rich vocabulary, details, metaphors—to make the experience vivid to the reader.

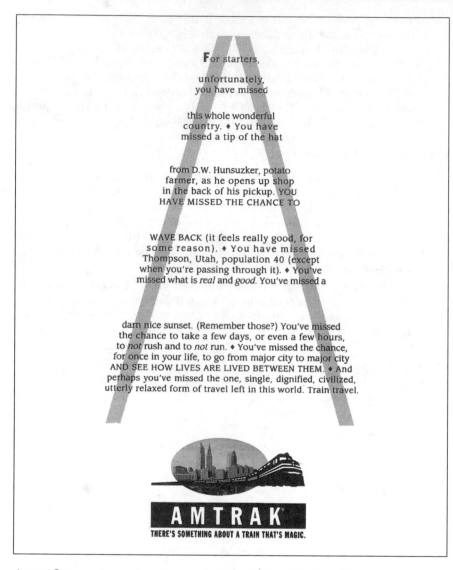

Amtrak® is a registered service mark of the National Railroad Passenger Corporation.

DISCUSSION QUESTIONS

1. What feelings does the advertiser want to evoke? Find words that make your answer clear.

2. The words *real* and *good* are italicized. Why are they so important? Is the advertiser making a contrast with something else?

3. How does the graphic design underscore the spirit and language of the ad?

Genetic Enhancement Allows for Even Greater Freedom

RONALD BAILEY

Enabling parents to genetically enhance their children is not going to be as easy as some of us might hope, nor will it happen as soon as we might wish, but Dinesh D'Souza is right when he claims in his article "Staying Human" (January 22) that one day it will be possible. This prospect frightens him. Why?

First, let's note that D'Souza is *not* against using genetic technology to cure genetic diseases, or using germline interventions to eliminate genetic diseases in future generations, or even using human cloning to overcome infertility; what he opposes is the use of "enhancement technologies to shape the destiny of others, and especially their children." D'Souza denounces such parents as "totalitarians" engaging in "despotism" and "tyranny."

But his opposition to this practice is fundamentally misconceived. First of all, he asserts that those of us who see no moral objection to genetic enhancements "speak about freedom and choice, although what [they] advocate is despotism and human bondage." This is nonsense. D'Souza has evidently adopted a notion of hard genetic determinism that is simply not warranted by biology. A gene that enhances one's capacity for music doesn't mean that its possessor must become another Scott Joplin or Keith Jarrett; genes simply don't work that way. D'Souza, like all of us, has many capacities stemming from his specific genetic endowment. He could, for example, have become a professional rugby player or a computer engineer, but he chose not to develop those particular abilities despite the fact that his specific complement of genes could have allowed him to.

Giving children such enhanced capacities as good health, stronger bodies, and cleverer brains, far from constraining them, would in fact give them greater freedom and more choices. It's a strange kind of despotism that enlarges a person's abilities and options in life.

But D'Souza is wrong even on his own terms. He has no objection to 5 fixing genetic diseases and disabilities, because one can assume that the

---

Ronald Bailey is the science correspondent for *Reason* magazine. His articles and reviews have appeared in the *Wall Street Journal*, the *Washington Post*, and the *New York Times Book Review*, among other publications. This colloquy appeared in the March 5, 2001, *National Review*.

beneficiary—the not-yet-born, possibly even-not-yet-conceived child—would happily have chosen to have those flaws corrected. Let's say a parent could choose genes that would guarantee her kid a twenty-point IQ boost. It is reasonable to presume that the kid would be happy to consent to this enhancement of his capacities. How about plugging in genes that would boost his immune system and guarantee that he would never get colon cancer, Alzheimer's, AIDS, or the common cold? Again, it seems reasonable to assume consent. These enhancements are general capacities that any human would reasonably want to have. In fact, lots of children already do have these capacities naturally, so it's hard to see that there is any moral justification for outlawing access to them for others.

Instead of submitting to the tyranny of random chance, which cruelly deals out futures blighted with ill health, stunted mental abilities, and early death, parents would be able to open more possibilities for their children to have fulfilling lives. Genetic enhancements to prevent these ills would not violate a child's liberty or autonomy, and certainly do not constitute the slavery depicted in D'Souza's overwrought analogy.

"The power they seek to exercise is not over 'nature,' but over *other human beings*," claims D'Souza. Actually, most of those who want access to genetic technologies for their children are motivated by exactly the opposite desire: What they seek is the power to defend their children against the manifold cruelties and indignities that "nature" so liberally dispenses, and thus make it possible for their children to have fulfilling lives. The good news is that would-be tyrannical parents who buy into D'Souza's erroneous notions of hard genetic determinism will be disappointed. Their children will have minds and inclinations all distinctly their own, albeit genetically enhanced.

Let's look briefly at some of D'Souza's other objections. He asserts with apparent alarm that "people living today can determine the genetic destiny of *all* future generations." This is true, but trivial: Our ancestors, too—through their mating and breeding choices—determined for us the complement of genes that we all bear today. They just didn't know which specific genes they were picking. The future will not be populated by robots who may look human but who are unable to choose for themselves their own destinies—genetic or otherwise.

D'Souza also has egalitarian worries that the "availability of enhancement technologies will create two classes in society": "Democratic societies can live with inequalities conferred by the lottery of nature, but can they countenance the deliberate introduction of biological alterations that give some citizens a better chance to succeed than others?" But D'Souza agrees that the type of genetic interventions contemplated here will likely become available to everyone as their prices go down. This seems to me to be a recipe for *eliminating* genetic inequalities rather than perpetuating them. Once inserting genes becomes routine and cheap, everyone will have access to it in fairly short order. As to whether our democratic society will be endangered by genetic engineering, I maintain that democracy and political equality are sustained chiefly by the principle that people are responsible moral agents who can distinguish between right and wrong, and deserve equal consideration before the law and a respected place in our political community. Having some citizens who take advantage of genetic technologies, and others who do not, will not change that.

D'Souza then accuses those who would allow access to genetic enhancements of not being "worried about diminishing the sanctity of human life." But who has a higher regard for the sanctity of life—those who fatalistically counsel us to live with the often bum hands that nature deals us, or those who want to use genetic technologies to ameliorate the ills that have afflicted humanity since time immemorial? Respecting the sanctity of life doesn't require that we take whatever random horrors nature dishes out.

Setting aside D'Souza's confusion over the philosophical issues surrounding consciousness, it is certain that it is our brains (conscious or not, awake or not), and not our genes, that make us individual human beings. The case of identical twins proves the point: They have precisely the same genes, but they are different, sometimes *very* different, people. That's why, in recent years, our society has legally defined death as brain death. Once our brains are gone, we are gone, even though our bodies— with all their genes—may live on. The fact is that we respect people, not their genes.

It is true for genetic engineering, as for all other technologies, that some people will misuse it; tragedies will occur. Given the sorry history of government-sponsored eugenics, control over genetic engineering must never be given to any government agency. But to use genetic engineering is not, by definition, to abuse it. This technology offers the prospect of ever greater freedom for individual human beings, and should be welcomed by everyone who cares about human life.

We Should Not Tamper with What Makes Us Human

DINESH D'SOUZA

The basic difference between Ron Bailey and me is that we have different views of human nature and human dignity. Bailey's argument, however, fails not only by my principles but by his own. He is so enamored of techno-utopian schemes that he is willing to sacrifice the core libertarian principle of individual autonomy to give children the "enhanced capacities" he is confident they will come to appreciate.

Dinesh D'Souza is a research scholar at the American Enterprise Institute and is the author of *The Virtue of Prosperity: Finding Values in an Age of Techno-Affluence* (2000).

My wife and I are blessed to have a six-year-old daughter. Had she suffered from a serious disease or disability, we would not have hesitated to take the necessary steps, including gene therapy, to cure her. Fortunately, our daughter is a normal child who doesn't suffer from any serious physical or mental disease. In our view, she is a gift, with her own distinctive potential and personality. Our job as parents is to help her develop her abilities and fulfill her promise. So we give her chess lessons and music lessons and so forth. But, like most parents, we would regard with horror the notion of redesigning her genetic structure.

Why? Because our children are not our property. We are entrusted with them, but we do not have the right to subject their distinctive nature to our will. It's strange that Bailey sees no problem in invoking a libertarian principle—the freedom to shape one's own life—in order to justify parents using scientific manipulation to regulate the genetic makeup of other people. What greater violation of individual autonomy is even conceivable? If I were to capture Bailey forcibly, take him to a lab in the Bahamas, and alter his brain to make him (let us say) more musical and give him ten extra IQ points, wouldn't he regard it as a profound violation of his autonomy and dignity? I suspect that Bailey would not be persuaded by my insistence that I was merely trying to expand his range of choices.

Bailey insists, however, that genetic engineering is benign because we can trust parents to look out for the welfare of their offspring. In general, this is true, but this presumption of the wisdom of paternalism is typically restricted to a child's years of dependence. My parents may give me piano lessons, but when I am older I can choose to give up the piano. My parents may want me to become a doctor, and thus force me to take biology—but I can choose to become a writer. By contrast, if parents are able to remake a child's genetic makeup, they are in a sense writing the genetic instructions that shape his entire life. If my parents give me blue eyes instead of brown eyes, if they make me tall instead of medium height, if they choose a passive over an aggressive personality, their choices will have a direct, lifelong effect on me. One need not be a genetic determinist to suggest that people lack the wisdom to "play God" in this sense. Would Bailey have wanted his parents to have designed him on a computer, selecting traits that they found desirable and eliminating those they didn't care for?

The greatest danger of genetic engineering is that we might become 5 arrogant enough to believe that we can not only remedy nature's defects but also improve on human nature itself. We should not have the right to try such experiments out on other people, even our own offspring. The children are human persons, and to tamper with their structure in the absence of a clear need—such as to avoid a specific disease—is a fundamental and impermissible violation of their integrity.

The ultimate goal of the techno-utopians is to straighten out the crooked timber of our humanity. This project is likely to fail, but its success would be even worse: It would mean that we will have ceased, in any meaningful sense, to be human.

DISCUSSION QUESTIONS

1. What is Bailey's response to D'Souza's accusation that genetic enhancement is "despotism" and "tyranny" (para. 2)? Point out at least two of Bailey's objections.
2. Both authors invoke moral principles in defense of their claims. What are they? Do you think one author has been more successful than the other in defending his use of these principles?
3. Both Bailey and D'Souza use hypothetical examples about themselves and each other. How effective are these examples?
4. D'Souza ends by saying that the success of the "techno-utopians . . . would mean that we will have ceased . . . to be human." Can you define what he means by "human"? Does his definition differ from Bailey's?

TAKING THE DEBATE ONLINE

For these and additional research URLs, see www.bedfordstmartins.com/rottenberg.

- *What Is Genetic Engineering?*
  http://dspace.dial.pipex.com/srtscot/geneng1.htm
  This site is a good place to start examining the issues surrounding genetic modification of humans. It is part of the Society, Religion, and Technology Project of the Church of Scotland.

- *The Human Genome Project: What It Means for You*
  http://thedoctorwillseeyounow.com/articles/other/genome_4/index.shtml
  This site examines some of the technical and scientific background needed to understand how genetic manipulation works.

- *Why Do We Fear Genetic Enhancement?*
  http://zolatimes.com/V5.1/genetic_enhancement.html
  This article by Matthew Ballin argues that we should not fear the manipulation of human genes.

- *Genetic Enhancement: The State of the Technology*
  http://www.bostontheological.org/fase/docs/ecrnewman.htm
  This essay by Stuart Newman looks at the complex issues surrounding genetic enhancement.

- *The Ethics of Human Genetic Engineering*
  http://www.uq.edu.au/~pdwgrey/pubs/geneth.html
  This paper, by William Grey, examines aspects of the ethical impact of advances in genetics and the difficulty of distinguishing between

therapeutic (or "corrective") and "enhancement" genetic engineering. Objections to genetic engineering are also considered.

EXERCISES

1. Select one or two related bumper stickers visible in your neighborhood. Examine the hidden warrants on which they are based, and assess their validity.

2. For a slogan found on a bumper sticker or elsewhere, supply the evidence to support the claim in the slogan. Or find evidence that disproves the claim.

3. Examine a few periodicals from fifty or more years ago. Select either an advertising or a political slogan in one of them, and relate it to beliefs or events of the period. Or tell why the slogan is no longer relevant.

4. Discuss the origin of a cliché or slogan. Describe, as far as possible, the backgrounds and motives of its users.

5. Make up your own slogan for a cause that you support. Explain and defend your slogan.

6. Discuss the appeal to needs and values of some popular advertising or political slogan.

7. Choose a cliché, and find evidence to support or refute it. *Examples:* People were much happier in the past. Mother knows best. Life was much simpler in the past. Money can't buy happiness.

8. Choose one of the statements in exercise 7 or another statement, and write a paper telling why you think such a statement has persisted as an explanation.

9. Select a passage, perhaps from a textbook, written largely in abstractions, and rewrite it using simpler and more concrete language.

CRITICAL LISTENING

10. In watching television dramas about law and medicine (*Law and Order, NYPD Blue, The Practice, ER*) do you find that the professional language, some of which you may not fully understand, plays a positive or negative role in your enjoyment of the show? Explain your answer.

11. Listen to a radio or television report of a sports event. Do the announcers use a kind of language, especially jargon, that would not be used in print reports? One critic thinks that sports broadcasting has had a "destructive effect . . . on ordinary American English." Is he right or wrong?

8

Induction, Deduction, and Logical Fallacies

Throughout the book we have pointed out the weaknesses that cause arguments to break down. In the vast majority of cases these weaknesses represent breakdowns in logic or the reasoning process. We call such weaknesses *fallacies,* a term derived from the Latin. Sometimes these false or erroneous arguments are deliberate; in fact, the Latin word *fallere* means "to deceive." But more often these arguments are either carelessly or unintentionally constructed. Thoughtful readers learn to recognize them; thoughtful writers learn to avoid them.

The reasoning process was first given formal expression by Aristotle, the Greek philosopher, almost 2,500 years ago. In his famous treatises, he described the way we try to discover the truth—observing the world, selecting impressions, making inferences, generalizing. In this process Aristotle identified two forms of reasoning: *induction* and *deduction.* Both forms, he realized, are subject to error. Our observations may be incorrect or insufficient, and our conclusions may be faulty because they have violated the rules governing the relationship between statements. The terms we've introduced may be unfamiliar, but the processes of reasoning, as well as the fallacies that violate these processes, are not. Induction and deduction are not reserved only for formal arguments about important problems; they also represent our everyday thinking about the most ordinary matters. As for the fallacies, they, too, unfortunately, may crop up anywhere, whenever we are careless in our use of the reasoning process.

In this chapter we examine some of the most common fallacies. First, however, a closer look at induction and deduction will make clear what happens when fallacies occur.

INDUCTION

Induction is the form of reasoning in which we come to conclusions about the whole on the basis of observations of particular instances. If you notice that prices on the four items you bought in the campus bookstore are higher than similar items in the bookstore in town, you may come to the conclusion that the campus store is a more expensive place to shop. If you also noticed that all three of the instructors you saw on the first day of school were wearing faded jeans and running shoes, you might say that your teachers are generally informal in their dress. In both cases you have made an *inductive leap,* reasoning from what you have learned about a few examples to what you think is true of a whole class of things.

How safe are you in coming to these conclusions? As we've noticed in discussing data and generalization warrants, the reliability of your conclusion depends on the quantity and quality of your observations. Were four items out of the thousands available in the campus store a sufficiently large sample? Would you come to the same conclusion if you chose fifty items? Might another selection have produced a different conclusion? As for the casually dressed instructors, perhaps further investigation would disclose that the teachers wearing jeans were all teaching assistants and that associate and full professors usually wore business clothes. Or the difference might lie in the academic discipline; anthropology teachers might turn out to dress less formally than business school teachers.

In these two situations, you could come closer to verifying your conclusions by further observation and experience—that is, by buying more items at both stores over a longer period of time and by coming into contact with a greater number of professors during a whole semester. Even without pricing every item in both stores or encountering every instructor on campus, you would be more confident of your generalization as the quality and quantity of your samples increased.

In some cases you can observe all the instances in a particular situation. For example, by acquiring information about the religious beliefs of all the residents of the dormitory, you can arrive at an accurate assessment of the number of Buddhists. But since our ability to make definitive observations about everything is limited, we must also make an inductive leap about categories of things that we ourselves can never encounter in their entirety. For some generalizations, as we have learned about evidence, we rely on the testimony of reliable witnesses who report that they have experienced or observed many more instances of the phenomenon. A television documentary may give us information about unwed teenage mothers in a city neighborhood; four girls are interviewed and followed for several days by the reporter. Are these girls typical of thousands of others? A sociologist on the program assures us that, in fact, they are. She herself has consulted with hundreds of other young mothers and can vouch for the fact that a conclusion about them, based on our observation of the four, will be sound. Obviously, though, our conclusion can only be probable, not certain. The sociologist's sample is large, but she can account only for hundreds, not thousands, and there may be unexamined cases that will seriously weaken our conclusions.

In other cases, we may rely on a principle known in science as "the uniformity of nature." We assume that certain conclusions about oak trees in the temperate zone of North America, for example, will also be true for oak trees growing elsewhere under similar climatic conditions. We also use this principle in attempting to explain the causes of behavior in human beings. If we discover that institutionalization of some children from infancy results in severe emotional retardation, we think it safe to conclude that under the same circumstances all children would suffer the same consequences. As in the previous example, we are aware that certainty about every case of institutionalization is impossible. With rare exceptions, the process of induction can offer only probability, not certain truth.

SAMPLE ANALYSIS:
AN INDUCTIVE ARGUMENT

True or False: Schools Fail Immigrants

RICHARD ROTHSTEIN

A common indictment of public schools is that they no longer offer upward mobility to most immigrants. It is said that in the first half of the twentieth century, children learned English, went to college, and joined the middle class but that many of today's immigrants are more likely to drop out, take dead-end jobs, or end up in prison.

Many true accounts reinforce these beliefs. But less noticed are equally valid anecdotes pointing to an opposite claim.

Richard Rothstein is a research associate of the Economic Policy Institute, a senior correspondent of the *American Prospect,* and the national education columnist of the *New York Times,* where this article appeared on July 4, 2001. He is the author of *The Way We Were: Myths and Realities of America's Student Achievement* (1997).

Policy by anecdote is flawed because too often we notice only what confirms our preconceptions. California's recent experience with Mexican immigrants provides ample material for stories about school failure. But on a day to celebrate the American promise, we might also turn to anecdotes of another kind.

Recent college commencements across California featured many immigrants from impoverished families whose first language was Spanish, who came through much-maligned bilingual education programs, learned English, and now head for graduate schools or professions.

At California State University at Fresno, for example, about 700 of   5
4,000 graduates this spring were Latino, typically the first in their families to attend college. Top-ranked were Pedro Nava and Maria Rocio Magaña, Mexican-born children of farm laborers and cannery workers.

Mr. Nava did not settle in the United States until the third grade. Before that, he lived in migrant labor camps during harvests and in Mexico the rest of the year. His California schooling was in Spanish until the fifth grade, when he was moved to English instruction. Now, with a college degree, he has enrolled in management and teacher training courses.

Ms. Magaña did not place into English classes until the second half of the eleventh grade. Now fluent in both academic and conversational English, she will soon begin a Ph.D. program in anthropology at the University of Chicago.

Their achievements are not unique. Both credit success to their mothers' emphasis on education. Both mothers enrolled in English and high school equivalency courses at the local community college.

Across California, these two-year institutions play an especially important role for immigrants.

Lourdes Andrade just finished her junior year at Brown University,   10
having transferred there after getting associate of arts degrees in history and liberal arts at Oxnard Community College, about forty miles northwest of Los Angeles.

Ms. Andrade arrived here at the age of four and all through elementary school worked with her mother making beds and cleaning bathrooms in hotels. Ms. Andrade, too, attributes her success to her mother's strong academic pressure and also to mentoring she received in a federally financed program to give extra academic support to migrant children.

The program's director, Lorenzo Moraza, also grew up speaking only Spanish. Now a school principal, Mr. Moraza estimates that about 30 percent of the immigrant children he has worked with acquired public school records that led them to college. Those who receive bachelor's degrees are many fewer, but Mr. Moraza says he thinks most drop out of college for economic reasons, not academic ones.

At the Fresno campus, nearly two-thirds of the immigrants and children of immigrants who enter as freshmen eventually graduate. The university operates special support services to help them do so.

You cannot spend time in California without noticing an extensive middle class of Latino schoolteachers, doctors, lawyers, and small-business people. Not all are recent immigrants, but many are. Some attended Catholic schools, but most are products of the public system. Many had bilingual education in the 1970s, 80s, and 90s. California has now banned such instruction, assuming it failed.

There are plenty of anecdotes to support a claim that schools fail im- 15
migrant children or an equally persuasive claim that schools serve them well. Getting better statistics should be a priority. Government numbers do not distinguish between students who are immigrants (or whose parents immigrated) from Hispanics with American roots for several generations.

To help interpret California's experience, the best federal data tell only that in 1996, there were 100,000 college students nationwide who were American citizens born in Mexico. This is less than 1 percent of all college students. But uncounted are even larger numbers of those born here to recent migrants.

Even a balanced collection of anecdotes that include successes as well as failures cannot determine whether California schools are less effective than we should expect, and whether wholesale change is needed to move more immigrants to the middle class. But the answer is certainly more complex than the stereotypes of systematic failure that pervade most accounts.

■ Analysis

An inductive argument proceeds by examining particulars and arriving at a generalization that represents a probable truth. The author of this article arrives at the truth he will defend—that public schools have been more successful than is often acknowledged in moving many immigrants into the middle class—by offering statistical data and a number of stories about immigrants from poor families who have entered graduate school or one of the professions.

Rothstein begins, as many arguers do, with a brief summary of the popular position with which he disagrees. At the end of the third paragraph, he announces that he will provide examples that point to a different conclusion.

The reader should ask three questions of an inductive argument: Is the evidence sufficient? Is it representative? Is it up-to-date? The evidence that Rothstein assembles consists of a series of anecdotes and statistical data about the performance of immigrant students. The success stories of five real persons are impressive, despite limitations imposed by the brevity of the essay, in part because they offer vivid examples of struggle that appeal to our emotions and bring to life an issue with which some of us may not be familiar. But five stories are hardly enough to prove a case; perhaps they are not representative. Rothstein, therefore, adds other data about the rate at which immigrant students graduate and the growing number of Latino professionals and businesspeople.

The reader has some reason to believe that the facts are up-to-date. First, Rothstein writes a regular column for a prestigious daily newspaper whose readers will be quick to find errors in arguments of which they're critical. Second, he refers to "recent college commencements," a graduation "this spring," bilingual education in the 1990s, and "the best federal data for California in 1996." At the same time, he does not claim that his argument is beyond debate, since the data are incomplete. Even the title suggests that the issue is still unsettled. Modesty in the arguer is always welcome and disposes the reader to view the argument more favorably.

DEDUCTION

While induction attempts to arrive at the truth, deduction guarantees sound relationships between statements. If each of a series of statements, called *premises,* is true, deductive logic tells us that the conclusion must also be true. Unlike the conclusions from induction, which are only probable, the conclusions from deduction are certain. The simplest deductive argument consists of two premises and a conclusion. In outline such an argument looks like this:

MAJOR PREMISE:	All students with 3.5 averages and above for three years are invited to become members of Kappa Gamma Pi, the honor society.
MINOR PREMISE:	George has had a 3.8 average for over three years.
CONCLUSION:	Therefore, he will be invited to join Kappa Gamma Pi.

This deductive conclusion is *valid* or logically consistent because it follows necessarily from the premises. No other conclusion is possible. Validity, however, refers only to the form of the argument. The argument itself may not be satisfactory if the premises are not true—if Kappa Gamma Pi has imposed other conditions or if George has only a 3.4 average. The difference between truth and validity is important because it alerts us to the necessity for examining the truth of the premises before we decide that the conclusion is sound.

One way of discovering how the deductive process works is to look at the methods used by Sherlock Holmes, that most famous of literary detectives, in solving his mysteries. His reasoning process follows a familiar pattern. Through the inductive process—that is, observing the particulars of the world—he came to certain conclusions about those particulars. Then he applied deductive reasoning to come to a conclusion about a particular person or event.

On one occasion Holmes observed that a man sitting opposite him on a train had chalk dust on his fingers. From this observation Holmes deduced that the man was a schoolteacher. If his thinking were outlined, it would take the form of the syllogism, the classic form of deductive reasoning:

MAJOR PREMISE: All men with chalk dust on their fingers are schoolteachers.

MINOR PREMISE: This man has chalk dust on his fingers.

CONCLUSION: Therefore, this man is a schoolteacher.

One dictionary defines *syllogism* as "a formula of argument consisting of three propositions." The first proposition is called the major premise and offers a generalization about a large group or class. This generalization has been arrived at through inductive reasoning or observation of particulars. The second proposition is called the minor premise, and it makes a statement about a member of that group or class. The third proposition is the conclusion, which links the other two propositions, in much the same way that the warrant links the support and the claim.

If we look back at the syllogism that summarizes Holmes's thinking, we see how it represents the deductive process. The major premise, the first statement, is an inductive generalization, a statement arrived at after observation of a number of men with chalk on their fingers. The minor premise, the second statement, assigns a particular member, the man on the train, to the general class of those who have dust on their fingers.

But although the argument may be logical, it is faulty. The deductive argument is only as strong as its premises. As Lionel Ruby pointed out, Sherlock Holmes was often wrong.[1] Holmes once deduced from the size of a large hat found in the street that the owner was intelligent. He obviously believed that a large head meant a large brain and that a large brain indicated intelligence. Had he lived one hundred years later, new information about the relationship of brain size to intelligence would have enabled him to come to a different and better conclusion.

In this case, we might first object to the major premise, the generalization that all men with chalk dust on their fingers are schoolteachers. Is it true? Perhaps all the men with dusty fingers whom Holmes had so far observed had turned out to be schoolteachers, but was his sample sufficiently large to allow him to conclude that all dust-fingered men, even those with whom he might never have contact, were teachers? Were there no other vocations or situations that might require the use of

[1] *The Art of Making Sense* (Philadelphia: Lippincott, 1954), ch. 17.

chalk? Draftsmen or carpenters or tailors or artists might have fingers just as white as those of schoolteachers. In other words, Holmes may have ascertained that all schoolteachers have chalk dust on their fingers, but he had not determined that *only* schoolteachers can be thus identified. Sometimes it is helpful to draw circles representing the various groups in their relation to the whole.

If a large circle (see the figure below) represents all those who have chalk dust on their fingers, we see that several different groups may be contained in this universe. To be safe, Holmes should have deduced that the man on the train *might* have been a schoolteacher; he was not safe in deducing more than that. Obviously, if the inductive generalization or major premise is false, the conclusion of the particular argument is also false or invalid.

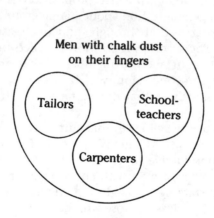

The deductive argument may also go wrong elsewhere. What if the minor premise is untrue? Could Holmes have mistaken the source of the white powder on the man's fingers? Suppose it was not chalk dust but flour or confectioner's sugar or talcum or heroin? Any of these possibilities would weaken or invalidate his conclusion.

Another example, closer to the kinds of arguments you will examine, reveals the flaw in the deductive process.

MAJOR
PREMISE: All Communists oppose organized religion.

MINOR
PREMISE: Robert Roe opposes organized religion.

CONCLUSION: Therefore, Robert Roe is a Communist.

The common name for this fallacy is "guilt by association." The fact that two things share an attribute does not mean that they are the same thing. The following diagram makes clear that Robert Roe and Communists do not necessarily share all attributes. Remembering that Holmes may have misinterpreted the signs of chalk on the traveler's fingers, we may also want to question whether Robert Roe's opposition to organized religion has been misinterpreted.

An example from history shows us how such an argument may be used. In a campaign speech during the summer of 1952, Senator Joseph McCarthy, who had made a reputation as a tireless enemy of communism, said, "I do not tell you that Schlesinger, Stevenson's number one man, number one braintrust, I don't tell you he's a Communist. I have no information on that point. But I do know that if he were a Communist he would also ridicule religion as Schlesinger has done."[2] This is an argument based on a sign warrant. Clearly the sign referred to by Senator McCarthy, ridicule of religion, would not be sufficient to characterize someone as a Communist.

Some deductive arguments give trouble because one of the premises, usually the major premise, is omitted. As in the warrants we examined in Chapter 6, a failure to evaluate the truth of the unexpressed premise may lead to an invalid conclusion. When only two parts of the syllogism appear, we call the resulting form an *enthymeme*. Suppose we overhear the following snatch of conversation:

"Did you hear about Jean's father? He had a heart attack last week."
"That's too bad. But I'm not surprised. I know he always refused to go for his annual physical checkups."

The second speaker has used an unexpressed major premise, the cause-and-effect warrant "If you have annual physical checkups, you can

[2]Joseph R. McCarthy, "The Red-Tinted Washington Crowd," speech delivered to a Republican campaign meeting at Appleton, Wisconsin, November 3, 1952.

avoid heart attacks." He does not express it because he assumes that it is unnecessary to do so. The first speaker recognizes the unspoken warrant and may agree with it. Or the first speaker may produce evidence from reputable sources that such a generalization is by no means universally true, in which case the conclusion of the second speaker is suspect.

A knowledge of the deductive process can help guide you toward an evaluation of the soundness of your reasoning in an argument you are constructing. The syllogism is often clearer than an outline in establishing the relations between the different parts of an argument.

Suppose you wanted to argue that your former high school should introduce a dress code. You might begin by asking these questions: What would be the purpose of such a regulation? How would a dress code fulfill that purpose? What reasons could you provide to support your claim?

Then you might set down part of your argument like this:

Dressing in different styles makes students more aware of social differences among themselves.

The students in this school dress in many different styles.

Therefore, they are more aware of differences in social status among the student body.

As you diagram this first part of the argument, you should ask two sets of questions:

1. Is the major premise true? Do differences in dress cause awareness of differences in social status? Has my experience confirmed this?

2. Is the minor premise true? Has my observation confirmed this?

The conclusion, of course, represents something that you don't have to observe. You can deduce with certainty that it is true if both the major and minor premises are true.

So far the testing of your argument has been relatively easy because you have been concerned with the testing of observation and experience. Now you must examine something that does not appear in the syllogism. You have determined certain facts about perceptions of social status, but you have not arrived at the policy you want to recommend: that a dress code should be mandated. Notice that the dress code argument is based on acceptance of a moral value.

Reducing awareness of social differences is a desirable goal for the school.

A uniform dress code would help to achieve that goal.

Therefore, students should be required to dress uniformly.

The major premise in this syllogism is clearly different from the previous one. While the premise in the previous syllogism can be tested by examining sufficient examples to determine probability, this statement, about the desirability of the goal, is a value judgment and cannot be proved by counting examples. Whether equality of social status is a desirable goal depends on an appeal to other, more basic values.

Setting down your own or someone else's argument in this form will not necessarily give you the answers to questions about how to support your claim, but it should clearly indicate what your claims are and, above all, what logical connections exist between your statements.

SAMPLE ANNOTATED ANALYSIS: A DEDUCTIVE ARGUMENT

Divorce and Our National Values

PETER D. KRAMER

Introduction:
The problem: a marital crisis caused by opposing views of marriage

How shall we resolve a marital crisis? Consider an example from the advice column of Ann Landers. An "Iowa Wife" wrote to ask what she should do about her husband's habit, after thirty years of marriage, of reading magazines at table when the couple dined out. Ann Landers advised the wife to engage her husband by studying subjects of interest to him.

Examples of opposing views

Readers from around the country protested. A "Fourteen-Year-Old Girl in Pennsylvania" crystallized the objections: "You told the wife to read up on sports or business, whatever he was interested in, even though it might be boring to her. Doesn't that defeat the basic idea of being your own self?" Chastened, Ann Landers changed course, updated her stance: Reading at table is a hostile act, perhaps even grounds for divorce.

When it comes to marriage, Ann Landers seems a reasonable barometer of our values. In practical terms, reading the sports pages might work for some Iowa wife—but we do not believe that is how spouses ought to behave. Only the second response, consider divorce, expresses our

Peter D. Kramer, a clinical professor of psychiatry at Brown University, is the author of *Listening to Prozac* (1993) and *Should You Leave?* (1997). This article appeared on the op-ed page of the *New York Times* on August 29, 1997.

Claim of fact or thesis
statement: Divorce
expresses respect for
the separate self.

A proposed solution to
the problem: "covenant
marriage"

overriding respect for autonomy, for the unique and separate self.

Look south now from Iowa and Pennsylvania to Louisiana, where a new law allows couples to opt for a "covenant marriage" — terminable only after a lengthy separation or because of adultery, abandonment, abuse, or imprisonment. The law has been praised by many as an expedient against the epidemic of divorce and an incarnation of our "traditional values."

Whether the law will lower the divorce rate is 5 an empirical question to be decided in the future, but it is not too soon to ask: Does covenant marriage express the values we live by?

Questioning the
covenant marriage
Development and
support:
(1) history and
philosophy of autonomy

History seems to say no. American literature's one great self-help book is *Walden,* a paean to self-reliance and an homage to Henry David Thoreau's favorite preacher, Ralph Waldo Emerson, who declaimed: "Say to them, O father, O mother, O wife, O brother, O friend, I have lived with you after appearances hitherto. Henceforward, I am the truth's. . . . I must be myself. I cannot break my self any longer for you, or you."

The economic philosophy we proudly export, fundamentalist capitalism, says that society functions best when members act in a self-interested manner. The nation's founding document is a bill of divorcement. Autonomy is the characteristic American virtue.

(2) autonomy as a goal
of psychotherapy

As a psychiatrist, I see this value embedded in our psychotherapy, the craft that both shapes and expresses the prevailing common sense. In the early 1970s, Carl Rogers, known as the "Psychologist of America," encapsulated the post–World War II version of our ideals: A successful marriage is one that increases the "self-actualization" of each member. Of a failed union, he wrote: "If Jennifer had from the first insisted on being her true self, the marriage would have had much more strife and much more hope."

Rogers was expressing the predominant viewpoint; for most of the past fifty years, enhanced autonomy has been a goal of psychotherapy. Erik Erikson began the trend by boldly proclaiming that the search for identity had become as important in his time as the study of sexuality was in Freud's. Later, Murray Bowen, a founder of family therapy, invoked a scale of maturity whose measure is a person's ability to maintain his or her beliefs in the face of family pressures. The useful response to crises within couples, Bowen suggested, is to hold fast to your values and challenge your partner to rise to meet your level of maturity.

But autonomy was a value for men only, and 10 largely it was pseudoautonomy, the successful man propped up by the indentured wife and overburdened mother. (No doubt Thoreau sent his clothes home for laundering.)

(3) autonomy extended to women

The self-help movement, beginning in the 1970s, extended this American ideal to women. Once both partners are allowed to be autonomous, the continuation of marriage becomes more truly voluntary. In this sense, an increase in divorce signals social progress.

It signals social progress, except that divorce is itself destructive. So it seems to me the question is whether any other compelling value counterbalances the siren song of self-improvement.

Another opposing view: mutuality as a preferable value

Turning again to psychotherapy, we do hear arguments for a different type of American value. Answering Erikson's call for individual identity, Helen Merrell Lynd, a sociologist at Sarah Lawrence College, wrote, "Nor must complete finding of oneself . . . precede finding oneself in and through other persons."

Her belief entered psychiatry through the writings of her pupil, Jean Baker Miller. A professor of psychiatry at Boston University, Dr. Miller faults most psychotherapy for elevating autonomy at the expense of qualities important to women, such as mutuality. To feel connected (when there is genuine give-and-take) is to feel worth. Miller wants a transformed culture in which mutuality "is valued as highly as, or more highly than, self-enhancement."

Refutation (the warrant): Americans do not value mutuality.

Mutuality is an ideal the culture believes it 15 should honor but does not quite. Ours is a society that does a half-hearted job of inculcating compromise, which is to say that we still teach these skills mainly to women. Much of psychotherapy addresses the troubles of those who make great efforts at compromise only to be taken advantage of by selfish partners.

Often the more vulnerable spouse requires rescue through the sort of move Ann Landers recommends, vigorous self-assertion, and even divorce.

Mutuality is a worthy ideal, one that might serve as a fit complement and counterbalance to our celebration of the self. But if we do not reward it elsewhere—if in the school and office and marketplace, we celebrate self-assertion—it seems worrisome to ask the institution of marriage to play by different rules.

Backing for the warrant: Self-assertion in school, office, and marketplace

What is insidious about Louisiana's covenant marriage is that, contrary to claims on its behalf, it is out of touch with our traditional values: self-expression, self-fulfillment, self-reliance.

The Louisiana law invites couples to lash themselves to a morality the broader culture does not support, an arrangement that creates a potential for terrible tensions.

Conclusion: restatement of the claim: Divorce reflects our national values.

Though we profess abhorrence of divorce, I suspect that the divorce rate reflects our national values with great exactness, and that conventional modern marriage—an eternal commitment with loopholes galore—expresses precisely the degree of loss of autonomy that we are able to tolerate.

20

■ Analysis

A deductive argument proceeds from a general statement that the writer assumes to be true to a conclusion that is more specific. Deductive reasoning is commonplace, although seldom so pure as the definition suggests. In Kramer's article the conclusion appears at the end of paragraph 3: "the second response, consider divorce, expresses our overriding respect for autonomy, for the unique and separate self." The major premise or general statement may be summed up as "Self-actualization is an important American value," and the minor premise as "Divorce is an expression of self-actualization."

Kramer's defense of the major premise is admirable. Despite its brevity, the article brims with significant quotations and instructive examples from literature, psychiatry, and social and economic history that began, as he reminds us, with a "bill of divorcement" (para. 7) from England in 1776.

Finding support for the minor premise is a more difficult exercise because the reader here confronts a *specific* consequence of self-fulfillment—divorce. In all arguments, details and examples test the strength of our generalizations, and while self-actualization is suitably vague, divorce is not. We know that it does not always represent liberation for both partners. Kramer is aware of the problem. In the same paragraph he has insisted both that divorce "signals social progress" and that it is "destructive" (para. 12). He knows that his critics will call on him to reconcile this contradiction.

So far Kramer's argument has been largely factual, proof of the existence of the American ideal. Now he advances onto shakier ground in an examination of values: "the question is whether any other compelling value counterbalances the siren song of self-improvement" (para. 12).

Kramer then responds to those therapists who value a different ideal—that of mutuality, cooperation, and compromise rather than self-assertion. He admires such virtues but finds them unlikely to prevail against the ideal of self-fulfillment that pervades all areas of American life. Divorce, he believes, is simply one expression of that ideal, and he rejects the proposition that we should "ask the institution of marriage to play by different rules" (para. 17).

In deductive argument the conclusion must be true. Questions of social behavior, however, are not so easily proved. We accept the conclusions in such cases if they are plausible—well supported and consistent with experience. Within the limits of this brief essay, Kramer's findings are convincing.

One other element is worth noting: Kramer's objectivity, his role as observer rather than advocate. For the most part, he has excluded himself from the argument. We suspect that, as a psychiatrist, he supports values of self-expression, but in this article he is describing not his own views but those of most Americans. He does not explicitly defend divorce; he explains it. On the whole, this is an effective strategy. We do not need to agree on the morality of self-fulfillment to accept his conclusion.

A NOTE ON THE SYLLOGISM AND THE TOULMIN MODEL

In examining the classical deductive syllogism, you may have noticed the resemblance of its three-part outline to the three-part structure of claim, support, and warrant that we have used throughout the text to illustrate the elements of argument. We mentioned that the syllogism was articulated over two thousand years ago by the Greek philosopher Aristotle. By contrast, the claim-support-warrant structure is based on the model of argument proposed by the modern British philosopher Stephen Toulmin.

Now, there is every reason to think that all models of argument will share some similarities. Nevertheless, the differences between the formal syllogism and the informal Toulmin model suggest that the latter is a more effective instrument for writers who want to know which questions to ask, both before they begin and during the process of developing their arguments.

The syllogism is useful for laying out the basic elements of an argument, as we have seen in several examples. It lends itself more readily to simple arguments. The following syllogism summarizes a familiar argument.

MAJOR PREMISE: Advertising of things harmful to our health should be legally banned.

MINOR PREMISE: Cigarettes are harmful to our health.

CONCLUSION: Therefore, advertising of cigarettes should be legally banned.

Cast in the form of a Toulmin outline, the argument looks like this:

CLAIM: Advertising of cigarettes should be legally banned.

SUPPORT (EVIDENCE): Cigarettes are harmful to our health.

WARRANT: Advertising of things harmful to our health should be legally banned.

or in diagram form:

Support ————————————→ *Claim*
Cigarettes are harmful   Advertising of cigarettes
to our health.   should be legally banned.

Warrant
Advertising of things harmful to our
health should be legally banned.

In both the syllogism and the Toulmin model the principal elements of the argument are expressed in three statements. You can see that the claim in the Toulmin model is the conclusion in the syllogism—that is, the proposition that you are trying to prove. The evidence (support) in the Toulmin model corresponds to the minor premise in the syllogism. And the warrant in the Toulmin model resembles the major premise of the syllogism.

But the differences are significant. One difference is the use of language. The syllogism represents an argument "in which the validity of the assumption underlying the inference 'leap' is uncontested."[3] That is, the words "major premise" seem to suggest that the assumption has been proved. They do not emphasize that an analysis of the premise—"Advertising of things harmful to our health should be legally banned"—is necessary before we can decide that the conclusion is acceptable. Of course, a careful arguer will try to establish the truth and validity of all parts of the syllogism, but the terms in which the syllogism is framed do not encourage him or her to examine the real relationship among the three elements. Sometimes the enthymeme (see p. 283), which uses only two elements in the argument and suppresses the third, makes analyzing the relationship even more difficult.

In the Toulmin model, the use of the term *warrant* indicates that the validity of the proposition must be established to *guarantee* the claim or make the crossing from support to claim. It makes clear that the arguer must ask *why* such advertising must be banned.

Nor is the term *minor premise* as useful to the arguer as "support." The word *support* instructs the arguer that he or she must take steps to provide the claim with factual evidence or an appeal to values.

A second difference is that while the syllogism is essentially static, with all three parts logically locked into place, the Toulmin model suggests that an argument is a *movement* from support to claim by way of the warrant, which acts as a bridge. Toulmin introduced the concept of warrant by asking "How do you get there?" (His first two questions, introducing the claim and support, were, "What are you trying to prove?" and "What have you got to go on?")

Lastly, recall that in addition to the three basic elements, the Toulmin model offers supplementary elements of argument. The *qualifier,* in the form of words like "probably" or "more likely," shows that the claim is not absolute. The *backing* offers support for the validity of the warrant. The *reservation* suggests that the validity of the warrant may be limited. These additional elements, which refine and expand the argument itself, reflect the real flexibility and complexity of the argumentative process.

COMMON FALLACIES

In this necessarily brief review it would be impossible to discuss all the fallacies listed by logicians, but we can examine the ones most likely to be found in the arguments you will read and write. Fallacies are

---

[3]Wayne E. Brockenreide and Douglas Ehninger, "Toulmin on Argument: An Interpretation and Application," *Contemporary Theories of Rhetoric: Selected Readings,* ed. Richard L. Johannesen (New York: Harper and Row, 1971), p. 245. This comparative analysis is indebted to Brockenreide and Ehninger's influential article.

difficult to classify, first, because there are literally dozens of systems for classifying, and second, because under any system there is always a good deal of overlap. Our discussion of the reasoning process, however, tells us where faulty reasoning occurs.

Inductive fallacies, as we know, result from the wrong use of evidence: That is, the arguer leaps to a conclusion on the basis of an insufficient sample, ignoring evidence that might have altered his or her conclusion. Deductive fallacies, on the other hand, result from a failure to follow the logic of a series of statements. Here the arguer neglects to make a clear connection between the parts of his or her argument. One of the commonest strategies is the introduction of an irrelevant issue, one that has little or no direct bearing on the development of the claim and serves only to distract the reader.

It's helpful to remember that, even if you cannot name the particular fallacy, you can learn to recognize it and not only refute it in the arguments of others but avoid it in your own as well.

■ 1. Hasty Generalization

In Chapter 5 (see pp. 163–64) we discussed the dangers in drawing conclusions on the basis of insufficient evidence. Many of our prejudices are a result of hasty generalization. A prejudice is literally a judgment made before the facts are in. On the basis of experience with two or three members of an ethnic group, for example, we may form the prejudice that all members of the group share the characteristics that we have attributed to the two or three in our experience. (See Gordon Allport, "The Nature of Prejudice," on p. 138.)

Superstitions are also based in part on hasty generalization. As a result of a very small number of experiences with black cats, broken mirrors, Friday the thirteenth, or spilled salt, some people will assume a cause-and-effect relation between these signs and misfortunes. *Superstition* has been defined as "a notion maintained despite evidence to the contrary." The evidence would certainly show that, contrary to the superstitious belief, in a lifetime hundreds of such "unlucky" signs are not followed by unfortunate events. To generalize about a connection is therefore unjustified.

■ 2. Faulty Use of Authority

Faulty use of authority—the attempt to bolster claims by citing the opinions of experts—was discussed in Chapter 5. Both writers and readers need to be especially aware of the testimony of authorities who may disagree with those cited. In circumstances where experts disagree, you are encouraged to undertake a careful evaluation and comparison of credentials.

■ 3. Post Hoc or Doubtful Cause

The entire Latin term for this fallacy is *post hoc, ergo propter hoc,* meaning, "After this, therefore because of this." The arguer infers that because one event follows another event, the first event must be the cause of the second. But proximity of events or conditions does not guarantee a causal relation. The rooster crows every morning at 5:00 and, seeing the sun rise immediately after, decides that his crowing has caused the sun to rise. A month after A-bomb tests are concluded, tornadoes damage the area where the tests were held, and residents decide that the tests caused the tornadoes. After the school principal suspends daily prayers in the classroom, acts of vandalism increase, and some parents are convinced that failure to conduct prayer is responsible for the rise in vandalism. In each of these cases, the fact that one event follows another does not prove a causal connection. The two events may be coincidental, or the first event may be only one, and an insignificant one, of many causes that have produced the second event. The reader or writer of causal arguments must determine whether another more plausible explanation exists and whether several causes have combined to produce the effect. Perhaps the suspension of prayer was only one of a number of related causes: a decline in disciplinary action, a relaxation of academic standards, a change in school administration, and changes in family structure in the school community.

In the previous section we saw that superstitions are the result not only of hasty generalization but also of the willingness to find a cause-and-effect connection in the juxtaposition of two events. A belief in astrological signs also derives from erroneous inferences about cause and effect. Only a very few of the millions of people who consult the astrology charts every day in newspapers and magazines have submitted the predictions to statistical analysis. A curious reader might try this strategy: Save the columns, usually at the beginning or end of the year, in which astrologers and clairvoyants make predictions for events in the coming year, allegedly based on their reading of the stars and other signs. At the end of the year evaluate the percentage of predictions that were fulfilled. The number will be very small. But even if some of the predictions prove true, there may be other less fanciful explanations for their accuracy.

In defending simple explanations against complex ones, philosophers and scientists often refer to a maxim called *Occam's razor,* a principle formulated by the medieval philosopher and theologian William of Occam. A modern science writer says this principle "urges a preference for the simplest hypothesis that does all we want it to do."[4] Bertrand Russell, the twentieth-century British philosopher, explained it this way:

> It is vain to do with more what can be done with fewer. That is to say,
> if everything in some science can be interpreted without assuming this

---

[4]Martin Gardner, *The Whys of a Philosophical Scrivener* (New York: Quill, 1983), p. 174.

or that hypothetical entity, there is no ground for assuming it. I have myself found this a most fruitful principle in logical analysis.[5]

In other words, choose the simpler, more credible explanation wherever possible.

We all share the belief that scientific experimentation and research can answer questions about a wide range of natural and social phenomena: evolutionary development, hurricanes, disease, crime, poverty. It is true that repeated experiments in controlled situations can establish what seem to be solid relations suggesting cause and effect. But even scientists prefer to talk not about cause but about an extremely high probability that under controlled conditions one event will follow another.

In the social sciences cause-and-effect relations are especially susceptible to challenge. Human experiences can seldom be subjected to laboratory conditions. In addition, the complexity of the social environment makes it difficult, even impossible, to extract one cause from among the many that influence human behavior.

■ 4. False Analogy

Many analogies are merely descriptive and offer no proof of the connection between the two things being compared. In recent years a debate has emerged between weight-loss professionals about the wisdom of urging overweight people to lose weight for health reasons. Susan Wooley, director of the eating disorders clinic at the University of Cincinnati and a professor of psychiatry, offered the following analogy in defense of her view that dieting is dangerous.

> We know that overweight people have a higher mortality rate than thin people. We also know that black people have a higher mortality rate than white people. Do we subject black people to torturous treatments to bleach their skin? Of course not. We have enough sense to know skin-bleaching will not eliminate sickle-cell anemia. So why do we have blind faith that weight loss will cure the diseases associated with obesity?"[6]

But it is clear that the false analogy between black skin and excessive weight does not work. The color of one's skin does not cause sickle-cell anemia, but there is an abundance of proof that excess weight influences mortality.

Historians are fond of using analogical arguments to demonstrate that particular circumstances prevailing in the past are being reproduced in the present. They therefore feel safe in predicting that the present course of history will follow that of the past. British historian Arnold

---

[5]*Dictionary of Mind, Matter and Morals* (New York: Philosophical Library, 1952), p. 166.

[6]*New York Times,* April 12, 1992, sec. C, p. 43.

Toynbee argues by analogy that humans' tenure on earth may be limited.

> On the evidence of the past history of life on this planet, even the extinction of the human race is not entirely unlikely. After all, the reign of man on the Earth, if we are right in thinking that man established his present ascendancy in the middle paleolithic age, is so far only about 100,000 years old, and what is that compared to the 500 million or 900 million years during which life has been in existence on the surface of this planet? In the past, other forms of life have enjoyed reigns which have lasted for almost inconceivably longer periods—and which yet at last have come to an end.[7]

Toynbee finds similarities between the limited reigns of other animal species and the possible disappearance of the human race. For this analogy, however, we need to ask whether the conditions of the past, so far as we know them, at all resemble the conditions under which human existence on earth might be terminated. Is the fact that human beings are also members of the animal kingdom sufficient support for this comparison?

■ 5. Ad Hominem

The Latin term *ad hominem* means "against the man" and refers to an attack on the person rather than on the argument or the issue. The assumption in such a fallacy is that if the speaker proves to be unacceptable in some way, his or her statements must also be judged unacceptable. Attacking the author of the statement is a strategy of diversion that prevents the reader from giving attention where it is due—to the issue under discussion.

You might hear someone complain, "What can the priest tell us about marriage? He's never been married himself." This ad hominem accusation ignores the validity of the advice the priest might offer. In the same way an overweight patient might reject the advice on diet by an overweight physician. In politics it is not uncommon for antagonists to attack each other for personal characteristics that may not be relevant to the tasks they will be elected to perform. They may be accused of infidelity to their partners, homosexuality, atheism, or a flamboyant social life. Even if certain accusations should be proved true, voters should not ignore the substance of what politicians do and say in their public offices.

This confusion of private life with professional record also exists in literature and the other arts. According to their biographers, the American writers Thomas Wolfe, Robert Frost, and William Saroyan—to name only a few—and numbers of film stars, including Charlie Chaplin, Joan

---

[7] *Civilization on Trial* (New York: Oxford University Press, 1948), pp. 162–163.

Crawford, and Bing Crosby, made life miserable for those closest to them. Having read about their unpleasant personal characteristics, some people find it hard to separate the artist from his or her creation, although the personality and character of the artist are often irrelevant to the content of the work.

Ad hominem accusations against the person do *not* constitute a fallacy if the characteristics under attack are relevant to the argument. If the politician is irresponsible and dishonest in the conduct of his or her personal life, we may be justified in thinking that the person will also behave irresponsibly and dishonestly in public office.

■ 6. False Dilemma

As the name tells us, the false dilemma, sometimes called the *black-white fallacy,* poses an either-or situation. The arguer suggests that only two alternatives exist, although there may be other explanations of or solutions to the problem under discussion. The false dilemma reflects the simplification of a complex problem. Sometimes it is offered out of ignorance or laziness, sometimes to divert attention from the real explanation or solution that the arguer rejects for doubtful reasons.

You may encounter the either-or situation in dilemmas about personal choices. "At the University of Georgia," says one writer, "the measure of a man was football. You either played it or worshiped those who did, and there was no middle ground."[8] Clearly this dilemma—"Love football or you're not a man"—ignores other measures of manhood.

Politics and government offer a wealth of examples. In an interview with the *New York Times* in 1975, the Shah of Iran was asked why he could not introduce into his authoritarian regime greater freedom for his subjects. His reply was, "What's wrong with authority? Is anarchy better?" Apparently he considered that only two paths were open to him — authoritarianism or anarchy. Of course, democracy was also an option, which, perhaps fatally, he declined to consider.

■ 7. Slippery Slope

If an arguer predicts that taking a first step will lead inevitably to a second, usually undesirable step, he or she must provide evidence that this will happen. Otherwise, the arguer is guilty of a slippery slope fallacy.

Asked by an inquiring photographer on the street how he felt about censorship of a pornographic magazine, a man replied, "I don't think any publication should be banned. It's a slippery slope when you start making decisions on what people should be permitted to read. . . . It's a dangerous precedent." Perhaps. But if questioned further, the man

[8]Phil Gailey, "A Nonsports Fan," *New York Times Magazine,* December 18, 1983, sec. 6, p. 96.

should have offered evidence that a ban on some things leads inevitably to a ban on everything.

Predictions based on the danger inherent in taking the first step are commonplace:

> Legalization of abortion will lead to murder of the old and the physically and mentally handicapped.
>
> The Connecticut law allowing sixteen-year-olds and their parents to divorce each other will mean the death of the family.
>
> If we ban handguns, we will end up banning rifles and other hunting weapons.

Distinguishing between probable and improbable predictions—that is, recognizing the slippery-slope fallacy—poses special problems because only future developments can verify or refute predictions. For example, in 1941 the imposition of military conscription aroused some opponents to predict that the draft was a precursor of fascism in this country. Only after the war, when 10 million draftees were demobilized, did it become clear that the draft had been an insufficient sign for a prediction of fascism. In this case the slippery-slope prediction of fascism might have been avoided if closer attention had been paid to other influences pointing to the strength of democracy.

More recently, the debate about cloning has raised fears of creation of genetic copies of adults. The *New York Times* reported that

> Many lawmakers today warned that if therapeutic cloning went forward, scientists would step onto a slippery slope that would inevitably lead to cloning people.[9]

Most scientists, however, reject this possibility for the foreseeable future.

Slippery slope predictions are simplistic. They ignore not only the dissimilarities between first and last steps but also the complexity of the developments in any long chain of events.

■ 8. Begging the Question

If the writer makes a statement that assumes that the very question being argued has already been proved, the writer is guilty of begging the question. In a letter to the editor of a college newspaper protesting the failure of the majority of students to meet the writing requirement because they had failed an exemption test, the writer said, "Not exempting all students who honestly qualify for exemption is an insult." But whether the students are honestly qualified is precisely the question that the exemption test was supposed to resolve. The writer has not proved that the students who failed the writing test were qualified for exemption. She has only made an assertion *as if* she had already proved it.

---

[9]August 1, 2001, p. A11.

In an effort to raise standards of teaching, some politicians and educators have urged that master teachers be awarded higher salaries. Opponents have argued that such a proposal begs the question because it assumes that the term *master teachers* can be or has already been defined.

Circular reasoning is an extreme example of begging the question: "Women should not be permitted to join men's clubs because the clubs are for men only." The question to be resolved first, of course, is whether clubs for men only should continue to exist.

■   **9. Straw Man**

The straw-man fallacy consists of an attack on a view similar to but not the same as the one your opponent holds. It is a familiar diversionary tactic. The name probably derives from an old game in which a straw man was set up to divert attention from the real target that a contestant was supposed to knock down.

One of the outstanding examples of the straw-man fallacy occurred in the famous Checkers speech of Senator Richard Nixon. In 1952 during his vice-presidential campaign, Nixon was accused of having appropriated $18,000 in campaign funds for his personal use. At one point in the radio and television speech in which he defended his reputation, he said:

> One other thing I probably should tell you, because if I don't they will probably be saying this about me, too. We did get something, a gift, after the election.
>
> A man down in Texas heard Pat on the radio mention the fact that our two youngsters would like to have a dog, and, believe it or not, the day before we left on this campaign trip we got a message from Union Station in Baltimore saying they had a package for us. We went down to get it. You know what it was?
>
> It was a little cocker spaniel dog, in a crate that he had sent all the way from Texas, black and white, spotted, and our little girl, Tricia, the six-year-old, named it Checkers.
>
> And, you know, the kids, like all kids, loved the dog, and I just want to say this, right now, that regardless of what they say about it, we are going to keep it.[10]

Of course, Nixon knew that the issue was the alleged misappropriation of funds, not the ownership of the dog, which no one had asked him to return.

■   **10. Two Wrongs Make a Right**

The two-wrongs-make-a-right fallacy is another example of the way in which attention may be diverted from the question at issue.

[10] Radio and television address of Senator Nixon from Los Angeles on September 23, 1952.

After President Jimmy Carter in March 1977 attacked the human rights record of the Soviet Union, Russian officials responded:

> As for the present state of human rights in the United States, it is characterized by the following facts: millions of unemployed, racial discrimination, social inequality of women, infringement of citizens' personal freedom, the growth of crime, and so on.[11]

The Russians made no attempt to deny the failure of *their* human rights record; instead they attacked by pointing out that the Americans are not blameless either.

■ 11. Non Sequitur

The Latin term *non sequitur,* which means "it does not follow," is another fallacy of irrelevance. An advertisement for a book, *Worlds in Collision,* whose theories about the origin of the earth and evolutionary development have been challenged by almost all reputable scientists, states:

> Once rejected as "preposterous"! Critics called it an outrage! It aroused incredible antagonism in scientific and literary circles. Yet half a million copies were sold and for twenty-seven years it remained an outstanding bestseller.

We know, of course, that the popularity of a book does not bestow scientific respectability. The number of sales, therefore, is irrelevant to proof of the book's theoretical soundness—a non sequitur.

Other examples sometimes appear in the comments of political candidates. Donald Trump, the billionaire real-estate developer, in considering a run for president of the United States in 2000, told an interviewer:

> My entire life, I've watched politicians bragging about how poor they are, how they came from nothing, how poor their parents and grandparents were. And I said to myself, if they can stay so poor for so many generations, maybe this isn't the kind of person we want to be electing to higher office. How smart can they be? They're morons. . . . Do you want someone who gets to be president and that's literally the highest paying job he's ever had?[12]

As a brief glance at U.S. history shows, it does not follow that men of small success in the world of commerce are unfit to make sound decisions about matters of state.

■ 12. Ad Populum

Arguers guilty of the *ad populum* fallacy make an appeal to the prejudices of the people (*populum* in Latin). They assume that their claim can be adequately defended without further support if they emphasize a belief

---

[11] *New York Times,* March 3, 1977, p. 1.
[12] *New York Times,* November 28, 1999, p. 11.

or attitude that the audience shares with them. One common form of ad populum is an appeal to patriotism, which may allow arguers to omit evidence that the audience needs for proper evaluation of the claim. In the following advertisement the makers of Zippo lighters made such an appeal in urging readers to buy their product.

> It's a grand old lighter. Zippo—the grand old lighter that's made right here in the good old U.S.A.
> We truly make an all-American product. The raw materials used in making a Zippo lighter are all right from this great land of ours.
> Zippo windproof lighters are proud to be Americans.

■ 13. Appeal to Tradition

In making an appeal to tradition, the arguer assumes that what has existed for a long time and has therefore become a tradition should continue to exist *because* it is a tradition. If the arguer avoids telling his or her reader *why* the tradition should be preserved, he or she may be accused of failing to meet the real issue.

The following statement appeared in a letter defending the membership policy of the Century Club, an all-male club established in New York City in 1847 that was under pressure to admit women. The writer was a Presbyterian minister who opposed the admission of women.

> I am totally opposed to a proposal which would radically change the nature of the Century. . . . A club creates an ethos of its own over the years, and I would deeply deplore a step that would inevitably create an entirely different kind of place.
> A club like the Century should surely be unaffected by fashionable whims. . . .[13]

■ 14. Faulty Emotional Appeals

In some discussions of fallacies, appeals to the emotions of the audience are treated as illegitimate or "counterfeit proofs." All such appeals, however, are *not* illegitimate. As we saw in Chapter 5 on support, appeals to the values and emotions of an audience are an appropriate form of persuasion. You can recognize fallacious emotional appeals if (1) they are irrelevant to the argument or draw attention from the issues being argued or (2) they appear to conceal another purpose. Here we treat two of the most popular appeals—to pity and to fear.

Appeals to pity, compassion, and natural willingness to help the unfortunate are particularly hard to resist. The requests for aid by most charitable organizations—for hungry children, victims of disaster, stray animals—offer examples of legitimate appeals. But these appeals to our sympathetic feelings should not divert us from considering other issues in a particular case. It would be wrong, for example, to allow a multiple

---

[13]David H. C. Read, letter to the *New York Times,* January 13, 1983, p. 14.

murderer to escape punishment because he or she had experienced a wretched childhood. Likewise, if you are asked to contribute to a charitable cause, you should try to learn how many unfortunate people or animals are being helped and what percentage of the contribution will be allocated to maintaining the organization and its officers. In some cases the financial records are closed to public review, and only a small share of the contribution will reach the alleged beneficiaries.

Appeals to fear are likely to be even more effective. But they must be based on evidence that fear is an appropriate response to the issues and that it can move an audience toward a solution to the problem. (Fear can also have the adverse effect of preventing people from taking a necessary action.) Insurance companies, for example, make appeals to our fears of destitution for ourselves and our families as a result of injury, unemployment, sickness, and death. These appeals are justified if the possibilities of such destitution are real and if the insurance will provide relief. It would also be legitimate to arouse fear of the consequences of drunk driving, provided, again, that the descriptions were accurate. On the other hand, it would be wrong to induce fear that fluoridation of public water supplies causes cancer without presenting sound evidence of the probability. It would also be wrong to instill a fear of school integration unless convincing proof were offered of undesirable social consequences.

An emotional response by itself is not always the soundest basis for making decisions. Your own experience has probably taught you that in the grip of a strong emotion like love or hate or anger you often overlook good reasons for making different and better choices. Like you, your readers want to be given the opportunity to consider all the available kinds of support for an argument.

READINGS FOR ANALYSIS

On Nation and Race

ADOLF HITLER

There are some truths which are so obvious that for this very reason they are not seen or at least not recognized by ordinary people. They sometimes pass by such truisms as though blind and are most astonished when someone suddenly discovers what everyone really ought to know. Columbus's eggs lie around by the hundreds of thousands, but Columbuses are met with less frequency.

Adolf Hitler (1889–1945) became the Nazi dictator of Germany in the mid-1930s. "On Nation and Race" (editor's title) begins Chapter 11 of *Mein Kampf* (*My Struggle*), vol. 1, published in 1925.

Thus men without exception wander about in the garden of Nature; they imagine that they know practically everything and yet with few exceptions pass blindly by one of the most patent principles of Nature's rule: the inner segregation of the species of all living beings on this earth.

Even the most superficial observation shows that Nature's restricted form of propagation and increase is an almost rigid basic law of all the innumerable forms of expression of her vital urge. Every animal mates only with a member of the same species. The titmouse seeks the titmouse, the finch the finch, the stork the stork, the field mouse the field mouse, the dormouse the dormouse, the wolf the she-wolf, etc.

Only unusual circumstances can change this, primarily the compulsion of captivity or any other cause that makes it impossible to mate within the same species. But then Nature begins to resist this with all possible means, and her most visible protest consists either in refusing further capacity for propagation to bastards or in limiting the fertility of later offspring; in most cases, however, she takes away the power of resistance to disease or hostile attacks.

This is only too natural.   5

Any crossing of two beings not at exactly the same level produces a medium between the level of the two parents. This means: The offspring will probably stand higher than the racially lower parent, but not as high as the higher one. Consequently, it will later succumb in the struggle against the higher level. Such mating is contrary to the will of Nature for a higher breeding of all life. The precondition for this does not lie in associating superior and inferior, but in the total victory of the former. The stronger must dominate and not blend with the weaker, thus sacrificing his own greatness. Only the born weakling can view this as cruel, but he after all is only a weak and limited man; for if this law did not prevail, any conceivable higher development of organic living beings would be unthinkable.

The consequence of this racial purity, universally valid in Nature, is not only the sharp outward delimitation of the various races, but their uniform character in themselves. The fox is always a fox, the goose a goose, the tiger a tiger, etc., and the difference can lie at most in the varying measure of force, strength, intelligence, dexterity, endurance, etc., of the individual specimens. But you will never find a fox who in his inner attitude might, for example, show humanitarian tendencies toward geese, as similarly there is no cat with a friendly inclination toward mice.

Therefore, here, too, the struggle among themselves arises less from inner aversion than from hunger and love. In both cases, Nature looks on calmly, with satisfaction, in fact. In the struggle for daily bread all those who are weak and sickly or less determined succumb, while the struggle of the males for the female grants the right or opportunity to propagate only to the healthiest. And struggle is always a means for improving a species' health and power of resistance and, therefore, a cause of its higher development.

If the process were different, all further and higher development would cease and the opposite would occur. For, since the inferior always predominates numerically over the best, if both had the same possibility of preserving life and propagating, the inferior would multiply so much more rapidly that in the end the best would inevitably be driven into the background, unless a correction of this state of affairs were undertaken. Nature does just this by subjecting the weaker part to such severe living conditions that by them alone the number is limited, and by not permitting the remainder to increase promiscuously, but making a new and ruthless choice according to strength and health.

No more than Nature desires the mating of weaker with stronger in- 10 dividuals, even less does she desire the blending of a higher with a lower race, since, if she did, her whole work of higher breeding, over perhaps hundreds of thousands of years, might be ruined with one blow.

Historical experience offers countless proofs of this. It shows with terrifying clarity that in every mingling of Aryan blood with that of lower peoples the result was the end of the cultured people. North America, whose population consists in by far the largest part of Germanic elements who mixed but little with the lower colored peoples, shows a different humanity and culture from Central and South America, where the predominantly Latin immigrants often mixed with the aborigines on a large scale. By this one example, we can clearly and distinctly recognize the effect of racial mixture. The Germanic inhabitant of the American continent, who has remained racially pure and unmixed, rose to be master of the continent; he will remain the master as long as he does not fall a victim to defilement of the blood.

The result of all racial crossing is therefore in brief always the following:

(a) Lowering of the level of the higher race;

(b) Physical and intellectual regression and hence the beginning of a slowly but surely progressing sickness.

To bring about such a development is, then, nothing else but to sin 15 against the will of the eternal creator.

And as a sin this act is rewarded.

When man attempts to rebel against the iron logic of Nature, he comes into struggle with the principles to which he himself owes his existence as a man. And this attack must lead to his own doom.

Here, of course, we encounter the objection of the modern pacifist, as truly Jewish in its effrontery as it is stupid! "Man's role is to overcome Nature!"

Millions thoughtlessly parrot this Jewish nonsense and end up by really imagining that they themselves represent a kind of conqueror of Nature; though in this they dispose of no other weapon than an idea, and at that such a miserable one, that if it were true no world at all would be conceivable.

But quite aside from the fact that man has never yet conquered Na- 20
ture in anything, but at most has caught hold of and tried to lift one or
another corner of her immense gigantic veil of eternal riddles and secrets, that in reality he invents nothing but only discovers everything,
that he does not dominate Nature, but has only risen on the basis of his
knowledge of various laws and secrets of Nature to be lord over those
other living creatures who lack this knowledge—quite aside from all
this, an idea cannot overcome the preconditions for the development
and being of humanity, since the idea itself depends only on man.
Without human beings there is no human idea in this world; therefore,
the idea as such is always conditioned by the presence of human beings
and hence of all the laws which created the precondition for their existence.

And not only that! Certain ideas are even tied up with certain men.
This applies most of all to those ideas whose content originates, not in
an exact scientific truth, but in the world of emotion, or, as it is so beau-
tifully and clearly expressed today, reflects an "inner experience." All
these ideas, which have nothing to do with cold logic as such, but represent only pure expressions of feeling, ethical conceptions, etc., are
chained to the existence of men, to whose intellectual imagination and
creative power they owe their existence. Precisely in this case the preservation of these definite races and men is the precondition for the existence of these ideas. Anyone, for example, who really desired the victory
of the pacifistic idea in this world with all his heart would have to fight
with all the means at his disposal for the conquest of the world by the
Germans; for, if the opposite should occur, the last pacifist would die out
with the last German, since the rest of the world has never fallen so
deeply as our own people, unfortunately, has for this nonsense so contrary to Nature and reason. Then, if we were serious, whether we liked it
or not, we would have to wage wars in order to arrive at pacifism. This
and nothing else was what Wilson, the American world savior, intended,
or so at least our German visionaries believed—and thereby his purpose
was fulfilled.

In actual fact the pacifistic-humane idea is perfectly all right perhaps
when the highest type of man has previously conquered and subjected
the world to an extent that makes him the sole ruler of this earth. Then
this idea lacks the power of producing evil effects in exact proportion as
its practical application becomes rare and finally impossible. Therefore,
first struggle and then we shall see what can be done. Otherwise
mankind has passed the high point of its development and the end is
not the domination of any ethical idea but barbarism and consequently
chaos. At this point someone or other may laugh, but this planet once
moved through the ether for millions of years without human beings
and it can do so again some day if men forget that they owe their higher
existence, not to the ideas of a few crazy ideologists, but to the knowledge and ruthless application of Nature's stern and rigid laws.

Everything we admire on this earth today—science and art, technology and inventions—is only the creative product of a few peoples and originally perhaps of *one* race. On them depends the existence of this whole culture. If they perish, the beauty of this earth will sink into the grave with them.

However much the soil, for example, can influence men, the result of the influence will always be different depending on the races in question. The low fertility of a living space may spur the one race to the highest achievements; in others it will only be the cause of bitterest poverty and final undernourishment with all its consequences. The inner nature of peoples is always determining for the manner in which outward influences will be effective. What leads the one to starvation trains the other to hard work.

All great cultures of the past perished only because the originally creative race died out from blood poisoning. 25

The ultimate cause of such a decline was their forgetting that all culture depends on men and conversely; hence that to preserve a certain culture the man who creates it must be preserved. This preservation is bound up with the rigid law of necessity and the right to victory of the best and stronger in this world.

Those who want to live, let them fight, and those who do not want to fight in this world of eternal struggle do not deserve to live.

Even if this were hard—that is how it is! Assuredly, however, by far the harder fate is that which strikes the man who thinks he can overcome Nature, but in the last analysis only mocks her. Distress, misfortune, and diseases are her answer.

The man who misjudges and disregards the racial laws actually forfeits the happiness that seems destined to be his. He thwarts the triumphal march of the best race and hence also the precondition for all human progress, and remains, in consequence, burdened with all the sensibility of man, in the animal realm of helpless misery.

It is idle to argue which race or races were the original representative 30 of human culture and hence the real founders of all that we sum up under the word *humanity*. It is simpler to raise the question with regard to the present, and here an easy, clear answer results. All the human culture, all the results of art, science, and technology that we see before us today, are almost exclusively the creative product of the Aryan. This very fact admits of the not unfounded inference that he alone was the founder of all higher humanity, therefore representing the prototype of all that we understand by the word *man*. He is the Prometheus of mankind from whose bright forehead the divine spark of genius has sprung at all times, forever kindling anew that fire of knowledge which illumined the night of silent mysteries and thus caused man to climb the path to mastery over the other beings of this earth. Exclude him—and perhaps after a few thousand years darkness will again descend on the earth, human culture will pass, and the world turn to a desert.

READING AND DISCUSSION QUESTIONS

1. Find places in the essay where Hitler attempts to emphasize the scientific objectivity of his theories.

2. Are some passages difficult to understand? (See, for example, para. 11.) How do you explain the difficulty?

3. In explaining his ideology, how does Hitler misinterpret the statement that "Every animal mates only with a member of the same species" (para. 3)? How would you characterize this fallacy?

4. Hitler uses the theory of evolution and his interpretation of the "survival of the fittest" to justify his racial philosophy. Find the places in the text where Hitler reveals that he misunderstands the theory in its application to human beings.

5. What false evidence about race does Hitler use in his assessment of the racial experience in North America? Examine carefully the last sentence of paragraph 11: "The Germanic inhabitant of the American continent, who has remained racially pure and unmixed, rose to be master of the continent; he will remain the master as long as he does not fall a victim to defilement of the blood."

6. What criticism of Jews does Hitler offer? How does this criticism help to explain Hitler's pathological hatred of Jews?

7. Hitler believes that pacifism is a violation of "Nature and reason" (para. 21). Would modern scientists agree that the laws of nature require unremitting struggle and conflict between human beings—until the master race conquers?

WRITING SUGGESTION

8. Do some research in early human history to discover the degree of truth in this statement: "All the human culture, all the results of art, science, and technology that we see before us today, are almost exclusively the creative product of the Aryan" (para. 30). You may want to limit your discussion to one area of human culture.

A Reasonable Life

FERENC MÁTÉ

A recent Department of Education report was released after extensively surveying nine million school kids. Eighth graders were asked how often in the last six months they had talked to a parent about their schoolwork. Half of them responded, "Once or twice, or not at all." And one-third responded, "Never." This is madness. What do we talk to them about? Haircuts? Sunglasses? Somebody's latest facial relocation? Do we talk at all? Or have we simply, under the relentless, crushing demand of longer and longer hours of commuting and work, and the grueling task of keeping up premises and appearances, become completely deaf and dumb, save for our prerecorded patter about the weather, baseball scores, and new weeds in the lawn? Have we taken a cue from junk bonds, junk food, junk mail, and junked our minds as well?

It is no mystery where our children learned not to use their minds: from us. According to a 1988 National Geographic survey, fully half of all Americans didn't know that the then Soviet Union was in the Warsaw Pact. In fact, one out of ten actually believed that America was. Six out of ten did not know the population of the United States, and half of them didn't know that Contras and Sandinistas had been fighting in Nicaragua. Now these might not have been life-and-death issues to them, but when the government had been spending nearly half of their tax dollars protecting them from the Warsaw Pact and the Sandinista devils, one would think that, if nothing else, simple curiosity about where their money is being flushed would keep them in touch with the outside world. The rest of their ignorance our children picked up on their own. They never had to think. From earliest childhood they have been *told* everything by television, advertising, teachers, and politicians.

I think most of us agree that fundamental social changes have to come. But those will take time. There are changes that we need to make at once before another generation of our children wastes away. Major social and physical menaces have bloomed in our society these last few decades to which our schools have reacted barely at all, while at the same time they have embraced all technical innovation as the newest savior. These threats have to be addressed and countered and the earlier we start the better. Call them Survival Studies, or Social Self-Defense. They should start in kindergarten.

Ferenc Máté was born in Hungary. Escaping at the age of eleven after the suppression of the Revolution of 1956, he has lived in Vancouver, New York, and Paris. Reprinted here are excerpts from his eighth book, *A Reasonable Life: Toward a Simpler, Secure, More Humane Existence* (1997).

Livestock and Politicians   We should have a quick combined course in animal husbandry and government just so our kids could learn to distinguish good-for-the-garden bullshit from the other kind.

New-History   Given the devastation of our planet triggered by the greed and overconsumption of a relatively small number of ignorant, power-hungry "blobs," would it not make sense to teach our children not about demented kings and queens and princes of industry, and the grotesquely motivated pyramids and edifices they built in their own honor, but about the great gentle masses through the ages, the nameless, harmless humanity? Would it not make sense to teach our children how humble, simple people—the peasants, the craftsmen, the fishermen, the country doctor—managed to live through the centuries? They should be our heroes, for they have withstood endless misery at the hands of the well-remembered, with whose life stories we bore our children now.

Religious Studies   It is most curious that we leave the teachings of the kindest and wisest men of history to mostly ignored courses at universities. Would the wisdom of Buddha, Jesus, and Mohammed and the teachings of myriad native tribes, with their all-encompassing view of man, Nature, life, and the universe, not be an infinitely more sound foundation for our children than obscure details about which insecure, jingoistic runt defeated which rabid loony where?

It is this lack of an overview of life, this lack of an attempt to give an overall perspective to the relationship between man and man, man and the earth, man and history, that leads to a morally and philosophically hollow citizenry, led by men and women who are convinced that "A Philosophy of Life" is a long-running soap on the tube every morning.

The Environment   It is safe to say that there is no greater current threat to our children than the destruction by their elders of the world around them. To give them a broad understanding of the results of all of our actions is essential. They need to understand that no human action lives in isolation; it has a result that, in some small way, can affect us all. And small things add up.

It is time for a Children's Bill of Rights. Every child born on this Earth has a God-given right to clean air, clean water, clean food, tranquility, and unspoiled natural beauty. (And, on his birthday, all the rocky-road ice-cream he can eat.) Children should be taught that. Should be taught to demand it. Should be taught, if the need arises, to fight for it.

Along with their rights they should be taught a Bill of Responsibilities. As Solzhenitsyn so profoundly observed, "Western civilization has spent three hundred years demanding rights, with almost no mention of responsibilities." First responsibility: Think through completely what you plan to do. Second responsibility: Don't do it; there are too many people doing it already. You'll just end up making a mess and who'll clean up after you? You lived fine without it so far, so why bother? Have another beer.

Farming   Every child, by the time he leaves elementary school, should know first hand—*not from bloody video!*—how to grow his own food, raise chickens, and cook them, so that when this crack-a-joke, house-of-gadgets of a society crumbles, and the last investment banker lies dead of starvation in front of an empty deli, he can be happily whistling in the fields with his little hoe.

Building   And know how to build his own house out of wood, stone, sticks, and mud.

It is not difficult to figure out what constitutes a reasonable life. You can, if you like pain, do it by elimination, by listing your daily activities and asking yourself "How does it feel?"

1. Being shocked awake from a deep sleep in middream by a heartless gadget every morning. Answer: Torture.

2. Breaking Olympic records in the Career-Octathelon: rising, crawling, dumping, showering, shaving, clipping nose hairs, gray-suiting (or Nair-ing, spraying-hair-until-bullet-proof-helmet, clown-facing, and dressing), chomping, slurping, cursing, and dashing to car. Answer: Humiliating.

3. Lurching, stopping, bumping, gridlocking while holding back caffeine rush so you don't tear off your car roof and serial-kill the first hundred people you find. Answer: Trying.

4. Being locked in office or factory with the boss hovering over you, smiling when you need to scream, nodding politely when you want to smash his nose flat with your forehead. Answer: Unbearable.

5. Lunching lumpy tepid mush with the combined fragrance of Pine-Scent and puppy chow. Answer: Don't remind me.

6. Repeating all of the above 10,000 times before you die. Answer: No way!

Or you can simply ask yourself what you would like to do if you could retire today. Most people would say, "Get a little house with a garden in the country or in a small town and live happily ever after."

So what are you waiting for? Why not sell the house, pack up the kids, kiss the boss goodbye, and head for the hills?

For economic security, emotional calm, diversity of work, and living in complete harmony with nature, nothing can surpass the classic, mostly self-sufficient, country family. As John Berger said, "It is the only class of people with a built-in resistance to consumerism." And it also has a built-in resistance to unemployment, recessions, inflation, deflation, traffic jams, and crime. In other words, it is the only class with a built-in ability to tell the hectic, frantic world to drop dead! How can *anything* feel better than that?!

And the social strength of the self-sufficient family is even greater. There simply exists no tighter or more stable social unit than a country family and its neighbors, all of whom share the same problems, same hopes, same harvests, and same droughts. After a lifetime of research in both psychology and anthropology, Carl Jung found the hamlet or village to be the ideal human habitation. So did Lewis Mumford, who spent the last decades of his life in upstate New York in his beloved hamlet of Amenia.

Eventually society will change—it will have to. It will realize that neither environmental salvation nor our social happiness lies in monstrous, impersonal cities, but out in the country in close contact with Nature, real neighbors, and our real selves. But if we sit and wait for the sick behemoth of a world to awaken and change direction, we'll all die of old age before it turns its head. If you want to have a reasonable life you will have to go and find it for yourself. You won't have far to look.

Small towns in North America are dying—except for those that have become quaint shopping malls for the rich, and are already dead. Some of the others want to be revitalized so badly, welcome strangers with such open arms, that they even offer free housing for those who venture there. And as for good land, no place offers more than North America. Nor is there a broader choice of vegetation and climate anywhere.

I realize that most of you will recoil in mortal terror at the mere thought of having torn from you the wonders of the city—steady job, museums, operas, Dunkin' Donuts—but I assure you life goes on without them. And is better. Much more satisfying replacements await you in the country. . . .

It can be done.

Your immediate fearful cry will be that you are by profession a computer RAM-byter microfries boot-chipper—and how in God's name can you survive in the country? Easy. Because long before you became any of the above obscenities, you were a perfectly normal human being to whom digging, hoeing, gathering, and hammer-swinging come infinitely more naturally than does byting RAMs. And the best way to learn to do something is by doing it. You don't need a million magazines, books, or videos to teach you; the best book on each subject will do. But you will need some clear thinking, imagination, and good old-fashioned common sense. If you're stuck, look around. Go visit and ask questions. It's a good way to meet the neighbors and people love to help. And the more you can learn from those around you, especially those who have lived and worked on the land and know the soil, know the seasons, the more confident and comfortable you will be.

But no matter how expert you become at self-sufficiency, you will not be able to grow bathroom taps or light bulbs. Hence the need for supplementary cash. The most important step is to ween yourself off the things that cost money. Your TV should stay where it belongs—in the factory in Japan. Not only won't you waste money buying it, but you also won't be tempted by the tons of gaudy rubble it tries to sell. Try to make some of the simple things you need. It's a lot more fun than shelling out money at a store, you'll feel a lot prouder of it, and you will probably never replace it because you're much too vain to throw out your precious handiwork.

There is no need to go to extremes. You need not try to make a watch 30 from old car parts, nor eyeglasses from a pile of sand. But you can easily reinvent things that you now see only in old movies, like sewing on a button instead of throwing out the shirt, patching holes in clothes, or even sewing them from scratch, darning, knitting, toy-making, furniture-making, preserving fruit and vegetables, and, as a last resort, cooking.

The cash that you do need can be found both in small towns and in the country, although admittedly in smaller quantities than in the city, but, as I said, you will need much less. The most important thing to realize, especially for those who think the country has no jobs, is that there are a jillion jobs but not the kind that require eight hours a day until you die. So while there might be no room for an entire accountant, there will certainly be work for a tenth of one. And while a full-time notary or lawyer or mortician would starve, a fifth or a tenth of each would thrive. On Fred Smith's island, a desktop publisher drives the ambulance and is the local fax man. In other words, specialists beware, but generalists who can combine, say, brain surgery with a little tree pruning and sausage-making will get on just fine.

The best part of having a wide range of jobs is not only that variety is the spice of life, but also that in variety lies security. If the demand for brain surgery diminishes, the demand for sausages might rise, and so on. . . .

Some people would object on a historical basis, saying that country life has been a dead-end in the past. While that may have been true forty years ago, it is no more. We have made great leaps in small equipment such as inexpensive motor-tillers, more hardy varieties of plants, good organic pest-control information, excellent soil conservation information, speedy transportation to market (and the tourist market coming to your door), and the ever-growing demand for tasty, healthy, unpesti-cided food. And even more important are the new portable jobs made possible by fax machines, computers, modems, and general technology that provide today's country life with more potential and variety than was ever dreamed of in the past.

So there you have it—a few things to escape to. Of course there are others; cabins in the woods, fishing boats, sailboats, and desert islands. But if you find the notion of immediately cutting city ties and heading for the hills far-fetched, too drastic, too irreversible, then at least do this: dump the TV set; cut up all credit cards, coupons, green stamps, cross-word puzzles; cancel all subscriptions, prescriptions, addictions, member-ships, affiliations, commitments and obligations, aerobics classes, kung fu classes, shrink appointments, hair appointments, and the ten-part doggy-dancing lessons you gave Fido for Christmas, and go home after work, just sit there in the dark, and try to figure out what this madness is all about. And what, if anything, it has to do with you. You might just come up with a better, more reasonable life. . . .

In a reasonable world, the need for taxes would be greatly reduced, as 35 would the need for governments that spend them. With small communities nearly self-reliant, or reliant only on neighbors, and everyone known by and dependent on those around him, our million fatuous laws could be sent to museum shelves. Reasonable, decent human conduct would be taught and enforced by all. We could once again become like the truly democratic corners of 1800s America, where, "Each citizen developed his civic mores informally, through conversations on street corners or in the square; in the day-to-day encounters in the shops; on the walks that took him past public buildings and houses of worship and settings of great natural beauty—that took him, if only for a moment, out of his private self."

What central governments remained would no longer be led by the belligerent, mentally limited, and emotionally callow of recent history, who attained their posts only through zeal for power, political conniving, and vicious public relations. They would be led by the truly wise, who have shown ability and deep concern for humanity through their lives. Candidates would not emerge after years of favor-gaining, kowtowing, and vulgar fund-raising, which gives those who promised Big Money the most, an advantage. They would be nominated by a Nobel-type committee, made up of the nation's most thoughtful citizens, who would base their decisions on a life of merit. The candidates could skip the year of numbing travel, posing, grinning, raving, glad-handing, posturing, and, as Bill Clinton said, "Learning nothing." They would instead, as we all had to do in school, write a simple, clear, easy-to-read essay (without the aid of speechwriters and hucksters) which, before being presented to the nation, would be examined by an esteemed, knowledgeable academy, judged for comprehension of problems and the feasibility of offered remedies. In other words, the academy would edit out the bullshit. This short and lucid essay, in point form if need be, conspicuously free of resonating moronities such as "It's morning in America" and "A thousand points of light," could then be presented to all, before election time. They could be discussed point by point, in family circles, on front porches, hamlet greens, shops, or village squares, without confounding advertising that, along with special interest and lobby groups, would be exiled to Saint Helena. An oral test would make sure the candidates comprehend their duties. We would then no longer have photo-op celebrities as leaders but true public *servants,* whose concentrated efforts go to making our schools and hospitals as sacred as banks and malls, and to keeping our streets swept and the sewers flowing. No less and no more.

READING AND DISCUSSION QUESTIONS

1. Find examples in paragraphs 25 to 36 of the following logical fallacies and other weaknesses of argumentation: (1) exaggeration, (2) name-

calling, (3) false dilemma, (4) slippery slope, (5) failure to define terms, (6) selective use of examples and quotations.

2. What aspects of American life does Máté criticize? Pick the specific aspects with which you agree and disagree, and provide examples from your own experience.

3. What is your reaction to the author's humor, or attempts at humor? Is it effective as argument? Why or why not?

4. Does the school curriculum described in paragraphs 3 to 12 sound practical? Can you point out strengths and weaknesses?

5. How would you characterize the election process described in paragraphs 35 and 36? Does it represent an improvement over today's practices? What would you include in a "simple, clear, easy-to-read essay" (para. 36) that would satisfy a knowledgeable academy and help ensure your election? How long would it have to be?

6. At times the author seems indifferent to history, science, and art. Where are "the great gentle masses" (para. 5)? Were food and air in the past always "clean" (para. 9)? If life on the farm or in the village was so satisfying, why have many millions of people deserted that life for the city? How would the author answer the economists who can explain the advantages of division of labor? Why does he lump museums and operas together with Dunkin' Donuts?

WRITING SUGGESTIONS

7. *A Reasonable Life* describes one man's ideal society. For more than two thousand years people have written about ideal societies or utopias. (*Utopia*, a word coined by Sir Thomas More in 1516 to describe such a community, means "nowhere" in Greek.) What aspects of present-day life would be very different in a utopia of your own creation? Among many other things, writers and filmmakers who design utopias treat education, courtship and marriage, child rearing, religion, form of government, and personal freedom. Describe your ideal version of something you feel strongly about.

8. *Dystopia* is the opposite of the ideal society. You may be familiar with *Nineteen Eighty-Four* by George Orwell, *Brave New World* by Aldous Huxley, and *Walden Two* by B. F. Skinner—books about societies created by behavioral engineering. Many contemporary science fiction novels and films also describe a world gone terribly wrong. If you have read or seen any of these works, choose one (or more), and tell how it reflects our fears of certain trends and changes in modern life.

9. The author of *A Reasonable Life* thinks that life in the country or a village is superior in almost every way to life in the city. Write an argument defending your own preference.

CHERYL SILAS had a highway collision, was hit twice from behind, and then sold three cars for us.

When Cheryl unbuckled her shoulder harness and lap belt, it took her a moment to realize her Saturn coupe was really a mess. And that, remarkably, she wasn't. That's when she decided to get another SC.

Several other people arrived at similar conclusions. A policeman at the accident scene came in soon after and ordered himself a sedan. As did a buddy of his, also on the force. Then Cheryl's brother, glad he still had a sister, bought yet another Saturn in Illinois.

Now, good referrals are important to any product. And we're always glad to have them. But we'd be more than happy if our customers found less dramatic ways to help spread the word.

A DIFFERENT KIND of COMPANY. A DIFFERENT KIND of CAR.

© 1991 Saturn Corporation. M.S.R.P. of 1992 Saturn SC shown is $12,415, including retailer prep and optional sunroof. Tax, license, transportation and other options additional. If you'd like to know more about Saturn, and our new sedans and coupe, please call us at 1-800-522-5000.

DISCUSSION QUESTIONS

1. What example of inductive reasoning does the advertiser use? How would you evaluate the probability of the conclusion?

2. To what extent does the use of an alleged real person in a narrative contribute to the effectiveness of the advertiser's pitch? Should the ad have contained more factual information?

DEBATE: Should We Have a National Identification Card to Fight Terrorism?

National IDs Won't Work

LORRAINE WOELLERT

With the public still shaken by the World Trade Center attack and spooked by a growing number of anthrax scares, the clamor for tighter security is growing. Suitcase searches, closed streets, and a cop on every corner just aren't enough to settle jittery psyches. So we keep looking for ways to reassure ourselves and to soothe complicated new fears.

One idea — a national identification card that presumably would separate law-abiding citizens from dangerous infiltrators — is being promoted as a tool to reduce the threat of terrorism. But it's no silver bullet. A national ID card would rip at the fabric of our constitutional freedoms. It would cost billions and be technologically imperfect. Most troubling, it would lull the populace into a false sense of security.

First off, what would you need to get an ID card? A birth certificate and driver's license? Anyone — including terrorists — can obtain or alter such documents. Several of the men suspected of the September 11 attacks had forged identities. What would have prevented them from obtaining ID cards? And what of domestic terrorists Theodore Kaczynski and Timothy McVeigh?

To guard against counterfeiting, the card would need to be encoded with biometric data such as a fingerprint, retinal scan, or blood sample — yet these come with high failure rates. "Biometrics are fallible," says Professor David J. Farber, a technology expert at the University of Pennsylvania. He says fingerprints are reasonably good if you have an expensive reader. But hand readers fail frequently, facial recognition is new and buggy, and retinal scans are costly. "If this is a first-line defense, you can afford a lot of errors, but only if they're errors that reject. If they're errors that accept, [the cards are] useless," he says. In any case, these systems count on a nonforgeable ID card, and the technology involved for that can be prohibitively expensive, adds Farber.

Even simple data-storage cards, at $10 to $35, don't come cheap. 5 Multiply that by 280 million Americans. Add the cost of card readers. Pay staff and overhead. The bottom line: a multibillion-dollar system that will take years to deploy and a well-funded bureaucracy to operate.

Then there's the Big Brother problem. A national ID card would eventually become as ubiquitous as the Social Security number and could

Lorraine Woellert covers politics from *BusinessWeek*'s Washington, D.C., bureau. This article and the one following appeared in the November 5, 2001, issue of *BusinessWeek*.

be required for everyday life in the new age of terror. Want to enter the Lincoln Tunnel to New York? Send a package? Register for school? Buy a computer? No can do without an ID card. "This will quickly become a mandatory system," says Barry Steinhardt, associate director of the American Civil Liberties Union.

Checks

Taken to the extreme, a smart card could record your ethnicity, religion, political leanings, or favorite cereal. And at every turn, government agencies, employers, banks, insurance and health-care companies, and grocery stores would pressure you to add data to your life-on-a-chip. A prospective employer using the card to check your citizenship might notice that you vote in Democratic primaries—since the ID is required when you go to the polls. Hmm, maybe you aren't a good fit for this company. What about that prescription you're taking to control schizophrenia—part of the medical record that your health-care provider insists must be on your card? Airport security might decide you're unfit to fly. "We need to very carefully think through what our objective is," says William P. Crowell, former director of the National Security Agency and head of Cylink Corp., a Santa Clara (Calif.) technology company. "Let's make sure . . . use of the card is limited to [that] purpose before moving ahead."

Therein lies the irony: The more robust the card is, the more faith the public will put in it. That, in turn, increases its vulnerability. "The more people assume the card is good, the less they will check you out, and the easier it becomes to slip someone past the system," says Professor Jonathan S. Shapiro of Johns Hopkins University. In other words, that false sense of security might only leave us more vulnerable to further terrorist attacks.

Yes, They Certainly Will

PAUL MAGNUSSON

Sorry, Lorraine, but the great debate over a national ID card has already been decided. We have fifty different varieties of driver's licenses. They're already required to cash checks, get a post office box, board an airplane, buy beer, register to vote, enroll in college, and even drive a car.

Paul Magnusson covers international trade and economics in Washington, D.C., for *BusinessWeek*.

But our makeshift system isn't working very well. Most licenses are easily altered or counterfeited. They're dumb, too: Little or no information is encoded in bar codes, magnetic strips, or smart computer chips. They're a necessary nuisance, basically.

In the wake of September 11, people are being asked for a picture ID so often that the real question is no longer whether to have a national ID card. Rather, it's how to improve on our haphazard system, without encountering huge expense or encouraging Big Brother to trample on the Bill of Rights.

Raising Questions

The defense against terrorism provides a compelling argument for national ID cards that could be required for various transactions. At least two of the September 11 terrorists were on an Immigration and Naturalization Service watch list of suspects, and still they flew around the United States, used credit cards, had bank accounts, cell phones, and frequent-flier memberships, and took flying lessons. National IDs might well have raised questions when the hijackers were buying airline tickets, since some had apparently overstayed their visas.

Ingenious new technologies could make ID cards more secure, useful, 5 and palatable to civil libertarians. Smart chips similar to those embedded in subway fare cards can hold digital photographs, thumbprints, or even retinal scans for foolproof identification. That's useful for a leasing company being careful about renting its new crop duster. And while the company is running your card through its reader, it can check to see if your private pilot's license is up to date. You have thoughtfully included that information as an option in order to save time. In fact, much of the information on a national ID card could be voluntary.

Actually, a national ID card is where emerging smart-chip technology, consumer convenience, and the fight against terrorism can all come together. Having trouble remembering your blood type or medical-insurance provider? Put it on the card for hospital emergency-room personnel to download on a reader employing a special encryption program for sensitive medical information. You might also include drug allergies and data concerning your next of kin. All this is "technologically easy," insists Oracle Corp. CEO Lawrence J. Ellison.

Protection

Why not have a voluntary ID card and keep the government out of it entirely? Because to be secure, the government needs to be involved, just as the Bureau of Engraving and Printing adds those special features to $50 bills to make them so hard to duplicate. Seven percent of Americans say their personal identification papers have been stolen at one time or another. But a national ID card, protected by a 1,024-bit key code, is impossible to break "without a supercomputer working away for a hundred years," says Avivah Litan, a consultant at GartnerGroup in Stamford,

Conn. "So a national ID card would actually enhance privacy by protecting against identity theft."

In Finland, for example, the government provides smart cards to authenticate the identity of someone transacting business over the Internet. The cost: just $37, including a reader that connects to a computer in your home or office. Finns can add medical information to the cards, as well as use them to access their company's Intranet or to do their banking on the Internet.

The government also should be allowed to demand some data be included on the card. National IDs could be used to screen out felons attempting to purchase guns if criminal records were added. And smart ID cards could be required of all immigrants admitted temporarily on student, business, or tourist visas.

All this security can be had for a surprisingly small investment. 10 GartnerGroup puts the cost per card at about $8, while a commercial reader might run around $50—well worth the cost to a business the first time it detects check or identity fraud.

The trick now is to fashion a national ID system that serves security while maintaining Americans' civil liberties. Thanks to technology, that's easier than ever.

DISCUSSION QUESTIONS

1. Woellert says that an ID "would lull the populace into a false sense of security" (para. 2). What proof has she provided to support this claim?

2. How does Magnusson answer the objection that ID cards are easy to forge or alter? Are his data persuasive?

3. Both Woellert and Magnusson use expert testimony to support their arguments. How effective are these references? Do some seem more trustworthy than others?

4. Would you feel that your civil liberties were threatened if you were forced to provide the data mentioned by both authors? Is Magnusson's argument about safety reassuring? Or would you want to place limits on the information encrypted in an ID card?

TAKING THE DEBATE ONLINE

For these and additional research URLs, see www.bedfordstmartins.com/rottenberg.

- *The American Civil Liberties Union: "Why Does the ACLU Oppose a National I.D. Card System?"*
  http://www.aclu.org/library/aaidcard.html

  The ACLU has vigorously opposed the creation of a national employee I.D. number and/or card as a misplaced, superficial "quick fix" that poses serious threats to our civil liberties and civil rights.

- *New York Times: Letters to the Editor*
  http://www.nytimes.com/2001/10/16/opinion/L16DERS.html
  Readers weigh in on the merits of national identification cards.

- *New York Times: National I.D. Cards: One Size Fits All*
  http://www.nytimes.com/2001/10/07/weekinreview/07WAKI.html
  This article examines the use of national identity cards in countries other than the United States.

- *Privacy International: National I.D.*
  http://www.privacy.org/pi/activities/idcard
  This organization, devoted to raising awareness of government surveillance and privacy issues, weighs in on the identity card debate.

- *Gemplus: National Identification Cards*
  http://www.gemplus.com/app/identity/nat_id.htm
  A company that manufactures "smart" identity cards outlines the benefits of their use.

EXERCISES

Decide whether the reasoning in the following examples is faulty. Explain your answers.

1. The presiding judge of a revolutionary tribunal, on being asked why people were being executed without trial: "Why should we put them on trial when we know that they're guilty?"

2. Since good nutrition is essential to the health of its citizens, the government should punish people who eat junk food.

3. Children who watch *Frasier* rather than *Friends* receive higher grades in school. So it must be true that *Frasier* is more educational than *Friends*.

4. The meteorologist predicted the wrong amount of rain for May. Obviously the meteorologist is unreliable.

5. Women ought to be permitted to serve in combat. Why should men be the only ones to face death and danger?

6. If Cher uses Equal, it must taste better than Sweet 'n Low.

7. People will gamble anyway, so why not legalize gambling in this state?

8. Because so much money was spent on public education in the last decade while educational achievement declined, more money to improve education can't be the answer to reversing the decline.

9. He's a columnist for the campus newspaper, so he must be a pretty good writer.

10. We tend to exaggerate the need for standard English. You don't need much standard English for most jobs in this country.

11. It's discriminatory to mandate that police officers must conform to a certain height and weight.

12. A doctor can consult books to make a diagnosis, so a medical student should be able to consult books when being tested.

13. Because this soft drink contains so many chemicals, it must be unsafe.

14. Core requirements should be eliminated. After all, students are paying for their education, so they should be able to earn a diploma by choosing the courses they want.

15. We should encourage a return to arranged marriages in this country since marriages based on romantic love haven't been very successful.

16. I know three redheads who have terrible tempers, and since Annabel has red hair, I'll bet she has a terrible temper, too.

17. Supreme Court Justice Byron White was an All-American football player while at college, so how can you say that athletes are dumb?

18. Benjamin H. Sasway, a student at Humboldt State University in California, was indicted for failure to register for possible conscription. Barry Lynn, president of Draft Action, an antidraft group, said, "It is disgraceful that this administration is embarking on an effort to fill the prisons with men of conscience and moral commitment."

19. You know Jane Fonda's exercise videos must be worth the money. Look at the great shape she's in.

20. James A. Harris, former president of the National Education Association: "Twenty-three percent of schoolchildren are failing to graduate, and another large segment graduate as functional illiterates. If 23 percent of anything else failed—23 percent of automobiles didn't run, 23 percent of the buildings fell down, 23 percent of stuffed ham spoiled—we'd look at the producer."

21. A professor at Rutgers University: "The arrest rate for women is rising three times as fast as that of men. Women, inflamed by the doctrines of feminism, are pursuing criminal careers with the same zeal as business and the professions."

22. Physical education should be required because physical activity is healthful.

23. George Meany, former president of the AFL-CIO, in 1968: "To these people who constantly say you have got to listen to these younger people, they have got something to say, I just don't buy that at all. They smoke more pot than we do and if the younger generation are the hundred thousand kids that lay around a field up in Woodstock, New York, I am not going to trust the destiny of the country to that group."

24. That candidate was poor as a child, so he will certainly be sympathetic to the poor if he's elected.

25. When the federal government sent troops into Little Rock, Arkansas, to enforce integration of the public school system, the governor of Arkansas attacked the action, saying that it was as brutal an act of intervention as Russia's sending troops into Hungary to squelch the Hungarians' rebellion. In both cases, the governor said, the rights of a freedom-loving, independent people were being violated.

26. Governor Jones was elected two years ago. Since that time constant examples of corruption and subversion have been unearthed. It is time to get rid of the man responsible for this kind of corrupt government.

27. Are we going to vote a pay increase for our teachers, or are we going to allow our schools to deteriorate into substandard custodial institutions?

28. You see, the priests were right. After we threw those virgins into the volcano, it quit erupting.

29. The people of Rome lost their vitality and desire for freedom when their emperors decided that the way to keep them happy was to provide them with bread and circuses. What can we expect of our own country now that the government gives people free food and there is a constant round of entertainment provided by television?

30. From Mark Clifton, "The Dread Tomato Affliction" (proving that eating tomatoes is dangerous and even deadly): "Ninety-two point four percent of juvenile delinquents have eaten tomatoes. Fifty-seven point one percent of the adult criminals in penitentiaries throughout the United States have eaten tomatoes. Eighty-four percent of all people killed in automobile accidents during the year have eaten tomatoes."

31. From Galileo, *Dialogues Concerning Two New Sciences*: "But can you doubt that air has weight when you have the clear testimony of Aristotle affirming that all elements have weight, including air, and excepting only fire?"

32. Robert Brustein, artistic director of the American Repertory Theatre, commenting on a threat by Congress in 1989 to withhold funding from an offensive art show: "Once we allow lawmakers to become art critics, we take the first step into the world of Ayatollah Khomeini, whose murderous review of *The Satanic Verses* still chills the heart of everyone committed to free expression." (The Ayatollah Khomeini called for the death of the author, Salman Rushdie, because he had allegedly committed blasphemy against Islam in his novel.)

CRITICAL LISTENING

33. Listen carefully to a speech by a candidate for public office. Note any fallacies or lapses in logical thinking. Do some kinds of fallacies seem more common than others?

PART TWO

Writing, Researching, and Presenting Arguments

9

Writing an Argumentative Paper

The person who understands how arguments are constructed has an important advantage in today's world. Television commercials, political speeches, newspaper editorials, and magazine advertisements, as well as many communications between individuals, all draw on the principles we have examined in the preceding chapters. By now you should be fairly adept at picking out claims, support, and warrants (explicit or unstated) in these presentations. The next step is to apply your skills to writing an argument of your own. The process of using what you have learned will enhance your ability to analyze critically the marketing efforts with which we are all bombarded every day. Mastering the writing of arguments also gives you a valuable tool for communicating with other people in school, on the job, and even at home.

In this chapter we move through the various stages involved in creating an argumentative paper: choosing a topic, defining the issues, organizing the material, writing the essay, and revising. We also consider the more general question of how to use the principles already discussed in order to convince a real audience. The more carefully you follow the guidelines set out here and the more thought you give to your work at each point, the better you will be able to utilize the art of argument when this course is over.

FINDING AN APPROPRIATE TOPIC

An old British recipe for jugged hare is said to begin, "First, catch your hare." To write an argumentative paper, you first must choose your topic. This is a relatively easy task for someone writing an argument as part of his or her job—a lawyer defending a client, for example, or an advertising executive presenting a campaign. For a student, however, it can be daunting. Which of the many ideas in the world worth debating would make a good subject?

Several guidelines can help you evaluate the possibilities. Perhaps your assignment limits your choices. If you have been asked to write a research paper, you obviously must find a topic on which research is available. If your assignment is more open-ended, you need a topic that is worth the time and effort you expect to invest in it. In either case, your subject should be one that interests you. Don't feel you have to write about what you know—very often finding out what you don't know will turn out to be more satisfying. You should, however, choose a subject that is familiar enough for you to argue about without fearing you're in over your head.

■ Invention Strategies

As a starting point, think of conversations you've had in the past few days or weeks that have involved defending a position. Is there some current political issue you're concerned about? Some dispute with friends that would make a valid paper topic? One of the best sources is controversies in the media. Keep your project in mind as you watch TV, read, or listen to the radio. You may even run into a potential subject in your course reading assignments or classroom discussions. Fortunately for the would-be writer, nearly every human activity includes its share of disagreement.

As you consider possible topics, write them down. One that looks unlikely at first glance may suggest others or may have more appeal when you come back to it later. Further, simply putting words on paper has a way of stimulating the thought processes involved in writing. Even if your ideas are tentative, the act of converting them into phrases or sentences can often help in developing them.

■ Evaluating Possible Topics

Besides interesting you, your topic must interest your audience. Who is the audience? For a lawyer it is usually a judge or jury; for a columnist, anyone who reads the newspaper in which his or her column appears. For the student writer, the audience is to some extent hypothetical. You should assume that your paper is directed at readers who are reasonably intelligent and well informed, but who have no specific knowledge of the subject. It may be useful to imagine you are writing for a local or school publication—this may be the case if your paper turns out well.

Be sure, too, that you choose a topic with two sides. The purpose of an argument is to defend or refute a thesis, which means the thesis must be debatable. In evaluating a subject that looks promising, ask yourself: Can a case be made for the opposing view? If not, you have no workable ground for building your own case.

Finally, check the scope of your thesis. Consider how long your paper will be, and whether you can do justice to your topic in that amount of space. For example, suppose you want to argue in favor of worldwide nuclear disarmament. Is this a thesis you can support persuasively in a short paper? One way to find out is by listing the potential issues or points about which arguers might disagree. Consider the thesis: "The future of the world is in danger as long as nuclear weapons exist." Obviously this statement is too general. You would have to specify what you mean by the future of the world (the continuation of human life? of all life? of the earth itself?) and exactly how nuclear weapons endanger it before the claim would hold up. You could narrow it down: "Human beings are error-prone; therefore as long as nuclear weapons exist there is the chance that a large number of people will be killed accidentally." Though this statement is more specific and includes an important warrant, it still depends on other unstated warrants: that one human being (or a small group) is in the position to discharge a nuclear weapon capable of killing a large number of people; that such a weapon could, in fact, be discharged by mistake, given current safety systems. Can you expect to show sufficient evidence for these assumptions in the space available to you?

By now it should be apparent that arguing in favor of nuclear disarmament is too broad an undertaking. A more workable approach might be to defend or refute one of the disarmament proposals under consideration by the U.S. Congress, or to show that nuclear weapons pose some specific danger (such as long-term water pollution) that is sufficient reason to strive for disarmament.

Can a thesis be too narrow? Certainly. If this is true of the one you have chosen, you probably realized it when you asked yourself whether the topic was debatable. If you can prove your point convincingly in a paragraph, or even a page, you need a broader thesis.

At this preliminary stage, don't worry if you don't know exactly how to word your thesis. It's useful to write down a few possible phrasings to be sure your topic is one you can work with, but you need not be precise. The information you unearth as you do research will help you to formulate your ideas. Also, stating a thesis in final terms is premature until you know the organization and tone of your paper.

■ To This Point

Let's assume you have surveyed a range of possible topics and chosen one that provides you with a suitable thesis for your paper. Before you go on, check your thesis against the following questions:

1. Is this topic one that will interest both me and my audience?
2. Is the topic debatable?
3. Is my thesis appropriate in scope for a paper of this length?
4. Do I know enough about my thesis to have a rough idea of what ideas to use in supporting it and how to go about finding evidence to back up these ideas?

DEFINING THE ISSUES

■ Preparing an Initial Outline

An outline, like an accounting system or a computer program, is a practical device for organizing information. Nearly every elementary and high school student learns how to make an outline. What will you gain if you outline your argument? Time and an overview of your subject. The minutes you spend organizing your subject at the outset generally save at least double the time later, when you have few minutes to spare. An outline also enables you to see the whole argument at a glance.

Your preliminary outline establishes an order of priority for your argument. Which supporting points are issues to be defended, which are warrants, and which are evidence? Which supporting points are most persuasive? By constructing a map of your territory, you can identify the research routes that are likely to be most productive. You can also pinpoint any gaps in your reasoning.

List each issue as a main heading in your outline. Next, write below it any relevant support (or sources of support) that you are aware of. Then reexamine the list and consider which issues appear likely to offer the strongest support for your argument. You should number these in order of importance.

■ Computers in the Outlining Process

Word-processing software can make outlining simpler by providing an automatic outlining function. If you begin an outline with the roman numeral *I* followed by a period, many word-processing systems automatically supply *II* when you hit the enter key and move to the next line. If you have subtopics (marked by *A*s or *1*s), the outlining function will also automatically supply the next letters or numbers when you hit "Enter." This function is a simple but useful tool that can help you create hierarchies of ideas and skeletal texts.

Even more useful is the cut-and-paste function that is a part of all word-processing software because outlines are typically revised as writers discover new information and ideas or new connections between information and ideas. Revising outlines—experimenting with the order of ideas or with whether an idea should be a major or subpoint, for example—is easier with a computer, and the speed of cutting and pasting makes the revision process central to every part of the writing process, including outlining.

Finally, word-processing software also makes outlining done after a draft is completed much simpler. One way to see how a draft of a paper is working, for example, is to take the first (or topic) sentence of each paragraph and to put them in a list. Seeing how these individual sentences build from each other and connect to each other can help you see how the paper as a whole is working. If done with a pen, such a process can be time-consuming, but cutting and pasting by computer makes this helpful strategy easy.

■ Case Study: Coed Bathrooms

To see how we raise and evaluate issues in a specific context, let's look at a controversy that surfaced recently at a large university. Students living in coed dorms elected to retain their coed bathrooms. The university administration, however, withdrew its approval, in part because of growing protests from parents and alumni.

The students raised these issues:

1. The rights of students to choose their living arrangements
2. The absence of coercion on those who did not wish to participate
3. The increase in civility between the sexes as a result of sharing accommodations
4. The practicality of coed bathrooms, which preclude the necessity for members of one sex to travel to a one-sex bathroom on another floor
5. The success of the experiment so far

On the other side, the administration introduced the following issues:

1. The role of the university *in loco parentis*
2. The necessity for the administration to retain the goodwill of parents and alumni
3. The dissatisfaction of some students with the arrangement
4. The inability of immature students to respect the right of others and resist the temptation of sexual activity

Now let's analyze these issues, comparing their strengths and weaknesses.

1. It is clear that not all the issues in this dispute were equally important. The arguers decided, therefore, to give greater emphasis to the issues that were most likely to be ultimately persuasive to their audiences and less attention to those that were difficult to prove or narrower in their appeal. The issue of convenience, for example, seemed a minor point. How much cost is imposed in being required to walk up or down a flight of stairs?

2. It was also clear that, as in several of the other cases we have examined, the support consisted of both factual data and appeals to values. In regard to the factual data, each side reported evidence to prove that

a. The experiment was or was not a success.

b. Civility had or had not increased.

c. The majority of students did or did not favor the plan.

d. Coercion had or had not been applied.

The factual data were important. If the administration could prove that the interests of some students had been injured, then the student case for coed bathrooms would be weakened.

But let us assume that the factual claims either were settled or remained in abeyance. We now turn our attention to a second set of issues, a contest over the values to be served.

3. Both sides claimed adherence to the highest principles of university life. Here the issues, while no easier to resolve, offered greater opportunity for serious and fruitful discussion.

The first question to be resolved was that of democratic control. The students asserted, "We should be permitted to have coed bathrooms because we can prove that the majority of us want them." The students hoped that the university community would agree with the implied analogy: that the university community should resemble a political democracy and that students should have full rights as citizens of that community. (This is an argument also made in regard to other areas of university life.)

The university denied that it was a democracy in which students had equal rights and insisted that it should not be. The administration offered its own analogical proof: Students are not permitted to hire their own teachers or to choose their manner of instruction, their courses of study, their grades, or the rules of admission. The university, they insisted, represented a different kind of community, like a home, in which the experienced are required to lead and instruct the inexperienced.

Students responded by pointing out that coed bathrooms or any other aspect of their living arrangements were areas in which *they* were experts and that freedom to choose living arrangements was not to be confused with a demand for equal participation in academic matters. Moreover, it was also true that in recent years the verdict had increasingly been rendered in favor of rights of special groups as against those of institutions. Students' rights have been among those that have benefited from the movement toward freedom of choice.

4. The second issue was related to the first but introduced a practical consideration, namely, the well-being of the university. The administration argued that more important than the wishes of the students in this essentially minor dispute was the necessity for retaining the support and goodwill of parents and alumni, who are ultimately responsible for the very existence of the university.

The students agreed that this support was necessary but felt that parents and alumni could be persuaded to consider the good reasons in the students' argument. Some students were inclined to carry the argument over goals even further. They insisted that if the university could maintain its existence only at the cost of sacrificing principles of democracy and freedom, then perhaps the university had forfeited its right to exist.

In making our way through this debate, we have summarized a procedure for tackling the issues in any controversial problem.

1. Raise the relevant issues and arrange them in order of importance. Plan to devote more time and space to issues you regard as crucial.

2. Produce the strongest evidence you can to support your factual claims, knowing that the opposing side or critical readers may try to produce conflicting evidence.

3. Defend your value claims by finding support in the fundamental principles with which most people in your audience would agree.

4. Argue with yourself. Try to foresee what kinds of refutation are possible. Try to anticipate and meet the opposing arguments.

ORGANIZING THE MATERIAL

Once you are satisfied that you have identified all the issues that will appear in your paper, you should begin to determine what kind of organization will be most effective for your argument. Now is the time to organize the results of your thinking into a logical and persuasive form. If you have read about your topic, answered questions, and acquired some evidence, you may already have decided on ways to approach your subject. If not, you should look closely at your outline now, recalling your purposes when you began your investigation, and develop a strategy for using the information you have gathered to achieve those purposes.

The first point to establish is what type of thesis you plan to present. Is your intention to make readers aware of some problem? To offer a solution to the problem? To defend a position? To refute a position held by others? The way you organize your material will depend to a great extent on your goal. With that goal in mind, look over your outline and reevaluate the relative importance of your issues. Which ones are most convincing? Which are backed up by the strongest support? Which ones relate to facts, and which concern values?

With these points in mind, let us look at various ways of organizing an argumentative paper. It would be foolish to decide in advance how many paragraphs a paper ought to have; however, you can and should choose a general strategy before you begin writing. If your thesis presents an opinion or recommends some course of action, you may choose simply to state your main idea and then defend it. If your thesis argues against an opposing view, you probably will want to mention that view and then refute it. Both these organizations introduce the thesis in the first or second paragraph (called the *thesis paragraph*). A third possibility is to start establishing that a problem exists and then introduce your thesis as the solution; this method is called *presenting the stock issues*. Although these three approaches sometimes overlap in practice, examining each one individually can help you structure your paper. Let's take a look at each arrangement.

■ Defending the Main Idea

All forms of organization will require you to defend your main idea, but one way of doing this is simple and direct. Early in the paper state the main idea that you will defend throughout your argument. You can also indicate here the two or three points you intend to develop in support of your claim; or you can raise these later as they come up. Suppose your thesis is that widespread vegetarianism would solve a number of problems. You could phrase it this way: "If the majority of people in this country adopted a vegetarian diet, we would see improvements in the economy, in the health of our people, and in moral sensitivity." You would then develop each of the claims in your list with appropriate data and warrants. Notice that the thesis statement in the first (thesis) paragraph has already outlined your organizational pattern.

Defending the main idea is effective for factual claims as well as policy claims, in which you urge the adoption of a certain policy and give the reasons for its adoption. It is most appropriate when your thesis is straightforward and can be readily supported by direct statements.

■ Refuting the Opposing View

Refuting an opposing view means to attack it in order to weaken, invalidate, or make it less credible to a reader. Since all arguments are dialogues or debates—even when the opponent is only imaginary—refutation of the other point of view is always implicit in your arguments. As you write, keep in mind the issues that an opponent may raise.

You will be looking at your own argument as an unsympathetic reader may look at it, asking yourself the same kinds of critical questions and trying to find its weaknesses in order to correct them. In this way every argument you write becomes a form of refutation.

How do you plan a refutation? Here are some general guidelines.

1. If you want to refute the argument in a specific essay or article, read the argument carefully, noting all the points with which you disagree. This advice may seem obvious, but it cannot be too strongly emphasized. If your refutation does not indicate scrupulous familiarity with your opponent's argument, he or she has the right to say, and often does, "You haven't really read what I wrote. You haven't really answered my argument."

2. If you think that your readers are sympathetic to the opposing view or are not familiar with it, summarize it at the beginning of your paper, providing enough information to give readers an understanding of exactly what you plan to refute. When you summarize, it's important to be respectful of the opposition's views. You don't want to alienate readers who might not agree with you at first.

3. If your argument is long and complex, choose only the most important points to refute. Otherwise the reader who does not have the original argument on hand may find a detailed refutation hard to follow. If the argument is short and relatively simple—a claim supported by only two or three points—you may decide to refute all of them, devoting more space to the most important ones.

4. Attack the principal elements in the argument of your opponent.

a. Question the evidence. (See pp. 163–69 in the text.) Question whether your opponent has proved that a problem exists.

b. Attack the warrants or assumptions that underlie the claim. (See pp. 201–02 in the text.)

c. Attack the logic or reasoning of the opposing view. (Refer to the discussion of fallacious reasoning on pp. 291–301 in the text.)

d. Attack the proposed solution to a problem, pointing out that it will not work.

5. Be prepared to do more than attack the opposing view. Supply evidence and good reasons in support of your own claim.

■ Finding the Middle Ground

Although an argument, by definition, assumes a difference of opinion, we know that opposing sides frequently find accommodation somewhere in the middle. As you mount your own argument about a controversial issue, you need not confine yourself to support of any of the differing positions. You may want to acknowledge that there is some justice on all sides and that you understand the difficulty of resolving the issue.

Consider these guidelines for an argument that offers a compromise between competing positions:

1. Early in your essay explain the opposing positions. Make clear the major differences separating the two (or more) sides.

2. Point out, whenever possible, that the opposing sides already agree to some exceptions to their stated positions. Such evidence may prove that the opposing sides are not so extreme as their advocates insist. Several commentators, writing about the budget conflict between Democrats and Republicans in late 1998, adopted this strategy, suggesting that compromise was possible because the differences were narrower than the public believed.

3. Make clear your own moderation and sympathy, your own willingness to negotiate. An example of this attitude appears in an essay on abortion in which the author infers how Abraham Lincoln might have treated the question of abortion rights.

> In this debate I have made my own position clear. It is a pro-life position (though it may not please all pro-lifers), and its model is Lincoln's position on slavery from 1854 until well into the Civil War: tolerate, restrict, discourage. Like Lincoln's, its touchstone is the common good of the nation, not the sovereign self. Like Lincoln's position, it accepts the legality but not the moral legitimacy of the institution that it seeks to contain. It invites argument and negotiation; it is a gambit, not a gauntlet.[1]

4. If you favor one side of the controversy, acknowledge that opposing views deserve to be considered. For example, in another essay on abortion, the author, who supports abortion rights, says,

> Those of us who are pro-choice must come to terms with those thoughtful pro-lifers who believe that in elevating the right to privacy above all other values, the most helpless form of humanity is left unprotected and is, in fact, defined away. They deserve to have their views addressed with sympathy and moral clarity.[2]

5. Provide evidence that accepting a middle ground can offer marked advantages for the whole society. Wherever possible, show that continued polarization can result in violence, injustice, and suffering.

6. In offering a solution that finds a common ground, be as specific as possible, emphasizing the part that you are willing to play in reach-

---

[1] George McKenna, "On Abortion: A Lincolnian Position," *The Atlantic Monthly,* September 1995, p. 68. (A gauntlet or glove is flung down in order to challenge an opponent to combat; a gambit is the opening move in a chess game, or in the words of one dictionary, "a concession that invites discussion." —ED.)

[2] Benjamin C. Schwarz, "Judge Ginsburg's Moral Myopia," *New York Times,* July 30, 1993, sec. A, p. 27.

ing a settlement. In an essay titled "Pro-Life and Pro-Choice? Yes!" the author concludes with this:

> Must those of us who abhor abortion, then, reconcile ourselves to seeing it spread unchecked? By no means. We can refuse to practice it ourselves—or, if we are male, beseech the women who carry our children to let them be born, and promise to support them, and mean it and do it. We can counsel and preach to others; those of us who are religious can pray. . . . What we must not do is ask the state to impose our views on those who disagree.[3]

On a different subject, a debate on pornography, the author, who is opposed to free distribution of obscene material, nevertheless refuses to endorse censorship.

> I think that, by enlarging the First Amendment to protect, in effect, freedom of expression, rather than freedom of speech and of the press, the courts made a mistake. The courts have made other mistakes, but I do not know a better way of defining the interests of the community than through legislation and through the courts. So I am willing to put up with things I think are wrong in the hope that they will be corrected. I know of no alternative that would always make the right decisions.[4]

■ Presenting the Stock Issues

Presenting the stock issues, or stating the problem before the solution, is a type of organization borrowed from traditional debate format. It works for policy claims when an audience must be convinced that a need exists for changing the status quo (present conditions) and for introducing plans to solve the problem. You begin by establishing that a problem exists (need). You then propose a solution (plan), which is your thesis. Finally, you show reasons for adopting the plan (advantages). These three elements—need, plan, and advantages—are called the stock issues.

For example, suppose you wanted to argue that measures for reducing acid rain should be introduced at once. You would first have to establish a need for such measures by defining the problem and providing evidence of damage. Then you would produce your thesis, a means for improving conditions. Finally you would suggest the benefits that would follow from implementation of your plan. Notice that in this organization your thesis paragraph usually appears toward the middle of your paper, although it may also appear at the beginning.

■ Ordering Material for Emphasis

Whichever way you choose to work, you should revise your outline to reflect the order in which you intend to present your thesis and supporting

---

[3] George Church, *Time*, March 6, 1995, p. 108.

[4] Ernest van den Haag, *Smashing Liberal Icons: A Collection of Debates* (Washington, D.C.: Heritage Foundation, 1981), p. 101.

ideas. Not only the placement of your thesis paragraph but also the wording and arrangement of your ideas will determine what points in your paper receive the most emphasis.

Suppose your purpose is to convince the reader that cigarette smoking is a bad habit. You might decide to concentrate on three unpleasant attributes of cigarette smoking: (1) it is unhealthy; (2) it is dirty; (3) it is expensive. Obviously, these are not equally important as possible deterrents. You would no doubt consider the first reason the most compelling, accompanied by evidence to prove the relationship between cigarette smoking and cancer, heart disease, emphysema, and other diseases. This issue, therefore, should be given greater emphasis than the others.

There are several ways to achieve emphasis. One is to make the explicit statement that you consider a certain issue the most important.

> Finally, and *most importantly*, human culture is often able to neutralize or reverse what might otherwise be genetically advantageous consequences of selfish behavior.[5]

This quotation also reveals a second way—placing the material to be emphasized in an emphatic position, either first or last in the paper. The end position, however, is generally more emphatic.

A third way to achieve emphasis is to elaborate on the material to be emphasized, treating it at greater length, offering more data and reasons for it than you give for the other issues.

■ Considering Scope and Audience

With a working outline in hand that indicates the order of your thesis and claims, you are almost ready to begin turning your notes into prose. First, however, it is useful to review the limits on your paper to be sure your writing time will be used to the best possible advantage.

The first limit involves scope. As mentioned earlier, your thesis should introduce a claim that can be adequately supported in the space available to you. If your research has opened up more aspects than you anticipated, you may want to narrow your thesis to one major subtopic. Or you could emphasize only the most persuasive arguments for your position (assuming these are sufficient to make your case) and omit the others. In a brief paper (three or four pages), three issues are probably all you have room to develop. On the other hand, if you suspect your thesis can be proved in one or two pages, look for ways to expand it. What additional issues might be brought in to bolster your argument? Alternatively, is there a larger issue for which your thesis could become a supporting idea?

Other limits on your paper are imposed by the need to make your points in a way that will be persuasive to an audience. The style and tone

[5] Peter Singer, *The Expanding Circle* (New York: New American Library, 1982), p. 171.

you choose depend not only on the nature of the subject but also on how you can best convince readers that you are a credible source. *Style* in this context refers to the elements of your prose—simple versus complex sentences, active versus passive verbs, metaphors, analogies, and other literary devices. *Tone* is the approach you take to your topic—solemn or humorous, detached or sympathetic. Style and tone together compose your voice as a writer.

Many students assume that every writer has only one voice. In fact, a writer typically adapts his or her voice to the material and the audience. Perhaps the easiest way to appreciate this is to think of two or three works by the same author that are written in different voices. Or compare the speeches of two different characters in the same story, novel, or film. Every writer has individual talents and inclinations that appear in most or all of his or her work. A good writer, however, is able to amplify some stylistic elements and diminish others, as well as to change tone, by choice.

It is usually appropriate in a short paper to choose an *expository* style, which emphasizes the elements of your argument rather than your personality. You may want to appeal to your readers' emotions as well as their intellects, but keep in mind that sympathy is most effectively gained when it is supported by believable evidence. If you press your point stridently, your audience is likely to be suspicious rather than receptive. If you sprinkle your prose with jokes or metaphors, you may diminish your credibility by detracting from the substance of your case. Both humor and analogy can be useful tools, but they should be used with discretion.

You can discover some helpful pointers on essay style by reading the editorials in newspapers such as the *New York Times,* the *Washington Post,* or the *Wall Street Journal.* The authors are typically addressing a mixed audience comparable to the hypothetical readers of your own paper. Though their approaches vary, each writer is attempting to portray himself or herself as an objective analyst whose argument deserves careful attention.

Again, remember your goals. You are trying to convince your audience of something; an argument is, by its nature, directed at people who may not initially agree with its thesis. Therefore, your voice as well as the claims you make must be convincing.

■ To This Point

The organizing steps that come between preparation and writing are often neglected. Careful planning at this stage, however, can save much time and effort later. As you prepare to start writing, you should be able to answer the following questions:

1. Is the purpose of my paper to persuade readers to accept a potentially controversial idea, to refute someone else's position, or to propose a solution to a problem?

2. Can or should my solution also incorporate elements of compromise and negotiation?

3. Have I decided on an organization that is likely to accomplish this purpose?

4. Does my outline arrange my thesis and issues in an appropriate order to emphasize the most important issues?

5. Does my outline show an argument whose scope suits the needs of this paper?

6. What questions of style and tone do I need to keep in mind as I write to ensure that my argument will be persuasive?

WRITING

■ Beginning the Paper

Having found a claim you can defend and the voice you will adopt toward your audience, you must now think about how to begin. An introduction to your subject should consist of more than just the first paragraph of your paper. It should invite the reader to give attention to what you have to say. It should also point you in the direction you will take in developing your argument. You may want to begin the actual writing of your paper with the thesis paragraph. It is useful to consider the whole paragraph rather than simply the thesis statement for two reasons. First, not all theses are effectively expressed in a single sentence. Second, the rest of the paragraph will be closely related to your statement of the main idea. You may show why you have chosen this topic or why your audience will benefit from reading your paper. You may introduce your warrant, qualify your claim, and in other ways prepare for the body of your argument. Because readers will perceive the whole paragraph as a unit, it makes sense to approach it that way.

Consider first the kind of argument you intend to present. Does your paper make a factual claim? Does it address values? Does it recommend a policy or action? Is it a rebuttal of some current policy or belief? The answers to those questions will influence the way you introduce the subject.

If your thesis makes a factual claim, you may be able to summarize it in one or two opening sentences. "Whether we like it or not, money is obsolete. The currency of today is not paper or coin, but plastic." Refutations are easy to introduce in a brief statement: "Contrary to popular views on the subject, the institution of marriage is as sound today as it was a generation ago."

A thesis that defends a value is usually best preceded by an explanatory introduction. "Some wars are morally defensible" is a thesis that can be stated as a simple declarative opening sentence. However, readers who disagree may not read any further than the first line. Someone defending this claim is likely to be more persuasive if he or she first gives an example of a situation in which war is or was preferable to peace or presents the thesis less directly.

One way to keep such a thesis from alienating the audience is to phrase it as a question. "Are all wars morally indefensible?" Still better would be to prepare for the question:

> Few if any of us favor war as a solution to international problems. We are too vividly aware of the human suffering imposed by armed conflict, as well as the political and financial turmoil that inevitably result. Yet can we honestly agree that no war is ever morally defensible?

Notice that this paragraph gains appeal from use of the first person *we*. The author implies that he or she shares the readers' feelings but has good reasons for believing those feelings are not sufficient grounds for condemning all wars. Even if readers are skeptical, the conciliatory phrasing of the thesis should encourage them to continue reading.

For any subject that is highly controversial or emotionally charged, especially one that strongly condemns an existing situation or belief, you may sometimes want to express your indignation directly. Of course, you must be sure that your indignation can be justified. The author of the following introduction, a physician and writer, openly admits that he is about to make a case that may offend readers.

> Is there any polite way to introduce today's subject? I'm afraid not. It must be said plainly that the media have done about as sorry and dishonest a job of covering health news as is humanly possible, and that when the media do not fail from bias and mendacity, they fail from ignorance and laziness.[6]

If your thesis advocates a policy or makes a recommendation, it may be a good idea, as in a value claim, to provide a short background. The following paragraph introduces an argument favoring relaxation of controls in high schools.

> "Free the New York City 275,000" read a button worn by many young New Yorkers some years ago. The number was roughly the total of students enrolled in the City's high schools.
>
> The condition of un-freedom which is described was not, however, unique to the schools of one city. According to the Carnegie Commission's comprehensive study of American public education, *Crisis in the Classroom,* public schools across the country share a common characteristic, namely, "preoccupation with order and control." The result is that students find themselves the victims of "oppressive and petty rules which give their schools a repressive, almost prison-like atmosphere."[7]

---

[6]Michael Halberstam, "TV's Unhealthy Approach to Health News," *TV Guide,* September 20–26, 1980, p. 24.

[7]Alan Levine and Eve Carey, *The Rights of Students* (New York: Avon Books, 1977), p. 11.

There are also other ways to introduce your subject. One is to begin with an appropriate quotation.

> "Reading makes a full man, conversation makes a ready man, and writing makes an exact man." So Francis Bacon told us around 1600. Recently I have been wondering how Bacon's formula might apply to present-day college students.[8]

Or you may begin with an anecdote. In the following introduction to an article about the relation between cancer and mental attitude, the author recounts a personal experience.

> Shortly after I moved to California, a new acquaintance sat in my San Francisco living room drinking rose-hip tea and chainsmoking. Like so many residents of the Golden West, Cecil was "into" all things healthy, from jogging to *shiatsu* massage to kelp. Tobacco didn't seem to fit, but he told me confidently that there was no contradiction. "It all has to do with energy," he said. "Unless you have a lot of negative energy about smoking cigarettes, there's no way they can hurt you; you won't get cancer."[9]

Finally, you may introduce yourself as the author of the claim.

> I wish to argue an unpopular cause: the cause of the old, free elective system in the academic world, or the untrammeled right of the undergraduate to make his own mistakes.[10]

> My subject is the world of Hamlet. I do not of course mean Denmark, except as Denmark is given a body by the play; and I do not mean Elizabethan England, though this is necessarily close behind the scenes. I mean simply the imaginative environment that the play asks us to enter when we read it or go to see it.[11]

You should, however, use such introductions with care. They suggest an authority about the subject that you shouldn't attempt to assume unless you can demonstrate that you are entitled to it.

■ Guidelines for Good Writing

In general, the writer of an argument follows the same rules that govern any form of expository writing. Your style should be clear and readable, your organization logical, your ideas connected by transitional phrases and sentences, your paragraphs coherent. The main difference between an argument and other kinds of expository writing, as noted earlier, is the need

[8] William Aiken, "The Conversation on Campus Today Is, Uh . . . ," *Wall Street Journal,* May 4, 1982, p. 18.

[9] Joel Guerin, "Cancer and the Mind," *Harvard Magazine,* November–December 1978, p. 11.

[10] Howard Mumford Jones, "Undergraduates on Apron Strings," *Atlantic Monthly,* October 1955, p. 45.

[11] Maynard Mack, "The World of Hamlet," *Yale Review,* June 1952, p. 502.

to persuade an audience to adopt a belief or take an action. You should assume your readers will be critical rather than neutral or sympathetic. Therefore, you must be equally critical of your own work. Any apparent gap in reasoning or ambiguity in presentation is likely to weaken the argument.

As you read the essays in this book and elsewhere, you will discover that good style in argumentative writing shares several characteristics:

- Variety in sentence structure: a mixture of both long and short sentences, different sentence beginnings

- Rich but standard vocabulary: avoidance of specialized terms unless they are fully explained, word choice appropriate to a thoughtful argument

- Use of details and examples to illustrate and clarify abstract terms, principles, and generalizations

You should take care to avoid the following:

- Unnecessary repetition: making the same point without new data or interpretation

- Exaggeration or stridency, which can create suspicion of your fairness and powers of observation

- Short paragraphs of one or two sentences, which are common in advertising and newspaper writing to get the reader's attention but are inappropriate in a thoughtful essay

In addition to these stylistic principles, seven general points are worth keeping in mind:

1. Although *you*, like *I*, should be used judiciously, it can be found even in the treatment of weighty subjects. Here is an example from an essay by the distinguished British mathematician and philosopher, Bertrand Russell.

> Suppose you are a scientific pioneer and you make some discovery of great scientific importance and suppose you say to yourself, "I am afraid this discovery will do harm": you know that other people are likely to make the same discovery if they are allowed suitable opportunities for research; you must therefore, if you do not wish the discovery to become public, either discourage your sort of research or control publication by a board of censors.[12]

Don't be afraid to use *you* or *I* when it is useful to emphasize the presence of the person making the argument.

2. Don't pad. This point should be obvious; the word *pad* suggests the addition of unnecessary material. Many writers find it tempting,

---

[12] "Science and Human Life," in *What Is Science?* edited by James R. Newman (New York: Simon and Schuster, 1955), p. 12.

however, to enlarge a discussion even when they have little more to say. It is never wise to introduce more words into a paper that has already made its point. If the paper turns out to be shorter than you had hoped, it may mean that you have not sufficiently developed the subject or that the subject was less substantial than you thought when you selected it. Padding, which is easy to detect in its repetition and sentences empty of content, weakens the writer's credibility.

3. For any absolute generalization—a statement containing words such as *all* or *every*—consider the possibility that there may be at least one example that will weaken the generalization. Such a precaution means that you won't have to backtrack and admit that your generalization is not, after all, universal. A student who was arguing against capital punishment for the reason that all killing was wrong suddenly paused in her presentation and added, "On the other hand, if given the chance, I'd probably have been willing to kill Hitler." This admission meant that she recognized important exceptions to her rule and that she would have to qualify her generalization in some significant way.

4. When offering an explanation, especially one that is complicated or extraordinary, look first for a cause that is easier to accept, one that doesn't strain credibility. (In Chapter 8, we called attention to this principle. See pp. 293–94.) For example, years ago a great many people were bemused by reports about the mysterious Bermuda Triangle, which had apparently swallowed up ships and planes since the mid-nineteenth century. The forces at work were variously described as space-time warps, UFOs that transported earthlings to other planets, and sea monsters seeking revenge. But a careful investigation revealed familiar, natural causes. A reasonable person interested in the truth would have searched for more conventional explanations before accepting the bizarre stories of extraterrestrial creatures. He or she would also exercise caution when confronted by conspiracy theories that try to account for controversial political events, such as the assassination of John F. Kennedy.

5. Check carefully for questionable warrants. Your outline should specify your warrants. When necessary, these should be included in your paper to link claims with support. Many an argument has failed because it depended on an unstated warrant with which the reader did not agree. If you were arguing for a physical education requirement at your school, you might make a good case for all the physical and psychological benefits of such a requirement. But you would certainly need to introduce and develop the warrant on which your claim was based—that it is the proper function of a college or university to provide the benefits of a physical education. Many readers would agree that physical education is valuable, but they might question the assumption that an academic institution should introduce a nonintellectual enterprise into the curriculum. At any point where you draw a controversial or tenuous conclusion, be sure your reasoning is clear and logical.

6. Avoid conclusions that are merely summaries. Summaries may be needed in long technical papers, but in brief arguments they create endings that are without force or interest. In the closing paragraph you should find a new idea that emerges naturally from the development of the whole argument.

7. Strive for a paper that is unified, coherent, and emphatic where appropriate. A *unified* paper stays focused on its goal and directs each claim, warrant, and piece of evidence toward that goal. Extraneous information or unsupported claims impair unity. *Coherence* means that all ideas are fully explained and adequately connected by transitions. To ensure coherence, give especially close attention to the beginnings and ends of your paragraphs: Is each new concept introduced in a way that shows it following naturally from the one that preceded it? *Emphasis,* as we have mentioned, is a function partly of structure and partly of language. Your most important claims should be placed where they are certain of receiving the reader's attention: key sentences at the beginning or end of a paragraph, key paragraphs at the beginning or end of your paper. Sentence structure can also be used for emphasis. If you have used several long, complex sentences, you can emphasize a significant point by stating it briefly and simply. You can also create emphasis with verbal flags, such as "The primary issue to consider . . ." or "Finally, we cannot ignore. . . ."

All clear expository prose will exhibit the qualities of unity, coherence, and emphasis. But the success of an argumentative paper is especially dependent on these qualities because the reader may have to follow a line of reasoning that is both complicated and unfamiliar. Moreover, a paper that is unified, coherent, and properly emphatic will be more readable, the first requisite of an effective argument.

REVISING

The final stage in writing an argumentative paper is revising. The first step is to read through what you have written for mistakes. Next, check your work against the guidelines listed under "Organizing the Material" and "Writing." Have you omitted any of the issues, warrants, or supporting evidence on your outline? Is each paragraph coherent in itself? Do your paragraphs work together to create a coherent paper? All the elements of the argument—the issues raised, the underlying assumptions, and the supporting material—should contribute to the development of the claim in your thesis statement. Any material that is interesting but irrelevant to that claim should be cut. Finally, does your paper reach a clear conclusion that reinforces your thesis?

Be sure, too, that the style and tone of your paper are appropriate for the topic and the audience. Remember that people choose to read an argument because they want the answer to a troubling question or the solution to a recurrent problem. Besides stating your thesis in a way that invites the reader to join you in your investigation, you must retain your audience's interest through a discussion that may be unfamiliar or contrary to their convictions. The outstanding qualities of argumentative prose style, therefore, are clarity and readability.

Style is obviously harder to evaluate in your own writing than organization. Your outline provides a map against which to check the structure of your paper. Clarity and readability, by comparison, are somewhat abstract qualities. Two procedures may be helpful. The first is to read two or three (or more) essays by authors whose style you admire and then turn back to your own writing. Awkward spots in your prose are sometimes easier to see if you get away from it and respond to someone else's perspective than if you simply keep rereading your own writing.

The second method is to read aloud. If you have never tried it, you are likely to be surprised at how valuable this can be. Again, start with someone else's work that you feel is clearly written, and practice until you achieve a smooth rhythmic delivery that satisfies you. And listen to what you are reading. Your objective is to absorb the patterns of English structure that characterize the clearest, most readable prose. Then read your paper aloud, and listen to the construction of your sentences. Are they also clear and readable? Do they say what you want them to say? How would they sound to a reader? According to one theory, you can learn the rhythm and phrasing of a language as you learn the rhythm and phrasing of a melody. And you will often *hear* a mistake or a clumsy construction in your writing that has escaped your eye in proofreading.

PREPARING THE MANUSCRIPT

Print your typed essay on one side of $8^1/2$-by-11-inch white computer paper, double-spacing throughout. Leave margins of 1 to $1^1/2$ inches on all sides, and indent each paragraph one-half inch or five spaces. Unless a formal outline is part of the paper, a separate title page is unnecessary. Instead, beginning about one inch from the top of the first page and flush with the left margin, type your name, the instructor's name, the course title, and the date, each on a separate line; then double-space and type the title, capitalizing the first letter of the words of the title except for articles, prepositions, and conjunctions. Double-space and type the body of the paper.

Number all pages at the top right corner, typing your last name before each page number in case pages are mislaid. If an outline is included, number its pages with lowercase roman numerals.

Use the spell-check and grammar-check functions of your word-processing program, and proofread the paper carefully for other mistakes.

Correct the errors, and reprint the pages in question. If you have used a typewriter, make corrections with liquid correction fluid, or, if there are only a few mistakes, cross them out and neatly write the correction above the line.

REVIEW CHECKLIST FOR ARGUMENTATIVE PAPERS

A successful argumentative paper meets the following criteria:

1. It presents a thesis that is of interest to both the writer and the audience, is debatable, and can be defended in the amount of space available.

2. Each statement offered in support of the thesis is backed up with enough evidence to give it credibility. Data cited in the paper come from a variety of sources. All quotations and direct references to primary or secondary sources are fully documented.

3. The warrants linking claims to support are either specified or implicit in the author's data and line of reasoning. No claim should depend on an unstated warrant with which skeptical readers might disagree.

4. The thesis is clearly presented and adequately introduced in a thesis paragraph, which indicates the purpose of the paper.

5. Supporting statements and data are organized in a way that builds the argument, emphasizes the author's main ideas, and justifies the paper's conclusions.

6. All possible opposing arguments are anticipated and refuted.

7. The paper is written in a style and tone appropriate to the topic and the intended audience. The author's prose is clear and readable.

8. The manuscript is clean, carefully proofed, and typed in an acceptable format.

10

Researching an Argumentative Paper

The success of any argument, short or long, depends in large part on the quantity and quality of the support behind it. Research, therefore, can be crucial for any argument outside your own experience. Most papers will benefit from research in the library and elsewhere because development of the claim requires facts, examples, statistics, and informed opinions that are available only from primary and secondary research sources. This chapter offers information and advice to help you work through the steps of writing a research paper, from getting started to preparing the finished product.

GETTING STARTED

The following guidelines will help you keep your research on track:

1. Focus your investigation on building your argument, not merely on collecting information about the topic. Do follow any promising leads that turn up from the sources you consult, but don't be diverted into general reading that has no direct bearing on your thesis.

2. Look for at least two pieces of evidence to support each point you make. If you cannot find sufficient evidence, you may need to revise or abandon the point.

3. Use a variety of sources. Seek evidence from different kinds of sources (books, magazines, Web sites, government reports, even personal interviews with experts) and from different fields.

4. Be sure your sources are authoritative. We have already pointed out elsewhere the necessity for examining the credentials of sources. Although it may be difficult or impossible for those outside the field to conclude that one authority is more trustworthy than another, some guidelines are available. Articles and essays in scholarly journals are probably more authoritative than articles in college newspapers. Authors whose credentials include many publications and years of study at reputable institutions are probably more reliable than newspaper columnists and the so-called man in the street. However, we can judge reliability much more easily if we are dealing with facts and inferences than with values and emotions.

5. Don't let your sources' opinions outweigh your own. Your paper should demonstrate that the thesis and ideas you present are yours, arrived at after careful reflection and supported by research. The thesis need not be original, but your paper should be more than a collection of quotations or a report of the facts and opinions you have been reading. It should be clear to the reader that the quotations and other materials support *your* claim and that *you* have been responsible for finding and emphasizing the important issues, examining the data, and choosing between strong and weak opinions.

6. Prepare for research by identifying potential resources and learning how they work. Make sure you know how to use the library's catalog and other databases available either in the library or through the campus network. For each database that looks useful, explore how to execute a subject search, how to refine a search, and how to print out or download results. Make sure you know how to find books, relevant reference materials, and journals. Find out whether interlibrary loan is an option and how long it takes. If you plan to use government publications, find out if your library is a depository for federal documents. Identify relevant organizions using the *Encyclopedia of Associations* and visit their Web sites. Finally, discuss your topic with a librarian at the reference desk to make sure you haven't overlooked anything.

MAPPING RESEARCH: A SAMPLE OUTLINE

To explore a range of research activities, let's suppose that you are preparing a research paper, six to ten pages long. You have chosen to defend the following thesis: *Conventional zoos should be abolished because they are cruel to animals and cannot provide the benefits to the public that they promise.* To keep your material under control and give direction to your reading, you would sketch a preliminary outline, which might look like this:

Why We Don't Need Zoos

I. Moral Objection: Animals have fundamental right to liberty
   A. Must prove animals are negatively affected by captivity
      1. research?
      2. research?
   B. Must refute claims that captivity is not detrimental to animals
      1. Brownlee's description of dolphin: "seeming stupor"; eating "half-heartedly"; not behaving like wild dolphins
      2. Personal experience: watching leopards running in circles in cages for hours
II. Practical Objection: Zoos can't accomplish what they claim to be their goals
   A. "Educational benefits" zoo provides are inaccurate at best: Public is not learning about wild animals at all but about domesticated descendants of same (support with research from [I.A] above)
   B. Conservation programs at zoos are ineffective
      1. It's difficult to breed animals in zoos
      2. Resultant offspring, when there is any, is victim of inbreeding. Leads to inferior stock that will eventually die out (research?)

Now you need to begin the search for the materials that will support your argument. There are two principal ways of gathering the materials — primary research and secondary research. Most writers will not want to limit themselves to one kind of research, but one method may work better than another for a particular project.

USING SOURCES: PRIMARY RESEARCH

Primary research involves looking for firsthand information. By *firsthand* we mean information taken directly from the original source, including field research (interviews, surveys, personal observations, or experiments). If your topic relates to a local issue involving your school or community, or if it focuses on a story that has never been reported by others, field research may be more valuable than anything available in the library. However, the library can be a source of firsthand information. Memoirs and letters written by witnesses to past events, photographs, contemporary news reports of historical events, or expert testimony presented at congressional hearings are all primary sources that may be available in your library. The Internet, too, can be a source of primary data. A discussion list, newsgroup, or chat room focused on your topic may give you a means to converse with activists and contact experts. Web sites of certain organizations provide documentation of their views, unfiltered by others' opinions. The text of laws, court opinions, bills, debates in Congress, environmental impact statements, and even selected declassified FBI files can be found through government-sponsored Web sites. Other sites present statistical data or the text of historical or political documents.

One of the rewards of primary research is that it often generates new information, which in turn produces new interpretations of familiar conditions. It is a favored method for anthropologists and sociologists, and most physical and natural scientists use observation and experiment at some point as essential tools in their research.

Consider the sample thesis that *zoos should be abolished*. Remember that you need to prove that *zoos are cruel to animals* and that *they cannot provide the benefits to the public that they promise*. It is possible to go directly to primary sources without consulting books or journals. For example:

- Phone the local area chapter of any animal rights group and ask to interview members on their opinions concerning zoos.

- Talk to the veterinarian on call at your local zoo and ask about animal injuries, illnesses, neuroses, and so forth.

- Search the World Wide Web for sites sponsored and developed by the groups associated with the animal rights movement. Many such informational sites will provide the text of current or proposed laws concerning this issue.

- Locate Internet newsgroups or discussion lists devoted to animal rights and identify experts in the field such as animal scientists who would be willing to provide authoritative opinions for your paper.

The information gleaned from primary research can be used directly to support your claim, or can provide a starting point for secondary research at the library.

USING SOURCES: SECONDARY RESEARCH

Secondary research involves locating commentary and analysis of your topic. In addition to raw evidence found through primary research, secondary sources provide a sense of how others are examining the issues and can provide useful information and analysis. Secondary sources may be written for a popular audience, ranging from news coverage, to popular explanations of research findings, to social analysis, to opinion pieces. Or they may be scholarly publications—experts presenting their research and theories to other researchers. These sources might also come in the form of analytical reports written to untangle possible courses of action, such as a report written by staff members for a congressional committee or an analysis of an issue by a think tank that wants to use the evidence it has gathered to influence public opinion.

Whatever form it may take, be sure when you use a secondary source that you consider the author's purpose and the validity of the material presented to ensure that it is useful evidence for your argument. An opinion piece published in a small-town paper, for example, may be a less impressive source for your argument than an analysis written by a former cabinet member. A description of a scientific discovery published in a magazine will carry less weight as evidence than the article written by the scientists making the discovery, presenting their research findings in a scientific journal.

The nature of your topic will determine which route you follow to find good sources. If the topic is current, you may find it more important to use articles than books and might bypass the library catalog altogether. If the topic has to do with social policy or politics, government publications may be particularly useful, though they would be unhelpful for a literary paper. If the topic relates to popular culture, the Internet may provide more information than more traditional publications. Consider what kinds of sources will be most useful as you choose your strategy. If you aren't certain which approaches fit your topic best, consult with a librarian at the reference desk.

■ Selecting and Searching Databases

You will most likely use one or more *databases* (online catalogs of reference materials) to locate books and articles on your topic. The library catalog is a database of books and other materials owned by the library; other databases may cover articles in popular or specialized journals and may even provide the full text of articles. Some databases may be available only in the library; others may be accessible all over campus. Here are some common features that appear in many databases.

Keyword or Subject Searching. You might have the option of searching a database by *keyword*—using the words that you think are most relevant to your search—or by subject. Typically, a keyword search will search for any occurrence of your search term in titles, notes, or the descriptive headings provided by database catalogers or indexers. The advantage to keyword searching is that you can use terms that come naturally to you to cast your net as widely as possible. The disadvantage is that there may be more than one way to express your topic and you may not capture all the relevant materials unless you use the right keywords.

With *subject searching,* you use search terms from a list of subject headings (sometimes called *descriptors*) established by the creators of the database. To make searching as efficient as possible, they choose one word or phrase to express a subject. Every time a new source is entered into the database, the indexers describe it using words from the list of subject headings: When you use the list to search the database, you retrieve every relevant source. You might find that a database lists these subject headings through a thesaurus feature. The sophisticated researcher will always pay attention to the subject headings or descriptors generally listed at the bottom of a record for clues to terms that might work best and for related terms that might be worth trying.

Searching for More Than One Concept. Most database searches allow you to combine terms using the connectors *and, or,* and *not.* These connectors (also known as *Boolean operators*) group search terms in different ways. If you search for zoos *and* animal rights, for example, the resulting list of sources will include only those that deal with both zoos and animal rights, leaving out any that deal with only one subject and not the other. If you connect terms with *or,* your list will contain sources that deal with either concept: A search for dogs *or* cats will create a list of sources that cover either animal. *Not* excludes concepts from a search. A search for animal rights *not* furs will search for the concept animal rights and then cut out any sources that deal with furs.

Limiting a Search. Most databases have some options for limiting a search by a number of variables, such as publication date, language, or format. If you find a large number of sources in a database search, you might limit your search to sources published in English in the past three years. If you need a visual aid for a presentation, you might limit a search of the library's catalog to videos, and so on.

Truncating Search Terms with Wild Cards. At times you will search for a word that has many possible endings. A wild card is a symbol that, placed at the end of a word root, allows for any possible ending for a word. For example, *animal** will allow a search for *animal* or *animals.*

Options for Saving Records. You may have the opportunity to print, download to a disk, or e-mail to yourself the citations you find in a database. Many databases have a feature for marking just the records you want so you save only those of interest.

Help Screens. Most databases offer some kind of online help that explains how to use the database effectively. If you invest five minutes getting familiar with the basics of a database, it may save you twenty minutes later.

■ Types of Databases

The Library Catalog. If you want to search for books, videos, or periodical publications, the library catalog is the database to search. Most libraries now have computerized catalogs, but some still have a card catalog. In either case, the type of information provided is the same.

Sample Online Catalog Record

You searched for the TITLE—animal rights movement

```
CALL #        Z7164.C45 M38 1994.
AUTHOR        Manzo, Bettina, 1943-
TITLE         The animal rights movement in the United States, 1975-
              1990 : an annotated bibliography / by Bettina Manzo.
IMPRINT       Metuchen, N.J. : Scarecrow Press, 1994.
PHYS DESCR    xi, 296 p. ; 23 cm.
NOTE          Includes indexes.
CONTENTS      Animal rights movement -- Activists and organizations --
              Philosophy, ethics, and religion -- Law and legislation
              -- Factory farming and vegetarianism -- Trapping and
              fur industry -- Companion animals -- Wildlife -- Cir-
              cuses, zoos, rodeos, dog
SUBJECT       Animal rights movement --United States --Bibliography.
              Animal rights --United States --Bibliography.
              Animal experimentation --United States --Bibliography.
OCLC #        30671149.
ISBN/ISSN     GB95-17241.
```

Every book in the library has an entry in the catalog that gives its author, title, publisher, date, length, and subject headings and perhaps some notes about its contents. It also gives the call number or location on the shelf and often some indication as to whether it is currently available. You can search the catalog for an author, title, subject, or keyword. Most online catalogs have ways of combining and limiting searches and for printing results. Remember when searching the catalog, though, that entries are created for whole books and not for specific parts of them. If you use too narrow search terms, you may not find a book that has a chapter that includes exactly what you are looking for. Use broad search terms, and check the subject headings for search terms that will work best. Plan to browse the shelves and examine the tables of contents of the books that you find through the catalog to see which, in fact, are most helpful for your topic.

General Periodical Databases. If you want to search for articles, you can find a number of options at your library. Most libraries have a generalized database of periodical articles that may include citations, citations with abstracts (brief summaries), or the entire text of articles. *EBSCOhost, Infotrac, Searchbank, Readers' Guide Abstracts,* and *ProQuest* are all online indexes of this type. Ask a librarian what is available in your library. These are particularly good for finding current information in fairly non-specialized sources, though they may include some scholarly journals. If you are looking for articles published before the 1980s — say, for news accounts published when the atomic bomb was dropped on Hiroshima — you would most likely need to use a print index such as the *Readers' Guide to Periodical Literature,* which began publication in 1900.

Specialized Databases. In addition to these general databases, you may find you need to delve deeper into a particular subject area. Every academic discipline has some sort of in-depth index to its research, and though the materials they cover tend to be highly specialized, they can provide more substantial support for your claims because they tend to cover sources written by experts in their fields. These resources may be available in electronic or print form:

Art Index

Biological Abstracts (the online version is known as *Biosis*)

Business Periodicals Index

ERIC (focused on education research)

Index Medicus (*Medline* or *PubMed* online)

Modern Languages Association International Bibliography (*MLA Bibliography* online)

Psychological Abstracts (*PsychInfo* or *PsychLit* online)

Sociological Abstracts (*Sociofile* online)

Check with a librarian to find out which specialized databases or indexes that relate to your topic are available in your library.

Database Services. In addition to individual databases, many libraries subscribe to database services that provide access to a number of databases from one search screen. *FirstSearch,* for example, provides access to a variety of subject-specific databases as well as *WorldCat,* a massive database of library catalogs. *Lexis/Nexis* is a collection of databases to over a billion texts, most of them available in full text; it is a strong source for news coverage, legal research, and business information. These may be available to you through the Web anywhere on campus. Again, a visit with a librarian will help you quickly identify what your library has available.

■ Encyclopedias

General and specialized encyclopedias offer quick overviews of topics and easy access to factual information. They also tend to have excellent selective bibliographies, pointing you toward useful sources. You will find a wide variety of encyclopedias in your library's reference collection; you may also have an online encyclopedia, such as *Britannica Online,* available through the Web anywhere on campus. Some specialized encyclopedias include the following:

Encyclopedia of African American History and Culture

Encyclopedia of American Social History

Encyclopedia of Bioethics

Encyclopedia of Educational Research

Encyclopedia of Hispanic Culture in the United States

Encyclopedia of International Relations

Encyclopedia of Philosophy

Encyclopedia of Sociology

Encyclopedia of the United States in the Twentieth Century

Encyclopedia of World Cultures

International Encyclopedia of Communications

McGraw-Hill Encyclopedia of Science and Technology

Political Handbook of the World

■ Statistical Resources

Often statistics are used as evidence in an argument. If your argument depends on establishing that one category is bigger than another, that the majority of people hold a certain opinion, or that one group is more affected by something than another group, statistics can provide the evidence you need. Of course, as with any other source, you need to be sure that your statistics are as reliable as possible and that you are reporting them responsibly.

It isn't always easy to find things counted the way you want. If you embark on a search for numbers to support your argument, be prepared to spend some time locating and interpreting data. Always read the fine print that explains how and when the data were gathered. Some sources for statistics include these:

U.S. Bureau of the Census. This government agency produces a wealth of statistical data, much of it available on CD-ROM or through the Web at <http://www.census.gov>. A handy compilation of their most useful tables is found in the one-volume annual handbook, *Statistical Abstract of the United States,* which also includes statistics from other government sources.

Other Federal Agencies. Numerous federal agencies gather statistical data. Among these are the National Center for Education Statistics, the National Center for Health Statistics, the National Bureau of Labor Statistics, and the Federal Bureau of Investigation, which annually compiles national crime statistics. One handy place to find a wide variety of federal statistics is a Web site called *FedStats* at <http://www.fedstats.gov>.

United Nations. Compilations of international data published by the United Nations include the *Demographic Yearbook* and *Statistical Yearbook.* Some statistics are also published by U.N. agencies such as the Food and Health Organization. Some are available from the U.N. Web site at <http://www.un.org>.

Opinion Polls. Several companies conduct opinion polls, and some of these are available in libraries. One such compilation is the Gallup Poll series, which summarizes public opinion polling from 1935 to the present. Other poll results are reported by the press. Search a database that covers news publications by using your topic and *polls* as keywords to help you locate some summaries of results.

■ Government Publications

Beyond statistics, government agencies compile and publish a wealth of information. For topics that concern public welfare, health, education, politics, foreign relations, earth sciences, the environment, or the economy, government documents may provide just the information you need.

The U.S. federal government is the largest publisher in the world. Its publications are distributed free to libraries designated as document depositories across the country. If your library is not a depository, chances are there is a regional depository somewhere nearby. Local, state, and foreign governments are also potential sources of information.

Federal documents distributed to depository libraries are indexed in *The Monthly Catalog of U.S. Government Documents,* available in many libraries as an electronic database. These include congressional documents such as hearings and committee reports, presidential papers, studies conducted by the Education Department or the Centers for Disease Control, and so on. Many government documents are available through the Internet. If you learn about a government publication through the news media, chances are you will be able to obtain a copy at the Web site of the sponsoring agency or congressional body. In fact, government publications are among the most valuable of resources available on the Web because they are rigorously controlled for content. You know you are looking at a U.S. federal government site when you see the domain suffix *.gov* in the URL.

■ Searching the Web

The World Wide Web is becoming an increasingly important resource for researchers. It is particularly helpful if you are looking for information about organizations, current events, political debates, popular culture, or government-sponsored research and activities. It is not an especially good place to look for literary criticism, historical analysis, or scholarly research articles, which are still more likely to be published in traditional ways. Biologists reporting on an important experiment, for example, are more likely to submit an article about it to a prestigious journal in the field than simply post their results on the Web.

Because anyone can publish whatever they like on the Web, searching for good information can be frustrating. Search engines operate by means of automated programs that gather information about sites and match search terms to whatever is out there, regardless of quality. A search engine may locate thousands of Web documents on a topic, but most are of little relevance and dubious quality. The key is to know in advance what information you need and who might have produced it. For example, if your topic has to do with some aspect of free speech and you know that the American Civil Liberties Union is involved in the issue, a trip to the ACLU home page may provide you with a wealth of information, albeit from a particular perspective. If your state's pollution control agency just issued a report on water quality in the area, you may find the report published at their Web site or the e-mail address of someone who could send it to you. The more you know about your topic before you sit down to surf, the more likely you will use your time productively.

If you have a fairly broad topic and no specific clues about where it might be covered, you may want to start your search using a selective guide to good sites. For example, the University of Texas maintains an excellent directory to sites relating to Latin America. Subject guides that selectively list valuable sites can be found at the *Argus Clearinghouse* at <http://www.clearinghouse.net>, the University of California's *Infomine* at <http://infomine.ucr.edu>, and the *World Wide Web Virtual Library* project at <http://www.vlib.org/Home.html>. Reference librarians will also be able to point you to quality sites that relate to your topic.

If you have a fairly specific topic in mind or are looking for a particular organization or document on the Web, a search engine can help you find it. *Google* is one of the best. No matter what search engine you choose, find out how it works, how it ranks results, and how deeply it indexes Web pages. Some search engines will retrieve more results than others simply because of the way the program gathers information from sites. As with databases, there are usually ways to refine a search and improve your results. Many search engines offer an advanced search option that may provide some useful options for refining and limiting a search.

It is important to know what will not be retrieved by a search engine. Because publishing and transmitting texts on the Web is relatively easy, it is becoming more common for libraries to subscribe to databases and electronic journals that are accessed through a Web browser. You may have *Britannica Online* and *Lexis/Nexis* as options on your library's home page. However, the contents of those subscriptions will be available only to your campus community and will not be searched by general Web search engines.

READING WITH A PURPOSE

When you begin studying your sources, read first to acquire general familiarity with your subject. Make sure that you are covering both sides of the question—in this case arguments both for and against the existence of zoos—as well as facts and opinions from a variety of sources. In investigating this subject, you will encounter data from biologists, ecologists, zoo directors, anthropologists, animal-rights activists, and ethical philosophers; their varied points of view will contribute to the strength of your claim.

As you read, look for what seem to be the major issues. They will probably be represented in all or most of your sources. For the claim about zoos the major issues may be summarized as follows: (1) the fundamental right wild animals have to liberty; (2) the harm done to animals who are denied this right and kept in captivity. On the other side, these issues will emerge: (1) the lack of concrete evidence that animals suffer or are harmed by being in zoos; (2) the benefits, in terms of entertainment, education, and conservation efforts that the public derives from zoos. The latter two, of course, are the issues you will have to refute. Your note taking should emphasize these important issues.

Record questions as they occur to you in your reading. Why do zoos exist? What are their major goals, and how well do they meet them? What happens to animals who are removed from the wild and placed in zoos? What happens to animals born and reared in captivity? How do these groups compare with their wild counterparts, who are free to live in their natural habitats? Do animals really have a right to liberty? What are the consequences of denying them this right? Are there consequences to humanity?

■ Evaluating Print Sources

The sources you find provide useful information that you need for your paper and help you support your claims. One key to supporting claims effectively is to make sure you have the best evidence available. It is tempting when searching a database or the Web to take the first sources that look good, print them or copy them, and not give them another thought until you are sitting down to compose your argument—only to discover that the sources aren't as valuable as they could be. Sources that looked pretty good at the beginning of your research may turn out to be less useful once you have learned more about the topic. And a source that seems interesting at first glance may turn out to be a rehash or digest of a much more valuable source, something you realize only when you sit down and look at it carefully.

To find the right stuff, be a critical thinker from the start of your research process. Scan and evaluate the references you encounter throughout your search. As you examine options in a database, choose sources that use relevant terms in their titles, seem directed to an appropriate audience, and are published in places that will look good in your Works Cited list. For example, a Senate Foreign Relations Committee report will be more impressive as a source than a comparable article in *Good Housekeeping*. An article from the scholarly journal *Foreign Affairs* will carry more clout than an article from *Reader's Digest*, even if they are on the same subject.

Skim and quickly evaluate each source that looks valuable.

- Is it relevant to your topic?
- Does it provide information you haven't found elsewhere?
- Can you learn anything about the author, and does what you learn inspire confidence?

As you begin to learn more about your topic and develop an outline, you can use sources to help direct your search. If a source mentions an organization, for example, you may use that clue to run a search on the Web for that organization's home page. If a newspaper story refers to a study published in a scientific journal, you may want to seek out that study to see the results of the research firsthand. And if you have a source that includes references to other publications, scan through them, and see which might also prove helpful to you. When you first started your research, chances are you weren't quite sure what you were looking for. Once you are familiar with your topic, you need to concentrate on finding sources that will best support the claims you want to make, and your increasing familiarity with the issue will make it easier to identify the best sources. That may mean a return trip to the library.

Once you have selected some useful sources to support your claims, make a more in-depth evaluation to be sure you have the best evidence available.

- Is it current enough? Have circumstances changed since this text was published?
- Is the author someone I want to call on as an expert witness? Does the author have the experience or credentials to make a solid argument that carries weight with my readers?
- Is it reliable information for my purposes? It may be highly opinionated, but are the basic facts it presents confirmed in other sources? Is the evidence presented in the text convincing?

These questions are not always easy to answer. In some cases, articles will include some information about the author, such as where he or she works. In other cases, no information or even an author's name is given. In that case, it may help to evaluate the publication and its reputation. If you aren't familiar with a publication and don't feel confident making your own judgment, see if it is described in Katz's *Magazines for Libraries,* which evaluates the reputation and quality of periodicals.

■ Evaluating Web Sources

Web sites pose challenges and offer unique opportunities for researchers, for one reason because they are part of a developing genre of writing. When evaluating a Web site, first examine what kind of site you are reading. Is the Web page selling or advertising goods or services (a business site)? Is it advocating a point of view (an advocacy site) or providing relatively neutral information, such as that found in the yellow pages (an informative or educational site)? Is the Web site addressing the interests of people in a particular organization or with common interests (an information-sharing site)? Is it reporting up-to-the-minute news (a news site) or appealing to some aspect of an individual's life and interests (a personal site)? Useful information for a research paper may be obtained from any of these kinds of Web pages, but it is helpful to know what the main purpose of the site is — and who its primary audience is — when determining how productive it will be for your research.

As you weigh the main purpose of the site, evaluate its original context. Does the site originate in a traditional medium, such as a print journal or an encyclopedia? Is the site part of an online journal, in which case its material had to go through a screening process? Or is the site the product of one individual's or organization's desire to create a Web page, which means the work may not have been screened or evaluated by any outside agency? In that case, the information may still be valuable, but you must be even more careful when evaluating it.

Answering preliminary questions like these help you before you begin a more specific evaluation of the site's content. To find answers to many of these questions, make a brief overview of the site itself, by looking, for example, at the clues contained in the Web address. That is, *.com* in the address means a business or commercial site; *.edu,* a site sponsored by a university or college; *.k12* is a site associated with a primary or secondary school; *.gov* indicates that the federal government sponsored the site; and *.org,* suggests that the site is part of a nonprofit or noncommercial group. Sites originating outside the United States have URLs that end with a two-letter country abbreviation, such as *.uk* for United Kingdom. Although these address clues can reveal a great deal about the origins and purposes of a Web site, remember that personal Web sites may also contain some of these abbreviations. Institutions such as schools and businesses sometimes sponsor individuals' personal Web sites (which are often unscreened by the institution) as well as official institutional sites. One possible key to determining whether a Web site is a personal page, however, is to look for a tilde (~) plus a name or part of a name in the address. Finally, if you are unsure of the sponsoring organization of a page, try erasing all the information in the URL after the first slash (/) and pressing the "Enter" key. Doing so often brings you to the main page of the organization sponsoring the Web site.

Most Web sites include a way to contact the author or sponsoring organization of the site, usually through e-mail. This is often a quick and easy way to get answers to the preliminary questions. If the site contains an address or phone number as part of its contact information, this means the organization or individual is available and probably willing to stand behind the site's content. If you can't find contact information the site may not be suitable to use as a primary resource. The information is not necessarily invalid, but such clues should alert you that information found on that page needs to be verified.

For the next step—that of more closely evaluating the contents of any Web site—Web researchers generally agree on the importance of five criteria: the authority, accuracy, objectivity, currency, and coverage of the site.[1] These criteria are just as important in evaluating traditional print texts, but electronic texts require special care. To understand how these criteria work, let's look at a specific example.

■ Evaluating a Web Page: One Example

Your latest assignment for a course in argumentation is to research and write on a topic of significance to you and your future. You are a woman thinking about a career in technology, and you want to know how women fare in such careers. You remember hearing that many women don't choose technology as a career path, despite the opportunities for personal and financial enrichment. You decide to research the subject so that you can write an argument that addresses this issue, maybe one that encourages women to enter computer science. Ultimately, though, your argument will depend on what facts, statistics, and debates you unearth about the broader issue of women following careers in technology. As you research, then, you have at least two competing goals in mind: first, to learn as much as you can about a topic that you find interesting and may affect your professional aspirations, and second, to gather data for a tentative argument you want to make, in this case counteracting the apparent tendency of women to avoid careers in technology.

You begin by using the databases of academic and nonacademic articles typically located through your college's or university's library Web page. These databases direct you to both academic and less formal

---

[1] Wolfram Memorial Library Web site.

GirlTECH Home Page

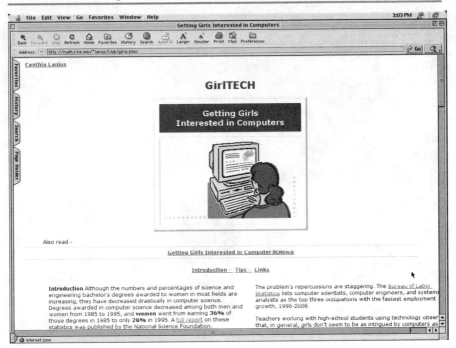

articles stored in journals that are kept either online or as print materials in your library. You also check the library's catalog for books on the subject. These texts likely will result in a range of sources for your search, and comparing a number of them will give you an idea of what the existing published research about women in technology covers. These kinds of sources—published online or in print—also can provide in-depth coverage of your topic, something that your average Web page found through *Yahoo!* or *Google* does not. The different issues covered also will make you realize how important it will be to narrow your topic about women and technology so that you can write an argument on a manageable piece of a complex subject.

After your initial foray into your library's traditional research materials, you want to explore World Wide Web resources. Can women find support on the Web in any online organizations for their choice of a technological career? What resources about this topic are available to someone who may have access to a computer but not to a research library?

You begin searching for answers through at least two of the standard search engines (*Lycos, Ask Jeeves,* or *Yahoo!,* for example). Because each search engine has different strengths and weaknesses, you are likely to find different sources on each. Searches on "Women and Technology"

Cynthia Lanius's Personal Web Page

and "Women and Computers" lead to a site titled "Getting Girls Interested in Computers" (the home page of which is reproduced here). When the page first comes up, you notice the title underneath the linked name *Cynthia Lanius* in the upper left corner and the heading "GirlTECH."

Scrolling down, you notice a few paragraphs of text about women in technology (not an in-depth analysis but some potentially useful statistics and resources). You also see a list of tips for engaging girls in technology and further references to Cynthia Lanius, including her contact information. Although you probably have guessed by now, the information at the very bottom of the page confirms that Lanius is the author of this Web site since she is identified as copyright owner.

Before you closely examine the page to evaluate its content, pay attention to the site's URL <http://math.rice.edu/~lanius/club/girls.html>. The *.edu* means that an educational institution sponsors the site, that the institution is Rice University, and even more specifically, that the mathematics department of Rice University sponsors the site. All of this information is determined by erasing the information after *.edu* in the URL. It is also important to note *~lanius* in the URL because it signifies a personal Web page representing the ideas of Cynthia Lanius rather than those of Rice University as an institution. That in itself doesn't disqualify the site as a source of useful information, but it does remind careful readers to examine Cynthia Lanius's credentials and why she created the site. Her exact affiliation with Rice University cannot be told from this opening page and requires further investigation.

A quick review of the whole page shows no sign that it originates from an existing publication or is part of an online journal. This, then, is another reason for the reader to take care in evaluating this site's content. Such a review also reveals that the page is concerned with advocacy as well as with education.

After this preliminary work is completed, you can apply the five criteria for evaluating Web sites: authority, accuracy, objectivity, currency, and coverage.

Authority

You have already begun to wonder about the authority of the author Cynthia Lanius. (The word *author* is the root for *authority*. Think about how these words became connected and how that connection is sometimes abused; not all authors are authorities.) Click on the link Lanius provides at the top of the page, which leads to her home page. This page contains Lanius's picture and professional title (Executive Director for the Center for Excellence and Equity in Education), both of which help a Web reader see her as a real person. The page also includes a variety of links, including sample lessons in science and math that Lanius has created for girls and a variety of reference sources. Most important for an evaluation of the site authority, however, are the lists of publications, presentations, and awards Lanius provides in her biography. The link to some of her presentations, for example, shows that Lanius has given numerous presentations on girls, science, math, technology, and education. Clearly serious organizations and individuals value her ideas and research, which suggests that Lanius's site is potentially useful and that she carries authority as an expert on women and technology.

Lanius's biography also lists the committees she is a member of and the programs she directs, among other things. The Web makes it easy to verify much of this information. Going to Rice's home page and looking up Lanius through the math department or the Center for Excellence and Equity in Education, for example, will verify her employment and status within this institution. Obviously you will not be able to verify every detail from every source, but the Web can help you check an authority's credentials and background.

Accuracy

Lanius's GirlTECH Web site includes many different kinds of information: statistics regarding the number of women who received computer science degrees in U.S. universities from 1985 to 1995, statistics that suggest a serious gap between the number of men studying computer science and the number of women pursuing this field, and statistics about the number of boys and girls in high schools taking advanced placement classes and

Another Page on the GirlTECH Site

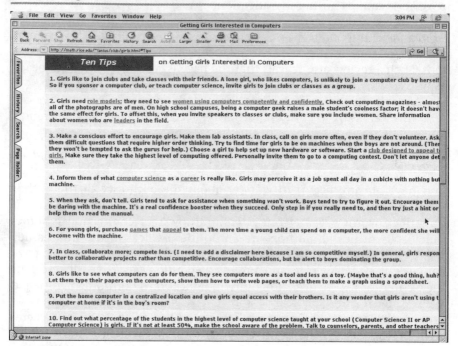

File Edit View Go Favorites Window Help   3:04 PM

Getting Girls Interested in Computers

Back Forward Stop Refresh Home Favorites History Search AutoFill Larger Smaller Print Mail Preferences

Address: http://math.rice.edu/~lanius/club/girls.html#Tips

Ten Tips on Getting Girls Interested in Computers

1. Girls like to join clubs and take classes with their friends. A lone girl, who likes computers, is unlikely to join a computer club by herself. So if you sponsor a computer club, or teach computer science, invite girls to join clubs or classes as a group.

2. Girls need role models; they need to see women using computers competently and confidently. Check out computing magazines - almost all of the photographs are of men. On high school campuses, being a computer geek raises a male student's coolness factor; it doesn't have the same effect for girls. To offset this, when you invite speakers to classes or clubs, make sure you include women. Share information about women who are leaders in the field.

3. Make a conscious effort to encourage girls. Make them lab assistants. In class, call on girls more often, even if they don't volunteer. Ask them difficult questions that require higher order thinking. Try to find time for girls to be on machines when the boys are not around. (Then they won't be tempted to ask the gurus for help.) Choose a girl to help set up new hardware or software. Start a club designed to appeal to girls. Make sure they take the highest level of computing offered. Personally invite them to go to a computing contest. Don't let anyone deter them.

4. Inform them of what computer science as a career is really like. Girls may perceive it as a job spent all day in a cubicle with nothing but a machine.

5. When they ask, don't tell. Girls tend to ask for assistance when something won't work. Boys tend to try to figure it out. Encourage them to be daring with the machine. It's a real confidence booster when they succeed. Only step in if you really need to, and then try just a hint or help them to read the manual.

6. For young girls, purchase games that appeal to them. The more time a young child can spend on a computer, the more confident she will become with the machine.

7. In class, collaborate more; compete less. (I need to add a disclaimer here because I am so competitive myself.) In general, girls respond better to collaborative projects rather than competitive. Encourage collaborations, but be alert to boys dominating the group.

8. Girls like to see what computers can do for them. They see computers more as a tool and less as a toy. (Maybe that's a good thing, huh?) Let them type their papers on the computers, show them how to write web pages, or teach them to make a graph using a spreadsheet.

9. Put the home computer in a centralized location and give girls equal access with their brothers. Is it any wonder that girls aren't using the computer at home if it's in the boy's room?

10. Find out what percentage of the students in the highest level of computer science taught at your school (Computer Science II or AP Computer Science) is girls. If it's not at least 50%, make the school aware of the problem. Talk to counselors, parents, and other teachers.

Internet zone

exams in science and math. Since Lanius's Web site — and much of her career — is based on combating statistics such as these, finding out more about these numbers is critical. Statistics come from many sources and are presented (and manipulated) in many ways; understanding their sources and how they compare to other statistics on the same or related issues is imperative. On the GirlTECH home page, Lanius provides a link to the National Science Foundation and the Bureau of Labor Statistics, two governmental resources that can help confirm the numbers. As you continue researching, be on the lookout for further statistics and compare them with Lanius's. What larger story about women and technology can you create based on statistical studies and reports?

Below the statistical evidence on the GirlTECH home page is a list of ten tips for encouraging girls to get interested in computers and technology careers. Because these tips are not verifiable facts but are instead suggestions based on Lanius's years of teaching girls and studying groups underrepresented in education, they cannot be evaluated for accuracy in the same way as can statistics. To evaluate these tips, a thoughtful reader should put him- or herself into the role of a student who feels shut out of technology classes or careers and consider whether the strategies Lanius offers would help alleviate insecurities or difficulties. A reader could also compare Lanius's ideas with those in literature on education and margin-alized groups. Most important, though, a reader should recognize that anecdotal information (which may be supported by research but does not represent universal fact) is different from statistical information and must be evaluated using different strategies. Go to the GirlTECH Web site and read through more of its content and the content of some of the links provided. How many kinds of knowledge (facts, opinions, arguments, etc.) are represented? What kinds of strategies will be needed to determine their accuracy?

Objectivity

Objectivity is an especially important and difficult factor to determine for a Web site such as "Getting Girls Interested in Computers." The site is concerned both with education and advocacy and is making an argument for a specific issue. The question, then, is not whether the site has any biases; it admits to a clear bias: that of greater inclusion of girls and women in the world of technology. In fact, all sites, even the most neutral ones, have biases; it is not possible to create a perfectly inclusive, objective, value-free text.

For most sites, then, the job of the research writer is to determine the nature of the biases and the degree to which they interfere with the information provided. This process involves analyzing the assumptions, or *warrants,* underlying the argument of a Web page and determining the basis for these warrants.

Lanius's site takes at least three things for granted, that is, it operates from three basic warrants. First, Lanius's site assumes that the number of women in technology-related fields is too low. Second, the site assumes that this low number represents a problem and not simply a difference between the genders that we should accept. Third, the site assumes that early intervention through education can change this trend and help girls see technological fields as options.

The first warrant is easy to analyze. By looking at several studies of women in technological fields (including the government sites Lanius links to), we can determine that, indeed, the number of women in technological careers is significantly lower than we might expect based on the number of women in the workforce. More difficult is evaluating the objectivity of the second warrant: that this underrepresentation is a problem all educators and, in fact, all people should be concerned about. Such an assumption will provoke a variety of interpretations. Some readers, for example, may believe the low number of women in technological fields to be a reflection of where women's interests lie. Others may view professional career choices as a matter of individual choice and not something that schools or educators should address directly. Still others may assume that any discussion about inclusion of underrepresented groups automatically means quotas or reverse discrimination. It is important for the discriminating reader to understand why Lanius and Rice

University would conclude that the low number of women in technological fields is a problem. Similarly, in evaluating the objectivity of Lanius's third warrant, it is important to ask why she believes education is a key to changing this situation.

Only when readers carefully examine issues such as these, while trying to put themselves into Lanius's shoes, can they determine whether an unfair bias makes the information, opinions, and suggestions that Lanius offers tainted or suspect. Such work can be done only when Lanius's work is compared with other research on girls, women, technology, and education, which she, helpfully, has provided access to on her Web site.

Currency

Currency is critical when evaluating Web sites. When a site was first created and when it was last updated influence the way you read the site and how you assess the other four criteria. Take the first criteria of authority, for example. If you go to the Rice University math department page, you find Lanius's name on the home page and on the Resources and Projects page.

Suppose that this was not the case, and you didn't find Lanius's credentials on the Rice University site. Explanations (aside from the unlikely possibility of fraud) are that the site had not updated its pages since Lanius joined the staff, or that she had left Rice and the GirlTECH site was not yet updated. Either way, further research would be necessary to determine Lanius's university status and expertise on women and technology and would also help you make informed decisions about Lanius as an authority.

Currency plays an equally important role in the second criterion, accuracy. Statistics, for example, change rapidly, and what were cutting-edge numbers a few years ago might now be completely different (for example, the number of Internet users has changed dramatically over the past decade and even in the last few years). It is always useful to analyze how current the statistics and arguments being offered on a Web site may be and to compare the dates of statistics such as the ones Lanius offers to the dates of other studies you encounter. Close analysis helps assure that you can present the most accurate research in your argument and are able to counter arguments based on less current information.

Coverage

Finally, readers of a Web site must evaluate the site's coverage, another difficult issue since no one text or Web site can cover a topic as large and complex as girls and women in technology. One way to gauge the coverage of a Web site is to look carefully at its primary topic and to examine other positions and opinions not represented by the site. Search for these perspectives in other forms of research, both Web-based and print, and think about why the author of the Web site chose not to include them in the text. Are they not of primary importance to the author's ideas? Is it possible that he or she may not be familiar with these alternative perspectives? Is it possible that they are not very reliable? How do you think the author would respond to such perspectives?

Analyzing the variety, quality, and number of links a Web site provides is also important. "Getting Girls Interested in Computers" is a successful Web site because it offers a long list of resources and links to other academic centers and professional organizations that promote technological fields for girls and women. It also includes links to online articles describing women in technology and sites that have been specifically created for girls. You may still want to pursue other research that takes the contrary view that the small number of women in technological professions is not the problem that Lanius sees. Nevertheless, this site does provide an excellent, well-rounded coverage of girls, women, and technology.

Conclusion

Evaluating Web sites as sources of information—indeed, evaluating any research text—is a difficult process. The five criteria we've used to evaluate Cynthia Lanius's "Getting Girls Interested in Computers" overlap. Starting with any one of the five criteria almost inevitably leads to the others: The accuracy of the information, for example, is clearly related to the authority of the Web site's author, to the biases present in the site, and to the coverage of the information offered. For some sites, one of these criteria will be most important; for others you may have to address all five in detail. You will not be able to analyze every Web site the way we have, but do subject the most important Web sites you encounter to this analysis before you tap them for information central to your work.

■ Taking Notes

While everyone has methods of taking notes, here are a few suggestions that should be useful to research writers who need to read materials quickly, comprehend and evaluate the sources, use them as part of a research paper assignment, and manage their time carefully.

When taking notes from a source, summarize instead of quoting long passages. Summarizing as you read saves time. If you feel that a direct quote is more effective than anything you could write and provides crucial support for your argument, copy the material word for word. Leave all punctuation exactly as it appears and insert ellipsis points ("...") if you delete material. Enclose all quotations in quotation marks and copy complete information about your source, including the author's name, the title of the book or article, the journal name if appropriate, page numbers, and publishing information. If you quote an article that appears in an anthology, record complete information about the book itself.

Note Card with
Quotation

Hediger   25

"The wild animal, with its marked tendency
to escape, is notorious for the fact that it is
never completely released from that all-
important activity, avoiding enemies, even
during sleep, but is constantly on alert."

Note Card with
Summary

Hediger   25

Animals who live in the wild have to be on
the watch for predators constantly.

If you aren't sure whether you will use a piece of information later, don't copy the whole passage. Instead, make a note of its bibliographic information so that you can find it again if you need it. Taking too many notes, however, is preferable to taking too few, a problem that will force you to go back to the library for missing information.

Record complete bibliographical information for each source that you intend to use in your paper (as well as for those sources you may use). This ensures that you will have all the information necessary to document your paper. Some researchers keep two sets of note cards: one set for the bibliographical information and one set for the notes themselves. Each source then appears on a card by itself, ready to be arranged in alphabetical order for the Works Cited or References page of the paper.

Use the note-taking process as a prewriting activity. Often when you summarize an author's ideas or write down direct quotes, you see or understand the material in new ways. Freewrite about the importance of these quotes, paraphrases, or summaries, or at least about those that seem especially important. If nothing else, take a minute to justify in writing why you chose to record the notes. Doing so will help you clarify and develop your thoughts about your argument.

Note Card with Statistics

Reiger   32

By end of decade, worldwide extinction
rate will be one species per hour.

Other statistics, too, in Reiger, "The Wages
of Growth," Field and Stream, July 1981:32.

Bibliography Note Card

Hediger, Heini. The Psychology and
Behavior of Animals in Zoos and Circuses.
Trans. Geoffrey Sircom. New York: Dover,
1968.

Taking this prewriting step seriously will help you analyze the ideas you record from outside sources. You will then be better prepared for the more formal (and inevitable) work of summarizing, paraphrasing, and composing involved in thinking critically about your topic and writing a research paper. Maybe most important, such work will help with that moment all writers face when they realize they "know what they want to say but can't find the words to say it." Overcoming such moments does not depend on finding inspiration while writing the final draft of a paper. Instead, successfully working through this common form of writer's block depends more on the amount of prewriting and thoughtful consideration of the notes done early in the research process.

As you take notes, also remember to refer to your outline to ensure that you are acquiring sufficient data to support all the points you intend to raise. Of course, you will be revising your outline during the course of your research as issues are clarified and new ideas emerge, but the outline will serve as a rough guide throughout the writing process. Keeping close track of your outline will also prevent you from recording material that is interesting but not relevant.

Relying on the knowledge of others is an important part of doing research; expert opinions and eloquent arguments help support your claims when your own expertise is limited. But remember, this is *your* paper. Your ideas and insights into other people's ideas are just as important as the information you uncover at the library. When writing an argument, do not simply regurgitate the words and thoughts of others in your essay. Work to achieve a balance between providing solid information from expert sources and offering your own interpretation of the argument and the evidence that supports it.

Using word-processing software can invigorate the process of note taking and of outlining (see p. 328). Taking notes using a computer gives you more flexibility than using pen and paper alone. For example, you can save your computer-generated notes and your comments on them in numerous places (at home, school, or work, or on a disk); you can cut and paste the text into various documents; you can add to the notes or modify them and still revert to the originals with ease. (Be sure not to delete or save over your original files, by always using the Save As function when modifying your original files.)

If your computer allows access to the World Wide Web, you can link notes to background material that may be useful once you begin writing drafts of your paper. For example, you could create links to an author's Web page or to any of his or her other works published on the Web. You could create a link to a study or an additional source cited in your notes, or you could link to the work of other researchers who support or argue against the information you recorded.

Because you can record information in any number of ways on your computer, your notes act as tools in the writing process. One of the best ways to start is to open a file for each source; enter the bibliographic information; directly type into the file a series of potentially useful quotations, paraphrases, and summaries; and add your initial ideas about the source. (For each entry, note the correct page references as you go along and indicate clearly whether you are quoting, paraphrasing, or summarizing.) You can then use the capabilities of your computer to aid you in the later stages of the writing process. For example, you can collect all your research notes into one large file in which you group like sources, evaluate whether you have too much information about one issue or one side of an argument, or examine sources that conflict with one another. You can imagine various organizational schemes for your paper based on the central themes and issues of the notes you have taken, and you can more clearly determine which quotes and summaries are essential to your paper and which may not be needed.

When you're ready to begin your first draft, the computer allows you to readily integrate material from your source notes into your research paper by cutting and pasting, thus eliminating the need to retype and reducing the chance of error. You can also combine all the bibliographic materials you have saved in separate files and then use the computer to alphabetize your sources for your final draft.

Although word processors do not dramatically change the research process, they do highlight the fact that taking notes, prewriting, drafting a paper, and creating bibliographies are integrated activities that should build from one another. When you take notes from a journal, book, or Web site, you develop your note-taking abilities so that they help with the entire writing process.

■ Quoting

You may want to quote passages or phrases from your sources if they express an idea in words more effective than your own. In this particular project, you might come across a statement that provides succinct, irrefutable evidence for an issue you wish to support. If the author of this statement is a professional in his or her field, someone with a great deal of authority on the subject, it would be appropriate to quote that author. Suppose, during the course of your research for the zoo paper, you find that many sources agree that zoos don't have the money or space necessary to maintain large enough animal populations to ensure successful captive breeding programs. But so far you only have opinions to that effect. You have been unable to find any concrete documentation of this fact until you come across Ulysses S. Seal's address to the National Zoological Park Symposia for the Public, September 1982. Here is how you could use Seal's words in your paper (using reference citation style of the American Psychological Association):

> Bear in mind that "none of these [zoo] budgets is allocated specifically for species preservation. Zoos have been established primarily as recreational institutions and are only secondarily developing programs in conservation, education and research" (Seal, 1982, p. 74).

Notice the use of brackets (not parentheses) in the first sentence, which enclose material that did not appear in the original source but is necessary for clarification. Brackets must be used to indicate any such changes in quoted material.

Quotations should be introduced logically and gracefully in your text. Make sure that the quoted material either supports or illustrates the point you have just made or the point you are about to make and that your writing remains grammatically correct once the quotation is introduced.

Quotations are an important tool for establishing your claims, but it is important not to overuse them. If you cannot say most of what you want to say in your own words, you probably haven't thought hard enough about what it is you want to say.

■ Paraphrasing

Paraphrasing involves restating the content of an original source in your own words. It is most useful when the material from your source is too long for your paper, can be made clearer to the reader by rephrasing, or is written in a style markedly different from your own.

A paraphrase should be as true to the original source as you can make it: Do not change the tone or the ideas, or even the order in which the ideas are presented. Take care not to allow your own opinions to creep into your paraphrase of someone else's argument. Your readers should always be aware of which arguments belong to you and which belong to outside sources.

Like a quotation, a paraphrase must *always* include documentation, or you will be guilty of plagiarism. Even though you are using your own words, the ideas in a paraphrase belong to someone else, and that person deserves credit for them. One final caveat: When putting a long passage into your own words, beware of picking up certain expressions and turns of phrase from your source. If you do end up using your source's exact words, make sure to enclose them in quotation marks.

Below is a passage from Shannon Brownlee's "First It Was 'Save the Whales,' Now It's 'Free the Dolphins'" (*Discover*, December 1986, pp. 70–72), along with a good paraphrase of the passage and two unacceptable paraphrases.

ORIGINAL PASSAGE

But are we being good caretakers by holding a dolphin or a sea lion in a tank? Yes, if two conditions are met: that they're given the best treatment possible and, no less important, that they're displayed in a way that educates and informs us. Captive animals must be allowed to serve as ambassadors for their species (Brownlee, 1986, p. 72).

A PARAPHRASE THAT PLAGIARIZES

In "First It Was 'Save the Whales,' Now It's 'Free the Dolphins,'" Shannon Brownlee (1986) argues that it's all right for people to hold animals in captivity as long as (1) the animals are treated as well as possible, and (2) the animals are displayed in a way that educates the public. Brownlee insists that animals be allowed to serve as "ambassadors for their species" (p. 72).

A PARAPHRASE THAT ALTERS THE MEANING OF THE ORIGINAL PASSAGE

According to Shannon Brownlee (1986), a captive animal is being treated fairly as long as it's kept alive and its captivity gives people pleasure. In her essay, "First It Was 'Save the Whales,' Now It's 'Free the Dolphins,'" she argues that people who keep animals in cages are responsible to the animals in only two ways: (1) they should treat their captives as well as possible (even if a small tank is all that can be provided), and (2) they should make sure that the spectators enjoy watching them (p. 72).

A GOOD PARAPHRASE

Shannon Brownlee (1986) holds that two criteria are necessary in order for the captivity of wild animals to be considered worthwhile. First, the animals should be treated as well as possible. Second, their captivity should have educational value for the people who come to look at them. "Captive animals," Brownlee claims, "must be allowed to serve as ambassadors for their species" (p. 72).

■ Summarizing

A summary, like a paraphrase, involves shortening the original passage as well as putting it in your own words. It gives the gist of the passage, including the important points while leaving out details. What makes summarizing difficult is that it requires you to capture often long and complex texts in just a few lines or a short paragraph. To do such work, you must be able to comprehend a variety of materials (see page 26 on "Responding as a Critical Reader" and specifically the section on "Comprehending Arguments" for further advice on this issue). To summarize well, you need to imagine yourself as the author of the piece you are summarizing and be true to the ideas that the author is expressing, even when those ideas conflict with your point of view. You must then move smoothly from being a careful reader to being a writer who, in your own words, recreates another's thoughts.

We summarize for many reasons: to let our boss know the basics of what we have been doing or to tell a friend why she should or should not see a movie. In your classes you are often asked to summarize articles or books, and even when this is not an explicit part of an assignment, the ability to summarize is usually expected. That is, when you are instructed to analyze an essay or to compare and contrast two novels, central to this work is the ability to carefully comprehend and recreate authors' ideas. Summarizing is the cornerstone on which all other critical reading and writing tasks are built.

When writing a research paper, the ability to summarize effectively is especially critical, because sources, though useful for your argument, will simply be too long to include in your text. It is up to you, then, to summarize those points and ideas that are most critical for your argument either because they support that argument or because they represent a counter point of view.

For instance, in the paper at the end of this chapter, "Why Zoos Should Be Eliminated," the statement, "It is generally acknowledged that it is difficult to breed zoo animals," is not a direct quotation. The idea comes from Jon Luoma's article in *Audubon* magazine (the writer of this essay acknowledges that this idea comes from Luoma). Returning to the original source makes it clear that neither quoting nor fully paraphrasing would have been suitable choices because the writer was able to reduce the following passage from Luoma's article to one sentence.

> But the successful propagation of entire captive species poses awesome management problems. . . . Sanford Friedman, the Minnesota Zoo's

director of biological programs, had explained to me that long-term maintenance of a species in captivity demands solutions to these fundamental problems. "First, we have to learn *how* to breed them. Second, we have to decide *who* to breed. And third, we have to figure out *what* to do with them and their offspring once we've bred them."

This passage is far too long to include in a brief research paper but is easily summarized without losing any of its effectiveness.

When summarizing long or difficult texts, try some of the following strategies to help you comprehend the essential points of the text.

1. Before you summarize, analyze the text following the strategies given in the section on "Responding as a Critical Reader" (p. 26). For example, you should always utilize prereading strategies by looking over the text as a whole before you read it carefully. Such work will often yield clues about the central ideas of the text from the title, the subheadings, and the introduction. Also, use your pen once you begin to read the text so that you link the acts of reading and writing. Underline important ideas, ask questions in the margins about difficult or significant ideas, and highlight topic sentences. Take a few minutes after reading the essay to jot down the essential ideas and any questions you have about the reading.

2. Reread the introduction and conclusion after you have read the essay once or twice. These two sections should complement each other and offer clues to the most significant issues of the text. An introduction or conclusion is often more than one paragraph; therefore, it is important that you read the first and last few paragraphs of an essay to understand what the author is trying to impress upon the reader. If you are summarizing a book, look especially at the preface, the first and last chapters, and any reviewers' comments. These sections will not tell you everything you need to know to summarize an entire book, but they will help you decide which points matter.

3. For a difficult essay, you may want to list all the subheadings (if they are used) or the topic sentence of each paragraph. These significant guideposts will map the piece as a whole: What do they tell you about the central ideas and the main argument the author is making? After reviewing the subheads or topic sentences, can you reread the essay and engage more easily with its finer points? For a book, you can do the same thing with chapter headings to break down the essential ideas. Remember that when you summarize, you must put another's words into your own (and cite the original text as well), so do not simply let a list of the subheadings or chapter titles stand in for your summary. They likely won't make sense when put together in paragraph form, but they will provide you with valuable ideas regarding the central points of the text.

4. Remember that summarizing requires attention to overall meaning and not to specific details. Therefore, avoid including many specific examples or concrete details from the text you are summarizing and try

to let your reader know what these examples and details add up to. Some of the specificity and excitement of the original text will be lost, but when summarizing, the goal is not to recreate all that is interesting about the original text. Rather, the writer's goal is to let the reader know the essential meaning of the original text in a clear, straightforward way.

■ Avoiding Plagiarism

Plagiarism is the use of someone else's words or ideas without adequate acknowledgment—that is, presenting such words or ideas as your own. Putting something in your own words is not in itself a defense against plagiarism; the source of the ideas must be identified as well. Giving credit to the sources you use serves three important purposes: (1) it reflects your own honesty and seriousness as a researcher; (2) it enables the reader to find the source of the reference and read further, sometimes to verify that the source has been correctly used; and (3) it adds the authority of experts to your argument. Deliberate plagiarism is nothing less than cheating and theft, and it is an offense that deserves serious punishment. Accidental plagiarism can be avoided if you take a little care when researching and writing your papers.

The writer of the zoo paper, for instance, uses and correctly introduces the following direct quotation by James Rachels (para. 4):

> As James Rachels (1976) writes:
>
> Humans have a right to liberty because they have various other interests that will suffer if their freedom is unduly restricted. The right to liberty -- the right to be free of external constraints on one's actions -- may then be seen as derived from a more basic right not to have one's interests needlessly harmed. (p. 210)

If the writer of the zoo paper had chosen to state this idea more briefly, in her own words, the result might have been something like this: "Human beings believe in their fundamental right to liberty because they all agree that they would suffer without it. The right to liberty, then, stems from the right not to suffer unnecessarily." Although the wording has been significantly altered, if this statement appeared as is, undocumented, the author of the paper would be guilty of plagiarism because the ideas are not original. To avoid plagiarism, the author needs to include a reference to James Rachels at the beginning of the summary and a citation of the page number at the end. Taking care to document sources is an obvious way to avoid plagiarism. You should also be careful in taking notes and, when writing your paper, indicating where your ideas end and someone else's ideas begin.

When taking notes, make sure either to quote word-for-word *or* to paraphrase: one or the other, not a little bit of both. If you quote, enclose any language that you borrow from other sources in quotation marks.

That way, when you look back at your note cards weeks later, you won't mistakenly assume that the language is your own. If you know that you aren't going to use a particular writer's exact words in your paper, then take the time to summarize that person's ideas right away. That will save you time and trouble later.

When using someone else's ideas in your paper, always let the reader know where that person's ideas begin and end. Here is an example from the zoo paper (para. 11):

> When zoo animals do mate successfully, the offspring is often weakened by inbreeding. According to geneticists, this is because a population of 150 breeder animals is necessary in order to "assure the more or less permanent survival of a species in captivity" (Ehrlich & Ehrlich, 1981, p. 211).

The phrase "according to geneticists" indicates that the material to follow comes from another source, cited parenthetically at the end of the borrowed material. If the student had not included the phrase "according to geneticists," it might look as if she only borrowed the passage in quotation marks, and not the information that precedes that passage.

Material that is considered common knowledge—that is, familiar or at least accessible to the general public—does not have to be documented. The author of *Hamlet,* the date the Declaration of Independence was signed, or the definition of *misfeasance,* while open to dispute (some scholars, for example, claim that William Shakespeare did not write *Hamlet*) are indisputably considered to be common knowledge in our culture. Unfortunately, it is not always clear whether a particular fact *is* common knowledge. Although too much documentation can clutter a paper and distract the reader, it's still better to cite too many sources than to cite too few and risk being accused of dishonesty. In general, if you are unsure whether or not to give your source credit, you should document the material.

■ Keeping Research under Control

Your preliminary outline provides guideposts for your research. You will need to revise it as you go along to make room for new ideas and evidence and for the questions that come up as you read. Rather than try to fit each new piece of information into your outline, you can use the numbering or lettering system in your outline to cross-reference your notebooks or file cards.

As much as possible, keep all materials related to the same point in the same place. You might do this by making a separate pile of file cards for each point and its support and questions or by reserving several pages in your notebook for information bearing on each point.

How do you know when you have done enough research? If you have kept your outline updated, you have a visual record of your progress. Check this against the guidelines on pages 346–47. Is each point backed by at least two pieces of support? Do your sources represent a range of authors and of types of data? If a large proportion of your support comes from one book, or if most of your references are to newspaper articles, you probably need to keep working. On the other hand, if your notes cite five different authorities making essentially the same point, you may have collected more data than you need. It can be useful to point out that more than one authority holds a given view and to make notes of examples that are notably different from one another. But it is not necessary to take down all the passages or examples expressing the same idea.

■ To This Point

Before you leave the library or your primary sources and start writing, check to make sure your research is complete.

1. Does your working outline show any gaps in your argument?
2. Have you found adequate data to support your claim?
3. Have you identified the warrants linking your claim with data and ensured that these warrants too are adequately documented?
4. If you intend to quote or paraphrase sources in your paper, do your notes include exact copies of all statements you may want to use and complete references?
5. Have you answered all the relevant questions that have come up during your research?
6. Do you have enough information about your sources to document your paper?

COMPILING AN ANNOTATED BIBLIOGRAPHY

An annotated bibliography is a list of sources that includes the usual bibliographic information followed by a paragraph describing and evaluating each source. Its purpose is to provide information about each source in a bibliography so that the reader has an overview of the resources related to a given topic.

For each source in an annotated bibliography, the same bibliographic information included in a Works Cited or References list is provided, alphabetized by author. Each reference also has a short paragraph that describes the work, its main focus, and, if appropriate, the methodology used in or the style of the work. An annotation might note special features such as tables or illustrations. Usually an annotation evaluates the source by analyzing its usefulness, reliability, and overall significance for understanding the topic. An annotation might include some information on the credentials of the author or the organization that produced it.

A SAMPLE ANNOTATION USING THE MLA CITATION STYLE

Warner, Marina. "Pity the Stepmother." New York Times. 12 May 1991, late ed.: D17. Lexis/Nexis Universe 12 Dec. 1998 <http://web .lexis-nexis.com/universe/form/academic/univ_gennews.html>.

The author asserts that many fairy tales feature absent or cruel mothers, transformed by romantic editors such as the Grimm brothers into step-mothers because the idea of a wicked mother desecrated an ideal. She argues that figures in fairy tales should be viewed in their historical con-text and that social conditions often affected the way that motherhood figured in fairy tales. Warner, a novelist and author of books on the images of Joan of Arc and the Virgin Mary, writes persuasively about the social roots of a fairy-tale archetype.

A SAMPLE ANNOTATION USING THE APA CITATION STYLE

"Don't Zoos Contribute to the Saving of Species from Extinction?" Animal Rights Resource Site. Envirolink Network. 14 Dec. 1998 <http://arrs .envirolink.org/Faqs+Ref/ar-faq/Q68.html>.

This Web site provides arguments against the idea that zoos save species from extinction. Breeding in captivity doesn't always work, and the limited gene pool creates problems. Habitat restoration is difficult, and until the problems of poaching and pollution are solved, the habitat will be dangerous for reintroduced species. Meanwhile, the individual animals living in zoos lose their freedom because of an abstract and possibly faulty concept. This Web site, part of the Animal Rights Resource Site sponsored by the Envirolink organization, is brief but outlines the major arguments against zoos' role in preserving species.

MLA SYSTEM FOR CITING PUBLICATIONS

One of the simplest methods of crediting sources is the Modern Language Association (MLA) in-text system, which is used in the research paper on immigration in this chapter. In the text of your paper, immediately after any quotation, paraphrase, or anything else you wish to document, simply insert a parenthetical mention of the author's last name and the page num-ber on which the material appeared. You don't need a comma after the author's name or an abbreviation of the word "page" or "p." For example, the following sentence appears in the fairy tale paper:

Famines in the seventeenth century often reduced the peasantry to a diet of "bad black bread, acorns, and roots" (Weber 96).

The parenthetical reference tells the reader that the information in this sentence came from page 96 of the book or article by Eugen Weber that appears in the Works Cited, at the end of the paper. The complete reference on the Works Cited page provides all the information readers need to locate the original source in the library:

Weber, Eugen. "Fairies and Hard Facts: The Reality of Folktales." Journal of the History of Ideas 42 (1981): 93-113.

If the author's name is mentioned in the same sentence, it is also acceptable to place only the page numbers in parentheses; it is not necessary to repeat the author's name. For example,

Bettelheim sees symbolic meaning in every motif and element in the story, and assumes that children interpret these symbolically as well (159-66).

Some sources do not name an author. To cite a work with an unknown author, give the title, or a recognizable shortened form, in the text of your paper. If the work does not have numbered pages, often the case in Web pages or nonprint sources, do not include page numbers. For example,

In some cases Sephardic Jews, "converted" under duress, practiced Christianity openly and Judaism in secret until recently ("Search for the Buried Past").

The list of works cited includes all material you have used to write your research paper. This list appears at the end of your paper and always starts on a new page. Center the title Works Cited, double-space between the title and the first entry, and begin your list, which should be arranged alphabetically by author. Each entry should start at the left margin; indent all subsequent lines of the entry five spaces. Number each page, and double-space throughout.

Another method of documenting sources is to use notes, either footnotes (at the foot of the page) or endnotes (on a separate page at the end of the paper). The note method is not as commonly used today as the in-text system because reference notes repeat almost all the information already given on the Works Cited page. If footnotes or endnotes are used, most word-processing programs have functions that make the insertion of these notes convenient.

Nevertheless, it is a valid method, so we illustrate it here. Superscript numbers go at the end of the sentence or phrase being referenced:

Roman authors admit to borrowing frequently from earlier Greek writers for their jokes, although no joke books in the original Greek survive today.[1]

The reference note for this citation would be

[1]Alexander Humez and Nicholas Humez, Alpha to Omega (Boston: Godine, 1981) 79.

On the Works Cited page this reference would be:

> Humez, Alexander, and Nicholas Humez. <u>Alpha to Omega</u>. Boston: Godine, 1981.

Notice that the page number for a book citation is given in the note but not the reference and that the punctuation differs. Otherwise the information is the same. Number the notes consecutively throughout your paper.

One more point: *Content notes,* which provide additional information not readily worked into a research paper, are also indicated by superscript numbers. Susan Middleton's paper on fairy tales features four such notes, included on a Notes page before the list of Works Cited.

Following are examples of the citation forms you are most likely to need as you document your research. In general, for both books and magazines, information should appear in the following order: author, title, and publication information. Each item should be followed by a period. When using as a source an essay that appears in this book, follow the citation model for "Material reprinted from another source," unless your instructor indicates otherwise. Consult the *MLA Handbook for Writers of Research Papers,* Fifth Edition, by Joseph Gibaldi (New York: Modern Language Association of America, 1999) for other documentation models and a list of acceptable shortened forms of publishers.

■ Print Sources

A BOOK BY A SINGLE AUTHOR

Gubar, Susan. <u>Racechanges: White Skin, Black Face in American Culture</u>. New York: Oxford UP, 1997.

AN ANTHOLOGY OR COMPILATION

Dark, Larry, ed. <u>Prize Stories 1997: The O. Henry Awards</u>. New York: Anchor, 1997.

A BOOK BY TWO AUTHORS

Alderman, Ellen, and Caroline Kennedy. <u>The Right to Privacy</u>. New York: Vintage, 1995.

Note: This form is followed even for two authors with the same last name.

Ehrlich, Paul, and Anne Ehrlich. <u>Extinction: The Causes and Consequences of the Disappearance of Species</u>. New York: Random, 1981.

A BOOK BY TWO OR MORE AUTHORS

Heffernan, William A., Mark Johnston, and Frank Hodgins. <u>Literature: Art and Artifact</u>. San Diego: Harcourt, 1987.

If there are more than three authors, name only the first and add: "et al." (and others).

A BOOK BY A CORPORATE AUTHOR

Poets & Writers, Inc. The Writing Business: A Poets & Writers Handbook. New York: Poets & Writers, 1985.

A WORK IN AN ANTHOLOGY

Head, Bessie. "Woman from America." Wild Women: Contemporary Short Stories by Women Celebrating Women. Ed. Sue Thomas. Woodstock: Overlook, 1994. 45-51.

AN INTRODUCTION, PREFACE, FOREWORD, OR AFTERWORD

Callahan, John F. Introduction. Flying Home and Other Stories. By Ralph Ellison. Ed. John F. Callahan. New York: Vintage, 1996. 1-9.

MATERIAL REPRINTED FROM ANOTHER SOURCE

Diffie, Whitfield, and Susan Landau. "Privacy: Protections and Threats." Privacy on the Line: The Politics of Wiretapping and Encryption. Cambridge, MA: MIT P, 1998. Rpt. in Elements of Argument: A Text and Reader. Annette T. Rottenberg. 7th ed. Boston: Bedford/St. Martin's, 2003. 554.

A MULTIVOLUME WORK

Skotheim, Robert Allen, and Michael McGiffert, eds. Since the Civil War. Vol. 2 of American Social Thought: Sources and Interpretations. 2 vols. Reading: Addison, 1972.

AN EDITION OTHER THAN THE FIRST

Charters, Ann, ed. The Story and Its Writer: An Introduction to Short Fiction, 5th ed. Boston: Bedford/St. Martin's, 1999.

A TRANSLATION

Allende, Isabel. The House of the Spirits. Trans. Magda Bogin. New York: Knopf, 1985.

A REPUBLISHED BOOK

Weesner, Theodore. The Car Thief. 1972. New York: Vintage-Random, 1987.

Note: The only information about original publication you need to provide is the publication date, which appears immediately after the title.

A BOOK IN A SERIES

Eady, Cornelius. Victims of the Latest Dance Craze. Omnation Press Dialogues on Dance Series 5. Chicago: Omnation, 1985.

AN ARTICLE FROM A DAILY NEWSPAPER

Doctorow, E. L. "Quick Cuts: The Novel Follows Film into a World of Fewer Words." New York Times 15 Mar. 1999, sec. B: 1+.

AN ARTICLE FROM A PERIODICAL

Schulhofer, Stephen. "Unwanted Sex." Atlantic Monthly Oct. 1998: 55-66.

AN UNSIGNED EDITORIAL

"Medium, Message." Editorial. Nation 28 Mar. 1987: 383-84.

ANONYMOUS WORKS

"The March Almanac." Atlantic Mar. 1995: 20.

Citation World Atlas. Maplewood: Hammond, 1987.

AN ARTICLE FROM A JOURNAL WITH SEPARATE PAGINATION FOR EACH ISSUE

Brewer, Derek. "The Battleground of Home: Versions of Fairy Tales." Encounter 54.4 (1980): 52-61.

AN ARTICLE IN A JOURNAL WITH CONTINUOUS PAGINATION THROUGHOUT THE VOLUME

McCafferty, Janey. "The Shadders Go Away." New England Review and Bread Loaf Quarterly 9 (1987): 332-42.

Note that the issue number is not mentioned here; because the volume has continuous pagination throughout the year, only the volume number 9 is needed.

A REVIEW

Walker, David. Rev. of A Wave, by John Ashbery. Field 32 (1985): 63-71.

AN ARTICLE IN A REFERENCE WORK

"Bylina." The Princeton Encyclopedia of Poetry and Poetics. Ed. Alex Preminger. Enlarged ed. Princeton: Princeton UP, 1974.

A GOVERNMENT DOCUMENT

United States. National Endowment for the Arts. 1989 Annual Report. Washington: Office of Public Affairs, 1990.

Frequently the Government Printing Office (GPO) is the publisher of federal government documents.

REPORTS

Gura, Mark. The Gorgeous Mosaic Project: A Work of Art by the Schoolchildren of the World. Teacher's packet. East Brunswick: Children's Atelier, 1990. ERIC ED 347 257.

Kassebaum, Peter. Cultural Awareness Training Manual and Study Guide. ERIC, 1992. ED 347 289.

The ERIC number at the end of the entry indicates that this source is available through ERIC (Educational Resource Information Center); some libraries have these available on microfiche. The number indicates which report to look for. Some ERIC documents were published elsewhere, as in the first example. If no other publishing information is given, treat ERIC (with no city given) as the publisher, as shown in the second entry. Reports are also published by NTIS (National Technical Information Service), state geological surveys, organizations, institutes within universities, and so on and may be called "technical reports," or "occasional papers." Be sure to include the source and the unique report number, if given.

AN UNPUBLISHED MANUSCRIPT

Leahy, Ellen. "An Investigation of the Computerization of Information Systems in a Family Planning Program." Unpublished master's degree project. Div. of Public Health, U of Massachusetts, Amherst, 1990.

A LETTER TO THE EDITOR

Flannery, James W. Letter. New York Times Book Review 28 Feb. 1993: 34.

PERSONAL CORRESPONDENCE

Bennett, David. Letter to the author. 3 Mar. 1993.

A CARTOON

Henley, Marian. "Maxine." Cartoon. Valley Advocate 25 Feb. 1993: 39.

■ Electronic Sources

A WEB SITE

Fairy Tales: Origins and Evolution. Ed. Christine Daaé. 12 Dec. 1998 <http://www.darkgoddess.com/fairy>.

Include the title if available; the author's name if available or, if not, a generic description such as "Home page"; the sponsoring organization or institution except in the case of commercial sponsorship; date of access; and URL in angle brackets.

A PAGE WITHIN A WEB SITE

"Don't Zoos Contribute to the Saving of Species from Extinction?" Animal Rights Resource Site. Envirolink Network. 14 Dec. 1998 <http://arrs.envirolink .org/faqs+Ref/ar-faq/Q68.html>.

A BOOK AVAILABLE ON THE WEB

Kramer, Heinrich, and James Sprenger. The Malleus Maleficarum. Trans.
　　Montague Summers. New York: Dover, 1971. 14 Dec. 1998 <http://www
　　.geocities.com/Athens/2962/witchcraze/malleus_2_ii_html>.

In this case the book had been previously published, and information
about its original publication was included at the site.

AN ARTICLE FROM AN ELECTRONIC JOURNAL

Minow, Mary. "Filters and the Public Library: A Legal and Policy Analysis." First
　　Monday 2.12 (1 Dec. 1997). 28 Nov. 1998 <http:www.firstmonday.dk/
　　issues/issue2_12/minow/index.html>.

MATERIAL ACCESSED THROUGH A COMPUTER SERVICE

Boynton, Robert S. "The New Intellectuals." Atlantic Monthly Mar. 1995.
　　Atlantic Unbound. America Online. 3 Mar. 1995. Keyword: Atlantic.

A CD-ROM

Corcoran, Mary B. "Fairy Tale." Grolier Multimedia Encyclopedia. CD-ROM.
　　Danbury: Grolier, 1995.

AN ARTICLE FROM A FULL-TEXT DATABASE AVAILABLE THROUGH THE WEB

Warner, Marina. "Pity the Stepmother." New York Times. 12 May 1991, late ed.:
　　D17. Lexis/Nexis Universe 12 Dec. 1998. <http://web.lexis-nexis.com/
　　universe/form/academic/univ_gennews.html>.

Include the original source information and the name of the database,
access date, and URL.

AN ARTICLE FROM A CD-ROM FULL-TEXT DATABASE

"Tribal/DNC Donations." News from Indian Country. (Dec. 1997). Ethnic
　　Newswatch. CD-ROM. Softline. 12 Oct. 1998.

Include the original source information and the name of the database,
the designation *CD-ROM,* the publisher of the CD-ROM, and the electronic publication data, if available.

AN ARTICLE FROM AN ELECTRONIC REFERENCE WORK

"Folk Arts." Britannica Online. Encyclopaedia Britannica. 14 Dec. 2002.
　　<http://www.eb.com:180>.

A PERSONAL E-MAIL COMMUNICATION

Franz, Kenneth. "Re: Species Reintroduction." E-mail to the author. 12 Oct.
　　2001.

AN E-MAIL COMMUNICATION POSTED TO A DISCUSSION LIST

Lee, Constance. "Re: Mothers and Stepmothers." Online posting. 10 Sept. 2002.
Folklore Discussion List <mglazer@panam.edu>.

If the address of the discussion list archives is known, include that information in angle brackets; if not, place the moderator's e-mail address in angle brackets.

A POSTING TO A WEB FORUM

DeYoung, Chris. Online posting. 12 Dec. 1998. Issues: Gay Rights. 14 Dec. 1998
<http://community.cnn.com/cgi-bin/WebX?14@52.7bmLaPoSc49^0@
.ee7239c/12479>.

Include the author, header (if any) in quotation marks, the designation *Online posting,* the date of the posting, the name of the forum, the date of access, and the URL.

A NEWSGROUP POSTING

Vining, Philip. "Zoos and Infotainment." Online posting. 16 Oct. 2002. 12 Dec.
2002. <news: alt.animals.ethics.vegetarian>.

Include the author, header in quotation marks, the designation *Online posting,* the date of posting, the date of access, and the name of the newsgroup.

A SYNCHRONOUS COMMUNICATION

Krishnamurthi, Ashok. Online discussion of cyberlaw and the media. "Reinventing Copyright in a Digital Environment." 25 Oct. 2002. MediaMOO. 25 Oct.
2002 <telnet://purple-crayon.media.mit.edu:8888>.

To cite a synchronous communication from a MUD or a MOO, include the name of the speaker, a description of the event, the date, the forum, the date of access, and the electronic address.

Other Sources

A LECTURE

Calvino, Italo. "Right and Wrong Political Uses of Literature." Symposium on European Politics. Amherst College, Amherst. 25 Feb. 1976.

A FILM

The Voice of the Khalam. Prod. Loretta Pauker. Perf. Leopold Senghor, Okara,
Birago Diop, Rubadiri, and Francis Parkes. Contemporary Films/McGraw-Hill,
1971. 16 mm, 29 min.

Other pertinent information to give in film references, if available, is the writer and director (see model for radio/television program for style).

A TELEVISION OR RADIO PROGRAM

The Shakers: Hands to Work, Hearts to God. Narr. David McCullough. Dir. Ken
    Burns and Amy Stechler Burns. Writ. Amy Stechler Burns, Wendy Tilghman,
    and Tom Lewis. PBS. WGBY, Springfield. 28 Dec. 1992.

A VIDEOTAPE

Style Wars! Videotape. Prod. Tony Silver and Henry Chalfont. New Day Films,
    1985. 69 min.

DVD

Harry Potter and the Sorcerer's Stone. DVD. Prod. Chris Columbus. Warner Bros.,
    2001. 152 min.

A PERFORMANCE

Quilters: A Musical Celebration. By Molly Newman and Barbara Damashek. Dir.
    Joyce Devlin. Musical dir. Faith Fung. Mt. Holyoke Laboratory Theatre,
    South Hadley, MA. 26 Apr. 1991. Based on The Quilters: Women and Domes-
    tic Art by Patricia Cooper and Norma Bradley Allen.

AN INTERVIEW

Hines, Gregory. Interview. With D. C. Denison. Boston Globe Magazine 29 Mar.
    1987: 2.

Note: An interview conducted by the author of the paper would be documented as follows:

Hines, Gregory. Personal interview. 29 Mar. 1987.

SAMPLE RESEARCH PAPER (MLA STYLE)

The following paper, prepared in the MLA style, was written for an advanced composition course. Told to compose a research paper on a literary topic, Susan Middleton chose to write on fairy tales—a subject
literary enough to satisfy her instructor, yet general enough to encom-
pass her own interest in developmental psychology. But as she explored
the subject, she found herself reading in a surprising array of disciplines,
including folklore, anthropology, and history. Although she initially
expected to report on the psychological importance of fairy tales,
Middleton at last wrote an argument about the importance of their historical and cultural roots. Her paper, as is typical for literary papers, an-
chors its argument in the events and details of its chosen text, "Hansel
and Gretel." But it also makes effective use of sources to help readers understand that there is more to the tale than a story that sends children
happily off to sleep.

When a Fairy Tale Is Not Just a Fairy Tale

By
Susan Middleton

Professor Herrington
English 2A
October 2002

Include a title page if an outline is part of the paper. If no outline is required, include name, instructor's name, course name, and date at the upper left corner of page 1.

Writer's name; page number

Middleton   ii

Topic outline. Some instructors require a thesis statement under "Outline" heading and before the outline itself.

Outline

I. Introduction:
   A. Dictionary definition of "fairy tale"
   B. Thesis: "Hansel and Gretel" has historical roots
II. Origin and distribution of tale
III. Historical basis of motifs
   A. Physical and economic hardship
      1. Fear of the forest
      2. Poverty and starvation
      3. Child abandonment
      4. Fantasies of finding treasure
   B. Cruel stepmother
   C. Wicked witch
      1. Eating meat associated with cannibalism and upper classes
      2. Elderly caretaker for unwanted children
      3. Witches in community
      4. Witchcraft as remnant of ancient fertility religion
IV. Rebuttals to historical approach
   A. Motivation for telling realistic tales
   B. Psychological interpretations
      1. Fairy tales dreamlike, not literal
      2. Freudian interpretation
V. Conclusion

Middleton   1

When a Fairy Tale Is Not Just a Fairy Tale

"Hansel and Gretel" is a well-known fairy tale, beloved of many children in both Europe and North America.[1] Although it has no fairies in it, it conforms to the definition of "fairy tale" given in Merriam-Webster's Collegiate Dictionary, Tenth Edition: "a story (as for children) involving fantastic forces and beings (as fairies, wizards, and goblins)." As anyone familiar with this tale will remember, Hansel and Gretel are two children on an adventure in the woods, where they encounter a wicked witch in a gingerbread house, who plans to fatten and eat them. Through their ingenuity they outsmart her, burn her up in her own oven, and return home triumphantly with a hoard of riches found in her house.

We think of fairy tales as being lighthearted fantasies that entertain but don't have much relevance to daily life. We often borrow the word to describe a movie with an unlikely plot, or a person not quite grounded in reality: "Oh, he's living in a fairy tale world; he hasn't got his head on his shoulders." In fact, the second definition of "fairy tale" in Webster's is "a made-up story usually designed to mislead."

So what is the meaning of "Hansel and Gretel"? Is it simply a story of make-believe, or something more? Fairy tales are told, read, and heard in the context of a time and place. Today we are exposed to them through illustrated storybooks, cartoons, and film. But in Europe, before technologies in printing made mass publishing possible, folktales were passed on orally. Women were the primary tellers of folktales, though they were later gathered and published by male writers such as Charles Perrault and the Grimm Brothers ("Tales"). They were told by adults mostly for adult audiences, although people often first heard them as children. They served to entertain and to relieve the boredom of repetitive work in the fields during the day and in the home in the evening (Weber 93, 113). In peasant and aboriginal communities, that is often still the case (Taggart 437).

I believe that "Hansel and Gretel" has historical meaning. Embedded in this simple narrative is a record of the experiences and events once common in the lives of the people who first told and listened to it.

Title centered

*Raised, super-
script number
refers to notes
giving infor-
mation at the
end of the
paper.*

*Writer briefly
summarizes
tale to orient
readers.*

*In-text citation
of author and
pages; citation
appears at the
end of the sen-
tence before
the period.*

*Thesis with
claim of fact
that the writer
must support*

Middleton   2

Where did "Hansel and Gretel" come from? We do not
know for certain. In oral form this tale shows wide distribution. Different versions have been recorded all over Europe,
India, Japan, Africa, the Caribbean, Pacific Islands, and among
native North and South Americans ("Hansel and Gretel"). As
with all folktales, there is no agreement among folklorists[2]
about whether all these versions migrated from one place to
another, sprang up independently, or derive from some combination of the two ("Hansel and Gretel"). Most oral versions of
it have been recorded in Europe (Aarne 117). This does not
prove that the tale originated there--it may simply reflect the
eagerness of people in Europe during the nineteenth and
twentieth centuries to record their own folk history--but it is
the best guideline for now.

Reference to dictionary article — page number not necessary

The tale may be very ancient, since folktales can be
passed on faithfully from one generation to another without
change. (The origins of "Cinderella," for example, can be
traced back to China in the ninth century [Thompson,
Folktale 126].) But we can't know that for sure. So, even
though "Hansel and Gretel" may have originated hundreds or
even thousands of years ago, it probably is only safe to compare a tale with the historical period when the tale was first
recorded. For "Hansel and Gretel" this means Europe in the
seventeenth to nineteenth centuries.[3]

Square brackets used to represent parentheses within parentheses

Eugen Weber is one historian who sees direct parallels between the characters and motifs in "Hansel and Gretel" (and
other Grimms' fairy tales) and the social and economic conditions in Europe during this period. One of the central themes
in the tale is poverty and abandonment. Recall how the tale
begins: Hansel and Gretel live with their parents near a huge
forest; their father is a woodcutter. The family is facing starvation because there is a famine. Twice their parents abandon
them in the woods to save themselves. The first time the children are able to find their way home, but the second time
they get lost.

Specific support from the tale cited

As Weber points out, until the middle of the nineteenth
century, the forest, especially for northern Europeans, carried
the real potential for encountering danger in the form of rob-

Middleton   3

bers, wild animals, and getting lost (96-97). Moreover, conditions of poverty, starvation, early death, and danger from unknown adults were common throughout Europe for peasants
and the working class (96). The majority of Europeans at the
beginning of the eighteenth century were farmers, and the
average life expectancy was about twenty-five years (Treasure
660, 667). Famines in the seventeenth century often reduced
the peasantry to a diet of "bad black bread, acorns, and roots"
(Weber 96). Hansel and Gretel are treated by the witch to a
dinner of pancakes and sugar, milk, nuts, and apples (101).
This may not sound particularly nourishing to our ears because we assume a healthy dinner must have vegetables
and/or meat. But when you're starving, anything is likely to
taste good; this would have been a sumptuous meal for Hansel
and Gretel.

Consecutive references immediately following an identified source ("Weber") cite only the pages within the source without repeating the source.

Narrative details linked to historical facts

Childhood was thought of differently then than today.
"Valued as an extra pair of hands or deplored as an extra
mouth to feed, the child belonged to no privileged realm of
play and protection from life's responsibilities" (Treasure
664). Social historian John Boswell estimates that anywhere
from 10 to 40 percent of children in towns and cities were
abandoned during the eighteenth century. Parental motivation included removing the stigma of illegitimate or physically
deformed children, being unable to support their children and
hoping to give them a better life with strangers, desiring to
promote one child's inheritance over another's, or simply lacking interest in raising the child (48, 428).

Source cited after direct quotation

Weber points out that peasants had very little cash and
didn't use banks. Hiding and finding treasure--gold, silver,
and jewelry--was a much more common occurrence two centuries ago than it is today (101), a kind of lottery for the
poor. In this light, the riches the children find in the witch's
house could reflect the common person's fantasy of striking it
rich.

Writer's interpretation of one aspect of the story

A central motif in the story is the stepmother who wants
to abandon the children to keep herself and her husband from
starving. (The father, at first reluctant, eventually gives in to
his wife's plan.) As Weber and others have noted, stepmothers

Middleton   4

were not unusual in history. The death rate among childbearing women was much higher in past centuries than it is today.
When women died in childbirth, there was strong economic
motivation for fathers to remarry. In the seventeenth and
eighteenth centuries, 20 to 80 percent of widowers remarried
within the year of their wife's death. By the mid-nineteenth
century, after life expectancy rose, only 15 percent of widowers did so (94, 112).

Reference to a
newspaper

What accounts for the stereotype of the heartless stepmother? Warner argues that mothers, not stepmothers, actually appeared in many of the tales in their original forms,
until romantic editors, like the Grimm brothers, "rebelled
against this desecration of motherhood and changed mothers
into wicked stepmothers" (D17). Weber suggests that stepmothers were assigned the role of doing evil to children for
economic reasons: The family would risk losing its good name
and perhaps its land if a biological parent killed a child (107).
There is also the issue of inheritance from the stepmother's
point of view: If her husband dies, her husband's children, not
she, would inherit the land and property. Literary and legal
evidence of stepmothers plotting to eliminate stepchildren,
especially stepsons, shows up in European literature as far
back as two millennia ago (Boswell 128).

Transition to
new topic:
witches

Another major theme in "Hansel and Gretel" is the wicked
witch, which also shows up in lots of other fairy tales. One of
the common beliefs about witches was that they ate children.
According to the words of a purported witch in the <u>Malleus
Maleficarum</u>, a treatise on witchcraft published originally
around 1486, "[we] cook them in a cauldron until the whole
flesh comes away from the bones to make a soup that may be
easily drunk" (Kramer and Sprenger, ch. 2, para. 12). The authors of this work were alarmists, describing in sometimes improbable terms the evil behavior of witches, but the question
remains: Were there witches in European history, and if so,
where did the reputation for eating children come from?

Weber notes that in fairy tales only evil figures eat meat
of any kind, whether animal or human flesh. Before the
middle of the nineteenth century the peasantry rarely ate meat,

but the aristocracy and bourgeoisie did. This discrepancy may
be the origin of the motif in some fairy tales of evil figures of
upper-class background wanting to eat children (112, 101).
Weber seems to imply that child-eating witches symbolized to
the peasantry either resentment of or paranoia about the aristocracy.

Although the witch's cottage in "Hansel and Gretel" is
not described as grand or large, there are other allusions to
wealth and comfort. The witch puts the two children to bed
between clean sheets, a luxury for much of the peasantry,
who slept on straw and for whom bed lice were a common reality (Treasure 661-62). And of course there is the hoard of
coin money and jewelry the children later discover there. Perhaps more significantly, the witch herself has a lot of power,
just as the aristocracy was perceived to have, including the
power to deceive and take away life.

David Bakan suggests that the historical basis for the
witch is the unmarried elderly woman in the community who
took in unwanted, illegitimate children and was often paid to
do this (66-67). There is also evidence that witchcraft, ranging from white magic to sorcery (black magic), was practiced
by both individual women and men among the peasantry during this time. For example, "the 'cunning folk' were at least as
numerous in sixteenth-century England as the parish clergy.
Moreover, in their divinatory, medical, and religious functions
they were far more important in peasant society than were
the official clergy" (Horsley 697). Witches were called on to
influence the weather, provide love potions, find lost objects,
midwife, identify thieves, and heal illnesses (698). Some services performed by witches were ambiguous: "Apparently
some peasants would conjure the storms or weather spirits to
avoid striking their own fields--but to strike someone else's
instead," but for the most part the wisewomen and sorcerers
were different people (698).

The idea that an organized witch cult, as portrayed by
the Catholic Church during the Middle Ages, actually existed
is dismissed today by most social historians. Jesse Nash thinks
we should reconsider the possibility that some of the behavior

Middleton   6

witches were accused of, including ritual cannibalism and sexual orgies in the woods, actually occurred in some form (12).
He sees witchcraft as "a surviving remnant of a religion which
was concerned with the fertility of crops, animals, humans,
and with the alteration of seasons and with the identification
of humans with animals" (13). These practices date back to a
matriarchal goddess religion which flourished in Europe 5,000
to 7,000 years ago, before invasion of the patriarchal cultures
from India (Marija Gimbutas in Nash 12). This religion included human sacrifice and was based on the concept of maintaining balance in the universe: The goddess of life was at the
same time the goddess of death. Wood-wives and fairies, who
lived in the forest, "were mediators of sacred knowledge to
their communities" (16).

*Source within
a source cited*

Nash suggests that in Europe, although Christianity became the official way of thinking about the world, it did not
replace the old beliefs entirely, despite strong attempts by
the Church to eliminate them. Religious beliefs and practices
can persist hidden for generations if need be.[4] The peasants
were able to live with and practice both Christianity and pa-
ganism in combination for centuries (25).

So we have seen there is validity to the claim that many
of the motifs of "Hansel and Gretel" have historical roots.
However, one might well ask why people would want to hear
stories so close to their own experiences. If oral tales during
this time were meant as entertainment mostly for adults,
wouldn't they want something to take their minds off their
troubles? Weber suggests a couple of motivations for telling
fairy tales. One was to experience "the delights of fear" (97).
Fairy tales were told along with ghost stories, gossip, jokes,
and fables. I suspect it was similar to the thrill some people
get today watching scary movies with happy endings.

*Having sup-
ported her
major claim,
the writer
continues by
anticipating
and addressing
possible
rebuttals.*

Second, fairy tales helped to explain how the world
worked. To most people not able to read, the world of cause
and effect was mysterious and could only be explained
through symbolism and analogy. Folktales had been used in
church sermons since the fourteenth century (Weber 110,
Zipes 22).

*Two sources
cited at once*

Middleton   7

But the industrial age ushered in the scientific revolution, and with it came the concept of explaining the unknown
by breaking it down into working parts (Weber 113). Reading
became available to large numbers of people. By this time
fairy tales were no longer meaningful ways to explain the
world for ordinary adults, so they became the province of
children's entertainment (113).

Folklorist Alan Dundes thinks it is naive to assume fairy
tales have literal meaning. In recent years he and a number of
other people have looked to psychology to explain the origin
of fairy tales. "Fairy tales are like dreams--can you find the
historic origin of dreams?" (Dundes). In their structure and
characters fairy tales do have a number of dreamlike aspects:
They rarely state the feelings of the hero directly, and all
inner experiences of the hero are projected outward into objects in nature and other people (Tatar 91). The other characters seem not to have separate lives of their own; all their
actions and intentions relate to the hero (Brewer 55). Also,
magical things happen: Elements of nature speak, granting favors to the hero or threatening success or even life. In one
version of "Hansel and Gretel," for example, a white duck
talks to the children and carries them across a lake on their
way home.

Competing theories presented

Telephone interview—no page numbers

The symbolic nature of fairy tales, however, doesn't deny
the validity of examining them for historical origins. As anyone who has recorded their own dreams knows, people and
objects from mundane, daily life show up regularly in them.
Sometimes these elements are disguised as symbols, but other
times they are transparently realistic. Similarly, the talking
duck and the gingerbread house in "Hansel and Gretel" may
be unreal, but other themes have more literal counterparts in
history.

One of the most quoted interpreters of fairy tales is psychologist Bruno Bettelheim, whose The Uses of Enchantment
analyzes fairy tales in Freudian terms. In his view, "Hansel
and Gretel" represents the task each of us as children must
face in coming to terms with anxiety--not the anxiety of facing starvation and being literally abandoned in the woods, but

Middleton   8

the ordinary fear of separating from our parents (especially mother) in the process of growing up to become independent adults. Bettelheim sees symbolic meaning in every motif and element in the story, and assumes that children interpret these symbolically as well (159-66).

Partial validity of competing theories acknowledged

Undeniably, there are themes in "Hansel and Gretel"--as in many of our most common fairy tales--that strike deep psychological chords with both children and adults. The wicked stepmother is a good example: Children often fantasize they are really stepchildren or adopted as a way to account for feeling victimized and abused by their parents. "In real life this fantasy occurs among children with a very high frequency" (Bakan 76).

Having qualified her major claim in light of other theories, student goes on to reiterate the support of her major claim in her conclusion.

These themes help to explain the enduring popularity of fairy tales among middle-class children over the last two centuries. But we cannot treat fairy tales as if they spring full-blown from the unconscious and tell us nothing about the past. For the people who told and heard "Hansel and Gretel" in the seventeenth to nineteenth centuries in Europe, the tale was describing events and phenomena that happened, if not to them, then to someone they knew. Everyone in rural communities was likely to have been exposed, whether in person or by hearsay, to some elderly woman claiming powers to alter weather patterns, heal the sick, cast spells, midwife, or take in illegitimate babies. Stepmothers were common, poverty and famine ongoing, and abandonment and child abuse very real. In addition to providing entertainment, tales like "Hansel and Gretel" reassured teller and listener alike that the ordinary physical hardships, which for most of us today are fictions, were possible to overcome.

Notes

1 We in the United States know it primarily in printed form, as it has come to us from Germany. Between 1812 and 1857, the Grimm brothers, Jacob and Wilhelm, published several editions of <u>Kinder und Hausmarchen</u> (<u>Children's and Household Tales</u>) (Zipes 6, 41, 79). In addition to "Hansel and Gretel," this book included over 200 other folktales (though not all of them were fairy tales). The anthology increased in popularity until by the turn of the twentieth century it outsold all other books in Germany except the Bible (Zipes 15). To date it has been translated into some seventy languages (Denecke).

2 Folklorists collect folktales from around the world and analyze them. Tales are categorized according to <u>type</u> (basic plot line) and <u>motifs</u> (elements within the tale). Two widely used references for folklorists are Antti Aarne's <u>Types of the Folklore</u> and Stith Thompson's <u>Motif-index</u>. "Hansel and Gretel" is type 327A in the Aarne classification.

3 The Grimms were the first to record tale type 327A in 1812 (see note 1). A related tale about Tom Thumb (tale type 327B) was first recorded by Charles Perrault from France in 1697 (Thompson, <u>Folktale</u> 37, 182).

4 Consider the example of Sephardic Jews who "converted" to Christianity under duress in Spain in the fifteenth century. Some of them moved to North America, and their descendants continued to practice Christianity openly and Judaism in secret until recently ("Search for the Buried Past").

Content notes appear at the end of the paper, before Works Cited.

Space included between superscript number and beginning of note

Indent five spaces to superscript number; rest of note is flush left.

Middleton   10

Works Cited

Sources arranged alphabetically by author's last name or by title

Aarne, Antti. The Types of the Folktale: Classification and Bibliography. Trans. and ed. Stith Thompson. 2nd rev. ed. FF Communications 184. Helsinki: Suomalainen Tiedeakatemia, 1964.

First line flush left in citation, rest indented five spaces

Bakan, David. Slaughter of the Innocents. Toronto: Canadian Broadcasting System, 1971.

Bettelheim, Bruno. The Uses of Enchantment: The Meaning and Importance of Fairy Tales. 1976. New York: Vintage, 1977.

Book

Boswell, John. The Kindness of Strangers: The Abandonment of Children in Western Europe from Late Antiquity to the Renaissance. New York: Pantheon, 1988.

Periodical

Brewer, Derek. "The Battleground of Home: Versions of Fairy Tales." Encounter 54.4 (1980): 52-61.

Encyclopedia article

Denecke, Ludwig. "Grimm, Jacob Ludwig Carl and Wilhelm Carl." Encyclopaedia Britannica: Macropaedia. 1992 ed.

Interview

Dundes, Alan. Telephone interview. 10 Feb. 1993.

"Fairy tale." Merriam-Webster's Collegiate Dictionary. 10th ed. 1993.

"Hansel and Gretel." Funk & Wagnalls Standard Dictionary of Folklore, Mythology, and Legend. Ed. Maria Leach. New York: Funk & Wagnalls, 1949.

Horsley, Richard A. "Who Were the Witches? The Social Roles of the Accused in the European Witch Trials." Journal of Interdisciplinary History 9 (1979): 689-715.

An online book

Kramer, Heinrich, and James Sprenger. The Malleus Maleficarum. Trans. Montague Summers. New York: Dover, 1971. 14 Dec. 1998. <http://www.geocities.com/Athens/2962/witchcraze/malleus_2_ii_html>.

Nash, Jesse. "European Witchcraft: The Hidden Tradition." Human Mosaic 21.1-2 (1987): 10-30.

Radio broadcast

"Search for the Buried Past." The Hidden Jews of New Mexico. Prod. Nan Rubin. WFCR, Amherst, MA. 13 Sept. 1992.

Taggart, James M. " 'Hansel and Gretel' in Spain and Mexico." Journal of American Folklore 99 (1986): 435-60.

Middleton   11

"The Tales and Their Tellers." Ed. Christine Daaé. <u>Fairy Tales:
   Origins and Evolution</u>. 12 Dec. 1998. <http://www
   .darkgoddess.com/fairy/tellers.htm>.

Tatar, Maria. "Folkloristic Phantasies: Grimm's Fairy Tales and
   Freud's Family Romance." <u>Fairy Tales as Ways of Knowing:
   Essays on Marchen in Psychology, Society and Literature</u>.
   Ed. Michael M. Metzger and Katharina Mommsen. <u>Ger-
   manic Studies in America</u> 41. Berne: Lang, 1981. 75-98.

Thompson, Stith. <u>The Folktale</u>. New York: Holt, 1946.

---. <u>Motif-index of Folk-literature: A Classification of Narrative
   Elements in Folktales, Ballads, Myths, Fables, Mediaeval
   Romances, Exempla, Fabliaux, Jest-books, and Local Leg-
   ends</u>. Rev. ed. 6 vols. plus index. Bloomington: Indiana
   UP, 1957.

Treasure, Geoffrey R. R. "European History and Culture: The
   Emergence of Modern Europe, 1500-1648." <u>Encyclopaedia
   Britannica: Macropaedia</u>. 1992 ed. 657-83.

Warner, Marina. "Pity the Stepmother." <u>New York Times</u>. 12
   May 1991, late ed.: D17. <u>Lexis/Nexis Universe</u> 12 Dec.
   1998. <http://web.lexis-nexis.com/universe/form/
   academic/univ_gennews.html>.

Weber, Eugen. "Fairies and Hard Facts: The Reality of Folktales." <u>Journal of the History of Ideas</u> 42 (1981): 93-113.

Zipes, Jack. <u>The Brothers Grimm: From Enchanted Forests to
   the Modern World</u>. New York: Routledge, 1988.

A page within a Web site

Article in an edited anthology

Two consecutive works by the same author

Volume in a multivolume revised edition

Newspaper online from a computer service

APA SYSTEM FOR CITING PUBLICATIONS

Instructors in the social sciences might prefer the citation system of the American Psychological Association (APA). Like the MLA system, the APA system calls for a parenthetical citation in the text of the paper. Unlike the MLA system, the APA system includes the year of publication in the parenthetical reference. Here is an example:

> Even though many South American countries rely on the drug trade for their economic survival, the majority of South Americans disapprove of drug use (Gorriti, 1989, p. 72).

The complete publication information for Gorriti's article will appear at the end of your paper, on a page titled "References." (Sample citations for the "References" page follow.)

If your list of references includes more than one work written by the same author in the same year, cite the first work as *a* and the second as *b*. For example, Gorriti's second article of 1989 would be cited in your paper as (Gorriti, 1989b).

Following are examples of the citation forms you are most likely to use. If you need the format for a type of publication not listed here, consult the *Publication Manual of the American Psychological Association*, Fifth Edition (2001).

■ Print Sources

A BOOK BY A SINGLE AUTHOR

Briggs, J. (1988). *Fire in the crucible: The alchemy of creative genius.* New York: St. Martin's Press.

MULTIPLE WORKS BY THE SAME AUTHOR IN THE SAME YEAR

Gardner, H. (1982a). *Art, mind, and brain: A cognitive approach to creativity.* New York: Basic.

Gardner, H. (1982b). *Developmental psychology: An introduction* (2nd ed.). Boston: Little, Brown.

AN ANTHOLOGY OR COMPILATION

Gioseffi, D. (Ed.). (1988). *Women on war.* New York: Simon & Schuster.

A BOOK BY TWO OR MORE AUTHORS OR EDITORS

Atwan, R., & Roberts, J. (Eds.). (1996). *Left, right, and center: Voices from across the political spectrum.* Boston: Bedford Books.

Note: List the names of *all* the authors or editors, no matter how many.

A BOOK BY A CORPORATE AUTHOR

International Advertising Association. (1977). *Controversy advertising: How advertisers present points of view on public affairs.* New York: Hastings House.

A WORK IN AN ANTHOLOGY

Mukherjee, B. (1988). The colonization of the mind. In Gioseffi, D. (Ed.) *Women on war* (pp. 140-142). New York: Simon & Schuster.

AN INTRODUCTION, PREFACE, FOREWORD, OR AFTERWORD

Hemenway, R. (1984). Introduction. In Z. N. Hurston, *Dust tracks on a road.* Urbana: University of Illinois Press, ix-xxxix.

AN EDITION OTHER THAN THE FIRST

Gumpert, G., & Cathcart, R. (Eds.). (1986). *Inter/media: Interpersonal communication in a media world* (3rd ed.). New York: Oxford University Press.

A TRANSLATION

Sartre, J. P. (1962). *Literature and existentialism.* (B. Frechtman, Trans.). New York: Citadel Press. (Original work published 1949.)

A REPUBLISHED BOOK

James, W. (1969). *The varieties of religious experience: A study in human nature.* London: Collier Books. (Original work published 1902.)

A BOOK IN A SERIES

Berthrong, D. J. (1976). *The Cheyenne and Arapaho ordeal: Reservation and agency life in the Indian territory, 1875-1907. Vol. 136. The civilization of the American Indian series.* Norman: University of Oklahoma Press.

A MULTIVOLUME WORK

Mussen, P. H. (Ed.). (1983). *Handbook of child psychology* (4th ed., Vols. 1-4). New York: Wiley.

AN ARTICLE FROM A DAILY NEWSPAPER

Hottelet, R. C. (1990, March 15). Germany: Why it can't happen again. *Christian Science Monitor,* p. 19.

AN ARTICLE FROM A PERIODICAL

Gorriti, G. A. (1989, July). How to fight the drug war. *Atlantic Monthly,* 70-76.

AN ARTICLE IN A JOURNAL WITH CONTINUOUS PAGINATION THROUGHOUT THE VOLUME

Cockburn, A. (1989). British justice, Irish victims. *The Nation, 249,* 554-555.

AN ARTICLE FROM A JOURNAL WITH SEPARATE PAGINATION FOR EACH ISSUE

Mukerji, C. Visual language in science and the exercise of power: The case of cartography in early modern Europe. *Studies in Visual Communication,* 10(3), 30-45.

AN ARTICLE IN A REFERENCE WORK

Frisby, J. P. (1990). Direct perception. In M. W. Eysenck (Ed.), *Blackwell dictionary of cognitive psychology* (pp. 95-100). Oxford: Basil Blackwell.

A GOVERNMENT PUBLICATION

United States Dept. of Health, Education, and Welfare. (1973). *Current ethical issues in mental health.* Washington, DC: U.S. Government Printing Office.

AN ABSTRACT

Fritz, M. (1990/1991). A comparison of social interactions using a friendship awareness activity. *Education and Training in Mental Retardation, 25,* 352-359. (From *Psychological Abstracts,* 1991, 78, Abstract No. 11474)

When the dates of the original publication and of the abstract differ, give both dates separated by a slash.

AN ANONYMOUS WORK

The status of women: Different but the same. (1992-1993). *Zontian, 73*(3), 5.

If the primary contributors to developing the program are known, begin the reference with those as the author(s) instead of the corporate author. If you are citing a documentation manual rather than the program itself, add the word "manual" before the closing bracket. If there is additional information needed for retrieving the program (such as report and/or acquisition numbers), add this at the end of the entry, in parentheses after the last period.

A REVIEW

Harris, I. M. (1991). [Review of the book *Rediscovering masculinity: Reason, language, and sexuality*]. *Gender and Society, 5,* 259-261.

Give the author of the review, not the author of the book being reviewed. Use this form for a film review also. If the review has a title, place it before the bracketed material, and treat it like an article title.

A LETTER TO THE EDITOR

Pritchett, J. T., & Kellner, C. H. (1993). Comment on spontaneous seizure activity [Letter to the editor]. *Journal of Nervous and Mental Disease, 181,* 138-139.

PERSONAL CORRESPONDENCE

B. Ehrenreich (personal communication, August 7, 1992).

(B. Ehrenreich, personal communication, August 7, 1992.)

Cite all personal communications to you (such as letters, memos, e-mails, and telephone conversations) in text only, *without* listing them among the references. The phrasing of your sentences will determine which of the two above forms to use.

AN UNPUBLISHED MANUSCRIPT

McIntosh, P. (1988). *White privilege and male privilege: A personal account of coming to see correspondences through work in women's studies.* Working

Paper 189. Unpublished manuscript, Wellesley College, Center for Research on Women, Wellesley, MA.

PROCEEDINGS OF A MEETING, PUBLISHED

Guerrero, R. (1972/1973). Possible effects of the periodic abstinence method. In W. A. Uricchio & M. K. Williams (Eds.), *Proceedings of a Research Conference on Natural Family Planning* (pp. 96-105). Washington, DC: Human Life Foundation.

If the date of the symposium or conference is different from the date of publication, give both, separated by a slash. If the proceedings are published annually, treat the reference like a periodical article.

■ Electronic Sources

AN ARTICLE FROM AN ONLINE PERIODICAL

Palya, W., Walter, D., Kessel, R., & Lucke, R. (2001). Linear modeling of steady-state behavioral dynamics [Electronic version]. *Journal of the Experimental Analysis of Behavior, 77,* 3-27.

If the article duplicates the version which appeared in a print periodical, use the same basic primary journal reference. See "An Article from a Periodical." If you have viewed the article only in its electronic form, add in brackets [Electronic version].

Riordan, V. (2001, January 1). Verbal-performance IQ discrepancies in children attending a child and adolescent psychiatry clinic. *Child and Adolescent Psychiatry On-Line.* Retrieved August 9, 2002, from http://www.priory.com/psych/iq.htm

If the article does not have a corresponding print version, include the date of access and the URL.

A NONPERIODICAL WEB DOCUMENT

Munro, K. (2001, February). *Changing your body image.* Retrieved February 5, 2002, from http://www.kalimunro.com/article_changing_body_image.html

In general, follow this format: author's name, the date of publication (if no publication date is available, use "n.d."), the title of the document in italics, date of access, and the source's URL.

A CHAPTER OR SECTION IN A WEB DOCUMENT

National Council of Welfare, Canada. (1998). Other issues related to poverty lines. In *A new poverty line: Yes, no or maybe?* (chap. 5). Retrieved July 9, 2002, from http://www.ncwcnbes.net/htmdocument/reportnewpovline/chap5.htm

AN E-MAIL

Do not include personal communications such as e-mails in your list of references. See "Personal Correspondence."

A MESSAGE POSTED TO A NEWSGROUP

Isaacs, K. (2002, January 20). Philosophical roots of psychology [Msg 1]. Message posted to news://sci.psychology.psychotherapy.moderated

Include an online posting in your reference list only if the posting is archived and is retrievable. Otherwise, cite an online posting as a personal communication and do not include it in the list of references. Care should be taken when citing electronic discussions. In general, they are not scholarly sources.

AN ARTICLE FROM A DATABASE

Lopez, F. G., Melendez, M. C., Sauer, E. M., Berger, E., & Wyssmann, J. (1998). Internal working models, self-reported problems, and help-seeking attitudes among college students. *Journal of Counseling Psychology, 45,* 79–83. Retrieved April 1, 2002, from PsycARTICLES database.

To cite material retrieved from a database, follow the format appropriate to the work retrieved and add the date of retrieval and the name of the database.

■ Other Sources

A FILM

Wachowski, A., & Wachowski L. (Writers/Directors). Silver, J. (Producer). (1999). *The matrix.* [Motion picture]. United States: Warner Bros.

Include the name and the function of the originator or primary contributor (director or producer). Identify the work as a motion picture. Include the country of origin and the studio. If the motion picture is of limited circulation, provide the name and address of the distributor in parentheses at the end of the reference.

A TELEVISION SERIES

Jones, R. (Producer). (1990). *Exploring consciousness.* [Television series]. Boston: WGBH.

SAMPLE RESEARCH PAPER (APA STYLE)

The following paper urges a change in our attitude toward zoos. Arguing the value claim that it is morally wrong for humans to exploit animals for entertainment, the student combines expert opinion gathered from research with her own interpretations of evidence. She is always careful to anticipate and represent the claims of the opposition before going on to refute them.

The student uses the APA style, modified to suit the preferences of her writing instructor. APA style requires a title page with a centered title, author, affiliation, and a short title that can be used as a "running head" on each page. An abstract page follows the title page and includes a one-paragraph abstract or summary of the article. Amanda Repp was told she could omit the title page and abstract recommended by the APA. A full description of APA publication conventions can be found in the *Publication Manual of the American Psychological Association,* Fifth Edition (2001).

Short title and page number, per APA style. Some instructors may prefer the student's name instead of the short title as a running head.

Amanda Repp   Zoos   1
English 102-G
Mr. Kennedy
Fall 2002

First paragraph ends with the thesis.

Citation includes author, year of publication, and page number. Ellipses (. . .) indicate omitted words; a period after ellipses indicates that the omission included the end of a sentence.

Why Zoos Should Be Eliminated

Zoos have come a long way from their grim beginnings. Once full of tiny cement-block steel cages, the larger zoos now boast simulated jungles, veldts, steppes, and rain forests, all in an attempt to replicate the natural habitats of the incarcerated animals. The attempt, however admirable, is misguided. It is morally wrong to keep wild animals in captivity, and no amount of replication, no matter how realistic, can compensate for the freedom these creatures are denied.

Peter Batten (1976) argues that a wild animal's life "is spent in finding food, avoiding enemies, sleeping, and in mating or other family activities. . . . Deprivation of any of these fundamentals results in irreparable damage to the individual" (p. 1). The fact that humans may be stronger or smarter than beasts does not give them the right to ambush and exploit animals for the purposes of entertainment.

We humans take our own liberty quite seriously. Indeed, we consider liberty to be one of our inalienable rights. But too many of us apparently feel no obligation to grant the same right to animals, who, because they cannot defend themselves against our sophisticated methods of capture and because they do not speak our language, cannot claim it for themselves.

But the right to liberty is not based on the ability to claim it, or even on the ability to understand what it is. As James Rachels (1976) writes:

Set long quotations of more than 40 words as block quotations. Indent all lines five spaces, double-space throughout, and put the page number of the quotations in parentheses after the final punctuation.

> Humans have a right to liberty because they have various other interests that will suffer if their freedom is unduly restricted. The right to liberty -- the right to be free of external constraints on one's actions -- may then be seen as derived from a more basic right not to have one's interests needlessly harmed. (p. 210)

Animals, like people, have interests that are harmed if they are kept in captivity: They are separated from their families and prevented from behaving according to their natural

instincts by being removed from the lives they know, which
are the lives they were meant to lead.

Some argue that animals' interests are not being harmed *Summary of*
when they are kept in zoos or aquariums -- that no damage is *an opposing*
being done to the individual -- but their claims are highly dis- *argument*
putable. For example, the Zurich Zoo's Dr. Heini Hediger
(1985) protests that it is absurd to attribute human qualities *Argument flaw*
to animals at all, but he nevertheless resorts to a human analogy: "Wild animals in the zoo rather resemble estate owners.
Far from desiring to escape and regain their freedom, they are
only bent on defending the space they inhabit and keeping it
safe from invasion" (p. 9). How can Dr. Hediger explain the *Refutation of*
actions of the leopards and cheetahs I have seen executing *opposing argu-*
figure eights off the walls and floors of their cages for hours *ment based on*
evidence from
on end? I have watched, spellbound by their grace but also *personal expe-*
horrified; it is impossible to believe that these animals do not *rience*
want their freedom. An estate owner would not spend his time
running frantically around the perimeters of his property.
These cats know they are not lords of any estate. The sense-
less repetition of their actions suggests that the cats know
that they are caged and that there is nothing to defend
against, no "estate" to protect.

Shannon Brownlee (1986) also believes that there is no *Summary of a*
concrete evidence that incarcerated animals are suffering or *second oppos-*
ing argument;
unhappy, but she weakens her own case in her description of *argument flaw*
Jackie, a dolphin in captivity who "spends the day in a seeming stupor" and "chews on the mackerel half-heartedly" at
feeding time (p. 70). Clearly there *is* something wrong with
Jackie; this becomes apparent when Brownlee contrasts
Jackie's lethargic behavior with that of wild dolphins
cavorting in the bay. Brownlee points out that Jackie has
never tried to escape through a hole in his enclosure, although he knows it is there. But this fact does not necessarily
mean that Jackie enjoys captivity. Instead, it may mean that *Challenge to*
Jackie's spirit has been broken and that he no longer remem- *an unstated*
warrant in the
bers or cares what his earlier days were like. Granted we have *argument*
no way of knowing what Jackie is really feeling, but does that
give us the right to *assume* that he is not feeling anything?

To be fair, Brownlee does not go that far. She does allow Jackie one emotional state, attributing his malaise to boredom. But perhaps if the author were removed from members of her family, as well as all other members of her species, and prevented from engaging in activities that most mattered to her, she would recognize Jackie's problems as something more than boredom. In any case, why should we inflict boredom on Jackie, or any other animal, just because we happen to have the means to do so?

The writer shifts to the second half of her argument.

Having registered these basic objections to zoos -- that keeping any creature in captivity is a fundamental infringement on that creature's right to liberty and dignity -- I want to take a closer look at the zoo as an institution, in order to assess fairly its goals and how it tries to meet them. Most zoo professionals today maintain that zoos exist for two main reasons: to educate humans and to conserve animal species.

Clarifying word in square brackets

These are both admirable goals, certainly, but as Seal (1985) notes, "none of these [zoo] budgets is allocated specifically for species preservation. Zoos have been established primarily as recreational institutions and are only secondarily developing programs in conservation, education, and research" (p. 74). The fact is most zoos do not have the money, space, or equipment required to make significant contributions in this area. The bulk of their money goes to the upkeep of the animals and exhibits -- that is, to put it crudely, to the displays.

Another opposing argument, with refutation

On behalf of the education a zoo provides, a common argument is that there is nothing like seeing the real thing. But what you see in the zoo is not a real thing at all. According to a statement from the Animal Rights Resource Site, "The conditions under which animals are kept in zoos typically distorts their behavior significantly" (How will people see). Many zoo and aquarium animals, like Jackie the dolphin, have been domesticated to the point of lethargy, in part because they are being exhibited alone or with only one other member of their species, when what they are used to is traveling in groups and finding their own food, instead of being fed. Anyone who wants to see the real thing would be better off watching some

Summary of two expert opinions that zoos do not help endangered species

Zoos   4

of the excellent programming about nature and wildlife that appears on public television.

As for conservation, it is clearly a worthwhile effort, but zoos are not effective agents of species preservation. It is generally acknowledged that it is difficult to breed zoo animals (Luoma, 1982, p. 104). Animals often do not reproduce at all -- quite possibly because of the artificial, and consequently unsettling, circumstances in which they live. When zoo animals do mate successfully, the offspring is often weakened by inbreeding. According to geneticists, this is because a population of 150 breeder animals is necessary in order to "assure the more or less permanent survival of a species in captivity" (Ehrlich & Ehrlich, 1981, p. 211). Few zoos have the resources to maintain populations that size. When zoos rely on smaller populations for breeding (as many do), the species' gene pool becomes more and more limited, "vigor and fecundity tend to decline" (Ehrlich & Ehrlich, 1981, p. 212), and this can eventually lead to extinction. In other words, we are not doing these animals any favors by trying to conserve them in zoos. Indeed, Wilson (1995) writes that "all the zoos in the world today can sustain a maximum of only 2,000 species of mammals, birds, reptiles, and amphibians, out of about 24,000 known to exist" (p. 57). Reserves and preservations, which have room for the larger populations necessary for successful conservation efforts and which can concentrate on breeding animals rather than on displaying them, are much more suitable for these purposes.

For what purposes, then, are zoos suitable? Are they even necessary? At present, they must house the many generations of animals that have been bred there, since these animals have no place else to go. Most animals in captivity cannot go back to the wild for one of two reasons. The first is that the creatures would be unable to survive there, since their instincts for finding their own food and protecting themselves from predators, or even the weather, have been greatly diminished during their time spent in captivity (Morton, 1985, p. 155). Perhaps this is why Jackie the dolphin chooses to remain in his enclosure.

Author, date, page cited parenthetically

Source with two authors cited parenthetically

Paraphrase with source cited parenthetically

Zoos   5

The other reason animals cannot return to the wild is an even sadder one: In many cases, their natural habitats no longer exist. Thanks to deforesting and clearing of land for homes, highways, factories, and shopping malls -- which are continually being built with no regard for the plant and animal life around them -- ecosystems are destroyed constantly, driving increasing numbers of species from their homes. Air and water pollution and toxic waste, results of the ever-increasing urbanization and industrialization throughout the world, are just some of the agents of this change. It is a problem I wish to address in closing.

The writer closes by proposing a solution of her own.

If zoos were to leave breeding programs to more appropriate organizations and to stop collecting animals, the zoo as an institution would eventually be phased out. Animals would cease to be exhibits and could resume being animals, and the money previously used to run zoos could be put to much better use. Ideally it could be used to investigate why endangered species are endangered, and why so many of the original habitats of these species have disappeared. Most important, it could be used to explore how we can change our habits and reorient our behavior, attitudes, and priorities, so we can begin to address these issues.

The problem of endangered species does not exist in a vacuum; it is a symptom of a much greater predicament. Humankind is responsible for this predicament, and it is up to us to recognize this before it is too late. Saving a selected species here and there will do none of us any good if those species can exist only in isolated, artificial environments, where they will eventually breed themselves into extinction. The money that has been concentrated on such efforts should be devoted instead to educating the public about the endangered planet -- not just its animals -- or, like the animals, none of us will have any place to go.

Zoos   6

References

Batten, P. (1976). *Living trophies.* New York: Crowell.

Brownlee, S. (1986, December). First it was "save the whales," now it's "free the dolphins." *Discover,* 70-72.

Ehrlich, P., & Ehrlich, A. (1981). *Extinction: The causes and consequences of the disappearance of species.* New York: Random House.

Hediger, H. (1985). From cage to territory. In R. Kirchschofer (Ed.), *The world of zoos: A survey and gazetteer* (pp. 9-20). New York: Viking.

How will people see wild animals and learn about them without zoos? (n.d.). In *Animal Rights Resource Site.* Retrieved December 14, 1998, from http://arrs.envirolink.org/faqs+Ref/ar-faq/Q70.html

Luoma, J. (1982, November). Prison or ark? *Audubon,* 102-109.

Morton, E. S. (1985). The realities of reintroducing species to the wild. In J. R. Hoage (Ed.), *Animal extinctions: What everyone should know* (pp. 147-158). National Zoological Park Symposia for the Public series. Washington, DC: Smithsonian Institution.

Rachels, J. (1976). Do animals have a right to liberty? In T. Regan & P. Singer (Eds.), *Animal rights and human obligations* (pp. 205-223). Englewood Cliffs, NJ: Prentice-Hall.

Seal, U. S. (1985). The realities of preserving species in captivity. In J. R. Hoage (Ed.), *Animal extinctions: What everyone should know* (pp. 147-158). National Zoological Park Symposia for the Public series. Washington, DC: Smithsonian Institution.

Wilson, E. (1995, October 30). Wildlife: Legions of the doomed. *Time,* 57-62. Retrieved December 12, 1999, from *Lexis/Nexis Universe.*

References start a new page.

A book with two authors

A work in an anthology

An article from a periodical

For each reference, flush left on first line, and indent three spaces on subsequent lines.

An article online from a database

11

Presenting an Argument Orally

Speech is the basic skill overlooked by many who urge a return to the Three R's. The ability to speak clearly and persuasively, and to think on one's feet can be as vital to success as reading and writing. Beginning with the job interview, speech classifies a person.[1]

You already know a good deal about the power of persuasive speech. You've not only listened to it from parents, teachers, preachers, coaches, friends, and enemies; you've practiced it yourself with varying degrees of success.

A classics scholar points out that the oratorical techniques we use today were "invented in antiquity and have been used to great effect ever since."[2] But history is not our only guide to the principles of public speaking. Much of what we know about the power of persuasive speech is knowledge based on lifelong experience — things we learn in everyday discourse with different kinds of people who respond to different appeals. Early in life you learned that you did not use the same language or the same approach to argue with your mother or your teacher as you used with your sibling or your friend. You learned, or tried to learn, how to convince people to listen to you and to trust you because you were truthful and knew

[1] Fred M. Hechinger, "About Education," *New York Times,* May 11, 1988, sec. B, p. 7.
[2] Mary Lefkowitz, "Classic Oratory," *New York Times,* January 24, 1999, sec. W, p. 15.

what you were talking about. And perhaps equally important, if you won the argument, you wanted to make it clear that your victory would not mean hardship for the loser (no obvious gloating). Although speeches to a larger, less familiar audience will require much more preparation, many of the rules of argument that guided you in your personal encounters can be made to work for you in more public arenas.

You will often be asked to make oral presentations in your college classes. Many jobs, both professional and nonprofessional, will call for speeches to groups of fellow employees or prospective customers, to community groups, and even government officials. Wherever you live, there will be controversies and public meetings about schooling and political candidates, about budgets for libraries and road repairs and pet control. The ability to rise and make your case before an audience is one that you will want to cultivate as a citizen of a democracy. Great oratory is probably no longer the most powerful influence in our society, and computer networks have usurped the role of oral communication in many areas of public life. But whether it's in person or on television there is still a significant role for a live presenter, a real human being to be seen and heard.

Some of your objectives as a writer will also be relevant to you as a speaker: making the appropriate appeal to an audience, establishing your credibility, finding adequate support for your claim. But other elements of argument will be different: language, organization, and the use of visual and other aids.

Before you begin a brief examination of these elements, keep in mind the larger objectives of the speechmaker. A good introduction to the process of influencing an audience is *the motivated sequence*.[3] This outline, created by a professor of speech communication, lists the five steps that must be taken in order to motivate an audience to adopt a policy, an action, or a belief.

1. Getting attention (attention step)

2. Showing the need: describing the problem (need step)

3. Satisfying the need: presenting the solution (satisfaction step)

4. Visualizing the results (visualization step)

5. Requesting action or approval (action step)

Perhaps you noticed that these steps resemble the steps taken by advertisers. (That list appears in the sample analysis of an ad in Chapter 2.) The resemblance is not accidental. According to the author of the motivated sequence, this is a description of the way "people systematically think their way through to a decision."

---

[3] Alan H. Monroe and Douglas Ehninger, *Principles of Speech Communication* (Glenview, Ill.: Scott, Foresman, 1969), p. 261.

As you read the following discussions of audience, credibility, language, organization, support, and visual and aural aids, try to think of occasions in your own experience when you were aware of these elements in spoken argument, formal or informal.

THE AUDIENCE

Most speakers who confront a live audience already know something about the members of that audience. They may know why the audience is assembled to hear the particular speaker, their vocations, their level of education, and their familiarity with the subject. They may know whether the audience is friendly, hostile, or neutral to the views that the speaker will express. Analyzing the audience is an essential part of speech preparation. If speakers neglect it, both audience and speaker will suffer. At some time all of us have been trapped as members of an audience, forced to listen to a lecture, a sermon, an appeal for action when it was clear that the speaker had little or no idea what we were interested in or capable of understanding. In such situations the speaker who seems indifferent to the needs of the audience will also suffer because the audience will either cease to listen or reject his claim outright.

In college classes students who make assigned speeches on controversial topics are often encouraged to first survey the class. Questionnaires and interviews can give the speaker important clues to the things he should emphasize or avoid: They will tell him whether he should give both sides of a debatable question, introduce humor, use simpler language, and bring in visual or other aids.

But even where such specific information is not immediately available, speakers are well advised to find out as much as they can about the beliefs and attitudes of their audience from other sources. They will then be better equipped to make the kinds of appeals—to reason and to emotion—that the audience is most responsive to. For example, two young evangelists for a religious group (not students at the university) were invited to visit a speech class and present an argument for joining their group. The visitors knew that the class was learning the principles of persuasive speaking; they had no other information about the listeners. After the speech, the students in the class asked questions about some practices of the religious group which had received unfavorable media attention, but the speakers turned aside all questions, saying they did not engage in argument but were instructed only to describe the rewards of joining their group. Before some other audience, such a strategy might have been emotionally satisfying and ultimately persuasive. For this class, however, which was prepared to look for hard evidence, logic, and valid assumptions, the refusal to answer questions suggested evasion and indifference to the interests of their audience. Class evaluations of the speech revealed, to no one's surprise, that the visitors had failed to motivate their listeners.

If you know something about your audience, ask yourself what impression your clothing, gestures and bodily movements, voice, and general demeanor might convey. It might be worth pointing out here that the visitors cited above arrived dressed in three-piece suits and sporting crew cuts to confront an audience in tee shirts, torn jeans, and long hair. The fact that both speakers and listeners were the same age was not quite enough to overcome an impression of real differences. Make sure, too, that you understand the nature of the occasion — is it too solemn for humor? too formal for personal anecdotes? — and the purpose of the meeting, which can influence your choice of language and the most effective appeal.

CREDIBILITY

The evaluation of audience and the presentation of your own credibility are closely related. In other words, what can you do to persuade this particular audience that you are a reliable exponent of the views you are expressing? Credibility, as you learned in Chapter 1, is another name for *ethos* (the Greek word from which the English word *ethics* is derived) and refers to the honesty, moral character, and intellectual competence of the speaker.

Public figures, whose speeches and actions are reported in the media, can acquire (or fail to acquire) reputations for being endowed with those characteristics. And there is little doubt that a reputation for competence and honesty can incline an audience to accept an argument that would be rejected if offered by a speaker who lacks such a reputation. One study, among many that report similar results, has shown that the same speech will be rated highly by an audience that thinks the Surgeon General of the United States has delivered it but treated with much less regard if they hear it delivered by a college sophomore.

How, then, does a speaker who is unknown to the audience or who boasts only modest credentials convince his listeners that he is a responsible advocate? From the moment the speaker appears before them, members of the audience begin to make an evaluation, based on external signs, such as clothing and mannerisms. But the most significant impression of the speaker's credibility will be based on what the speaker says and how he says it. Does the speaker give evidence that he knows the subject? Does he seem to be aware of the needs and values of the audience? Especially if he is arguing an unpopular claim, does he seem modest and conciliatory?

An unknown speaker is often advised to establish his credentials in the introduction to his speech, to summarize his background and experience as proof of his right to argue the subject he has chosen. A prize-winning and widely reprinted speech by a student begins with these words:

> When you look at me, it is easy to see several similarities between us. I have two arms, two legs, a brain, and a heart just like you. These are my hands, and they are just like yours. Like you, I also have wants and desires; I am capable of love and hate. I can laugh and I can cry. Yes, I'm just like you, except for one very important fact—I am an ex-con.[4]

This is a possibly risky beginning—not everybody in the audience will be friendly to an ex-con—but it signifies that the speaker brings some authority to his subject, which is prison reform. It also attests to the speaker's honesty and may rouse sympathy among certain listeners. (To some in the audience, the speaker's allusions to his own humanity will recall another moving defense, the famous speech by Shylock, the Jewish moneylender, in Shakespeare's *The Merchant of Venice*.)

The speaker will often use an admission of modesty as proof of an honest and unassuming character. He presents himself not as an expert but as one well aware of his limitations. Such an appeal can generate sympathy in the audience (if they believe him) and a sense of identification with the speaker.

The professor of classics quoted earlier has analyzed the speech of a former senator who defended President Clinton at his impeachment trial. She found that the speaker "made sure his audience understood that he was one of them, a friend, on their level, not above them. He denied he was a great speaker and spoke of his friendship with Mr. Clinton." As the writer points out, this confession brings to mind the speech by Mark Antony in *Julius Caesar*:

> I am no orator, as Brutus is,
> But (as you know me all) a plain blunt man
> That loves my friend; (3.2.226–28)

The similarity of these attempts at credibility, separated by almost four hundred years (to say nothing of the fact that Aristotle wrote about *ethos* 2,500 years ago) tells us a good deal about the enduring influence of *ethos* or character on the speaker's message.

ORGANIZATION

Look at the student speech at the end of this chapter. The organization of this short speech—the usual length of speeches delivered in the classroom—is easily mastered and works for all kinds of claims.

---

[4]Richard M. Duesterbeck, "Man's Other Society," in Wil Linkugel, R. R. Allen, and Richard Johannesen, eds., *Contemporary American Speeches* (Belmont, Calif.: Wadsworth, 1965), p. 264.

At the end of the first paragraph the speaker states what he will try to prove, that a vegetarian diet contributes to prevention of chronic diseases. In the third paragraph the speaker gives the four points that he will develop in his argument for vegetarianism. Following the development of these four topics, the conclusion urges the audience to take action, in this case, to stop eating meat.

This basic method of organizing a short speech has several virtues. First, the claim or thesis statement that appears early in a short speech, if the subject is well chosen, can engage the interest of the audience at once. Second, the list of topics guides the speaker in planning and developing his speech. Moreover, it tells the audience what to listen for as they follow the argument.

A well-planned speech has a clearly defined beginning, middle, and end. The beginning, which offers the introduction, can take a number of forms, depending on the kind of speech and its subject. Above all, the introduction must win the attention of the audience, especially if they have been required to attend, and encourage them to look forward to the rest of the speech. The authors of the motivated sequence suggest seven basic attention-getters: (1) referring to the subject or occasion, (2) using a personal reference, (3) asking a rhetorical question, (4) making a startling statement of fact or opinion, (5) using a quotation, (6) telling a humorous anecdote, (7) using an illustration.[5]

The speeches by the ex-con and the vegetarian provide examples of two of the attention-getters cited above—using a personal reference and asking a rhetorical question. In another kind of argument, a claim of fact, the student speaker uses a combination of devices to introduce her claim that culturally deprived children are capable of learning:

> In Charles Schulz's popular cartoon depiction of happiness, one of his definitions has special significance for the American school system. The drawing shows Linus, with his eyes closed in a state of supreme bliss, a broad smile across two-thirds of his face and holding a report card upon which is a big bold "A." The caption reads: "Happiness is finding out you're not so dumb after all." For once, happiness is not defined as a function of material possessions, yet even this happiness is practically unattainable for the "unteachables" of the city slums. Are these children intellectually inferior? Are they unable to learn? Are they not worth the time and the effort to teach? Unfortunately, too many people have answered "yes" to these questions and promptly dismissed the issue.[6]

The middle or body of the speech is, of course, the longest part. It will be devoted to development of the claim that appeared at the beginning. The length of the speech and the complexity of the subject will

---

[5] Monroe and Ehninger, p. 206.
[6] Carolyn Kay Geiman, "Are They Really 'Unteachables'?" in Linkugel, Allen, and Johannesen, p. 123.

determine how much support you provide. Some points will be more important than others and should therefore receive more extended treatment. Unless the order is chronological, it makes sense for the speaker to arrange the supporting points in emphatic order, that is, the most important at the end because this may be the one that listeners will remember.

The conclusion should be brief; some rhetoricians suggest that the ending should constitute 5 percent of the total length of the speech. For speeches that contain several main points with supporting data, you may need to summarize. Or you may return to one of the attention-getters mentioned earlier. One writer recommends this as "the most obvious method" of concluding speeches, "particularly appropriate when the introduction has included a quotation, an interesting anecdote, a reference to an occasion or a place, an appeal to the self-interest of the audience, or a reference to a recent incident."[7]

An example of such an ending appears in a speech given by Bruce Babbitt, Secretary of the Interior, in 1996. Speaking to an audience of scientists and theologians, the Secretary defended laws that protected the environment. This is how the speech began:

> A wolf's green eyes, a sacred blue mountain, the words from Genesis, and the answers of children all reveal the religious values manifest in the 1977 Endangered Species Act.

(The children Babbitt refers to had written answers to a question posed at an "eco-expo" fair, "Why Save the Environment?")

And this is the ending of the speech:

> I conclude here tonight by affirming that those religious values remain at the heart of the Endangered Species Act, that they make themselves manifest through the green eyes of the grey wolf, through the call of the whooping crane, through the splash of the Pacific salmon, through the voices of America's children.
>
> We are living between the flood and the rainbow: between the threats to creation on the one side and God's covenant to protect life on the other.
>
> Why should we save endangered species?
>
> Let us answer this question with one voice, the voice of the child at that expo, who scrawled her answer at the very bottom of the sheet:
> "Because we can."[8]

The speaker must also ensure the smooth flow of his argument throughout. Coherence, or the orderly connections between ideas, is even more important in speech than in writing because the listener cannot go back to uncover these connections. The audience listens for ex-

---

[7] James C. McCroskey, *An Introduction to Rhetorical Communication* (Englewood Cliffs, N.J.: Prentice-Hall, 1968), p. 204.

[8] Calvin McLeod Logue and Jean DeHart, eds., *Representative American Speeches 1995–1996* (New York: Wilson, 1996), p. 70ff.

pressions that serve as guideposts—words, phrases, and sentences to indicate which direction the argument will take. The student speech on vegetarianism uses these words among others: *next, then, finally, here, first of all, whereas, in addition, secondly, in fact, now, in conclusion.* Other expressions can also help the listener to follow the development. Each of the following examples from real speeches makes a bridge from a previous idea to a new one: "Valid factual proof, right? No, wrong!" "Consider an illustration of this misinformation." "But there is another way." "Up to this point, I've spoken only of therapy." "And so we face this new challenge." "How do we make this clear?" "Now, why is this so important?"

LANGUAGE

It should be observed that each kind of rhetoric has its own appropriate style. That of written prose is not the same as that of spoken oratory.
—Aristotle

In the end, your speech depends on the language. No matter how accurate your analysis of the audience, how appealing your presentation of self, how deep your grasp of the material, if the language does not clearly and emphatically convey your argument, the speech will probably fail. Fortunately, the effectiveness of language does not depend on long words or complex sentence structure; quite the contrary. Most speeches, especially those given by beginners to small audiences, are distinguished by an oral style that respects the rhythms of ordinary speech and sounds spontaneous.

The vocabulary you choose, like the other elements of spoken discourse we have discussed, is influenced by the kind of audience you confront. A student audience may be entertained or moved to identification with you and your message if you use the slang of your generation; an assembly of elderly church members at a funeral may not be so generous. Use words that both you and your listeners are familiar with, language that convinces the audience you are sharing your knowledge and opinions, neither speaking down to them nor over their heads. As one writer puts it, "You never want to use language that makes the audience appear ignorant or stupid."

Make sure, too, that the words you use will not be considered offensive by some members of your audience. Today we are all sensitive, sometimes hypersensitive, to terms we once used freely if not wisely. One word, improperly used, can cause some listeners to reject the whole speech.

The short speeches you give will probably not be devoted to elaborating grand abstractions, but it is not only abstract terms that need definition. When you know your subject very well, you forget that others can be ignorant of it. Think whether the subject is one that the particular audience you are addressing is not likely to be familiar with. If this is the case, then explain even the basic terms. In one class a student who had chosen to discuss a subject about which he was extremely knowledgeable, betting on horse races, neglected to define clearly the words *exacta*, *subfecta*, *trifecta*, *parimutuel*, and others, leaving his audience fairly befuddled.

Wherever it is appropriate, use concrete language with details and examples that create images and cause the listener to feel as well as think. One student speaker used strong words to good effect in providing some unappetizing facts about hot dogs: "In fact, the hot dog is so adulterated with chemicals, so contaminated with bacteria, so puffy with gristle, fat, water, and lacking in protein, that it is nutritionally worthless."[9]

Another speech on a far more serious subject offered a personal experience with vivid details. The student speaker was a hemophiliac making a plea for blood donations.

> I remember the three long years when I couldn't even walk because repeated hemorrhages had twisted my ankles and knees to pretzel-like forms. I remember being pulled to school in a wagon while other boys rode their bikes and pushed to my table. I remember sitting in the dark empty classroom by myself during recess while the others went out in the sun to run and play. And I remember the first terrible day at the big high school when I came on crutches and built-up shoes carrying my books in a sack around my neck.[10]

As a rule, the oral style demands simpler sentences. That is because the listener must grasp the grammatical construction without the visual clues of punctuation available on the printed page. Simpler means shorter and more direct. Use subject-verb constructions without a string of phrases or clauses preceding the subject or interrupting the natural flow of the sentence. Use the active voice frequently. In addition to assuring clarity for the audience, such sentences are easier for the speaker to remember and to say. (The sentences in the paragraph above are long, but notice that the sentence elements of subject, verb, and subordinate clause are arranged in the order dictated by natural speech.)

Simpler, however, does not mean less impressive. A speech before any audience may be simply expressed without loss of emotional or intellectual power. "The Nature of Prejudice" in Chapter 4 is a noteworthy example. First delivered as a speech to an audience of experts, it nevertheless reflects the characteristics of conversation. One of the most elo-

---

[9] Donovan Ochs and Anthony Winkler, *A Brief Introduction to Speech* (New York: Harcourt, Brace, Jovanovich, 1979), p. 74.

[10] Ralph Zimmerman, "Mingled Blood," in Linkugel, Allen, and Johannesen, p. 200.

quent short speeches ever delivered in this country is the surrender speech in 1877 by Chief Joseph of the Nez Perce Tribe, which clearly demonstrates the power of simple words and sentences.

> I am tired of fighting. Our chiefs are killed. Looking Glass is dead. Toohulsote is dead. The old men are all dead. It is the young men who say no and yes. He who led the young men is dead. It is cold and we have no blankets. The little children are freezing to death. My people, some of them, have run away to the hills and have no blankets, no food. No one knows where they are — perhaps they are freezing to death. I want to have time to look for my children and see how many of them I can find. Maybe I shall find them among the dead. Hear me, my chiefs. I am tired. My heart is sad and sick. From where the sun now stands I will fight no more forever.[11]

If you are in doubt about the kind of language in which you should express yourself, you might follow Lincoln's advice: "Speak so that the most lowly can understand you, and the rest will have no difficulty."

A popular stylistic device — repetition and balance or parallel structure — can emphasize and enrich parts of your message. Look back to the balanced sentences of the passage from the student speaker on hemophilia, sentences beginning with "I remember." Almost all inspirational speeches, including religious exhortation and political oratory, take advantage of such constructions, whose rhythms evoke an immediate emotional response. It is one of the strengths of Martin Luther King Jr.'s "I Have a Dream." Keep in mind that the ideas in parallel structures must be similar and that, for maximum effectiveness, they should be used sparingly in a short speech. Not least, the subject should be weighty enough to carry this imposing construction.

SUPPORT

The support for a claim is essentially the same for both spoken and written arguments. Factual evidence, including statistics, and expert opinion, as well as appeals to needs and values, are equally important in oral presentations. But time constraints will make a difference. In a speech the amount of support that you provide will be limited to the capacity of listeners to digest and remember information that they cannot review. This means that you must choose subjects that can be supported adequately in the time allotted. The speech by Secretary Babbitt, for example, on saving the environmental protection laws, developed material on animals, national lands, water, his own history, religious tradition, and the history of environmental legislation, to name only the most

---

[11]M. Gidley, *Kopet: A Documentary Narrative of Chief Joseph's Last Years.* (Chicago: Contemporary Books, 1981), p. 31.

important. It would have been impossible to defend his proposition in a half-hour speech. Although his subject was far more limited, the author of the argument for vegetarianism could not do full justice to his claim for lack of time. Meat-eaters would find that some of their questions remain unanswered, and even those listeners friendly to the author's claim might ask for more evidence from authoritative sources.

While both speakers and writers use logical, ethical, and emotional appeals in support of their arguments, the forms of presentation can make a significant difference. The reasoning process demanded of listeners must be relatively brief and straightforward, and the supporting evidence readily assimilated. The ethical appeal or credibility of the speaker is affected not only by what he says but by his appearance, bodily movements, and vocal expressions. And the appeal to the sympathy of the audience can be greatly enhanced by the presence of the speaker. Take the excerpt from the speech of the hemophiliac. The written descriptions of pain and heartbreak are very moving, but place yourself in the audience, looking at the victim and imagining the suffering experienced by the human body standing in front of you. No doubt the effect would be deep and long-lasting, perhaps more memorable even than the written word.

Because the human instrument is so powerful, it must be used with care. You have probably listened to speakers who used gestures and voice inflections that had been dutifully rehearsed but were obviously contrived and worked, unfortunately, to undermine rather than support the speaker's message and credibility. If you are not a gifted actor, avoid gestures, body language, and vocal expressions that are not truly felt.

Some speech theorists treat support or proofs as *nonartistic* and *artistic*. The nonartistic support—factual data, expert opinion, examples—is considered objective and verifiable. Its acceptability should not depend on the character and personality of the speaker. It is plainly different from the artistic proof, which is subjective, based on the values and attitudes of the listener, and therefore more difficult for the speaker to control. This form of support is called artistic because it includes creative strategies within the power of the speaker to manipulate. In earlier parts of this chapter we have discussed the artistic proofs, ways of establishing credibility, and recognizing the values of the audience.

PRESENTATION AIDS

■ Charts, Graphs, Handouts

Some speeches, though not all, will be enhanced by visual and other aids: charts, graphs, maps, models, objects, handouts, recordings, and computer technology. These aids, however, no matter how visually or aurally exciting, should not overwhelm your own oral presentation. The objects are not the stars of the show. They exist to make your spoken argument more persuasive.

Charts and graphs, large enough and clear enough to be seen and understood, can illuminate speeches that contain numbers of any kind, especially statistical comparisons. You can make a simple chart yourself, on paper for use with an easel or a transparency for use with a slide projector. Enlarged illustrations or a model of a complicated machine—say, the space shuttle—would help a speaker to explain its function. You already know that photographs or videos are powerful instruments of persuasion, above all in support of appeals for humanitarian aid, for both people and animals.

Court cases have been won or lost on the basis of diagrams or charts that purport to prove the innocence or guilt of a defendant. Such aids do not always speak for themselves. No matter how clear they are to the designer, they may be misinterpreted or misunderstood by a viewer. Some critics have argued that the jury in the O. J. Simpson case failed to understand the graphs of DNA relationships that experts for the prosecution displayed during the trial. Before you show any diagrams or charts of any complexity to your audience, ask friends if they find them easy to understand.

The use of a handout also requires planning. It's probably unwise to put your speech on hold while the audience reads or studies a handout that requires time and concentration. Confine the subject matter of handouts to material that can be easily grasped as you discuss or explain it.

■ Audio

Audio aids may also enliven a speech or even be indispensable to its success. One student played a recording of a scene from *Romeo and Juliet*, spoken by a cast of professional actors, to make a point about the relationship between the two lovers. Another student chose to define several types of popular music, including rap, goth, heavy metal, and techno. But he used only words, and the lack of any musical demonstration meant that the distinctions remained unclear.

■ Video

With sight, sound, and movement, a video can illustrate or reinforce the main points of a speech. A speech warning people not to drink and drive will have a much greater effect if enhanced by a video showing the tragic and often gruesome outcome of car accidents caused by drunk driving. Schools that teach driver's education frequently rely on these bone-chilling videos to show their students that getting behind the wheel is a serious responsibility, not a game. If you want to use video, check to make sure that a VCR and television are available to you. Most schools have an audio-visual department that manages the delivery, setup, and return of all equipment.

■ Multimedia

Multimedia presentation software programs enable you to combine several different media such as text, charts, sound, and still or moving pictures into one unit. In the business world, multimedia presentations are commonly used in situations where you have a limited amount of time to persuade or teach a fairly large audience. For instance, the promotion director of a leading teen magazine is trying to persuade skeptical executives that a magazine Web site would increase sales and advertising revenue. Since the magazine is sold through newsstand and subscription, some executives question whether the cost of creating and maintaining a Web site outweighs the benefits. Using multimedia presentation software, the promotion director can integrate: demographic charts and graphs showing that steadily increasing numbers of teenagers surf the Web, a segment from a television news program reporting that many teens shop online (an attraction for advertisers), and downloaded pages from a competitor's Web site to demonstrate that others are already reaping the benefits of the Internet. With several studies reporting that people today are increasingly "visual" in their learning styles, multimedia software may be the most effective aid for an important presentation.

Though effective when done well, technically complicated presentations require large amounts of time and careful planning. First you must ensure that your computer is powerful enough to adeptly handle presentation software such as Microsoft PowerPoint, Lotus Freelance, Harvard Graphics, Adobe Persuasion, Cintel Charisma, and Asymetrix Compel. Then you need to familiarize yourself with the program. Most presentation software programs come equipped with helpful tutorials. If the task of creating your own presentation from scratch seems overwhelming, you can use one of the many preformatted presentation templates: You will simply need to customize the content. Robert Stephens, the founder of the Geek Squad, a Minneapolis-based business that provides on-site emergency response to computer problems, gives the following tips for multimedia presentations:

1. In case of equipment failure, always bring two of everything.

2. Back up your presentation not only on floppy disk, but on CD-ROM, or a Zip drive.

3. Avoid live visits to the Internet. Because connections can fail or be painfully slow, and sites can move or disappear, if you must visit the Internet in your presentation, download the appropriate pages onto your hard drive ahead of time. It will still look like a live visit.

4. In the end, technology cannot replace creativity. Make sure that you are using multimedia to reinforce not replace your main points.[12]

Make sure that any necessary apparatus will be available at the right time. If you have never used the devices you need for your presentation, practice using them before the speech. Few things are more disconcerting for the speechmaker and the audience than a speaker who is fumbling with his materials, unable to find the right picture or to make a machine work.

SAMPLE PERSUASIVE SPEECH

The following speech was delivered by C. Renzi Stone to his public speaking class at the University of Oklahoma. Told to prepare a persuasive speech, C. Renzi Stone chose to speak about the health benefits of vegetarianism. Note his attention-grabbing introduction.

Live Longer and Healthier: Stop Eating Meat!
C. RENZI STONE

What do Steve Martin, Dustin Hoffman, Albert Einstein, Jerry Garcia, Michael Stipe, Eddie Vedder, Martina Navratilova, Carl Lewis, and 12 million other Americans all have in common? All of these well-known people were or are vegetarians. What do they know that we don't? Consuming a regimen of high-fat, high-protein flesh foods is a sure-fire prescription for disaster, like running diesel fuel through your car's gasoline engine. In the book *Why Do Vegetarians Eat Like That?* David Gabbe asserts that millions of people today are afflicted with chronic diseases that can be directly linked to the consumption of meat. Eating a vegetarian diet can help prevent many of those diseases.

In 1996, 12 million Americans identified themselves as vegetarians. That number is twice as many as in the decade before. According to a recent National Restaurant Association poll found in *Health* magazine, one in five diners say they now go out of their way to choose restaurants that serve at least a few meatless entrees. Obviously, the traditionally American trait of a meat-dominated society has subsided in recent years.

In discussing vegetarianism today, first I will tell how vegetarians are perceived in society. Next, I will introduce several studies validating my

[12]Robert Stephens as paraphrased in "When Your Presentation Crashes . . . Who You Gonna Call?" by Eric Matson, *Fast Company*, February/March 1997, p. 130.

claim that a meatless diet is extraordinarily healthy. I will then show how a veggie diet can strengthen the immune system and make the meatless body a shield from unwanted diseases such as cancer and heart disease. Maintaining a strict vegetarian diet can also lead to a longer life. Finally, I will put an image into the audience's mind of a meatless society that relies on vegetables for the main course at breakfast, lunch, and dinner.

Moving to my first point, society generally holds two major misperceptions about vegetarians. First of all, society often perceives vegetarians as a radical group of people with extreme principles. In this view, vegetarians are seen as a monolithic group of people who choose to eat vegetables because they are opposed to the killing of animals for food. The second major misconception is that because vegetarians do not eat meat, they do not get the proper amounts of essential vitamins and minerals often found in meat.

Here is my response to these misconceived notions. First of all, vege- 5 tarians are not a homogeneous group of radicals. Whereas many vegetarians in the past did join the movement on the principle that killing animals is wrong, many join the movement today mainly for its health benefits. In addition, there are many different levels of vegetarianism. Some vegetarians eat nothing but vegetables. Others don't eat red meat but do occasionally eat chicken and fish.

Secondly, contrary to popular opinion, vegetarians get more than enough vitamins and minerals in their diet and generally receive healthier nourishment than meat eaters. In fact, in an article for *Health* magazine, Peter Jaret states that vegetarians actually get larger amounts of amino acids due to the elimination of saturated fats which are often found in meat products. Studies show that the health benefits of a veggie lifestyle contribute to increased life expectancy and overall productivity.

Hopefully you now see that society's perceptions of vegetarians are outdated and just plain wrong. You are familiar with many of the problems associated with a meat-based diet, and you have heard many of the benefits of a vegetarian diet. Now try to imagine how you personally can improve your life by becoming a vegetarian.

Can you imagine a world where people retire at age eighty and lead productive lives into their early 100s? Close your eyes and think about celebrating your seventieth wedding anniversary, seeing your great-grandchildren get married, and witnessing 100 years of world events and technological innovations. David Gabbe's book refers to studies that have shown a vegetarian diet can increase your life expectancy up to fifteen years. A longer life is within your reach, and the diet you eat has a direct impact on your health and how you age.

In conclusion, vegetarianism is a healthy life choice, not a radical cult. By eliminating meat from their diet, vegetarians reap the benefits of a vegetable-based diet that helps prevent disease and increase life expectancy. People, take heed of my advice. There are many more sources of information available for those who want to take a few hours to research the benefits of the veggie lifestyle. If you don't believe my comments, discover the whole truth for yourself.

Twelve million Americans know the health benefits that come with 10 being a vegetarian. Changing your eating habits can be just as easy as making your bed in the morning. Sure, it takes a few extra minutes and some thought, but your body will thank you in the long run.

You only live once. Why not make it a long stay?

PART THREE
Multiple
Viewpoints

The following section contains a variety of viewpoints on eight controversial questions. These questions generate conflict among experts and laypeople alike for two principal reasons. First, even when the facts are not in dispute, they may be interpreted differently by opposing sides. Second, and certainly more difficult to resolve, equally worthwhile values may be in conflict.

Multiple Viewpoints lends itself to classroom debates, both formal and informal. It can also serve as a useful source of informed opinions, which can lead to further research. First, read all the articles in one chapter of a Multiple Viewpoints section. Then select a topic for your research paper, either one suggested in this book (see Topics for Research at the end of each chapter) or another approved by your teacher. You may wish to begin your research by choosing material to support your claim from two or three articles in the text or by exploring recommended sources on the Web (see Taking the Debate Online at the end of each chapter).

Ask the following questions about each controversy:

1. Are there two — or more — different points of view on the subject? Do all sides make clear what they are trying to prove? Summarize their claims.
2. Do all sides share the same goals? If not, how are they different?
3. How important is definition of key terms? Do all sides agree on the definitions? If so, what are they? If not, how do they differ? Does definition become a significant issue in the controversy?
4. How important is evidence in support of the claims? Does the support fulfill the appropriate criteria? If not, what are its weaknesses? Do the authorities have convincing credentials?
5. Do the arguers base any part of their arguments on needs and values that their readers are expected to share? What are they? Do the arguers provide examples of the ways these values function? Is there a conflict of values? If so, which seem more important?
6. What warrants or assumptions underlie the claims? Are they implicit or explicit? Do the arguers examine them for the reader? Are the warrants acceptable? If not, point out their weaknesses.
7. What are the main issues? Is there a genuine debate — that is, does each side try to respond to arguments on the other side?
8. Do the arguers propose solutions to a problem? Are the advantages of their proposals clear? Are there obvious disadvantages?
9. Does each argument follow a clear and orderly organization, one that lends itself to a good outline? If not, what are the weaknesses?
10. Does language play a part in the argument? Are there any examples of misuse of language — slanted or loaded words, clichés, slogans?
11. Do the arguers show an awareness of audience? How would you describe the audience(s) for whom the various arguments are presented?
12. Do you think that one side won the argument? Can you find examples of negotiation and compromise, of attempts to establish a common ground? Explain your answer in detail.

12

Corporate
Responsibility

A corporation is defined in law as "an organization enjoying legal personality for the purposes of carrying on certain activities." The corporations mentioned in the following articles are all businesses for profit.
Typically, they raise capital by selling shares of stock to stockholders who
are nominally responsible for the decisions made by the corporation.

Corporations are not new. They existed in some form in ancient
Rome and in medieval England. Nor is the idea of corporate responsibility new. In 1890 the Sherman Anti-Trust Act was the first of several such
laws to prohibit business practices that restricted competition. In the first
half of the twentieth century social reformers expressed strong opposition to sweatshops, which employed women, children, and the elderly at
long hours and low wages in unsanitary conditions.

Now these concerns have reemerged as companies move operations to
developing countries where costs of production are much lower. Some of
the most popular American products are now made abroad under what
critics cite as "less than ideal labor conditions." But corporate responsibility has come to mean not only increased sensitivity to fair working conditions, including decent wages and a refusal to hire children, but also a
commitment to philanthropy and the support of social causes, like education. In addition, corporations are now asked to accept responsibility for
any damage their products might inflict. The 1997 tobacco settlement, in

which tobacco companies promised to pay billions of dollars in reparations to the states, may be only the beginning of a concerted attack on the manufacturers of guns and automobiles, which also injure people.

On the other side are those who argue that a corporation should not be held responsible for satisfying popular demand for a product. It is the users who should be held accountable for their choices. A number of economists insist that the corporation is obliged only to fulfill its commitment to its stockholders to make a profit. They argue that the private corporation is not bound to make social policy and should not do so — as a matter of democratic principle. Nor should corporations be routinely condemned for paying lower wages abroad to people who would otherwise be even less gainfully employed or not at all.

In the last few years lawsuits have taken the place of legislation by the Congress in a movement to control or punish tobacco companies and gun manufacturers. But experts disagree about the justice of litigation that replaces public policy. In 2000 and 2001 anticorporate forces called attention to their demands in widespread demonstrations. Meetings in Italy, France, Canada, and elsewhere of organizations concerned with the global economy were violently disrupted by groups claiming that giant corporations were exploiting poor people and natural resources all over the world.

The dilemma is summed up by a writer in *Newsweek* reporting on the ability of corporations to practice good works: "You can afford the luxury of goodness only if you make a buck or two for shareholders."

Nike's Power Game

SARAH EDITH JACOBSON

> BEFORE READING: From reading the headlines, can you guess what claim the writer will make? Do you have opinions about labor unions that might influence your judgment of this argument?

W hen Phil Knight, the chief executive of Nike, withdrew a promised $30 million donation to the University of Oregon last month, his announcement had the tone of an angry parent. He chastised the university for joining the Worker Rights Consortium, a group that monitors conditions in factories that make clothing with college logos. He accused the university of "inserting itself into the new global economy where I

Sarah Edith Jacobson was a senior at the University of Oregon and active in United Students against Sweatshops when she wrote this article for the *New York Times*. It appeared on May 16, 2000, along with the following essay by Jaime Sneider.

make my living" and doing so "on the wrong side, fumbling a teachable moment."

Mr. Knight, an Oregon graduate, was angry that the university had joined this consortium rather than the Fair Labor Association, a group that includes as members the same industries that have profited from sweatshop conditions in their production plants. The Worker Rights Consortium is based on the premise that work conditions will not be changed by codes and monitors that come from industry, but by involvement of workers, through collective bargaining with management.

In joining the consortium, the University of Oregon pledged to use its influence to improve conditions at factories producing clothes with the university logo. Mr. Knight, accusing his alma mater of shredding its "bonds of trust" with him, seemed offended that it had not asked his permission.

The university's decision was not made lightly. In March, a referendum sponsored by the student government yielded a three-fourths majority vote in support of membership. A committee accountable to the university president, David B. Frohnmayer, and made up of students, faculty, administrators, and alumni, voted unanimously the same month in favor of joining. Then the University Senate, composed of faculty and students, passed a resolution calling for membership. It was only after all these steps that President Frohnmayer signed the university into membership.

Mr. Knight's punitive reaction really questions the autonomy of the 5 university itself. If the voice of one alumnus held more weight than a year of university-wide deliberation, what role would there be for shared governance on campus? If donations from corporate America depended on toeing a corporate line, the university would be better off without the money.

The goal of students across the country who are organizing around sweatshop issues is to create widespread change in an industry where insufficient wages and mandatory overtime are common. In many third world and American apparel factories, there have been reports of intimidation of workers who try to speak out. And because it is easy for these factories to cut and run, vanishing across national borders and abandoning workers, many people are hesitant to organize unions or demand a living wage.

The Worker Rights Consortium and the student anti-sweatshop campaign challenge companies like Nike not only to let the public know the conditions in apparel factories, but to begin long-term change.

Will the debate about sweatshop conditions move beyond the specifics of monitoring and toward establishing the right to organize? Phil Knight's withdrawal of money from the University of Oregon sends the signal that his company is resisting a move in that direction.

Good Propaganda, Bad Economics

JAIME SNEIDER

BEFORE READING: What do you think "bad economics" means in a discussion of business practices?

College students continue to propagage the myth that Nike and other apparel companies contract out to foreign "sweatshops" where overworked and underpaid workers toil in unhealthful conditions. They are especially outraged by the recent decision by Philip Knight of Nike to withdraw a promised $30 million donation to the University of Oregon in protest of the school's decision to join the Worker Rights Consortium, a labor rights group.

Rather than condemn Mr. Knight, students should commend him.

The Worker Rights Consortium, which was established last fall by students, unions, and human rights groups, accuses Nike of failing to pay its workers a "living wage," ignoring safety concerns, and forcing employees to work overtime. But, comparatively speaking, conditions at third world factories where Nike goods are made are remarkably benevolent. For example, a number of the plants have air conditioning in countries where it is a rarity. Some factories also have clinics that can be used by employees' families, who otherwise would have little if any medical care. Several others even have schools where workers' children can learn everything from reading and writing to biology and physics.

A typical worker in a Nike factory in Vietnam makes about $564 a year, which may not seem like much, but is more than twice the country's average annual income. The employee turnover rate in Nike's factories in Indonesia is consistently below 2 percent, low even by American standards. Such loyalty suggests that workers do not have better prospects.

Many statistics cited by student activists are misleading and originate 5 with the A.F.L.-C.I.O., which has endorsed the Worker Rights Consortium. The A.F.L.-C.I.O. has a direct economic interest: the regulations advocated by the consortium would increase American companies' foreign manufacturing costs, thus encouraging them to abandon their operations abroad and manufacture products domestically instead—employing union labor.

Mr. Knight has agreed to an open monitoring of Nike factories through the Fair Labor Association, a group composed of consumer groups, corporations, and universities that has been endorsed by the

---

Jaime Sneider was editorial page editor of the *Columbia Daily Spectator* when this article was written. It was published in the *New York Times,* along with the preceding essay by Sarah Edith Jacobson, on May 16, 2000.

White House. Nike has said that many students have genuine concerns about working conditions abroad and that the company recognizes that there is always room for improvement.

But, according to a Nike spokeswoman, "the way to get true reform is to have all the players at the table." The Worker Rights Consortium, on the other hand, has not prescribed clear goals or monitoring procedures, and does not yet have legal status as a nonprofit organization. It has been reluctant to include companies like Nike in the dialogue, claiming that corporate participation of any kind threatens workers' rights.

While many students uncritically believe the Worker Rights Consortium, they ignore the fact that Phil Knight and Nike have championed the well-being of workers internationally. By trying to punish Nike, these students threaten to impoverish the workers they claim to protect.

"So that's where it goes! Well, I'd like to thank you fellows for bringing this to my attention."

Social Responsibility of Business and Labor

MILTON FRIEDMAN

BEFORE READING: Does the "social responsibility" of business and labor sound like a good thing? Can you think of arguments against it?

The view has been gaining widespread acceptance that corporate officials and labor leaders have a "social responsibility" that goes beyond serving the interest of their stockholders or their members. This view shows a fundamental misconception of the character and nature of a free economy. In such an economy, there is one and only one social responsibility of business — to use its resources and engage in activities designed to increase its profits so long as it stays within the rules of the game, which is to say, engages in open and free competition, without deception or fraud. Similarly, the "social responsibility" of labor leaders is to serve the interests of the members of their unions. It is the responsibility of the rest of us to establish a framework of law such that an individual in pursuing his own interest is, to quote Adam Smith again, "led by an invisible hand to promote an end which was no part of his intention. Nor is it always the worse for the society that it was no part of it. By pursuing his own interest, he frequently promotes that of the society more effectually than when he really intends to promote it. I have never known much good done by those who affected to trade for the public good."[1]

Few trends could so thoroughly undermine the very foundations of our free society as the acceptance by corporate officials of a social responsibility other than to make as much money for their stockholders as possible. This is a fundamentally subversive doctrine. If businessmen do have a social responsibility other than making maximum profits for stockholders, how are they to know what it is? Can self-selected private individuals decide what the social interest is? Can they decide how great a burden they are justified in placing on themselves or their stockholders to serve that social interest? Is it tolerable that these public functions of taxation, expenditure, and control be exercised by the people who happen at the moment to be in charge of particular enterprises, chosen for those posts by strictly private groups? If businessmen are civil servants rather than the employees of their stockholders, then in a democracy

---

[1] Adam Smith, *The Wealth of Nations* (1776), bk. IV, chapter ii, p. 421 (Cannan, ed., London, 1930).

Milton Friedman, winner of the Nobel Prize in economics, is a senior research fellow at the Hoover Institution, Stanford University, and Paul Snowden Russell Distinguished Service Professor Emeritus of Economics at the University of Chicago. This essay is excerpted from *Capitalism and Freedom* (1962).

they will, sooner or later, be chosen by the public techniques of election and appointment.

And long before this occurs, their decision-making power will have been taken away from them. A dramatic illustration was the cancellation of a steel price increase by U.S. Steel in April 1962 through the medium of a public display of anger by President Kennedy and threats of reprisals on levels ranging from antitrust suits to examination of the tax reports of steel executives. This was a striking episode because of the public display of the vast powers concentrated in Washington. We were all made aware of how much of the power needed for a police state was already available. It illustrates the present point as well. If the price of steel is a public decision, as the doctrine of social responsibility declares, then it cannot be permitted to be made privately.

The particular aspect of the doctrine which this example illustrates, and which has been most prominent recently, is an alleged social responsibility of business and labor to keep prices and wage rates down in order to avoid price inflation. Suppose that at a time when there was upward pressure on prices—ultimately of course reflecting an increase in the stock of money—every businessman and labor leader were to accept this responsibility and suppose all could succeed in keeping any price from rising, so we had voluntary price and wage control without open inflation. What would be the result? Clearly product shortages, labor shortages, gray markets, black markets. If prices are not allowed to ration goods and workers, there must be some other means to do so. Can the alternative rationing schemes be private? Perhaps for a time in a small and unimportant area. But if the goods involved are many and important, there will necessarily be pressure, and probably irresistible pressure, for governmental rationing of goods, a governmental wage policy, and governmental measures for allocating and distributing labor.

Price controls, whether legal or voluntary, if effectively enforced 5 would eventually lead to the destruction of the free-enterprise system and its replacement by a centrally controlled system. And it would not even be effective in preventing inflation. History offers ample evidence that what determines the average level of prices and wages is the amount of money in the economy and not the greediness of businessmen or of workers. Governments ask for the self-restraint of business and labor because of their inability to manage their own affairs—which includes the control of money—and the natural human tendency to pass the buck.

One topic in the area of social responsibility that I feel duty-bound to touch on, because it affects my own personal interests, has been the claim that business should contribute to the support of charitable activities and especially to universities. Such giving by corporations is an inappropriate use of corporate funds in a free-enterprise society.

The corporation is an instrument of the stockholders who own it. If the corporation makes a contribution, it prevents the individual stockholder from himself deciding how he should dispose of his funds. With the corporation tax and the deductibility of contributions, stockholders may of course want the corporation to make a gift on their behalf, since this would enable them to make a larger gift. The best solution would be the abolition of the corporate tax. But so long as there is a corporate tax, there is no justification for permitting deductions for contributions to charitable and educational institutions. Such contributions should be made by the individuals who are the ultimate owners of property in our society.

People who urge extension of the deductibility of this kind of corporate contribution in the name of free enterprise are fundamentally working against their own interest. A major complaint made frequently against modern business is that it involves the separation of ownership and control—that the corporation has become a social institution that is a law unto itself, with irresponsible executives who do not serve the interests of their stockholders. This charge is not true. But the direction in which policy is now moving, of permitting corporations to make contributions for charitable purposes and allowing deductions for income tax, is a step in the direction of creating a true divorce between ownership and control and of undermining the basic nature and character of our society. It is a step away from an individualistic society and toward the corporate state.

God versus GE

JOHN F. WELCH JR. AND
SISTER PATRICIA DALY

BEFORE READING: Does organized religion have something to say to big business? If so, what is it?

Sister Patricia Daly: Good morning, Mr. Welch, members of the board, and fellow shareholders. My name is Pat Daly. I am a Dominican sister, and I am here representing the Interfaith Center on Corporate Responsibility. ICCR has been raising very critical issues before U.S. corporations for almost thirty years. We represent about $90 billion of investment money.

These comments were published in *Harper's Magazine* in August 1998. The comments are from an exchange between John F. Welch Jr., CEO of General Electric, and Sister Patricia Daly that occurred during the April 22 GE shareholders' meeting. On June 3, the Environmental Protection Agency ordered GE to begin dredging the Housatonic River near GE's Pittsfield, Massachusetts, plant, citing PCB levels "among the highest" ever found in the United States.

Today, I would like to discuss the resolution on the necessity for public education about General Electric's pollution around the Hudson Valley. The Hudson River is the largest PCB spill on the planet. It is also the largest Superfund site in the country. Most of those PCBs are in the river because of the past practices of General Electric. We also have been contacted by GE employees in the beautiful Berkshires and along the Housatonic River watershed who are facing similar situations. This is a serious concern for people who have given their lives to General Electric and have been very grateful to be a part of the GE family.

Mr. Welch, we will probably never agree on the science of PCBs. We did agree last year that certainly PCB-contaminated fish should not be eaten by people along the Hudson Valley. We have asked, and we continue to ask, General Electric to work with us on a public-education program. So many people along the Hudson Valley depend on the river to feed their families. It is not common knowledge that people should not be fishing and feeding their families on a regular basis from the Hudson. So we are asking again that you join us in educating people about the hazards they face.

John F. Welch Jr.: Thank you. Before we have any more comments on this, I would like to put the company's position on PCBs in perspective for all of you.

PCB use by General Electric has always been lawful. It is criti-   5
cal to know that our use of PCBs, every day we ever used them, was lawful. We did not manufacture PCBs; we bought them. Starting in the 1940s, General Electric and every electrical manufacturer used PCBs in electrical equipment for a very important reason: safety. PCBs were used in capacitors and transformers to prevent fires. Government codes mandated the use of PCBs in electrical equipment. In the mid-1970s, the government changed its position and banned the continued production and use of PCBs. Our company complied immediately.

PCBs do not pose health risks. Based on the scientific evidence developed since the 1970s, we simply do not believe that there are any significant adverse health effects from PCBs. More than twenty studies show absolutely no link between workers and others with elevated PCBs in their blood, and cancer and other adverse health effects.

I want to make it very clear to all of you that we, your company, will base our discussion of PCBs, as we have for twenty years, on science, not on bad politics or shouting voices from a few activists. Science will decide this issue. Advocates can shout loudly. They can say anything. They are accountable to no one.

Daly: Mr. Welch, you are right. We are all accountable, and you know who I am accountable to.

Welch: No, I do not. I would like to—

Daly: I truly think my accountability is ultimately to God, which is   10
    why—

Welch: And I think mine is also.

Daly: I am not judging that. What I am saying, Mr. Welch, is that this is
    an issue of public education.

Welch: Sister, why not take public education right to the government
    and have them educate the public on the situation. It is not our job
    to educate.

Daly: It is, however. Let's get this absolutely straight. The EPA continues
    to list PCBs on its suspected-carcinogen list. For you to be saying
    that PCBs are perfectly harmless is not true. I really want our com-
    pany to be a credible mover on this. We all remember the images of
    the CEOs of the tobacco companies swearing that they were telling
    the truth. Do they have any credibility in the United States today?

Welch: That is an outrageous comparison.   15

Daly: That is an absolutely valid comparison, Mr. Welch.

Welch: It is outrageous.

Daly: Mr. Welch, I am sorry, but we need to have the independent sci-
    entific community decide this, not the GE scientific community.

Welch: Twenty-seven studies, twenty-one of them independent, have
    concluded that there is no correlation between PCB levels and can-
    cer, Sister. You have to stop this conversation. You owe it to God to
    be on the side of truth here.

Daly: I am on the side of truth. The other consideration here is that this   20
    is not just about carcinogens. We are talking about hormonal dis-
    ruptions, fertility issues, and developmental problems in children.
    Those are real issues, and certainly those are the issues that my sis-
    ters are seeing in schools all along the Hudson River. That is exactly
    what is going on here.

Welch: Thank you very much for coming, Sister. Let's move on to the
    next agenda item.

Victims of Everything

JACOB SULLUM

BEFORE READING: Cigarette advertising is banned from TV and radio. Should the government control other kinds of commercial advertising?

Like you, I've seen innumerable Calvin Klein ads featuring sallow, sullen, scrawny youths. Not once have I had an overwhelming urge to rush out and buy some heroin, and probably neither have you. Yet the death of Davide Sorrenti, a twenty-year-old fashion photographer who overdosed on heroin in February, is now being held up as proof that such images have the power to turn people into junkies.

On Wednesday President Clinton accused the fashion industry of "increasing the allure of heroin among young people" and urged it not

Jacob Sullum, a senior editor at *Reason* magazine, is the author of *For Your Own Good: The Anti-Smoking Crusade and the Tyranny of Public Health* (1998). This essay appeared in the *New York Times* on May 23, 1997.

to "glamorize addiction" to sell clothes. "We now see on college campuses and in neighborhoods heroin becoming increasingly the drug of choice," he said. "And we know that part of this has to do with the images that are finding their way to our young people."

In reality, heroin is not "the drug of choice" by any stretch of the imagination. In the government's 1995 National Household Survey on Drug Abuse, 0.1 percent of respondents reported that they had used the drug in the previous month. A nationwide study done in 1994 for the Department of Health and Human Services found about the same level of heroin use among nineteen- to twenty-eight-year-olds; marijuana use was 140 times as common, and alcohol was far and away the most popular intoxicant.

And there is no reason to expect that people attracted to the look promoted by Calvin Klein and other advertisers—a cynical, sanitized vision of drug use that pretends to reflect a gritty reality—will also be attracted to heroin any more than suburban teenagers who wear baggy pants and backward caps will end up shooting people from moving cars.

Nevertheless, the editors of the cutting-edge fashion magazines that 5 helped popularize the heroin-chic look are professing repentance. "With Davide's death," said Long Nguyen, *Detour*'s style director, "we realized how powerful fashion pictures are."

And how powerful is that? Leaving aside the point that Mr. Sorrenti, as a producer of these images, can hardly be seen as an unknowing victim of their influence, it is important to keep in mind what pictures can and cannot do. Clearly, they can provoke outrage. They can also pique curiosity, create awareness, and elicit a range of emotional reactions. But they cannot *make* anyone buy jeans or perfume, let alone take up heroin. Nor can they make kids smoke cigars, despite the claims of critics about the power of photos showing cigar-chomping celebrities. A conscious mind must intervene, deciding how to interpret the message and whether to act on it.

Blurring the distinction between persuasion and coercion is often the first step toward censorship. In the 1950s, John Kenneth Galbraith and Vance Packard argued that corporations used advertising to manipulate consumers and create an artificial desire for their products. The federal court that upheld the 1970 ban on broadcast advertising of cigarettes was clearly influenced by such ideas, citing "the subliminal impact of this pervasive propaganda."

We see the same line of thinking today. In calling for restrictions on Web sites promoting alcohol and tobacco, the Center for Media Education, a research group in Washington, warns that "interactivity has a hypnotic and addictive quality that some analysts believe could be stronger than television."

The aim of such arguments is to portray people not as independent moral agents but as mindless automatons. It's a view of human nature that encourages the flight from responsibility to victimhood that we see all around us: the smoker who blames a cigarette maker for his lung cancer, the heavy drinker who blames the liquor company for her baby's birth defects, the mass murderer who blames dirty magazines for inspiring his crimes.

So far no one has called for a ban on glassy-eyed waifs, and the critics of heroin chic have every right to decry the message they believe it sends. But they should be careful not to send a dangerous message themselves: that the dictates of fashion overwhelm our ability to choose. 10

Moral Tactics

DANIEL YANKELOVICH

BEFORE READING: You've seen many portrayals of business corporations and their executives on TV and in the movies. In general, are they treated fairly or unfairly?

Recently, companies have eased up on downsizing. This trend offers us an insight into how business responds to moral pressure. As government grows less powerful and the market economy more powerful, the moral stance of the business corporation becomes an issue of the utmost importance.

Those outside the business community—in academia, the media, and government—are quick to pressure business to exercise its "social responsibilities." More often than not, however, this appeal proves counterproductive. Business executives find it easy to brush aside these urgings, often with irritation.

The resentment comes from their suspicion that, as businesspeople, they are treated as if they had no moral concerns for the larger society (which is spectacularly untrue). Their resentment also comes from the fact that, most of the time, what they are asked to do sacrifices the interests of shareholders for some putative social goal.

Nevertheless, there is one form of pressure that does make sense to business: the reminder that the short-term and the long-term interests of business often conflict and that the morally right thing to do usually serves the long term better than the short term.

The shift in emphasis from social responsibility to this point of view may seem like mere semantics, but it is not. The social responsibility argument pits business interests against societal ones. The short-term vs. 5

Daniel Yankelovich is founder of one of the country's largest and most respected research and consulting firms. This essay was published in the July/August 1997 issue of *Mother Jones*.

long-term argument offers different strategies for achieving legitimate business goals.

One of the strengths of the market economy is that, in the long run, it is more likely to be self-corrective than institutions such as the government, the media, or universities. The winds of reality blow harder, and sooner or later competitive pressures — plus regulation — help to correct the worst abuses. This is what we now see happening in the moderating of the downsizing strategy.

Realistically we must recognize that there are limits to how well business can serve the moral needs of society, even when executives act with enlightened self-interest. But, as the shift from downsizing to the new emphasis on "people factors" reminds us, the opportunity for our market economy to serve the moral as well as the economic needs of the nation remains significant. But it requires taking a longer time horizon and keeping faith with one of the basic tenets of the traditional Protestant ethic — doing well by doing good.

Scotch the Ads? Absolut-ly!

JOHN LEO

BEFORE READING: Have you ever been aware that you as a teenager were being targeted by a beer or cigarette ad? Did any of the ads tempt you?

It could be a put-on, but *Adweek* magazine says liquor ads on television may be good for society. The magazine noted that the first booze ad shown on American TV in nearly fifty years celebrated fundamental American values. It was a Seagram commercial, placed on a station in Corpus Christi, Texas, and it featured two dogs.

One dog, labeled "obedience school graduate," carried a newspaper in its mouth. The other, carrying a bottle of Crown Royal, was labeled "valedictorian." *Adweek* said this positioned liquor as a reward for achievement and delayed gratification in a world sadly governed by instant gratification. Liquor flourished in the pre-'60s culture of self-restraint, said *Adweek,* and the impact of televised liquor ads "could well be salutary."

Maybe. But it's possible to doubt that the rapid spread of self-restraint is what the distillers have in mind. The more likely long-term result is a set of psychologically clever ads aimed at young people and resulting in another upward tick or two each year in the death rate from drunk driving.

Adweek's odd commentary contains a germ of truth—one genre of liquor and beer advertising does indeed stress authority, hard work, and sons following the lead of fathers. Many Scotch ads are filled with dogs, castles, and other emblems of tradition, the central message being, "We know Scotch tastes like iodine, but your dad drank it and you should too." This lives on in Dewar's current "Let's grow up and drink Scotch" campaign, and a Chivas Regal ad in which a grown man actually wishes his father would tell him what to do more often.

But these are upscale magazine ads aimed at the well off. Do not ex- 5 pect many dog and daddy ads once the booze industry gets revved up for the TV youth market and spots on *Seinfeld*. Instead we will see a lot of MTV imagery, Orwellian fantasies about sex and power, and Joe Camel-like appeals to the young.

The ad industry is very good at generating commercials that break down restraint and promote impulse. It's also important to know that the legal-drug business (tobacco and alcohol) accumulates a lot of private psychological research, the better to know which of our buttons to push.

John Leo is a columnist for *U.S. News & World Report,* where this article first appeared on December 9, 1996.

The generic stuff appears in marketing magazines, but the really potent findings, which result in all those manipulative and coded ads, aren't made public. No psychologist on the take has yet come forward to blow the whistle, à la Jeffrey Wigand. But now that the Federal Trade Commission is issuing subpoenas in connection with TV alcohol advertising, it surely should try to get the closely guarded research behind many beer and liquor ads.

The general rule of thumb is: the more dangerous the product, the more coded the ads are likely to be. Newport cigarettes' "Alive with pleasure" ads, for example, which seem much cleaned up nowadays, depended for years on coded themes of sexual hostility and violence running beneath all those merry scenes of outdoorsy couples at play. Among the egregious magazine ads for liquor, my favorite is the Bacardi Black "Taste of the night" campaign with its unmissable theme of night and liquor as liberators of the real you (and your darker side) from the bonds of civilized society. Just what we need in this troubled culture— more promotion of everyone's darker side. The booze industry as Darth Vader.

In dropping their self-imposed ban on TV ads, the distillers said they wouldn't target the young. We should be dubious. The liquor executives fear they won't be able to sell their brown drinks anymore—bourbon, Scotch, and brandy have not caught on among boomers or postboomers. The trend is toward white drinks—vodka and gin—and sweet-tasting or healthy-looking drinks that disguise alcoholic content. That's why Miller is testing "alcopops," a malt-based drink that looks and tastes like lemonade. Anheuser-Busch isn't far behind. Alcopops have been successfully marketed in Britain and Australia with ads featuring lovable cartoon characters—a way of conceding that the young are indeed being targeted.

The distillers' argument about beer ads has more merit. They say a can of beer has about as much alcohol as a mixed drink, so either ban beer from TV or let liquor ads on. In fact, some conspiracy theorists think the distillers' real goal is to drive beer off TV. That's extremely unlikely. Beer is so entrenched in TV economics that it's hard to imagine the sort of social upheaval necessary to drive it away. But if beer and liquor ads are going to be on TV, the ads should be regulated in the public interest. Alcohol is really a drug, and we have a long tradition of regulating drug ads to protect the public. The makers of Rogaine or Prozac aren't permitted to say whatever they wish in ads. Why should the good-tasting narcotics be exempted?

The regulation might cover TV only—our most emotional medium 10 and the one watched most closely by children. It could curb appeals to children as well as devious psychological manipulation of adults along the lines of Bacardi's Darth Vader print ad. We know that the televising of liquor ads will promote accelerated consumption, with predictable increases in addiction and drunk driving. If we can't stop it, let's at least set some sensible rules that reflect the true social costs involved.

Keep Guns out of Lawyers' Hands

JOHN R. LOTT JR.

BEFORE READING: Your views about gun ownership have probably been affected by TV shows, movies, news reports, and perhaps even by real-life experiences. How did you decide that gun ownership is a safety measure or a danger for the owner?

The state attorneys general and trial lawyers behind the temporarily derailed $516 billion tobacco settlement have opened up a Pandora's box of legal tricks. Long after the tobacco matter is in the past, these maneuvers could continue to be used against other unwitting industries that have nothing to do with cigarettes.

Much like states led the charge on tobacco, cities are spearheading the assault on the next target for a huge, amorphous product-liability suit—firearms companies. Chicago and Philadelphia are already threatening to sue gun makers. "The key is to get a lawsuit whereby the manufacturer is held liable, just like the smoking industry is held liable," said Chicago Mayor Richard Daley. Philadelphia Mayor Edward Rendell wants gun manufacturers to reimburse the city for all of its health-care expenses and police salaries that arise from gun violence.

These are not the only lawsuits facing gun makers. Last week the MacArthur Justice Center at the University of Chicago filed a suit accusing gun companies of knowingly aiding criminals in the commission of crimes. The case, filed on behalf of the estates of three dead people, claims that the gun companies "specifically geared" their weapons to make them attractive to gang members. Among the offending characteristics listed are low price, easy concealability, corrosion resistance, and high firepower. The fact that an industry is being sued for making affordable products shows how far the liability-litigation madness has gone.

As in the tobacco cases, the antigun plaintiffs acknowledge only the costs and not the benefits of the products. However, the case against gun manufacturers will be harder to make. The states' class-action suits against tobacco emphasized what the tobacco companies knew about their products, not whether smokers themselves knew the risks of smoking. The plaintiffs are essentially accusing the tobacco companies of fraud—not fully revealing the deadliness of their product. This strategy wouldn't work against the gun makers since everyone knows that guns can kill.

Tobacco companies had a response to the states' claim that smoking 5 cost taxpayers Medicaid money to pay for tobacco-related illnesses.

John R. Lott Jr. is a fellow at the University of Chicago Law School and is the author of *More Guns, Less Crime* (1998). His essay appeared in the *Wall Street Journal* on June 23, 1998.

When smokers get sick, they tend to die relatively quickly. While states must bear these health-care costs sooner, since smokers die younger than nonsmokers, the expenses are offset by shorter illnesses—indeed, by smokers' shorter lives. And once the long-term savings to state pension programs are taken into account, smoking actually saves states money.

Tobacco companies were never comfortable with this morbid argument and judges weren't sympathetic to it. This permitted the state attorneys general to make fantastical accounting arguments in which they cited the costs, but not the benefits, of smoking to state coffers.

But simply claiming that murders are committed with guns would not be enough for the cities to win. Unlike tobacco companies, gun makers also have powerful arguments about the benefits of gun ownership. Criminals tend to attack victims who they perceive as weak—and guns serve as an important deterrent against crime.

Americans use guns defensively about 2.5 million times a year, and 98 percent of the time merely brandishing the weapon is sufficient to stop an attack. Resistance with a gun is also the safest course of action when confronted by a criminal. For example, the chances of serious injury from an attack are 2.5 times greater for women offering no resistance than for those resisting with a gun. And guns help to bridge the strength differential between male criminals and their female victims, putting women on a more equal footing with men in terms of personal safety.

In my own recent research on gun ownership rates across states over time, I found that higher gun ownership rates are associated with lower crime rates. Further, poor people in the highest-crime areas benefit the most from gun ownership. Lawsuits against gun makers could raise the price of firearms, which would most severely reduce gun ownership among the law-abiding, much-victimized poor.

The cities' suits put Messrs. Daley and Rendell at odds with the wis- 10 dom of the very people whose job it is to keep the streets safe. The police cannot feasibly protect everybody all the time. Perhaps this is why police officers are sympathetic to law-abiding citizens owning guns. A 1996 survey of 15,000 chiefs of police and sheriffs conducted by the National Association of Chiefs of Police found that 93 percent of them thought law-abiding citizens should be able to purchase guns for self defense.

The cities would also face a credibility problem with their potential lawsuits: The towns themselves pay for police officers to carry guns. This makes it harder for them to deny that being armed has substantial benefits.

As for the MacArthur Justice Center, its charges represent the dangerous combination of counting costs but not benefits in legal arguments and of using courts to make public policy. Lightweight, concealable guns may help criminals, but they also help protect law-abiding citizens in the forty-three states that allow concealed handguns. States issuing the most carry permits have had the largest drops in violent crime. Criminals may value guns with firepower, but so do potential victims who want to stop an attacker.

Perhaps the next prey for the local government and trial lawyers will be automobile companies. After all, the state bears some health-care costs from car accidents and has to pay highway patrolmen to clean up the crashes.

Every product has illegitimate uses. Once legitimate products get assailed because they have a well-known downside, it's hard to see where the process will stop.

Revolution in the Air

BEFORE READING: How reasonable is it to expect wind power to replace fossil fuels?

TomPaine.common sense
A Journal of Opinion

Revolution in the Air

Wind Power Threatens the Dinosaur Lobby.

It's a quiet revolution. No slogans, masked mobs or smashed windows.

There's just a rhythmic *whoosh whoosh whoosh* – the hushed whir of windmills.

The wind-power revolution has arrived. Maybe just in time.

The grim reality of human-induced global warming... California's energy crisis... pollution-induced lung disease... ever more warning – **we must cope with our addiction to fossil-fuel "dinosaur power."**

Wind power can help.

It's growing 24 percent annually worldwide and could provide three million jobs by 2020, says the Worldwatch Institute (**www.Worldwatch.org**). Meanwhile, employment in the fossil-fuel industry is shrinking.

In Iowa, 257 windmills are helping farmers weather the farm crisis. Landowners earn $2,000 annually for each windmill they host. "We could easily have ten times the wind energy production we now have in Iowa," says one proponent.

The economic efficiency of wind power blows away dinosaur power. Once built, a windmill produces clean electricity with little additional expense or input. And besides dirty coal, it's now the cheapest power.

Fossil-fuel generators cost a lot to build. They demand constant feeding. We all pay twice: as ratepayers, and then as taxpayers, through government subsidies for industry, plus the cost of environmental damage and degraded public health.

All this makes wind power superior, yet political leaders resist the wind revolution. Why?

The Dinosaur Lobby – oil, gas and coal companies – prefer the status quo. They use their wealth to indenture public servants and twist public policy.

Just look at the energy plan from the Oil Patch President. It calls for more dirty power – and more nuclear, although bailing out that industry is costing Americans more than $100 billion. Clean energy gets short shrift.

But such willful ignorance will just delay the wind-power revolution, not stop it.

Common sense, like wind, finds its way through the cracks.

This week at TomPaine.com – Revolution in the Air. *Featuring "Going to Work for Wind Power" by Michael Renner... "Cleaner Than Cows" and "Do Windmills Kill Birds?" by David Case... and "A New Crop for U.S. Farmers" by Patrick Mazza, from Earth Island Journal (www.EarthIsland.org).*

TomPaine.com is an online journal.

THINKING AND WRITING ABOUT CORPORATE RESPONSIBILITY

QUESTIONS FOR DISCUSSION AND WRITING

1. The student authors of the articles about Nike are engaged in a debate. Jacobson introduces several issues which she says Nike has failed to address. Does Sneider respond directly to her accusations? Has he introduced new data that support Nike's management? Are these two arguments equally strong?

2. Friedman's claim that corporations have only one "social responsibility," to their stockholders, is based on a belief in individual freedom of choice. Point out places where he explains the connection.

3. Since both Daly and Welch claim scientific research as an ally, how can a reader determine the truth? What is Welch's principal defense against Daly's accusations? Is it convincing?

4. Summarize Sullum's view of the power of advertising. Do you agree? Can you cite examples from experience, as Sullum does, to support your conclusion?

5. According to Leo, advertisements by beer and liquor companies are full of subliminal or coded appeals. Were you surprised by any of his interpretations? Or do you think that most people are aware of them and able to resist them? Compare Sullum's conclusions about advertising.

6. What is the basis of the lawsuit against the gun makers? What is Lott's objection to it? What differences does Lott find between damages inflicted by cigarettes and those inflicted by guns? Lott points out that cigarettes also provide benefits to their users. What benefits of gun ownership are described? Do you think Lott is guilty of a slippery-slope fallacy at the end?

7. "Revolution in the Air" is an advertisement. Are there signs—for example, in the language or the format—that identify it as an ad? Are there statements that need further proof in a longer argument? How effective is it as a claim of policy?

TOPICS FOR RESEARCH

Corporate charity versus philanthropy by nonprofit organizations

Fashion industry advertising: socially responsible?

Wind power: the drawbacks

What socially responsible businesses do (Barbie, Levi Strauss, etc.)

TAKING THE DEBATE ONLINE

For these and additional research URLs, see www.bedfordstmartins.com/rottenberg.

- *FDA*
  www.fda.gov

  This site is maintained by the Food and Drug Administration, the nation's foremost consumer protection agency.

- *Just Stop It*
  http://www.caa.org.au/campaigns/nike/index1.html

  This is the page of a site attempting to "get Nike to take responsibility for the conditions in the factories where their shoes are made."

- *General Electric*
  http://www.hudsonvoice.com

  This site, maintained by General Electric, contains numerous articles arguing against dredging rivers contaminated with PCBs by GE.

- *A Citizen's Guide*
  http://www.toxicstargeting.com/ge/citizenguide.htm

  This site contains a map of sites which GE contaminated by PCBs.

- *Legal Information Institute*
  http://www.law.cornell.edu/topics/products_liability.html

  This site provides a brief overview of product liability law.

- *Alternative Energy Institute, Inc.*
  http://www.altenergy.org

  This site contains explanations of such renewable energy sources as solar, wind, hydroelectric, biomass energy, hydrogen and fuel cell, geothermal, and others.

- *Annual Report: Corporate Responsibility*
  http://www.nikebiz.com/

  This is a pro-Nike site on the company's corporate responsibility.

13

Criminal Justice: Trial by Jury

A trial by jury of one's peers, or equals, is guaranteed by three amendments in the U.S. Constitution's Bill of Rights. The Fifth and Sixth Amendments refer to capital or serious crimes that are punishable by prison or death. (The Seventh Amendment governs civil disputes about money or property, which can be settled by monetary awards.) The amendments require that trials be speedy, public, and fair, as opposed to trials in eighteenth-century Britain, which were often lengthy, secret, and arbitrary or prejudiced by special interests. Two rules are almost universally mandated, though not required by the Constitution—the number of jurors (twelve) and a unanimous vote for conviction or acquittal. (Two states do not observe these mandates.) The American jury system is based on English common law, but most European countries follow Roman law, in which a case is heard and decided not by a jury of one's peers but by professional and lay judges.

Since the beginning of the republic, the jury has functioned as a powerful instrument of democratic decision making. One judge points out that "a trial is not a search for the truth, but rather a mechanism for resolving a disagreement over facts."[1] But the system has come under attack when juries deliver verdicts that seem to ignore the rules of evidence

[1] Avern Cohn, *New York Times Book Review*, October 7, 2001, p. 4.

and the law. One such case was the highly publicized murder trial of O. J. Simpson, the African American football star who was acquitted of the murder of his white wife and her male friend. In this case the largely black jury was said by critics to have practiced "jury nullification"—that is, the right of a jury to disregard, or nullify, the evidence and the law if it believes that the law is unjust. The not guilty verdict was clearly influenced by the racist remarks of a white police officer who was a principal prosecution witness.

This case, in fact, prompted a widespread review of trial by jury in its present form. Lawyers, judges, and other observers of courtroom procedure have offered the following objections:

- Juries composed of people without training in the law are unable to fully understand the instructions of judges and to evaluate the sometimes dubious legal arguments of lawyers and their appeals to emotion.

- Juries composed of people without knowledge of science have difficulty understanding evidence provided by scientists and forensic experts.

- Juries are not representative of the whole community but only of those who can be found on voter rolls or in telephone directories or who do not seek exemption.

- The selection of an impartial jury is skewed by the rights of lawyers on both sides to choose (by peremptory challenge) jurors who will be sympathetic to their arguments.

- Some so-called "stealth" jurors lie about their impartiality in order to be chosen for jury duty.

Having watched many fictional trials on TV, where the camera pans the serious and attentive faces of the jurors, we still know little about what actually transpires when the jurors are deliberating. According to one scholar,

> The jury room is one more setting for the unequal exercise of power. Some of the members have more rhetorical skill, or personal charm, or moral force, or simple stubbornness than others, and they are more likely to determine the verdict.[2]

Despite criticism of some well-known cases, many legal scholars believe that no substantial changes to the jury system are needed. Others, however, claim that the efficiency and fairness of criminal justice can be improved by new rules for the selection and responsibilities of the jury. And an influential minority has argued that the jury system no longer serves its purpose, cannot be salvaged, and should be replaced by one or more professional judges.

---

[2] Michael Walzer, *Spheres of Justice* (New York: Basic Books, 1983), p. 308.

Unsung Heroes: Juries Offer True Justice

ALAN DERSHOWITZ

BEFORE READING: If trial by jury is seriously flawed, as its critics claim, why do you think Americans continue to support it as a preferred instrument of justice?

The American jury, one of the great bastions of liberty, is under increasing attack. Many lawyers regard it as, at best, a necessary evil. It slows the process of adjudication. Its outcomes are unpredictable. It is inexpert at deciding complex issues. It is subject to emotional, even bigoted, appeals. Its verdicts lack consistency, since different juries arrive at different conclusions in cases with similar facts. It seems anachronistic in our age of efficiency and specialization.

In England, where the jury originated, it has been all but abolished in civil cases. In the United States, where our Constitution forbids its abolition in most cases, it has been limited wherever possible. Moreover, the traditional size of juries has been reduced from twelve to six in many cases, and the requirement of unanimity has been changed in many states to a two-thirds majority.

At an even more fundamental level, the cumbersomeness of juries has resulted in relatively few cases actually being tried: The vast majority are settled before trial, in criminal cases by a plea bargain and in civil cases by a financial compromise. The expense and unpredictability of jury trials have also driven many institutional litigants such as stock brokerage firms to demand that their customers waive trial by jury and accept the more streamlined mechanism of arbitration.

In sum, it's fair to say that if our Constitution did not mandate the right to trial by jury in most criminal and civil cases, the jury would be in danger of becoming an endangered species of adjudication.

It's ironic, though not at all surprising, that as we Americans unappreciatively chip away at the right to trial by jury, reformers in several Eastern European nations are calling for its transplantation onto their foreign soil. Having experienced totalitarian judicial and political systems, they are searching for mechanisms that promise some popular checks on the abuse of governmental power. 5

They have seen enough of Communist efficiency, predictability, expertise, and objectivity. They understand, as some Americans seem not to, that making the judicial "trains run on time" is not the sole criterion by which to judge a legal system. For a trial to be fair, the adjudicator

Alan Dershowitz is a professor of law at the Harvard Law School and is the author of several books, including *Reversal of Fortune* (1990); *Contrary to Popular Opinion* (1992), the source of this selection; and *Supreme Injustice* (2001).

must be *independent* of the powers that be, willing and able to stand up to pressures to do the government's bidding.

The American jury has passed that difficult test with flying colors, from the colonial period when it acquitted John Peter Zenger of politically inspired charges of libel to recent juries that have ruled in favor of such unpopular defendants as John Hinkley, Peggy McMartin Buckey, Imelda Marcos, and John DeLorean.

Juries, unlike judges, do not become routinized: Every case is their first and only case. It is their opportunity to do justice, and most jurors take their role quite seriously.

Many judges, especially some who have been on the bench for years, regard criminal defendants as presumptively guilty, since most who have come before them have pleaded guilty or been convicted. Juries, on the other hand, really seem to believe in the presumption of innocence and require the prosecution to prove each case beyond a reasonable doubt.

Nor can anyone *whisper* to a jury. Everything said to them is said   10 openly and on the record. They hear only the evidence that is properly admissible. They do not learn that the prosecutor believes that the defendant is a bad or dangerous man—unless there is admissible evidence to support these assertions. The jurors are umpires, not fans.

The very independence and unaccountability of juries also make them a potentially dangerous institution in some settings. Racist juries in the pre–civil rights South routinely acquitted white killers of African Americans. Some contemporary jurors, who regard themselves as foot soldiers in the war against drugs, seem willing to convict anyone with a Colombian passport of drug charges.

But the jury is simply one part of our system of checks and balances. It, too, must be kept in check by other institutions of government, such as trial and appellate judges.

In addition to recent efforts at limiting the role of juries, there is another serious danger on the horizon. Sophisticated social scientists are becoming increasingly involved on behalf of wealthy litigants in trying to select jurors who will favor their side. Since the average litigant cannot afford this expensive luxury—he can barely scrape up the money for exorbitant legal fees—only the most powerful plaintiffs or defendants will be able to manipulate jury selection to their advantage. These "designer juries" threaten to skew the randomness of the jury and destroy its objectivity.

In the end, the jury system, like democracy itself, is the worst mechanism for achieving justice, "except," as Winston Churchill said about democracy, "for all the others." Even with its imperfections, the American jury serves as a powerful check on the abuses of governmental power.

Our system of checks and balances may not be the most efficient   15 mechanism for governing. But it is the envy of all who treasure liberty and believe in government by the people. American jurors are the people administering justice.

"I urge this jury not to let the evidence prejudice you against my client."

Trial by Jury Should Be Abolished

CHRISTIE DAVIES

BEFORE READING: If you were on trial, would you prefer to be tried by a jury of your peers — same age, same social class — or by a judge?

In all the wringing of hands about race, civil rights, and the relations between police and public occasioned by the Rodney King verdicts, no one has dared to criticize that sacred cow, "trial by jury." No institution competing in the marketplace would ever survive if at its core it had a system of decision making like this, one which is about as reliable as an examination of the entrails of a ritually sacrificed free-range rooster.

Behind each erroneous conviction there lies a muddled jury of twelve more or less good, supposedly true, men, women, and hobble-dehoys. Since most states do not demand any kind of qualification based on property or education, the dullest citizens may sit on a jury. Juries are also erratically skewed by the attempts by prosecution, and even more by

---

Christie Davies is a professor of sociology at the University of Reading in England and the coauthor of *Wrongful Imprisonment: Mistaken Convictions and Their Consequences* (1973). This essay first appeared in the *National Review* on May 24, 1993.

defense, lawyers to cross-examine, challenge, and choose individual jurors until they get the jury composition they want, a process made even easier if they can also choose *where* the trial is held. In so doing they undermine the very rationale of the jury as a random representation of the people at large. The very principle of the random selection of jurors is itself a dubious one for other reasons. No one in his senses would entrust an important decision in his life—where to live, what job to apply for, whether to have an operation, what shares to buy—to a random sample of twelve people, and yet we place our system of criminal justice in their uncertain hands. In some districts, no doubt, the jurors are above average, but in others they are stupid, feckless, illiterate, and felonious in thought and undetected deed. Does it really redress the balance if these same wretched jurors are mugged and raped on their way home by the villains they have just acquitted?

Jurors Make Wrong Decisions

Not only do jurors wrongly acquit, they also falsely convict, and there are many innocent men and women sitting in jails throughout America because a jury got it wrong. The studies of wrongful imprisonment by Edward Radin, Edwin M. Borchard, Jerome and Barbara Frank, E. S. Gardner, and E. B. Block cite a frightening number of such cases. In addition to the famous instances they discuss, there are many other unknown, not very articulate, wrongly imprisoned individuals whose plight is not going to gain the attention of legal crusaders or those with influence in the mass media. They are alleged rapists who have been set up by vindictive women whose favors they once enjoyed but later spurned. They are small-businessmen done for "serious" fraud who were quite incapable of keeping one set of account books let alone two. They are all unfashionable little people, and no newspaper or television station is going to invest substantial sums of money in investigating their cases. They are all in prison because juries are no shrewder or more experienced than you or I and usually a lot less so.

Should these unfortunates take their case to appeal, they will get nowhere, because appeals courts see their task as being to look for minor and irrelevant errors in legal procedure rather than to reexamine the facts, however flagrantly absurd the jury's verdict may have been. Appeals courts may be barred by the state constitution from considering questions of fact at all, and, even when they are allowed to do so, they are reluctant to declare that the jury got it wrong. Even if in private the appeals judges think that the jurors were dolts, they will not say so, but will scrabble around trying to find a minor procedural error that will allow them to set aside the verdict. The worst position for an innocent defendant to be in is for the trial to be conducted impeccably and for the jury then perversely to convict. The appeals judges are then unable to criticize the trial procedure and will not criticize the jury, so the defendant stays in prison.

The jury is quite unlike all other tribunals, which have to give rea- 5 sons for their decisions and to show how evidence is linked by logic to produce a conclusion. The jury is an oracle, a secret anonymous conclave swayed by unknown and unknowable prejudices and mental aberrations. Its decisions cannot be criticized or easily overturned because no one has any idea how it arrived at them. For appeals judges to speculate too much on the perceptions and reasoning of jurors would be to rob the jury of its primitive sacred quality. So they have no choice but to hide behind these bookless sibyls or to attack, sometimes unfairly, their judicial colleague's handling of the original trial.

If we are to have a rational method of reaching verdicts in criminal trials that also gives proper scope for appeal, then the jury must be replaced by a small team of experienced professional legal assessors. They would have to provide open, reasoned, and explicit reports saying how and why they reached their verdict.

Judge and Jury Should Swap Roles

The jury, however, ought to be retained in some capacity, as it is a part of democracy, a means of involving the ordinary citizen in the making of decisions within the criminal-justice system. The task for which the jury *is* eminently suited is that of sentencing. Juries should be entrusted with the task of deciding what penalty (within limits laid down by the state legislatures) should be imposed on those convicted by the new tribunals described above. Judge and jury should thus swap places.

Judges are by virtue of their training and experience better at deciding questions of fact as well as law than are the inexperienced members of a jury. However, when it comes to sentencing, judges are sometimes quirky and erratic and hand out bizarre sentences that indicate their ignorance of the moral priorities of the mass of the population. This situation can be rectified by letting the jury decide the sentence. The jury, being a random sample of the public, by definition represents the moral indignation of the community at large far better than any panel of judges, criminologists, or market researchers could ever do. Individual men and women differ enormously in intellectual capacity and thus in their ability to arrive at a correct decision, but they are democratically though arbitrarily equal in their power of telling right from wrong. In a democracy consciences are equal, however unequal brains may be. Not cloistered judges out of touch with popular sentiment but the people themselves should assess the heinousness of particular crimes and thus the appropriate sentence. Let the judges become the jury and the jury the judges.

Jury Nullification: Freedom's Last Chance

ROBERT ANTON WILSON

BEFORE READING: Would it be fair to serve on a jury if you disagreed with the law that the defendant was accused of violating (for example, using marijuana or blockading a health-care clinic that provides abortions)?

An old idea has resurfaced that may have major potential to slow or even reverse the terrifying erosion of the Bill of Rights under the Reagan-Bush team and their right-wing Supreme Court. I refer to the revival of the ancient Saxon doctrine of jury nullification, which has now become a projected Constitutional amendment under consideration in twenty-two states.

Since Mr. Justice Brennan, the last plumb-line defender of civil liberties, has retired, and the Supreme Court seems fated to move even further toward the authoritarian right-wing, only jury nullification can preserve what still remains in this perishing Republic of Anglo-American libertarianism.

Jury nullification rests upon an old common law principle (which Lysander Spooner in his scholarly "Essay on Trial by Jury" [1852] proved to underlie the jury clause of Magna Carta) — *viz., that the only way to prevent the government from imposing unjust or nefarious laws is to grant juries the right to negate such laws.* This right, as Spooner demonstrated, explains the tradition that a jury should consist of twelve citizens selected at random and thereby representing (as far as scientifically possible) the full range of common sense and common morality of the population in general (including the recalcitrants and cranks among us, upon whom liberty has always depended in bad times).

In a once popular formulation, the doctrine of jury nullification holds that "a jury may judge the law as well as the facts in the case." Since Magna Carta this has been repeatedly upheld by courts in both England and America, only occasionally denied by lower, and currently remains the law of both countries, although judges have no legal obligations to inform juries that they possess this right.

In fact, in one infamous decision, in the 1890s, the U.S. Supreme Court 5 upheld the right of jury nullification but simultaneously ruled that the judge not only doesn't have to tell the jury they have this right but can prevent the defense attorney from telling them. In other words, American juries have the right to nullify the law, but the judge, if so inclined, can do everything in her or his power to prevent them from knowing it.

Robert Anton Wilson is the coauthor, with Robert Shea, of *The Illuminatus! Trilogy* (1984). This piece originally appeared in Wilson's newsletter, *Trajectories,* in 2001.

In only one state out of the fifty—Maryland—does the state constitution oblige the judge to inform the jury that they have the right to acquit where the facts prove the defendant technically guilty but the sensibility of the jury holds that he or she did no real wrong. In the other forty-nine states, the right exists nebulously, like a ghost, haunting old parchments; judges do not talk about it, and juries, not knowing that they hold in their hands the final checkmate against tyranny, do not exercise the authority they possess.

As Lord Denman wrote (in *O'Connel v. Rex,* 1884): "Every jury in the land is tampered with and falsely instructed by the judge when it is told that it must accept as the law that which has been given to them, or that they must bring in a certain verdict, or that they can decide only the facts of the case." Outside Maryland, every jury in America is still tampered with and falsely instructed in this manner.

The Fully Informed Jury Amendment can change all this, since it would require judges to inform juries of their right to judge the law as well as the facts and to refuse to enforce any law they find repugnant, tyrannical, nefarious, or just plain idiotic.

Under the current government, we can expect abortion to become illegal again, and some women will die in back alleys the way they did before *Roe v. Wade.* But an informed jury can nullify any antiabortion law by refusing to convict doctors or patients or the counselors who send the patients to the doctors. They can nullify the law "in the teeth of the facts" of the case; and even one informed juror can hang the jury and cause a mistrial.

Similarly, the present idiotic "war" on drugs will continue indefi- 10
nitely, at a cost of billions, with further erosion of the Constitution, and with no tangible good results credible to anyone with more than half an inch of forehead. But an informed juror can again cause a mistrial. Certainly, the antipot law, the silliest of our drug laws, could not survive, in a nation with at least 70 million potheads, if juries knew they had the right of nullification.

In the landmark William Penn case in England in the 1670s, the state proved beyond doubt that Penn "was guilty"; i.e., he did consciously and deliberately violate the law by preaching in a public street a religion not that of the Anglican Church. The jury refused to convict, finding religious persecutions repugnant. The judge, in a fury, confined them to the Tower of London until they would agree to convict. After those twelve ordinary unheroic Englishmen had served enough time in the Tower, public opinion forced the judge to reverse himself and admit the jury had the right to decide the law as well as the facts. And that, children, is how religious liberty came to birth in the modern world after 200 years of bloody religious wars: twelve simple men who felt sick and tired of religious bigotry and refused to enforce an intolerant law.

Similarly, in the John Peter Zenger case (New York, 1734), the state proved conclusively that Zenger violated the law by printing antigovernment articles in his newspaper, the New York *Weekly Journal*. The jury simply refused to convict him and nullified the law. That was the beginning of freedom of the press in this country, even before the Revolution and the First Amendment.

As in Penn's and Zenger's day, Anglo-American juries today still have the right to cry "Halt!" to any government that tramples upon human liberty; and even if the FIJ Amendment does not pass all fifty states in the near future, the very fact that it exists and is receiving publicity means that some jurors at least will know their rights when they enter the jury box.

Jury Nullification Should Not Be Allowed

MARK S. PULLIAM

BEFORE READING: Is jury nullification a form of civil disobedience? (See a dictionary for a definition of *civil disobedience*.)

What do nineteenth-century anarchist Lysander Spooner,[1] the O. J. Simpson legal defense team, some elements of the militia movement,[2] the Los Angeles juries that failed to convict the Menendez brothers of murdering their parents and that acquitted the brutal assailants of Reginald Denny, and the activists who promote the idea of "fully informed juries"[3] have in common?

They all symbolize the notion that juries can and should refuse to heed the instructions given them by the trial judge and that jurors should instead follow their own consciences and "nullify" those instructions by doing what they personally feel is just.

Jury instructions are the applicable legal rules communicated to the jury by the trial judge. In virtually every jurisdiction, jurors take an oath at the beginning of the case that they will consider only the evidence presented and the instructions of the court. The "instructions" are, therefore, laws that society has duly enacted through either the legislative process or the common law judicial process. In either event, the laws derive legitimacy from our democratic political traditions.

---

[1] Lysander Spooner, *An Essay on the Trial by Jury* (1852). [All notes are Pulliam's unless noted otherwise.]

[2] "Militias Are Joining Jury-Power Activists to Fight Government," *Wall Street Journal* (May 25, 1995), p. A1 (hereinafter "Militias").

[3] Ibid.

Mark S. Pulliam is an attorney in San Diego, California. This piece first appeared in the March 1996 issue of *Freeman*.

As citizens, we may not agree with all the laws on the books, but in a system of representative government we are bound to follow them. It is inherent in the concept of the state that there will not be unanimity in all matters but that the views of the majority will prevail. This "coercion" or "oppression" of the dissenting minority has long perturbed anarchist philosophers such as the aforementioned Spooner, who objected to the "social compact" rationale for the state as well as the institution of the jury.[4] Jury-power activists sometimes cite Spooner as a proponent of "jury nullification," but he is best known for his more fundamental objection to constitutional government.

On what basis do advocates of jury nullification attempt to justify   5 the lawlessness that ignoring the court's instructions entails? Advocates advance two principal explanations, neither of which is persuasive: (1) civil disobedience, or the moral right or obligation to resist enforcement of an unjust law,[5] and (2) populist opposition to tyrannical actions by an unresponsive government.[6] Let's consider these explanations.

Civil Disobedience

Civil disobedience is a misnomer in the context of a seated juror refusing to follow the law. Civil disobedience, properly understood, is resistance to unjust government action as a last resort—when disobedience is the only alternative to becoming a participant in an objectionable act. This will never be the case with a seated juror. A potential juror who objected to service could refuse to report to court or serve on a jury. A person with a moral objection to enforcing a particular law (say, punishing a defendant charged with private drug use or blockading abortion clinics) could disclose that objection during voir dire[7] and be excused from serving in the case.

But, after a juror has reported for service, been screened through voir dire, been seated and sworn to follow the law according to the instructions of the court, there is no room for "civil disobedience." A juror reneging on his oath is an outlaw, a scofflaw. A renegade juror cheats the parties to the case out of their right to have the matter decided according to the law, on the basis of which the evidence and arguments have been presented.

Despite proponents' fondness of quoting Henry David Thoreau on civil disobedience,[8] a lawless juror is no more heroic than a rogue policeman violating the law or a politician accepting a bribe. If a juror (or any

---

[4] Lysander Spooner, *No Treason: The Constitution of No Authority* (1870).

[5] Michael Pierone, "Requiring Citizens to Do Evil," *The Freeman* (July 1993), p. 261.

[6] "Militias," p. A8; N. Stephan Kinsella, "Legislation and Law in a Free Society," *The Freeman* (September 1995), pp. 561, 563.

[7] **voir dire:** "To say the truth," an oath given by a witness that he will tell the truth in regard to questions concerning his competency. —Ed.

[8] Pierone, p. 262, note 5.

other member of the political community) feels that a particular law is unjust—and in a society as large and diverse as ours, we can assume that someone, somewhere, feels that every law on the books is unjust—the remedy is to petition the legislature for reform, not to infiltrate the jury and then ignore the law.

Populist Opposition

The other frequently cited justification for jury nullification—the need to rein in abusive government power—is even more specious. An honest anarchist such as Lysander Spooner would refuse to serve on a jury because he wouldn't believe in the concept of mandatory jury service or even governmental proceedings to enforce the law. Let's not forget that a trial, whether civil or criminal, *is* government action. Enforcing democratically enacted laws is one of the basic purposes of government. When a juror considers defying his oath and deciding a case based on his personal feelings rather than the court's instructions, the alternative is not between liberty and coercion but between coercion informed by the rule of law and coercion at the whim of twelve jurors.

And what is a jury acting outside the law but a twelve-person mob, 10 like modern-day vigilantes? Although the jury-power activists point to historical events where juries refused to enforce the Fugitive Slave Act,[9] there is no assurance that a jury operating outside the law would only acquit in a criminal case; it could just as easily "nullify" the instructions by convicting a person who was technically innocent. Moreover, there are no counterparts to the Fugitive Slave Law in a civil case. Furthermore, nullifying the law strips the individuals who comprise society of *their* right to have the laws enforced. Nothing could be more tyrannical or despotic than the arbitrary decision of a jury that has rejected the law.

It disturbs me to see libertarians and conservatives—whom I generally regard as allies—embrace the jury nullification cause. The rule of law is essential to the preservation of liberty. Friedrich Hayek, perhaps the twentieth century's preeminent theorist of classical liberalism—the political philosophy of freedom—believed that the defining characteristic of a free society is the rule of law, meaning legal rules stated in advance, uniformly applied, without excessive discretion.[10] In Hayek's words: "[W]hen we obey laws, in the sense of general abstract rules laid down irrespective of their application to us, we are not subject to another man's will and are therefore free."[11] Thus, it is the universal, nonselective nature of law that allows us to be free.[12] In Hayek's view, it is precisely

[9]Ibid.

[10]Friedrich A. Hayek, *The Road to Serfdom* (Chicago: University of Chicago Press, 1944), pp. 72–79.

[11]Friedrich A. Hayek, *The Constitution of Liberty* (Chicago: University of Chicago Press, 1960), p. 153.

[12]Ibid., pp. 153–54.

because judges and juries cannot pick and choose what laws to enforce in a particular case "that it can be said that laws and not men rule."[13] Jury-activist pamphleteers in front of the courthouse would do well to heed Hayek's admonition that "few beliefs have been more destructive of the respect for the rules of law and of morals than the idea that a rule is binding only if the beneficial effect of observing it in the particular instance can be recognized."[14]

Yet that is exactly what advocates of jury nullification espouse—following the law only if they agree with it in a particular case. I am not unsympathetic to concerns about unjust laws and government overreaching. The solution is grassroots political activism and reforms such as fewer federal mandates and expanded use of the initiative and recall devices, not shortsighted demagoguery in the form of jury nullification. Jurors ignoring the law accomplish nothing but anarchy in a microcosm—nullifying the rule of law.

"Your Honor, we're going to go with the prosecution's spin."

13Ibid., p. 153.
14Ibid., p. 159.

Juries on the Rampage

BURTON S. KATZ

BEFORE READING: Should jurors be allowed to decide matters of scientific fact?

> Send a message . . . to stop this cover-up! If you don't stop it who will?
> [I]t has to be stopped by you. [I]f you don't do what's right, this kind of
> conduct will continue on forever. —Johnnie Cochran, 1995

We love juries and we hate them. It has been so since the emergence of the modern jury in 1670. Our ambivalence about juries is a tension built right into the system. The whole problem is one of power. Jurors in criminal cases have power, and they have a lot of it.

We like it when our juries use their power to protect us against tyrannical government. The phrase *tyrannical government* is not just some political science catchphrase. The power to lock me up and throw me in jail is an awesome power, easy to abuse. Of all the constitutional protections that stand between me and overzealous prosecutors or judges who don't like the way I look, the right to trial by jury is the most important.

Juries really do bring a fresh sense of the values of the community into a musty, jaded courtroom. Judges and DAs have seen it all after a few years. Over and over. They lose their sense of outrage. Ho-hum, another murder case. Another guy the state of California or the state of Texas is trying to send to the gas chamber. Another day's work.

But there is a downside to juries. For them to protect us against tyrannical government, overzealous prosecutors, and bad judges, we have to give jurors power. A lot of power. We like it when the jurors bring *our* values into the courtroom. When the jury agrees with *us*. Throughout American history, and especially in the last five explosive years, we have seen stupid and bigoted juries render one bad decision after another. When that happens, we are not so certain we like *those* jurors to have all that power. *Their* community values don't seem so good.

As you can see, we both love and hate juries for precisely the same 5 reason. Jurors have lots of power: the power to prevent the government from abusing its power to imprison citizens; the power to do horrible injustice, to free murderers or to convict innocent people because they do not like their looks or the color of their skin.

Judge Burton S. Katz has been a defense attorney, television commentator, and teacher. He was also a prosecutor, most notably in the Charles Manson family murders. This selection comes from his book *Justice Overruled: Unmasking the Criminal Justice System* (1997).

Jurors decide the facts. Not judges. Not appellate courts. If jurors decide a criminal defendant has a good alibi, that's it, it doesn't matter how unbelievable or stupid the alibi may be. If jurors decide DNA typing, accurate to one in 1.6 billion, is not enough to prove the defendant was at the crime scene, that's it. There is *no* appeal when a jury wrongfully or incredibly acquits a criminal defendant.

Jurors can ignore the law completely. Even if everyone agrees on the facts, and the law is clear that the defendant is guilty on those facts, the jury may still acquit the defendant. This is known as *jury nullification.*

A jury in a criminal case may do pretty much as it pleases when it comes to acquitting a defendant or convicting a defendant of lesser charges. That tremendous power makes the modern Anglo-American jury system unique.

The jury system needs to be changed. Not the core of the system; the jury system has served us fairly well for many hundreds of years. Recently, however, jurors have increasingly run amuck, with the willing aid of shameless attorneys and the media. Judges have failed to control their courtrooms. Juries, attorneys, and judges need to be reined in without taking away the essential power of the jury.

Bushell's Case: Where It All Began

You may think complete independence of juries is a recent development. It is not. The modern jury emerged in 1670 in the famous Bushell's case. In 1670, recalcitrant jurors did not land lucrative book deals. Instead, jurors were under extreme pressure to convict in criminal cases. When I say pressure, I mean that angry judges, appointed by and beholden to the monarch, could *imprison, fine, or banish* a juror who refused to convict a criminal defendant. That is, until Bushell's case.

That is fascinating even today. The crown had arrested William Penn for preaching the tenets of the Quaker religion. Because England had an official church, preaching other religions was against the law. So William Penn *was* guilty of violating the law of England. At trial, Penn defiantly admitted preaching the word of God to an assemblage of people—a clear violation of the law. All that remained was for the jury to convict him. Or so the crown thought. Penn defiantly proclaimed to the jury that since people have the right to worship God, *any* assembly for such a purpose is legal. And any law to the contrary is wrong. The judge, however, had other ideas. He instructed the jury as follows:

> You have heard what the Indictment is. It is for preaching to the
> people, and drawing a tumultuous company after them, and Mr. Penn
> was speaking. . . . [If Penn is not punished], you see they will go on
> [preaching]. . . . [N]ow we are upon the matter of fact *which you are to
> keep to, and observe, as what hath been fully sworn at your [the jurors'] peril*
> (Emphasis added.)

At the jurors' peril! Quite a bit different from the situation today.

The jury attempted to return a partial verdict against Penn but refused to convict him of unlawful assembly or disturbing the peace. The jurors also acquitted a codefendant, William Mead. Both verdicts were clear violations of the court's instructions. The judge was angry. He ordered the jury to be locked up without "eat, drink, fire, and tobacco" and to resume deliberations. He ordered the jurors to follow the court's instructions and return a proper (i.e., guilty) verdict. (This is the true meaning of being sequestered!)

The jury again refused to change its verdict, and the furious court threatened to starve them. Their backs to the wall, the jury returned a unanimous verdict of not guilty. This was jury nullification, pure and simple. The jurors gave the fist to the law, refusing to acknowledge its moral or legal authority. But Bushell's case was far from over. In fact, it was just starting.

The furious judge fined the jurors. One of the jurors, Edward Bushell, 15 was an uncommonly stubborn man. He refused to pay his fine; the judge threw Bushell in jail. Bushell appealed his imprisonment to the Court of Common Pleas. Chief Justice Vaughan then made history by ruling that *jurors may not be fined nor imprisoned for their verdicts.* Stop and think about this for a minute. It seems so simple, it is easy to miss how important it is. Jurors can do pretty much whatever they want, and we cannot punish them.

The Right to Trial by Jury: A Defense
of Colonial America against King George

America enthusiastically adopted the English system of powerful juries. Before the American Revolution, the colonies saw jurors as a way to protect themselves against the tyranny of the English monarch. For example, in 1735 a jury refused to convict John Peter Zenger, a printer, of the crime of seditious libel against the New York colony's royal governor. Zenger had published a completely truthful article in his newspaper, the *Weekly Journal,* in which he revealed that the corrupt colonial governor had dismissed the chief justice of the New York Supreme Court for ruling against the governor in a court case. Although the article was truthful, the law still regarded it as criminal libel at that time.

The only real issue for the jury was whether Zenger had, in fact, published the article. Truth was no defense. Zenger's lawyer, Andrew Hamilton, argued that the jurors had the "right beyond all dispute to determine both the law and the fact, and where they do not doubt of the law, they ought to do so. [Jurors should] see with their own eyes, . . . hear with their own ears, and . . . make use of their consciences and understanding in judging of the lives, liberties or estate of their fellow subjects."

The jury acquitted Zenger, refusing to follow a law it felt was unjust.

Most of the colonies had enacted laws requiring trial by jury by the time of the American Revolution. The royal government in the colonies appointed judges who were lackeys for the crown and often denied defendants the right to jury trials—especially in politically significant cases. Our British overlords knew that American juries were not likely to convict Americans in political cases. This was such an incendiary issue that, in our Declaration of Independence, Thomas Jefferson wrote:

> The history of the present King of Great Britain is a history of repeated injuries and usurpations, all having in direct object the establishment of an absolute Tyranny over these States. To prove this, let the Facts be submitted to a candid world.
>
> He has made Judges dependent on his Will alone, for the tenure of their offices and payment of their salaries.
>
> He has . . . subject[ed] us to a jurisdiction foreign to our constitution . . . giving his Assent to their Acts of pretended Legislation. . . . For depriving us in many cases, of the benefits of Trial By Jury.

That says it all. The government appoints lackeys for judges, and we 20 need the common sense of the citizens to protect us from the government. As a result, in 1774 the First Continental Congress declared that all colonists were empowered with the right to the "great and inestimable privilege of being tried by their peers of the vicinage."

The Blessings of an Independent Jury System

I have seen every possible side of our independent jury system. Sometimes it is a great blessing, sometimes a curse. Not surprising, since jurors are but human. Of course, in the historic cases, an independent jury sounds wonderful—everyone ought to be protected from the tyranny of old King George, right? But even in modern times I have seen many examples of a jury genuinely serving as a protection against abusive government.

Consider the famous MacMartin Preschool case. I watched with horror as a politically ambitious district attorney brought utterly unsubstantiated claims of bizarre sexual molestation against Raymond Buckey and his mother and grandmother. The charges were made by schoolchildren, apparently egged on by their parents and therapists. I watched with incredulity as the therapists were caught on videotape, asking the children over and over if they had been touched "down there." The therapists would just not take no for an answer. Eventually the children said yes. Based on that evidence, and on claims by the preschoolers of secret tunnels and bus rides to churches where sexual rites were performed and animals were sacrificed (not one shred of which was ever confirmed by any physical evidence), the state of California undertook to put poor, hapless Raymond Buckey and his mother in jail. Raymond spent five years in jail and his mother over two years, awaiting the conclusion of the trial. Thank God for an independent jury. They acquitted the defendants rapidly after a preliminary hearing and a trial that lasted several years. (A few unresolved remaining counts were dismissed by the DA, but for the

Buckeys, justice came awfully late—long after their lives were smashed and wasted.). . .

The Curse of an Independent Jury System

So the independent jury system seems pretty good. Well, not always. Imagine how difficult it was in 1940 to convict a white man of raping a black woman or lynching a black man in the deep South. Or in 1950. Or in 1960. Or to convict KKK members for murdering civil rights protesters. That too is jury nullification, and it is not so pretty. Bigotry and hatred never are.

Take the 1991 murder of Yankel Rosenbaum in Crown Heights, in which an African American and Hispanic jury acquitted Rosenbaum's black killer, Lemrick Nelson. The murder took place during an emotionally charged race riot. Frankly, the race riot continued in the jury room. Here is how the United States Court of Appeals described the uncontested facts:

> An automobile driven by a Hasidic Jew struck two black children playing in the Crown Heights neighborhood of Brooklyn during the evening of August 19, 1991. One child was killed, and the other was seriously injured. Rumors spread throughout the community, during the course of the evening, that ambulance personnel responding to the scene of the accident first treated the Jewish driver rather than the two seriously injured children pinned beneath the automobile. A large crowd gathered at the accident scene. . . . [A crowd of black men, including the murderer, Nelson, headed for a nearby Jewish neighborhood.] Yankel Rosenbaum had the misfortune to be espied by Nelson and some ten other black individuals. One of them shouted, "There's a Jew, get the Jew," and they chased Rosenbaum across the street and attacked him. Rosenbaum, having been stabbed in the midsection of his body by Nelson, was left bleeding in the street.
>
> The police apprehended Nelson approximately one block away from the stabbing scene. They found in Nelson's pocket a bloody knife with the word "Killer" on the handle. When Rosenbaum confronted Nelson during a "show-up" identification, he positively identified Nelson as the person who had stabbed him. Rosenbaum died in the early morning hours of the following day at the hospital to which he had been taken following the incident. Shortly thereafter, Nelson orally admitted to the police that he had stabbed Rosenbaum.
>
> For causing the death of Yankel Rosenbaum, Nelson was charged as an adult with second degree murder under New York law on August 26, 1991. *After a six-week trial in Kings County Supreme Court, Nelson was acquitted in October 1992 of all charges arising out of the events of August 19, 1991.*

Ouch. It's payback time. (Nelson was subsequently retried under federal civil rights laws and convicted by a federal jury in 1996.). . . 25

The cases I have been talking about are the ones you have probably heard of—the notorious cases. But the rot goes much deeper in the system. In courthouses in predominantly African American neighborhoods of New York, Los Angeles, and other major cities, it is increasingly difficult to convict a black man for assault on, or murder of, a white man. I am sure the reverse is true today in other parts of America. Although no one wants to talk about it, that is another of the ugly little facts about our justice system today.

In each of the above cases, a jury refused to convict an obviously guilty person. It's thrilling to read about how Edward Bushell made history by refusing to convict William Penn for preaching the word of God or John Zenger for printing the truth about a corrupt colonial governor. Modern jury nullification is not so thrilling. . . . Modern defendants are getting away with murder and mayhem, and our powerful, independent juries are responsible. What is going on? Why the change?

One explanation may lie in the fact that the jury is supposed to bring the conscience of the community into the court system. A community conscience, as historically envisioned, probably no longer exists. That notion related to a homogeneous society where a single community more or less shared common values and mores. In England and colonial America, blacks, women, and minorities could not serve as jurors. Verdicts therefore reflected the conscience of white male landowners of a certain class standing. Today our multiethnic society makes it hard to define, let alone capture, the essence of the community conscience. It is far more difficult today to reach a community consensus of right and wrong, of shared values. Egregious verdicts or hung juries happen when jurors vote in accordance with their ethnic or religious affiliations or on the basis of the politics of special interests, without regard to the merits of the evidence. Political essayist George Will refers to this phenomenon as "group think."

Is the jury system dead? Should it be replaced? I still regard a powerful, independent jury as one of our most important protections against government tyranny. Juries can and do bring the conscience of the community into the judicial system. But what we are seeing are not isolated cases. The trend is clearly toward ever-increasing use of the jury system to "get even" with society for "past wrongs." To punish the system. Worse, to punish an entire society. The myth of the melting pot has long since died. There is a real danger that this nation of increasingly segregated and hostile cultures, each carrying baggage of perceived hurts, paranoia, and ill will, could become as polarized as the Serbs and the Croats.

Jurors are getting their say today, just as juries did in 1670. Too often, however, their "say" has all the judiciousness of a temper tantrum. Too often the modern conscience of the community allows murderers to walk free because of the color of their skin or because of the color of the skin of the person they murdered. Or because all cops are pigs and liars. Or because of past wrongs, real or imagined.

I regard this trend of acquitting dangerous criminals as the most serious assault on the integrity of the jury system since 1670, when the judge fined poor William Bushell for refusing to imprison William Penn. If this trend continues, and if juries continue to "group think" their way to injustice, the independent jury will not survive as an institution. It will not take many more Simpson or Rodney King verdicts to build a political consensus that the jury system needs major changes—and perhaps needs to be discarded altogether. This would be a tragedy. But the system can be repaired.

A Jury of Our Fears

HAROLD J. ROTHWAX

BEFORE READING: What reasons, apart from ill health, would cause so many people to refuse jury duty?

> We have a jury system that is superior to any in the world, and its efficacy is only marred by the difficulty of finding twelve men every day who don't know anything and can't read. —Mark Twain

> The man who wants a jury has a bad case. —Oliver Wendell Holmes

At a recent robbery trial, I noticed a female juror sitting with her eyes closed during the testimony of a crucial witness. I asked a court officer to tell her to sit with her eyes open, and during the recess, I called her in.

"Were you sleeping?" I asked.

She shrugged.

"It's necessary for you to hear this evidence," I warned her.

"I don't really have to listen to every word," she explained, to my 5 dismay. "I can tell whether someone is telling the truth by looking at the way he moves his eyebrows."

Fortunately, I learned this before the jury began to deliberate, and the juror was discharged. Yet it still troubled me. Every time I seat a jury, I fear that there is at least one person in the group who will simply not follow the rules of law. In New York, if a juror is dismissed after deliberations have started, she cannot be replaced by an alternate without the consent of the defendant—and a mistrial will almost certainly ensue. I got lucky when I caught this woman in time. . . .

For twenty-five years Harold J. Rothwax has been a judge on the New York State Supreme Court. He has also been a lecturer at Columbia University Law School and was a Guggenheim Fellow at the Yale Law School in 1984. This essay was originally published as a chapter of Rothwax's book *Guilty: The Collapse of Criminal Justice* (1996).

The jury is considered the jewel and the centerpiece of the American criminal justice system. It represents the people standing between a possibly oppressive government and the lonely, accused individual. No one can be convicted or condemned except by the judgment of his peers. By its verdict (which literally means "to speak the truth"), a community of citizens, drawn from a cross-section of the population, determines the validity of the government's charges. When we say that our system is the best in the world, we generally have the jury in mind.

But how well does the jury serve as a truth finder? How well does it serve as a voice of impartial justice? To what extent do our procedures and rules of evidence facilitate or impede the reliability of its findings?

The *rhetoric* that idealizes the jury and the *reality* of its operation are in conflict. Increasingly, we see high-profile cases of obviously guilty defendants who are acquitted by juries (the police in the Rodney King trial) or convicted of much lesser offenses (Reginald Denny). We see juries unable to reach a verdict even with the most overwhelming evidence (the Menendez brothers). Or, as in the case of O. J. Simpson, we see juries that simply fail to deliberate. And we must examine why.

Although attorneys and judges will often proclaim their admiration 10 of a jury's ability to reach the truth, privately they will acknowledge that a trial before a jury is a crapshoot, a roll of the dice, with all the randomness and uncertainty that implies.

To some extent this is a product of the exclusionary rules and rules of evidence that we have already discussed. But to a greater extent it is a comment on the procedures by which we recruit and select jurors, and the way that we manipulate them, orient them, instruct them, and condition their behavior.

It is also a comment on the jurors themselves.

Not too long ago I heard the following "joke" twice on TV: "Remember, if you get in trouble with the law and have to go to trial, your fate will be decided by twelve people so stupid they couldn't even get out of jury duty."

Juries may be getting dumber, but it's because attorneys (especially defense attorneys) want them that way. If, as I have argued, the overwhelming number of defendants who go to trial are guilty, then it is reasonable to expect that a defense attorney will seek jurors who will not or cannot intelligently evaluate evidence. He will want gullible, manipulable, emotional, suggestible jurors—and through our system of selection he will get them.

The lie we tell ourselves abut the sanctity of the jury begins with re- 15 cruitment. The jury is intended to be inclusive, widely representative, and a true cross section of the community. But it is not. Most commonly, we have sought the names of prospective jurors from voter registration rolls. In a time of public apathy and cynicism, however, many citizens do not register to vote. This excludes a large percentage of the population— in many areas more than 50 percent. To deal with this problem, a number of states have sought to enlarge the rolls by obtaining the names of nonvoters from welfare rolls, tax withholding lists, and registers of licensed drivers. Some even rely on telephone directories. While the impulse to widen the base of prospective jurors is admirable, one may question whether those who will not take the brief time to vote in their own interest will be prepared to set aside a much larger block of time to sit disinterestedly on a matter that does not directly affect their lives.

Increasingly, people summoned for jury duty have not been responding. They just don't show up. For example, in the last week of July 1995, only 10 percent of those summoned to appear in the Criminal Term of the Supreme Court in New York County responded. As a result, a number of serious felony cases that were ready to proceed to trial could not go forward. What happens to those citizens who fail to respond? Nothing at all. There are no jury service enforcement officers. To my knowledge, no person has *ever* been sanctioned for a failure to respond to a jury notice. G. Thomas Munsterman, a jury expert, has stated that the only way to be caught for ignoring a jury notice is to "write in and tell the court what they can do with their summons."

Of the small number of jurors who do appear, an increasingly large number seek to be excused for reasons of convenience or necessity—especially when the trial is scheduled to last for more than a brief period. A judge will often be reluctant to refuse to excuse a prospective juror who maintains that he or she cannot serve. To refuse may only provoke the untruthful response from the juror that he cannot be fair or impartial. Long experience has taught me that to insist on a juror serving when he clearly does not want to is to assure problems in the midst of the trial.

For years, many states have had jury exemption statutes, which exempted from service certain professions or other categories of workers (doctors, lawyers, clergy). To avoid the inconvenience of jury service, some associations have sought exemptions by using political weight when there was no apparent basis for exemption. Of late, many of the states (New York most recently) have done away with these exemptions, but, for the reasons stated above, I do not expect that this expansion of the juror base will result in a larger group of available prospective jurors. . . .

Once we have, with great difficulty, managed to scrape together a group of potential jurors who are willing to serve, the selection process is further complicated by the number of peremptory challenges (or challenges without cause) the lawyers are allowed. Too often, these challenges are used to "dumb down" the jury.

In 1994, I tried a case in which the defendant was charged with an [20] $800,000 Medicaid fraud. The case was complex; it involved a great many computer printouts and bank records. The defense attorney tried to challenge three prospective jurors for cause: one was an accountant, one was the treasurer of a corporation, and the third was a math teacher. The argument was that they would be *too* knowledgeable. I denied the lawyer's challenge for cause, but he simply got rid of them with peremptory challenges. As a result of this kind of game playing, unintelligent, unsophisticated jurors are often selected to determine the "truth." The voir dire[1] and the peremptory challenge demonstrate the basic mistrust of jurors that is held by trial lawyers.

At some level that is to be expected. The jury system requires us to entrust the fact-finding function, often in complex cases, to a group of untrained, frequently poorly educated, often reluctant and casually selected persons who are not repeat players, who do not have to give reasons or explanations for the results they reach, and who may allow extraneous considerations (the lateness of the hour, group dynamics, the appeal—or lack of it—of the lawyers) to affect their judgment.

But it is more than that. Although the Sixth Amendment requires an "impartial" jury, we have ceased in this day and age to *believe* in impartiality. And lawyers don't necessarily even want it.

In the United States, the process of jury selection is often protracted, sometimes as long as the trial itself—sometimes taking months. In the voir dire, the attorneys frequently pry into the most private areas of a juror's life. In the O. J. Simpson trial, the prospective jurors had to fill out an 80-page questionnaire with 294 questions—some calling for essay-type responses—inquiring into such compelling areas as:

- Have you ever written a letter to the editor of a newspaper or magazine?
- How important is religion in your life?
- Have you or anyone close to you undergone an amniocentesis?
- Have you ever asked a celebrity for an autograph?

Judge Lance Ito allowed the attorneys to ask whatever they wanted. These questions had nothing to do with whether a juror could be fair and impartial.

Even though it is clear that we cannot know how an individual juror 25 will vote in any given case, we use the voir dire to indoctrinate and to pry. For lawyers whose clients have deep pockets, "scientific jury consultants" are increasingly relied upon. It is now a growing industry—with polls and focus groups and shadow juries. And, increasingly, we are eliminating jurors on the basis of group biases.

I don't support the elimination of peremptory challenges altogether, for the simple reason that we need a way to dismiss a person who may be technically acceptable but whose tone, posture, or manner is just not right. Yet I feel strongly that we should limit these challenges to three for each side. . . .

---

[1] **voir dire:** "to say the truth," an oath given by a witness that he will tell the truth in regard to questions concerning his competency.—ED.

Erratic and irrational jury behavior make verdicts a crapshoot. But a jury trial is also a minefield where the search for truth can be waylaid and blown up by a multitude of rules that are arbitrary and serve no useful purpose—least of all to aid us in the search for the truth.

Evidence is admissible in a trial only if it is relevant. A judge determines relevance by asking whether the proffered evidence assists in establishing a fact in issue or in controverting it. But not all relevant evidence is admissible. Sometimes relevant evidence is highly prejudicial but only minimally probative.

If we had complete faith in the ability of the jury to function as mature, sophisticated, and intelligent fact finders, then we could submit to them *all* relevant evidence, but we don't have that faith.

So the judge serves as a gatekeeper. He decides not only what is rele- 30 vant but also whether the jury will be able to hear *all* of the relevant evidence. . . .

Because we do not trust the jury to sift that which is probative from that which is prejudicial, we exclude relevant evidence from the jury when the judge concludes that the prejudicial impact of the evidence exceeds its probative value.

Sometimes even when the evidence is *highly* probative, it is excluded because it is "too inflammatory." The case of *Johnson v. United States* is a good example.

The evidence showed that Johnson, after murdering one individual, went to the victim's apartment and shot the victim's thirteen-year-old son along with another child. The Federal District of Columbia Court of Appeals found this evidence more prejudicial than probative of Johnson being the first victim's killer and reversed his murder conviction.

Note, however, that the murder of the children tended in several ways to establish that Johnson was guilty of the first killing:

1. The same weapon was used to murder all three individuals.

2. Johnson was familiar with the apartment and its occupants.

3. A weapon taken from the victim's apartment was in Johnson's possession at the time of his arrest.

Nevertheless, the majority held that the trial court had erred in ad- 35 mitting the evidence. "The emotional impact of the heinous slaying of two innocent children, asleep and alone in an apartment" was simply too inflammatory. It was determined that the prejudicial impact of this evidence outweighed its probative value. It was, in my opinion, a maddening decision.

Contrast *Johnson* with the issue of the admissibility of the Fuhrman tapes in the O. J. Simpson case. You'll recall that Judge Ito allowed the playing of tapes from a past interview in which Fuhrman used racial slurs. The tendency in this area of the law to be more generous to the defendant than to the People is manifest. The People can't appeal an acquittal, but the defendant can appeal a conviction. Precisely because of this fact, the People ought to be given the benefit of the doubt on issues of law, and the defendant the benefit of the doubt on issues of fact.

The Fuhrman tapes were certainly more prejudicial than probative. They were not fundamental to the main proof of the case and would unduly prejudice a mostly African American jury. Yet Judge Ito deemed them relevant.

The necessity of unanimity from twelve jurors has continued to be a source of frustration in the court's ability to carry out justice. . . .

Although the U.S. Constitution does not require unanimous verdicts, and although thirty-three states permit nonunanimous verdicts in civil cases, forty-eight of our fifty states require unanimous verdicts in criminal cases, and so do the federal courts.

It's hard to know why this is so; it is simply a subject we don't discuss. It's a sacred cow. Two years ago the chief judge of the state of New York empaneled a commission to study the working of the jury system and to recommend changes. After much study the commission issued a lengthy report. When I looked at the report to see what it had to say about unanimity, it said that the subject had not been taken up because it was "controversial." One might argue that that is exactly why it *should* have been taken up! But the committee clearly wanted to avoid opening that particular can of worms.

Why can't we discuss the legitimacy of unanimous juries? What would happen if we allowed verdicts of ten to two or eleven to one? This is certainly far more than a bare majority. Would the search for truth be impaired? Would the jury system lose legitimacy and respect— more than it already has? Would the deliberative process be affected adversely?

Presumably, there would be fewer hung juries—so the system would be more efficient. Would it be less fair? Because jury deliberations are secret, exhaustive studies are not possible. The most highly regarded study was done by Harry Kalven Jr. and Hans Zeisel in their work *The American Jury,* published in 1966. Kalven and Zeisel concluded that deliberation had no significant effect on the final verdict in nine out of ten cases. "With very few exceptions the first ballot determines the outcome of the verdict . . . the real decision is often made before the deliberation begins." The authors also concluded that deliberation did not change votes through reasoning but rather through intimidation and peer pressure. In that sense, unanimity should not lead us to conclude that the verdict is more reliable.

A study by Dr. Deanna Kuhn of Columbia University Teachers College in New York, published in 1994 in the journal *Psychological Science,* showed that substantial numbers of jurors often jumped to conclusions early in the case and then tended to stick vehemently with those conclusions. These decision makers were largely immune to the deliberative process.

Justice Lewis Powell concluded that the unanimity rule put pressure on jurors to compromise, "despite the frequent absence of a rational basis for such compromise." So that in the end the requirement of unanimity led "not to full agreement among the twelve but to agreement by none and compromise by all." Greater accuracy might be obtained without a dissenter's veto, and without the need to compromise with one or two holdouts who resist reasoned argument.

My own experience as a trial judge leads me to agree with this assessment. In every instance that I can recall where the jury was split ten to two or eleven to one, in my judgment the holdout was *not* being rational. On the other hand, when the split was eight to four or seven to five, both sides had a reasoned basis for their positions. 45

In the interest of truth and efficiency, I would recommend permitting verdicts of eleven to one or ten to two. . . .

We have assigned awesome responsibility and power to this group of twelve "ordinary" citizens, whom we do not trust with the truth—and indeed strive to mislead. More and more, other factors outside the law are seeping into jury boxes and making the outcome of criminal trials more questionable as jurors assert their power without restraint.

Under our law, jurors are told by the judge that they are *only* finders of fact and that they are obliged by their oath to accept the law as the judge gives it to them, to apply that law to the facts they have found, and thereby reach their verdict.

In fact, jurors have the power to ignore a judge's instructions and to do whatever they please. Judges don't tell them this, and they don't permit the attorneys to tell them either. But jury deliberations are secret, and jurors can never be punished for the way they vote (or don't vote)— and many jurors know of this power. Of late, an organization called the Fully Informed Jury Association (FIJA) has begun to lobby for laws protecting the "right" of nullification—and, more importantly, to advise citizens and prospective jurors of that power. Many who are involved in violating one law or another are expected to respond favorably to such an initiative.

The problem is especially urgent and a matter of concern now when we appear to be witnessing racial line-drawing during jury deliberations. Although jury nullification has been employed to restrain a tyrannical government, it is a double-edged sword, one that has been used to exonerate Southern whites who killed or injured blacks and civil rights workers and also to condemn blacks in the South and elsewhere on insufficient evidence. When the government is democratic and not oppressive, nullification mocks the rule of law. 50

Although, when we speak of nullification, we generally have in mind the action of the *entire* jury, we should also understand that isolated jurors can also act to nullify without regard to the law or the evidence. The unanimity requirement enhances their power and enlarges their role.

Whatever the demographic makeup of a community may be, the law does not require that the final jury of twelve reflect the exact proportion of each group in the population. (In polyglot New York City, we would probably need a jury of fifty to serve that end.) The law has aimed to be inclusive, and no group can reasonably claim that it is being excluded.

But, increasingly, our search for a jury that is truly representative of the community has involved us in issues of race, gender, national origin, and religion. The theory behind the jury was that through a cross section of the population we obtain diverse and enriching perspectives—and that the jurors, once selected, would impartially, disinterestedly, and objectively seek the truth.

The large number of peremptory challenges has always imperiled that goal and has allowed its discriminatory impact to skew the composition of the final group of twelve. Only the abolition of the peremptory challenge, or its substantial reduction, can deal with the consequences of its abuse.

But we are also at another crossroads. We must examine whether the 55 jury will be a deliberative body or a representative one; whether its members will see themselves as part of a group, proportionately represented and designated to vote a certain way, or whether they will see themselves as impartial, disinterested, and focused entirely on the evidence.

The divisions in a multiethnic society cannot be resolved by the criminal justice system—just as conditions outside of the criminal justice system provide us with the defendants who inhabit it. If the racial, cultural, and class divisions continue to multiply and intensify, there can be no doubt that they will impact on the jury to its lasting detriment.

Ours is the only system in the world that gives such absolute power to a jury of ordinary citizens.

Japan, for example, had a jury system for a while and dropped it. Israel has never had one. Germany, France, and most of the rest of Europe rely on small panels of professional and lay judges. India inherited the British jury system from its former colonizers, but dropped it in 1961.

Shortly before Mikhail Gorbachev left office, at the invitation of the Lawyers Committee for Human Rights, I and two federal judges went to the then U.S.S.R. We found an enormous interest in our jury system from the judges, lawyers, and academics that we met. Although Russia had a jury system under the tsars, it had been abandoned under the Bolsheviks in favor of a mixed panel of professional and lay judges. The professionals with whom we met admired the jury system and considered it a protection against the tyranny from which they were just then emerging. I understand that Russia is now experimenting with a jury system.

England has a jury system. But it seems to be plagued by some of the same problems we face in America. Consider how a London jury resolved the issues in a recent murder case. 60

After being unable to reach a decision on the first day of deliberation, the jury was sent to a hotel. While there, four jurors convened and used a Ouija board to make contact with the murder victim. (Since they didn't have a Ouija board in the room, they fashioned one by printing letters of the alphabet on scraps of paper and using a glass instead of a pointer.) The jurors each put a finger on the glass, which then purportedly moved toward a succession of letters, revealing it was claimed, a message from the deceased: "Vote guilty tomorrow."

At breakfast the following morning the matter was discussed with other members of the jury. The result was a unanimous verdict to convict. The conviction was later reversed on appeal and the defendant was retried and convicted again—this time in the conventional manner. Judging from what I see every day in the courtroom, jurors might just as well use Ouija boards to reach their decisions.

Love and Death in New Jersey

STEPHEN J. ADLER

BEFORE READING: How good do you think you are in determining whether someone is telling the truth? How did you arrive at your criteria for judging?

On Friday, March 15, 1991, police answering a call at 36 Sunnyslope Road in Millington, New Jersey, found Fabio Hernandez, bloodied and groaning in pain, on the floor of the master bedroom. He had been shot in the chest and was also bleeding from a laceration near his left eye. He was dressed only in a pair of khaki pants, open at the belt, with the zipper down. Police officers found a 9 mm shell casing under his body. He was rushed to Morristown Memorial Hospital, where he died the next day during surgery.

Other than Hernandez, who gave no statement before he died, there had been two witnesses to the shooting. One had been Kevin Schneider, a Newark narcotics detective who had lived in the house before his divorce from Marisol Schneider a few months earlier and who owned the gun that had shot Hernandez. The other witness had been Marisol, who still lived in the house and had been Hernandez's lover both before and after the divorce. Kevin's and Marisol's versions of events contradicted

---

Stephen J. Adler is the law editor of the *Wall Street Journal* and author of *The Jury: Trial and Error in the American Courtroom* (1994), the source of this selection.

each other on most important details. Physical evidence was inconclusive. It would be up to a jury, after Kevin was charged with murder, to decide who was telling the truth about this triangle of love and death.

This is the kind of case in which juries are supposed to excel. There's no legal gobbledygook to parse, no complicated finances to follow, and little apparent room for prejudice to squeeze out reason. Here the common sense of the common man, the jury system's most treasured asset, can take over. And jurors do bring a lifetime of experience to judging whether other people's words square with their deeds. In their daily lives jurors make hundreds of such calculations: whether the used-car dealer is telling the truth about the mileage; whether the job applicant is lying about his experience; whether the child is concocting a tall tale about the missing homework; whether the spouse is working late or playing around. A knack for knowing whom to trust, whom to believe, whom to shun is the essence of common sense. Collectively twelve jurors would seem likely to have a great deal more of it than any single judge, no matter how well versed in law or experienced in life.

Yet for the most part the Schneider deliberations do not support this upbeat hypothesis. The jury in this case was a good deal more alert, sophisticated, and well educated than most. Nonetheless, . . . the jurors' various lapses, oversights, and unsupported assumptions raise questions about whether juries do anything well enough to justify our continuing reliance on them. Moreover, academic studies suggest that the traps the Schneider jurors fell into as they assessed the witnesses' credibility are, depressingly, all too common.

Indeed, in the last decade or so a startling consensus has emerged 5 among researchers that observers without special training, such as jurors, are egregiously bad at determining when someone is telling the truth, inadvertently giving false testimony, or lying. This, of course, contradicts the cherished folklore about jurors' common sense and powers of observation. It also helps explain why it's so difficult to find ways to help jurors such as those in the Schneider case do a more effective job. . . .

. . . [In] the jurors' first chance to get a good look at Marisol Schneider, . . . some of the men were clearly disappointed with how the leading lady had been cast. Marisol was a plain, almost mousy young woman with big teeth and long, kinky hair. She wore a blazer, slacks, and a white silk blouse, standard demure-witness attire. Juror Bill Westerfield, a sixty-one-year-old retired telephone company engineer, didn't think she was someone who'd be able to bewitch *him.* "Why would Kevin be so obsessed with her that he'd want to kill someone?" he wondered. Juror Rick Smith, forty-five, a truck mechanic and national guardsman with a military crew cut, also was surprised. "I expected she would be a foxy-looking lady that Kevin couldn't resist," Smith recalled after the trial. "But she wasn't so foxy; she didn't have a great body; she was an average-looking girl. I figured, why make such a fuss about her?"

Doreen Morgan, a meticulously well-dressed and carefully groomed woman of thirty, whose long nails were painted in two pale shades, also noticed immediately that Marisol was plainly dressed and not very good-looking. In addition, Marisol had a don't-mess-with-me demeanor that suggested an unpleasant toughness. Wendy Meadows, a nineteen-year-old bank teller who was the youngest of the jurors, thought the witness seemed kind of snobby. Marisol had already made a strong and negative impression on both the men and the women, and she hadn't even begun to speak. Could the jurors disregard their personal impressions of her in assessing her testimony? Or were their personal impressions of value? The academic research was unequivocal on the subject: Though a witness's likability bears no relation to whether he or she is telling the truth, jurors overwhelmingly believe that an unappealing witness is more likely to be dishonest. . . .

It [also] jarred some of them, for example, that Marisol appeared so unemotional, even when she described the death of her lover and then identified various blood-splattered articles of his clothing. "Latins are emotional," thought computer specialist Doreen Morgan, herself part Italian, "and here she shows no emotion. She's cold." For Mike Poremba, a hard-charging forty-eight-year-old Dean Witter Trust vice president, the cool demeanor also created suspicion, in his case not because of his preconceptions about Latins but because of his view that women typically are highly emotional, demonstrative beings. Yet here was Marisol, with not a tear in her eye or a crack in her voice, giving almost sterile descriptions of the most tragic, traumatic events. . . .

On Wednesday, February 26, Critchley [the defense attorney] called his client to the stand. And once again Critchley got the jurors to focus less on probability than on likability. Unlike Marisol, Kevin looked right at the jurors when he talked, as if he were speaking with them in their living rooms, Mike Poremba thought. It was such a simple thing, yet jurors always seemed to notice it. To them it signified trustworthiness. It also was a sign of good coaching. The best lawyers and trial consultants always drill their witnesses to make eye contact with jurors, and Critchley, of course, had done so with Kevin as they had prepared for trial together in the basement conference room of Critchley's office in an old clapboard house in West Orange. In any event, as a narcotics detective Kevin had had substantial experience testifying at trials and appealing to jurors.

The defendant also had the good fortune of being clean-cut and pleasant-looking, with a certain air of sadness. Numerous academic studies, usually involving trial simulations rather than actual cases, confirm that appearance counts in the courtroom. According to the researchers, good-looking defendants are convicted at lower rates and, when convicted, given shorter sentences than unattractive ones. Additionally, one study of criminal cases involving juvenile defendants found that defendants who look sad or distressed are less likely to be convicted than those who look happy or angry. Other research indicates that convicted criminals who appear to be suffering, whether from remorse or physical injury, receive shorter sentences than those who don't seem to be in pain. . . .

Decision time for the jurors had arrived. Each of them had had two 10 weeks in which to absorb the testimony, observe the key players, reflect on their behavior and on their demeanor now.

Doreen Morgan, even more than some of the others, had structured her analysis of the case around the question of which players she liked, trusted, and respected and which she didn't. This calculus included the lawyers, and she strongly preferred prosecutor O'Reilly to defense counsel Critchley. Indeed, O'Reilly's apparently sincere, apparently deeply held belief that Kevin was guilty was the best thing the prosecution had going for it, as far as she was concerned. But because she thought Kevin was a decent man and Marisol was "a sleaze," she was quick to pick up on the various holes in her story.

Without subjecting Kevin's story to the same level of scrutiny, she forgot that he had first claimed self-defense, then asserted the factually different—and legally cleaner—defense that the gun had gone off accidentally. She didn't consider at all why Marisol would have fabricated a story that Fabio had been leaning over to put his pants on when he'd been shot. It was enough that Marisol had been shown, in general, to be a liar. She gave only passing thought to whether it was plausible that Kevin would be unable to use his street-fighting skills, including karate and judo, to overcome any assault by Fabio. "I don't know karate," she later explained that she had reasoned. "Would I throw down my gun if I was a Newark cop and use karate? I don't know." She fell back, finally, on her affinity for Kevin, the hardworking man who had been wronged. "I was relieved he had a good excuse for what happened," she admitted later. "I liked him. I felt bad for him and all he'd been through. I didn't want to believe that he did it in cold blood." She also liked his friends, many of whom had testified on his behalf and many others of whom had sat in the spectator seats each day and offered him moral support. Marisol's cheering section had been decidedly smaller. Doreen Morgan had noted the disparity. . . .

Jurors in posttrial interviews almost never admit that they reached their decision out of sympathy or hate; even unsophisticated jurors know that this isn't an answer that reflects well on them. But jurors' sound bite responses to quick interviews often obscure, rather than illuminate, what goes on in the jury room. In longer or repeated conversations and in the comments of other jurors on the same panel, one often uncovers the messier, less logical dimension to people's decision making.

In Meadows's case, the anti-Marisol rhetoric she'd heard inside the courtroom—and outside, during the jurors' lunchtime tirades—hadn't made much of an impact. "Maybe because I'm so young, I didn't mind that she was cheating," Wendy reflected later. "I told them that she's not on trial." She'd listened to Marisol with some sympathy and receptivity. She couldn't understand why Marisol had bothered to deny staying in contact with Kevin after the divorce, but overall she'd found Marisol's story of the shooting credible. Kevin was the final witness, though, and his three days of impassioned testimony had won her heart. He'd looked and sounded gentle, as if he "couldn't hurt a fly," as she put it later. She also remembered eleven-year-old Jennifer, who had cried so hard the first day of trial, and imagined that having a stepfather in jail would create hardships for the girl. Protecting Jennifer made emotional sense to Wendy, and the lottery of jury duty had dealt her the splendid power to wipe away the girl's tears. When Critchley cried during his closing argument, Meadows melted. Kevin's lawyer never would have let a client get so close to him if the client wasn't innocent, she figured. To her, tears signified sincerity—a supposition for which the academic research, not surprisingly, offers no support. She wanted to hug Kevin. She certainly had no intention of sending him away. . . .

The jury had been out for less than two hours. The room was small, 15 and the heat was on full blast, making everyone uncomfortable. The jurors were anxious to vote. But one juror, church secretary Sue McNamara, suggested that it would look unseemly if the jury came back too quickly. So the jurors dutifully read each charge, discussed it, and voted—just to slow down the process a bit. After deliberating, if that was the right word, for barely three hours, they returned with their not-guilty verdict. . . .

The jurors' obsessions with Kevin's likability, Marisol's adultery, and a series of minimally relevant events long before the shooting had turned out to shape their decision as much as any evidence directly related to the murder charge. And their off-the-point concerns had obscured the vital question of how Marisol, if lying, could have foreseen minutes after the shooting what was the right lie to tell in order to get Kevin convicted.

Barring interviews with these jurors would have left their deliberations a mystery and perhaps lent the verdict more credibility. But it also would have obscured a problem with juries that must be confronted in order to be overcome: If mystery is all that jury verdicts have going for them, the jury system is surely in deep trouble.

The truth is, cases such as Schneider bolster, rather than undermine, the argument for a strong, effective system of trial by jury. He-said, she-said cases such as this one pose a problem for any decision maker, whether professional or amateur, because the truth about what happened can never truly be known. In science, history, and even biography, truth can be provisional, and new truths can rise and fall in turn. We shift easily from diets high in iron to those low in cholesterol, from the celebration of the discovery of America to the repudiation of conquest and slavery, from adulation of a slain ex-president to revulsion and back again. But in order for any system of justice to attach consequences to wrongful acts, it has to rely on some official version of events. The question isn't who knows the truth (because no one does) but whose version of the truth we should prefer.

Having a judge or panel of judges decide what's true, as most countries do, wouldn't guarantee a better result than a jury, and these professional decision makers would bring their own different limitations and prejudices to the table. A judge might not have cared that Critchley had cried during his closing statement; indeed, such showboating might have been held against him. But a judge also might not have had Doreen Morgan's useful insights into working-class life, or Ed Zawada's possibly helpful knowledge of guns, or Mike Poremba's distinctive experience with taking a hard punch from an overweight man.

A judge, hardened by his many past experiences with mendacious 20 defendants, also might not have made an honest effort to consider whether Kevin's defense might possibly be truthful. Judges have heard every phony alibi dozens of times; they are certainly correct in assuming that it's usually not true that the dog ate the homework, or that the murder defendant was with his parents the entire night, or that the deadly mix of chemicals was intended to create a miracle drug rather than a bomb. But sometimes the excuse is true. And a judge may miss the clues because he has heard it all before and has lost sight of the awful court of judgment, something a jury, for all its faults, almost never does.

Another reason to prefer a jury over a judge in cases of great public concern is that if the jury system is working properly, a jury's verdict should be more acceptable to the community. This is a logical assumption when one considers that juries spring from the community and then return to it. Indeed, assuring the community that justice has been done is a core function of the jury system. Juries, rather than judges, became the primary triers of factual disputes in medieval England in part because they offered a credible and civilized alternative to vigilante justice and trial by combat.

If a judge had found Schneider not guilty, people could have speculated that it was just a matter of a cop getting a sweetheart deal from a fellow government employee. Ideally, the jury system protects against the accumulation of such corrosive conclusions. At least, with the jury, in the absence of certainty, we have democracy. The fact that this comforting thought didn't prevent the rioting that followed the first Rodney King verdict[1] may partly reflect our declining faith in the quality of

---

[1] In 1991 Rodney King, a black man, was severely beaten by four white Los Angeles police officers when he resisted arrest. The officers were tried for assault with a deadly weapon but acquitted by a white jury. The verdict, widely regarded as unfair, incited four days of riots by predominantly African American and Latino groups. —ED.

jurors' decisions. More than this, though, it reflects particular problems with that case, including its location along the nation's most volatile racial fault line, the jury's apparent disregard of videotaped proof, and the unfortunate choice of a suburban venue far from the scene of the crime.

Despite the King case, Judge John J. Gibbons's rationale for trial by jury remains a powerful one. "It is often said that the judicial process involves the search for objective truth," the federal appeals court judge once observed in an opinion. "We have no real assurance, however, of objective truth whether the trial is to [a judge] or to a jury. The judicial process can do no more than legitimize the imposition of sanctions by requiring that some minimum standards of fair play, which we call due process, are adhered to. . . . In the process of gaining public acceptance for the imposition of sanctions, the role of the jury is highly significant."

If one appreciates the advantages of letting jurors decide he-said, she-said cases, the main issue raised by the Schneider case becomes how to ensure that jurors are trained, or at least instructed, to become more discerning judges of witnesses' credibility.

Certainly, much is already known within the academic community 25 that would be useful to anyone trying to make an intelligent choice between witnesses' contradictory stories. The research, usually done in an experimental setting using college students as subjects, shows that people tend to believe one witness over another on the basis of who is more likable, assertive, secure, and capable of sticking to his story under intense cross-examination. Here, it seems, was Kevin Schneider's big advantage over Marisol.

The most reliable indications that a person is lying turn out to be quite different. Studies show that compared with truth tellers, liars typically make fewer hand gestures, move their heads less, speak more slowly, and sit more rigidly, but that they betray their anxiety by shifting their feet or tapping their fingers. In addition, liars tend to relax their facial muscles and affect pleasant expressions, as if aware that observers will be watching their faces for signs of deceit. Partly because untrained observers seem to watch for the wrong signals, they often reach the wrong results. In one often cited academic study of 715 observers, a truthful speaker was judged to be lying by 74.3 percent of the subjects, and a lying witness was judged truthful by 73.7 percent.

As if liars don't create enough trouble for the earnest juror, witnesses who intend to provide accurate testimony but whose memories are faulty also can present serious obstacles. The problem is that human memory isn't like a videotape recording that stays constant each time it's replayed. Rather, as psychologist Elizabeth Loftus has put it, "Memory may be changed—colored by succeeding events, other people's recollections or suggestions, increased understanding, or a new context. Truth and reality, when seen through the filter of our memories, are not objective facts but subjective, interpretive realities." The point: that a witness may think he is telling the truth but may actually be recalling the event inaccurately. Conceivably Marisol or Kevin might have actually believed aspects of their stories that were objectively untrue.

Social science research has shown that the accuracy of testimony decreases as the stress level of the person at the time of the remembered event increases. Specifically the presence of a weapon at the crime scene markedly reduces the witness's later ability to say what really happened. The witness tends to focus attention on the weapon and become inattentive to surrounding details.

Another reason for inaccurate testimony might be that the witness has been coached after the event and has actually come to believe the postevent version over his original memory. In one experiment that illustrates this point, a group of students listened to a teacher's lecture, about which the student newspaper then wrote an intentionally inaccurate story. Those who read the story later remembered the lecture differently from, and less accurately than, those who hadn't. Further, contrary to many lawyers' and jurors' instincts, independent studies show that the stress of cross-examination, rather than forcing truth to the surface, impairs memory and reduces the accuracy of testimony.

Judges usually share very little of these data with juries. Indeed, most jury instructions provide only the most pro forma advice on how to tell whether a witness is telling the truth. A standard instruction used by many judges is this: "In weighing the testimony of a witness, you should consider his relationship to the plaintiff or to the defendant; his interest, if any, in the outcome of the case; his manner of testifying; his opportunity to observe or acquire knowledge concerning the facts about which he testified; his candor, fairness, and intelligence; and the extent to which he has been supported or contradicted by other credible evidence." The simplest way to provide more detailed and useful information, such as that gleaned from the academic studies, would be for judges to incorporate it into their legal instructions, preferably at both the start and the end of the trial. Some judges already do so on their own initiative. . . . More ambitiously, state judicial officials could collaborate on a set of standard jury instructions that reflect not an eighteenth- or nineteenth-century faith in raw common sense but a late-twentieth-century understanding of how the senses can deceive.

Such instructions might have alerted the Schneider jury to avoid irrelevant considerations and to ask the right questions about the witnesses. For example, might stress and the presence of a weapon—not to mention a week of intensive pretrial preparation by prosecutors—have affected the accuracy of Marisol's testimony, however honest her intent? Might wishful thinking and the coaxing of a savvy defense lawyer have led Kevin to believe his version, even if untrue? Whose body language and facial expressions appeared more consistent with those of someone telling the truth?

Getting jurors to consider such questions means acknowledging that left to their own devices, many juries go astray. And that requires us to embrace, rather than run from, the lessons we have learned from opening the jury room door to reporters, scholars, and other observers. To improve juries and to realize the hope for a more reliable, trustworthy system that deserves to be preserved and venerated, we need to sacrifice the mystery of jury deliberations for a while, see the jury clearly, and then make changes.

THINKING AND WRITING ABOUT CRIMINAL JUSTICE: TRIAL BY JURY

QUESTIONS FOR DISCUSSION AND WRITING

1. What are Davies's objections to trial by jury? Does Dershowitz answer any of his objections?

2. Davies says that professional legal assessors would provide "open, reasoned, and explicit reports saying how and why they reached their verdict" (para. 6). Would it be a good idea for juries to provide defenses of their verdicts? Why, or why not?

3. Wilson mentions several actions that juries can take to "nullify" laws they object to. What are they? Does his argument refute any of Pulliam's objections?

4. What dangers to democratic government does Pulliam foresee if jury nullification prevails? If you don't recognize his references to court trials of the 1980s and 1990s, look them up, and decide if you agree with Pulliam's assessment of their verdicts.

5. Katz says, "Jurors can do pretty much whatever they want, and we cannot punish them" (para. 15). Does he suggest any remedies for limiting the independence of juries?

6. Rothwax, like Katz, believes that juries have too much power. (Perhaps it's relevant that both Rothwax and Katz are judges.) What evidence does Rothwax provide to support his claim? Can you suggest specific remedies for the deficiencies that Rothwax describes?

7. Adler argues that a trial by a jury of one's peers is superior to a trial by a judge alone. Summarize the main points of his argument. Are some claims stronger than others?

TOPICS FOR RESEARCH

The acquittal of the Menendez brothers

Early jury nullification: the Zenger case

The appeal to the jury: some famous closing arguments

The Fully Informed Jury amendment

TAKING THE DEBATE ONLINE

For these and additional research URLs, see www.bedfordstmartins.com/rottenberg.

- *Fully Informed Jury Association*
  http://www.fija.org

  The Fully Informed Jury Association is a nonprofit educational association whose mission is to inform all Americans about their rights, powers, and responsibilities when serving as trial jurors.

- *Jurors' Handbook: A Citizens Guide to Jury Duty*
  http://www.fija.org/juror-handbook.htm

  This site outlines the rights and responsibilities of jurors.

- *Judge or Jury Trial: Which Is Better?*
  http://www.nolo.com/lawcenter/faqs/detail.cfm/objectID/
  E075E38B-3046-4439-AA0268D01238370B

  This online legal encyclopedia considers whether a defendant's interests are better served with a jury or a judge.

- *No More Jury Trials for Terrorists*
  http://www.townhall.com/columnists/michellemalkin/
  mm20011024.shtml

  According to this essay, "The Founding Fathers' constitutional pledge to 'provide for the common defense' was meant to protect liberty-loving Americans—not evil terrorists looking for victims to pay their legal expenses and clean their filthy, blood-stained robes."

- *The American Jury: Bulwark of Democracy*
  http://www.crfc.org/americanjury

  This is an online resource guide for teachers, students, and citizens devoted to explaining the American jury system and its role in American legal, social, and political life.

- *Trial by Jury*
  http://www.cato.org/dailys/12-09-98.html

  This article, by Clay S. Conrad, argues that "the purpose of trial by jury, as the Supreme Court itself has noted, is to prevent 'oppression by the government.'"

14

The Family

The traditional family is still alive but growing weaker. As depicted in Norman Rockwell paintings and the movies and TV series of more than a generation ago, this idyllic family lived in a white house with a picket fence and consisted of a breadwinner father, a homemaker mother, two or three lively but dutiful children, and a friendly dog. In 1998 a research group found that only 26 percent of American households consisted of married couples with children. The director of the survey observed that Americans seem to be accepting of "the modern family," and to be more tolerant of separation and divorce, whether or not there are children.

Some of the socioeconomic forces behind these changes are not hard to find: a wider endorsement of the values of individualism and personal freedom, a relaxation of divorce laws, vastly increased numbers of women in the workforce, even the movement of young people to colleges away from home. Perhaps it is not surprising that the importance of biological kinship itself has come under attack. The legal correspondent of the *New York Times* wrote that a court case in 2000 "opened the door to a profound debate over the definition of family."[1] Can someone not related to a child be given visiting rights if the family court con-

---

[1] Linda Greenhouse, "Case on Visitation Rights Hinges on Defining Family," *New York Times,* January 4, 2001, sec. A, p. 11.

cludes that "visitation would be in the best interests of the child"? A gay rights organization argued that "the quality and security of the relationship between individual children and adults rather than blood ties or labels" should govern legal decisions.

In fact, it is not only the legal definition of family that is a source of controversy. We have always debated the influence of family in shaping our lives. One of the reasons for a range of opinions is that everyone is a member of a family, and each member may experience the family differently. An expert on family law asks:

> Are families havens of love, care, attention, and affection? Or are they hells of manipulation, guilt, and oppression? Are families natural preserves, where social and legal rules follow biology and passion? Or are they social institutions created and regulated by government to serve specific public purposes?[2]

We know, of course, that traditional families are not necessarily happy and fulfilled. Often they are bound only by marriage and blood — what the poet Stephen Spender called "loveless intimacy." The family of the past sometimes remained intact because release was difficult or impossible.

But freedom from family does not come without a price. A prominent psychoanalyst has warned that the tradeoff for freedom from the commitments and responsibilities of family may be loneliness and insecurity. And the emotional and economic consequences for broken families, especially for women and children, are often devastating. Folk wisdom has it that "the past is prologue," but it's not clear how much the history of the family so far can tell us about the direction the family will take in an American society that keeps changing. (See also "Divorce and Our National Values" by Peter D. Kramer, p. 285).

[2] Martha Minow, *Family Matters* (New York: New Press, 1993), p. 1.

Why I Hate "Family Values"

KATHA POLLITT

BEFORE READING: When you read the term *family values*, what ideas come to mind? Do you find them comforting or oppressive?

That there is something called "the family"—Papa Bear, Mama Bear, Brother Bear, and Sister Bear—that is the best setting for raising children, and that it is in trouble because of a decline in "values," are bromides accepted by commentators of all political stripes. The right blames a left-wing cultural conspiracy: obscene rock lyrics, sex education, abortion, prayerless schools, working mothers, promiscuity, homosexuality, decline of respect for authority and hard work, welfare, and, of course, feminism. (On the *Chicago Tribune* op-ed page, Allan Carlson, president of the ultraconservative Rockford Institute, found a previously overlooked villain: federal housing subsidies. With all that square footage lying around, singles and unhappy spouses could afford to live on their own.) The left blames the ideology of postindustrial capitalism: consumerism, individualism, selfishness, alienation, lack of social supports for parents and children, atrophied communities, welfare, and feminism. The center agonizes over teen sex, welfare moms, crime, and divorce, unsure what the causes are beyond some sort of moral failure—probably related to feminism. Interesting how that word keeps coming up.

I used to wonder what family values are. As a matter of fact, I still do. If abortion, according to the right, undermines family values, then single motherhood (as the producers of *Murphy Brown* were quick to point out) must be in accord with them, no? No. Over on the left, if gender equality, love, and sexual expressivity are desirable features of contemporary marriage, then isn't marriage bound to be unstable, given how hard those things are to achieve and maintain? Not really.

Just say no, says the right. Try counseling, says the left. Don't be so lazy, says the middle. Indeed, in its guilt-mongering cover story "Legacy of Divorce: How the Fear of Failure Haunts the Children of Broken Marriages," *Newsweek* was unable to come up with any explanation for the high American divorce rate except that people just didn't try hard enough to stay married.

When left, right, and center agree, watch out. They probably don't know what they're talking about. And so it is with "the family" and "family values." In the first place, these terms lump together distinct

---

Katha Pollitt has written about controversial moral and political issues for *The Nation, The New Yorker,* and the *New York Times.* This selection is excerpted from her book *Reasonable Creatures: Essays on Women and Feminism* (1995).

social phenomena that in reality have not very much to do with one another. The handful of forty-something professionals like Murphy Brown who elect to have a child without a male partner have little in common with the millions of middle- and working-class divorced mothers who find themselves in desperate financial straits because their husbands fail to pay court-awarded child support. And neither category has much in common with inner-city girls like those a teacher friend of mine told me about the other day: a thirteen-year-old and a twelve-year-old, impregnated by boyfriends twice their age and determined to bear and keep the babies—to spite abusive parents, to confirm their parents' low opinion of them, to have someone to love who loves them in return.

Beyond that, appeals to "the family" and its "values" frame the discussion as one about morals instead of consequences. In real life, for example, teen sex—the subject of endless sermons—has little relation with teen childbearing. That sounds counterfactual, but it's true. Western European teens have sex about as early and as often as American ones but are much less likely to have babies. Partly it's because there are far fewer European girls whose lives are as marked by hopelessness and brutality as those of my friend's students. And partly it's because European youth have much better access to sexual information, birth control, and abortion. Or consider divorce. In real life, parents divorce for all kinds of reasons, not because they lack moral fiber and are heedless of their children's needs. Indeed, many divorce because they *do* consider their kids and want to protect them from the poisonous effects of growing up in a household marked by violence, craziness, open verbal warfare or simple lovelessness.

Perhaps this is the place to say that I come to the family-values debate with a personal bias. I am recently separated myself. I think my husband and I would fall under *Newsweek*'s "didn't try harder" rubric, although we thought about splitting up for years, discussed it for almost a whole additional year, and consulted no fewer than four therapists, including a marital counselor who advised us that marriage was one of modern humanity's only means of self-transcendence (religion and psychoanalysis were the others, which should have warned me) and admonished us that we risked a future of shallow relationships if we shirked our spiritual mission, not to mention the damage we would "certainly" inflict on our daughter. I thought he was a jackass—shallow relationships? *moi?* But he got to me. Because our marriage wasn't some flaming disaster—with broken dishes and hitting and strange hotel charges showing up on the MasterCard bill. It was just unhappy, in ways that weren't going to change. Still, I think both of us would have been willing to trudge on to spare our child suffering. That's what couples do in women's magazines; that's what the Clintons say they did. But we realized it wouldn't work: As our daughter got older, she would see right through us, the way kids do. And, worse, no matter how hard I tried to put on a happy face, I would wordlessly communicate to her—whose favorite fairy tale is "Cinderella," and whose favorite game is Wedding, complete with bath-towel bridal veil—my resentment and depression and cynicism about relations between the sexes.

The family-values advocates would doubtless say that my husband and I made a selfish choice, which society should have impeded or even prevented. There's a growing sentiment in policy land to make divorce more difficult. In *When the Bough Breaks,* Sylvia Ann Hewlett argues that couples should be forced into therapy (funny how ready people are to believe that counseling, which even when voluntary takes years to modify garden-variety neuroses, can work wonders in months with resistant patients who hate each other). Christopher Lasch briefly supported a constitutional amendment forbidding divorce to couples with minor children, as if lack of a separation agreement would keep people living together (he's backed off that position, he told me recently). The Communitarians, who flood my mailbox with self-promoting worry-fests, furrow their brows wondering "How can the family be saved without forcing women to stay at home or otherwise violating their rights?" (Good luck.) But I am still waiting for someone to explain why it would be better for my daughter to grow up in a joyless household than to live as she does now, with two reasonably cheerful parents living around the corner from each other, both committed to her support and cooperating, as they say on *Sesame Street,* in her care. We may not love each other, but we both love her. Maybe that's as much as parents can do for their children and all that should be asked of them.

But, of course, civilized cooperation is exactly what many divorced parents find they cannot manage. The statistics on deadbeat and vanishing dads are shocking—less than half pay child support promptly and in full, and around half seldom or never see their kids within a few years of marital breakup. Surely, some of this male abdication can be explained by the very thinness of the traditional paternal role worshiped by the preachers of "values"; it's little more than breadwinning, discipline, and fishing trips. How many diapers, after all, has Dan Quayle changed? A large percentage of American fathers have never changed a single one. Maybe the reason so many fathers fade away after divorce is that they were never really there to begin with.

It is true that people's ideas about marriage are not what they were in the 1950s—although those who look back at the fifties nostalgically forget both that many of those marriages were miserable and that the fifties were an atypical decade in more than a century of social change. Married women have been moving steadily into the workforce since 1890; beginning even earlier, families have been getting smaller; divorce has been rising; sexual activity has been initiated ever earlier and marriage delayed; companionate marriage has been increasingly accepted as desirable by all social classes and both sexes. It may be that these trends have reached a tipping point, at which they come to define a new norm. Few men expect to marry virgins, and children are hardly "stigmatized" by divorce, as they might have been a mere fifteen or twenty years ago. But if people want different things from family life—if women, as Arlie Hochschild pointed out in *The Second Shift,* cite as a major reason for separation the failure of their husbands to share domestic labor; if both sexes are less willing to resign themselves to a marriage devoid of sexual pleasure, intimacy, or shared goals; if single women decide they want to be mothers; if teenagers want to sleep together—why shouldn't society adapt? Society is, after all, just us. Nor are these developments unique to the United States. All over the industrialized world, divorce rates are high, single women are having babies by choice, homosexuals are coming out of the closet, and infidelity, always much more common than anyone wanted to recognize, is on the rise. Indeed, in some ways America is behind the rest of the West: We still go to church, unlike the British, the French, and, now that Franco is out of the way, the Spanish. More religious than Spain! Imagine.

I'm not saying that these changes are without cost—in poverty, 10 loneliness, insecurity, and stress. The reasons for this suffering, however, lie not in moral collapse but in our failure to acknowledge and adjust to changing social relations. We still act as if mothers stayed home with children, wives didn't need to work, and men earned a "family wage." We'd rather preach about teenage "promiscuity" than teach young people—especially young women—how to negotiate sexual issues responsibly. If my friend's students had been prepared for puberty by schools and discussion groups and health centers, the way Dutch young people are, they might not have ended up pregnant, victims of what is, after all, statutory rape. And if women earned a dollar for every dollar earned by men, divorce and single parenthood would not mean poverty. Nobody worries about single fathers raising children, after all; indeed, paternal custody is the latest legal fad.

What is the point of trying to put the new wine of modern personal relations in the old bottles of the sexual double standard and lifelong miserable marriage? For that is what most of the current discourse on "family issues" amounts to. No matter how fallacious, the culture greets moralistic approaches to these subjects with instant agreement. Judith Wallerstein's travesty of social science, *Second Chances,* asserts that children are emotionally traumatized by divorce, and the fact that she had no control group is simply ignored by an ecstatic press. As it happens, a 1991 study in *Science* did use a control group. By following 17,000 children for four years, and comparing those whose parents split with those whose parents stayed in troubled marriages, the researchers found that the "divorce effect" disappeared entirely for boys and was very small for girls. Not surprisingly, this study attracted absolutely no attention.

Similarly, we are quick to blame poor unmarried mothers for all manner of social problems—crime, unemployment, drops in reading scores, teen suicide. The solution? Cut off all welfare for additional children. Force teen mothers to live with their parents. Push the women to marry in order to attach them to a male income. (So much for love—talk about marriage as legalized prostitution!)

New Jersey's new welfare reform law gives economic coercion a particularly bizarre twist. Welfare moms who marry can keep part of their dole, but only if the man is *not* the father of their children. The logic is that, married or not, Dad has a financial obligation to his kids, but Mr. Just Got into Town does not. If the law's inventors are right that welfare policy can micromanage marital and reproductive choice, they have just guaranteed that no woman on the dole will marry her children's father. This is strengthening the family?

Charles Murray, of the American Enterprise Institute, thinks New Jersey does not go far enough. Get rid of welfare entirely, he argued in the *New York Times:* Mothers should marry or starve, and if they are foolish enough to prefer the latter, their kids should be put up for adoption or into orphanages. Mickey Kaus, who favors compulsory low-wage employment for the poor, likes orphanages, too.

None of those punitive approaches will work. There is no evidence 15 that increased poverty decreases family size, and welfare moms aren't likely to meet many men with family-size incomes, or they'd probably be married already, though maybe not for long. The men who impregnated those seventh graders, for example, are much more likely to turn them out as prostitutes than to lead them to the altar. For one thing, those men may well be married already.

The fact is, the harm connected with the dissolution of "the family" is not a problem of values—at least not individual values—it's a problem of money. When there are no jobs and the poor are abandoned to their fates, people don't get to display "work ethic," don't feel good about themselves, and don't marry or stay married. The girls don't have anything to postpone motherhood for; the boys have no economic prospects that would make them reasonable marriage partners. This was true in the slums of eighteenth-century London, and it is true today in the urban slums of Latin America and Africa, as well as in those of the United States. Or take divorce. Of course divorce can be psychologically hard on children, and on their parents, too. But social policy can't do very much about that, any more than it can make a bad marriage a good one. What government can do something about is the economic consequences of divorce: It makes lots of women, and their children, poor. One reason, which has got a fair amount of attention recently, is the scandalously low level of child support, plus the tendency of courts to award a disproportionate share of the marital assets to the man. The other reason is that women earn much less than men, thanks to gender discrimination and the failure of the workplace to adapt to the needs of working mothers. Instead of moaning about "family values" we should be thinking about how to provide the poor with decent jobs and social services and about how to insure economic justice for working women. And let marriage take care of itself.

Family values and the cult of the nuclear family is, at bottom, just another way to bash women, especially poor women. If only they would get married and stay married, society's ills would vanish. Inner-city crime would disappear because fathers would communicate manly values to their sons, which would cause jobs to spring up like mushrooms after rain. Welfare would fade away. Children would do well in school. (Irene Impellizeri, anticondom vice president of the New York City Board of Education, recently gave a speech attributing inner-city children's poor grades and high dropout rates to the failure of their families to provide "moral models," the way immigrant parents did in the good old days—a dangerous argument for her, in particular, to make; doesn't she know that Italian American kids have dropout and failure rates only slightly lower than black and Latino teens?)

When pundits preach morality, I often find myself thinking of Samuel Johnson, literature's greatest enemy of cant and fatuity. What would the eighteenth-century moralist make of our current obsession with marriage? "Sir," he replied to Boswell, who held that marriage was a natural state, "it is so far from being natural for a man and woman to live in the state of marriage that we find all the motives which they have for remaining in that connection, and the restraints which civilized society imposes to prevent separation, are hardly sufficient to keep them together." Dr. Johnson knew what he was talking about: He and his wife lived apart. And what would he think of our confusion of moral preachments with practical solutions to social problems? Remember his response to Mrs. Thrale's long and flowery speech on the cost of children's clothes. "Nay, madam," he said, "when you are declaiming, declaim; and when you are calculating, calculate."

Which is it going to be? Declamation, which feeds no children, employs no jobless, and reduces gender relations to an economic bargain? Or calculation, which accepts the fact that the Berenstain Bears, like Murphy Brown, are fiction? The people seem to be voting with their feet on "the family." It's time for our "values" to catch up.

*"Well, now that the kids have grown up and left
I guess I'll be shoving along, too."*

Family Is One of the Few Certainties We Will Take with Us Far into the Future

CAROL SHIELDS

BEFORE READING: If unrelated people live, work, and play together, can they be defined as a family? Why, or why not?

Six-year-old Christopher spotted something from the rear window of his grandparents' car. Three great radio towers stood close together in a field, one of them immensely tall, one slightly shorter, and one just half the size of the second. "A family," Christopher mumbled nonchalantly against the glass.

Carol Shields, a novelist, won the 1995 Pulitzer Prize for her novel *The Stone Diaries*. Her latest book is *Dressing Up for the Carnival* (2002). This article comes from the *Wall Street Journal*, January 1, 2000.

Father, mother, and child—the iconography offered by these three steel structures was clear, even to a boy of six. Here they stood, shoulder to shoulder, breaking the line of the horizon and suggesting, with their bold, leggy presence, human creatures, nakedly acknowledging their spatial relationship.

My husband and I smiled, as we often do when Christopher comes up with one of his poetic stretches. This symbolic configuration of the family must live at the very front of his brain, an image so simplified, stylized, and accessible he can express it without a hint of self-consciousness or of misunderstanding. A family, yes. Or at least an archetypal representation. Its resolute triangularity has entered his primary imagination where it holds authority over wider society, whose circles of power and permanence he only dimly perceives.

By the year 2050, given good health, reasonable luck, and a peaceful society, Christopher will be a man in his mid-fifties. Chances are reasonably good that he will be a father by that time and perhaps even a grandfather. Almost certainly, though, he will be embedded in some form of family, traditional or otherwise. Human beings are social creatures, interdependent economically, linked to each other by emotional need, sexual desire, and the drive to perpetuate their species. This Darwinian truth may seem reductive, but it isn't so easily set aside.

Even now, this sometimes willful and stubbornly independent child 5 sitting in the back seat must sense he isn't yet able to stand outside the family rubric. He would perish. His existence would be without meaning.

Belonging to Someone

This weekend, the world passes an imaginary divide. Our clocks and calendars declare their own importance, adjuring us to pay attention, to celebrate or grieve or at the very least meditate upon our human arrangements and how they have served or failed us.

The condition of family is one of the few certainties we will take with us into the next thousand years; each of us is, and will continue to be, someone's son or daughter. The most wretchedly isolated street person occupies a twig on a branch of a family tree, however invisible. The solitarily inclined, the viciously misanthropic—these, too, share gene structures with a chain of forebears, known or unknown. St. Jerome clinging to his rocky isle is remembered as that extraordinarily rare individual who needed no one other than God. (God the father? It seems even our deities are arranged in familial groupings.) St. Jerome aside, the rest of us, whatever our considered choices, belong to others.

Evolution is a slow-grinding process, and millions of years would be required to redesign our basic regenerative mechanics, transforming us, in fact, into another species altogether. Men bearing offspring or communes of women reproducing by parthenogenesis will probably remain, for the time being, inhabitants of science fiction.

The specter of cloning, introduced in the last decade of our own century, may, on the other hand, offer serious alternatives and stir what has already become one of the prime philosophical arguments of our time. Yet even the specter of genetic manipulation will come down in the end to a specific mother's egg specifically stimulated.

But the family has proved particularly difficult to decode. It is, has al- 10
ways been, a walking, talking irony. We speak about the family being the bosom of love and comfort, romantic language that adheres to the word *family* without the least embarrassment. *Family* also is another word for *tyranny*. James Joyce called the family a snare, the ultimate and damaging intimacy of enemies, which must be confronted once the simple demands of infancy are satisfied.

Families imply care, expectation, control, or, on the other side of the wallpaper, neglect, and abuse. Almost no one is tutored in family courtesy, no one is given a list of rules. And very few are afforded a second chance to repair the lives with which they collide. Jane Austen wrote six splendid novels, each of which concludes with the ceremony of marriage and the implied continuation of family, and yet the happiness of all her families is deformed by sibling rivalry, parental ignorance, insensitivity, embarrassment, and economic expediency. Interestingly, she didn't marry or have a child, remaining with her blood family to the end.

It might be argued that all art is ultimately about family, the creation of structures—music, sculpture, poetry, dance—that reflect our immediate circle, what families do to us and how they can be reimagined or transcended. What is a novel but a story about the fate of a child? What is a play—think of Shakespeare, Ibsen, Shaw, Pinter, and Stoppard—but the interaction of those who are randomly thrown together, the testimony of the most (or least) reliable witnesses we are afforded: our families?

Less Fruitful

The family of the future will carry on its shoulders many of the changes we have seen in our own lifetime. We understand more and more about the ways in which poverty and family intersect. The relative ease of divorce has fractured our assumptions about the two-parent family.

Families are smaller now that we have the means to prevent conception, at least in modern industrial countries. Once, a large number of children was considered an economic benefit, but that is no longer the case. Concern about overpopulation, too, has limited procreation, so that social norms about family size have shifted. Child care has become a critical issue since the women's movement led to a reduction in the number of stay-at-home mothers.

And in the Western world we complain that we never have enough 15
time; yet the nurturing of children is the one thing that cannot be com-

pressed. The speed of milk flowing from a mother's nipple into the baby's mouth is fixed. The reading aloud of, say, *The Wind in the Willows,* even when summarized or excerpted, is dependent on narrative comprehension, which follows neurological laws—which demand sequencing, not multitasking.

There is no turning back from this knowledge. The notion of quality time has been exposed as a sham or else a fantasy—one of the many hopeful fantasies entertained about family and family life.

Diverse Forms

What is certain is that families will continue to exist in diverse forms, just as they always have. Sometimes this surprises us; sometimes we find it a relief from the various shades of guilt that attach to family membership.

The stereotypical family—malevolent or wholesome—has existed only as a diversion or a type of shorthand; each actual family gestures toward an infinite number of variations.

Medieval craftsmen living under the same roof with their apprentices formed ad hoc families, with, perhaps, subtly gauged degrees of intimacy or distance. Those large, bustling, prosperous Victorian families—almost certainly closer to being a fiction than a reality—came in their own variations, though usually dependent on servants who had their own very different, often concealed, family models. The so-called Boston marriage—two women living together, sexually connected or not—represents another experiment in family.

Of course, there always have been de facto families: gay families, 20 monastic families, gatherings of friends or acquaintances who have agreed to share a roof, a kitchen, a bed. Couples who consider themselves a family must be resentful when asked whether they have "any family." But can a single person constitute a "family"? I wouldn't dismiss the notion.

We can't really talk about abstract families; family studies may be the darling of sociologists, psychologists and Freudians, statistical extrapolations, and conclusions, but there is no such thing as *the* family. Geography, class, culture, historical time, perception—all these interfere with an overall notion of what the family is.

It may be true, after all, that Ozzie and Harriet invented the standard modern family, something that scarcely existed outside of radio land: two cheerful, committed parents, bumbling but well-intentioned, and a couple of healthy kids who test them and sometimes teach them new pieties. The fact is, families are more protected than almost any other institution by a veil of secrecy, their domestic moments hidden from view. And it may well be that the questions posed within families are as cloaked as those that come from outside, and the answers as subversive or evasive or pointless.

The best we can do is look into our individual histories and hope we can back far enough away, squinting, peering, in order to get a little perspective—even though we know that distancing ourselves from family is a challenging, and perhaps impossible, assignment.

The "Normal" Family

Oak Park, Illinois, where I was born, seemed intent in the 1940s and 1950s on projecting an image of homogeneity. This was where the "taverns leave off and church steeples begin." It was assumed that this safe and prosperous and progressive community (they called themselves a village, even though the population exceeded 70,000) operated from a secure nexus of white families: each household provided with a mother (at home), a father (with an office job in downtown Chicago), and children (healthy, intelligent, enrolled in one of the excellent public schools, each named after an American poet, Hawthorne, Longfellow, Whittier).

I believed this narrative, even though everything I saw belied it.   25

Next door to us on Emerson Avenue lived the Ollershaws with their four children, all of whom attended the local Catholic school where, we were told, the teachers were brides of Jesus. Mr. Ollershaw was intermittently unemployed, and the second child, Patsy, went into frequent and dramatic epileptic seizures, even while we played hopscotch, jump rope, or kick-the-can in the early evening.

On the other side of us was Mrs. Anderson, a widow, a witch, or so we believed, able to cast spells. Next to her was the Shavaughan family with their two children, the oldest of whom was, for some mysterious reason, unable to ride a bicycle. What was the matter with Bobby Shavaughan?

Mrs. Dastas, next to the Shavaughans, lived with her husband, dyed her hair, grew dahlias, and spoke to no one. Next to her was a house split into apartments. The first floor was occupied by an elderly man and his young son, Teddy Woolhouse. There was no mother, no woman in this family. How did they manage? We couldn't imagine. Upstairs, alone, lived Miss Spokie, who drew fashion illustrations for the *Chicago Tribune*. We never saw her, in fact, not even once. She must have come and gone after dark.

The Wiggens family further down the block had recently lost their head of household. It was said that he collapsed and died on the train platform, falling directly into the path of a commuter train. Years later the truth occurred to me: He jumped—of course, he jumped. The Worthingtons had a daughter in an upstairs bedroom who had been asleep for nine years. A coma, it was called. The Tomeks spoke with a foreign accent and ate pancakes for supper instead of breakfast. Mary Louise Fulton's mother stayed in bed all day while Mary Louise was at school. She was a beautiful woman, everyone said, as though her beauty might, after all, have sustained and heartened her.

Perhaps we—my mother, father, brother, sister, and I—were the   30 only true family in our little American neighborhood, healthy, thriving, "normal." But I didn't think that, growing up. I felt, as perhaps all children do, that we were the ones who were different. I longed to enter the wholly untroubled world of Dick and Jane: Dick who never picked on little kids, Jane with her clean white socks, sunny Sally, even the cheerful, housebroken Spot.

What I've come to understand, and with surprising relief, is that we existed as a part of that enormous diversity we call the family, not "normal" at all, but fragile, self-created, provisional, and eager to avoid concerning ourselves with the arrangements of others.

Diversity is both our reality and our hope. There is a sense in which the creation of families is the ultimate opportunity for freedom (although the Chinese experiment with the one-child family seems a denial of this truth).

Gender option in our own society may tighten the pattern of openness, but we will, one hopes, remain aware in the next century, perhaps the next millennium, of our essential dependence on the knit of family structure, caught up in the surprise of love we feel for those who surround us, their randomness, their uniqueness, their ability to give definition to us—their family.

Why Do We Marry?

JANE SMILEY

> BEFORE READING: Reflect on the families of friends and relatives in which the parents have divorced. Did some family members gain and others lose as the result of the divorce?

My guinea-pig child, now twenty-one, was home from her senior year in college for Christmas vacation. This child was not by temperament suited to be the unbuffered firstborn of a literary, free-thinking mother and an anxiety-prone father, the child of divorce, joint custody, and stepparenting. Her whole life, she has been a girl who liked things steady and predictable. Thus it came as a surprise to me when she disclosed her ideal family, the one she aims to have when she is the matriarch. The word she used was *welcoming*. Should you want to be in her family, whoever you are, well, she is going to be happy to have you. Her house will have plenty of beds and plenty of dishes and plenty of congenial people sitting around discussing issues like women's health care and

---

Jane Smiley is the author of nine novels, among them *A Thousand Acres*, which won a Pulitzer Prize in 1992. Her most recent is *Horse Heaven* (2000). Her essay is reprinted from the *Utne Reader* for September/October 2000.

the third wave of feminism. I liked it. It sounded quite like the home she has grown up in, of which I have been the matriarch.

The last night before my daughter went back to college, we had another one of those family dinners—you know, me, my boyfriend, his daughter and son by his second wife, my daughters by my second husband, and my seven-year-old son by my third husband. The topic of conversation was how my son came to walk home from school—more than a mile up a steep, winding road on a very warm day. "What did you do when cars went by?" I asked.

"I stepped to the side of the road!" he answered. He was laughing at the success of his exploit. Not only had he been a very bold boy who had accomplished something he had been wanting to do; he had been impressively disobedient. We all laughed, and my boyfriend and I squeezed each other's hands, pleased and seduced by that happy-family idea, everyone safe and well-fed, getting along, taken care of.

But we are not married, and we have no plans to blend our families. I come to the theory and practice of marriage at the start of the new millennium with a decidedly checkered past and an outsider's view. But, I admit, I'm still paying attention, implicated, at least, by the fact that my children assume they will get married. I see the breakdown of the traditional family not as a dark and fearsome eventuality but rather as something interesting to observe, something that I have endured, survived, and actually benefited from, something that will certainly be part of the material from which my children build their lives.

High-Tech Parenting

AMITAI ETZIONI

BEFORE READING: How much have technical innovations affected your family? Do you regard some changes as undesirable?

The parental crisis is over. Salvation has arrived in the form of technology that opens up a whole new world of Remote Parenting. One pioneer of the movement is attorney Mary Croft. Too busy to talk with her twelve-year-old daughter about the happenings of a school day, boy-and-girl things, or permission to stop over at a friend's house, Ms. Croft purchased a pair of beepers so the child could cue her mom "talk needed" as

Amitai Etzioni is university professor at George Washington University. He is the author of nineteen books, including *The New Golden Rule: Community and Morality in a Democratic Society* (1996). His essay appeared in the January/February 1998 issue of *The American Enterprise*.

the mother-attorney raced around taking care of her clients. Alas, the beepers didn't prove efficient enough. The elder Croft often found that when her daughter needed a response, the phone booths on street corners or in airport stalls were occupied. So a pair of cellular phones were added to the mother-daughter relationship.

Parents are not to worry that beep-and-ring relations are less affectionate than old-fashioned talks-and-hugs on the way to Little League or while stacking dishes in the washer. Reassuring experts ranging from professors to electronic device-makers insist that "teleparenting"—or, more advanced yet, "virtual parenting"—is the wave of the future. For long-distance parenting to succeed, psychologists promise, children need only have clear routines. Once those are in place, parents can click in to check that the TV has been turned off as scheduled and homework turned on; that the wholesome tuna sandwich has been prepared; and that the dog (who does not get the beep-and-ring thing yet) has been let out. Those who fear that children will learn to game the system—turning off the idiot box when the phone rings, claiming to be home on the third beep while they are actually in a friend's liquor cabinet—need not panic. Surely the industry is hard at work designing cellular picture phones armed with place-identifiers, using satellites to verify the exact location of the speaker.

"Quality time" has long since replaced quantity time in many high-powered homes. The notion that a child opens up to parental guidance at unpredictable times—during a long walk, a prolonged conversation—is discounted by careerist parents. Many now seem to believe that they and their children can "relate" on demand, during times set aside for that purpose. Today's new twist is that even the truncated face-to-face "quality time" is being replaced—by quality phone calls. Tax accountant Jane Maddow says cellular phones are an indispensable part of her parenting. Almost every day, even at the busy peak of tax season, she will push other things aside so that she can talk for as long as *five minutes,* to each of her two boys when they return home from school.

Computer scientists at Rice University are working on something called the cyborg blanket, with the aim of freeing parents from the heavy responsibility of tending infants. The "blanket" will play soothing music or prerecorded warm words from mother or father when an infant engages in "low-intensity" crying. High-intensity crying will lead to a beep being broadcast to parents.

Parents had better keep these marvelous gizmos in good repair, be- 5 cause family get-togethers may soon be replaced by conference calls. Expect a beep and a ring at future wedding anniversaries or other big days. Cost will be no problem, because the children have been well trained to keep phone calls short, constantly reminded by the clicks of call-waiting that others compete with them for their parents' time. And as parents grow old and find themselves installed in a nursing home, they had better take a modem with them; e-mails from their children are sure to follow. As time allows.

"Before we begin this family meeting, how about we go around and say our names and a little something about ourselves."

The Sting of Divorce

WILLIAM S. POLLACK
WITH TODD SHUSTER

BEFORE READING: How has divorce affected some of the young people you know?

I don't know why they got divorced. They were a happy couple.
—Garcia, twelve, from a city in the Northeast

I felt like someone had put a hundred daggers in my heart. I never before knew what divorce really meant or what went with it. . . . My dad moved out less than a month later.
—Bruce, fourteen, from a suburb in northern New England

Not Simple by Any Means: Chip, fifteen, from a Small Town in New England

There are some things in life that we just don't want to deal with, accept, or even acknowledge as existing.

Almost a month ago—and it seems like a lot less—I found out that my parents would be getting a divorce. That sounds simple, sounds common, sounds like something that would be accepted and possibly even expected, as one-half of all marriages end in divorce.

It doesn't matter what it sounds like! If it sounds simple, then believe me when I tell you that it is not. If it sounds common, then believe me that I have never had anything remotely close to this happen in my family. If it sounds like something acceptable, then, by God, believe me when I say it is not. As for being expected, there was no hint, no warning, no smoke before everything went up in flames. It was sudden, harsh, cold, and impersonal; and worst of all, it was my family that it was happening to.

The divorce process is not simple by any means. Trust me, I've done my homework, I've done research, and I've found out everything that is supposed to happen. I've been blessed with a very caring girlfriend who went through the same process when she was five. Although her circumstances were vastly different from mine, she has helped me tremendously by telling me what is supposed to happen, and what I'm going to feel like as it is happening. That's the worst part of a divorce, by the way— it's the *not knowing*, the feeling that you're being left behind, that the

William S. Pollack, a clinical psychologist, is assistant clinical professor of psychology at Harvard Medical School and director of the Center for Men at McLean Hospital in Belmont, Massachusetts. Todd Shuster is a journalist. This selection is taken from *Real Boys' Voices* (2000).

divorce is not a subject to be discussed, that it's just something which is supposed to happen on its own. It's a feeling of indescribable loneliness.

It's such an emptiness, such a hole in your very soul which can't be   5
filled; at times you will be doing some routine mechanical thing, like homework, and you'll think, "Oh, I don't know how to do this, I'll just ask my dad. . ." and things trail off as you realize that you don't have a dad who will be coming home that evening. You have a dad who lives down the street, or in the next town, or around the world; it doesn't matter. The important thing is that you have a dad who doesn't live at home. This is the hardest part, recognizing the change in the normal routine. Recognizing and realizing that from now on you will be split between two parents, or will not see one except on weekends, or will not see one again. I don't know which of these things is worse.

Although statistically half of all marriages end in divorce, that doesn't mean anything. Saying that is like saying, "You have a one in five thousand chance of having a fatal accident while driving." That means that one of those other five thousand people driving home *will* have a wreck, not you. Numbers, statistics, percentages, while they never lie, make lousy condolences and even worse reminders. I never thought at all, ever, not once, that something like this would happen in my family.

There is no history of divorce on either side of my family, and I've checked. Both sets of grandparents have very detailed genealogy records dating back literally hundreds of years, and nowhere in either one will you find a dashed line, which represents a divorce. This is something completely new, completely wrong that is happening to my family. This was never supposed to happen to the little kid with the funny mom and the really tall dad. This was not supposed to happen!

As for this being acceptable, allow me to quote with great emphasis that bald guy from *Apollo 13:* "Failure is not, *ever,* an option!" This is giving up, this is quitting, and this is failure on the grandest scale. That is divorce, simply and bluntly. Quitting. What a disgusting, dishonorable, and altogether deplorable act.

Talking or thinking about or even feeling all that the word *divorce* encompasses is difficult. In fact, this is the most difficult thing that has ever happened in my fifteen years of life. I have overcome many obstacles in my hopes of one day walking on the ocean floor, once diving deeper than all the safe limits to save a friend. I have jumped off cliffs with nothing but a thin rope dangling in the air to hold me to this earth. I have done things that other men only imagine. Yet dealing with my parents' divorce is more difficult, more challenging, and more taxing on me mentally and physically than all of these feats combined.

The only advice I can offer to anyone else going through this is the   10
advice which my girlfriend gave me: "Hang in there, baby. Hang in there."

E-mail: The Future of the Family Feud?

CANDY SCHULMAN

BEFORE READING: Think about how e-mail has affected your relationships with your family. Would these relationships change if e-mail were no longer available?

A few months ago I had my first e-mail argument. I've heard about e-mail romances, but I didn't know how common e-mail fighting is—until I mentioned it to friends, who readily confessed their own on-line tiffs. My foray into Internet madness began with a disagreement between one of my relatives and me. We had never bickered before. As our barbs zapped through cyberspace, I became increasingly alarmed at how modern technology is affecting human relationships.

My twentysomething relative, a.k.a. quarrel 2000@gripemail.com, was born A. C. (after computers) with a mouse in his hand. I am a bit of a technophobe, viewing computers with trepidation but knowing I must log on if I am to move forward in this fast-changing world.

Our fight was a misunderstanding involving ego, self-esteem, you-hurt-my-feelings, I'm-right-you're-wrong. The altercation began over the antiquated telephone. We both hung up in a huff. Disturbed that issues were unresolved, I transferred our argument onto the Internet, where our family does almost everything these days, from sending birthday cards to sharing recipes.

We all know that e-mail makes communication immediate, but in the modern e-mail argument, discourse is actually slowed down—with painful consequences. When my first e-mail went unanswered, I wrote a second the next day. No new mail! Then a third, with a plea, "I can't believe we can't talk about this. I've been crying every night."

I couldn't know whether quarrel2000's lack of response meant he 5 was angrier than I'd imagined. Or was he simply nonplused about my hurt feelings? Or had my e-mail disappeared someplace in cyberspace and not even reached its destination?

And then, I logged on at 12:06 p.m. and there was mail from quarrel2000! My fingers shook as I clicked on READ NEW MAIL. Quarrel wrote, "This isn't something to cry over. I don't even care anymore." "You don't care about my hurt feelings?" I typed. SEND MAIL. Click.

Eighteen hours later: "I meant I don't care about whatever it is we were fighting about. I'm over it. You should be too."

Oh. Misunderstandings and days of delay before clarifications can be heard make these conversations (if I dare to call them that) very

---

Candy Schulman lives in New York City. She wrote this piece for the December 18, 2000, edition of *Newsweek*.

unsatisfying. As a writing professor, I've often felt optimistic about e-mail because it makes writers out of everyone, renewing our enthusiasm for the moribund written word. But as a family member with hurt feelings, I can't always read messages with emotional clarity. Not to mention the risk of screen words' being misinterpreted. Is the writer of this e-mail argument taking on an angry tone? An ironic one? Conciliatory? Only the most highly skilled writers can make these nuances clear.

When arguments occur face to face, we're more likely to hear each other, sit through silences and think about what's transpired. I don't know if quarrel2000 ever read my lengthy e-mails trying to justify my actions and words—he might have said, "Oh, no! Not another angry e-mail from my obstinate relative!" and simply pressed DELETE.

I've watched people's interpersonal skills steadily decline since the 10 advent of answering machines. Rather than having conversations with each other, we leave one-way messages, never risking retribution. Talk into a recording and you expediently do the job: cancel a dinner reservation, terminate an employee, send a message of condolence after a death. Nobody says "It's Susan, call me back" anymore. Now it's "I can't go out with you Saturday night . . ." Beep! End of message.

And now, we don't even fight in person anymore. I can imagine a new dot-com company being launched to sell accouterments to online arguments: written scripts to download into your computer with guarantees to prove your point of view, flower services for making up with your loved one.

Right now, my online argument with Q2000 is in remission. We e-mail each other in polite, concise, guarded messages. Our altercation briefly spread, however, through our family on the Web, as other family members heard about our feud and began sending their own commentaries back and forth to one another. As our disagreement catapulted into a multigenerational group e-mail debate, its original premise became increasingly unclear, even distorted.

As we move further away from human interaction, I am making a resolution that the next time words between relatives or friends explode in anger, I'm going to demand that, whenever possible, we climb in the ring together and spar it out in person. It might sting, but there's a prize at the end of the match: we can hear each other say "I'm sorry," then fall into each other's arms in a reassuring, forgiving hug.

THINKING AND WRITING ABOUT THE FAMILY

QUESTIONS FOR DISCUSSION AND WRITING

1. What does Pollitt mean by family values? Why does she hate them? How does she define her own values?

2. What is Shields's definition of a family? Do you think her definition is too broad? (Notice that the word *normal* is in quotation marks in paragraph 30.) Explain your answer.

3. Would Jane Smiley agree with Pollitt? Why does she welcome the breakdown of the traditional family? Does her family arrangement seem attractive or unsettling?

4. What aspects of family life is Etzioni satirizing? This article was written in 1998. As you read this four or five years later, can you tell if some of the author's predictions have become facts of family life? If so, are the changes good or bad?

5. What are the sources of Chip's suffering in the wake of his parents' divorce? Do Pollitt and Smiley have arguments that might console him?

6. Do you agree with Schulman that the replacement of face-to-face and telephone conversation by e-mail can damage personal relationships? Or does it enhance them?

TOPICS FOR RESEARCH

The family on TV

Welfare: good or bad for the family?

The case for or against having children

The legacy of divorce

Unconventional families

TAKING THE DEBATE ONLINE

For these and additional research URLs, see www.bedfordstmartins.com/rottenberg.

- *The American Family Association*
  http://www.afa.net

  The American Family Association defends traditional family values, particularly against what it sees as assaults in the entertainment media.

- *Facts for Families*
  http://www.aacap.org/info_families/index.htm

  Presented by the American Academy of Child and Adolescent Psychiatry, the Facts for Families Web site includes fifty-one fact sheets covering many of the issues faced by families today. Among the topics covered in the collection are children and divorce, eating disorders, TV violence, learning disabilities, sexual abuse, AIDS, lead exposure, and anxiety.

- *Gay and Lesbian Family Values*
  http://www.angelfire.com/co/GayFamilyValues

  This site defines the family as "a unit of love, with one or more consenting adults regardless of gender, creed, or color."

- *Research Forum on Children, Families, and the New Federalism*
  http://www.researchforum.org

  The Research Forum offers a comprehensive database of research projects that explore welfare reform, child well-being, and links to other important research and advocacy groups.

- *U.S. Census Bureau American Fact Finder*
  http://factfinder.census.gov/java_prod/dads.ui.homePage.HomePage

  The Census Bureau's Fact Finder provides authoritative maps, tables, and statistics on who lives together in the United States, including information on race, gender, and income.

15

Freedom of Speech

The First Amendment to the Constitution of the United States reads, "Congress shall make no laws respecting an establishment of religion, or prohibiting the free expression thereof; or abridging the freedom of speech, or of the press; or the right of the people peaceably to assemble, and to petition the Government for a redress of grievances." (The first ten amendments were ratified on December 15, 1791, and form what is known as the Bill of Rights.) The arguments in this section will consider primarily the issue of "abridging the freedom of speech, or of the press."

The limits of free speech in the United States are constantly being adjusted as social values change and new cases testing those limits emerge. Several prominent areas of controversy are emphasized in the following selection of essays.

One of the most hotly debated issues has been played out on college campuses. Following federal law, a number of colleges and universities have formulated codes of conduct which define the "correct" ways of naming certain persons, groups, or activities in order to avoid offense to those who have historically been most vulnerable to "hate" speech—African Americans, Jews, women, and gays and lesbians. These policies have frequently provoked opposition from members of the college community on both sides of the political spectrum. Their disagreement is based on a principle enunciated in 1929 by Justice Oliver Wendell Holmes: "the principle of free thought—not free thought for those who agree with us but freedom for the thought that we hate." A few students who have been harshly punished for using "racist, sexist, and homophobic" speech have taken their cases to court. In several cases the courts decided that the policies enforcing strict speech codes were in violation of the First Amendment. College and university officials are now drafting new codes that would define the prohibited language and conduct in narrower and more specific terms.

Probably more controversial and vastly more difficult to control is speech in cyberspace. Congress and the states have begun to enact legislation that would prohibit dissemination of material regarded as offensive. But defenders of free speech argue that cyberspace communication should be private, like posted mail and conversation.

Freedom of speech is also a central issue in arguments over the lyrics of rap songs, which have been accused of advocating violence against police officers and women. Parents have raised concerns about the effects of such lyrics on young listeners and proposed rating labels for some albums. The language in one rap song in the early 1990s, calling for murder of police officers, led to appeals for censorship and boycotts of the record company.

Even nonverbal art forms whose creators express views that offend large groups of people are not immune to issues of free speech. Controversial movies, photography, painting, and sculpture, as well as religious displays on public land and even nude dancing, have all been defended as forms of speech protected by the Constitution.

On Racist Speech

CHARLES R. LAWRENCE III

BEFORE READING: Have you ever heard students use racist speech in conversation? Did you ever make any objections? Why, or why not?

I have spent the better part of my life as a dissenter. As a high school student, I was threatened with suspension for my refusal to participate in a civil defense drill, and I have been a conspicuous consumer of my First Amendment liberties ever since. There are very strong reasons for protecting even racist speech. Perhaps the most important of these is that

---

Charles R. Lawrence III is a professor of law at Georgetown University. His article appeared in the October 25, 1989, *Chronicle of Higher Education,* when Lawrence was teaching law at Stanford University. It is adapted from a speech given at a conference of the American Civil Liberties Union.

such protection reinforces our society's commitment to tolerance as a value, and that by protecting bad speech from government regulation, we will be forced to combat it as a community.

But I also have a deeply felt apprehension about the resurgence of racial violence and the corresponding rise in the incidence of verbal and symbolic assault and harassment to which blacks and other traditionally subjugated and excluded groups are subjected. I am troubled by the way the debate has been framed in response to the recent surge of racist incidents on college and university campuses and in response to some universities' attempts to regulate harassing speech. The problem has been framed as one in which the liberty of free speech is in conflict with the elimination of racism. I believe this has placed the bigot on the moral high ground and fanned the rising flames of racism.

Above all, I am troubled that we have not listened to the real victims, that we have shown so little understanding of their injury, and that we have abandoned those whose race, gender, or sexual preference continues to make them second-class citizens. It seems to me a very sad irony that the first instinct of civil libertarians has been to challenge even the smallest, most narrowly framed efforts by universities to provide black and other minority students with the protection the Constitution guarantees them.

The landmark case of *Brown v. Board of Education* is not a case that we normally think of as a case about speech. But *Brown* can be broadly read as articulating the principle of equal citizenship. *Brown* held that segregated schools were inherently unequal because of the *message* that segregation conveyed—that black children were an untouchable caste, unfit to go to school with white children. If we understand the necessity of eliminating the system of signs and symbols that signal the inferiority of blacks, then we should hesitate before proclaiming that all racist speech that stops short of physical violence must be defended.

University officials who have formulated policies to respond to incidents of racial harassment have been characterized in the press as "thought police," but such policies generally do nothing more than impose sanctions against intentional face-to-face insults. When racist speech takes the form of face-to-face insults, catcalls, or other assaultive speech aimed at an individual or small group of persons, it falls directly within the "fighting words" exception to First Amendment protection. The Supreme Court has held that words which "by their very utterance inflict injury or tend to incite an immediate breach of the peace" are not protected by the First Amendment.

If the purpose of the First Amendment is to foster the greatest amount of speech, racial insults disserve that purpose. Assaultive racist speech functions as a preemptive strike. The invective is experienced as a blow, not as a proffered idea, and once the blow is struck, it is unlikely that a dialogue will follow. Racial insults are particularly undeserving of First Amendment protection because the perpetrator's intention is not to discover truth or initiate dialogue but to injure the victim. In most situations, members of minority groups realize that they are likely to lose if they respond to epithets by fighting and are forced to remain silent and submissive.

Courts have held that offensive speech may not be regulated in public forums such as streets where the listener may avoid the speech by moving on, but the regulation of otherwise protected speech has been permitted when the speech invades the privacy of the unwilling listener's home or when the unwilling listener cannot avoid the speech. Racist posters, fliers, and graffiti in dormitories, bathrooms, and other common living spaces would seem to clearly fall within the reasoning of these cases. Minority students should not be required to remain in their rooms in order to avoid racial assault. Minimally, they should find a safe haven in their dorms and in all other common rooms that are a part of their daily routine.

I would also argue that the university's responsibility for ensuring that these students receive an equal educational opportunity provides a compelling justification for regulations that ensure them safe passage in all common areas. A minority student should not have to risk becoming the target of racially assaulting speech every time he or she chooses to walk across campus. Regulating vilifying speech that cannot be anticipated or avoided would not preclude announced speeches and rallies — situations that would give minority-group members and their allies the chance to organize counter-demonstrations or avoid the speech altogether.

The most commonly advanced argument against the regulation of racist speech proceeds something like this: we recognize that minority groups suffer pain and injury as the result of racist speech, but we must allow this hate mongering for the benefit of society as a whole. Freedom of speech is the lifeblood of our democratic system. It is especially important for minorities because often it is their only vehicle for rallying support for the redress of their grievances. It will be impossible to formulate a prohibition so precise that it will prevent the racist speech you want to suppress without catching in the same net all kinds of speech that it would be unconscionable for a democratic society to suppress.

Whenever we make such arguments, we are striking a balance on the 10 one hand between our concern for the continued free flow of ideas and the democratic process dependent on that flow, and, on the other, our desire to further the cause of equality. There can be no meaningful discussion of how we should reconcile our commitment to equality and our commitment to free speech until it is acknowledged that there is real harm inflicted by racist speech and that this harm is far from trivial.

To engage in a debate about the First Amendment and racist speech without a full understanding of the nature and extent of that harm is to risk making the First Amendment an instrument of domination rather than a vehicle of liberation. We have not all known the experience of victimization by racist, misogynist, and homophobic speech, nor do we equally share the burden of the societal harm it inflicts. We are often quick to say that we have heard the cry of the victims when we have not.

The *Brown* case is again instructive because it speaks directly to the psychic injury inflicted by racist speech by noting that the symbolic message of segregation affected "the hearts and minds" of Negro children "in a way unlikely ever to be undone." Racial epithets and harassment often cause deep emotional scarring and feelings of anxiety and fear that pervade every aspect of a victim's life.

Brown also recognized that black children did not have an equal opportunity to learn and participate in the school community if they bore the additional burden of being subjected to the humiliation and psychic assault contained in the message of segregation. University students bear an analogous burden when they are forced to live and work in an environment where at any moment they may be subjected to denigrating verbal harassment and assault. The same injury was addressed by the Supreme Court when it held that sexual harassment that creates a hostile or abusive work environment violates the ban on sex discrimination in employment of Title VII of the Civil Rights Act of 1964.

Carefully drafted university regulations would bar the use of words as assault weapons and leave unregulated even the most heinous of ideas when those ideas are presented at times and places and in manners that provide an opportunity for reasoned rebuttal or escape from immediate injury. The history of the development of the right to free speech has been one of carefully evaluating the importance of free expression and its effects on other important societal interests. We have drawn the line between protected and unprotected speech before without dire results. (Courts have, for example, exempted from the protection of the First Amendment obscene speech and speech that disseminates official secrets, that defames or libels another person, or that is used to form a conspiracy or monopoly.)

Blacks and other people of color are skeptical about the argument 15 that even the most injurious speech must remain unregulated because, in an unregulated marketplace of ideas, the best ones will rise to the top and gain acceptance. Our experience tells us quite the opposite. We have seen too many demagogues elected by appealing to America's racism. We have seen too many good liberal politicians shy away from the issues that might brand them as being too closely allied with us.

Whenever we decide that racist speech must be tolerated because of the importance of maintaining societal tolerance for all unpopular speech, we are asking blacks and other subordinated groups to bear the burden for the good of all. We must be careful that the ease with which we strike the balance against the regulation of racist speech is in no way influenced by the fact that the cost will be borne by others. We must be certain that those who will pay that price are fairly represented in our deliberations and that they are heard.

At the core of the argument that we should resist all government regulation of speech is the ideal that the best cure for bad speech is good, that ideas that affirm equality and the worth of all individuals will ultimately prevail. This is an empty ideal unless those of us who would fight racism are vigilant and unequivocal in that fight. We must look for ways to offer assistance and support to students whose speech and political participation are chilled in a climate of racial harassment.

Civil rights lawyers might consider suing on behalf of blacks whose right to an equal education is denied by a university's failure to ensure a nondiscriminatory educational climate or conditions of employment. We must embark upon the development of a First Amendment jurisprudence grounded in the reality of our history and our contemporary experience. We must think hard about how best to launch legal attacks against the most indefensible forms of hate speech. Good lawyers can create exceptions and narrow interpretations that limit the harm of hate speech without opening the floodgates of censorship.

Everyone concerned with these issues must find ways to engage actively in actions that resist and counter the racist ideas that we would have the First Amendment protect. If we fail in this, the victims of hate speech must rightly assume that we are on the oppressors' side.

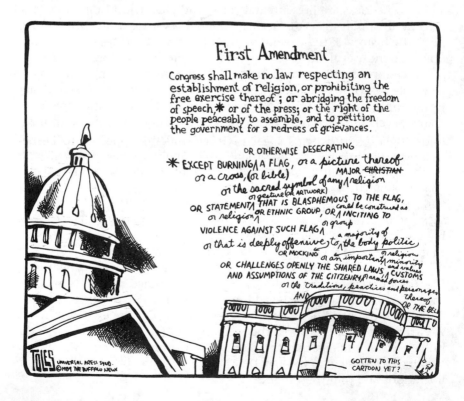

Bethel School District No. 403 v. Fraser

SUPREME COURT OF THE UNITED STATES

BEFORE READING: Should school officials censor in any way a speech delivered by a student at a school assembly? Give reasons why or why not.

Chief Justice Burger delivered the opinion of the Court.
We granted certiorari to decide whether the First Amendment prevents a school district from disciplining a high school student for giving a lewd speech at a school assembly.

I:A

On April 26, 1983, respondent Matthew N. Fraser, a student at Bethel High School in Pierce County, Washington, delivered a speech nominating a fellow student for student elective office. Approximately 600 high school students, many of whom were fourteen-year-olds, attended the assembly. Students were required to attend the assembly or to report to the study hall. The assembly was part of a school-sponsored educational program in self-government. . . . During the entire speech, Fraser referred to his candidate in terms of an elaborate, graphic, and explicit sexual metaphor.

Two of Fraser's teachers, with whom he discussed the contents of his speech in advance, informed him that the speech was "inappropriate and that he probably should not deliver it" and that his delivery of the speech might have "severe consequences."

During Fraser's delivery of the speech, a school counselor observed 5 the reaction of students to the speech. Some students hooted and yelled; some by gestures graphically simulated the sexual activities pointedly alluded to in respondent's speech. Other students appeared to be bewildered and embarrassed by the speech. One teacher reported that on the day following the speech, she found it necessary to forgo a portion of the scheduled class lesson in order to discuss the speech with the class.

A Bethel High School disciplinary rule prohibiting the use of obscene language in the school provides:

> Conduct which materially and substantially interferes with the educational process is prohibited, including the use of obscene, profane language or gestures.

This selection comes from Jamin B. Raskin's 2000 book *We the Students*. Raskin is professor of constitutional law at American University Washington College of Law.

The morning after the assembly, the Assistant Principal called Fraser into her office and notified him that the school considered his speech to have been a violation of this rule. Fraser was presented with copies of five letters submitted by teachers, describing his conduct at the assembly; he was given a chance to explain his conduct, and he admitted to having given the speech described and that he deliberately used sexual innuendo in the speech. Fraser was then informed that he would be suspended for three days and that his name would be removed from the list of candidates for graduation speaker at the school's commencement exercises.

Fraser sought review of this disciplinary action through the School District's grievance procedures. The hearing officer determined that the speech given by respondent was "indecent, lewd, and offensive to the modesty and decency of many of the students and faculty in attendance at the assembly." The examiner determined that the speech fell within the ordinary meaning of "obscene," as used in the disruptive-conduct rule, and affirmed the discipline in its entirety. Fraser served two days of his suspension and was allowed to return to school on the third day.

I:B

. . . [Fraser] alleged a violation of his First Amendment right to freedom of speech and sought both injunctive relief and monetary damages. . . . The District Court held that the school's sanctions violated respondent's right to freedom of speech under the First Amendment to the United States Constitution, that the school's disruptive-conduct rule is unconstitutionally vague and overbroad, and that the removal of respondent's name from the graduation speaker's list violated the Due Process Clause of the Fourteenth Amendment because the disciplinary rule makes no mention of such removal as a possible sanction. The District Court awarded [Fraser] $278 in damages, $12,750 in litigation costs and attorney's fees, and enjoined the School District from preventing [him] from speaking at the commencement ceremonies. [Fraser], who had been elected graduation speaker by a write-in vote of his classmates, delivered a speech at the commencement ceremonies on June 8, 1983.

The Court of Appeals for the Ninth Circuit affirmed the judgment of the District Court, holding that [Fraser's] speech was indistinguishable from the protest armband in *Tinker v. Des Moines Independent Community School District.* . . .[1]

We granted certiorari. We reverse. . . .

III

[Following is the decision of the U.S. Supreme Court overturning the decision of the State Court of Appeals.]

---

[1] The high school students in the *Tinker* case wore black armbands to protest American involvement in the Vietnam War. — ED.

. . . The undoubted freedom to advocate unpopular and controversial views in schools and classrooms must be balanced against the society's countervailing interest in teaching students the boundaries of socially appropriate behavior. Even the most heated political discourse in a democratic society requires consideration for the personal sensibilities of the other participants and audiences.

In our Nation's legislative halls, where some of the most vigorous political debates in our society are carried on, there are rules prohibiting the use of expressions offensive to other participants in the debate. Senators have been censured for abusive language directed at other Senators. . . . Can it be that what is proscribed in the halls of Congress is beyond the reach of school officials to regulate?

The First Amendment guarantees wide freedom in matters of adult 15 public discourse. A sharply divided Court upheld the right to express an antidraft viewpoint in a public place, albeit in terms highly offensive to most citizens. It does not follow, however, that simply because the use of an offensive form of expression may not be prohibited to adults making what the speaker considers a political point, the same latitude must be permitted to children in a public school. . . .

Surely it is a highly appropriate function of public school education to prohibit the use of vulgar and offensive terms in public discourse. . . . The determination of what manner of speech in the classroom or in school assembly is inappropriate properly rests with the school board. . . .

The pervasive sexual innuendo in Fraser's speech was plainly offensive to both teachers and students—indeed to any mature person. By glorifying male sexuality, and in its verbal content, the speech was acutely insulting to teenage girl students. The speech could well be seriously damaging to its less mature audience, many of whom were only fourteen years old and on the threshold of awareness of human sexuality. Some students were reported as bewildered by the speech and the reaction of mimicry it provoked. . . .

We hold that petitioner School district acted entirely within its permissible authority in imposing sanctions upon Fraser in response to his offensively lewd and indecent speech. Unlike the sanctions imposed on the students wearing armbands in *Tinker*, the penalties imposed in this case were unrelated to any political viewpoint. The First Amendment does not prevent the school officials from determining that to permit a vulgar and lewd speech such as respondent's would undermine the school's basic educational mission. A high school assembly or classroom is no place for a sexually explicit monologue directed towards an unsuspecting audience of teenage students. Accordingly, it was perfectly appropriate for the school to disassociate itself to make the point to the pupils that vulgar speech and lewd conduct is wholly inconsistent with the "fundamental values" of public school education. . . .

Reversed.

Justice Marshall, dissenting.   20

. . . I dissent from the Court's decision . . . because in my view the School District failed to demonstrate that respondent's remarks were indeed disruptive. The District Court and Court of Appeals conscientiously applied *Tinker v. Des Moines Independent Community School District* and concluded that the School District had not demonstrated any disruption of the educational process. I recognize that the school administration must be given wide latitude to determine what forms of conduct are inconsistent with the school's educational mission; nevertheless, where speech is involved, we may not unquestioningly accept a teacher's or administrator's assertion that certain pure speech interfered with education.

Ice-T: The Issue Is Creative Freedom

BARBARA EHRENREICH

BEFORE READING: To what extent are fantasies of violence — killing, torture, sexual assault — dangerous either to the individual or to society?

ce-T's song "Cop Killer" is as bad as they come. This is black anger — raw, rude, and cruel — and one reason the song's so shocking is that in postliberal America, black anger is virtually taboo. You won't find it on TV, not on the *McLaughlin Group* or *Crossfire,* and certainly not in the placid features of Arsenio Hall or Bernard Shaw. It's been beaten back into the outlaw subcultures of rap and rock, where, precisely because it is taboo, it sells. And the nastier it is, the faster it moves off the shelves. As Ice-T asks in another song on the same album, "Goddamn what a brotha gotta do / To get a message through / To the red, white, and blue?"

But there's a gross overreaction going on, building to a veritable paroxysm of white denial. A national boycott has been called, not just of the song or Ice-T, but of all Time Warner products. The president himself has denounced Time Warner as "wrong" and Ice-T as "sick." Ollie North's Freedom Alliance has started a petition drive aimed at bringing Time Warner executives to trial for "sedition and anarchy."

Much of this is posturing and requires no more courage than it takes to stand up in a VFW hall and condemn communism or crack. Yes, "Cop Killer" is irresponsible and vile. But Ice-T is as right about some things as

---

Barbara Ehrenreich, honorary chair of Democratic Socialists of America, is the author of numerous books, including *Blood Rites: Origins and History of the Passions of War* (1997). This article is from the July 20, 1992, issue of *Time*.

he is righteous about the rest. And ultimately, he's not even dangerous — least of all to the white power structure his songs condemn.

The "danger" implicit in all the uproar is of empty-headed, suggestible black kids, crouching by their boom boxes, waiting for the word. But what Ice-T's fans know and his detractors obviously don't is that "Cop Killer" is just one more entry in pop music's long history of macho hyperbole and violent boast. Flip to the classic-rock station, and you might catch the Rolling Stones announcing "the time is right for violent revoloo-shun!" from their 1968 hit "Street Fighting Man." And where were the defenders of our law-enforcement officers when a white British group, the Clash, taunted its fans with the lyrics: "When they kick open your front door / How you gonna come / With your hands on your head / Or on the trigger of your gun?"

"Die, Die, Die Pig" is strong speech, but the Constitution protects 5 strong speech, and it's doing so this year more aggressively than ever. The Supreme Court has just downgraded cross burnings to the level of bonfires and ruled that it's no crime to throw around verbal grenades like "nigger" and "kike." Where are the defenders of decorum and social stability when prime-time demagogues like Howard Stern deride African Americans as "spear chuckers"?

More to the point, young African Americans are not so naive and suggestible that they have to depend on a compact disc for their sociology lessons. To paraphrase another song from another era, you don't need a rap song to tell which way the wind is blowing. Black youths know that the police are likely to see them through a filter of stereotypes as miscreants and potential "cop killers." They are aware that a black youth is seven times as likely to be charged with a felony as a white youth who has committed the same offense, and is much more likely to be imprisoned.

They know, too, that in a shameful number of cases, it is the police themselves who indulge in "anarchy" and violence. The U.S. Justice Department has received 47,000 complaints of police brutality in the past six years, and Amnesty International has just issued a report on police brutality in Los Angeles, documenting forty cases of "torture or cruel, inhuman, or degrading treatment."

Menacing as it sounds, the fantasy in "Cop Killer" is the fantasy of the powerless and beaten down — the black man who's been hassled once too often ("A pig stopped me for nothin'!"), spread-eagled against a police car, pushed around. It's not a "responsible" fantasy (fantasies seldom are). It's not even a very creative one. In fact, the sad thing about "Cop Killer" is that it falls for the cheapest, most conventional image of rebellion that our culture offers: the lone gunman spraying fire from his AK-47. This is not "sedition"; it's the familiar, all-American, Hollywood-style pornography of violence.

Which is why Ice-T is right to say he's no more dangerous than George Bush's pal Arnold Schwarzenegger, who wasted an army of cops in *Terminator 2*. Images of extraordinary cruelty and violence are marketed every day, many of far less artistic merit than "Cop Killer." This is our free market of ideas and images, and it shouldn't be any less free for a black man than for other purveyors of "irresponsible" sentiments, from David Duke to Andrew Dice Clay.[1]

Just, please, don't dignify Ice-T's contribution with the word *sedition*. The past masters of sedition—men like George Washington, Toussaint L'Ouverture, Fidel Castro, or Mao Zedong, all of whom led and won armed insurrections—would be unimpressed by "Cop Killer" and probably saddened. They would shake their heads and mutter words like "infantile" and "adventurism." They might point out that the cops are hardly a noble target, being, for the most part, honest working stiffs who've got stuck with the job of patrolling ghettos ravaged by economic decline and official neglect.

There is a difference, the true seditionist would argue, between a revolution and a gesture of macho defiance. Gestures are cheap. They feel good, they blow off some rage. But revolutions, violent or otherwise, are made by people who have learned how to count very slowly to ten.

Free Speech on the Internet: Opinion on the Constitutionality of the Communications Decency Act

STEWART DALZELL

BEFORE READING: Did your parents try to protect you from pornography on the Internet? If so, do you consider their action to have been reasonable or overprotective?

The Internet is a far more speech-enhancing medium than print, the village green, or the mails. Because it would necessarily affect the Internet itself, the CDA would necessarily reduce the speech available for adults on the medium. This is a constitutionally intolerable result.

Some of the dialogue on the Internet surely tests the limits of conventional discourse. Speech on the Internet can be unfiltered, unpol-

---

[1]David Duke, an advocate of white supremacy, was defeated in his bid for governor of Louisiana in 1991. Andrew Dice Clay is a stand-up comedian known for his use of offensive language against women and minorities.

Stewart Dalzell is a judge for the United States Court of Appeals for the Third Circuit. Reprinted here are excerpts from his opinion in striking down major parts of the Communications Decency Act (CDA). The excerpts were published in the *New York Times* on June 13, 1996.

ished, and unconventional, even emotionally charged, sexually explicit, and vulgar—in a word, "indecent" in many communities. But we should expect such speech to occur in a medium in which citizens from all walks of life have a voice. We should also protect the autonomy that such a medium confers to ordinary people as well as media magnates.

Moreover, the CDA will almost certainly fail to accomplish the government's interest in shielding children from pornography on the Internet. Nearly half of Internet communications originate outside the United States, and some percentage of that figure represents pornography. Pornography from, say, Amsterdam will be no less appealing to a child on the Internet than pornography from New York City, and residents of Amsterdam have little incentive to comply with the CDA.

My analysis does not deprive the government of all means of protecting children from the dangers of Internet communication. The government can continue to protect children from pornography on the Internet through vigorous enforcement of existing laws criminalizing obscenity. . . . As we learned at the hearing, there is also a compelling need for public education about the benefits and dangers of this new medium, and the government can fill that role as well. In my view, our action today should only mean that the government's permissible supervision of Internet content stops at the traditional line of unprotected speech.

Parents, too, have options available to them. As we learned at the 5 hearing, parents can install blocking software on their home computers or they can subscribe to commercial online services that provide parental controls. It is quite clear that powerful market forces are at work to expand parental options to deal with these legitimate concerns. More fundamentally, parents can supervise their children's use of the Internet or deny their children the opportunity to participate in the medium until they reach an appropriate age. . . .

Cutting through the acronyms and argot that littered the hearing testimony, the Internet may fairly be regarded as a never-ending world-wide conversation. The government may not, through the CDA, interrupt that conversation. As the most participatory form of mass speech yet developed, the Internet deserves the highest protection from governmental intrusion.

True it is that many find some of the speech on the Internet to be offensive, and amid the din of cyberspace many hear discordant voices that they regard as indecent. The absence of governmental regulation of Internet content has unquestionably produced a kind of chaos, but as one of the plaintiffs' experts put it with such resonance at the hearing: "What achieved success was the very chaos that the Internet is. The strength of the Internet is that chaos." Just as the strength of the Internet is chaos, so the strength of our liberty depends upon the chaos and cacophony of the unfettered speech the First Amendment protects.

For these reasons, I without hesitation hold that the CDA is unconstitutional on its face.

*"It's only fair to warn you that my conversation contains
adult language that you may find offensive."*

"Cultural Vandals" Hide behind Free Speech

JEFF DURSTEWITZ

BEFORE READING: The authors of the Bill of Rights probably never envisioned the kinds of images we see and dialogue and lyrics we listen to today. In some of the music and computer games that you're familiar with, has the right to free expression gone too far?

In his June 11 Politics & People column "Teen Violence Spawned by Guns and Cultural Rot," Al Hunt got it half right: Teen violence is spawned by cultural rot. But the gun issue is really a red herring. Guns, by themselves, do nothing at all. And the focus on "teen" violence—as opposed to the terrible intellectual, emotional, and spiritual harm we are doing all our children in this country—is far too specific.

Jeff Durstewitz's letter to the editor appeared in the *Wall Street Journal* on June 29, 1998.

As Bill Bennett says, we do indeed live in a society that seems dedicated to corrupting our children and stealing their innocence. Nine-year-olds and younger are watching *South Park,* even though its Brechtian sensibility is geared toward college students. A whole subgenre of "action" movies link and equate mayhem (i.e., body count) with humor and camaraderie. Steven Spielberg said he wouldn't take his ten-year-old to see *Jurassic Park,* yet he knew many parents would. Music, computer games, the Internet—the evidence of moral and cultural degradation is almost inescapable. Under the guise of "free speech," merchandisers are aggressively doing violence to our kids. They, in turn, are doing violence to each other. If Socrates was executed in ancient Athens for "corrupting the youth," what punishment should we contemplate for today's cultural vandals?

It's about time we all acknowledged a basic fact: The First Amendment doesn't mean that anything goes, anytime. We have the right to set standards and limits where children—who are essentially defenseless—are concerned. The Constitution should not be a ready license to rob our kids of their precious childhood, not to mention submerging their minds and souls in an endless, demoralizing, and deepening flood of dreck.

A Case the Scouts Had to Win

STEFFEN N. JOHNSON

> BEFORE READING: Should college fraternities and sororities be permitted to limit their membership to certain races and religions? Are these practices an example of free association guaranteed by the First Amendment?

To the dismay of gay rights groups and some civil libertarians, the Supreme Court ruled on Wednesday that it is unconstitutional for the state to require a Boy Scout troop to admit a gay scoutmaster. The court's decision, however, goes to the heart of the First Amendment's guarantee of free association. It may be a civil right to have access to employment, or to transportation, or to hotels and restaurants. But it is not a civil right to assist in raising other people's children.

In the past, the court had understandably ruled that society's interest in ensuring access to certain opportunities like jobs, school, and other basic necessities must sometimes override the right to associate with whomever one pleases. Everyone needs to make a living. Everyone needs

Steffen N. Johnson is a lawyer and a lecturer at the University of Chicago Law School. His article was published in the June 30, 2000, edition of the *New York Times.*

an education. Thus, the court ruled that businesses or commercial gath-erings like the Rotary Club cannot exclude women from their ranks.

But serving as a role model for young children whose parents share common values is not the same sort of privilege as a job or an education. It is a service, and one entrusted to few people.

To extend the reach of anti-discrimination laws to private groups whose purpose is not to make a profit but to bring together people with similar values, would destroy the nation's diverse tradition of voluntary collaboration for common causes. And a world in which the government could declare which causes and which moral positions benefit society, and which do not, could only be described as Orwellian.

The case arose when the Scouts informed James Dale that he could 5 not serve as a leader of a troop in Monmouth County, New Jersey. Mr. Dale sued, claiming that the Scouts had unlawfully discriminated against him because he was gay, and the New Jersey courts agreed. But the Supreme Court, in a five to four ruling, said that forcing a group to accept certain members may impair its ability to "express those views, and only those views, that it intends to express."

Exercising the right to exclude others may seem intolerant, but such a right is indispensable to private groups seeking to define them-selves, to chart their own moral course, and to work together for common ends. If the Boy Scouts were required to admit leaders who advocated a position contrary to its own, then men could assert the right to lead the Girl Scouts, gentiles could assert the right to head Jewish groups, and heterosexuals could assert the right to lead gay groups.

Mr. Dale's supporters said that the case was about status-based dis-crimination and that enforcing anti-discrimination laws against volun-tary groups like the Scouts was valid because antigay beliefs are not what brought the Scouts together. But a group should not need to have an antigay agenda to hold the view that homosexual behavior is wrong. Many churches, for example, teach that homosexual activity is immoral while affirming that gay people should be treated with equal dignity and respect. That does not mean that they have given up their right not to appoint homosexuals to leadership.

Like many Americans, the Boy Scouts attempt to walk the line be-tween tolerance of everyone and disapproval of certain types of conduct. That they wish to express their view by example or by quiet persuasion, rather than an outspoken campaign, does not diminish their right to take a position on moral issues.

As the court's majority understood, people's rights to hold moral po-sitions, to associate with others who share the same views, and to instill those views in their children without threat of outside interference are liberties that belong as much to gay men and lesbians as to the Boy Scouts, as much to those who advocate alternative lifestyles as to those who advocate traditional morality.

THINKING AND WRITING ABOUT FREEDOM OF SPEECH

QUESTIONS FOR DISCUSSION AND WRITING

1. How does Lawrence relate *Brown v. Board of Education* to issues of free speech? What principle does he invoke in defense of restrictive speech codes on campus?

2. In *Bethel School District No. 403 v. Fraser,* the U.S. Supreme Court ruled that children in a public school—in this case, high school students—do not have the same rights as adults to use sexual speech in a public forum. What reasons did the Court give for making a distinction? What reason did Justice Marshall give for his dissent? This case was argued in 1986. Do you think that the lewd speech at a school graduation would be treated in the same way today?

3. Can you think of circumstances in which creative freedom should bow to social responsibility? What evidence does Ehrenreich use to prove that "Cop Killer" is not dangerous? Is it convincing?

4. Dalzell acknowledges the dangers to children from pornographic material on the Internet. What is his solution? What reasons does Dalzell give for thinking it is important to protect speech on the Internet?

5. Do you think Durstewitz's complaints about cultural corruption are justified? Can you give other examples of "intellectual, emotional, and spiritual harm" to which children are exposed?

6. What distinction does Johnson make between the right to a job or an education and the right to associate with particular people? Explain why Johnson believes that the Scouts are protected by the First Amendment.

TOPICS FOR RESEARCH

Lyrics in rock music: How dangerous are they?

Codes of speech conduct at some colleges and universities: goals and effects

Religious displays on public land

Freedom of speech on the Internet

Prayer in public schools

Free speech issues in school newspapers

TAKING THE DEBATE ONLINE

For these and additional research URLs, see www.bedfordstmartins.com/rottenberg.

- *Freedom of Speech and Privacy in the Information Age*
  http://qsilver.queensu.ca/law/sopinka.htm

A faculty of law from Queen's University writes about the freedom of speech and privacy in the information age.

- *American Civil Liberties Union*
  www.aclu.org/issues/freespeech/hmfs.html
  The ACLU's site condemns censorship in cinema, literature, and life.

- *Massachusetts Music Industry Coalition*
  http://www.massmic.com
  This site condemns the censorship of musical expression.

- *Trinity College of Vermont: Jeff Haig*
  www.trinityvt.edu/jhaig/censor.htm
  This site lists useful sources in the study of censorship past, present, and future, including groups that are in favor of censorship.

- *Internet Free Expression Alliance*
  http://www.ifea.net/mission.html
  This mission of this organization is to ensure the continuation of the Internet as a forum for open, diverse, and unimpeded expression and to oppose any governmental effort to promote, coerce, or mandate the rating or filtering of online content.

- *Scouting for All*
  http://www.scoutingforall.org
  This group advocates allowing the Boy Scouts of America to accept gay and atheist scouts.

16

Privacy in the Information Age

Although the word *privacy* is nowhere mentioned in the Constitution, the right to privacy has been inferred from the intent of several Amendments: the First, the Third, the Ninth, and the Fourteenth. Needless to say, the makers of that document could not have foreseen the worldwide dissemination of information, private as well as public, which the development of technology would make possible at the end of the twentieth century. Today the courts, wrestling with charges that the right to privacy is being violated, must try to strike a balance between the right to privacy and the right to know and to speak freely.

Electronic purveyors of information can make our financial records, our medical history, our buying habits, and other data available to those who are interested. Television talk shows encourage people to divulge intimate secrets to millions of viewers. Employers test their employees for drug use and demand information about personal habits and life choices. On computer Web sites strangers are invited to enter our homes and share our lives. Even in the open air we are being watched. In an effort to control crime, more than two thousand surveillance cameras have been mounted in the streets and parks of Manhattan to monitor public activity.

One disturbing result of this information explosion has been the exposure of children to adult knowledge. Neil Postman, author of *The Disappearance of Childhood*, says,

> With the new technologies, television being at the forefront, there are fewer and fewer secrets, medical secrets, sexual secrets, political secrets. Adults used to reveal secrets to you, the child, in stages, in school, in books. When you knew all the secrets, you became an adult. But now all of that is available on the Internet or TV.[1]

But the capacity of machines to provide information would not be enough to make us vulnerable to public scrutiny. Changes in the social and moral climate of the last four decades have removed many of our defenses. "Letting it all hang out" strikes millions of people as an acceptable guide to behavior. It may be hard to believe that in the not-so-distant past extramarital pregnancy, homosexuality, even a diagnosis of cancer were deeply held secrets. Now we express ourselves far more freely in our language, both in everyday speech and in literature, in our clothing, and in our sexual relationships. Births have been televised; so has a death.

Some observers, however, think that today's absence of privacy is no more serious than that experienced by earlier generations who lived in small towns and villages where everybody's activities were a matter of common knowledge. In the city people can and often do remain anonymous. Even the decline of the extended family, in which personal behavior was closely watched and evaluated by an army of relatives, has contributed to a greater sense of privacy.

Nevertheless, the questions surrounding this issue will multiply as public and private places become increasingly interchangeable. If people value the convenience of having wide access to information, services, and entertainment, as well as the right to express themselves freely, are they justified in thinking that they will also be able to guard their privacy? Do they perhaps regard the loss of privacy as a price they are willing to pay for admission to the global village? If not, how can their privacy be protected?

---

[1] Anthony Ramirez, "Lolitas Don't Shock Anymore, but *Lolita* Still Does," *New York Times*, August 2, 1998, p. Wk 5.

Remote Control

AVRAHAM BALABAN

BEFORE READING: Do you prefer conversation by e-mail or telephone? Explain your preference.

Recently I needed to call a friend and colleague to find out the deadline for proposals for a comparative-literature conference that we both planned to attend. A moment before calling, I hesitated: isn't a telephone call an intrusion? An imposition? Isn't it more appropriate to send her an e-mail, so that she can answer when it's convenient?

In the good old days, in nice weather people sat on their front porches. If you wanted to talk to them or spend a leisurely hour in their company, all you had to do was walk down the street, exchange pleasantries, and be invited for tea or coffee.

Once air-conditioning closed people off in their homes, porch life disappeared, and the idea that people could simply stop by unannounced vanished. The order of the day changed. We now call ahead and set up an appointment before visiting. The idea that once upon a time people would show up uninvited is hard to imagine. "What do you mean the Goldmans are here? Why didn't they call ahead?"

In 1984, I was a visiting scholar at Harvard, coming all the way from Tel Aviv. A week or so after we moved into our house, I saw my new neighbor over the fence. We introduced ourselves, and he invited my wife and me to stop by sometime. So we did. The rest of the year he was careful to stay clear of these newcomers who were not familiar with the local code.

The telephone used to be how Americans communicated while 5 maintaining their privacy and controlling whom they wanted to see. The advent of e-mail has added a new dimension to the game. You send an e-mail to your friend, your colleague, or your dean, who replies when he or she has an answer or has a minute between other urgent e-mails. Your correspondent has the luxury of finding the right information before responding but also has control over the length of the answer and the length of the communicative act itself.

Next to e-mail, the telephone suddenly feels like an invasion. Can I simply call my colleague and ask her for the deadline for our proposals? Maybe it's not a good time for her. Maybe she's racing to an appointment or brushing her teeth. Maybe she doesn't like to answer on the

Avraham Balaban is chair of the Department of African and Asian Languages and Literature of the University of Florida. "Remote Control" was printed in the *New York Times* on March 22, 1999.

spot, doesn't like to be cornered. E-mail would be so much neater, more considerate, more respectful of privacy.

Yes, e-mail gives us the cocoon we have always dreamed of; now we can be as alienated as we want to be.

Can Anything Be Done to Protect Your Privacy in Cyberspace?

MARK MAREMONT

BEFORE READING: Have you ever suffered as a result of an invasion of your privacy? Did the experience change your behavior in any way?

It's 2005, and within hours of booking a flight to Las Vegas online, your e-mail inbox is spilling over with messages from hotels offering room specials. Knowing you subscribe to an online newsletter for heart-bypass patients, one hotel trumpets its in-room defibrillators. A nearby casino, tipped off that you recently have surfed pornography Web sites, touts its lap dancing. The car-rental company you attempted to book rejects you after a database reveals you've had a recent accident.

So much for a private getaway.

The digital age has brought people instant access to information, given consumers more choices, and helped speed communications. But for most people, the era of near-ubiquitous computers is also eroding privacy. Vast amounts of electronic information are being collected each day from credit cards, e-mail, Web surfing, and even highway toll passes. Technically, the Las Vegas scenario would require nothing more than tying several databases together.

And that's just the beginning. With access to your genetic profile, insurance companies could predict your likelihood of contracting certain diseases. Potential employers could examine the political opinions you expressed online years earlier. Ubiquitous surveillance cameras matched with pattern-recognition technology could track your movements almost anywhere.

"The technological capacity to reduce privacy to a nonexistent level 5 is already there," says Reg Whitaker, a political scientist at York University in Toronto and author of a recent book on the subject.

It's the leading source of future dread in America. For all the obvious benefits conferred by the unimpeded flow of information, Americans

---

Mark Maremont is a staff reporter in the *Wall Street Journal*'s Boston bureau. This article appeared in that newspaper on January 1, 2000.

cited loss of personal privacy as their number 1 concern about the twenty-first century, ahead of overpopulation, terrorism, and global warming, in a *Wall Street Journal*/NBC poll.

But don't mourn for privacy just yet.

Already, some of the same technologies that threaten privacy are being used to defend it, and the arms race has only begun. There's also a growing sense among privacy gurus that individuals will not just complain about invasive technologies but will rebel against them, exhibiting biologically encoded human yearning for privacy.

"A Deep Drive"

"People have a deep drive to develop their privacy and their space," says Harvard University sociobiologist Edward O. Wilson, who likens the human desire for privacy to the territorial instinct of all animals. Even in primitive societies where people live in close quarters, he says, individuals always insist on a minimum distance from others. Dr. Wilson believes highly personal information such as financial and medical records have become part of our individual space, something we instinctively defend.

Individual companies perceived to be violating privacy rights have   10 come in for a barrage of criticism. Consider the recent case of Image Data LLC, a Nashua, New Hampshire, outfit that collected digitized driver's license photos from three states for a commercial database. Public outrage over the plan, intended to combat check and credit-card fraud, forced the states to cancel the arrangement.

Marc Rotenberg, executive director of the Electronic Privacy Information Center, Washington, sees parallels with the environmental movement. Initially, many companies argued they could never abandon certain practices, such as toxic dumping. Yet most such outfits have changed those practices under pressure of public opinion and new legal standards.

The popular perception, fueled by George Orwell's classic *1984*, is that technological advancement automatically causes the loss of privacy. But technology itself is already playing a strong role in the defense of privacy.

Just as junk e-mail, or digital spam, became a problem, technologies emerged to block it from e-mail inboxes. Powerful encryption programs have made it easier for people to surf the Internet anonymously, and digital cash helps mask buyers' profiles. Alan F. Westin, an emeritus professor of law at Columbia University who has studied privacy issues for decades, believes that technology advances will continue to aid privacy.

Unwanted solicitations could be halted with filtering software that permits consumers to specify what types of solicitations they want, he says. The filtering tools could be equipped with a "privacy preference" feature, which would screen out transmissions from senders that don't comply with certain privacy standards, while the standards would be monitored by independent agencies.

Privacy Seal

The Council of Better Business Bureaus, Arlington, Virginia, earlier 15 this year took a first step in this direction by announcing an online-privacy "seal" program, in which participating companies agree to adhere to a code of privacy practices. Among other things, the code requires a site to disclose how it intends to use the information being collected, mandates that consumers be allowed to opt out of data collection, and requires site operators to obtain parental permission to collect data on children. More than 100 companies have signed up already.

Dr. Westin believes that managing our privacy will become an everyday activity in the twenty-first century and beyond, requiring as much energy and thought as managing finances has in the twentieth century. "My grandchildren will be absolutely conscious of privacy management," he adds, including knowing their privacy rights and what their personal information is worth to a marketer.

Sensing a market opportunity, a host of small companies are developing privacy-enhancement tools and services. One, Zero Knowledge Systems of Montreal, is testing software that encrypts outgoing Internet traffic, including e-mail, and sends it through a series of electronic detours to conceal its origins. The software also makes it easier for users to employ pseudonyms to conduct disparate activities on the Web, for, say, political activities or job searching.

Another theoretically popular concept, still in infancy, is the so-called infomediary, a vendor that defends privacy by acting as a middleman between consumers and marketers. A consumer shopping for a new car, for example, might supply the infomediary with buying specifications, such as features and price range. The infomediary would release selected information to car dealers, which would in turn communicate with the middleman and not the consumer.

But the infomediary model is fraught with challenges. Funneling transactions through third parties or electronic aliases may add time and hassle. Many people may not bother because of the inconvenience or cost. Cell phones, for example, are vastly less private than land lines, yet millions use them without thinking twice.

Some technologists also believe that privacy will be impossible to de- 20 fend against a determined and well-funded intrusion. "Privacy will be a technology race, and the winner will be the side with more money," says Bruce Schneier, a cryptography expert and chief technology officer of Counterpane Internet Security Inc., San Jose, California. He says technology is likely to give people some protection against their fellow citizens but not against big government agencies or anybody really intent on digging out private information.

Some types of information might not be protectable at all. Arthur Caplan, director of the Center for Bioethics at the University of Pennsylvania, predicts that a person's genetic information will be easily extracted from a Kleenex or urinal or even through a rapid body scan that could be undetectable to the subject. "Biological information will be so readily available to so many people, personal privacy will go right out the window," he says.

Information All Around?

The prospect that laws and technology might not be enough to preserve any real measure of privacy has led David Brin, a physicist and science-fiction author, to propose a radical solution: complete transparency. In a recent book, he argues that it will be impossible to keep any information truly private. Instead, he proposes to open nearly all information to everyone. This, he argues, would help ensure that information is not misused.

If a corporate boss can monitor the keystrokes of telemarketing employees, Mr. Brin suggests, then those employees ought to have the legal right to watch what the boss does, perhaps with video cameras following him everywhere. This will make the boss think twice about how much information he really needs on the employees, he says.

As peculiar as Mr. Brin's proposition may seem, it addresses an unassailable truth: For all the power of public outrage and for all the technology power marshaled by individuals, we will never be as private in the future as we are now, just as we're not as private now as we were a century ago. The question is not whether we can retain privacy, but what we can do to keep it from disappearing entirely.

"A crisis point for privacy is facing us now," says Austin Hill, presi- 25
dent of Zero Knowledge. "If we don't make sure privacy is really around, it will be gone, and the next thousand years will be very scary."

TWO-WAY STREET

Too Much Privacy Is a Health Hazard

THOMAS LEE

BEFORE READING: Is there anything in your life that you would prefer not to tell your doctor? Suppose the secret posed a danger to your health.

Most patients like what they see on the computer monitor on my desk. There are lists of their medications and medical problems, laboratory results, and reminders to do mammograms. They are impressed that all the doctors at our hospital work with the same information about them. They are amused that I can check their test results from a laptop computer on an airplane. But more than a few people find cause to worry in this cutting-edge system. Could their diagnosis of diabetes leak to employers? Insurers? Companies making products for diabetics? A few years from now, will their genetic codes be flying around the Internet?

These are not paranoid fantasies. Threats to our medical privacy are proliferating as technology speeds the flow of information—and people are fighting back. Patients are increasingly reluctant to release their health records, and states are passing laws to restrict access to them. Unfortunately, these efforts can backfire. In Maine lawmakers tried earlier this year to bar the release of any information without a patient's written consent. The law seemed reasonable at first, but the result was chaos. Doctors caring for the same patient couldn't compare notes without first seeking permission. Clinical labs had to stop giving patients their results over the phone. You couldn't even call a local hospital to find out if a loved one had been admitted. Confidentiality is a vital component of the trust between patients and physicians, and protecting it is worth some inconvenience. But information is the lifeblood of good health care. In short, privacy can be hazardous to your health.

Consider what happens when a doctor writes you a prescription. If that doctor doesn't know about every other drug you're using, the results can be disastrous. Patients have died because one doctor prescribed Viagra for impotence and another ordered nitroglycerin for angina—a combination that causes dangerous drops in blood pressure. Fatal reactions have also occurred when patients on Prozac or Zoloft were given monoamine oxidase inhibitors (another type of antidepressant). Most deaths from drug interactions could be prevented by databases that show every prescription written for a particular patient. But insurers usually withhold that information, for fear of offending subscribers. The result is that physicians have to rely on what patients remember or choose to disclose.

Thomas Lee is the medical director of Partners Community HealthCare, Inc., in Boston. His article was published in *Newsweek* on August 16, 1999.

Drug interactions are not the only potential hazard. Suppose a person whose records are on file at one hospital shows up in the emergency room of another. Even if the records can be transferred, state law may bar the release of information about mental illness or HIV status, forcing the ER physician to fly halfblind. A laceration on a patient with a history of severe depression may warrant more than sutures — it may have been a suicide gesture. Likewise, pneumonia in a patient with HIV requires different tests and treatments than it would in someone else.

Even when privacy advocates concede that doctors need unfettered access to patients' records, most favor shielding them from HMO administrators. But a responsible health plan can put clinical information to good use. As part of a "disease management" program, an HMO may use computer software to determine whether patients with a chronic condition, such as asthma or hypertension, are filling their prescriptions and showing up for appointments. Those who fall behind may get a reminder by mail or phone. These programs can measurably improve people's health, but patients often miss out on them by refusing to authorize access to their records. Some plans hesitate even to launch such programs. One Massachusetts HMO is now debating whether to send flu-shot reminders to members with HIV. The program would almost surely save lives, but it would just as surely draw criticism as a breach of confidentiality. 5

Privacy advocates are especially wary of electronic data. If we can't keep tabs on nuclear secrets at Los Alamos, they ask, how likely are we to keep computerized medical records out of hostile hands? But electronic record keeping may actually reduce the risk, even while making information more accessible. No one can tell who has looked at a paper chart, but anyone who opens a secure electronic record leaves a computerized fingerprint. A psychiatrist at a New England teaching hospital was recently fined for peeking at an acquaintance's medical records seven times. The bad news is that it was so easy for the psychiatrist to gain access. The good news is that she was so easily caught.

The real challenge is not just to detect such breaches but to prevent them. The doctors in my network will soon have to answer a series of questions before opening a patient's computerized record. We'll have to explain how we're involved in the patient's care, and how long our need for access will continue. And logging on to our system requires not only a password but also a smart card that generates new access codes every thirty seconds. Anyone who stole my smart card would also need my password, and vice versa. These safeguards cost money and time, and doctors will grumble about the extra keystrokes. But with a little creativity and common sense, we'll find a way to protect privacy while ensuring that doctors have the information they need to take good care of people.

What Privacy Rights?

BOB HERBERT

BEFORE READING: If you drafted a law to protect the right to privacy, what personal information would the law make it illegal to distribute? Think of all the places where information about you is on file.

A recent report out of Washington tells a story about Dr. Louis Hafken, a psychiatrist in Providence, Rhode Island, who received a letter from a company that reviews prescription drug benefits for insurers and employers.

The letter contained what should have been confidential information about one of Dr. Hafken's patients, including a printout of her prescription records. It noted that she was taking Ativan, an antianxiety drug. The company wanted to know why. Was the patient depressed, or suffering from panic disorder, or experiencing alcohol withdrawal? Did the doctor plan to continue giving her Ativan?

The doctor did not provide the requested information. "Frankly," he was quoted as saying, "it's none of their business."

The patient was naturally upset to learn that her employer had examined the records of her psychiatric treatment. The implications of such snooping are obvious. Dr. Hafken said many of his patients "are afraid to be completely honest in therapy" because they fear that people other than their doctors will learn of matters that were supposed to have remained secret.

They have reason to be worried. We are very close to the day when 5 strangers will know, or will be able to know, anything they want about you.

Your financial profile and buying habits have long since been catalogued and traded like baseball cards. Your medical records, supposedly secure, are not. Your boss may well be monitoring your telephone conversations and e-mail. Hidden video cameras have been installed—sometimes legally and sometimes not—in dressing rooms and public bathrooms. Thieves armed with your social security number can actually hijack your identity.

"Nothing Sacred: The Politics of Privacy" is a report released last month by the Center for Public Integrity, a highly regarded nonpartisan research organization. The report warned that the privacy of Americans "is being compromised and invaded from many angles" and asserted that Congress has not done nearly enough to slow the assault.

Bob Herbert is a columnist for the *New York Times*. This article appeared in his In America column on September 27, 1998.

"Time and again," said Charles Lewis, director of the center, "Congress has put the economic interests of various privacy invaders ahead of the privacy interests of the American public."

According to the report, Congress first heard testimony that there were problems keeping medical records confidential in 1971. But it still has not passed legislation designed to curb the abuses.

So you still get cases like that of Mark Hudson, a former insurance 10 company employee who told the *Times* in 1996 that he was shocked to find during his computer training that he could call up the records of any of the company's subscribers, including information about his own psychiatric treatment and the antidepressant medication he was taking.

"I can tell you unequivocally that patient confidentiality is not eroding," he said. "It can't erode because it's simply nonexistent."

The right to privacy in the workplace is virtually nonexistent as well.

"Most people assume that Federal laws protect Americans from being spied upon in the workplace," said the report. "To the contrary, over the years Congress has rejected legislation spelling out basic privacy protections for employees."

In addition to the possible monitoring of telephone conversations and e-mail, workers are frequently subjected to the scrutiny of hidden video cameras, can be required to type at computers that monitor the number of errors they make and the number of breaks they take, and often are compelled to provide urine samples and submit to psychological exams.

For some jobs, the scrutiny is reasonable. For others, it is not. In all 15 cases it should be properly regulated, and the guidelines should be clear. That is not what is happening. As the center's report noted, Congress has gone out of its way to preserve the right of employers to eavesdrop and otherwise spy upon and collect personal data on their employees.

For decades, privacy advocates have called for legislation that would spell out and guarantee a citizen's basic right to privacy. But tremendous amounts of money are being made from the rampant transfer of the most personal types of information. The huge corporate interests and others that benefit from that gold mine do not want it sealed.

Talk Show Telling versus Authentic Telling: The Effects of the Popular Media on Secrecy and Openness

EVAN IMBER-BLACK

BEFORE READING: Are you surprised that people are so willing to disclose their secrets on TV talk shows? Is such a development good or bad?

> Well, my guests today say that they can't bear to keep their secrets locked inside of them any longer. And they've invited their spouse or lover to come on national television to let them hear the secrets for the first time.
> — Montel Williams

The young woman entered my therapy room slowly, with the usual hesitation of a new client. I settled her in a chair, expecting to begin the low-key question-and-answer conversation that usually takes the entire first session. Almost before she could pronounce my name, she began telling me a deeply personal and shameful secret. In an effort to slow her down and start to build a relationship that might be strong enough to hold her enormous pain, I gently asked her what made her think it was all right to tell me things so quickly. "I see people doing it on *Oprah* all the time," she replied.

Throughout history human beings have been fascinated by other people's secrets. In great literature, theater, and films we view how people create and inhabit secrets and cope with the consequences of planned or unplanned revelation. Life-changing secrets are central to such ancient dramas such as *Oedipus* or Shakespeare's *Macbeth* as well as to twentieth-century classics such as Ibsen's *A Doll's House,* Eugene O'Neill's *Long Day's Journey into Night,* Arthur Miller's *Death of a Salesman* and *All My Sons,* or Lorraine Hansberry's *A Raisin in the Sun.* Like me, you may remember the poignancy of the sweet secrets in the O. Henry tale "Gift of the Magi," where a wife secretly cuts and sells her hair to buy her husband a watch chain for Christmas, while he, unbeknownst to her, sells his watch in order to buy silver combs for her hair. Contemporary popular films, such as *Ordinary People, The Prince of Tides,* or *The Wedding*

Evan Imber-Black, Ph.D., is director of program development at the Ackerman Institute for the Family in New York City and a professor of psychiatry at the Albert Einstein College of Medicine. Her published work includes *Rituals for Our Times* (with Janine Roberts, Ed.D., 1992) and *Secrets in Families and Family Therapy* (1993). Printed here is an excerpt from her book *The Secret Life of Families: Truth-Telling, Privacy, and Reconciliation in a Tell-All Society* (1998).

Banquet, also illustrate the complexity of secrets and their impact on every member of a family. Literary and dramatic portrayals of perplexing secrets and their often complicated and messy resolutions help us to remember that keeping and opening secrets is not simple. Perhaps most important, they help us appreciate our own deep human connection to the dilemmas of others.

Since the advent of television, however, we have begun to learn about other people's secrets and, by implication, how to think about our own secrets in a very different way. Exploiting our hunger for missing community, both afternoon talk shows and evening magazine shows have challenged all of our previously held notions about secrecy, privacy, and openness. While such shows have been around for nearly thirty years, in the 1980s something new began to appear: celebrities began to open the secrets in their lives on national television.[1] As we heard about Jane Fonda's bulimia, Elizabeth Taylor's drug addiction, or Dick Van Dyke's alcoholism—formerly shameful secrets spoken about with aplomb—centuries of stigma seemed to be lifting. Other revelations enabled us to see the pervasiveness of wife battering and incest. The unquestioned shame and secrecy formerly attached to cancer, adoption, homosexuality, mental illness, or out-of-wedlock birth began to fall away.

This atmosphere of greater openness brought with it many benefits. In my therapy practice I experienced an important shift as the people I worked with displayed a greater ease in raising what might never have been spoken about a decade earlier. Frightening secrets lost some of their power to perpetuate intimidation. Those who had been silenced began to find their voices and stake their claim as authorities on their own lives.

But as the arena of the unmentionable became smaller and smaller, a 5 more dangerous cultural shift was also taking place: the growth of the simplistic belief that telling a secret, regardless of context, is automatically beneficial. This belief, promulgated by television talk shows and media exposés, has ripped secrecy and openness away from their necessary moorings in connected and empathic relationships. Painful personal revelations have become public entertainment, used to sell dish soap and to manufacture celebrity.

If cultural norms once made shameful secrets out of too many happenings in human life, we are now struggling with the reverse assumption: that opening secrets—no matter how, when, or to whom—is morally superior and automatically healing. The daily spectacle of strangers opening secrets in our living rooms teaches us that no distinctions need be drawn, no care need be taken, no thought given to consequences.

---

[1] For a complete discussion of the history of talk television and the wider context in which it is embedded, see J. A. Heaton and N. L. Wilson, *Tuning In Trouble: Talk TV's Destructive Impact on Mental Health* (San Francisco: Jossey-Bass, 1995).

Talk Show Telling

From a Sally Jessy Raphael show in 1994, we hear and see the following conversation:

> *Sally*: Let's meet David and Kelly. They're newlyweds. They got married in December. . . . As newlyweds, what would happen if he cheated on you? What would you do?
>
> *Kelly*: I don't know.
>
> *[Before David begins to speak, the print at the bottom of the screen reads, "Telling Kelly for the first time that he's cheating on her," thus informing the audience of the content of the secret before Kelly is told.]*
>
> *David*: I called Sally and told the producer of the show that I was living a double life. . . . I had a few affairs on her.
>
> *Sally (to Kelly)*: Did you know about that?
>
> *[Camera zooms in on Kelly's shocked and pained expression; she is speechless and in tears, and she shakes her head while members of the audience chuckle.]*
>
> *Sally*: Kelly, how do you feel? On the one hand, listen to how awful and bad this is. On the other hand, he could have just not ever told you. He loves you so much that he wanted to come and get this out. . . .

In the late 1960s the *Phil Donahue Show* began a new media format for sharing interesting information and airing issues. This shifted in the late 1970s and 1980s to celebrity confessions and the destruction of taboos. In the 1990s talk TV brings us the deliberate opening of secrets that one person in a couple or a family has never heard before. In a cynical grab for ratings and profits, the format of such shows has changed rapidly from one where guests were told ahead of time that they were going to hear a secret "for the first time on national television" to one where guests are invited to the show under some other ruse. These programs are referred to as "ambush" shows.

According to former talk show host Jane Whitney, "Practically anyone willing to 'confront' someone—her husband's mistress, his wife's lover, their promiscuous best friend—in a televised emotional ambush could snare a free ticket to national notoriety. *Those who promised to reveal some intimate secret to an unsuspecting loved one got star treatment*" (italics added).[2] Presently there are over thirty talk shows on every weekday. Forty million Americans watch these shows, and they are syndicated in many other countries.[3] Even if you have never watched a talk show, you live in an environment where assumptions about secrets have been affected by talk show telling.

---

[2]J. Whitney, "Why I Simply Had to Shut Up," *New York Daily News*, June 11, 1995, p. 6.

[3]Talk television is extremely profitable. A typical show costs about $200,000 a week to produce, compared to an average $1 million a week for a drama. In 1992, for instance, Oprah Winfrey's show earned $157 million, Phil Donahue's show $90 million, and Sally Jessy Raphael's show $60 million (Heaton and Wilson, *Tuning In Trouble*).

Opening painful secrets on talk TV shows promotes a distorted sense   10
of values and beliefs about secrecy and openness. While viewers are
drawn into the sensational content of whatever secret is being revealed,
the impact on relationships after the talk show is over is ignored. Indeed,
when there has been severe relationship fallout, or even tragedy following the opening of a secret, talk show hosts and producers claim they
have no responsibility, intensifying the belief that secrets can be reck-
lessly opened without any obligation to be concerned about the aftermath. Consider the following:

- In one notorious incident in 1995, a young man named Jonathon
  Schmitz murdered an acquaintance, Scott Amedure, following an
  unwelcome revelation on the *Jenny Jones* show.[4] Schmitz had been
  told that he was coming on the show to meet a "secret admirer." He
  was *not* told that the show was about "men who have secret crushes
  on men."[5] When his shock and humiliation resulted in Amedure's
  murder, the host and producers insisted they had no responsibility.

- On the *Montel Williams* show, a woman heard for the first time that her
  sister had been sleeping with her boyfriend for several years. She came
  on the show after being told it was a show about "old boyfriends."

- Former talk show host Jane Whitney describes a show she did called
  "Revealing Your Double Life." A mother was invited on who had no
  idea why her son had cut himself off from her for two years.
  Whitney, of course, knew that the son was about to reveal his
  pending sexual reassignment surgery. When she met the mother
  just before the show, the woman implored her, "Do you know
  what's wrong? We were always so close. I don't know what's happened. Is he sick? Does he have AIDS?" Assuring the mother that
  "everything would be all right," Whitney lied and kept the secret
  in order to maximize its revelation on the show.[6]

- Ricki Lake invited on a man who had been keeping his homosexuality a secret from his family. His roommate announced that he had
  taken it upon himself to tell the man's family this secret.[7]

When such actions occur over and over again on talk TV, we lose our
capacity to ask a critical question—namely, under what circumstances
do we have the right to open another person's secret?

[4]*Newsweek*, March 20, 1995, p. 30; *New York Times*, March 12, 1995, p. A22, and
March 14, 1995, pp. A1, A10.

[5]The tragedy attached to this particular show distracts our attention from an important dimension of many of these programs, which is that they commonly pander
to feelings of homophobia, racism, and sexism. See Heaton and Wilson, *Tuning In
Trouble*, for a full discussion of this issue.

[6]Whitney, "Why I Simply Had to Shut Up."

[7]J. A. Heaton, and N. L. Wilson, "Tuning In to Trouble," *Ms.* magazine, Septem-
ber/October 1995, 6(2), pp. 45–48.

On talk television, husbands hear for the first time that their wives want a divorce; mothers are told the secret of their daughters' sexual abuse; wives discover that their husbands tell friends about their sexual relationship. And all of this occurs in a context in which the host disingenuously denies any responsibility for what is set in motion in the complex ecology of family relationships.

Talk show telling ignores the importance of committed relationships. Telling can be anonymous and disguised. A studio audience and a viewing audience consisting of strangers hear the previously hidden details of our lives. Commercial breaks cavalierly interrupt the opening and hearing of a painful secret. Eavesdropping stands in for sincere listening. Voyeurism substitutes for witnessing. The host's pseudo-intimate hugs and caresses replace genuine healing.

When secrets are opened on television, several peculiar triangles are created. The relationship between the person telling the secret and the person hearing the secret is immediately invaded by the audience, the host, and the "expert," each with a calculated and repetitious role. These roles are imbued with arrogance: the belief that one knows what is best for other people to do about the secrets in their lives. Talk show telling involves opening secrets to a huge group of uninvolved, faultfinding listeners who have no responsibility for the relationship after the talk show ends.

When a secret is about to be revealed, captions are placed below the   15 image of the person who has not yet heard it. The audience sees such words as "About to hear that his wife just had an abortion" or "Jim is not Ellen's biological father." Thus the audience knows the content of the secret before the person whose life the secret affects. A context of humiliation is constructed. Often the audience laughs or gasps while the camera catches a close-up of the perplexed face of the listener. The recipient of the secret is, in fact, the last to know. This structure reduces empathy and enables the audience to feel separate from and superior to the ambushed guest.

The audience encourages further revelations through applause.[8] As viewers, we get the message over and over that opening a secret, regardless of consequences, gains attention and approval. Loudly applauded, cheered, jeered, and fought over, secrets are in fact trivialized. On talk shows, a secret of sexual abuse equals a secret about family finances equals a secret about being a Nazi equals a secret of paternity.

Once a secret is revealed, both the teller and the recipient are immediately vulnerable to the judgmental advice and criticism of strangers. Blaming and taking sides abound. Not a moment elapses for reflection on the magnitude and gravity of what has occurred. Every secret is instantly reduced to a one-dimensional problem that will yield to simplistic solutions.

---

[8]See R. Cialdini, *Influence: How and Why People Agree to Things* (New York: William Morrow, 1984), for a discussion regarding studies on compliance showing that once people agree to participate in something, they often go along with much more than they originally intended.

Soon after a secret is opened, the host goes into high gear with some variation of the message that opening the secret can have only good results. Sally Jessy Raphael tells the young wife who has just discovered the secret of her husband's affairs in front of millions of unasked-for snoopers, "He loves you so much that he wanted to come and get this out." The message to all is that telling a secret, in and of itself, is curative. There is no place for ambivalence or confusion. Indeed, guests are often scolded for expressing doubt or hesitation about the wisdom of national disclosure of the intimate aspects of their lives.

The host's position as a celebrity can frame the content of a given secret and the process of telling as either normal or abnormal, good or bad. When Oprah Winfrey joins guests who are exposing secrets of sexual abuse or cocaine addiction with revelations of her own, the telling becomes hallowed. No distinctions are drawn between what a famous person with a lot of money and power might be able to speak about without consequences and what an ordinary person who is returning to their family, job, and community after the talk show might be able to express. Conversely, some hosts display initial shock, dismay, and negativity toward a particular secret, its teller, or its recipient. When a guest on the *Jerry Springer Show* who has just discovered that a woman he had a relationship with is a transsexual hides in embarrassment and asks the host what he would do, Springer responds, "Well, I certainly wouldn't be talking about it on national TV!" A context of disgrace is created, only to be transformed at the next commercial break into a context of understanding and forgiveness.

Toward the end of any talk show on which secrets have been re- 20
vealed, a mental health therapist enters. A pseudo-therapeutic context is created. The real and difficult work that is required after a secret opens disappears in the smoke and mirrors of a fleeting and unaccountable relationship with an "expert" who adopts a position of superiority and assumed knowledge about the lives of people he or she has just met.[9] While we are asked to believe that there are no loose ends when the talk show is over, the duplicitousness of this claim is evident in the fact that many shows now offer "aftercare," or real therapy, to deal with the impact of disclosing a secret on television.[10]

The time needed even to begin to deal adequately with any secret is powerfully misrepresented on talk television. In just under forty minutes

[9]See L. Armstrong, *Rocking the Cradle of Sexual Politics* (New York: Addison-Wesley, 1994), for a thoughtful discussion of the impact of such "experts" on talk television when the topic is incest. According to Armstrong, such a structure diminishes the issue, reducing it from one with crucial political implications to simply a matter of personal opinion.

[10]Jamie Diamond, "Life after Oprah," *Self*, August 1994, pp. 122–125, 162; also see Heaton and Wilson, *Tuning In Trouble*, for a thoughtful critique of the questionable quality of such "aftercare."

on a single *Montel Williams* show, a man told his wife he was in a homosexual relationship; a woman told her husband she was having an affair with his boss; another woman told her boyfriend that she was a transsexual; a wife revealed to her husband that they were $20,000 in debt; and a woman told her boyfriend that she had just aborted their pregnancy. An ethos of "just blurt it out" underpins these shows.

Talk show telling also erases age-appropriate boundaries between parents and children. Children are often in the audience hearing their parents' secrets for the first time. On one show an eight-year-old boy heard his aunt reveal that he had been abandoned by his mother because she "didn't want" him. Children may also be onstage revealing a secret to one parent about the other parent, without a thought given to the guilt children experience when they are disloyal to a parent.[11] The impact on these children, their sense of shame and embarrassment, and what they might encounter when they return to school the next day is never considered.

Ultimately, talk show telling transforms our most private and intimate truths into a commodity. Shows conclude with announcements: "Do you have a secret that you've never told anyone? Call and tell us"; "Have you videotaped someone doing something they shouldn't do? Send us the tape." A juicy secret may get you a free airplane trip, a limousine ride, an overnight stay in a fancy hotel. While no one forces anyone to go on a talk show, the fact that most guests are working-class people who lack the means for such travel makes talk show telling a deal with the devil.

[11] *Sally Jessy Raphael Show*, November 29, 1994, "We Want Mom to Leave Her Cheating Husband"; transcript by Journal Graphics.

"You have the right to remain silent. Anything you say may be used against you in a court of law, newspapers, periodicals, radio, television, all electronic media, and technologies yet to be invented."

Privacy Rights: The New Employee Relations Battlefield

WILLIAM S. HUBBARTT

BEFORE READING: If you were seeking employment, are there some kinds of questions that you would refuse to answer — questions about sexual preference, religion, or use of prescribed drugs, for example — because you doubted their relevance to the job?

Can an employee be dismissed for dating a fellow employee?

Can a manager monitor conversations in his employees' break room?

Does a drug test invade privacy, or is it a reasonable safeguard against accidents on the job?

Is e-mail private correspondence?

These and other questions strike at the heart of the conflict between an employer's concern for managing the safety and security of the workplace and an employee's privacy interest.

The news media are filled with reports of employers who routinely conduct locker searches, monitor telephone calls, mount video cameras that watch employees on the job, and monitor computers and electronic mail systems. Many of these stories emerge when a lawsuit is filed by an outraged employee seeking redress for a perceived violation of his or her privacy.

I say "perceived" because an employee's right to privacy in the private-sector workplace is *not* fundamentally guaranteed by the Constitution or federal laws, even though many employees believe this to be the case. On the other hand, employers do not have carte blanche. Some federal and state laws do afford certain limited privacy protections for employees. But in their desire to control their businesses, some employers clearly cross the boundary between reasonable management practices and outrageous personal violations.

Why are conflicts over privacy increasing?

Companies don't set out to spy on employees or break into desks 5 and lockers. But as companies have watched losses caused by theft and drug abuse soar, they have responded by instituting controls to protect their assets and interests. Such common deterrents as drug testing and

---

William S. Hubbartt is the founder and president of Hubbartt and Associates, a human resources consulting firm, and the author of five books, including *The New Battle over Workplace Privacy* (1998), from which this excerpt is taken.

workplace surveillance are extremely sensitive and can offend employees if they are not explained adequately and implemented with care.

Another "hot spot" is workplace technology. Sophisticated computer and communications technology allows managers to monitor performance by monitoring conversations or counting keystrokes. Again, if such procedures are instituted with little explanation or respect, employees will have strong negative reactions.

Their reactions are understandable. Most of us regard the right to privacy as one of the fundamental freedoms of a democratic society. Our history lessons taught us that the American colonists sought privacy protections and freedom from colonial rule of the English government. Our founding fathers sought to include privacy protections in our Constitution and our government. We grew up believing that individuals should be protected from unwanted prying into their personal lives and activities and that information about one's private life should not be subject to scrutiny by others, by the government, or by one's employer.

With these expectations, it's natural that both employers and employees wonder whether there are laws against employer spying and just what privacy rights employees are entitled to on the job. In truth, there *is* no comprehensive privacy statute. Yes, there is a constitutional provision that limits certain search and seizure actions by the government. And yes, there are laws that limit certain forms of monitoring and specify how an employer can use or release private information. But most of the constitutional protections we enjoy as private citizens vanish when we go to work. While the government, as an employer, is subject to constitutional privacy limitations, laws impose few limitations on the private employer.

Our privacy rights on the job are much more limited than most of us believe. The Constitution affords only limited privacy protections. . . . Local laws vary from state to state and, like federal laws, are subject to judicial interpretation. Many areas of privacy are new and have yet to be legislated. Other laws are so recent that cases that hinge on their interpretation are only now making their way through the court system, so it may be months or years before an employer can see the significance of a ruling. In the meantime, employers and employees find themselves clashing on privacy in a number of areas, as the following summary reveals.

Preemployment Tests

Arlene Kurtz learned that workplace privacy concerns begin at the start   10 of the employment process when she applied for a job as a clerk typist with the city of North Miami, Florida. The city had developed a policy that all job applicants must sign an affidavit stating that they had not used tobacco products for one year before seeking city employment. The city had implemented a no-smoking policy in 1990, claiming that smokers create higher health costs, as much as $4,611 per year more than nonsmokers. When Kurtz refused to sign the affidavit, she was not hired. She then filed suit against the city alleging that the no-smoking rule was an invasion of privacy.

In her suit, Kurtz claimed that the rule interfered with an aspect of her personal life in which she had a legitimate expectation of privacy. She alleged that if the city's ban against the hiring of smokers was permitted, it would allow employers to further regulate personal lives of employees on other matters, such as when to go to bed at night, what to drink on weekends, where to take vacations, or what hobbies to engage in. In evaluating the facts of the case, the courts sided with the city, indicating that the city's concern for protecting employees' health and for controlling health care costs justified the no-smoking rule.[1]

In *Kurtz*, the city was able to justify its preemployment smoking rule. But other kinds of preemployment tests also have been subject to privacy invasion or other legal claims:

Physical exams. Many firms use physical exams in prehire placement and during employment. Improper use of this information can result in a privacy invasion or violate employment laws.

Drug/alcohol screening. Record numbers of firms are conducting drug/alcohol screening tests. The intrusive nature of these tests prompts many privacy invasion claims.

Background checks. Improper handling or disclosure of information gathered from education, credentials, credit, driving, or criminal records can result in privacy claims or other labor law violations.

Reference checks. Résumé fraud and other employee relations problems have led employers to seek verification of employment information provided by job candidates. Careless use of this information can result in privacy or defamation claims.

15

Testing. Employer use of psychological testing, polygraph testing, and other kinds of paper-and-pencil measuring instruments are subject to legal restrictions. Improper inquiries of handling of test results can lead to privacy invasion claims.

After-Hours Activities

What an employee does off the job is his or her business—or is it? Employer intrusions into personal lives of employees create many questions. Can an employer regulate or prevent employees from taking a second job? Can an employee be fired because he was arrested off the job? What should an employer do if an employee refuses to work because of religious beliefs? Is it lawful for an employer to regulate an employee's drinking or smoking off the job? Is it a privacy invasion when the em-

---

[1] *Kurtz v. City of North Miami,* 11 IER Cases 480, US, No. 95-545 (1996).

ployer limits dating between employees? These kinds of issues have created many privacy invasion claims.

Consider the case of Robin Joy Brown, who applied to the State of Georgia for a position as a state's attorney.

> Brown had all the prerequisites: a Phi Beta Kappa undergraduate, she had received a law scholarship, edited the law review, received her law degree, and completed law clerk experience. After being offered a job by the Georgia state's attorney's office, she accepted. But prior to starting her employment she advised a deputy state's attorney of her plans for an upcoming wedding and that she would be changing her name from Brown to Shahar. She did not tell the deputy that she planned to marry another woman.
>
> When Georgia Attorney General Bowers learned that the planned wedding was to another woman, he withdrew the job offer stating in a letter that the purported marriage would "jeopardize the proper function of this office." Brown went ahead with her marriage plans, changed her name to Shahar, and filed suit for loss of job. In her suit, Shahar alleged that she was "fired" because of her participation in a private religious ceremony of marriage. The U.S. Court of Appeals ultimately heard the case and found that the employer's action violated the Shahars' constitutional right of intimate association.[2]

Employer involvement in off-the-job conduct usually occurs in one of the following areas:

> *Criminal and other off-duty misconduct.* Some individuals just can't seem to stay out of trouble. Inappropriate collection or release of this information can lead to privacy claims and other liabilities.
>
> *Secondary employment.* Employees may feel that secondary employment is a private affair, but when it affects the employer's business, the employer may have a say. [20]
>
> *Smoking and use of other lawful products off the job.* Off-the-job use of lawful products is generally the employee's business. On some issues, an employer may have justification to regulate off-duty conduct, but privacy claims frequently occur when employers try to control this kind of conduct.
>
> *Employee dating.* Regulation of dating may seem beyond the employer's purview, but sexual harassment claims as well as privacy invasion claims make this a sensitive subject.
>
> *Personal beliefs and lifestyles.* Employee beliefs and lifestyles may be related to religion, marital status, or sexual preference. These issues are highly personal, and improper handling of them can lead to privacy invasion or other legal claims.

---

[2] *Shahar v. Bowers,* 11 IER Cases 521 (1994).

Conclusion

In all aspects of our lives, certain individual freedoms are given up in order to accommodate the greater needs of the public, the government, or an organization such as an employer. Because of terrorism and hijacking, our society readily submits to use of metal detector screens and searches of personal belongings when boarding commercial aircraft at the airport. Upon return from overseas trips, travelers customarily accept luggage searches because of the recognized need to control the unauthorized influx of drugs into the country.

Freedom of speech does not protect the calling out of "fire" in a 25 crowded theater. As a society, we tolerate the increased presence of security cameras at banks, retail stores, and other places where cash is handled because we recognize that the use of these devices to deter crime is more important than the loss of certain aspects of our privacy. But privacy rights seem to be diminishing, and employer prying seems to be growing.

Privacy: Protections and Threats

WHITFIELD DIFFIE AND SUSAN LANDAU

BEFORE READING: Have the terrorist attacks on September 11, 2001, changed American beliefs about privacy? Explain.

Protecting the national security and enforcing the laws are basic societal values. Often they stand in competition with another basic societal value: privacy. The competition is hardly an equal contest. National security and law enforcement not only have political constituencies, they are represented by major societal organizations. Privacy has no such muscle behind it. As a result, although an attachment to privacy endures and at times grows, privacy is often violated.

The Dimensions of Privacy

Two hundred years ago, if you chose to speak to a colleague about private matters, you had to do it in person. Others might have seen the two of you walk off together, but to overhear your conversation an eaves-

---

Whitfield Diffie is the inventor of public-key cryptography, which allows the use of a public key to create a document in codes to be decoded by the recipient with a private key. Susan Landau is a former professor of computer science at the University of Massachusetts, Amherst. Both work at Sun Microsystems. Excerpted here is a chapter from their book *Privacy on the Line: The Politics of Wiretapping and Encryption* (1998). The original notes have been omitted, and bibliographic footnotes inserted.

dropper would have had to follow closely and would likely have been observed. Today, the very communication links that have made it possible to converse at a distance have the potential to destroy the privacy such conversations previously enjoyed.

From video cameras that record our entries into shops and buildings to supermarket checkout tapes that list every container of milk and package of cigarettes we buy, privacy is elusive in modern society. There are records of what we do, with whom we associate, where we go. Insurance companies know who our spouses are, how many children we have, how often we have our teeth cleaned. The increasing amount of transactional information—the electronic record of when you left the parking lot, the supermarket's record of your purchase—leaves a very large public footprint and presents a far more detailed portrait of the individual than those recorded at any time in the past. Furthermore, information about individuals is no longer under the control of the person to whom the information pertains; such loss of control is loss of privacy.

Privacy as a Fundamental Human Right

Privacy is at the very soul of being human. Legal rights to privacy appeared two thousand years ago in Jewish laws such as this: "[If one man builds a wall opposite his fellow's] windows, whether it is higher or lower than them . . . it may not be within four cubits [If higher, it must be four cubits higher, for privacy's sake]."[1] The Talmud explains that a person's neighbor "should not peer and look into his house."

Privacy is the right to autonomy, and it includes the right to be let   5 alone. Privacy encompasses the right to control information about ourselves, including the right to limit access to that information. The right to privacy embraces the right to keep confidences confidential and to share them in private conversation. Most important, the right to privacy means the right to enjoy solitude, intimacy, and anonymity.[2]

Not all these rights can be attained in modern society. Some losses occur out of choice. (In the United States, for example, candidates for office make public much personal information, such as tax and medical records, that private citizens are allowed to keep private.) Some losses are matters of convenience. (Almost no one pays bills in cash anymore.) But the maintenance of some seclusion is fundamental to the human soul. Accordingly, privacy is recognized by the international community as a basic human right. Article 12 of the 1948 Universal Declaration of Human Rights states:

> No one shall be subjected to arbitrary interference with his privacy,
> family, home or correspondence, nor to attacks upon his honour and

[1] Herbert Danby, *The Mishnah* (Oxford: Oxford UP, 1933), p. 367.
[2] David Flaherty, *Protecting Privacy in Surveillance Societies: The Federal Republic of Germany, Sweden, France, Canada, and the United States* (Chapel Hill: U of North Carolina P, 1989), p. 8.

reputation. Everyone has the right to the protection of the law against such interference or attacks.[3]

The 1967 International Covenant on Human Rights makes the same point.

The Soviet Union, East Germany, and other totalitarian states rarely respected the rights of individuals, and this includes the right to privacy. Those societies were permeated by informants, telephones were assumed to be tapped and hotel rooms to be bugged: life was defined by police surveillance. Democratic societies are supposed to function differently.

Privacy in American Society

Privacy is essential to political discourse. The fact is not immediately obvious because the most familiar political discourse is public. History records political speeches, broadsides, pamphlets, and manifestos, not the quiet conversations among those who wrote them. Without the opportunity to discuss politics in private, however, the finished positions that appear in public might never be formulated.

Democracy requires a free press, confidential lawyer-client relations, and the right to a fair trial. The foundations of democracy rest upon privacy, but in various democratic societies the protection of privacy is interpreted in varying ways. Britain, for example, has much looser laws regarding wiretaps than the United States. A number of European nations extend more protection to individuals' data records than the United States does.

Privacy is culture dependent. Citizens of crowded countries such as India and the Netherlands hold very different views of what constitutes privacy than citizens of the United States. The American concept developed in a land with a bountiful amount of physical space and in a culture woven from many disparate nationalities. 10

In the 1970s, as rapid computerization brought fear of a surveillance society, some nations sought to protect individuals from the misuse of personal data. Sweden, Germany, Canada, and France established data-protection boards to protect the privacy and the integrity of records on individual citizens. When the U.S. congress passed a Privacy Act with a similar goal, President Gerald Ford objected to the creation of another federal bureaucracy, and no U.S. data-protection commission was ever established.[4] Ten states have data-protection laws, and California includes a right to privacy in its state constitution. New York is the only state that attempts any oversight (ibid.). It would, however, be a mistake to view the lack of a major regulatory apparatus in the United States as a lack of legal protection of privacy.

[3] Academy on Human Rights, *Handbook of Human Rights* (1993), p. 3.
[4] Flaherty, p. 305.

Privacy Protection in the United States

Most Americans believe that privacy is a basic right guaranteed by the Constitution. The belief has some truth to it, but not nearly as much as some believe. Nowhere is the word privacy mentioned in the Constitution, nor is a right to privacy explicit in any amendment. Privacy is nonetheless implicit to the Constitution.

The First Amendment protects the individual's freedoms of expression, religion, and association. The Third Amendment protects the private citizen against the state's harboring an army in his home, the Fourth against unreasonable search or seizure. The Fifth Amendment ensures that an individual cannot be compelled to provide testimony against himself. The Ninth Amendment reserves to "the people" those rights that are not enumerated in the Constitution. And "the Fourteenth Amendment's guarantee that no person can be deprived of life, liberty or property without due process of law, provides an additional bulwark against governmental interference with individual privacy."[5] . . .

Why Privacy?

Despite strictures to prevent abuses, the U.S. government has invaded citizens' privacy many times over the last fifty years, in many different political situations, targeting individuals and political groups. Politicians have been wiretapped, and lawyers' confidential conversations with clients have been eavesdropped upon by FBI investigators.

Sometimes invasion of privacy has been government policy; sometimes a breach has occurred because an individual within the government misappropriated collected information. The history of the last five decades shows that attacks on privacy are not an anomaly. When government has the power to invade privacy, abuses occur.

Conflict between protecting the security of the state and the privacy of its individuals is not new, but technology has given the state much more access to private information about individuals than it once had. As Justice Louis Brandeis so presciently observed in his dissenting opinion in *Olsmstead,*

> "in the application of a constitution, our contemplation cannot be only of what has been but of what may be." The progress of science in furnishing the government with means of espionage is not likely to stop with wiretapping. Ways may some day be developed by which the Government, without removing papers from secret drawers, can reproduce them in court, and by which it will be enabled to expose to a jury the most intimate occurrences of the home. Advances in the psychic and related sciences may bring means of exploring unexpressed beliefs,

15

[5] United States Senate, Committee on the Judiciary, Subcommittee on Constitutional Rights, *Federal Data Banks and Constitutional Rights,* Vol. I (Washington, D.C.: U.S. Government Printing Office, Ninety-Third Congress, Second Session, 1974), p. ix.

thoughts and emotions. . . . Can it be that the Constitution affords no protection against such invasions of individual security?[6]

Preservation of privacy is critical to a democratic political process. Change often begins most tentatively, and political discussion often starts in private. Journalists need to operate in private when cultivating sources. Attorneys cannot properly defend their clients if their communications are not privileged. As the Church Committee observed:

> Personal privacy is protected because it is essential to liberty and the pursuit of happiness. Our Constitution checks the power of Government for the purpose of protecting the rights of individuals, in order that all our citizens may live in a free and decent society. Unlike totalitarian states, we do not believe that any government has a monopoly on truth.
>
> When Government infringes those rights of nurturing and protecting them, the injury spreads far beyond the particular citizens targeted to untold numbers of other Americans who may be intimidated.
>
> Persons most intimidated may well not be those at the extremes of the political spectrum, but rather those nearer the middle. Yet voices of moderation are vital to balance public debate and avoid polarization of our society.[7]

What type of society does the United States seek to be? The incarceration of Japanese Americans during World War II began with an invasion of privacy and ended in the tyrannical disruption of many individual lives. Could the roundup of Japanese Americans have occurred so easily if the Census Bureau's illegal cooperation had not made the process so efficient? The purpose of the Bill of Rights is to protect the rights of the people against the power of the government. In an era when technology makes the government ever more efficient, protection of these rights becomes ever more important.

Citizens of the former Eastern Bloc countries attest to the corruption of society that occurs when no thought or utterance is private. No one suggests that people living in the United States face imminent governmental infringements of this type, but in 1972 congressional staffers wrote that "what separates military intelligence in the United States from its counterparts in totalitarian states, then, is not its capabilities, but its intentions."[8] Electing officials we believe to be honest, trusting them to

---

[6] Louis Brandeis, Dissenting opinion in *Olmstead* v. *United States* (277 U.S. 438, 1928), p. 474.

[7] United States Senate, Senate Select Committee to Study Governmental Operations with Respect to Intelligence Activities, *Intelligence Activities and the Rights of Americans, Final Report, Book II*, Report 94–755, (Ninety-Fourth Congress, Second Session, April 23, 1976), pp. 290–91.

[8] United States Senate, Committee on the Judiciary, Staff of the Subcommittee on Constitutional Rights, *Army Surveillance of Civilians: A Documentary Analysis* (Ninety-Second Congress, Second Session, 1972), p. 96.

appoint officials who will be fair, and insulating the civil service from political abuse, we hope to fill the government with people of integrity. Recent history is replete with examples of abuse of power. Relying solely on
intentions is dangerous for any society, and the Founding Fathers were
careful to avoid it.

The right to be let alone is not realistic in modern society. But in a 20
world that daily intrudes upon our personal space, privacy and confidentiality in discourse remain important to the human psyche. Thoughts and
values still develop in the age-old traditions of talk, reflection, and argument, and trust and privacy are essential. Our conversations may be with
people who are at a distance, and electronic media may transmit discussions that once might have occurred over a kitchen table or on a walk to
work. But confidentiality—and the perception of confidentiality—are as
necessary for the soul of mankind as bread is for the body.

THINKING AND WRITING ABOUT PRIVACY IN THE INFORMATION AGE

QUESTIONS FOR DISCUSSION AND WRITING

1. Balaban argues that e-mail has made our lives more private—and more
   distant from the lives of others. Many people would argue the opposite—that e-mail has drawn us closer to each other. Do you think
   Balaban has proved his claim?

2. In Maremont's article a physicist proposes "complete transparency"
   (para. 22). Would this solve the problem of preserving privacy or create
   more problems? (In many schools students are under surveillance in the
   corridors and rest rooms. Should teachers and administrators also be on
   camera? Elaborate on the warrant underlying your claim.)

3. Has Lee convinced you that making medical records available to qualified personnel is a good thing? If so, what were the most effective elements of his argument?

4. Herbert wants "legislation that would spell out and guarantee a citizen's
   basic right of privacy" (para. 16). Does he suggest what legislation he
   would advise? What feelings do you think Herbert is trying to evoke in
   his readers?

5. Do you think that talk show telling should be controlled? If so, to what
   extent should it be controlled and by whom?

6. How far should employers be permitted to go in acquiring information
   about employees? Summarize Hubbartt's views on the subject. Does the
   type of work make a difference? Make a list of reasonable and unreasonable requirements. Explain the reasons for your choices.

7. What, according to Diffie and Landau, are the moral and spiritual di-
   mensions of privacy? (Many scholars have noted that three great

religions were born in the desert.) Do you feel that you have suffered from a lack of privacy in your life? If so, what were the consequences?

TOPICS FOR RESEARCH

Privacy in student dormitories

Surveillance in reducing crime

Privacy in Orwell's *Nineteen Eighty-Four*

Legal efforts to guarantee electronic privacy

TAKING THE DEBATE ONLINE

For these and additional research URLs, see www.bedfordstmartins.com/rottenberg.

- *Electronic Privacy Information Center*
  http://www.epic.org

  EPIC, a public-interest research center in Washington, D.C., includes some of the latest developments in Internet privacy issues, links to many online resources, and policy archives.

- *The Privacy Page*
  http://www.privacy.org

  This site offers more than two dozen links to privacy-related articles in several online magazines, as well as a resource archive and links to other privacy organizations.

- *Privacy Law in the USA*
  http://www.rbs2.com/privacy.htm

  Created by attorney Ronald B. Standler, this essay covers the history of privacy law, modern privacy laws, the privacy of businesses, invasions of privacy by journalists, and more.

- *The Privacy Forum*
  http://www.vortex.com/privacy.html

  The Privacy Forum includes a moderated digest for the discussion and analysis of issues relating to the general topic of privacy in the information age. Topics include a wide range of telecommunications, information, and database collecting and sharing that pertains to the privacy concerns of individuals, groups, businesses, and government.

- *Privacy International*
  http://www.privacyinternational.org

  Privacy International is a human rights group formed in 1990 as a watchdog on surveillance by governments and corporations. It is based in London and has an office in Washington, D.C. PI has conducted campaigns throughout the world on issues ranging from wiretapping and national security activities, to ID cards, video surveillance, data matching, police information systems, and medical privacy.

- *Online Privacy Alliance*
  http://www.privacyalliance.org

  The Online Privacy Alliance is a cross-industry coalition of more than eighty global companies and associations committed to promoting the privacy of individuals online.

17

Reparations for Slavery

Two hundred and forty-six years of slavery in the United States began in 1619 when slaves were first brought to America from Africa and ended in 1865 with the passage of the Thirteenth Amendment to the Constitution. Claims for reparation are not new, but they have gained momentum in recent years with the repeated introduction of legislation in Congress — so far, not acted on — to create a commission to study slavery and recommend ways to make reparations to the descendants of slaves. The remedy most often suggested is monetary compensation. As of May 2002, suits have been brought against several corporations that profited from slavery. Randall Robinson, a participant in a forthcoming suit, explains the rationale:

> When government participates in a crime against humanity, and benefits from it, then that government is under the law obliged to make the victim whole.[1]

The advocates of reparations find a precedent in payments made by Germany to Holocaust survivors and by the United States government to

[1] Tamar Lewin, "Calls for Slavery Restitution Getting Louder," *New York Times*, June 4, 2001, sec. A, p. 17.

the Japanese in America who were interned in camps during World War II. Damages paid by the tobacco companies have also been cited. Advocates insist that the legacy of slavery continues to victimize its descendants and to reward those—insurance companies, for example—who derived benefits from an economy created in large part by slavery.

Those who oppose reparations argue that the payments made in the twentieth century compensated the living who were direct victims of internment and physical suffering. The African Americans who would receive money today are several generations removed from the original victims, and those who would pay were not owners of slaves. Moreover, to pursue reparations is to perpetuate a myth of victimhood when African Americans have, in fact, made enormous progress.

As the lawsuit proceeds, it seems certain that those accused of profiting from slavery will not be limited to traditional Southern plantation owners. Long ago Harriet Beecher Stowe, the author of *Uncle Tom's Cabin,* claimed that New Englanders were equally guilty of slavery and slave trading. As if to confirm her judgment, in August 2001 two researchers reported that they had uncovered connections between Yale University and the slave trade.

The questions, both moral and practical, to be debated in the coming months are already clear: Who would be eligible for reparations for slavery? What form would reparations take? If monetary, how much would they cost? Who would pay? The problems are not only enormously complicated but also deeply emotional. Needless to say, the issue is divisive. The vast majority of whites oppose reparations; almost all African Americans support them.

Ten Reasons Why Reparations for Slavery Is a Bad Idea— and Racist Too

DAVID HOROWITZ

BEFORE READING: The title says that reparations for slavery is a bad idea. Can you think of any support for this claim?

I. There is no single group responsible for the crime of slavery.

While white Europeans conducted the trans-Atlantic slave trade, Arabs and black Africans were responsible for enslaving the ancestors of African Americans. There were 3,000 black slaveowners in the antebellum United States. Are reparations to be paid by *their* descendants too? There were white slaves in colonial America. Are their descendents going to receive payments?

II. There is no single group that benefited exclusively from slavery.

The claim for reparations is premised on the false assumption that only whites have benefited from slavery. If slave labor has created wealth for Americans, then obviously it has created wealth for black Americans as well, including the descendants of slaves. The GNP of black America makes the African American community the tenth most prosperous "nation" in the world. American blacks *on average* enjoy per capita incomes in the range of twenty to fifty *times* that of blacks living in any of the African nations from which they were kidnapped.

III. Only a minority of white Americans owned slaves, while others gave their lives to free them.

Only a tiny minority of Americans ever owned slaves. This is true even for those who lived in the antebellum South where only one white in five was a slaveholder. Why should *their* descendants owe a debt? What about the descendants of the 350,000 Union soldiers who died to free the slaves? They gave their lives. What morality would ask their descendants to pay again? If paying reparations on the basis of skin color is not racism, *what is?*

David Horowitz is editor of *Front Page* magazine and the author of several books including *Hating Whitey and Other Progressive Causes* (1999) and *The Art of Political War and Other Radical Pursuits* (2000). This article appeared as a paid advertisement in the Brown University *Daily Herald* on March 13, 2001.

IV. Most living Americans have no connection (direct or indirect) to slavery.

The two great waves of American immigration occurred after 1880 and then after 1960. What logic would require Vietnamese boat people, Russian refuseniks, Iranian refugees, Armenian victims of the Turkish persecution, Jews, Mexicans, Greeks, or Polish, Hungarian, Cambodian, and Korean victims of Communism to pay reparations to American blacks?

V. The historical precedents used to justify the reparations claim do not apply, and the claim itself is based on race not injury.

The historical precedents generally invoked to justify the reparations 5 claim are payments to Jewish survivors of the Holocaust, Japanese Americans, and African American victims of racial experiments in Tuskegee or racial outrages in Rosewood and Oklahoma City. But in each case, the recipients of reparations were the direct victims of the injustice or their immediate families. This would be the only case of reparations to people who were not immediately affected and whose sole qualification to receive reparations would be racial. During the slavery era, many blacks were free men or slaveowners themselves, yet the reparations claimants make no attempt to take this fact into account. If this is not racism, what is?

VI. The reparations argument is based on the unsubstantiated claim that all African Americans suffer from the economic consequences of slavery and discrimination.

No scientific attempt has been made to prove that living individuals have been adversely affected by a slave system that was ended nearly 150 years ago. But there is plenty of evidence that the hardships of slavery were hardships that individuals could and did overcome. The black middle class in America is a prosperous community that is now larger in absolute terms than the black underclass. Its existence suggests that present economic adversity is the result of failures of individual character rather than the lingering aftereffects of racial discrimination or a slave system that ceased to exist well over a century ago. West Indian blacks in America are also descended from slaves but their average incomes are equivalent to the average incomes of whites (and nearly 25 percent higher than the average incomes of American-born blacks). How is it that slavery adversely affected one large group of descendants but not the other? How can government be expected to decide an issue that is so subjective?

VII. The reparations claim is one more attempt to turn African Americans into victims. It sends a damaging message to the African American community and to others.

The renewed sense of grievance—which is what the claim for reparations will inevitably create—is not a constructive or helpful message for black leaders to send to their communities and to others. To focus the social passions of African Americans on what some other Americans may have done to their ancestors fifty or a hundred-and-fifty years ago is to burden them with a crippling sense of victimhood. How are the millions of nonblack refugees from tyranny and genocide who are now living in America going to receive these claims, moreover, except as demands for special treatment—an extravagant new handout that is only necessary because some blacks can't seem to locate the ladder of opportunity within reach of others, many of whom are less privileged than themselves?

VIII. Reparations to African Americans have already been paid.

Since the passage of the Civil Rights Acts and the advent of the Great Society in 1965, trillions of dollars in transfer payments have been made to African Americans in the form of welfare benefits and racial preferences (in contracts, job placements and educational admissions)—all under the rationale of redressing historic racial grievances. It is said that reparations are necessary to achieve a healing between African Americans and other Americans. If trillion-dollar restitutions and a wholesale rewriting of American law (in order to accommodate racial preferences) is not enough to achieve a "healing," *what is?*

IX. What about the debt blacks owe to America?

Slavery existed for thousands of years before the Atlantic slave trade and in all societies. But in the thousand years of slavery's existence, there never was an antislavery movement until white Anglo-Saxon Christians created one. If not for the antislavery beliefs and military power of white Englishmen and Americans, the slave trade would not have been brought to an end. If not for the sacrifices of white soldiers and a white American president who gave his life to sign the Emancipation Proclamation, blacks in America would *still* be slaves. If not for the dedication of Americans of all ethnicities and colors to a society based on the principle that all men are created equal, blacks in America would not enjoy the highest standard of living of blacks anywhere in the world and indeed one of the highest standards of living of any people in the world. They would not enjoy the greatest freedoms and the most thoroughly protected individual rights anywhere. Where is the acknowledgment of black America and its leaders for *those* gifts?

X. The reparations claim is a separatist idea that sets African Americans against the nation that gave them freedom.

Blacks were here before the *Mayflower*. Who is more American than   10 the descendants of African slaves? For the African American community to isolate itself from America is to embark on a course whose implications are troubling. Yet the African American community has had a long-running flirtation with separatists, nationalists, and the political left, who want African Americans to be no part of America's social contract. African Americans should reject this temptation.

For all America's faults, African Americans have an enormous stake in this country and its heritage. It is this heritage that is really under attack by the reparations movement. The reparations claim is one more assault on America, conducted by racial separatists and the political left. It is an attack not only on white Americans, but on all Americans—especially African Americans.

America's African American citizens are the richest and most privileged black people alive, a bounty that is a direct result of the heritage that is under assault. The American idea needs the support of its African American citizens. But African Americans also need the support of the American idea. For it is the American idea that led to the principles and created the institutions that have set African Americans—and all of us—free.

Thoughts about Restitution

RANDALL ROBINSON

BEFORE READING: Have you ever read a book or seen a movie in which the lives of slaves played a part (*Roots, Gone with the Wind, Uncle Tom's Cabin*)? What did the fictional treatment suggest about the reality of these lives?

M ore than twenty years ago, black activist James Foreman interrupted the Sunday morning worship service of the largely white Riverside Church in New York City and read a *Black Manifesto* which called upon American churches and synagogues to pay $500 million as "a beginning of the reparations due us as people who have been exploited and degraded, brutalized, killed, and persecuted." Foreman followed by promising to penalize poor response with disruptions of the churches' program agency operations. Though Foreman's tactics were broadly criticized in the mainstream press, the issue of reparations itself elicited almost no thoughtful response. This had been the case by then for nearly a century, during which divergent strains of black thought had offered a variety of reparations proposals. The American white community had turned a deaf ear almost uniformly.

Randall Robinson is president of TransAfrica Forum, an organization that provides commentary and scholarship on policy issues related to Africa and the Caribbean and that educates Americans on topics such as human rights, democracy, and global economic policy. The excerpt here comes from *The Debt: What America Owes to Blacks* (2000).

Gunnar Myrdal, a widely respected thinker, wrote of dividing up plantations into small parcels for sale to ex-slaves on long-term installment plans. He theorized that American society's failure to secure ex-slaves with an agrarian economic base had led ultimately to an entrenched segregated society, a racial caste system. But while Myrdal had seen white landowners being compensated for their land, he never once proposed recompense of any kind for the ex-slave he saw as in need of an economic base. In fact, in his book on the subject, *An American Dilemma*, Myrdal never once uses the words *reparation, restitution, indemnity,* or *compensation.*

In the early 1970s Boris Bittker, a Yale Law School professor, wrote a book, *The Case for Black Reparations,* which made the argument that slavery, Jim Crow, and a general climate of race-based discrimination in America had combined to do grievous social and economic injury to African Americans. He further argued that sustained government-sponsored violations had rendered distinctions between *de jure* and *de facto* segregation meaningless for all practical purposes. Damages, in his view, were indicated in the form of an allocation of resources to some program that could be crafted for black reparations. The book evoked little in the way of scholarly response or follow-up.

The slim volume was sent to me by an old friend who once worked for me at TransAfrica, Ibrahim Gassama, now a law professor at the University of Oregon. I had called Ibrahim in Eugene to talk over the legal landscape for crafting arguments for a claim upon the federal and state governments for restitution or reparations to the derivative victims of slavery and the racial abuse that followed in its wake.

"It's the strangest thing," Ibrahim had said to me. "We law professors 5 talk about every imaginable subject, but when the issue of reparations is raised among white professors, many of whom are otherwise liberal, it is met with silence. Clearly, there is a case to be made for this as an unpaid debt. Our claim may not be enforceable in the courts because the federal government has to agree to allow itself to be sued. In fact, this will probably have to come out of the Congress as other American reparations have. Nonetheless, there is clearly a strong case to be made. But, I tell you, the mere raising of the subject produces a deathly silence, not unlike the silence that greeted the book I'm sending you."

Derrick Bell, who was teaching at Harvard Law School while I was a student there in the late 1960s, concluded his review of Bittker's book in a way that may explain the reaction Ibrahim got from his colleagues:

> Short of a revolution, the likelihood that blacks today will obtain direct payments in compensation for their subjugation as slaves before the Emancipation Proclamation, and their exploitation as quasi-citizens since, is no better than it was in 1866, when Thaddeus Stevens recognized that his bright hope of "forty acres and a mule" for every freedman had vanished "like the baseless fabric of a vision."

If Bell is right that African Americans will not be compensated for the massive wrongs and social injuries inflicted upon them by their government, during and after slavery, then there is *no* chance that America can solve its racial problems—if solving these problems means, as I believe it must, closing the yawning economic gap between blacks and whites in this country. The gap was opened by the 246-year practice of slavery. It has been resolutely nurtured since in law and public behavior. It has now ossified. It is structural. Its framing beams are disguised only by the counterfeit manners of a hypocritical governing class.

For twelve years Nazi Germany inflicted horrors upon European Jews. And Germany paid. It paid Jews individually. It paid the state of Israel. For two and a half centuries, Europe and America inflicted unimaginable horrors upon Africa and its people. Europe not only paid nothing to Africa in compensation but followed the slave trade with the remapping of Africa for further European economic exploitation. (European governments have yet even to accede to Africa's request for the return of Africa's art treasures looted along with its natural resources during the century-long colonial era.)

While President Lincoln supported a plan during the Civil War to compensate slave owners for their loss of "property," his successor, Andrew Johnson, vetoed legislation that would have provided compensation to ex-slaves.

Under the Southern Homestead Act, ex-slaves were given six months 10 to purchase land at reasonably low rates without competition from white southerners and northern investors. But, owing to their destitution, few ex-slaves were able to take advantage of the homesteading program. The largest number that did were concentrated in Florida, numbering little more than three thousand. The soil was generally poor and unsuitable for farming purposes. In any case, the ex-slaves had no money on which to subsist for months while waiting for crops or the scantest wherewithal to purchase the most elementary farming implements. The program failed. In sum, the United States government provided no compensation to the victims of slavery. . . .

The issue here is not whether or not we can, or will, win reparations. The issue rather is whether we will fight for reparations, because we have decided for ourselves that they are our due. In 1915, into the sharp teeth of southern Jim Crow hostility, Cornelius J. Jones filed a lawsuit against the United States Department of the Treasury in an attempt to recover sixty-eight million dollars for former slaves. He argued that, through a federal tax placed on raw cotton, the federal government had benefited financially from the sale of cotton that slave labor had produced and for which the black men, women, and children who had produced the cotton had not been paid. Jones's was a straightforward proposition. The monetary value of slaves' labor, which he estimated to be sixty-eight million dollars, had been appropriated by the United States government. A debt existed. It had to be paid to the, by then, ex-slaves or their heirs.

Where was the money?

A federal appeals court held that the United States could not be sued without its consent and dismissed the so-called Cotton Tax case. But the court never addressed Cornelius J. Jones's question about the federal government's appropriation of property—the labor of blacks who had worked the cotton fields—that had never been compensated.

Let me try to drive the point home here: through keloids of suffering, through coarse veils of damaged self-belief, lost direction, misplaced compass, shit-faced resignation, racial transmutation, black people worked long, hard, killing days, years, centuries—and they were never *paid.* The value of their labor went into others' pockets—plantation owners, northern entrepreneurs, state treasuries, the United States government.

Where was the money?

Where *is* the money?

There is a debt here.

I know of no statute of limitations either legally or morally that would extinguish it. Financial quantities are nearly as indestructible as matter. Take away here, add there, interest compounding annually, over the years, over the whole of the twentieth century.

Where is the money?

Jews have asked this question of countries and banks and corporations and any who had been discovered at the end of the slimy line holding in secret places the gold, the art, the money that was the rightful property of European Jews before the Nazi terror. Jews have demanded what was their due and received a fair measure of it.

Clearly, how blacks respond to the challenge surrounding the simple demand for restitution will say a lot more about us *and do a lot more for us* than the demand itself would suggest. We would show ourselves to be responding as any normal people would to victimization were we to assert collectively in our demands for restitution that, for 246 years and with the complicity of the United States government, hundreds of millions of black people endured unimaginable cruelties—kidnapping, sale as livestock, deaths in the millions during terror-filled sea voyages, backbreaking toil, beatings, rapes, castrations, maimings, murders. We would begin a healing of our psyches were the most public case made that whole peoples lost religions, languages, customs, histories, cultures, children, mothers, fathers. It would make us more forgiving of ourselves, more self-approving, more self-understanding to see, *really see,* that on three continents and a string of islands, survivors had little choice but to piece together whole new cultures from the rubble shards of what theirs had once been. And they were never made whole. And never compensated. Not one red cent.

Left behind to gasp for self-regard in the vicious psychological wake of slavery are history's orphans played by the brave black shells of their ancient forebears, people so badly damaged that they cannot *see* the damage or how their government may have been partly, if not largely, responsible for the disabling injury that by now has come to seem normal and unattributable.

Until America's white ruling class accepts the fact that the book never closes on massive unredressed social wrongs, America can have no future as one people. Questions must be raised, to American private, as well as public, institutions. Which American families and institutions, for instance, were endowed in perpetuity by the commerce of slavery? And how do we square things with slavery's modern victims from whom all natural endowments were stolen? What is a fair measure of restitution for this, the most important of all American human rights abuses? . . .

The enslavement of black people was practiced in America for 246 years. In spite of and because of its longevity, it would not be placed on the list by either the Americans or the Europeans who had played a central role in slavery's business operations. Yet the black holocaust is far and away the most heinous human rights crime visited upon any group of people in the world over the last five hundred years.

There is oddly no inconsistency here.   25

Like slavery, other human rights crimes have resulted in the loss of millions of lives. But only slavery, with its sadistic patience, asphyxiated memory, and smothered cultures, has hulled empty a whole race of people with intergenerational efficiency. Every artifact of the victims' past cultures, every custom, every ritual, every god, every language, every trace element of a people's whole hereditary identity, wrenched from them and ground into a sharp choking dust. It is a human rights crime without parallel in the modern world. For it produces its victims *ad infinitum,* long after the active stage of the crime has ended. . . .

On April 27, 1993, under the auspices of the Organization of African Unity (a body comprised of African governments), the first pan-African conference on the subject of reparations was convened in Abuja, Nigeria. . . . The delegation at the end of their deliberations drafted a declaration that was later unanimously adopted by Africa's heads of state at a summit meeting.

I should like to quote for you parts of that declaration, for it accomplishes at least two important purposes. First, it makes known the victim's (in other words, Africa's) very public witness, which has been long suppressed. Second, it introduces what I believe to be a just and legitimate claim against the United States and the countries of western Europe for restitution:

> Recalling the establishment by the Organization of African Unity of a machinery for appraising the issue of reparations in relation to the damage done to Africa and to the Diaspora by enslavement, colonialism, and neo-colonialism; convinced that the issue of reparations is an important question requiring the united action of Africa and its Diaspora and worthy of the active support of the rest of the international community;

Fully persuaded that the damage sustained by the African peoples is not a theory of the past but is painfully manifested from Harare to Harlem and in the damaged economies of Africa and the black world from Guinea to Guyana, from Somalia to Surinam;

Aware of historic precedents in reparations varying from German payments of restitution to the Jews, to the question of compensating Japanese Americans for the injustice of internment by the Roosevelt administration in the United States during World War II;

Cognizant of the fact that compensation for injustice need not necessarily be paid entirely in capital transfer but could include service to the victims or other forms of restitution and readjustment of the relationship agreeable to both parties;

Emphasizing that an admission of guilt is a necessary step to reverse this situation;

Emphatically convinced that what matters is not the guilt but the responsibility of those states whose economic evolution once depended on slave labor and colonialism and whose forebears participated either in selling and buying Africans, or in owning them, or in colonizing them;

Convinced that the pursuit of reparations by the African peoples on the continent and in the Diaspora will be a learning experience in self-discovery and in uniting political and psychological experiences;

Calls upon the international community to recognize that there is a unique and unprecedented moral debt owed to the African peoples which has yet to be paid—the debt of compensation to the Africans as the most humiliated and exploited people of the last four centuries of modern history.

The declaration was ignored by American media. . . . I cannot say that I was surprised that American media had not covered the conference. News decision makers no doubt decided that such deliberations were unimportant, even though they had for years heaped attention upon the appeals of other groups in the world for compensation as wronged parties. As you can see, such claims were hardly unique in the world, and many had been pursued successfully, resulting in billions of dollars in compensation.

After World War I the allies made successful claims against Germany, as would Jews after World War II. The Poles also laid claims against the Germans after being used by the Nazis during the Second World War as slave labor. Japanese Americans recovered from the United States government. The Inuit recovered from the Canadian government. Aborigines recovered money and large areas of land from the Australian government. Korean women, forced into prostitution by Japan during World War II, were compensated as well.

According to Dudley Thompson, international law in this area is replete with precedents.

Not only is there a moral debt, but there is clearly established precedence in law based on the principle of unjust enrichment. In law if a party unlawfully enriches himself by wrongful acts against another, then the party so wronged is entitled to recompense. There have been some fifteen cases in which the highest tribunals including the International Court at the Hague have awarded large sums as reparations based on this law.

Only in the case of the black people have the claims, the claimants, the crime, the law, the precedents, the awful contemporary social consequences all been roundly ignored. The thinking must be that the case that cannot be substantively answered is best not acknowledged at all. Hence, the United States government and white society generally have opted to deal with this *debt* by forgetting that it is owed. The crime—246 years of an enterprise murderous both of a people and their culture—is so unprecedentedly massive that it would require some form of collective insanity not to see it and its living victims.

But still many, if not most, whites cannot or will not see it (a behavior that is accommodated by all too many uncomplaining blacks). This studied white blindness may be a modern variant of a sight condition that afflicted their slaveholding forebears who concocted something called *drapetomania,* the so-called mental disorder that slaveholders seriously believed caused blacks to run away to freedom. America accepts responsibility for little that goes wrong in the world, least of all the contemporary plight of black Americans. And until America can be made to do so, it is hard to see how we can progress significantly in our race relations.

Don't Waste Your Breath

JACK E. WHITE

BEFORE READING: Is there any point in pursuing the subject of reparations if there is little or no chance that payments will be made? If so, explain the reasons for continuing to argue the case.

The idea that the government should pay African Americans reparations to compensate for the suffering of their slave ancestors has been kicking around for as long as I can remember. It hit the front pages last week, thanks to David Horowitz, a right-wing commentator with whom I've tangled in the past. Following his familiar MO of attracting publicity

Jack E. White was the first African American journalist to become a columnist for *Time* magazine, where this article appeared on April 2, 2001. He is a national correspondent for that publication and is based in Washington, D.C.

by attacking causes espoused by civil rights leaders, Horowitz took out tendentious ads in college newspapers around the country, listing ten reasons why reparations are "a bad idea for blacks." Predictably, a rumpus ensued on campuses from Duke to Wisconsin. At Brown University in Rhode Island—whose founders include a prominent slave trader—students offended by the *Brown Daily Herald*'s decision to publish the ad seized all 4,000 copies of the paper. At the University of California, Berkeley, a forum on reparations degenerated into a shouting match after Horowitz delivered a characteristically pugnacious speech. But once they have finished railing at Horowitz, reparations supporters ought to applaud him. The fuss he started is just the kind of highly visible wrangling they need to prove that reparations is an issue worth fighting about, not a pipe dream. If an archconservative like Horowitz is so down on the idea, it must have merit.

Or does it?

I've always thought the fight for reparations was a waste of time—not out of principle, but for practical reasons. Like nearly every black person I've discussed it with, I consider the moral case for compensating African Americans for the crimes committed against their forebears during 244 years of slavery to be unassailable. I even wrote a column about how much it would take to settle our claim—$24 trillion for the pain, suffering, and unpaid labor of millions of slaves, deposited in a trust fund that would underwrite education and economic development in impoverished black areas. With funding like that, none of us would need affirmative action. Talk about freedom!

There's just one stumbling block: no matter how strong our arguments are, we'll never get white folks to pay up. Most white Americans are descended from people who immigrated here after the Civil War, so they feel no need to atone. Heck, we couldn't even persuade Bill Clinton, who is practically kin, to apologize for slavery, much less pony up any cash. Is there any reason to think George W. Bush—let alone a majority in Congress—would be more receptive?

As for going to court, we would first have to get past all sorts of legal   5 hurdles, such as the doctrine of sovereign immunity, under which the government can be sued only if it allows itself to be sued. Eventually we would bang heads with Clarence Thomas and his like-minded colleagues on the Supreme Court. I'd rather take my chances speeding on the New Jersey Turnpike in a BMW with Rodney King at the wheel and a blond hanging out the window.

My pessimism isn't shared by Charles Ogletree, a Harvard law professor who has put together a Reparations Coordinating Committee to plot possible legal strategies. Or by Randall Robinson, head of the Washington-based lobbying group TransAfrica, which led the battle to impose the economic sanctions that helped topple white rule in South Africa. Robinson, who jump-started the reparations campaign last year with his book *The Debt: What America Owes to Blacks,* predicts that once blacks are unified behind the idea, whites can be persuaded to support reparations by an appeal to their sense of justice. "I don't think among rational people that you can argue that a graver crime has occurred than slavery," Robinson told *Time*'s Elaine Rivera. "Whites will come to recognize for moral and practical reasons that reparations benefit the whole of society."

He has a lot more faith in human nature than I do.

The reparations movement, to be sure, has won some scattered victories. In 1994, Florida Governor Lawton Chiles signed a law providing $2.1 million to the survivors of a 1923 rampage by a white mob on the mostly black hamlet of Rosewood. The Oklahoma legislature is considering reparations for the survivors of a 1921 race riot in Tulsa in which as many as 300 people were murdered. California has enacted a law crafted by state senator Tom Hayden that will force insurance companies to disclose whether they issued policies that paid slave owners in the event of a slave's death.

That's great. I'm all for identifying companies that profited from slavery and paying damages to victims of racial brutality, but that's a long way from collecting the century-old debt that reparations proponents are seeking. Sure, the money from reparations would help solve present-day problems like the black education gap, AIDS, and the high incarceration rate among black youths—but we'll never see it. We've got too many real issues to deal with to waste resources on a glorious lost cause.

"The only solution I can see is to hold a series of long and costly hearings in order to put off finding a solution."

Slavery, Justice, and Reparations

ALAN MILES, JEFFREY DEKRO,
AND PEGGY DE STEFANO

BEFORE READING: What do you think are the worst legacies of slavery? Have white Americans also suffered as a result?

To the Editor:

It may be true, as Randall N. Robinson, an advocate of reparations, suggests, that the United States government participated in a crime against humanity when it sanctioned slavery. But it is also true that the United States government and its people acted decisively to end slavery, at the great cost of civil war.

If we are to pay reparations to the heirs of slaves, must we not also pay reparations to the heirs of those who lost their lives ending slavery?

Alan Miles

To the Editor:

In the Jewish tradition, repentance is never complete without the sharing of wealth to create justice.

In 1952, Germany agreed to pay $845 million in money and goods to Israel, of which $110 million went to Jewish organizations for the resettlement and rehabilitation of Jewish survivors of the Holocaust. Some viewed the agreement as an insult to the memory of six million murdered Jews, but the moral currency of Israel and the Jewish people received a tremendous boost.

Most supporters of reparations for African Americans advocate simi- 5 lar institution-building payments that would uplift all Americans. On this issue, our country is long overdue on both repentance and justice.

Jeffrey Dekro

To the Editor:

While the issue of reparations to African Americans deserves investigation and resolution, I resist the characterization offered by Professor Charles Ogletree, who said that if the idea of paying reparations for slavery makes Americans uneasy, it is probably because for most whites, it is a new idea, based on a history they do not understand (news article, June 4).

Alan Miles lives in New York. Jeffrey Dekro is president of the Shefa Fund, a foundation that organizes Jewish institutional investments in community development. Peggy De Stefano lives in Bakersfield, California. Their letters were printed in the *New York Times* on June 7, 2001.

As an Italian American who traces her roots in this country to the arrival of grandparents from Naples in the early twentieth-century wave of immigration, I may not understand the history that Professor Ogletree refers to, but I certainly understand mine. None of my ancestors were involved in slavery. As we sort through this divisive issue, let's not forget who the profiteers were.

Peggy De Stefano

Righting the Wrongs of Slavery

JIM MYERS

> BEFORE READING: If reparations payments were voted into law, what reactions do you predict would follow?

I t is odd . . . —and some might say contemptible—for white Americans to speak habitually about race in terms that suggest black Americans have now, after all this tormented history, been "given" their rights and their fair share of opportunities. It is particularly insulting that the word *given* is so often used, as if whites have kindly shared from a bounty of privileges that do not otherwise extend to black people. Apparently, this alleged generosity would mean that whites gained rights from a higher authority, but blacks gain theirs from whites.

This issue involves more than semantic detail. It highlights an aspect of white thinking that needs readjustment. First, whites did not give rights to black people, if they also maintain that rights are God given. Whites may have denied black people their rights—against God's will— but they did not give black people their rights. Got that? Next, black people were not the only Americans who gained from the ending of segregation and the opening of American life to fuller black participation. Whites also gained, and to prove this we need only imagine what the South would now be like if our apartheid system had not ended.

A segregated South would surely have become ever more socially and economically isolated. Few industries would have located—or relocated—there; the new South would never have happened. The 1996 Olympics would have been held somewhere other than Atlanta. Nor would the Braves or any other big league sports teams play in Florida, Georgia, Louisiana, or Texas. Most likely, a racially segregated South

---

Jim Myers has written for *USA Today, The Atlantic Monthly,* and other publications and is the author of *Afraid of the Dark: What Whites and Blacks Need to Know about Each Other* (2000), the source of this selection. He is a white man married to a black woman.

would have become such a social and economic backwater, shunned, and disconnected from the rest of the world, that it would have collapsed under its own inefficiencies.

You don't believe this? Consider how a racially segregated Hartsfield International Airport would function — or not function. It could never be the world's second-busiest airport operating under the requirements of segregation — two waiting rooms, two restaurants, and two sets of restrooms. It barely operates at some moments under integration; the silly demands of segregation would quickly reduce Hartsfield to dysfunction. And would black people have had to sit in the back of planes flying in and out of the South, too? What airlines would accommodate this nonsense?

So it seems obvious that if blacks have been "given" anything, whites   5 have been "given" something, too. Whites in the South have been "given" the keys to inclusion in the twentieth-century world, to their own prosperity in the "new" South, and to their membership in civilized society. Indeed, whites in the South should be thankful that the civil rights movement rescued segregationists from their own foolishness.

Then, too, the civil rights movement also produced gains for women and other minorities. So many Americans gained that it sometimes seems that the civil rights movement left its originators behind in most of the markers of economic and social well-being. For this reason, among others, some black Americans do not easily relinquish the notion that justice is still owed them, now and for the centuries of slavery, too. Some black Americans firmly believe reparations should be paid for slavery.

Reparations are not a mainstream idea; you don't hear whites suggesting it very often. You hear about it most among black people. I have friends, relatives, and associates who believe reparations would be just, as were payments to Japanese citizens and others interred during World War II. My wife thinks it would be right. (And if a check came, would I ask her to send it back?)

But it is also equally clear — especially remembering the white reaction about an *apology* for slavery — that white Americans would oppose such a plan. The concept, moreover, is loaded with complexities that would be difficult to resolve. Would black skin alone be enough to qualify? Who would be considered black? Recent black immigrants? The descendants of slaves who are now considered white?

Still, white resistance to reparations might be such that some whites would surely riot if payments were made. And what would motivate whites to pay reparations in the first place? It is almost impossible to imagine circumstance in which such legislation could pass.

If any payments were made, whites would surely consider it *their*   10 money. And bitterness over blacks being paid off with white people's money would far exceed anything seen in the O. J. Simpson case. There might be no precedent for the white anger that could ensue except the violence of the early 1900s.

Imagine the frenzy, the outrage. Journalists would report on how the money was being spent. Celebrations, parties, and other extravagances in black neighborhoods would produce more anger and outcries across the color line. White car dealers and other merchants might hold sales and "Slavery Days" specials. But black drug addicts would inevitably be found spending their reparations with drug dealers who, by the way, might also be found to have gotten payments. And how long would whites stand for that?

White bitterness could become inescapable. Whites would examine every shopping cart a black person was pushing, every car a black American was driving. Eventually, whites would claim that black people get nothing through their own initiative and ability; everything black people have—their homes, clothes, whatever—would be seen to have come from the money whites gave up.

Imagine the white fury that would ensue, if rich, superstar athletes and entertainers got reparations payments. Imagine the bitterness whites might harbor toward black neighbors and coworkers who got payments. Yet all this potential for white bitterness might make no difference if reparations enabled black Americans to separate themselves from whites, creating an independent black America. And this idea has been seized by a few white supremacists or "racialists" who suggest the reparation be paid to encourage blacks to separate themselves into a black state.

Otherwise, blacks should consider the reaction reparations might produce: whites will still be the controlling majority in the land, only now they will be a very angry majority. And would paying reparations put the issue of slavery to rest?

The problem is that we can never right the wrongs of slavery. We   15 cannot diminish it or make it more acceptable by saying it was more benign; we cannot clear the shadow, especially if we view slavery as an issue that one or the other side is trying to use for political advantage. All that will continue is an argument.

It is obvious, too, that the mere presence of black people is an effect of slavery, and this fact adds to the complexity of the moral dilemma. A wrong that cannot be undone has produced a result we must embrace as good. We cannot reject the past so totally as to wish that black Americans were not here as Americans. So if we sense that the descendants of slaves enrich and enliven our culture, as they obviously do, or if we have friends or loved ones who are black, we are in a perverse way the distant beneficiaries of slavery.

Nor can blacks so totally reject the awful realities of slavery as to wish they were now someone else, a creation, physically, culturally, and spiritually of a totally different place. But who am I to say this? My own life is grandly enriched by the presence of people who would not be here if slavery had not been. Selfishly, I would not have it any other way.

Many Billions Gone: Is It Time to Reconsider the Case for Black Reparations?

ROBERT WESTLEY

BEFORE READING: What kind of reparations payments would most benefit all Americans, both black and white?

Compensation to blacks for the injustices suffered by them must first and foremost be monetary. It must be sufficient to indicate that the United States truly wishes to make blacks whole for the losses they have endured. Sufficient, in other words, to reflect not only the extent of unjust black suffering but also the need for black economic independence from societal discrimination. No less than with the freedmen, freedom for black people today means economic freedom and security. A basis for that freedom and security can be assured through group reparations in the form of monetary compensation, along with free provision of goods and services to black communities across the nation. The guiding principle of reparations must be self-determination in every sphere of life in which blacks are currently dependent.

To this end, a private trust should be established for the benefit of all black Americans. The trust should be administered by trustees popularly elected by the intended beneficiaries of the trust. The trust should be financed by funds drawn annually from the general revenue of the United States for a period not to exceed ten years. The trust funds should be expendable on any project or pursuit aimed at the educational and economic empowerment of the trust beneficiaries to be determined on the basis of need. Any trust beneficiary should have the right to submit proposals to the trustees for the expenditure of trust funds.

The above is only a suggestion about how to use group reparations for the benefit of blacks as a whole. In the end, determining a method by which all black people can participate in their own empowerment will require a much more refined instrument than it would be appropriate for me to attempt to describe here. My own beliefs about what institutions black people need most certainly will not reflect the views of all black people, just as my belief that individual compensation is not the best way to proceed probably does not place me in the majority. Everybody who could just get a check has many reasons to believe that it would be best to get a check. On this point, I must subscribe to the wisdom that

---

Robert Westley is an associate professor at Tulane University Law School. His article first appeared in the *Boston College Law Review*, December 1998.

holds, if you give a man a loaf, you feed him for a day. It is for those blacks who survive on a "bread concern level" that the demand for reparations assumes its greatest importance.

"Well, if there's not going to be any bonus, how about some reparations?"

The Future of Slavery's Past

HENRY LOUIS GATES JR.

BEFORE READING: Can you think of any reasons why African nations should receive compensation for the benefits that Americans derived from slavery?

Near the end of the millennium, Mathieu Kérékou, president of Benin, made a pilgrimage to the Church of the Great Commission in Baltimore to apologize on his knees to African Americans for the African role in the slave trade. Then, in December 1999, during a reconciliation conference at which Africans (including Ghana's former president Jerry Rawlings), Americans, and Europeans acknowledged and

---

Henry Louis Gates Jr. is chair of the Afro-American Studies Department and director of the W. E. B. Du Bois Institute for Afro-American Research at Harvard University. His essay was published on July 29, 2001, in the *New York Times*.

apologized for their ancestors' culpability in the slave trade, Mr. Kérékou said all parties, buyers and sellers, "must confess our responsibility before history for this shameful trade." The kingdom of Dahomey, precolonial ancestor to Benin, profited handsomely from the traffic in black slaves.

The candor of Mr. Kérékou and Mr. Rawlings stands in refreshing contrast to the reluctance of Western leaders to treat honestly, or even to mention, the problem of slavery. In 1998 Bill Clinton was roundly criticized in the United States for suggesting that slavery might conceivably have been an obstacle to the development of a healthy relationship between the United States and the nations of Africa. Shocking! Did anyone think less of Pope John Paul II when he apologized for the Vatican's complicity in the Holocaust? Did anyone think less of Tony Blair when he acknowledged Britain's inaction before the Irish famines that also did so much to populate America? Of course not; those were bold and honest assertions, the kind we forlornly expect our leaders to make, all the more bracing for the fact we hear them so rarely.

At the same time, the stakes involved in such recognitions with regard to the slave trade are vastly different for African leaders than for their Western equivalents. The profits of slave trading did not lead to expansion (or diversification) of economies in Africa on any significant scale. The export of human beings from Africa led mainly to more such exporting and to a dramatic net economic loss to exporting nations as a whole. By contrast, in the West—in Europe and European colonies in America—imported slave labor, given certain political, economic, and geographical conditions, did greatly enable the building of what we now consider modern economies.

In short, many Western nations reaped large and lasting benefits from African slavery, while African nations did not. African regrets, profound indeed, do not have to be other than regrets because the results of African slave trading have, in Africa, been negative, an economic curse. The results in many parts of the West, and spectacularly in the English North American colonies, later the United States, have been economically positive. So Western regrets about slavery have a different character because here the responsibility for slavery is carried forward from past to present in the form of wealth. Slavery is embedded in American prosperity. That will not go away.

This fact materially increases the possibilities for Western countries 5 to advance the reconciliation of Africa, Europe, and the Americas—it provides a context for the call last month by Secretary General Kofi Annan of the United Nations for annual contributions of $7 billion to $10 billion to a fund uniting rich and poor nations in a global effort against AIDS. It is a magnificent goal, emphasizing prevention and treatment, linking private and public sectors, and stressing short-term goals along with the urgent need to build enduring health care systems. The fund could save millions of children around the world, but it will be aimed especially at Africa, where seven out of 10 AIDS victims live.

This is the answer that so many of us have been waiting for, from Bishop Desmond Tutu of South Africa, who believes we need a Marshall Plan against AIDS, to Americans like me who have long hoped for a truly grand gesture by the United States toward Africa. Combined with a generous package of debt relief for African nations, it would save an entire generation.

The United States originally committed $200 million to the AIDS fund, and it hiccupped another $100 million last weekend in Genoa, Italy. This is grossly out of scale with the size of the American economy and the global responsibility that America's leaders so often invoke when it is in their interest.

Our recognition of our responsibility will make or break the success of Secretary General Annan's fund. Already, other nations and organizations have given generously to the fund—and made the American contribution look paltry in comparison. The Gates Foundation alone has given $100 million. Japan and Britain have each given $200 million. The G-8 summit in Genoa offered smoke and mirrors and some imaginative relabeling of other aid commitments, but at the end of the weekend the fund was still far short of its goal.

The United States should give not less than $2 billion annually to the fund. That amounts to $1,750 for each person taken from Africa and brought in the New World. A gesture of this magnitude will be far more than an exercise in altruism. By fighting seriously against diseases that take millions of African lives a year, Americans will be protecting their own lives and drawing from Africa's hard-won expertise in a brutal struggle. More and more of our recent progress against AIDS has been based on discoveries made in Africa. On July 3, an article in the *New York Times* described the high incidence of AIDS in the Mississippi Delta— one of America's most African regions. One of the top specialists treating patients there was a young Nigerian doctor, Hamza O. Brimah.

Vigorous American participation in the United Nations effort would, 10 among other benefits, recognize the links that join all families long after the simplest link of physical presence is broken. It will allow Africans to see Americans as I know them to be—people of all colors and backgrounds who often pursue selfish ends but can be motivated to unite when extraordinary circumstances demand it. In other words, people just like Africans.

The more we come to realize these truths about ourselves, the more we will bridge gulfs that once seemed unbridgeable: the gulf between the continents and the gulf between the centuries. Slavery will not disappear from our common history, but it may be mitigated by this type of reparation. In the end, you can't relive the past, but you can do a lot to live with it. And sometimes you can a build a future while doing so.

A Childish Illusion of Justice?

SHELBY STEELE

BEFORE READING: Why would an African American object to reparations?

My father was born in the last year of the nineteenth century. His father was very likely born into slavery, though there are no official records to confirm this. Still, from family accounts, I can plausibly argue that my grandfather was born a slave.

When I tell people this, I worry that I may seem conceited, like someone claiming a connection to royalty. The extreme experience of slavery—its commitment to broken-willed servitude—was so intense a crucible that it must have taken a kind of genius to survive it. In the jaws of slavery and segregation, blacks created a life-sustaining form of worship, rituals for every human initiation from childbirth to death, a rich folk mythology, a world-famous written literature, a complete cuisine, a truth-telling comic sensibility, and, of course, some of the most glorious music the world has ever known.

Like the scion of an aristocratic family, I mention my grandfather to stand a little in the light of the black American genius. So my first objection to reparation for slavery is that it feels like selling our birthright for a pot of porridge. There is a profound esteem that comes to us from having overcome four centuries of oppression.

This esteem is an irreplaceable resource. In Richard Wright's *Black Boy,* a black elevator operator makes pocket money by letting white men kick him in the behind for a quarter. Maybe reparations are not quite this degrading, but when you trade on the past victimization of your own people, you trade honor for dollars. And this trading is only uglier when you are a mere descendant of those who suffered but nevertheless prevailed.

I believe the greatest problem black America has had over the past 5 thirty years has been precisely a faith in reparational uplift—the idea that all the injustice we endured would somehow translate into the means of uplift. We fought for welfare programs that only subsidized human inertia, for cultural approaches to education that stagnated skill development in our young, and for affirmative-action programs that removed the incentive to excellence in our best and brightest.

Today 70 percent of all black children are born out of wedlock. Sixty-eight percent of all violent crime is committed by blacks, most often

---

Shelby Steele is a research fellow at the Hoover Institution who specializes in the study of race relations, multiculturalism, and affirmative action. His most recent book is *A Dream Deferred: The Second Betrayal of Black Freedom in America* (1998). His essay here is from *Newsweek* on August 27, 2001.

against other blacks. Sixty percent of black fourth graders cannot read at grade level. And so on. When you fight for reparational uplift, you have to fit yourself into a victim-focused, protest identity that is at once angry and needy. You have to locate real transformative power in white society and then manipulate white guilt by seducing it with neediness and threatening it with anger. And you must nurture in yourself, and pass on to your own children, a sense of aggrieved entitlement that sees black success as an impossibility without the intervention of white compassion.

The above statistics come far more from this crippling sense of entitlement than from racism. And now the demand for reparations is yet another demand for white responsibility when today's problem is a failure of black responsibility.

When you don't know how to go forward, you find an excuse to go backward. You tell yourself that if you can just get a little justice for past suffering, you will feel better about the challenges you face. So you make justice a condition of your going forward. But of course, there is no justice for past suffering, and to believe there is only guarantees more suffering.

The worst enemy black America faces today is not white racism but white guilt. This is what encourages us to invent new pleas rather than busy ourselves with the hard work of development. So willing are whites to treat us with deference that they are a hard mark to pass up. The entire civil-rights establishment strategizes to keep us the wards of white guilt. If these groups had to rely on black money rather than white corporate funding, they would all go under tomorrow.

An honest black leadership would portray our victimization as only a 10 condition we faced and nurture a black identity around the ingenuity by which we overcame it. It would see reparations as a childish illusion of perfect justice. I can't be repaid for my grandfather. The point is that I owe him a great effort.

THINKING AND WRITING ABOUT REPARATIONS FOR SLAVERY

QUESTIONS FOR DISCUSSION AND WRITING

1. Horowitz's advertisement, which appeared in several college newspapers, aroused the intense anger of many students and teachers. Horowitz maintains he wrote the ad to show another point of view. Why do you think he characterizes the call for reparations as racist? Do some of his claims seem inflammatory? If so, does use of language contribute to the effect? Are any of his claims defensible? Which arguments among the other essays in this section take issue with some of Horowitz's claims?

2. Robinson speaks at length about the psychological rewards for both blacks and whites if reparations are made. What are they? Contrast the predictions of Myers, who foresees outrage and bitterness on the part of whites. Does your knowledge of history or psychology suggest which outcome is more likely?

3. Only Robinson describes the physical and mental suffering caused by slavery. To what extent do these descriptions contribute to the strength of his argument? Are they too "literary," as some critics have suggested?

4. What reason does White offer for believing that white Americans will never agree to reparations?

5. What does Myers mean when he says that the end of slavery also "gave" whites something? Is this gift the same as the reward that Robinson describes?

6. Many whites apparently oppose monetary reparations because they fear that some recipients will use the money for frivolous purposes. Do you think that Westley's proposals for distributing the money would reassure them? What specific safeguards does he suggest?

7. Gates makes a connection between slavery in America and a moral debt that Americans owe to Africans today. Explain his reasons for urging the United States to give at least $2 billion annually to a U.N. fund to prevent and treat AIDS in Africa. Do you think that Americans would find this form of reparation more acceptable than direct payments to African Americans here?

8. Although Shelby Steele is African American, his approach to reparations for slavery differs from that of most other African Americans. Point out the differences. What does he emphasize that the others do not? Explain the meaning of the title to his essay.

TOPICS FOR RESEARCH

Recent actions on reparations by the states and private corporations

Slavery and slave trading in the North

Uncle Tom's Cabin and other antislavery novels

The antislavery movement in the United States

TAKING THE DEBATE ONLINE

For these and additional research URLs, see www.bedfordstmartins.com/ rottenberg.

- *Talking Reparations with Charles Ogletree*
  http://www.africana.com/DailyArticles/index_20010828_1.htm

  This page has an interview with Charles Ogletree, a Harvard Law School professor and prominent legal theorist who is heading a legal team seeking reparations for the descendants of American slaves by suing the U.S.

government and specific American corporations and individuals who directly benefited from slavery and its aftermath of Jim Crow segregation.

- *Self-Determination Committee*
  http://www.directblackaction.com

  The Self-Determination Committee works to educate descendants of African slaves and demands reparations from the United States of America for them.

- *David A. Love: U.S. Needs to Pay Reparations for Slavery*
  http://www.progressive.org/mpbvlo00.htm

  This essay from the Progressive Media Project makes the case for reparations paid to descendants of slaves.

- *The World & I: An Apology and Reparations for Slavery?*
  http://205.178.185.71/public/2000/April/REPCON.html

  The *World & I* is a monthly publication of the *Washington Times*. This article asserts that "the fact is that the problem facing black Americans has nothing to do with a legacy of slavery and, as a result, can hardly be ameliorated by 'reparations.'"

- *Daily Policy Digest: Reparations for Slavery*
  http://www.ncpa.org/pi/internat/pd091001a.html

  This brief article by Bruce Bartlett argues against U.S. reparations to African countries, asserting that "very few Africans were kidnapped by European slave traders. The vast majority were sold into slavery by African leaders of the time" and other countries were much more deeply involved in the slave trade than was the United States.

- *Thomas Sowell: Reparations for Slavery?*
  http://www.jewishworldreview.com/cols/sowell071700.asp

  "Why then are they demanding something that they know they are not going to get? Because the demagogues themselves will benefit, even if nobody else does."

18

Responding to Terror

On the morning of September 11, 2001, three American passenger planes were seized by terrorists and flown into the two World Trade Center Towers in New York and the Pentagon outside Washington, D.C. Two hours later both towers had collapsed in a horrendous firestorm, killing more than three thousand people, including hundreds of police and firefighters who had started rescue operations. Several hundred federal employees were also killed at the Pentagon, which was severely damaged. A fourth plane, apparently headed for the White House, crashed in Pennsylvania after several passengers on board overpowered the hijackers.

The suicide hijackers were identified as Islamic fundamentalists, members of a global network known as Al-Qaeda, based in Afghanistan and led by Osama bin Laden, a wealthy Saudi Arabian exile.

The purpose of the hijackers was clear—to terrorize and punish the United States, in part for its support of the state of Israel and sanctions against Iraq but, above all, for what one writer called its "secular modernity." The expressions of modernity which have pervaded cultures around the world— freedoms of speech and religion, the full participation of women in public and social life, the open display of sexuality in popular music, television, and movies—are regarded as intolerable threats to a civilization governed by an austere interpretation of Islam. Hostility to the United States had expressed itself earlier in attacks by Islamic radicals on American targets overseas.

Early in October the United States and Great Britain launched a counterattack from the air and on the ground to destroy the Taliban, the repressive rulers of Afghanistan and protectors of bin Laden. Other governments, in Europe, the Middle East, and Asia, offered support. Two months later the Taliban had been defeated, and a new government was being formed. (At this writing the hunt for bin Laden continues. His capture, however, will not mean the extinction of terrorist cells still scattered throughout the world.)

The effects of the attacks on the United States have been deep and wide-ranging. Some of the most serious are psychological, an anxiety about what may happen next. In addition, both in the United States and in Europe governments have taken actions which might have been unimaginable a few months ago: surveillance at airports and places of public assembly, such as concert halls and ball parks; interrogation of Muslim students; closed immigration hearings; roving wiretaps. Because most Americans believe that the terrorist attacks were acts of war and that further attacks, perhaps biological or chemical, are not only possible but probable, there has been little protest against these measures.

Nevertheless, objections have been raised to racial and ethnic profiling (in this case, of Arabs), more restrictive immigration policies, detentions without trial, and, especially, to military tribunals for terrorists who may be brought to trial. The critics of military justice argue that the attacks were crimes, not acts of war, a crucial distinction. If bin Laden is guilty of a *crime*, he must be tried not in a military court but in a civil court before a jury of civilians, with all the rights accorded a citizen of the United States.

However these acts of hatred are defined, one thing seems certain: We must sacrifice some of our freedoms in defense of our lives. "One of the most important decisions the nation faces," writes an American historian, "is how we balance the security measures we need to forestall future attacks with America's much-cherished doctrine of civil liberties."[1]

---

[1] Jay Winik, "Security Comes before Liberty," *Wall Street Journal*, October 23, 2001, p. A26.

The Case for Rage and Retribution

LANCE MORROW

BEFORE READING: What were your feelings when you first heard of the September 11 attacks? Have these feelings changed? If so, in what way?

For once, let's have no "grief counselors" standing by with banal consolations, as if the purpose, in the midst of all this, were merely to make everyone feel better as quickly as possible. We shouldn't feel better.

For once, let's have no fatuous rhetoric about "healing." Healing is inappropriate now, and dangerous. There will be time later for the tears of misfortune.

A day cannot live in infamy without the nourishment of rage. Let's have rage. What's needed is a unified, unifying, Pearl Harbor sort of purple American fury—a ruthless indignation that doesn't leak away in a week or two, wandering off into Prozac-induced forgetfulness or into the next media sensation (O.J. . . . Elián . . . Chandra . . .) or into a corruptly thoughtful relativism (as has happened in the recent past, when, for example, you might hear someone say, "Terrible what he did, of course, but, you know, the Unabomber does have a point, doesn't he, about modern technology?").

Let America explore the rich reciprocal possibilities of the fatwa. A policy of focused brutality does not come easily to a self-conscious, self-indulgent, contradictory, diverse, humane nation with a short attention span. America needs to relearn a lost discipline, self-confident relentlessness—and to relearn why human nature has equipped us all with a weapon (abhorred in decent peacetime societies) called hatred.

As the bodies are counted, into the thousands and thousands, hatred 5 will not, I think, be a difficult emotion to summon. Is the medicine too strong? Call it, rather, a wholesome and intelligent enmity—the sort that impels even such a prosperous, messily tolerant organism as America to act. Anyone who does not loathe the people who did these things, and the people who cheer them on, is too philosophical for decent company.

It's a practical matter, anyway. In war, enemies are enemies. You find them and put them out of business, on the sound principle that that's what they are trying to do to you. If what happened on Tuesday does not give Americans the political will needed to exterminate men like Osama bin Laden and those who conspire with them in evil mischief, then nothing ever will, and we are in for a procession of black Tuesdays.

Lance Morrow has been covering national affairs for *Time* magazine since 1965. This column appeared the day after the September 11, 2001, terrorist attacks.

This was terrorism brought to near perfection as a dramatic form. Never has the evil business had such production values. Normally, the audience sees only the smoking aftermath—the blown-up embassy, the ruined barracks, the ship with a blackened hole at the waterline. This time the first plane striking the first tower acted as a shill. It alerted the media, brought cameras to the scene so that they might be set up to record the vivid surreal bloom of the second strike ("Am I seeing this?") and then—could they be such engineering geniuses, so deft at demolition?—the catastrophic collapse of the two towers, one after the other, and a sequence of panic in the streets that might have been shot for a remake of *The War of the Worlds* or for *Independence Day*. Evil possesses an instinct for theater, which is why, in an era of gaudy and gifted media, evil may vastly magnify its damage by the power of horrific images.

It is important not to be transfixed. The police screamed to the people running from the towers, "Don't look back!"—a biblical warning against the power of the image. Terrorism is sometimes described (in a frustrated, oh-the-burdens-of-great-power tone of voice) as "asymmetrical warfare." So what? Most of history is a pageant of asymmetries. It is mostly the asymmetries that cause history to happen—an obscure Schickelgruber nearly destroys Europe; a mere atom, artfully diddled, incinerates a city. Elegant perplexity puts too much emphasis on the "asymmetrical" side of the phrase and not enough on the fact that it is, indeed, real warfare. Asymmetry is a concept. War is, as we see, blood and death.

It is not a bad idea to repeat a line from the nineteenth-century French anarchist thinker Pierre-Joseph Proudhon: "The fecundity of the unexpected far exceeds the prudence of statesmen." America, in the spasms of a few hours, became a changed country. It turned the corner, at last, out of the 1990s. The menu of American priorities was rearranged. The presidency of George W. Bush begins now. What seemed important a few days ago (in the media, at least) became instantly trivial. If Gary Condit is mentioned once in the next six months on cable television, I will be astonished.

During World War II, John Kennedy wrote home to his parents from 10 the Pacific. He remarked that Americans are at their best during very good times or very bad times; the in-between periods, he thought, cause them trouble. I'm not sure that is true. Good times sometimes have a tendency to make Americans squalid. The worst times, as we see, separate the civilized of the world from the uncivilized. This is the moment of clarity. Let the civilized toughen up, and let the uncivilized take their chances in the game they started.

Military Tribunals Are Necessary in Times of War

DOUGLAS W. KMIEC

BEFORE READING: Should the September 11, 2001, attacks be defined as acts of war or as crimes committed by individuals? How did you arrive at your definition?

Having successfully overseen the rout of the Taliban from Kabul, President Bush has now directed the creation of special military tribunals. These courts would try foreign nationals the president considers to be part of the terrorist group al Qaeda and others who aid and abet terrorists, as well as those who knowingly harbor such people. Predictably, the American Civil Liberties Union has rushed to decry this logical exercise of war powers as "deeply disturbing" and in contravention of ideas "central to our democracy." In fact, the president's order is well-grounded in constitutional text, statute, and past practice and is more likely to preserve civil liberty than undermine it.

Terrorism is not ordinary crime within an ordered society. It is the indiscriminate killing of innocents and the destruction of property. As such, it is the quintessential crime against humanity; it is not a social or cultural dysfunction capable of rehabilitation or rectification by means of ordinary law enforcement and prosecution.

Past experience with trying terrorist acts within the regular criminal justice system has been unsatisfactory largely because standards of proof and rules of evidence appropriate to peacetime are ill-suited to the effective punishment and deterrence of terrorism. The presumption of innocence, the requirement of proof beyond reasonable doubt, Miranda rights, and privileges against self-incrimination all make sense in the delicate context of the balance between a citizen's rights and society's interests in protecting its physical and material security. However, when Congress has authorized a president to respond with all necessary force to events like those of September 11 and "any future act" of international terrorism, the state of war requires the balance to be different.

The standard applied in military tribunals is simple and pragmatic. If those perpetrating war crimes are not disposed of upon the field of battle, military tribunals may be empowered to ascertain with evidence that is "probative to a reasonable man"—that is, more probable than not—that a given person or organization is guilty of what Sir Edward Coke called, centuries ago, a "crime committed by the enemies of mankind."

Douglas W. Kmiec is dean of the Catholic University of America. Formerly, he was a legal counsel in the Reagan administration. His article comes from the *Wall Street Journal* on November 15, 2001.

This will mean that neither the hearsay rule (which has bedeviled prior 5 terrorist trials in federal courts because of the disappearance, or inaccessibility, of direct witnesses) nor ill-fitting exclusionary rules that have no deterrence-based relevance to this setting would derail the admission of evidence obtained under the interrogation authorized by the president. The president has specifically provided as well that the interrogation be humane, and "without any adverse distinction based on race, color, religion, gender, birth, wealth, or similar criteria." ACLU charges of "racial and ethnic profiling" thus find no support within the scope of the directive. As in past cases, the actual composition and procedures of these tribunals—which can sit either in the United States or elsewhere—are left to be determined by the secretary of defense and military commanders subordinate to the president, subject, however, to the provision of a "full and fair trial," with conviction and sentencing needing two-thirds of the tribunal.

While the rules and regulations are yet to come, we can get some inkling of their content by examining those promulgated by military commanders, such as Dwight Eisenhower in the European theater of World War II and Douglas MacArthur in the Pacific. And while there are subtle differences, both commanders specified greater evidentiary latitude, including allowing secondary evidence where witnesses are unavailable, and copies of documents and confessions to be admitted without undue delay.

Is all this just an elaborate denial of due process and an example of sham proceedings? Hardly. The use of military tribunals was commonplace in World War II, and those appearing before them were both exonerated and executed. The same is likely now. The "fair trial" mandated by the Bush order should become reality simply because the disciplined, legally trained military personnel sitting in judgment are likely to be evenhanded. In contrast, consider how difficult it would be to find a jury capable of being dispassionate about the mass murder at the World Trade Center and the Pentagon.

Most importantly, military tribunals have the virtue of allowing evidence to be considered without forcing the disclosure of classified information in open court or the identification of intelligence personnel and sources. And here, the point of military tribunals, and their appropriateness, becomes plain. These bodies are not primarily for purposes of punishment. They are extensions of the military campaign and of the efforts of the president to "protect the United States and its citizens, and for the effective conduct of military operations and prevention of terrorist attacks."

Perhaps that is why the creation of these tribunals in wartime—for the trial of war crimes—is so well fixed and unassailable in constitutional precedent. The Supreme Court does not sit in ultimate review of the tribunal's work, beyond assuring itself that the commission was properly impaneled. It is also why the jurisdiction of these bodies depends upon Congress's war powers and on the individual who, with

however much reluctance he must surely have, acts as our commander-
in-chief.

"I thought I'd never laugh again. Then I saw your jacket."

Poking Holes in the Constitution

ROBERT KUTTNER

BEFORE READING: Timothy McVeigh, an American terrorist whose truck-bomb destroyed the Oklahoma City federal building, was tried in a civilian court. Should foreign
terrorists be accorded the same rights?

The biggest menace to the personal security of Americans may not be
terrorism but government's response to it.

The administration has already rammed through an antiterrorism
bill that allows normal due process and privacy protections to be waived
if a prosecutor thinks some potential suspect has some remote connection to terrorism. Now the president has decided that terrorism suspects

Robert Kuttner is coeditor of the *American Prospect.* His column appears regularly in the
Boston Globe, where this selection was published on November 26, 2001.

can be tried before special military tribunals, which do away with the inconvenience of constitutional niceties.

The CIA, which is not supposed to use third-degree tactics itself, has been collaborating with foreign governments all too willing to use torture, such as Egypt and Albania. The CIA has knowingly turned terrorism suspects over to the agents of such governments to keep its own hands nominally clean.

Here at home, at least a thousand legal foreign residents have been rounded up and detained, often without formal charges being lodged against them. This would be illegal for U.S. citizens. But noncitizens, even legal permanent resident aliens, are said to be in America at the government's sufferance. No ordinary due process for them.

Law-abiding Americans are supposed to be reassured. We, after all, 5 are not terrorists. These extraordinary measures are directed at them, not at us. But these waivers of constitutional rights tend not to stay bottled up. The Constitution was written not to protect the guilty but to protect the innocent. Hundreds of entirely innocent bystanders have already been rounded up in FBI and INS[1] dragnets.

History shows that special Star Chamber[2] tactics justified by war or cold war conditions slop over and harm ordinary people because zealous police and prosecutors often overreach their bounds and often make mistakes. History also shows that even in the United States and other democracies, police agencies often yield to the temptation of using third-degree tactics unless they are restrained by laws and judges.

Even before September 11, government was eroding a variety of rights in the name of fighting crime, drugs, or terror. Legal foreign residents lost due-process protections under Clinton-era legislation. Both parties have supported summary justice measures allowing the seizure of property of drug suspects, with the police department getting to keep the loot.

Remember the Rodney King beatings? Until the rulings of the Warren Supreme Court protecting the rights of criminal suspects, beatings and coerced confessions, often false confessions, were common. During the cold war, the FBI and CIA mounted secret operations to disrupt constitutionally protected dissent, much of it surrounding the Vietnam War.

There is no evidence that any of this made us any more secure as a nation. Fifteen years after the United States ignominiously withdrew from Vietnam, supposedly a crucial domino in the battle against world communism, the Soviet Union collapsed largely from internal rot.

Nobody has shown why constitutional criminal justice is powerless 10 to investigate and bring to justice people accused of terrorist activities. One stated concern—that public trials might expose intelligence sources

---

[1] Immigration and Naturalization Service.—ED.
[2] A seventeenth-century English court of law that arbitrarily enforced the king's will. Now used to mean any secret and arbitrary legal proceeding.—ED.

and police methods—speaks volumes. The framers of the Constitution were all too familiar with police methods. They lived in the era of the Star Chamber in England.

That's why they mandated speedy and public trials before independent judges. Even without special legislation, current law allows for sealed testimony in special circumstances to be divulged to a judge but not to be made public. Narrowly drawn extensions of this process can be used in cases when a judge—not a prosecutor—certifies that probable cause exists to believe that a terrorist crime has been committed.

The other stated concern—that putting terrorists on trial would risk making martyrs of them—is more a statement of our own insecurity in the court of world public opinion. The Israelis did not flinch from putting Adolf Eichmann on trial for fear of fanning the flames of anti-Semitism, nor did the United States hesitate to try Nazis at Nuremberg. If an international criminal court is good enough for Slobodan Milosevic, it should be good enough for Osama bin Laden.

Police and prosecutors, in democracies and dictatorships alike, tend to see constitutional strictures as inconveniences. That's why criminal justice and the protection of individual rights are too important to be left to the sole discretion of police agencies.

Americans have surmounted worse challenges than this one without giving up liberties. It is hard to know which is more frightening—the administration's wish list of extraconstitutional shortcuts or the resounding lack of opposition from most members of Congress. Long after al Qaeda and bin Laden are defeated, Americans will suffer from this rush to militarize justice.

Terror on Trial: An American Test

TAD BLAIR, JONATHAN SHERWOOD,
ALLEN BODNER, RICHARD W. LYMAN,
AND ERIK A. LUCKEY

BEFORE READING: Can an accused foreign terrorist receive a fair trial in the United States in either a civil or military court?

To the Editor:
President Bush defends the use of military tribunals for trying non-citizens by arguing that "we must not let foreign enemies use the forums of liberty to destroy liberty itself." But by repealing civil liberties in response to terror, isn't the administration doing exactly that?

Terrorists can kill Americans, but they can make only idle threats against our freedom. Leave it to our own government to deliver the knockout punch.

Tad Blair

To the Editor:
Many Americans are complaining that the military tribunals for terrorists would be unfair ("President Defends Military Tribunals in Terrorist Cases," front page, November 30). It's time for these people to wake up.

This is not some storybook we live in. These terrorists do not care at all for our civil liberties or our lives, and they would probably just as soon kill any American trying to stand up for their rights. The idea that we should be fair to them is utopian at best and foolish at worst.

These people view themselves as soldiers at war, so let's treat them as 5
such. It would be a terrible shame if a terrorist were on trial in a civilian court and got off on some technicality. It is better to put these people away for good. I couldn't care less about their "rights." Remember, they don't care about ours.

Jonathan Sherwood

To the Editor:
In "Martial Justice, Full and Fair" (Op-Ed, November 30), Alberto R. Gonzales, President Bush's counsel, tries to justify the executive order establishing military tribunals for accused terrorists. But the very language he uses subverts the fairness element and illustrates the potential dangers inherent in this process.

Mr. Gonzales describes the military commissions as being established to "try enemy belligerents who commit war crimes" and the executive

---

These letters appeared in the December 1, 2001, *New York Times*.

order as covering only "foreign war criminals." The order itself speaks to individuals *alleged* to have committed offenses, but Mr. Gonzales seems to have largely assumed the guilt of the defendants even as he extols the fairness of the process.

Allen Bodner

To the Editor:

In "Wake Up, America," by Anthony Lewis (column, November 30), a former deputy attorney general, George J. Terwilliger III, is quoted as saying that the authors of the September 11 outrages "don't deserve constitutional protection." But constitutional protection is not some sort of reward for good conduct. When this protection is reserved for those thought to be deserving, it ceases to be real protection. We lose our constitutional rights *after* it has been established by the courts that we no longer deserve them, not before.

American society is strengthened by our constitutional protections. To forfeit them weakens our social fabric and damages our standing in the world when we can least afford it.

Richard W. Lyman

The writer is president emeritus of Stanford University.

To the Editor:

Anthony Lewis (column, November 30) argues that citizens do not 10 understand the "dangerous breadth" of President Bush's executive order empowering military tribunals to dispense justice to noncitizens. What seems more dangerous to me is the strange notion that protection under the Constitution somehow extends to noncitizens.

That sort of logic leads one to conclude that every person on earth is both bound and protected by the Constitution. In addition to devaluing United States citizenship, that argument makes virtually all our military actions illegal and threatens our national sovereignty.

Erik A. Luckey

Security versus Civil Liberties

RICHARD A. POSNER

BEFORE READING: Based on the state of national safety today, do you think the government has overreacted — gone too far — in restricting some of our liberties?

In the wake of the September 11 terrorist attacks have come many proposals for tightening security; some measures to that end have already been taken. Civil libertarians are troubled. They fear that concerns about national security will lead to an erosion of civil liberties. They offer historical examples of supposed overreactions to threats to national security. They treat our existing civil liberties—freedom of the press, protections of privacy and of the rights of criminal suspects, and the rest—as sacrosanct, insisting that the battle against international terrorism accommodate itself to them.

I consider this a profoundly mistaken approach to the question of balancing liberty and security. The basic mistake is the prioritizing of liberty. It is a mistake about law and a mistake about history. Let me begin with law. What we take to be our civil liberties—for example, immunity from arrest except upon probable cause to believe we've committed a crime and from prosecution for violating a criminal statute enacted after we committed the act that violates it—were made legal rights by the Constitution and other enactments. The other enactments can be changed relatively easily, by amendatory legislation. Amending the Constitution is much more difficult. In recognition of this the Framers left most of the constitutional provisions that confer rights pretty vague. The courts have made them definite.

Concretely, the scope of these rights has been determined, through an interaction of constitutional text and subsequent judicial interpretation, by a weighing of competing interests. I'll call them the public-safety interest and the liberty interest. Neither, in my view, has priority. They are both important, and their relative importance changes from time to time and from situation to situation. The safer the nation feels, the more weight judges will be willing to give to the liberty interest. The greater the threat that an activity poses to the nation's safety, the stronger will the grounds seem for seeking to repress that activity, even at some cost to liberty. This fluid approach is only common sense.

Supreme Court Justice Robert Jackson gave it vivid expression many years ago when he said, in dissenting from a free-speech decision he thought doctrinaire, that the Bill of Rights should not be made into a

---

Richard A. Posner, a former professor of law at the University of Chicago, is a judge of the U.S. Court of Appeals. *The Atlantic Monthly* published his article in December 2001.

suicide pact. It was not intended to be such, and the present contours of the rights that it confers, having been shaped far more by judicial inter- pretation than by the literal text (which doesn't define such critical terms as "due process of law" and "unreasonable" arrests and searches), are alterable in response to changing threats to national security.

If it is true, therefore, as it appears to be at this writing, that the events of September 11 have revealed the United States to be in much greater jeopardy from international terrorism than had previously been believed—have revealed it to be threatened by a diffuse, shadowy enemy that must be fought with police measures as well as military force—it stands to reason that our civil liberties will be curtailed. They *should* be curtailed, to the extent that the benefits in greater security outweigh the costs in reduced liberty. All that can reasonably be asked of the respon- sible legislative and judicial officials is that they weigh the costs as care- fully as the benefits.

It will be argued that the lesson of history is that officials habitually exaggerate dangers to the nation's security. But the lesson of history is the opposite. It is because officials have repeatedly and disastrously un- derestimated these dangers that our history is as violent as it is. Consider such underestimated dangers as that of secession, which led to the Civil War, of a Japanese attack on the United States, which led to the disaster at Pearl Harbor, of Soviet espionage in the 1940s, which accelerated the Soviet Union's acquisition of nuclear weapons and emboldened Stalin to encourage North Korea's invasion of South Korea; of the installation of Soviet missiles in Cuba, which precipitated the Cuban missile crisis; of political assassinations and outbreaks of urban violence in the 1960s; of the Tet Offensive of 1968; of the Iranian revolution of 1979 and the subsequent taking of American diplomats as hostages; and, for that matter, of the events of September 11.

It is true that when we are surprised and hurt, we tend to overreact— but only with the benefit of hindsight can a reaction be separated into its proper and excess layers. In hindsight we know that interning Japanese Americans did not shorten World War II. But was this known at the time? If not, shouldn't the Army have erred on the side of caution, as it did? Even today we cannot say with any assurance that Abraham Lincoln was wrong to suspend habeas corpus during the Civil War, as he did on several occasions, even though the Constitution is clear that only Con- gress can suspend this right. (Another of Lincoln's wartime measures, the Emancipation Proclamation, may also have been unconstitutional.) But Lincoln would have been wrong to cancel the 1864 presidential election, as some urged: by November of 1864 the North was close to victory, and canceling the election would have created a more dangerous precedent than the wartime suspension of habeas corpus. This last example shows that civil liberties remain part of the balance even in the most dangerous of times, and even though their relative weight must then be less.

Lincoln's unconstitutional acts during the Civil War show that even legality must sometimes be sacrificed for other values. We are a nation under law, but first we are a nation. I want to emphasize something else, however: the malleability of law, its pragmatic rather than dogmatic character. The law is not absolute, and the slogan *"Fiat iustitia ruat caelum"* ("Let justice be done though the heavens fall") is dangerous nonsense. The law is a human creation rather than a divine gift, a tool of government rather than a mandarin mystery. It is an instrument for promoting social welfare, and as the conditions essential to that welfare change, so must it change.

Civil libertarians today are missing something else—the opportunity to challenge other public-safety concerns that impair civil liberties. I have particularly in mind the war on drugs. The sale of illegal drugs is a "victimless" crime in the special but important sense that it is a consensual activity. Usually there is no complaining witness, so in order to bring the criminals to justice the police have to rely heavily on paid informants (often highly paid and often highly unsavory), undercover agents, wiretaps and other forms of electronic surveillance, elaborate sting operations, the infiltration of suspect organizations, random searches, and monitoring of airports and highways, the "profiling" of likely suspects on the basis of ethnic or racial identity or national origin, compulsory drug tests, and other intrusive methods that put pressure on civil liberties. The war on drugs has been a big flop; moreover, in light of what September 11 has taught us about the gravity of the terrorist threat to the United States, it becomes hard to take entirely seriously the threat to the nation that drug use is said to pose. Perhaps it is time to redirect law-enforcement resources from the investigation and apprehension of drug dealers to the investigation and apprehension of international terrorists. By doing so we may be able to minimize the net decrease in our civil liberties that the events of September 11 have made inevitable.

Don't Sacrifice Our Liberties

CAIT MURPHY

BEFORE READING: Suppose that, in the struggle against terrorism, you had to sacrifice some privacy — of your e-mail, your locker, your telephone conversations, among others. Would you object?

I was living in London in 1994, when the Irish Republican Army declared its first ceasefire. Naturally, after twenty-five years of intermittent outrages, people were wary of the promise. For weeks after the announcement, life was not significantly different. People still looked at you incredulously if you asked them to watch your bag. Libraries still kept their book-return slots closed; they were vulnerable to bomb attacks. Only after months with no new atrocities did daily life grow easier and more pleasant.

The following year I was visiting Paris, whose rail and subway stations had for the past few months been devastated by terrorist hits. All the garbage bins, which had been used to hide bombs, were shuttered. Parisians with litter placed it neatly under the bins, the mounds of rubbish making a distinctive and smelly trail. A small thing, perhaps, but disturbing to a people and country that take pride in their public places.

Now it is America's turn to react to terrorism. In one blow, the United States has almost certainly suffered more casualties than Northern Ireland has experienced in thirty-two years of its wretched troubles. This was not, of course, only an attack on Americans. Some three million New Yorkers were born in another country, and the World Trade Center was as polyglot as any place on earth. Whoever the terrorists are, their slaughter of innocents is certain to have included people of their own race, religion, or nation.

There are two challenges now. One is to deliver us from the evil people who did this. The second is subtler. It is to not change our society in ways that will ultimately damage it.

There will, no question, be some loss of personal liberty in the wake 5 of this tragedy. Air travel will never be the same; security checks will be more stringent, time-consuming, and invasive. That is a price we will pay every time we board a plane or perhaps even enter an airport.

But let's carefully consider such costs before we incur them. America has a bad habit of taking a tragedy, like Columbine, and then going overboard to combat it, such as instituting zero-tolerance policies for nursery school kids roughhousing. There is going to be a temptation, in the wake

---

Cait Murphy is a journalist who has written for *The Economist* and *The Atlantic Monthly*. This opinion piece was printed in the October 2001 issue of *Fortune*.

of this disaster, to treat every prominent building or area as a fortress under permanent, dire threat. It is easy enough to imagine pressure for, say, metal detectors in state parks, national identity cards, limiting the public's access to official places, bulletproof shields in post offices, or extraordinary powers for the police or military. But turning America into an armed and fearful camp in response to the events of September 11 would simply give those who wish us ill another victory.

The price of liberty, the saying goes, is eternal vigilance. That surely means vigilance against the kind of people who would fly planes into crowded skyscrapers. But it also means vigilance against exercising excessive zeal in our own determination not to let such terror happen again.

The human cost of this terrorism is unfathomable; the economic cost, incalculable. But we do have the power, and the responsibility, to determine the cost to our freedom.

War at Home

DENIS JOHNSON

BEFORE READING: Do you believe that the United States bears some responsibility for the terrorist attacks?

Several times during the 1990s I did some reporting from what we generally call trouble spots, and witnessing the almost total devastation of some of these places (Somalia, Afghanistan, the southern Philippines, Liberia) had me wondering if I would ever see such trouble in my own country: if I would ever feel it necessary to stay close to the radio or television; if I would sleep with the window wide open in order to hear the approach of the engines of war or to smell the smoke of approaching fires or to stay aware of the movements of emergency teams coping with the latest enormity; if I would one day see American ground heaped with the ruins of war; if I would ever hear Americans saying, "They're attacking the Capitol! The Pentagon! The White House!"; if I would stand in the midst of an American crowd witnessing the kind of destruction that can be born of the wickedness of the human imagination, or turn to examine American faces a few seconds after their eyes had taken it in; if I would one day see American streets choked with people who don't know exactly where they're going but don't feel safe where they are; and if I would someday feel uncontrollably grateful to be able to get my laundry done and to find simple commerce persisting in spite of madness. I wondered if the wars I'd gone looking for would someday come looking for us.

Traveling in the Third World, I've found that to be an American sometimes means to be wondrously celebrated, to excite a deep, instantaneous loyalty in complete strangers. In the southern Philippines, a small delegation headed by a village captain once asked that I take steps to have their clan and their collection of two dozen huts placed under the protection of the United States. Later, in the same region, a teenage Islamic separatist guerrilla among a group I'd been staying with begged me to adopt him and take him to America. In Afghanistan, I encountered men who, within minutes of meeting me, offered to leave their own worried families and stay by my side as long as I required it, men who found medicine somewhere in the ruins of Kabul for me when I needed it, and who never asked for anything back—all simply because I was American.

Denis Johnson writes poetry, novels, and short stories. His books include the poetry collections *The Man among the Seals* and *Inner Weather* and the novel *Angels*. He is also a correspondent for *The New Yorker,* where this article was printed on September 24, 2001; *Esquire,* and other magazines.

On the other hand, I think we sense—but don't care always to apprehend—the reality that some people hate America. To many suffering souls, we must seem incomprehensibly aloof and self-centered, or worse. For nearly a century, war has rolled lopsidedly over the world, crushing the innocent in their homes. For half that century, the United States has been seen, by some people as keeping the destruction rolling without getting too much in the way of it—has been seen, by some people, to lurk behind it. And those people hate us. The acts of terror against this country—the hijackings, the kidnappings, the bombings of our airplanes and barracks and embassies overseas, and now these mass atrocities on our own soil—tell us how much they hate us. They hate us as people hate a bad God, and they'll kill themselves to hurt us.

On Thursday, as I write in New York City, which I happened to be visiting at the time of the attack, the wind has shifted, and a sour electrical smoke travels up the canyons between the tall buildings. I have now seen two days of war in the biggest city in America. But imagine a succession of such days stretching into years—years in which explosions bring down all the great buildings, until the last one goes, or until bothering to bring the last one down is just a waste of ammunition. Imagine the people who have already seen years like these turn into decades—imagine their brief lifetimes made up only of days like these we've just seen in New York.

It's Not All America's Fault

HAZEM SAGHIYEH

BEFORE READING: What do you think are the distinguishing characteristics of modern societies such as the United States and western Europe?

Millions of Arabs and Muslims hold U.S. foreign policy responsible for the calamity of September 11. Is it? The answer is: yes, but also no.

The yes has been widely articulated. Yes, there was and is a deep sense of frustration because of the bias shown by the United States to Israel and because of America's cruel insistence on continued sanctions against Iraq. Plus, for historical reasons, Muslims and Arabs can always feel bitterness toward America: in the early 1950s, the CIA helped topple the elected government of Iran to reinstall the Shah. In the late 1980s, the United States left Afghanistan very messy after using it as a battleground against the Soviets.

Hazem Saghiyeh is a journalist for London's Arabic newspaper *al-Hayat*. This article was printed in *Time* on October 15, 2001.

But there is a no here as well, which hasn't been voiced much in the Arab world. Certainly the international community has a responsibility to address the political grievances of Muslim societies, especially the Palestinian question, and try to reduce the poverty and inequality endemic in most of the Middle East. But no effort at redress by the West will work unless the Muslim world as a whole rethinks its relation to modernity. Why is it that Africa, though poorer and more hurt by the West, did not create a terrorist phenomenon? Why did Latin America export its "purest" terrorist product, Carlos the Jackal, to the Middle East?

The reasons lie in the fact that we in the Muslim world have not been able to overcome the trauma caused by colonialism. We could not open up to the tools that modernity suggested, for the simple reason that they were introduced by way of colonialism. Our oil wealth allowed us to import the most expensive consumer commodities, but we could not overcome our suspicions of outside political and ideological goods: democracy, secularism, the state of law, the principle of rights, and, above all, the concept of the nation-state, which was seen as a conspiracy to fragment our old empire.

A certain fixation on the past took hold alongside a deep uneasiness   5
with the present. Religious reform did not take off. The Muhammad Abdu project to renew Islam the way Martin Luther reformed Christianity ended at the turn of the nineteenth century in disarray, opening the way to more extreme versions of the religion. Efforts to modernize the Arab language and bridge the gap between the spoken vernaculars and the written classical did not materialize. Public spheres—such as a free press, trade unions, civil societies—for debating matters related to the common good were not established. And most important, Muslims and Arabs never resolved the question of political legitimacy. They failed to develop workable models, which has made every attempt at political change long and dangerous.

The question of legitimacy is flagrant in Iran, where President Mohammed Khatami and his supporters won all the popular elections but could not win real power, which instead resides with Ayatullah Ali Khamemei. In Syria it seems there is no way out of Hafez Assad's authoritarian legacy. If Saddam Hussein finally falls from power in Iraq, heaven knows who might replace him, so ruthless has he been in suppressing rivals. Yasser Arafat's lack of a mandate has made him unable to make historic decisions in the peace process, so he instead alternates between directions.

The weak legitimacy of local regimes leaves the most essential themes of social and political destiny hanging, creating a vacuum to be filled only by populist politicians and extremist groups, by wars and civil wars. By failing to establish effective polities, we have perpetuated our impotence, making it all the harder to catch up with the West. Lebanon, the only pluralistic example in the Arab world, was destroyed by its own religious sects and its neighbors. Among the states in the area that don't work or barely do so are Iraq, Sudan, Pakistan, Algeria, and Lebanon.

Arab intellectuals, who ought to encourage change, have largely failed in that role. For the most part, they did not detach themselves from the tribal tradition of defending "our" causes in the face of the "enemy." Their priority has not been to criticize the incredible shortcomings that they live with. They tend ceaselessly to highlight their "oneness." Thus they help stereotype themselves before being stereotyped by any enemy. It is in this particular history and this particular culture, and not in any alleged clash of civilizations, that the roots of our wretched present lie.

THINKING AND WRITING ABOUT RESPONDING TO TERROR

QUESTIONS FOR DISCUSSION AND WRITING

1. Morrow uses references that you may need to look up: "a day . . . in infamy" (para. 3); "the Unabomber" (para. 3); "fatwa" (para. 4); "Schickelgruber" (para. 8); "Gary Condit" (para. 9). He expresses "ruthless indignation" (para. 3) and advocates the cultivation of hatred. What warrant underlies his claim? Do you think his argument would be more — or less — persuasive if the tone were more moderate?

2. If you aren't already familiar with some legal terms from reading crime novels or viewing law and police dramas on TV, look up the following terms before discussing the essays by Kmiec and Kuttner on military trials: *probable cause, Star Chamber, Miranda rights, probative, exclusionary rules, secondary evidence.* Briefly summarize the arguments on both sides of the debate. Does Kmiec refute any of Kuttner's criticisms? Be specific. Do the letters in "Terror on Trial" add anything new to the argument?

3. In several places Judge Posner disagrees with the conventional wisdom about war, liberty, and legality. Point out his differences. How effective are his examples from history as support for his claim? How does Posner connect his references to the drug war with the events on September 11, 2001?

4. Go over Murphy's examples of excessive vigilance in paragraph 6. Do you agree that her fear of "loss of personal liberty" (para. 5) following the terrorist attacks is justified? Or is it exaggerated? Explain.

5. What is Johnson referring to when he says, "But imagine a succession of such days stretching into years" (para. 4)? Find examples of language that emphasizes the emotional treatment of his argument.

6. Saghiyeh, like the writer quoted in the chapter introduction, speaks of the failure of the Muslim world to achieve "modernity." What examples does he provide? What responsibility do *you* think America has "to address the political grievances of Muslim societies . . . and try to reduce the poverty and inequality endemic in most of the Middle East" (para. 3)?

7. Look at the essay "The Case for Torture" by Michael Levin in Chapter 6 (p. 202). Does his argument seem more relevant after the attacks of September 11? Why, or why not?

TOPICS FOR RESEARCH

What the Koran says about violence

Wartime restrictions on civil liberties in U.S. history

A definition of terrorism

Psychology of the terrorist

The case against retaliation

TAKING THE DEBATE ONLINE

For these and additional research URLs, see www.bedfordstmartins.com/ rottenberg.

- *After September 11*
  http://www.bedfordstmartins.com/september11

  This site is designed to provide teachers and students with a starting point in their discussions, research, and writing about these unfolding events. It includes links to some of the most interesting and provocative commentaries that have emerged post–September 11. Commentaries represent a variety of perspectives, as well as questions and suggestions for pursuing more deeply the issues these essays raise.

- *Research and Reference Resources on the Events of September 11, 2001*
  http://www.freepint.com/gary/91101.html

  This comprehensive collection of materials about September 11 was compiled by Gary Price. It includes many government documents.

- *September 11, 2001*
  http://www.howstuffworks.com/sept-eleven.htm

  This article answers basic questions about the September 11 terrorist attack, such as how and when the World Trade Center Towers collapsed.

- *Resources for September 11, 2001*
  http://www.researchbuzz.com/911

  This page is a collection of links on various topics related to September 11, such as news coverage, terrorism, and memorials.

- *September 11 Archive*
  http://september11.archive.org

  This site is a collection of Web materials that are expressions of "individual people, groups, the press, and institutions from around the world in the aftermath of the attacks in the U.S. on September 11, 2001." The creators of the site "hope the archive provides resources for many kinds of reflection on the meanings of these events."

19

Sex and Violence in Popular Culture

The ongoing controversy about explicit sex and violence in movies, television, and rap music has surfaced again with particular urgency. A 1995 *New York Times* article found that "nine out of ten of those polled could think of something bad to say about popular culture, with a large proportion mentioning too much sex, violence, and vulgar language."[1] The reasons for the renewed attacks are not hard to find. Crime and sexual activity among the young have energized the search for a cause, and popular culture is a perennial target. But the extraordinary accessibility of this culture raises new alarms. Never has commercial entertainment been so widely and easily available to the young, the population thought to be most susceptible to its influence.

The debate begins with claims about the nature and extent of that influence. Are some forms of popular entertainment necessarily dangerous and immoral? How much are viewers affected by continued exposure to depictions of explicit sex and violence? Researchers have argued the point for years, but today a majority consensus believes that long-term viewing does, in fact, alter the behavior of certain audiences. In recent years what appear to be copy-cat crimes have followed the showing of

[1] Elizabeth Kolbert, "Americans Despair of Popular Culture," *New York Times*, August 20, 1995, sec. H, p. 1.

particularly violent films. Experts also debate the relative effects of fictional and real-life images: Which are more corrupting—the graphic creations in movies or the daily reports of real-life horrors in the news?

Not surprisingly, even where agreement exists on the nature of the problem, there is disagreement about solutions. However strongly some critics feel about the dangers of exposure, they argue that the dangers of government censorship may, in the long run, be greater. But if government intervention is rejected, can other solutions—a rating system for television shows and music albums, a V-chip in the TV set allowing parents to block undesirable programs, respect by producers for the so-called family hour, and above all, closer monitoring by parents—guarantee that young people will be insulated from exposure to sex and violence in the media? Most Americans are not optimistic. The *New York Times* poll shows that 63 percent of those questioned believe that ratings alone, for example, will not "keep children from seeing or listening to inappropriate material."

Of course, popular culture is not the only source of exposure. Movies, television, and music reflect the activities, tastes, fantasies, and prejudices of a larger society. Reducing the amount of sex and violence in the media is certainly easier than reforming a whole society. Still, the question remains: To what extent can any reform in popular entertainment successfully address the problems of teenage crime and sexual activity?

Sex, Violence, and Videotape

IRVING KRISTOL

BEFORE READING: Did your parents ever restrict your viewing of certain TV shows or movies when you were younger? What was the reason for their decision?

On March 31, Britain experienced an unexpected cultural shock. That was when Professor Elizabeth Newson, head of the child development unit at Nottingham University, issued a report on violence-rich videos (known in the United Kingdom as "video nasties") and their effect on children. The report was signed by twenty-five psychologists and pediatricians, all known to be of the liberal persuasion. Its gist is summed up by the following quotations:

"Many of us hold our liberal ideals of freedom of expression dear, but now begin to feel that we were naive in our failure to predict the extent of damaging material and its all-too-free availability to children."

Irving Kristol, a fellow of the American Enterprise Institute, coedits *The Public Interest*. This essay appeared in the May 31, 1994, issue of the *Wall Street Journal*.

It then went on: "By restricting such material from home viewing, society must take on a necessary responsibility in protecting children from this, as from other forms of child abuse."

A storm of controversy ensued, which the American press largely ignored. A Labour member of Parliament introduced legislation to limit the availability of such "video nasties." The movie industry was naturally outraged, since so much of their profits come from the subsequent sale of videotapes, and they cried "Censorship!"—which, of course, is what was being advocated. More surprising was the reaction of the Tory Home Minister, Michael Howard, who turned out to be "wet" (we would say "soft") on this whole issue. He was very worried about all those households without children, whose freedom to watch "video nasties" would be circumscribed.

Both True and False

And then, inevitably, there were the unreconstructed liberal aca- 5
demics, who kept insisting that no one had ever proved a causal relation between TV violence and aggressive behavior by the young. This was both true and false. It was true in the sense that such clear-cut, causal relations are beyond the reach of social science—there are simply too many other factors that influence youthful behavior. It was false because there is an abundance of circumstantial evidence that points to the existence of such a relation—circumstantial evidence so strong as to raise no reasonable doubt in the minds of ordinary people, and of parents especially.

In the Spring 1993 issue of *The Public Interest,* Brandon Centerwall, a professor of epidemiology at the University of Washington, summarizes much of this circumstantial evidence. He focuses on research findings on the effect of television when it was introduced to rural, isolated communities in Canada and when English-language TV came to South Africa in 1975, having previously been banned by the Afrikaans-speaking government. In all such instances there was a spectacular increase in violent crime, most especially among the young.

Professor Centerwall also notes that when TV was introduced in the United States after World War II, the homicide rate among whites, who were the first to buy sets, began to rise, while the black homicide rate didn't show any such increase until four years later.

Statistical studies of the relation between youthful aggressiveness and TV can be deceptive, Professor Centerwall explains, if they focus on the overall, average response—which, indeed, seems weak. But aggressive impulses, like most human phenomena, are distributed along a bell-shaped curve, and it is at the margin where the significant effect is to be observed: "It is an intrinsic property of such 'bell curve' distributions that small changes in the average imply major changes at the extremes. Thus, if an exposure to television causes 8 percent of the population to shift from below-average aggression to above-average aggression, it follows that the homicide rate will double."

Professor Centerwall concludes that "the evidence indicates that if, hypothetically, television technology had never been developed, there would today be 10,000 fewer homicides each year in the United States, 70,000 fewer rapes, and 700,000 fewer injurious assaults. Violent crime would be half what it is."

So the evidence for some kind of controls over television (and tapes) 10 is strong enough to provoke popular and political concern. It is certainly true that any such controls will involve some limitations on the freedom of adults to enjoy the kind of entertainment they might prefer. But modest limits on adult liberties ought to be perfectly acceptable if they prevent tens of thousands of our children from growing up into criminal adults. And it is the children we should be focusing on. The violence-prone adults, especially at the pathological fringe, are beyond our reach and, in most cases, beyond all possibility of redemption. It is the young people—especially those who have not yet reached adolescence—who are most affected by television, as all the studies agree.

Something will surely be done about this problem, despite the American Civil Liberties Union and other extreme interpreters of the First Amendment. In Britain, Mr. Howard has reluctantly agreed to propose appropriate legislation, propelled by a powerful consensus among Tories, the Labour Party, the Liberal Party, the media, and popular opinion. There is little doubt that, in the United States, a momentum for similar action is building up. How politicians will respond to it remains to be seen. But the idea that our popular culture can have malignant effects upon our young, and upon our society in its entirety, seems to be an idea whose coming cannot be long delayed.

And if there is a connection between our popular culture and the plague of criminal violence we are suffering from, then is it not reasonable to think that there may also be such a connection between our popular culture and the plagues of sexual promiscuity among teenagers, teenage illegitimacy, and, yes, the increasing number of rapes committed by teenagers? Here again, we don't really need social science to confirm what common sense and common observations tell us to be the case.

Can anyone really believe that soft porn in our Hollywood movies, hard porn in our cable movies, and violent porn in our "rap" music is without effect? Here, the average, overall impact is quite discernible to the naked eye. And at the margin, the effects, in terms most notably of illegitimacy and rape, are shockingly visible.

Clearly, something must be done to lower the temperature of the sexual climate in which we live. And whatever is done, it will of necessity limit the freedoms of adults to indulge their sexual fantasies. Most of us will not mourn the loss of such freedoms, but—as with violence—there are those who will loudly protest any such rude "violation" of our "civil liberties."

Censorship, we will be told, is immoral—though no moral code of 15 any society that has ever existed has ever deemed it so. Besides, we will be told further, it is ineffectual. Well, those of us who have lived in a slightly chillier sexual climate have survived as witnesses to the fact that it is not so ineffectual after all. True, censorship makes a difference only at the margin. But, and this cannot be repeated too often, it is at the margin where the crucial action is. This is as true for sexual activity as it is for economic activity.

Invitation to Promiscuity

The most common (hypocritical and politically cowardly) response to the problems generated by our overheated sexual climate is that these are something parents have to do something about. But parents cannot do it on their own. They never have been able to do it on their own. Parents have always relied on churches, schools, and the popular culture for help. Today, no such reliance is possible.

The mainline churches, still intoxicated with a vulgarized Freudianism, have discovered that sex is good and repression is bad. The schools hand out condoms to adolescents while timidly suggesting that they ought to limit their activity to "responsible sex." This is nothing less than an official invitation to promiscuity. The culture, meanwhile, is busy making as much money as possible out of as much sex as possible.

No, the government, at various levels, will have to step in to help the parents. And it will do so despite the anticipated cries of outrage from libertarians, liberal or conservative. The question, and it is no easy question, is just how to intervene. That is the issue that is now up for serious discussion.

TV Isn't Violent Enough

MIKE OPPENHEIM

BEFORE READING: Think about some of the violent movies or TV shows you have seen recently. Were you genuinely frightened by their depictions of violence? Did the pictures of the destruction of the World Trade Center towers on September 11, 2001, frighten you in a different way?

Caught in an ambush, there's no way our hero (Matt Dillon, Eliot Ness, Kojak, Hoss Cartwright . . .) can survive. Yet, visibly weakening, he blazes away, and we suspect he'll pull through. Sure enough, he's around for the final clinch wearing the traditional badge of the honorable but harmless wound: a sling.

When this essay was published in the February 11, 1984, issue of *TV Guide*, Mike Oppenheim was a freelance writer and physician practicing medicine in California.

As a teenager with a budding interest in medicine, I knew this was nonsense and loved to annoy my friends with the facts.

"Aw, the poor guy! He's crippled for life!"

"What do you mean? He's just shot in the shoulder."

"That's the worst place! Vital structures everywhere. There's the blood supply for the arm: axillary artery and vein. One nick and you can bleed to death on the spot." 5

"So he was lucky."

"OK. If it missed the vessels it hit the brachial plexus: the nerve supply. Paralyzes his arm for life. He's gotta turn in his badge and apply for disability."

"So he's *really* lucky."

"OK. Missed the artery. Missed the vein. Missed the nerves. Just went through the shoulder joint. But joint cartilage doesn't heal so well. A little crease in the bone leaves him with traumatic arthritis. He's in pain the rest of his life — stuffing himself with codeine, spending his money on acupuncture and chiropractors, losing all his friends because he complains all the time. . . . Don't ever get shot in the shoulder. It's the end. . . ."

Today, as a physician, I still sneer at TV violence, though not because of any moral objection. I enjoy a well-done scene of gore and slaughter as well as the next viewer, but "well-done" is something I rarely see on a typical evening in spite of the plethora of shootings, stabbings, muggings, and brawls. Who can believe the stuff they show? Anyone who remembers high-school biology knows the human body can't possibly respond to violent trauma as it's usually portrayed. 10

On a recent episode, Matt Houston is at a fancy resort, on the trail of a vicious killer who specializes in knifing beautiful women in their hotel rooms in broad daylight. The only actual murder sequence was in the best of taste: all the action off screen, the flash of a knife, moans on the sound track.

In two scenes, Matt arrives only minutes too late. The hotel is alerted, but the killer's identity remains a mystery. Absurd! It's impossible to kill someone instantly with a knife thrust — or even render him unconscious. Several minutes of strenuous work are required to cut enough blood vessels so the victim bleeds to death. Tony Perkins in *Psycho* gave an accurate, though abbreviated, demonstration. Furthermore, anyone who has watched an inexperienced farmhand slaughter a pig knows that the resulting mess must be seen to be believed.

If consulted by Matt Houston, I'd have suggested a clue: "Keep your eyes peeled for someone panting with exhaustion and covered with blood. That might be your man."

Many Americans were puzzled at the films of the assassination attempt on President Reagan. Shot in the chest, he did not behave as TV had taught us to expect ("clutch chest, stagger backward, collapse").

Only after he complained of a vague chest pain and was taken to the hospital did he discover his wound. Many viewers assumed Mr. Reagan is some sort of superman. In fact, there was nothing extraordinary about his behavior. A pistol is certainly a deadly weapon, but not predictably so. Unlike a knife wound, one bullet can kill instantly—provided it strikes a small area at the base of the brain. Otherwise, it's no different: a matter of ripping and tearing enough tissue to cause death by bleeding. Professional gangland killers understand the problem. They prefer a shotgun at close range.

The trail of quiet corpses left by TV's good guys, bad guys, and as- 15 sorted ill-tempered gun owners is ridiculously unreal. Firearms reliably produce pain, bleeding, and permanent, crippling injury (witness Mr. Reagan's press secretary, James Brady: shot directly in the brain but very much alive). For a quick, clean death, they are no match for Luke Skywalker's light saber.

No less unreal is what happens when T. J. Hooker, Magnum, or a Simon brother meets a bad guy in manly combat. Pow! Our hero's fist crashes into the villain's head. Villain reels backward, tipping over chairs and lamps, finally falling to the floor, unconscious. Handshakes all around. . . . Sheer fantasy! After hitting the villain, our hero would shake no one's hand. He'd be too busy waving his own about wildly, screaming with the pain of a shattered fifth metacarpal (the bone behind the fifth knuckle), an injury so predictable it's called the "boxer's fracture." The human fist is far more delicate than the human skull. In any contest between the two, the fist will lose.

The human skull is tougher than TV writers give it credit. Clunked with a blunt object, such as the traditional pistol butt, most victims would not fall conveniently unconscious for a few minutes. More likely, they'd suffer a nasty scalp laceration, be stunned for a second or two, then be extremely upset. I've sewn up many. A real-life, no-nonsense criminal with a blackjack (a piece of iron weighing several pounds) has a much better success rate. The result is a large number of deaths and permanent damage from brain hemorrhage.

Critics of TV violence claim it teaches children sadism and cruelty. I honestly don't know whether or not TV violence is harmful, but if so the critics have it backward. Children can't learn to enjoy cruelty from the neat, sanitized mayhem on the average series. There isn't any! What they learn is far more malignant: that guns or fists are clean, efficient, exciting ways to deal with a difficult situation. Bang!—you're dead! Bop!—you're unconscious (temporarily)!

"Truth-in-advertising" laws eliminated many absurd commercial claims. I often daydream about what would happen if we had "truth in violence"—if every show had to pass scrutiny by a board of doctors who had no power to censor but could insist that any action scene have at least a vague resemblance to medical reality ("Stop the projector! . . . You have your hero waylaid by three Mafia thugs who beat him brutally before he struggles free. The next day he shows up with this cute little Band-aid over his eyebrow. We can't pass that. You'll have to add one eye swollen shut, three missing front teeth, at least twenty stitches over the lips and eyes, and a wired jaw. Got that? Roll 'em . . .").

Seriously, real-life violence is dirty, painful, bloody, disgusting. It 20 causes mutilation and misery, and it doesn't solve problems. It makes them worse. If we're genuinely interested in protecting our children, we should stop campaigning to "clean up" TV violence. It's already too antiseptic. Ironically, the problem with TV violence is: It's not violent enough.

Hollow Claims about Fantasy Violence

RICHARD RHODES

> BEFORE READING: As you grow older, does violence in the media appeal to you more — or less? Can you account for your reactions?

The moral entrepreneurs are at it again, pounding the entertainment industry for advertising its Grand Guignolesque[1] confections to children. If exposure to this mock violence contributes to the development of violent behavior, then our political leadership is justified in its indignation at what the Federal Trade Commission has reported about the marketing of violent fare to children. Senators John McCain and Joseph Lieberman have been especially quick to fasten on the FTC report as they make an issue of violent offerings to children.

But is there really a link between entertainment and violent behavior?

The American Medical Association, the American Psychological Association, the American Academy of Pediatrics, and the National Institutes of Mental Health all say yes. They base their claims on social science research that has been sharply criticized and disputed within the social science profession, especially outside the United States. In fact, no direct, causal link between exposure to mock violence in the media and subsequent violent behavior has ever been demonstrated, and the few claims of modest correlation have been contradicted by other findings, sometimes in the same studies.

History alone should call such a link into question. Private violence has been declining in the West since the media-barren late Middle Ages, when homicide rates are estimated to have been ten times what they are in Western nations today. Historians attribute the decline to improving social controls over violence—police forces and common access to courts of law—and to a shift away from brutal physical punishment in child-rearing (a practice that still appears as a common factor in the background of violent criminals today).

The American Medical Association has based its endorsement of 5 the media violence theory in major part on the studies of Brandon Centerwall, a psychiatrist in Seattle. Dr. Centerwall compared the murder rates for whites in three countries from 1945 to 1974 with numbers for

[1] Grand Guignol, a popular theater founded in Paris in 1897 to present graphic performances of crimes.—ED.

Richard Rhodes is the author of more than two dozen books, including *The Making of the Atomic Bomb* (1986), which won a Pulitzer Prize for nonfiction, and, most recently, *Why They Kill: The Discoveries of a Maverick Criminologist* (1999). The *New York Times* printed this article on September 17, 2000.

television set ownership. Until 1975, television broadcasting was banned in South Africa, and "white homicide rates remained stable" there, Dr. Centerwall found, while corresponding rates in Canada and the United States doubled after television was introduced.

A spectacular finding, but it is meaningless. As Franklin E. Zimring and Gordon Hawkins of the University of California at Berkeley subsequently pointed out, homicide rates in France, Germany, Italy, and Japan either failed to change with increasing television ownership in the same period or actually declined, and American homicide rates have more recently been sharply declining despite a proliferation of popular media outlets—not only movies and television, but also video games and the Internet.

Other social science that supposedly undergirds the theory, too, is marginal and problematic. Laboratory studies that expose children to selected incidents of televised mock violence and then assess changes in the children's behavior have sometimes found more "aggressive" behavior after the exposure—usually verbal, occasionally physical.

But sometimes the control group, shown incidents judged not to be violent, behaves more aggressively afterward than the test group; sometimes comedy produces the more aggressive behavior; and sometimes there's no change. The only obvious conclusion is that sitting and watching television stimulates subsequent physical activity. Any kid could tell you that.

As to those who claim that entertainment promotes violent behavior by desensitizing people to violence, the British scholar Martin Barker offers this critique: "Their claim is that the materials they judge to be harmful can only influence us by trying to make us be the same as them. So horrible things will make us horrible—not horrified. Terrifying things will make us terrifying—not terrified. To see something aggressive makes us feel aggressive—not aggressed against. This idea is so odd, it is hard to know where to begin in challenging it."

Even more influential on national policy has been a twenty-two year 10 study by two University of Michigan psychologists, Leonard D. Eron and L. Rowell Huesmann, of boys exposed to so-called violent media. The Telecommunications Act of 1996, which mandated the television V-chip, allowing parents to screen out unwanted programming, invoked these findings, asserting, "Studies have shown that children exposed to violent video programming at a young age have a higher tendency for violent and aggressive behavior later in life than children not so exposed."

Well, not exactly. Following 875 children in upstate New York from third grade through high school, the psychologists found a correlation between a preference for violent television at age eight and aggressiveness at age eighteen. The correlation—0.31—would mean television accounted for about 10 percent of the influences that led to this behavior. But the correlation only turned up in one of three measures of aggression: the assessment of students by their peers. It didn't show up in students' reports about themselves or in psychological testing. And for girls, there was no correlation at all.

Despite the lack of evidence, politicians can't resist blaming the media for violence. They can stake out the moral high ground confident that the First Amendment will protect them from having to actually write legislation that would be likely to alienate the entertainment industry. Some use the issue as a smokescreen to avoid having to confront gun control.

But violence isn't learned from mock violence. There is good evidence—causal evidence, not correlational—that it's learned in personal violent encounters, beginning with the brutalization of children by their parents or their peers.

The money spent on all the social science research I've described was diverted from the National Institute of Mental Health budget by reducing support for the construction of community mental health centers. To this day there is no standardized reporting system for emergency-room findings of physical child abuse. Violence is on the decline in America, but if we want to reduce it even further, protecting children from real violence in their real lives—not the pale shadow of mock violence—is the place to begin.

"Bang": Guns, Rap, and Silence

JAY NORDLINGER

BEFORE READING: Do you think music can influence behavior as well as emotion?

A lot of people were interested in the Sean "Puffy" Combs trial: fans of rap music; celebrity-watchers; connoisseurs of popular culture. But one group of people showed no interest whatsoever: gun-control activists. This was rather strange—a dog that didn't bark. The Combs case was awash in guns; so is Combs's world—that of rap, or "hip-hop." But the gun-controllers prefer to ignore this dark corner. Their indifference, or passivity, may be taken to represent a broader failure of liberalism to confront ghetto culture—to look it in the eye and cry, "No!"

Combs—known as "Puff Daddy"—is a major figure in rap, the boss of a record label called "Bad Boy." (Another label is called "Murder, Inc."—one refreshing thing about the rappers is their lack of pretense.) The Combs case dominated New York at the beginning of this year, the

Jay Nordlinger is the managing editor of the *National Review*, where this article appeared on April 16, 2001.

trial of a century that is still very young. What happened is this: In December 1999, Combs visited a nightclub with his girlfriend (the pop star Jennifer Lopez), a few "associates," and several of his guns. Someone insulted Combs. Shooting broke out. Three people were injured, two of them badly. Then Combs and his group fled the scene. When the police finally caught up with the getaway car—or rather, the getaway Lincoln Navigator SUV—they found two guns. Combs was subsequently charged with illegal weapons possession and bribery (he had tried to get his driver to accept responsibility for the guns). The rapper's guilt seemed clear, but he denied everything.

In a now-de rigueur move, Combs hired Johnnie Cochran, the O.J. lawyer, who composed a few new rhymes and flashed his smile at the jury. Combs got off. One of those "associates," however, was not so lucky: Jamal "Shyne" Barrow—a rapper described as Combs's protégé—was found guilty of first-degree assault. He now faces twenty-five years in prison.

So, another day, another rap case—this time, no one died. It's easy to look away from rap and its nature. But it should not be so, and it certainly shouldn't be so for gun-controllers. Thug rappers should be their worst nightmare (and a lot of other people's). Yet the antigun activists would rather go after Charlton Heston, rednecks, and other soft targets. It's far more comfortable to torment the NRA, which advocates not only gun rights but gun safety, than to get in the faces of "gangsta" rappers, who glory in guns and gun violence in song after song after song. Most people, by now, are familiar with rap's hideous and constant degradation of women (where are the feminists, incidentally?). They are less familiar with rap's celebration of the gun. Back in 1992, there was a brief furor over a rap called "Cop Killer." The idea of gunning down policemen is certainly an attention-getter. But if rappers are enthusing only about killing one another, that seems to be another matter, something to be swept under the rug.

Liberals have occasionally been interested in this subject. Tipper and   5
Al Gore were, before Hollywood bit their heads off. Usually, though, when you try to interest liberals in the horrors of today's worst music, they roll their eyes and recall how their parents railed against "Elvis's pelvis." Ah, the two magic words: "Elvis's pelvis." Say them, and you shut down any discussion about, for example, rap's effects on the young. And doesn't every generation murmur, with a sigh and a shake of the head, "Kids today . . ."? But any sensate being can see that "gangsta" rap—with its sanction, even urging, of rape, murder, and other abuse—has nothing at all in common with Elvis Presley's swaying hips. It must be, in part, a fear of uncoolness—of fogeydom—that keeps many people from coming to grips with rap. They are perfectly happy to claim that the sight of Joe Camel causes millions of young'uns to smoke cigarettes; but they are reluctant to consider what rap—poured constantly into young ears—might do.

The Object of Their Affections

Rappers sing of guns with almost lascivious glee. They express close to an erotic feeling about their "pieces": "glocks" (for the Austrian manufacturer), "gats" (short for Gatlings), "nines" or "ninas" (for 9-mm pistols), and so on in a long and chilling lexicon. Bullets and clips are lingered over as eyes and lips might be in love songs. Here's a sample from "Trigga Gots No Heart" by the rapper Spice 1: "Caps [bullets] peel from gangsters in my 'hood. You better use that nina 'cause that deuce-deuce [.22-caliber weapon] ain't no good, and I'm taking up a hobby, maniac murderin', doin' massacre robbery." There is no end of material like this. The rapper Notorious B.I.G., slain by gun in 1997, sang, "Somebody's gotta die. Let the gunshots blow. Somebody's gotta die. Nobody gotta know that I killed yo' a** in the midst, kid." And, "Don't fill them clips too high. Give them bullets room to breathe. Damn, where was I?" Dr. Dre had a hit called "Rat-Tat-Tat-Tat," whose refrain went, "Never hesitate to put a nigga on his back. Rat-tat-tat-tat to the tat like that, and I never hesitate to put a nigga on his back."

During the Combs trial, some thought that Shyne Barrow's lyrics would do the young man no good. They are horrible, but since millions of kids drink them in, their parents might as well know them, too. In "Bad Boyz," Barrow raps, "Now tell me, who wanna f*** with us? Ashes to ashes, dust to dust. I bang—and let your f***in' brains hang. . . . My point is double-fours [a .44 magnum] at your f***in' jaws, pointed hollow point sh** [this is bullet terminology], four point six [?], need I say more? Or do you get the point, b**ch?" In another track—"Bang"—he says, "Niggas wanna bang. We could bang out till the clip's done, or your vital arteries hang out." And: "Got my mind right, like Al Pacino and Nino. I head to Capitol Hill to kidnap Janet Reno. Words droppin' and shockin', guns cockin' and poppin', somebody call Cochran" (that would be the lawyer Johnnie—life imitating art, or is it the other way around?). Barrow continues, "No time to waste, nine in my waist, ready for war, any time, any place. F*** it, just another case."

Are these words meant to be taken seriously, or are they just play—disturbing, maybe, but basically harmless? Shyne Barrow did, indeed, have a "nine in his waist" at that nightclub, and it appears to have been luck that he didn't kill the people he hit. Moral relativism, however, is rife in discussion about rap (such as it is). Barrow's lawyer, Murray Richman, made the following, delicious comment to the *New York Post* last December: "Dostoyevsky wrote about murder—does that implicate him as a murderer?" Or "when Eartha Kitt salaciously sings "Santa, Baby,' does that mean she really wants to sleep with Santa Claus?" This sort of statement is meant to be a conversation-stopper, like "Elvis's pelvis." You know: Dostoyevsky, Eartha Kitt, Shyne Barrow—artists all, and liable to be misunderstood by the conservative and hung-up. "Kids today . . ."—ha ha.

Now, gun-control groups are concerned—and why shouldn't they be?—with laws and loopholes and gun shows and accidents in homes and Charlton Heston and, of course, school shootings, out of which they make hay. They say nothing about hip-hop culture, and next to nothing about popular culture generally. The groups put out a steady stream of press releases: praising states' "safety initiatives," trying to shame manufacturers, worrying about "children's health." In fact, they seem to burrow into every nook and cranny of American life—but keep mum about the ghetto and its anthems.

Nancy Hwa is spokesman for Handgun Control, Inc. (the Jim and 10 Sarah Brady group). She says that her organization has "called on people in the creative industry not to glamorize guns" but has not dealt with hip-hop in particular. "Other targets have a more direct relationship with getting your hands on guns," she says—for example, "sales at gun shows." And no one group, she sensibly points out, can cover everything. Plus, "when it comes right down to it, you can listen to rap or Marilyn Manson or country music, and, in the end, as long as the young person can't get their hands on a gun, all they're guilty of is questionable taste in music." For Handgun Control, Inc., the issue is "access," plain and simple.

Ted Pascoe speaks for Do It for the Kids!, a gun-control group in Colorado. "We don't address it," he says of the rap issue. "We have enough trouble with the Second Amendment without attacking the First as well." Meaning? "Well, there is a perception in this country that individuals enjoy the protections conferred by the Second Amendment. But that amendment only confers on states the right to maintain militias. So the individual has no standing in court to make Second Amendment claims. However, Americans tend to believe they *do* have the right to bear arms. So, it's troublesome, because whenever you start talking about passing stronger gun laws, a lot of folks—even if they're not involved in the issue, or vested in it—can invoke the Second Amendment and sometimes effectively take the wind out of your sails." A stance against rap, says Pascoe, would only bring trouble: "The large number of gun-control groups don't want to be seen as attacking every element in the Constitution, or more than one. I think that the First Amendment contains rights that we *do* enjoy—that individuals have First Amendments rights."

The confusion of rights and responsibilities of "what you got a right to do and what is right to do," as the supreme fogey Bill Bennett puts it—is an old one.

Andy Pelosi, who represents New Yorkers against Gun Violence, says that his group "really focuses on legislative issues—we've done a little bit of violence in the media, but not rap." He makes the point that "it would be unfair to look at one genre without looking at the others. You could make a case about heavy metal, alternative rock—you wouldn't want to single out just rap." This would, indeed, be a painful step for most liberals. It would involve a clash of their pieties: gun control—outright demonization of the gun—and a taboo against taking issue with black culture in any of its aspects. The old "No enemies to the left" might mingle with a new slogan: "No enemies among blacks" (with Clarence Thomas and the other Toms excepted, of course).

"Silence Kills"

The country is engaged in a great debate over gun control; but there should be no disagreement about the awfulness—why not go all the way? the evil—of the most violent, dehumanizing, and desensitizing rap. The inner city is bleeding from gun crime. White America should probably think harder about the perpetual Columbines taking place in ghettos. Of course, many excuse rap on grounds that it merely reflects life on the mean streets. And whether this stuff has bloody consequences is an open question. In 1993, a rapper called Masta Ace, talking to the *St. Petersburg Times,* said, "It's like a Schwarzenegger movie—you don't come out wanting to shoot anybody." But he quickly had a second thought: "I think it does shape mentalities and helps develop a callousness to where you could really shoot somebody and not think twice about it."

Sure: There's only so much a gun-control group or conservative alarm-raisers or anyone else can do about (what might be termed) hate rap. But activists, who love to talk—it is their principal activity—might at least talk. A group called the Campus Alliance to End Gun Violence proclaims as its number-one position, "Gun violence disproportionately preys on the young. Silence kills. We must speak." Well, all right: Minus a right-wing militia or two, there is only one class of people—an extremely wealthy and popular class of people—that actually *exalts* gun violence. So . . . ?

Violence Never Solved Anything, but It's Entertaining

HOLMAN W. JENKINS JR.

BEFORE READING: In watching a violent TV show or movie, would your pleasure be reduced if the bad guys won? Why?

The stock market is jittery. Poverty stares us in the face. At least we still have violent programming on TV, but some would take even this solace away from us.

A debatable sociological wisdom crept into the law with the 1996 Telecommunications Act. Children who watch violent television are at

Holman W. Jenkins Jr. writes the Business World column for the *Wall Street Journal.* This column appeared on October 28, 1998.

risk of becoming aggressive and violent themselves. Adults who steep themselves in the local news develop an exaggerated fear of the world, the so-called mean world syndrome.

As one of the many scholars plying this vein has noted approvingly, "policymakers are taking the position that television programmers should provide warnings to make viewers aware of the risks of watching certain shows." Because we are programmed by TV, we need the V-chip to reprogram our programmer.

Certainly television has wrought changes in the world, but before asking how it has reshaped human nature, how has human nature shaped television?

Since it became popular to denounce the "wasteland" in the early 5 1950s, surprisingly few have asked basic questions about the supply and demand for violent programming. The standard critique assumes supply without demand: The audience is dumbly trapped before the show, which is calculated to lift them to a higher state of "arousal" in order to become more receptive to the messages of advertisers.

Now we have the benefit of an economist looking at all this, James Hamilton of Duke, whose new book is *Channeling Violence: The Economic Market for Violent Television Programming.*

It turns out that broadcasters are neither as dumb nor as smart as the standard critique paints them. Pollsters constantly reiterate that Americans find TV "too violent," but combing more finely through the data one finds a substantial minority of dissenters, the people who actually watch violent TV. In Nielsen speak, these are males age eighteen to thirty-four, females age eighteen to thirty-four, and then males age thirty-five to forty-nine. There is demand after all, and it comes from young adults of both sexes.

That broadcasters are prepared to oblige them is no mystery. These viewers are advertisers' most valuable and elusive demographic group. Young adults are out building lives and careers. They are just developing the brand attachments that will last a lifetime but are seldom to be found in front of a TV where marketers can reach them.

Advertisers pay richly to reach youthful consumers. Ted Turner, who can often be heard denouncing television violence from a podium, has given us Saturday Night Nitro on TNT—whole evenings of delicious violence aimed at young adult viewers. Even when competing against *Monday Night Football,* 65 percent of the movies on TNT contained violence. The rest of the year 92 percent contained violence.

Mr. Hamilton says broadcasters don't aim their violence at younger 10 children, and advertisers don't reward broadcasters for young children in the audience. Their viewing is an "externality," like pollution. But someone might have said the same about adult viewers back when the Big Three networks forced everyone to sit through the same programs.

Thanks to technology and the proliferation of channels, audiences have been freed to go their separate ways. Cable, especially premium cable, has become the violence medium, while violence has dropped steeply on the major networks.

The action-adventure genre has all but disappeared, with the sorry exceptions of CBS's *Walker, Texas Ranger* and ABC's new *Vengeance Unlimited*. The networks base their survival hopes on compiling the last large audiences in television-land, so they fill up our evenings with news-magazines and sitcoms—shows that attract young people without driving other viewers out of the room.

Why does the younger demographic have a special taste for violent programming? We can at least speculate.

Dolf Zillmann, a psychologist at the University of Alabama, has been one of the few paying attention to the viewer's perspective. Among his several contributions, he has shown that teenagers swarm to horror flicks so the boys can demonstrate their manly unflappability and girls can demonstrate their vulnerable desirability. Boys and girls who fulfill these roles are rated as more sexually desirable by their peers.

Young people, as they set about making room for themselves in the world, are especially full of anxiety about whether good guys or bad guys triumph in the end. Nor are they burdened unduly by a sense of proportionality. Mr. Zillmann points to a program in which a lawyer cheats an old lady out of her savings. The audience's sense of poetic justice is no less fulfilled by "seeing him burn and die in a crash" than seeing him receive a fine and disbarment. 15

Mr. Hamilton, the economist, supplies buttressing evidence when you consider that the young are less discriminating in matters of taste. Unsurprisingly, the more stars *TV Guide* awards a film, the less violent the film is likely to be. Violent shows are often bad shows. A lousy producer working with a bunch of mediocre writers and actors is going to resort to cloddish violence to dramatize what would otherwise have to be rendered by more literary means.

Criminologists have long noted that homicide becomes rarer among elite social groups as those groups make greater use of lawyers. TV seems to be evolving in the same direction. Lawyer shows are proliferating on the networks. Boilerplate courtroom drama may be replacing shoot-em-up as the preferred formula for resolving conflict.

Those who worry about television may sincerely dream of society becoming a nicer, less competitive place. Children do sometimes mow down their school chums, acting out a scene they may have seen on cable. But claiming we have to reprogram the media watched by 99.99 percent of us to influence the behavior of 0.01 percent is to be rendered helpless by a much smaller problem.

Only sick minds are interested in plotless violence. A British censor once explained his methods by saying he made certain cuts "because we were worried about a very few people who might be vulnerable to being influenced by playing one particular scene in that video repeatedly in their home."

These "very few people" surely exist in the audience, but making 20 television the issue only avoids the question of how we could be doing a better job of identifying the homicidally mentally ill before someone gets hurt.

A Desensitized Society Drenched in Sleaze

JEFF JACOBY

BEFORE READING: What's the difference between the violence depicted in popular movies and described in the lyrics of some rap songs and the violence portrayed in *Macbeth* or a classic Greek play like *Oedipus Rex?*

I was seventeen years old when I first saw an X-rated movie. It was Thanksgiving in Washington, D.C. My college dorm had all but emptied out for the holiday weekend. With no classes, no tests, and nobody around, I decided to scratch an itch that had long been tormenting me.

I used to see these movies advertised in the old *Washington Star,* and — like any seventeen-year-old boy whose sex life is mostly theoretical — I burned with curiosity. I wondered what such films might be like, what awful, thrilling secrets they might expose.

And so that weekend I took myself to see one. Full of anticipation, nervous and embarrassed, I walked to the Casino Royale at 14th Street and New York Avenue. At the top of a long flight of stairs, a cashier sat behind a cage. "Five dollars," he demanded — steep for my budget, especially since a ticket to the movies in the late seventies usually cost $3.50. But I'd come this far and couldn't turn back. I paid, I entered, I watched.

For about twenty minutes. The movie, I still remember, was called *Cry for Cindy,* and what I saw on the screen I'd never seen — I'd never even imagined — before. A man and a woman, oral sex, extreme close-ups. The sheer gynecological explicitness of it jolted me. Was *this* the forbidden delight hinted at by those ads? This wasn't arousing, it was repellent. I was shocked. More than that: I was ashamed.

I literally couldn't take it. I bolted the theater and tumbled down the 5 steps. My heart was pounding and my face was burning. I felt dirty. Guilty. I was conscience-stricken.

All that — over a dirty movie.

Well, I was an innocent at seventeen. I was naive and inexperienced, shy with girls, the product of a parochial-school education and a strict upbringing. Explicit sex — in the movies, music, my social life — was for-

---

Jeff Jacoby is a columnist for the *Boston Globe,* where this essay appeared on June 8, 1995.

eign to me. Coming from such an environment, who *wouldn't* recoil from *Cry for Cindy* or feel repelled by what it put up on that screen?

But here's the rub: Dirty movies don't have that effect on me anymore. I don't make a practice of seeking out skin flicks or films with explicit nudity, but in the years since I was seventeen, I've certainly seen my share. Today another sex scene is just another sex scene. Not shocking, not appalling, nothing I feel ashamed to look at. Writhing bodies on the screen? Raunchy lyrics in a song? They may entertain me or they may bore me, but one thing they no longer do is make me blush.

I've become jaded. And if a decade and a half of being exposed to this stuff can leave *me* jaded — with my background, my religious schooling, my disciplined origins — what impact does it have on kids and young adults who have never been sheltered from anything? What impact does it have on a generation growing up amid dysfunctional families, broken-down schools, and a culture of values-free secularism?

If sex- and violence-drenched entertainment can desensitize me, it 10 can desensitize anyone. It can desensitize a whole society. It can drag us to the point where nothing is revolting. Where nothing makes us blush.

And what happens to an unblushing society? Why, everything. Central Park joggers get raped and beaten into comas. Sixth-graders sleep around. Los Angeles rioters burn down their neighborhood and murder dozens of their neighbors. The Menendez boys blow off their parents' heads. Lorena Bobbitt mutilates her husband in his sleep. "Artists" sell photographs of crucifixes dunked in urine. Prolife fanatics open fire on abortion clinics. Daytime TV fills up with deviants. The U.S. Naval Academy fills up with cheaters. The teen suicide rate goes through the roof.

And we get used to all of it. We don't blush.

The point isn't that moviegoers walk out of Oliver Stone's latest grotesquerie primed to kill. Or that Geto Boys' sociopathic lyrics ("Leavin' out her house, grabbed the bitch by her mouth / Drug her back in, slam her down on the couch. / Whipped out my knife, said, 'If you scream I'm cutting,' / Open her legs and . . .") cause rape. The point is that when blood and mayhem and sleazy sex drench our popular culture, we get accustomed to blood and mayhem and sleazy sex. We grow jaded. Depravity becomes more and more tolerable because less and less scandalizes us.

Of course, the entertainment industry accepts no responsibility for any of this. Time Warner and Hollywood indignantly reject the criticisms heaped on them in recent days. We don't cause society's ills, they say, we only reflect them. "If an artist wants to deal with violence or sexuality or images of darkness and horror," said film director Clive Barker, "those are legitimate subjects for artists."

They are, true. Artists have dealt with violence and sexuality and 15 horror since time immemorial. But debauchery is not art. There is nothing ennobling about a two-hour paean to bloodlust. To suggest that Snoop Doggy Dogg's barbaric gang-rape fantasies somehow follow in the tradition of Sophocles' tragic drama, Chaucer's romantic poetry, or Solzhenitsyn's moral testimony is to suggest that there is no difference between meaning and meaninglessness.

For Hollywood and Time Warner, perhaps there no longer is. The question before the house is, what about the rest of us?

Gore for Sale

EVAN GAHR

BEFORE READING: Did you enjoy violent video games when you were younger? Can you explain why they did or did not appeal to you?

F resh corpses litter the ground. Blood is everywhere. Victims moan and beg for mercy. Others scream for help.

This may sound like a horrific scene from the Littleton, Colorado, shooting. But players of the computer game Postal just call it fun. They assume the role of Postal Dude, who snaps one day and mows down

Evan Gahr is the Washington correspondent for *Jewish World Review* and an adjunct scholar at the Washington-based Center for Equal Opportunity. This article appeared in the *Wall Street Journal* on April 30, 1999.

everyone in sight. For added realism, as the Web site of the developer (Running with Scissors) proudly states: "Corpses stay where they fall for the duration of the game—no mysterious disappearing bodies." But they do not fall right away. First "watch your victims run around on fire."

If you have a perverse fascination with violence, it's no longer necessary to skulk around in search of underground entertainments. Just visit your neighborhood electronics store. At the Wiz on Manhattan's Upper East Side, the notorious game Grand Theft Auto is smack in the middle of a display rack behind the cashier. The game's story line: As either a "gansta" or "psycho bitch" you will be "running over innocent pedestrians, shooting cops, and evading the long arm of the law."

In another game, Duke Nukem (manufactured by GT Interactive), sex and violence combine. Determined to expel from Los Angeles the aliens who are kidnapping scantily clad women, Duke Nukem trolls the seedy quarters of the city and shoots anyone who gets in his way. He even kicks his victims' decapitated heads through goalposts to celebrate.

In Doom, one of the most popular among violent video games and a 5 favorite of one of the Littleton murderers, the player wanders through a maze of rooms, corridors, and halls killing everything in sight. Survive and you make it to the next level. For lethal power you can choose among a pistol, shot gun, rocket launcher, and chainsaw. The aliens and monsters don't go down easily. Bodily fluid spurts all over the walls; aliens are left to lie in pools of blood, their limbs sometimes dangling in the air.

The manufacturer of Doom, id Software, advises that you should "prepare for the most intense mutant-laden, blood-spattered action ever. You don't just play Doom—you live it." You certainly do.

A more advanced version of Doom, called Quake, is an "ultra-violent gorefest," as one online reviewer called it. Players wander through a maze and use every weapon imaginable to slay aliens. (The nail gun is a big hit.) There's heightened realism because you can view any part of the game from an endless number of angles. For example, it's possible to bounce a grenade off a wall to hit someone around the corner. Lucky you.

What is going on here? Well, for one thing entrepreneurship. Violent computer games are a small but influential part of the $6.2 billion video- and computer-game market. They have proliferated in recent years and are now deeply embedded in youth culture. They are played either on play stations (Nintendo or Sony), PCs, or the Internet, where you battle it out with other players.

With each new release players are promised seemingly endless amounts of blood and gore. The more people you kill and maim the better. It is an entire subculture that uses 3D graphics, spectacular sound effects, and other computer-driven bells and whistles to blur the distinction between reality and fantasy—and to celebrate criminality. The game titles speak for themselves: Blood, Bedlam, Death Rally, and Redneck Rampage.

The idea is not just to kill but to kill with glee. Last year, a new joy-   10
stick system promised: "You get better accuracy and control, but what
are you going to do with all the extra bodies? Be the first on your block
to make your neighbors say, 'What's that smell?'" Another manufacturer, Interplay Productions, celebrates "the sheer ecstasy of crunching
bones against their bumper" in its game Carmageddon. "Drive whatever
you want, wherever you want, and over whoever you want. You make
the rules. Your motto. Just kill, baby." And watch the blood spatter on
the windshield.

Video-game violence is not new. As Eric Rozenman noted in a recent
Washington Times article, one of the earlier games, Death Race, caused
quite a commotion in the mid-1970s: "The game involved an automobile driver running down pedestrians. The latter expired with unconvincing moans, the skilled motorists recording a tally of crucifixes."

Even Space Invaders was considered too violent when it was released
in the late 1970s. But the games have become progressively more violent
ever since—and vivid. The most remarkable breakthrough came in 1992,
when a first-person shooter game called Wolfenstein 3-D hit the market.

Previously, players looked at the screen as if from above. With
Wolfenstein 3-D, however, you see the action from the on-screen char-
acter's point of view. You become the character. The following year
Doom was introduced. A deluge of first-person shooter games followed.

These caught the attention of Senator Joseph Lieberman (Democrat,
Connecticut). He and Senator Herb Kohl (Democrat, Wisconsin) held
hearings on the games in 1993. Prodded by the senators, the industry
adopted a voluntary rating system. Yet the ratings are not even enforced
by stores, and incredibly violent games are often rated suitable for kids.
More important, parents don't seem to realize what their kids are
playing.

Should they be concerned? What message, for example, does Grand   15
Theft Auto send? Jayson Bernstein, spokesman for the manufacturer,
American Softworks Corp., says, "It's just a game." Industry spokesmen
also defend their products by contending that there are no studies that
conclusively link computer games to violence.

Some academics, too, say the games get a bum rap. The real problem
is—big surprise here—social injustice. Henry Jenkins, director of Comparative Media Studies at MIT, recently argued that the focus on video-
game violence seems to be the most recent strategy of our culture to shift
focus away from the obvious root causes of violence: urban conditions,
poverty and the ready availability of guns.

And so on. Luckily, for those who worry about a culture in which
these games thrive, a small backlash is evident. In January, the city of
Stanton, California, allowed a new arcade to open only after it promised
not to use violent or sexually charged games. The Minnesota Legislature
is considering banning the sale of violent games to children under eighteen. In Chicago, about fifty people recently demanded that Toys "Я" Us

stop selling violent video games and toys. The protesters, from a partnership of several churches, held a mock funeral outside the store. The store ignored them. In the wake of Littleton, how will such protests play?

Like other refuse that litters the cultural landscape, these computer games didn't just magically appear one day. They have flourished in a cultural milieu in which most anything goes. These days, to paraphrase FDR, it sometimes seems that we have nothing left to stigmatize but stigma itself. When parents and community members try to fight such garbage, or even quarantine it, they are derided in certain quarters as intolerant zealots or enemies of the First Amendment.

But if twelve-year-olds wake up one day and discover they no longer have such easy access to Redneck Rampage, free speech will survive. And everyone else might even be a bit safer.

THINKING AND WRITING ABOUT SEX AND VIOLENCE IN POPULAR CULTURE

QUESTIONS FOR DISCUSSION AND WRITING

1. Kristol defends a limited censorship of popular culture. Summarize his reasons. Would any of the writers in Chapter 15, Freedom of Speech, agree with him?

2. Although Oppenheim is writing about violence and Jacoby is writing about sex, both their claims are based on a shared assumption. Explain it, and decide whether it is valid.

3. What evidence do you find in these essays that establishes a cause-and-effect relationship between TV violence and youthful crime?

4. Rhodes provides evidence from several studies to prove that TV and movie violence do not influence youthful behavior. How convincing is it? Does Rhodes answer the claims of Nordlinger, Jenkins, or Jacoby?

5. Nordlinger accuses antigun activists of being unwilling to attack rappers who "sing of guns with almost lascivious glee" (para. 6). But antigun groups protest that rappers are protected by the First Amendment. What is Nordlinger's response to that argument? Do you think there might be other reasons for the lack of protest?

6. Why does Jenkins think we should resist trying to "reprogram the media" (para. 18)? Do you agree with his explanation for teenage attraction to violent films? If not, do you have other explanations?

7. Several authors contend that TV or movie violence is not to blame for youthful crime. What causes do they suggest?

8. You are probably familiar with some of the games Gahr describes or others like them. Do you agree with the manufacturers that they are harmless? How does Gahr answer objections about violations of "freedom of speech"?

TOPICS FOR RESEARCH

Violence in selected TV shows: justified or unjustified?

Sex on TV: what message?

The significance of gangsta rap

Survey of studies on the effect of TV and movie violence

Influence of music videos and sports events on youthful behavior

TAKING THE DEBATE ONLINE

For these and additional research URLs, see www.bedfordstmartins.com/rottenberg.

- *Profits or Prestige: Sex and Violence in Feature Films*
  http://web.syr.edu/~jlmcquiv/film_sv.html

  This thoroughly researched essay by James McQuivey at Syracuse University explores some of the reasons that film producers in Hollywood rely on sexual and violent content. It ends with a series of charts and graphs that try to track and analyze box office receipts, Academy Award nominations, and violent content.

- *Media Scope: Media Policy Clearinghouse*
  http://mediascope.org

  This site contains an extensive collection of resources about media, including film, television, the Internet, electronic interactive games, and music.

- *Media Watch*
  http://www.mediawatch.com

  Media Watch, an organization whose goal is to challenge abusive stereotypes and other biased images commonly found in the media, provides these links to media-related news stories, videos, and an archive of past content.

- *NCTV: National Coalition on Television Violence*
  http://www.nctvv.org

  The National Coalition on Television Violence provides information on blocking devices, community action, recent news briefs, and a list of links to other organizations whose mission is to end TV violence.

- *Federal Communications Commission Consumer Facts: Obscene and Indecent Broadcasts*
  http://www.fcc.gov/cib/consumerfacts/obscene.html

  This page explains what the FCC considers to be obscene broadcasts and explains how standards are enforced.

PART FOUR
Classic
Arguments

From Crito

PLATO

Socrates: . . . Ought a man to do what he admits to be right, or ought he to betray the right?

Crito: He ought to do what he thinks right.

Socrates: But if this is true, what is the application? In leaving the prison against the will of the Athenians, do I wrong any? Or rather do I not wrong those whom I ought least to wrong? Do I not desert the principles which are acknowledged by us to be just — what do you say?

Crito: I cannot tell, Socrates; for I do not know.

Socrates: Then consider the matter in this way: — Imagine that I am 5 about to play truant (you may call the proceeding by any name which you like), and the laws of the government come and interrogate me: "Tell us, Socrates," they say: "what are you about? Are you not going by an act of yours to overturn us — the laws, and the whole state, as far as in you lies? Do you imagine that a state can subsist and not be overthrown, in which the decisions of law have no power, but are set aside and trampled upon by individuals?" What will be our answer, Crito, to these and the like words? Any one, and especially a rhetorician, will have a good deal to say on behalf of the law which requires a sentence to be carried out. He will argue that this law should not be set aside; and shall we reply, "Yes, but the state has injured us and given an unjust sentence." Suppose I say that?

Crito: Very good, Socrates.

Socrates: "And was that our agreement with you?" the law would answer; "or were you to abide by the sentence of the state?" And if I were to express my astonishment at their words, the law would probably add: "Answer, Socrates, instead of opening your eyes — you are in the habit of asking and answering questions. Tell us, — What complaint have you to make against us which justifies you in attempting to destroy us and the state? In the first place did we not bring you into existence? Your father married your mother by our aid and begat you. Say whether you have any objection to urge against those of us who regulate marriage?" None, I should reply. "Or against those of us who after birth regulate the nurture and education of children, in which you also were trained? Were not the laws, which have the charge of education, right in commanding your father to train you in

---

Plato, who died in 347 B.C., was one of the greatest Greek philosophers. He was a student of the Greek philosopher Socrates, whose teachings he recorded in the form of dialogues between Socrates and his pupils. In this dialogue, Crito visits Socrates — who is in prison, condemned to death for corrupting the youth of Athens — and tries to persuade him to escape. Socrates, however, refuses, basing his decision on his definition of justice and virtue. From Plato's *Crito,* trans. Benjamin Jowett, 3rd ed. (New York: Dial Press, 1982).

music and gymnastics?" Right, I should reply. "Well then, since you were brought into the world and nurtured and educated by us, can you deny in the first place that you are our child and slave, as your fathers were before you? And if this is true you are not on equal terms with us; nor can you think that you have a right to do to us what we are doing to you. Would you have any right to strike or revile or do any other evil to your father or your master, if you had one, because you have been struck or reviled by him, or received some other evil at his hands?—you would not say this? And because we think right to destroy you, do you think that you have any right to destroy us in return, and your country as far as in you lies? Will you, O professor of true virtue, pretend that you are justified in this? Has a philosopher like you failed to discover that our country is more to be valued and higher and holier far than mother or father or any ancestor, and more to be regarded in the eyes of the gods and of men of understanding? Also to be soothed, and gently and reverently entreated when angry, even more than a father, and either to be persuaded, or if not persuaded, to be obeyed? And when we are punished by her, whether with imprisonment or stripes, the punishment is to be endured in silence, and if she leads us to wounds or death in battle, thither we follow as is right; neither may any one yield or retreat or leave his rank, but whether in battle or in a court of law, or in any other place, he must do what his city and his country order him; or he must change their view of what is just: and if he may do no violence to his father or mother, much less may he do violence to his country." What answer shall we make to this, Crito? Do the laws speak truly, or do they not?

Crito: I think that they do.

Socrates: Then the laws will say, "Consider, Socrates, if we are speaking truly that in your present attempt you are going to do us an injury. For, having brought you into the world, and nurtured and educated you, and given you and every other citizen a share in every good which we had to give, we further proclaim to any Athenian by the liberty which we allow him, that if he does not like us when he has become of age and has seen the ways of the city, and made our acquaintance, he may go where he pleases and take his goods with him. None of us laws will forbid him or interfere with him. Any one who does not like us and the city, and who wants to emigrate to a colony or to any other city, may go where he likes, retaining his property. But he who has experience of the manner in which we order justice and administer the state, and still remains, has entered into an implied contract that he will do as we command him. And he who disobeys us is, as we maintain, thrice wrong; first, because in disobeying us he is disobeying his parents; secondly, because we are the authors of his education; thirdly, because he has made an agreement with us that he will duly obey our commands; and he neither obeys them nor convinces us that our commands are unjust; and we do not rudely impose them, but give him the alternative of obeying or convincing us;—that is what we offer, and he does neither.

"These are the sort of accusations to which, as we were saying, you, 10
Socrates, will be exposed if you accomplish your intentions; you, above
all other Athenians." Suppose now I ask, why I rather than anybody else?
They will justly retort upon me that I above all other men have acknowledged the agreement. "There is clear proof," they will say, "Socrates, that
we and the city were not displeasing to you. Of all Athenians you have
been the most constant resident in the city, which, as you never leave,
you may be supposed to love. For you never went out of the city either to
see the games, except once when you went to the Isthmus, or to any
other place unless when you were on military service; nor did you travel
as other men do. Nor had you any curiosity to know other states or their
laws: your affections did not go beyond us and our state; we were your
special favorites, and you acquiesced in our government of you; and here
in this city you begat your children, which is a proof of your satisfaction.
Moreover, you might in the course of the trial, if you had liked, have
fixed the penalty at banishment; the state which refuses to let you go
now would have let you go then. But you pretended that you preferred
death to exile, and that you were not unwilling to die. And now you
have forgotten these fine sentiments, and pay no respect to us the laws,
of whom you are the destroyer; and are doing what only a miserable
slave would do, running away and turning your back upon the compacts
and agreements which you made as a citizen. And first of all answer this
very question: Are we right in saying that you agreed to be governed according to us in deed, and not in word only? Is that true or not?" How
shall we answer, Crito? Must we not assent?

Crito: We cannot help it, Socrates.

Socrates: Then will they not say: "You, Socrates, are breaking the
covenants and agreements which you made with us at your leisure, not
in any haste or under any compulsion or deception, but after you have
had seventy years to think of them, during which time you were at liberty to leave the city, if we were not to your mind, or if our covenants appeared to you to be unfair. You had your choice, and might have gone
either to Lacedaemon or Crete, both which states are often praised by
you for their good government, or to some other Hellenic or foreign
state. Whereas you, above all our Athenians, seemed to be so fond of
the state, or, in other words, of us her laws (and who would care about a
state which has no laws?), that you never stirred out of her; the halt, the
blind, the maimed were not more stationary in her than you were. And
now you run away and forsake your agreements. Not so, Socrates, if you
will take our advice; do not make yourself ridiculous by escaping out of
the city.

"For just consider, if you transgress and err in this sort of way, what
good will you do either to yourself or to your friends? That your friends
will be driven into exile and deprived of citizenship, or will lose their
property, is tolerably certain; and you yourself, if you fly to one of the
neighboring cities, as, for example, Thebes or Megara, both of which are

well governed, will come to them as an enemy, Socrates, and their government will be against you, and all patriotic citizens will cast an evil eye upon you as a subverter of the laws, and you will confirm in the minds of the judges the justice of their own condemnation of you. For he who is a corrupter of the laws is more than likely to be a corrupter of the young and foolish portion of mankind. Will you then flee from well-ordered citizens and virtuous men? And is existence worth having on these terms? Or will you go to them without shame, and talk to them, Socrates? And what will you say to them? What you say here about virtue and justice and institutions and laws being the best things among men? Would that be decent of you? Surely not. But if you go away from well-governed states to Crito's friends in Thessaly, where there is a great disorder and licence, they will be charmed to hear the tale of your escape from prison, set off with ludicrous particulars of the manner in which you were wrapped in a goatskin or some other disguise, and metamorphosed as the manner is of runaways; but will there be no one to remind you that in your old age you were ashamed to violate the most sacred laws from a miserable desire of a little more life? Perhaps not, if you keep them in a good temper; but if they are out of temper you will hear many degrading things; you will live, but how?—as the flatterer of all men, and the servant of all men; and doing what?—eating and drinking in Thessaly, having gone abroad in order that you may get a dinner. And where will be your fine sentiments about justice and virtue? Say that you wish to live for the sake of your children—you want to bring them up and educate them—will you take them into Thessaly and deprive them of Athenian citizenship? Is this the benefit which you will confer upon them? Or are you under the impression that they will be better cared for and educated here if you are still alive, although absent from them; for your friends will take care of them? Do you fancy that if you are an inhabitant of Thessaly they will take care of them, and if you are an inhabitant of the other world that they will not take care of them? Nay: but if they who call themselves friends are good for anything, they will—to be sure they will.

"Listen, then, Socrates, to us who have brought you up. Think not of life and children first, and of justice afterwards, but of justice first, that you may be justified before the princes of the world below. For neither will you nor any that belong to you be happier or holier or juster in this life, or happier in another, if you do as Crito bids. Now you depart in innocence, a sufferer and not a doer of evil; a victim, not of the laws of men. But if you go forth, returning evil for evil, and injury for injury, breaking the covenants and agreements which you have made with us, and wronging those whom you ought least of all to wrong, that is to say, yourself, your friends, your country, and us, we shall be angry with you while you live, and our brethren, the laws in the world below, will receive you as an enemy; for they will know that you have done your best to destroy us. Listen, then, to us and not to Crito."

This, dear Crito, is the voice which I seem to hear murmuring in my 15 ears, like the sound of the flute in the ears of the mystic; that voice, I say, is humming in my ears, and prevents me from hearing any other. And I know that anything more which you may say will be vain. Yet speak, if you have anything to say.

Crito: I have nothing to say, Socrates.

Socrates: Leave me then, Crito, to fulfill the will of God, and to follow whither he leads.

DISCUSSION QUESTIONS

1. What debt to the law and his country does Socrates acknowledge? Mention the specific reasons for which he owes obedience. Is the analogy of the country to parents a plausible one? Why, or why not?

2. Explain the nature of the implied contract that exists between Socrates and the state. According to the state, how has Socrates forfeited his right to object to punishment?

3. What appeal does that state make to Socrates' sense of justice and virtue?

WRITING SUGGESTIONS

4. Socrates bases his refusal to escape the death penalty on his definition of justice and virtue. Basing your own argument on other criteria, make a claim for the right of Socrates to try to escape his punishment. Would some good be served by his escape?

5. The analogy between one's country and one's parents is illustrated at great length in Socrates' argument. In the light of modern ideas about the relationship between the state and the individual in a democracy, write a refutation of the analogy. Perhaps you can think of a different and more fitting one.

A Modest Proposal

JONATHAN SWIFT

I t is a melancholy object to those who walk through this great town[1] or travel in the country, when they see the streets, the roads, and cabin doors, crowded with beggars of the female sex, followed by three, four, or six children, all in rags and importuning every passenger for an alms. These mothers, instead of being able to work for their honest livelihood, are forced to employ all their time in strolling to beg sustenance for their helpless infants, who, as they grow up, either turn thieves for want of work, or leave their dear native country to fight for the Pretender in Spain, or sell themselves to the Barbados.[2]

I think it is agreed by all parties that this prodigious number of children in the arms, or on the backs, or at the heels of their mothers, and frequently of their fathers, is in the present deplorable state of the kingdom a very great additional grievance; and therefore whoever could find out a fair, cheap, and easy method of making these children sound, useful members of the commonwealth would deserve so well of the public as to have his statue set up for a preserver of the nation.

But my intention is very far from being confined to provide only for the children of professed beggars; it is of a much greater extent, and shall take in the whole number of infants at a certain age who are born of parents in effect as little able to support them as those who demand our charity in the streets.

As to my own part, having turned my thoughts for many years upon this important subject, and maturely weighed the several schemes of other projectors,[3] I have always found them grossly mistaken in their computation. It is true, a child just dropped from its dam may be supported by her milk for a solar year, with little other nourishment; at most not above the value of two shillings, which the mother may certainly

---

[1] Dublin. — ED. [All notes are the editor's.]

[2] The Pretender was James Stuart, who was exiled to Spain. Many Irish men had joined an army attempting to return him to the English throne in 1715. Others had become indentured servants, agreeing to work for a set number of years in Barbados or other British colonies in exchange for their transportation out of Ireland.

[3] Planners.

This essay is acknowledged by almost all critics to be the most powerful example of irony in the English language. (*Irony* means saying one thing but meaning another.) In 1729 Jonathan Swift, prolific satirist and dean of St. Patrick's Cathedral in Dublin, was moved to write in protest against the terrible poverty in which the Irish were living under British rule. Notice that the essay is organized according to one of the patterns outlined in Part Two of this book (see Presenting the Stock Issues, Chapter 9, p. 335). First, Swift establishes the need for a change, then he offers his proposal, and finally, he lists its advantages.

get, or the value in scraps, by her lawful occupation of begging; and it is exactly at one year that I propose to provide for them in such a manner as instead of being a charge upon their parents or the parish, or wanting food and raiment for the rest of their lives, they shall on the contrary contribute to the feeding, and partly to the clothing, of many thousands.

There is likewise another great advantage in my scheme, that it will prevent those voluntary abortions, and that horrid practice of women murdering their bastard children, alas, too frequent among us, sacrificing the poor innocent babes, I doubt, more to avoid the expense than the shame, which would move tears and pity in the most savage and inhuman breast.

The number of souls in this kingdom being usually reckoned one million and a half, of these I calculate there may be about two hundred thousand couples whose wives are breeders; from which number I subtract thirty thousand couples who are able to maintain their own children, although I apprehend there cannot be so many under the present distress of the kingdom; but this being granted, there will remain an hundred and seventy thousand breeders. I again subtract fifty thousand for those women who miscarry, or whose children die by accident or disease within the year. There only remain an hundred and twenty thousand children of poor parents annually born. The question therefore is, how this number shall be reared and provided for, which, as I have already said, under the present situation of affairs, is utterly impossible by all the methods hitherto proposed. For we can neither employ them in handicraft or agriculture; we neither build houses (I mean in the country) nor cultivate land. They can very seldom pick up a livelihood by stealing till they arrive at six years old, except where they are of towardly parts;[4] although I confess they learn the rudiments much earlier, during which time they can however be looked upon only as probationers, as I have been informed by a principal gentleman in the county of Cavan, who protested to me that he never knew above one or two instances under the age of six, even in a part of the kingdom so renowned for the quickest proficiency in that art.

I am assured by our merchants that a boy or a girl before twelve years old is no salable commodity; and even when they come to this age they will not yield above three pounds, or three pounds and a half a crown at most on the Exchange; which cannot turn to account either to the parents or the kingdom, the charge of nutriment and rags having been at least four times that value.

I shall now therefore humbly propose my own thoughts, which I hope will not be liable to the least objection.

I have been assured by a very knowing American of my acquaintance in London, that a young healthy child well nursed is at a year old a most delicious, nourishing, and wholesome food, whether stewed, roasted,

[4]Innate talents.

baked, or boiled; and I make no doubt that it will equally serve in a fricassee or a ragout.[5]

I do therefore humbly offer it to public consideration that of the 10 hundred and twenty thousand children, already computed, twenty thousand may be reserved for breed, whereof only one fourth part to be males, which is more than we allow to sheep, black cattle, or swine; and my reason is that these children are seldom the fruits of marriage, a circumstance not much regarded by our savages, therefore one male will be sufficient to serve four females. That the remaining hundred thousand may at a year old be offered in sale to the persons of quality and fortune through the kingdom, always advising the mother to let them suck plentifully in the last month, so as to render them plump and fat for a good table. A child will make two dishes at an entertainment for friends; and when the family dines alone, the fore or hind quarter will make a reasonable dish, and seasoned with a little pepper or salt will be very good boiled on the fourth day, especially in winter.

I have reckoned upon a medium that a child just born will weigh twelve pounds, and in a solar year if tolerably nursed increaseth to twenty-eight pounds.

I grant this food will be somewhat dear, and therefore very proper for landlords, who, as they have already devoured most of the parents, seem to have the best title to the children.

Infant's flesh will be in season throughout the year, but more plentiful in March, and a little before and after. For we are told by a grave author, an eminent French physician,[6] that fish being a prolific diet, there are more children born in Roman Catholic countries about nine months after Lent than at any other season; therefore, reckoning a year after Lent, the markets will be more glutted than usual, because the number of popish infants is at least three to one in this kingdom; and therefore it will have one other collateral advantage, by lessening the number of Papists among us.

I have already computed the charge of nursing a beggar's child (in which list I reckon all cottagers, laborers, and four-fifths of the farmers) to be about two shillings per annum, rags included; and I believe no gentleman would repine to give ten shillings for the carcass of a good fat child, which, as I have said, will make four dishes of excellent nutritive meat, when he hath only some particular friend or his own family to dine with him. Thus the squire will learn to be a good landlord, and grow popular among the tenants; the mother will have eight shillings net profit, and be fit for work till she produces another child.

---

[5]Stew.

[6]A reference to Swift's favorite French writer, François Rabelais (1494?–1553), who was actually a broad satirist known for his coarse humor.

Those who are more thrifty (as I must confess the times require) may   15
flay the carcass; the skin of which artificially[7] dressed will make admirable gloves for ladies, and summer boots for fine gentlemen.

As to our city of Dublin, shambles[8] may be appointed for this purpose in the most convenient parts of it, and butchers we may be assured
will not be wanting; although I rather recommend buying the children
alive, and dressing them hot from the knife as we do roasting pigs.

A very worthy person, a true lover of his country, and whose virtues I
highly esteem, was lately pleased in discoursing on this matter to offer a
refinement upon my scheme. He said that many gentlemen of his kingdom, having of late destroyed their deer, he conceived that the want of
venison might be well supplied by the bodies of young lads and maidens,
not exceeding fourteen years of age nor under twelve, so great a number
of both sexes in every county being now ready to starve for want of work
and service; and these to be disposed of by their parents, if alive, or otherwise by their nearest relations. But with due deference to so excellent a
friend and so deserving a patriot, I cannot be altogether in his sentiments; for as to the males, my American acquaintance assured me from
frequent experience that their flesh was generally tough and lean, like
that of our schoolboys, by continual exercise, and their taste disagreeable; and to fatten them would not answer the charge. Then as to the females, it would, I think with humble submission, be a loss to the public,
because they soon would become breeders themselves; and besides, it is
not improbable that some scrupulous people might be apt to censure
such a practice (although indeed very unjustly) as a little bordering upon
cruelty; which, I confess, hath always been with me the strongest objection against any project, how well soever intended.

But in order to justify my friend, he confessed that this expedient
was put into his head by the famous Psalmanazar,[9] a native of the island
Formosa, who came from thence to London above twenty years ago, and
in conversation told my friend that in his country when any young person happened to be put to death, the executioner sold the carcass to persons of quality as a prime dainty; and that in his time the body of a
plump girl of fifteen, who was crucified for an attempt to poison the em-
peror, was sold to his Imperial Majesty's prime minister of state, and
other great mandarins of the court, in joints from the gibbet, at four
hundred crowns. Neither indeed can I deny that if the same use were
made of several plump young girls in this town, who without one single
groat to their fortunes cannot stir abroad without a chair, and appear at

---

[7]With art or craft.
[8]Butcher shops or slaughterhouses.
[9]Georges Psalmanazar was a Frenchman who pretended to be Japanese and wrote an
entirely imaginary *Description of the Isle Formosa*. He had become well known in
gullible London society.

the playhouse and assemblies in foreign fineries which they never will pay for, the kingdom would not be the worse.

Some persons of a desponding spirit are in great concern about that vast number of poor people who are aged, diseased, or maimed, and I have been desired to employ my thoughts what course may be taken to ease the nation of so grievous an encumbrance. But I am not in the least pain upon that matter, because it is very well known that they are every day dying and rotting by cold and famine, and filth and vermin, as fast as can be reasonably expected. And as to the younger laborers, they are now in almost as hopeful a condition. They cannot get work, and consequently pine away for want of nourishment to a degree that if any time they are accidentally hired to common labor, they have not strength to perform it; and thus the country and themselves are happily delivered from the evils to come.

I have too long digressed, and therefore shall return to my subject. I think the advantages by the proposal which I have made are obvious and many, as well as of the highest importance. 20

For first, as I have already observed, it would greatly lessen the number of Papists, with whom we are yearly overrun, being the principal breeders of the nation as well as our most dangerous enemies; and who stay at home on purpose to deliver the kingdom to the Pretender, hoping to take their advantage by the absence of so many good Protestants, who have chosen rather to leave their country than to stay at home and pay tithes against their conscience to an Episcopal curate.

Secondly, the poorer tenants will have something valuable of their own, which by law may be made liable to distress,[10] and help to pay their landlord's rent, their corn and cattle being already seized and money a thing unknown.

Thirdly, whereas the maintenance of an hundred thousand children, from two years old and upwards, cannot be computed at less than ten shillings a piece per annum, the nation's stock will be thereby increased fifty thousand pounds per annum, besides the profit of a new dish introduced to the tables of all gentlemen of fortune in the kingdom who have any refinement in taste. And the money will circulate among ourselves, the goods being entirely of our own growth and manufacture.

Fourthly, the constant breeders, besides the gain of eight shillings sterling per annum by the sale of their children, will be rid of the charge of maintaining them after the first year.

Fifthly, this food would likewise bring great custom to taverns, where 25 the vintners will certainly be so prudent as to procure the best receipts for dressing it to perfection, and consequently have their houses frequented by all the fine gentlemen, who justly value themselves upon their knowledge in good eating; and a skillful cook, who understands how to oblige his guests, will contrive to make it as expensive as they please.

---

[10]Subject to possession by lenders.

Sixthly, this would be a great inducement to marriage, which all wise nations have either encouraged by rewards or enforced by laws and penalties. It would increase the care and tenderness of mothers toward their children, when they were sure of a settlement for life to the poor babes, provided in some sort by the public, to their annual profit instead of expense. We should see an honest emulation among the married women, which of them could bring the fattest child to the market. Men would become as fond of their wives during the time of their pregnancy as they are now of their mares in foal, their cows in calf, or sows when they are ready to farrow; nor offer to beat or kick them (as is too frequent a practice) for fear of a miscarriage.

Many other advantages might be enumerated. For instance, the addition of some thousand carcasses in our exportation of barreled beef, the propagation of swine's flesh, and improvements in the art of making good bacon, so much wanted among us by the great destruction of pigs, too frequent at our tables, which are no way comparable in taste or magnificence to a well-grown, fat, yearling child, which roasted whole will make a considerable figure at a lord mayor's feast or any other public entertainment. But this and many others I omit, being studious of brevity.

Supposing that one thousand families in this city would be constant customers for infants' flesh, besides others who might have it at merry meetings, particularly weddings and christenings, I compute that Dublin would take off annually about twenty thousand carcasses, and the rest of the kingdom (where probably they will be sold somewhat cheaper) the remaining eighty thousand.

I can think of no one objection that will possibly be raised against this proposal, unless it should be urged that the number of people will be thereby much lessened in the kingdom. This I freely own, and it was indeed one principal design in offering it to the world. I desire the reader will observe, that I calculate my remedy for this one individual kingdom of Ireland and for no other that ever was, is, or I think ever can be upon earth. Therefore let no man talk to me of other expedients: of taxing our absentees at five shillings a pound: of using neither clothes nor household furniture except what is of our own growth and manufacture: of utterly rejecting the materials and instruments that promote foreign luxury: of curing the expensiveness of pride, vanity, idleness, and gaming in our women: of introducing a vein of parsimony, prudence, and temperance: of learning to love our country, in the want of which we differ even from Laplanders and the inhabitants of Topinamboo:[11] of quitting our animosities and factions, nor acting any longer like the Jews, who were murdering one another at the very moment their city was taken:[12] of being a little cautious not to sell our country and conscience

[11]District of Brazil.
[12]During the Roman siege of Jerusalem (A.D. 70), prominent Jews were charged with collaborating with the enemy and put to death.

for nothing: of teaching landlords to have at least one degree of mercy toward their tenants: lastly, of putting a spirit of honesty, industry, and skill into our shopkeepers; who, if a resolution could now be taken to buy only our native goods, would immediately unite to cheat and exact upon us in the price, the measure, and the goodness, nor could ever yet be brought to make one fair proposal of just dealing, though often and earnestly invited to it.

Therefore I repeat, let no man talk to me of these and the like expedi- 30 ents, till he hath at least some glimpse of hope that there will ever be some hearty and sincere attempt to put them in practice.

But as to myself, having been wearied out for many years with offering vain, idle, visionary thoughts, and at length utterly despairing of success, I fortunately fell upon this proposal, which, as it is wholly new, so it hath something solid and real, of no expense and little trouble, full in our own power, and whereby we can incur no danger in disobliging England. For this kind of commodity will not bear exportation, the flesh being of too tender a consistence to admit a long continuance in salt, although perhaps I could name a country which would be glad to eat up our whole nation without it.

After all, I am not so violently bent upon my own opinion as to reject any offer proposed by wise men, which shall be found equally innocent, cheap, easy, and effectual. But before something of that kind shall be advanced in contradiction to my scheme, and offering a better, I desire the author or authors will be pleased maturely to consider two points. First, as things now stand, how they will be able to find food and raiment for an hundred thousand useless mouths and backs. And secondly, there being a round million of creatures in human figure throughout this kingdom, whose sole subsistence put into a common stock would leave them in debt two millions of pounds sterling, adding those who are beggars by profession to the bulk of farmers, cottagers, and laborers, with their wives and children who are beggars in effect; I desire those politicians who dislike my overture, and may perhaps be so bold to attempt an answer, that they will first ask the parents of these mortals whether they would not at this day think it a great happiness to have been sold for food at a year old in this manner I prescribe, and thereby have avoided such a perpetual scene of misfortunes as they have since gone through by the oppression of landlords, the impossibility of paying rent without money or trade, the want of common sustenance, with neither house nor clothes to cover them from the inclemencies of the weather, and the most inevitable prospect of entailing the like of greater miseries upon their breed forever.

I profess, in the sincerity of my heart, that I have not the least personal interest in endeavoring to promote this necessary work, having no other motive than the public good of my country, by advancing our trade, providing for infants, relieving the poor, and giving some pleasure to the rich. I have no children by which I can propose to get a single penny; the youngest being nine years old, and my wife past childbearing.

DISCUSSION QUESTIONS

1. What implicit assumption about the treatment of the Irish underlies Swift's proposal? Do expressions such as "just dropped from its dam" (para. 4) and "whose wives are breeders" (para. 6) give the reader a clue?

2. In this essay Swift assumes a persona; that is, for the purposes of the proposal he makes, he pretends to be a different person. Describe the characteristics of that person. Point out the places in the essay that reveal them.

3. In several places, however, Swift reveals himself as the outraged witness of English cruelty and indifference. Note the language that seems to reflect his own feelings.

4. Throughout the essay Swift recites lists of facts, many of them in the form of statistics. How do these facts contribute to the persuasiveness of his argument? How do they affect the reader?

5. What social practices and attitudes of both the Irish and the English does Swift condemn?

6. Does Swift offer any solutions for the problems he attacks? How do you know?

7. When this essay first appeared in 1729, some readers took it seriously and accused Swift of monstrous cruelty. Can you think of reasons that these readers failed to recognize the ironic intent?

WRITING SUGGESTIONS

8. Try an ironical essay of your own. Choose a subject that clearly lends itself to such treatment. As Swift did, use logic and restraint in your language.

9. Choose a problem for which you think you have a solution. Defend your solution by using the stock issues as your pattern of organization.

Civil Disobedience

HENRY DAVID THOREAU

I heartily accept the motto, — "That government is best which governs least"; and I should like to see it acted up to more rapidly and systematically. Carried out, it finally amounts to this, which also I believe, — "That government is best which governs not at all"; and when men are prepared for it, that will be the kind of government which they will have. Government is at best but an expedient; but most governments are usually, and all governments are sometimes, inexpedient. The objections which have been brought against a standing army, and they are many and weighty, and deserve to prevail, may also at last be brought against a standing government. The standing army is only an arm of the standing government. The government itself, which is only the mode which the people have chosen to execute their will, is equally liable to be abused and perverted before the people can act through it. Witness the present Mexican war, the work of comparatively a few individuals using the standing government as their tool; for, in the outset, the people would not have consented to this measure.

This American government, — what is it but a tradition, though a recent one, endeavoring to transmit itself unimpaired to posterity, but each instant losing some of its integrity? It has not the vitality and force of a single living man; for a single man can bend it to his will. It is a sort of wooden gun to the people themselves. But it is not the less necessary for this; for the people must have some complicated machinery or other, and hear its din, to satisfy that idea of government which they have. Governments show thus how successfully men can be imposed on, even impose on themselves, for their own advantage. It is excellent, we must all allow. Yet this government never of itself furthered any enterprise, but by the alacrity with which it got out of its way. *It* does not keep the country free. *It* does not settle the West. *It* does not educate. The character inherent in the American people has done all that has been accomplished; and it would have done somewhat more, if the government had not sometimes got in its way. For government is an expedient by which men would fain succeed in letting one another alone; and, as has been said, when it is most expedient, the governed are most let alone by it. Trade and commerce, if they were not made of India-rubber, would never

---

Henry David Thoreau (1817–1862), philosopher and writer, is best known for *Walden,* an account of his solitary retreat to Walden Pond, near Concord, Massachusetts. Here he remained for more than two years in an effort to "live deliberately, to front only the essential facts of life." "Civil Disobedience" was first given as a lecture in 1848 and published in 1849. It was widely read and influenced both Mahatma Gandhi in the passive-resistance campaign he led against the British in India and Martin Luther King Jr. in the U.S. civil rights movement.

manage to bounce over the obstacles which legislators are continually putting in their way; and, if one were to judge these men wholly by the effects of their actions, and not partly by their intentions, they would deserve to be classed and punished with those mischievous persons who put obstructions on the railroads.

But, to speak practically and as a citizen, unlike those who call themselves no-government men, I ask for, not at once no government, but *at once* a better government. Let every man make known what kind of government would command his respect, and that will be one step toward obtaining it.

After all, the practical reason why, when the power is once in the hands of the people, a majority are permitted, and for a long period continue, to rule, is not because they are most likely to be in the right, nor because this seems fairest to the minority, but because they are physically the strongest. But a government in which the majority rule in all cases cannot be based on justice, even as far as men understand it. Can there not be a government in which majorities do not virtually decide right and wrong, but conscience?—in which majorities decide only those questions to which the rule of expediency is applicable? Must the citizen ever for a moment, or in the least degree, resign his conscience to the legislator? Why has every man a conscience, then? I think that we should be men first, and subjects afterward. It is not desirable to cultivate a respect for the law, so much as for the right. The only obligation which I have a right to assume, is to do at any time what I think right. It is truly enough said, that a corporation has no conscience; but a corporation of conscientious men is a corporation *with* a conscience. Law never made men a whit more just; and, by means of their respect for it, even the well-disposed are daily made the agents of injustice. A common and natural result of an undue respect for law is, that you may see a file of soldiers, colonel, captain, corporal, privates, powder-monkeys, and all, marching in admirable order over hill and dale to the wars, against their wills, aye, against their common sense and consciences, which makes it very steep marching indeed, and produces a palpitation of the heart. They have no doubt that it is a damnable business in which they are concerned; they are all peaceably inclined. Now, what are they? Men at all? or small moveable forts and magazines, at the service of some unscrupulous man in power? Visit the Navy-Yard, and behold a marine, such a man as an American government can make, or such as it can make a man with its black arts,—a mere shadow and reminiscence of humanity, a man laid out alive and standing, and already, as one may say, buried under arms with funeral accompaniments, though it may be,—

Not a drum was heard, nor a funeral note,
As his corse to the rampart we hurried;
Not a soldier discharged his farewell shot
O'er the grave where our hero we buried.

The mass of men serve the state thus, not as men mainly, but as ma- 5 chines, with their bodies. They are the standing army, and the militia, jailers, constables, posse comitatus, &c. In most cases there is no free exercise whatever of the judgment or of the moral sense; but they put themselves on a level with wood and earth and stones; and wooden men can perhaps be manufactured that will serve the purpose as well. Such command no more respect than men of straw, or a lump of dirt. They have the same sort of worth only as horses and dogs. Yet such as these even are commonly esteemed good citizens. Others, — as most legislators, politicians, lawyers, ministers, and office-holders, — serve the State chiefly with their heads; and, as they rarely make any moral distinctions, they are as likely to serve the Devil, without *intending* it, as God. A very few, as heroes, patriots, martyrs, reformers in the great sense, and *men*, serve the state with their consciences also, and so necessarily resist it for the most part, and they are commonly treated as enemies by it. A wise man will only be useful as a man, and will not submit to be "clay," and "stop a hole to keep the wind away," but leave that office to his dust at least: —

> I am too high-born to be propertied,
> To be a secondary at control,
> Or useful serving-man and instrument
> To any sovereign state throughout the world.

He who gives himself entirely to his fellow-men appears to them useless and selfish; but he who gives himself partially to them is pronounced a benefactor and philanthropist.

How does it become a man to behave toward this American government today? I answer that he cannot without disgrace be associated with it. I cannot for an instant recognize that political organization as *my* government which is the *slave's* government also.

All men recognize the right of revolution; that is, the right to refuse allegiance to, and to resist, the government, when its tyranny or its inefficiency are great and unendurable. But almost all say that such is not the case now. But such was the case, they think, in the Revolution of '75. If one were to tell me that this was a bad government because it taxed certain foreign commodities brought to its ports, it is most probable that I should not make an ado about it, for I can do without them. All machines have their friction; and possibly this does enough good to counterbalance the evil. At any rate, it is a great evil to make a stir about it. But when the friction comes to have its machine, and oppression and robbery are organized, I say, let us not have such a machine any longer. In other words, when a sixth of the population of a nation which has undertaken to be the refuge of liberty are slaves, and a whole country is unjustly overrun and conquered by a foreign army, and subjected to military law, I think that it is not too soon for honest men to rebel and revolutionize. What makes this duty the more urgent is the fact, that the country so overrun is not our own, but ours is the invading army.

Paley, a common authority with many on moral questions, in his chapter on the "Duty of Submission to Civil Government," resolves all civil obligation into expediency; and he proceeds to say, "that so long as the interest of the whole society requires it, that is, so long as the established government cannot be resisted or changed without public inconveniency, it is the will of God that the established government be obeyed, and no longer. . . . This principle being admitted, the justice of every particular case of resistance is reduced to a computation of the quantity of the danger and grievance on the one side, and of the probability and expense of redressing it on the other." Of this, he says, every man shall judge for himself. But Paley appears never to have contemplated those cases to which the rule of expediency does not apply, in which a people, as well as an individual, must do justice, cost what it may. If I have unjustly wrested a plank from a drowning man, I must restore it to him though I drown myself. This, according to Paley, would be inconvenient. But he that would save his life, in such a case, shall lose it. This people must cease to hold slaves, and to make war on Mexico, though it cost them their existence as a people.

In their practice, nations agree with Paley; but does any one think   10
that Massachusetts does exactly what is right at the present crisis?

> A drab of state, a cloth-'o-silver slut,
> To have her train borne up, and her soul trail in the dirt.

Practically speaking, the opponents to a reform in Massachusetts are not a hundred thousand politicians at the South, but a hundred thousand merchants and farmers here, who are more interested in commerce and agriculture than they are in humanity, and are not prepared to do justice to the slave and to Mexico, *cost what it may.* I quarrel not with far-off foes, but with those who, near at home, cooperate with, and do the bidding of, those far away, and without whom the latter would be harmless. We are accustomed to say, that the mass of men are unprepared; but improvement is slow, because the few are not materially wiser or better than the many. It is not so important that many should be as good as you, as that there be some absolute goodness somewhere; for that will leaven the whole lump. There are thousands who are *in opinion* opposed to slavery and to the war, who yet in effect do nothing to put an end to them; who, esteeming themselves children of Washington and Franklin, sit down with their hands in their pockets, and say that they know not what to do, and do nothing; who even postpone the question of freedom to the question of free-trade, and quietly read the prices-current along with the latest advice from Mexico, after dinner, and, it may be, fall asleep over them both. What is the price-current of an honest man and patriot today? They hesitate, and they regret, and sometimes they petition; but they do nothing in earnest and with effect. They will wait, well disposed, for others to remedy the evil, that they may no longer have it to regret. At most, they give only a cheap vote, and a feeble countenance and God-speed, to the right, as it goes by them. There are nine hundred and ninety-nine patrons of virtue to one virtuous man; but it is easier to deal with the real possessor of a thing than with the temporary guardian of it.

All voting is a sort of gaming, like checkers or backgammon, with a slight moral tinge to it, a playing with right and wrong, with moral questions; and betting naturally accompanies it. The character of the voters is not staked. I cast my vote, perchance, as I think right; but I am not vitally concerned that that right should prevail. I am willing to leave it to the majority. Its obligation, therefore, never exceeds that of expediency. Even voting *for the right* is *doing* nothing for it. It is only expressing to men feebly your desire that it should prevail. A wise man will not leave the right to the mercy of chance, nor wish it to prevail through the power of the majority. There is but little virtue in the action of masses of men. When the majority shall at length vote for the abolition of slavery, it will be because they are indifferent to slavery, or because there is but little slavery left to be abolished by their vote. *They* will then be the only slaves. Only *his* vote can hasten the abolition of slavery who asserts his own freedom by his vote.

I hear of a convention to be held at Baltimore, or elsewhere, for the selection of a candidate for the presidency, made up chiefly of editors, and men who are politicians by profession; but I think, what is it to any independent, intelligent, and respectable man what decision they may come to? Shall we not have the advantage of his wisdom and honesty, nevertheless? Can we not count upon some independent votes? Are there not many individuals in the country who do not attend conventions? But no: I find that the respectable man, so called, has immediately drifted from his position, and despairs of his country, when his country has more reason to despair of him. He forthwith adopts one of the candidates thus selected as the only *available* one, thus providing that he is himself *available* for any purposes of the demagogue. His vote is of no more worth than that of any unprincipled foreigner or hireling native, who may have been bought. O for a man who is *a man,* and, as my neighbor says, has a bone in his back which you cannot pass your hand through! Our statistics are at fault: The population has been returned too large. How many *men* are there to a square thousand miles in this country? Hardly one. Does not America offer any inducement for men to settle here? The American has dwindled into an Odd Fellow, — one who may be known by the development of his organ of gregariousness, and a manifest lack of intellect and cheerful self-reliance; whose first and chief concern, on coming into the world, is to see that the Almshouses are in good repair; and, before yet he has lawfully donned the virile garb, to collect a fund for the support of the widows and orphans that may be;

who, in short, ventures to live only by the aid of the Mutual Insurance company, which has promised to bury him decently.

It is not a man's duty, as a matter of course, to devote himself to the eradication of any, even the most enormous wrong; he may still properly have other concerns to engage him; but it is his duty, at least, to wash his hands of it, and, if he gives it no thought longer, not to give it practically his support. If I devote myself to other pursuits and contemplations, I must first see, at least, that I do not pursue them sitting upon another man's shoulders. I must get off him first, that he may pursue his contemplations too. See what gross inconsistency is tolerated. I have heard some of my townsmen say, "I should like to have them order me out to help put down an insurrection of the slaves, or to march to Mexico;—see if I would go"; and yet these very men have each, directly by their allegiance, and so indirectly, at least, by their money, furnished a substitute. The soldier is applauded who refuses to serve in an unjust war by those who do not refuse to sustain the unjust government which makes the war; is applauded by those whose own act and authority he disregards and sets at nought; as if the State were penitent to that degree that it hired one to scourge it while it sinned, but not to that degree that it left off sinning for a moment. Thus, under the name of Order and Civil Government, we are all made at last to pay homage to and support our own meanness. After the first blush of sin, comes its indifference; and from immoral it becomes, as it were, *un*moral, and not quite unnecessary to that life which we have made.

The broadest and most prevalent error requires the most disinterested virtue to sustain it. The slight reproach to which the virtue of patriotism is commonly liable, the noble are most likely to incur. Those who, while they disapprove of the character and measures of a government, yield to it their allegiance and support, are undoubtedly its most conscientious supporters, and so frequently the most serious obstacles to reform. Some are petitioning the State to dissolve the Union, to disregard the requisitions of the President. Why do they not dissolve it themselves,—the union between themselves and the State,—and refuse to pay their quota into its treasury? Do not they stand in the same relation to the State, that the State does to the Union? And have not the same reasons prevented the State from resisting the Union which have prevented them from resisting the State?

How can a man be satisfied to entertain an opinion merely, and 15 enjoy *it*? Is there any enjoyment in it, if his opinion is that he is aggrieved? If you are cheated out of a single dollar by your neighbor, you do not rest satisfied with knowing that you are cheated, or with saying that you are cheated, or even with petitioning him to pay you your due; but you take effectual steps at once to obtain the full amount, and see that you are never cheated again. Action from principle, the perception and the performance of right, changes things and relations; it is essentially revolutionary, and does not consist wholly with anything which was. It not only divides states and churches, it divides families; ay, it divides the *individual,* separating the diabolical in him from the divine.

Unjust laws exist: Shall we be content to obey them, or shall we endeavor to amend them, and obey them until we have succeeded, or shall we transgress them at once? Men generally, under such a government as this, think that they ought to wait until they have persuaded the majority to alter them. They think that, if they should resist, the remedy would be worse than the evil. But it is the fault of the government itself that the remedy *is* worse than the evil. *It* makes it worse. Why is it not more apt to anticipate and provide for reform? Why does it not cherish its wise minority? Why does it cry and resist before it is hurt? Why does it not encourage its citizens to be on the alert to point out its faults, and *do* better than it would have them? Why does it always crucify Christ, and excommunicate Copernicus and Luther, and pronounce Washington and Franklin rebels?

One would think, that a deliberate and practical denial of its authority was the only offence never contemplated by government; else, why has it not assigned its definite, its suitable and proportionate penalty? If a man who has no property refuses but once to earn nine shillings for the State, he is put in prison for a period unlimited by any law that I know, and determined only by the discretion of those who placed him there; but if he should steal ninety times nine shillings from the State, he is soon permitted to go at large again.

If the injustice is part of the necessary friction of the machine of government, let it go, let it go: Perchance it will wear smooth,—certainly the machine will wear out. If the injustice has a spring, or a pulley, or a rope, or a crank, exclusively for itself, then perhaps you may consider whether the remedy will not be worse than the evil; but if it is of such a nature that it requires you to be the agent of injustice to another, then, I say, break the law. Let your life be a counter friction to stop the machine. What I have to do is to see, at any rate, that I do not lend myself to the wrong which I condemn.

As for adopting the ways which the State has provided for remedying the evil, I know not of such ways. They take too much time, and a man's life will be gone. I have other affairs to attend to. I came into this world, not chiefly to make this a good place to live in, but to live in it, be it good or bad. A man has not everything to do, but something; and because he cannot do *everything,* it is not necessary that he should do *something* wrong. It is not my business to be petitioning the Governor or the Legislature any more than it is theirs to petition me; and, if they should not hear my petition, what should I do then? But in this case the State has provided no way: Its very Constitution is the evil. This may seem to be harsh and stubborn and unconciliatory; but it is to treat with the utmost kindness and consideration the only spirit that can appreciate or deserves it. So is all change for the better, like birth and death, which convulse the body.

I do not hesitate to say, that those who call themselves Abolitionists 20 should at once effectually withdraw their support, both in person and property, from the government of Massachusetts, and not wait till they constitute a majority of one, before they suffer the right to prevail through them. I think that it is enough if they have God on their side, without waiting for that other one. Moreover, any man more right than his neighbors, constitutes a majority of one already.

I meet this American government, or its representative, the State government, directly, and face to face, once a year—no more—in the person of its tax-gatherer; this is the only mode in which a man situated as I am necessarily meets it; and it then says distinctly, Recognize me; and the simplest, the most effectual, and, in the present posture of affairs, the indispensablest mode of treating with it on this head, of expressing your little satisfaction with and love for it, is to deny it then. My civil neighbor, the tax-gatherer, is the very man I have to deal with,—for it is, after all, with men and not with parchment that I quarrel,—and he has voluntarily chosen to be an agent of the government. How shall he ever know well what he is and does as an officer of the government, or as a man, until he is obliged to consider whether he shall treat me, his neighbor, for whom he has respect, as a neighbor and well-disposed man, or as a maniac and disturber of the peace, and see if he can get over this obstruction to his neighborliness without a ruder and more impetuous thought or speech corresponding with his action? I know this well, that if one thousand, if one hundred, if ten men whom I could name,— if ten *honest* men only,—aye, if *one* HONEST man, in this State of Massachusetts, *ceasing to hold slaves,* were actually to withdraw from this copartnership, and be locked up in the county jail therefor, it would be the abolition of slavery in America. For it matters not how small the beginning may seem to be: What is once well done is done forever. But we love better to talk about it: That we say is our mission. Reform keeps many scores of newspapers in its service, but not one man. If my esteemed neighbor, the State's ambassador, who will devote his days to the settlement of the question of human rights in the Council Chamber, instead of being threatened with the prisons of Carolina, were to sit down the prisoner of Massachusetts, that State which is so anxious to foist the sin of slavery upon her sister,—though at present she can discover only an act of inhospitality to be the ground of a quarrel with her,—the Legislature would not wholly waive the subject the following winter.

Under a government which imprisons any unjustly, the true place for a just man is also a prison. The proper place today, the only place which Massachusetts has provided for her freer and less desponding spirits, is in her prisons, to be put out and locked out of the State by her own act, as they have already put themselves out by their principles. It is there that the fugitive slave, and the Mexican prisoner on parole, and the Indian come to plead the wrongs of his race, should find them; on that separate, but more free and honorable ground, where the State places those who are not *with* her, but *against* her,—the only house in a slave State in which a free man can abide with honor. If any think that their influence would be lost there, and their voices no longer afflict the ear of the State, that they would not be as an enemy within its walls, they do not know by how much truth is stronger than error, nor how much more eloquently and effectively he can combat injustice who has experienced a little in his own person. Cast your whole vote, not a strip of paper merely, but your whole influence. A minority is powerless while it conforms to the majority; it is not even a minority then; but it is irresistible when it clogs by its whole weight. If the alternative is to keep all just men in prison, or give up war and slavery, the State will not hesitate which to choose. If a thousand men were not to pay their tax-bills this year, that would not be a violent and bloody measure, as it would be to pay them, and enable the State to commit violence and shed innocent blood. This is, in fact, the definition of a peaceable revolution, if any such is possible. If the tax-gatherer, or any other public officer, asks me, as one has done, "But what shall I do?" my answer is, "If you really wish to do any thing, resign your office." When the subject has refused allegiance, and the officer has resigned his office, then the revolution is accomplished. But even suppose blood should flow. Is there not a sort of blood shed when the conscience is wounded? Through this wound a man's real manhood and immortality flow out, and he bleeds to an everlasting death. I see this blood flowing now.

I have contemplated the imprisonment of the offender, rather than the seizure of his goods,—though both will serve the same purpose,—because they who assert the purest right, and consequently are most dangerous to a corrupt State, commonly have not spent much time in accumulating property. To such the State renders comparatively small service, and a slight tax is wont to appear exorbitant, particularly if they are obliged to earn it by special labor with their hands. If there were one who lived wholly without the use of money, the State itself would hesitate to demand it of him. But the rich man,—not to make any invidious comparison,—is always sold to the institution which makes him rich. Absolutely speaking, the more money, the less virtue; for money comes between a man and his objects, and obtains them for him; and it was certainly no great virtue to obtain it. It puts to rest many questions which he would otherwise be taxed to answer; while the only new question which it puts is the hard but superfluous one, how to spend it. Thus his moral ground is taken from under his feet. The opportunities of living are diminished in proportion as what are called the "means" are increased. The best thing a man can do for his culture when he is rich is to endeavor to carry out those schemes which he entertained when he was poor. Christ answered the Herodians according to their condition. "Show me the tribute-money," said he;—and one took a penny out of his pocket;—if you use money which has the image of Cæsar on it, and which he has made current and valuable, that is, *if you are men of the State,* and gladly enjoy the advantages of Cæsar's government, then pay him back some of his own when he demands it; "Render therefore to Cæsar that which is Cæsar's, and to God those things which are God's,"—leaving them no wiser than before as to which was which; for they did not wish to know.

When I converse with the freest of my neighbors, I perceive that, whatever they may say about the magnitude and seriousness of the question, and their regard for the public tranquility, the long and the short of the matter is, that they cannot spare the protection of the existing government, and they dread the consequences to their property and families of disobedience to it. For my own part, I should not like to think that I ever rely on the protection of the State. But, if I deny the authority of the State when it presents its tax-bill, it will soon take and waste all my property, and so harass me and my children without end. This is hard. This makes it impossible for a man to live honestly, and at the same time comfortably, in outward respects. It will not be worth the while to accumulate property; that would be sure to go again. You must hire or squat somewhere, and raise but a small crop, and eat that soon. You must live within yourself, and depend upon yourself always tucked up and ready for a start, and not have many affairs. A man may grow rich in Turkey even, if he will be in all respects a good subject of the Turkish government. Confucius said: "If a state is governed by the principles of reason, poverty and misery are subjects of shame; if a state is not governed by the principles of reason, riches and honors are the subjects of shame." No: Until I want the protection of Massachusetts to be extended to me in some distant southern port, where my liberty is endangered, or until I am bent solely on building up an estate at home by peaceful enterprise, I can afford to refuse allegiance to Massachusetts, and her right to my property and life. It costs me less in every sense to incur the penalty of disobedience to the State, than it would to obey. I should feel as if I were worth less in that case.

Some years ago, the State met me in behalf of the Church, and com- 25 manded me to pay a certain sum toward the support of a clergyman whose preaching my father attended, but never I myself. "Pay," it said, "or be locked up in the jail." I declined to pay. But, unfortunately, another man saw fit to pay it. I did not see why the schoolmaster should be taxed to support the priest, and not the priest the schoolmaster; for I was not the State's schoolmaster, but I supported myself by voluntary subscription. I did not see why the lyceum should not present its tax-bill, and have the State to back its demand, as well as the Church. However, at the request of the selectmen, I condescended to make some such statement as this in writing:—"Know all men by these presents, that I, Henry Thoreau, do not wish to be regarded as a member of any incorporated society which I have not joined." This I gave to the town clerk; and he has it. The State, having thus learned that I did not wish to be regarded as a member of that church, has never made a like demand on me since; though it said that it must adhere to its original presumption that time. If I had known how to name them, I should then have signed off in detail from all the societies which I never signed on to; but I did not know where to find a complete list.

I have paid no poll-tax for six years. I was put into a jail once on this account, for one night; and, as I stood considering the walls of solid stone, two or three feet thick, the door of wood and iron, a foot thick, and the iron grating which strained the light, I could not help being struck with the foolishness of that institution which treated me as if I were mere flesh and blood and bones, to be locked up. I wondered that it should have concluded at length that this was the best use it could put me to, and had never thought to avail itself of my services in some way. I saw that, if there was a wall of stone between me and my townsmen, there was a still more difficult one to climb or break through, before they could get to be as free as I was. I did not for a moment feel confined, and the walls seemed a great waste of stone and mortar. I felt as if I alone of all my townsmen had paid my tax. They plainly did not know how to treat me, but behaved like persons who are underbred. In every threat and in every compliment there was a blunder; for they thought that my chief desire was to stand the other side of that stone wall. I could not but smile to see how industriously they locked the door on my meditations, which followed them out again without let or hindrance, and *they* were really all that was dangerous. As they could not reach me, they had resolved to punish my body; just as boys, if they cannot come at some person against whom they have a spite, will abuse his dog. I saw that the State was half-witted, and it was timid as a lone woman with her silver spoons, and that it did not know its friends from its foes, and I lost all my remaining respect for it, and pitied it.

Thus the State never intentionally confronts a man's sense, intellectual or moral, but only his body, his senses. It is not armed with superior wit or honesty, but with superior physical strength. I was not born to be forced. I will breathe after my own fashion. Let us see who is the strongest. What force has a multitude? They only can force me who obey a higher law than I. They force me to become like themselves. I do not hear of *men* being *forced* to live this way or that by masses of men. What sort of life were that to live? When I meet a government which says to me, "Your money or your life," why should I be in haste to give it my money? It may be in a great strait, and not know what to do: I cannot help that. It must help itself; do as I do. It is not worth the while to snivel about it. I am not responsible for the successful working of the machinery of society. I am not the son of the engineer. I perceive that, when an acorn and a chestnut fall side by side, the one does not remain inert to make way for the other, but both obey their own laws, and spring and grow and flourish as best they can, till one, perchance, over-shadows and destroys the other. If a plant cannot live according to its nature, it dies; and so a man.

The night in prison was novel and interesting enough. The prisoners in their shirt-sleeves were enjoying a chat and the evening air in the doorway, when I entered. But the jailer said, "Come, boys, it is time to lock up"; and so they dispersed, and I heard the sound of their steps re-turning into the hollow apartments. My roommate was introduced to me by the jailer, as "a first-rate fellow and a clever man." When the door was locked, he showed me where to hang my hat, and how he managed mat-ters there. The rooms were white-washed once a month; and this one, at least, was the whitest, most simply furnished, and probably the neatest apartment in the town. He naturally wanted to know where I came from, and what brought me there; and, when I had told him, I asked him in my turn how he came there, presuming him to be an honest man, of course; and, as the world goes, I believe he was. "Why," said he, "they ac-cuse me of burning a barn; but I never did it." As near as I could discover, he had probably gone to bed in a barn when drunk, and smoked his pipe there; and so a barn was burnt. He had the reputation of being a clever man, had been there some three months waiting for his trial to come on, and would have to wait as much longer; but he was quite domesticated and contented, since he got his board for nothing, and thought that he was well-treated.

He occupied one window, and I the other; and I saw, that if one stayed there long, his principal business would be to look out the win-dow. I had soon read all the tracts that were left there, and examined where former prisoners had broken out, and where a grate had been sawed off, and heard the history of the various occupants of that room; for I found that even here there was a history and a gossip which never circulated beyond the walls of the jail. Probably this is the only house in the town where verses are composed, which are afterward printed in a circular form, but not published. I was shown quite a long list of verses which were composed by some young men who had been detected in an attempt to escape, who avenged themselves by singing them.

I pumped my fellow-prisoner as dry as I could, for fear I should never   30
see him again; but at length he showed me which was my bed, and left me to blow out the lamp.

It was like travelling into a far country, such as I had never expected to behold, to lie there for one night. It seemed to me that I never had heard the town-clock strike before, nor the evening sounds of the village; for we slept with the windows open, which were inside the grating. It was to see my native village in the light of the Middle Ages, and our Con-cord was turned into a Rhine stream, and visions of knights and castles passed before me. They were the voices of old burghers that I heard in the streets. I was an involuntary spectator and auditor of whatever was done and said in the kitchen of the adjacent village-inn, — a wholly new and rare experience to me. It was a closer view of my native town. I was fairly inside of it. I never had seen its institutions before. This is one of its peculiar institutions; for it is a shire town. I began to comprehend what its inhabitants were about.

In the morning, our breakfasts were put through the hole in the door, in small oblong-square tin pans, made to fit, and holding a pint of chocolate, with brown bread, and an iron spoon. When they called for the vessels again, I was green enough to return what bread I had left; but my comrade seized it, and said that I should lay that up for lunch or dinner. Soon after, he was let out to work at haying in a neighboring field, whither he went every day, and would not be back till noon; so he bade me good-day, saying that he doubted if he should see me again.

When I came out of prison, — for some one interfered, and paid that tax, — I did not perceive that great changes had taken place on the common, such as he observed who went in a youth, and emerged a tottering and gray-headed man; and yet a change had to my eyes come over the scene, — the town, and State, and country, — greater than any that mere time could effect. I saw yet more distinctly the State in which I lived. I saw to what extent the people among whom I lived could be trusted as good neighbors and friends; that their friendship was for summer weather only; that they did not greatly propose to do right; that they were a distinct race from me by their prejudices and superstitions, as the Chinamen and Malays are; that, in their sacrifices to humanity, they ran no risks, not even to their property; that, after all, they were not so noble but they treated the thief as he had treated them, and hoped, by a certain outward observance and a few prayers, and by walking in a particular straight though useless path from time to time, to save their souls. This may be to judge my neighbors harshly; for I believe that many of them are not aware that they have such an institution as the jail in their village.

It was formerly the custom in our village, when a poor debtor came out of jail, for his acquaintances to salute him, looking through their fingers, which were crossed to represent the grating of a jail window, "How do ye do?" My neighbors did not thus salute me, but first looked at me, and then at one another, as if I had returned from a long journey. I was put into jail as I was going to the shoemaker's to get a shoe which was mended. When I was let out the next morning, I proceeded to finish my errand, and having put on my mended shoe, joined a huckleberry party, who were impatient to put themselves under my conduct; and in half an hour, — for the horse was soon tackled, — was in the midst of a huckleberry field, on one of our highest hills, two miles off, and then the State was nowhere to be seen.

This is the whole story of "My Prisons." 35

I have never declined paying the highway tax, because I am as desirous of being a good neighbor as I am of being a bad subject; and, as for supporting schools, I am doing my part to educate my fellow-countrymen now. It is for no particular item in the tax-bill that I refuse to pay it. I simply wish to refuse allegiance to the State, to withdraw and stand aloof from it effectually. I do not care to trace the course of my dollar, if I could, till it buys a man, or a musket to shoot one with,—the dollar is innocent,—but I am concerned to trace the effects of my allegiance. In fact, I quietly declare war with the State, after my fashion, though I will still make what use and get what advantage of her I can, as is usual in such cases.

If others pay the tax which is demanded of me, from a sympathy with the State, they do but what they have already done in their own case, or rather they abet injustice to a greater extent than the State requires. If they pay the tax from a mistaken interest in the individual taxed, to save his property or prevent his going to jail, it is because they have not considered wisely how far they let their private feelings interfere with the public good.

This, then, is my position at present. But one cannot be too much on his guard in such a case, lest his action be biased by obstinacy, or an undue regard for the opinions of men. Let him see that he does only what belongs to himself and to the hour.

I think sometimes, Why, this people mean well; they are only ignorant; they would do better if they knew how: why give your neighbors this pain to treat you as they are inclined to? But I think again, this is no reason why I should do as they do, or permit others to suffer much greater pain of a different kind. Again, I sometimes say to myself, When many millions of men, without heat, without ill will, without personal feelings of any kind, demand of you a few shillings only, without the possibility, such is their constitution, of retracing or altering their present demand, and without the possibility, on your side, of appeal to any other millions, why expose yourself to this overwhelming brute force? You do not resist cold and hunger, the winds and the waves, thus obstinately; you quietly submit to a thousand similar necessities. You do not put your head into the fire. But just in proportion as I regard this as not wholly a brute force, partly a human force, and consider that I have relations to those millions as to so many millions of men, and not of mere brute or inanimate things, I see that appeal is possible, first and instantaneously, from them to the Maker of them, and, secondly, from them to themselves. But, if I put my head deliberately into the fire, there is no appeal to fire or to the Maker of fire, and I have only myself to blame. If I could convince myself that I have any right to be satisfied with men as they are, and to treat them according, and not according, in some respects, to my requisitions and expectations of what they and I ought to be, then, like a good Mussulman and fatalist, I should endeavor to be satisfied with things as they are, and say it is the will of God. And, above all, there is this difference between resisting this and a purely brute or natural force, that I can resist this with some effect; but I cannot expect, like Orpheus, to change the nature of the rocks and trees and beasts.

I do not wish to quarrel with any man or nation. I do not wish to 40
split hairs, to make fine distinctions, or set myself up as better than my
neighbors. I seek rather, I may say, even an excuse for conforming to the
laws of the land. I am but too ready to conform to them. Indeed, I have
reason to suspect myself on this head; and each year, as the tax-gatherer
comes round, I find myself disposed to review the acts and position of
the general and State governments, and the spirit of the people, to discover a pretext for conformity.

> We must affect our country as our parents;
> And if at any time we alienate
> Our love or industry from doing it honor,
> We must respect effects and teach the soul
> Matter of conscience and religion,
> And not desire of rule or benefit.

I believe that the State will soon be able to take all my work of this sort
out of my hands, and then I shall be no better a patriot than my fellow-
countrymen. Seen from a lower point of view, the Constitution, with all
its faults, is very good; the law and the courts are very respectable; even
this State and this American government are, in many respects, very admirable and rare things, to be thankful for, such as a great many have described them; but seen from a point of view a little higher, they are what
I have described them; seen from a higher still, and the highest, who
shall say what they are, or that they are worth looking at or thinking of
at all?

However, the government does not concern me much, and I shall
bestow the fewest possible thoughts on it. It is not many moments that I
live under a government, even in this world. If a man is thought-free,
fancy-free, imagination-free, that which *is not* never for a long time
appearing *to be* to him, unwise rulers or reformers cannot fatally interrupt him.

I know that most men think differently from myself; but those
whose lives are by profession devoted to the study of these or kindred
subjects, content me as little as any. Statesmen and legislators, standing
so completely within the institution, never distinctly and nakedly behold it. They speak of moving society, but have no resting-place without
it. They may be men of a certain experience and discrimination, and
have no doubt invented ingenious and even useful systems, for which we
sincerely thank them; but all their wit and usefulness lie within certain
not very wide limits. They are wont to forget that the world is not governed by policy and expediency. Webster never goes behind government, and so cannot speak with authority about it. His words are wisdom
to those legislators who contemplate no essential reform in the existing
government; but for thinkers, and those who legislate for all time, he
never once glances at the subject. I know of those whose serene and wise
speculations on this theme would soon reveal the limits of his mind's

range and hospitality. Yet, compared with the cheap professions of most reformers, and the still cheaper wisdom and eloquence of politicians in general, his are almost the only sensible and valuable words, and we thank Heaven for him. Comparatively, he is always strong, original, and, above all, practical. Still his quality is not wisdom, but prudence. The lawyer's truth is not Truth, but consistency, or a consistent expediency. Truth is always in harmony with herself, and is not concerned chiefly to reveal the justice that may consist with wrong-doing. He well deserves to be called, as he has been called, the Defender of the Constitution. There are really no blows to be given by him but defensive ones. He is not a leader, but a follower. His leaders are the men of '87. "I have never made an effort," he says, "and never propose to make an effort; I have never countenanced an effort, and never mean to countenance an effort, to disturb the arrangement as originally made, by which the various States came into the Union." Still thinking of the sanction which the Constitution gives to slavery, he says, "Because it was a part of the original compact,—let it stand." Notwithstanding his special acuteness and ability, he is unable to take a fact out of its merely political relations, and behold it as it lies absolutely to be disposed of by the intellect,—what, for instance, it behooves a man to do here in America today with regard to slavery, but ventures, or is driven, to make some such desperate answer as the following, while professing to speak absolutely, and as a private man,—from which what new and singular code of social duties might be inferred? "The manner," says he, "in which the governments of those States where slavery exists are to regulate it, is for their own consideration, under their responsibility to their constituents, to the general laws of propriety, humanity, and justice, and to God. Associations formed elsewhere, springing from a feeling of humanity, or any other cause, have nothing whatever to do with it. They have never received any encouragement from me, and they never will."[1]

They who know of no purer sources of truth, who have traced up its stream no higher, stand, and wisely stand, by the Bible and the Constitution, and drink at it there with reverence and humility; but they who behold where it comes trickling into this lake or that pool, gird up their loins once more, and continue their pilgrimage toward its fountainhead.

No man with a genius for legislation has appeared in America. They are rare in the history of the world. There are orators, politicians, and eloquent men, by the thousand; but the speaker has not yet opened his mouth to speak, who is capable of settling the much-vexed questions of the day. We love eloquence for its own sake, and not for any truth which it may utter, or any heroism it may inspire. Our legislators have not yet learned the comparative value of free-trade and of freedom, of union, and of rectitude, to a nation. They have no genius or talent for comparatively humble questions of taxation and finance, commerce and

---

[1]These extracts have been inserted since the Lecture was read.

manufactures and agriculture. If we were left solely to the wordy wit of legislators in Congress for our guidance, uncorrected by the seasonable experience and the effectual complaints of the people, America would not long retain her rank among the nations. For eighteen hundred years, though perchance I have no right to say it, the New Testament has been written; yet where is the legislator who has wisdom and practical talent enough to avail himself of the light which it sheds on the science of legislation?

The authority of government, even such as I am willing to submit 45
to, — for I will cheerfully obey those who know and can do better than I, and in many things even those who neither know nor can do so well, — is still an impure one: To be strictly just, it must have the sanction and consent of the governed. It can have no pure right over my person and property but what I concede to it. The progress from an absolute to a limited monarchy, from a limited monarchy to a democracy, is a progress toward a true respect for the individual. Even the Chinese philosopher was wise enough to regard the individual as the basis of the empire. Is a democracy, such as we know it, the last improvement possible in government? Is it not possible to take a step further towards recognizing and organizing the rights of man? There will never be a really free and enlightened State, until the State comes to recognize the individual as a higher and independent power, from which all its own power and authority are derived, and treats him accordingly. I please myself with imagining a State at last which can afford to be just to all men, and to treat the individual with respect as a neighbor; which even would not think it inconsistent with its own repose, if a few were to live aloof from it, not meddling with it, nor embraced by it, who fulfilled all the duties of neighbors and fellowmen. A State which bore this kind of fruit, and suffered it to drop off as fast as it ripened, would prepare the way for a still more perfect and glorious State, which also I have imagined, but not yet anywhere seen.

DISCUSSION QUESTIONS

1. Summarize briefly Thoreau's reasons for arguing that civil disobedience is sometimes a *duty*.

2. Thoreau, like Martin Luther King Jr. in "Letter from Birmingham Jail" (p. 692), speaks of "unjust laws" (para. 16). Do they agree on the positions that citizens should take in response to these laws? Are Thoreau and King guided by the same principles? In Plato's "Crito" (p. 635), what does Socrates say about obedience to unjust laws?

3. What examples of government policy and action does Thoreau use to prove that civil disobedience is a duty? Explain why they are — or are not — effective.

4. Why do you think Thoreau provides such a detailed account of one day in prison? (Notice that King does not give a description of his confine-

ment.) What observation about the community struck Thoreau when he emerged from jail?

WRITING SUGGESTIONS

5. Argue that civil disobedience to a school policy or action is justified. (Examples might include failure to establish an ethnic studies department, refusal to allow ROTC on campus, refusal to suspend a professor accused of sexual harassment.) Be specific about the injustice of the policy or action and the values that underlie the resistance.

6. Under what circumstances might civil disobedience prove to be dangerous and immoral? Can you think of cases of disobedience when *conscience,* as Thoreau uses the term, did not appear to be the guiding principle? Try to identify what you think is the true motivation for the resistance.

The Obligation to Endure

RACHEL CARSON

The history of life on earth has been a history of interaction between living things and their surroundings. To a large extent, the physical form and the habits of the earth's vegetation and its animal life have been molded by the environment. Considering the whole span of earthly time, the opposite effect, in which life actually modifies its surroundings, has been relatively slight. Only within the moment of time represented by the present century has one species—man—acquired significant power to alter the nature of his world.

During the past quarter century this power has not only increased to one of disturbing magnitude but it has changed in character. The most alarming of all man's assaults upon the environment is the contamination of air, earth, rivers, and sea with dangerous and even lethal materials. This pollution is for the most part irrecoverable; the chain of evil it initiates not only in the world that must support life but in living tissues is for the most part irreversible. In this now universal contamination of the environment, chemicals are the sinister and little-recognized partners of radiation in changing the very nature of the world—the very nature of its life. Strontium 90, released through nuclear explosions into the air, comes to earth in rain or drifts down as fallout, lodges in soil, enters into the grass or corn or wheat grown there, and in time takes up its abode in the bones of a human being, there to remain until his death. Similarly, chemicals sprayed on croplands or forests or gardens lie long in soil, entering into living organisms, passing from one to another in a chain of poisoning and death. Or they pass mysteriously by underground streams until they emerge and, through the alchemy of air and sunlight, combine into new forms that kill vegetation, sicken cattle, and work unknown harm on those who drink from once pure wells. As Albert Schweitzer[1] has said, "Man can hardly even recognize the devils of his own creation."

It took hundreds of millions of years to produce the life that now inhabits the earth—eons of time in which that developing and evolving and diversifying life reached a state of adjustment and balance with its surroundings. The environment, rigorously shaping and directing the life

[1] Alsatian-born physician, humanitarian, philosopher (1875–1965), Schweitzer was awarded the Nobel prize for peace in 1952. [ED.]

Rachel Carson (1909–1964) was a scientist with the U.S. Fish and Wildlife Service. She maintained a lifelong interest in preservation of the natural environment and the damage inflicted by chemicals used in agriculture and industry. Her book *Silent Spring* (1962), from which the following chapter is taken, was influential in the banning of DDT and other pesticides.

it supported, contained elements that were hostile as well as supporting. Certain rocks gave out dangerous radiation; even within the light of the sun, from which all life draws its energy, there were short-wave radiations with power to injure. Given time—time not in years but in millennia—life adjusts, and a balance has been reached. For time is the essential ingredient; but in the modern world there is no time.

The rapidity of change and the speed with which new situations are created follow the impetuous and heedless pace of man rather than the deliberate pace of nature. Radiation is no longer merely the background radiation of rocks, the bombardment of cosmic rays, the ultraviolet of the sun that have existed before there was any life on earth; radiation is now the unnatural creation of man's tampering with the atom. The chemicals to which life is asked to make its adjustment are no longer merely the calcium and silica and copper and all the rest of the minerals washed out of the rocks and carried in rivers to the sea; they are the synthetic creations of man's inventive mind, brewed in his laboratories, and having no counterparts in nature.

To adjust to these chemicals would require time on the scale that is 5 nature's; it would require not merely the years of a man's life but the life of generations. And even this, were it by some miracle possible, would be futile, for the new chemicals come from our laboratories in an endless stream; almost five hundred annually find their way into actual use in the United States alone. The figure is staggering and its implications are not easily grasped—five hundred new chemicals to which the bodies of men and animals are required somehow to adapt each year, chemicals totally outside the limits of biologic experience.

Among them are many that are used in man's war against nature. Since the mid-1940s over two hundred basic chemicals have been created for use in killing insects, weeds, rodents, and other organisms described in the modern vernacular as "pests"; and they are sold under several thousand different brand names.

These sprays, dusts, and aerosols are now applied almost universally to farms, gardens, forests, and homes—nonselective chemicals that have the power to kill every insect, the "good" and the "bad," to still the song of birds and the leaping of fish in the streams, to coat the leaves with a deadly film, and to linger on in soil—all this though the intended target may be only a few weeds or insects. Can anyone believe it is possible to lay down such a barrage of poisons on the surface of the earth without making it unfit for all life? They should not be called "insecticides" but "biocides."

The whole process of spraying seems caught up in an endless spiral. Since DDT was released for civilian use, a process of escalation has been going on in which ever more toxic materials must be found. This has happened because insects, in a triumphant vindication of Darwin's principle of the survival of the fittest, have evolved super races immune to the particular insecticide used, hence a deadlier one has always to be developed—and then a deadlier one than that. It has happened also because, for reasons to be described later, destructive insects often undergo a "flareback," or resurgence, after spraying, in numbers greater than before. Thus the chemical war is never won, and all life is caught in its violent crossfire.

Along with the possibility of the extinction of mankind by nuclear war, the central problem of our age has therefore become the contamination of man's total environment with such substances of incredible potential for harm—substances that accumulate in the tissues of plants and animals and even penetrate the germ cells to shatter or alter the very material of heredity upon which the shape of the future depends.

Some would-be architects of our future look toward a time when it 10 will be possible to alter the human germ plasm by design. But we may easily be doing so now by inadvertence, for many chemicals, like radiation, bring about gene mutations. It is ironic to think that man might determine his own future by something so seemingly trivial as the choice of an insect spray.

All this has been risked—for what? Future historians may well be amazed by our distorted sense of proportion. How could intelligent beings seek to control a few unwanted species by a method that contaminated the entire environment and brought the threat of disease and death even to their own kind? Yet this is precisely what we have done. We have done it, moreover, for reasons that collapse the moment we examine them. We are told that the enormous and expanding use of pesticides is necessary to maintain farm production. Yet is our real problem not one of *overproduction*? Our farms, despite measures to remove acreages from production and to pay farmers *not* to produce, have yielded such a staggering excess of crops that the American taxpayer in 1962 is paying out more than one billion dollars a year as the total carrying cost of the surplus-food storage program. And is the situation helped when one branch of the Agriculture Department tries to reduce production while another states, as it did in 1958, "It is believed generally that reduction of crop acreages under provisions of the Soil Bank[2] will stimulate interest in use of chemicals to obtain maximum production on the land retained in crops."

All this is not to say there is no insect problem and no need of control. I am saying, rather, that control must be geared to realities, not to mythical situations, and that the methods employed must be such that they do not destroy us along with the insects.

The problem whose attempted solution has brought such a train of disaster in its wake is an accompaniment of our modern way of life. Long before the age of man, insects inhabited the earth—a group of extraordi-

---

[2] A federal plan that encourages farmers to plant crops that will be beneficial to the soil. [Ed.]

narily varied and adaptable beings. Over the course of time since man's advent, a small percentage of the more than half a million species of insects have come into conflict with human welfare in two principal ways: as competitors for the food supply and as carriers of human disease.

Disease-carrying insects become important where human beings are crowded together, especially under conditions where sanitation is poor, as in time of natural disaster or war or in situations of extreme poverty and deprivation. Then control of some sort becomes necessary. It is a sobering fact, however, as we shall presently see, that the method of massive chemical control has had only limited success, and also threatens to worsen the very conditions it is intended to curb.

Under primitive agricultural conditions the farmer had few insect 15 problems. These arose with the intensification of agriculture—the devotion of immense acreages to a single crop. Such a system set the stage for explosive increases in specific insect populations. Single-crop farming does not take advantage of the principles by which nature works; it is agriculture as an engineer might conceive it to be. Nature has introduced great variety into the landscape, but man has displayed a passion for simplifying it. Thus he undoes the built-in checks and balances by which nature holds the species within bounds. One important natural check is a limit on the amount of suitable habitat for each species. Obviously then, an insect that lives on wheat can build up its population to much higher levels on a farm devoted to wheat than on one in which wheat is intermingled with other crops to which the insect is not adapted.

The same thing happens in other situations. A generation or more ago, the towns of large areas of the United States lined their streets with the noble elm tree. Now the beauty they hopefully created is threatened with complete destruction as disease sweeps through the elms, carried by a beetle that would have only limited chance to build up large populations and to spread from tree to tree if the elms were only occasional trees in a richly diversified planting.

Another factor in the modern insect problem is one that must be viewed against a background of geologic and human history: the spreading of thousands of different kinds of organisms from their native homes to invade new territories. This worldwide migration has been studied and graphically described by the British ecologist Charles Elton in his recent book *The Ecology of Invasions.* During the Cretaceous Period, some hundred million years ago, flooding seas cut many land bridges between continents and living things found themselves confined in what Elton calls "colossal separate nature reserves." There, isolated from others of their kind, they developed many new species. When some of the land masses were joined again, about 15 million years ago, these species began to move out into new territories—a movement that is not only still in progress but is now receiving considerable assistance from man.

The importation of plants is the primary agent in the modern spread of species, for animals have almost invariably gone along with the plants, quarantine being a comparatively recent and not completely effective innovation. The United States Office of Plant Introduction alone has introduced almost two hundred thousand species and varieties of plants from all over the world. Nearly half of the 180 or so major insect enemies of plants in the United States are accidental imports from abroad, and most of them have come as hitchhikers on plants.

In new territory, out of reach of the restraining hand of the natural enemies that kept down its numbers in its native land, an invading plant or animal is able to become enormously abundant. Thus it is no accident that our most troublesome insects are introduced species.

These invasions, both the naturally occurring and those dependent 20 on human assistance, are likely to continue indefinitely. Quarantine and massive chemical campaigns are only extremely expensive ways of buying time. We are faced, according to Dr. Elton, "with a life-and-death need not just to find new technological means of suppressing this plant or that animal"; instead we need the basic knowledge of animal populations and their relations to their surroundings that will "promote an even balance and damp down the explosive power of outbreaks and new invasions."

Much of the necessary knowledge is now available, but we do not use it. We train ecologists in our universities and even employ them in our governmental agencies, but we seldom take their advice. We allow the chemical death rain to fall as though there were no alternative, whereas in fact there are many, and our ingenuity could soon discover many more if given opportunity.

Have we fallen into a mesmerized state that makes us accept as inevitable that which is inferior or detrimental, as though having lost the will or the vision to demand that which is good? Such thinking, in the words of the ecologist Paul Shepard, "idealizes life with only its head out of water, inches above the limits of toleration of the corruption of its own environment. . . . Why should we tolerate a diet of weak poison, a home in insipid surroundings, a circle of acquaintances who are not quite our enemies, the noise of motors with just enough relief to prevent insanity? Who would want to live in a world which is just not quite fatal?"

Yet such a world is pressed upon us. The crusade to create a chemically sterile, insect-free world seems to have engendered a fanatic zeal on the part of many specialists and most of the so-called control agencies. On every hand there is evidence that those engaged in spraying operations exercise a ruthless power. "The regulatory entomologists . . . function as prosecutor, judge and jury, tax assessor and collector and sheriff to enforce their own orders," said Connecticut entomologist Neely Turner. The most flagrant abuses go unchecked in both state and federal agencies.

It is not my contention that chemical insecticides must never be used. I do contend that we have put poisonous and biologically potent chemicals indiscriminately into the hands of persons largely or wholly ignorant of their potentials for harm. We have subjected enormous numbers of people to contact with these poisons, without their consent and often without their knowledge. If the Bill of Rights contains no guarantee that a citizen shall be secure against lethal poisons distributed either by private individuals or by public officials, it is surely only because our forefathers, despite their considerable wisdom and foresight, could conceive of no such problem.

I contend, furthermore, that we have allowed these chemicals to be used with little or no advance investigation of their effect on soil, water, wildlife, and man himself. Future generations are unlikely to condone our lack of prudent concern for the integrity of the natural world that supports all life.

There is still very limited awareness of the nature of the threat. There is an era of specialists, each of whom sees his own problem and is unaware of or intolerant of the larger frame into which it fits. It is also an era dominated by industry, in which the right to make a dollar at whatever cost is seldom challenged. When the public protests, confronted with some obvious evidence of damaging results of pesticide applications, it is fed little tranquilizing pills of half truth. We urgently need an end to these false assurances, to the sugarcoating of unpalatable facts. It is the public that is being asked to assume the risks that the insect controllers calculate. The public must decide whether it wishes to continue on the present road, and it can do so only when in full possession of the facts. In the words of Jean Rostrand,[3] "The obligation to endure gives us the right to know."

DISCUSSION QUESTIONS

1. Explain the meaning of the title of this essay.
2. What is the principal object of Carson's attack? Cite examples of her claim.
3. What does Carson mean by "in the modern world there is no time" (para. 3)?
4. How does the survival of the fittest, as defined by Darwin, make necessary greater use of insecticides?
5. Carson calls the motives of those who use chemicals the control of "a few unwanted species." As far as you know, does this seem like a fair appraisal of their objectives?
6. Does Carson offer workable remedies for improving the situation she deplores? Explain.
7. Does Carson's language suggest an inflexible position or a moderate one? Or perhaps both in different parts of her argument? Find passages that support your view.

[3] French biologist and writer (1894–1977). [ED.]

8. What elements of Carson's prose style make her argument accessible to nonspecialists?

WRITING SUGGESTIONS

9. Choose a controversial subject concerned with the natural environment. (For example: global warming, offshore oil drilling, acid rain, human encroachment on animal habitats.) Choose two or three important points to develop either for or against the claim that serious harm has occurred or will occur.

10. If nature in some of her myriad forms—garden, mountain, water, shore, meadow, forest—has ever played a significant part in your life, describe your experience and explain why it was meaningful.

Warfare: An Invention— Not a Biological Necessity

MARGARET MEAD

Is war a biological necessity, a sociological inevitability, or just a bad invention? Those who argue for the first view endow man with such pugnacious instincts that some outlet in aggressive behavior is necessary if man is to reach full human stature. It was this point of view which lay back of William James's famous essay, "The Moral Equivalent of War," in which he tried to retain the warlike virtues and channel them in new directions. A similar point of view has lain back of the Soviet Union's attempt to make competition between groups rather than between individuals. A basic, competitive, aggressive, warring human nature is assumed, and those who wish to outlaw war or outlaw competitiveness merely try to find new and less socially destructive ways in which these biologically given aspects of man's nature can find expression. Then there are those who take the second view: warfare is the inevitable concomitant of the development of the state, the struggle for land and natural resources of class societies springing, not from the nature of man, but from the nature of history. War is nevertheless inevitable unless we change our social system and outlaw classes, the struggle for power, and possessions; and in the event of our success warfare would disappear, as a symptom vanishes when the disease is cured.

One may hold a compromise position between these two extremes; one may claim that all aggression springs from the frustration of man's biologically determined drives and that, since all forms of culture are frustrating, it is certain each new generation will be aggressive and the aggression will find its natural and inevitable expression in race war, class war, nationalistic war, and so on.

All three positions are very popular today among those who think seriously about the problems of war and its possible prevention, but I wish

---

Margaret Mead (1901–1978) was the first American anthropologist to study childhood, adolescence, and gender. Her work focused primarily on culture rather than biology or race as the primary factor in determining variations in human behavior and personality. As a graduate student, she conducted field research on adolescence and sexuality in Samoa. Her resulting work, the best-selling *Coming of Age in Samoa* (1928), made her a household name in the United States. She went on to publish forty-four books, including *Growing Up in New Guinea* (1930) and *Sex and Temperament* (1935), and hundreds of articles. Her early research in Samoa has been challenged by Derek Freeman, an anthropologist who characterizes Mead's work as being antievolutionary and fundamentally flawed in its portrayal of sexuality in the South Seas. Freeman's accusations, however, have been discredited by many scholars who recognize Mead's important contributions to the field. The following article, in which Mead argues that warfare is a cultural invention and not a biological necessity, was published in *Asia* in 1940.

to urge another point of view, less defeatist perhaps than the first and third, and more accurate than the second: that is, that warfare, by which I mean organized conflict between two groups as *groups,* in which each group puts an army (even if the army is only fifteen Pygmies) into the field to fight and kill, if possible, some of the members of the army of the other group—that warfare of this sort is an invention like any other of the inventions in terms of which we order our lives, such as writing, marriage, cooking our food instead of eating it raw, trial by jury, or burial of the dead, and so on. Some of this list any one will grant are inventions: trial by jury is confined to very limited portions of the globe; we know that there are tribes that do not bury their dead but instead expose or cremate them; and we know that only part of the human race has had a knowledge of writing as its cultural inheritance. But, whenever a way of doing things is found universally, such as the use of fire or the practice of some form of marriage, we tend to think at once that it is not an invention at all but an attribute of humanity itself. And yet even such universals as marriage and the use of fire are inventions like the rest, very basic ones, inventions which were perhaps necessary if human history was to take the turn it has taken, but nevertheless inventions. At some point in his social development man was undoubtedly without the institution of marriage or the knowledge of the use of fire.

The case for warfare is much clearer because there are peoples even today who have no warfare. Of these the Eskimo are perhaps the most conspicuous example, but the Lepchas of Sikkim are an equally good one. Neither of these peoples understands war, not even the defensive warfare. The idea of warfare is lacking, and this lack is as essential to carrying on war as an alphabet or a syllabary is to writing. But whereas the Lepchas are a gentle, unquarrelsome people, and the advocates of other points of view might argue that they are not full human beings or that they had never been frustrated and so had no aggression to expend in warfare, the Eskimo case gives no such possibility of interpretation. The Eskimo are not a mild and meek people; many of them are turbulent and troublesome. Fights, theft of wives, murder, cannibalism occur among them—all outbursts of passionate men goaded by desire or intolerable circumstance. Here are men faced with hunger, men faced with loss of their wives, men faced with the threat of extermination by other men, and here are orphan children, growing up miserably with no one to care for them, mocked and neglected by those about them. The personality necessary for war, the circumstances necessary to goad men to desperation are present, but there is no war. When a traveling Eskimo entered a settlement he might have to fight the strongest man in the settlement to establish his position among them, but this was a test of strength and bravery, not war. The idea of warfare, of one *group* organizing against another *group* to maim and wound and kill them, was absent. And without that idea passions might rage but there was no war.

But, it may be argued, isn't this because the Eskimo have such a low 5
and undeveloped form of social organization? They own no land, they
move from place to place, camping, it is true, season after season on the
same site, but this is not something to fight for as the modern nations of
the world fight for land and raw materials. They have no permanent possessions that can be looted, no towns that can be burned. They have no
social classes to produce stress and strains within the society which
might force it to go to war outside. Doesn't the absence of war among
the Eskimo, while disproving the biological necessity of war, just go to
confirm the point that it is the state of development of the society which
accounts for war, and nothing else?

We find the answer among the Pygmy peoples of the Andaman Islands in the Bay of Bengal. The Andamans also represent an exceedingly
low level of society: they are a hunting and food-gathering people; they
live in tiny hordes without any class stratification; their houses are simpler than the snow houses of the Eskimo. But they knew about warfare.
The army might contain only fifteen determined Pygmies marching in a
straight line, but it was the real thing none the less. Tiny army met tiny
army in open battle, blows were exchanged, casualties suffered, and the
state of warfare could only be concluded by a peacemaking ceremony.

Similarly, among the Australian aborigines, who built no permanent
dwellings but wandered from water hole to water hole over their almost
desert country, warfare—and rules of "international law"—were highly
developed. The student of social evolution will seek in vain for his obvious causes of war, struggle for lands, struggle for power of one group over
another, expansion of population, need to divert the minds of a populace restive under tyranny, or even the ambition of a successful leader to
enhance his own prestige. All are absent, but warfare as a practice remained, and men engaged in it and killed one another in the course of a
war because killing is what is done in wars.

From instances like these it becomes apparent that an inquiry into
the causes of war misses the fundamental point as completely as does an
insistence upon the biological necessity of war. If a people have an idea
of going to war and the idea that war is the way in which certain situations, defined within their society, are to be handled, they will sometimes go to war. If they are a mild and unaggressive people, like the
Pueblo Indians, they may limit themselves to defensive warfare; but they
will be forced to think in terms of war because there are peoples near
them who have warfare as a pattern, and offensive, raiding, pillaging
warfare at that. When the pattern of warfare is known, people like the
Pueblo Indians will defend themselves, taking advantage of their natural
defenses, the *mesa* village site, and people like the Lepchas, having no
natural defenses and no idea of warfare, will merely submit to the in-
vader. But the essential point remains the same. There is a way of behaving which is known to a given people and labeled as an appropriate form

of behavior. A bold and warlike people like the Sioux or the Maori may label warfare as desirable as well as possible; a mild people like the Pueblo Indians may label warfare as undesirable; but to the minds of both peoples the possibility of warfare is present. Their thoughts, their hopes, their plans are oriented about this idea, that warfare may be selected as the way to meet some situation.

So simple peoples and civilized peoples, mild peoples and violent, assertive peoples, will all go to war if they have the invention, just as those peoples who have the custom of dueling will have duels and peoples who have the pattern of vendetta will indulge in vendetta. And, conversely, peoples who do not know of dueling will not fight duels, even though their wives are seduced and their daughters ravished; they may on occasion commit murder but they will not fight duels. Cultures which lack the idea of the vendetta will not meet every quarrel in this way. A people can use only the forms it has. So the Balinese have their special way of dealing with a quarrel between two individuals; if the two feel that the causes of quarrel are heavy, they may go and register their quarrel in the temple before the gods, and, making offerings, they may swear never to have anything to do with each other again. Under the Dutch government they registered such mutual "not-speaking" with the Dutch government officials. But in other societies, although individuals might feel as full of animosity and as unwilling to have any further contact as do the Balinese, they cannot register their quarrel with the gods and go on quietly about their business because registering quarrels with the gods is not an invention of which they know.

Yet, if it be granted that warfare is after all an invention, it may 10 nevertheless be an invention that lends itself to certain types of personality, to the exigent needs of autocrats, to the expansionist desires of crowded peoples, to the desire for plunder and rape and loot which is engendered by a dull and frustrating life. What, then, can we say of this congruence between warfare and its uses? If it is a form which fits so well, is not this congruence the essential point? But even here the primitive material causes us to wonder, because there are tribes who go to war merely for glory, having no quarrel with the enemy, suffering from no tyrant within their boundaries, anxious neither for land nor loot nor women, but merely anxious to win prestige which within that tribe has been declared obtainable only by war and without which no young man can hope to win his sweetheart's smile of approval. But if, as was the case with the Bush Negroes of Dutch Guiana, it is artistic ability which is necessary to win a girl's approval, the same young man would have to be carving rather than going out on a war party.

In many parts of the world, war is a game in which the individual can win counters — counters which bring him prestige in the eyes of his own sex or of the opposite sex; he plays for these counters as he might, in our society, strive for a tennis championship. Warfare is a frame for such prestige-seeking merely because it calls for the display of certain skills and certain virtues; all of these skills—riding straight, shooting straight, dodging the missiles of the enemy, and sending one's own straight to the mark—can be equally well exercised in some other framework and, equally, the virtues—endurance, bravery, loyalty, steadfastness—can be displayed in other contexts. The tie-up between proving oneself a man and proving this by a success in organized killing is due to a definition which many societies have made of manliness. And often, even in those societies which counted success in warfare a proof of human worth, strange turns were given to the idea, as when the Plains Indians gave their highest awards to the man who touched a live enemy rather than to the man who brought in a scalp—from a dead enemy—because killing a man was less risky. Warfare is just an invention known to the majority of human societies by which they permit their young men either to accumulate prestige or avenge their honor or acquire loot or wives or slaves or sago lands or cattle or appease the blood lust of their gods or the restless souls of the recently dead. It is just an invention, older and more widespread than the jury system, but none the less an invention.

But, once we have said this, have we said anything at all? Despite a few instances, dear to the hearts of controversialists, of the loss of the useful arts, once an invention is made which proves congruent with human needs or social forms, it tends to persist. Grant that war is an invention, that it is not a biological necessity nor the outcome of certain special types of social forms, still, once the invention is made, what are we to do about it? The Indian who had been subsisting on the buffalo for generations because with his primitive weapons he could slaughter only a limited number of buffalo did not return to his primitive weapons when he saw that the white man's more efficient weapons were exterminating the buffalo. A desire for the white man's cloth may mortgage the South Sea Islander to the white man's plantation, but he does not return to making bark cloth, which would have left him free. Once an invention is known and accepted, men do not easily relinquish it. The skilled workers may smash the first steam looms which they feel are to be their undoing, but they accept them in the end, and no movement which has insisted upon the mere abandonment of usable inventions has ever had much success. Warfare is here, as part of our thought; the deeds of warriors are immortalized in the words of our poets; the toys of our children are modeled upon the weapons of the soldier; the frame of reference within which our statesmen and our diplomats work always contains war. If we know that it is not inevitable, that it is due to historical accident that warfare is one of the ways in which we think of behaving, are we given any hope by that? What hope is there of persuading nations to abandon war, nations so thoroughly imbued with the idea that resort to war is, if not actually desirable and noble, at least inevitable whenever certain defined circumstances arise?

In answer to this question I think we might turn to the history of other social inventions, inventions which must once have seemed as firmly entrenched as warfare. Take the methods of trial which preceded the jury system: ordeal and trial by combat. Unfair, capricious, alien as they are to our feeling today, they were once the only methods open to individuals accused of some offense. The invention of trial by jury gradually replaced these methods until only witches, and finally not even witches, had to resort to the ordeal. And for a long time the jury system seemed the one best and finest method of settling legal disputes, but today new inventions, trial before judges only or before commissions, are replacing the jury system. In each case the old method was replaced by a new social invention; the ordeal did not go out because people thought it unjust or wrong, it went out because a method more congruent with the institutions and feelings of the period was invented. And, if we despair over the way in which war seems such an ingrained habit of most of the human race, we can take comfort from the fact that a poor invention will usually give place to a better invention.

For this, two conditions at least are necessary. The people must recognize the defects of the old invention, and some one must make a new one. Propaganda against warfare, documentation of its terrible cost in human suffering and social waste, these prepare the ground by teaching people to feel that warfare is a defective social institution. There is further needed a belief that social invention is possible and the invention of new methods which will render warfare as out-of-date as the tractor is making the plow, or the motor car the horse and buggy. A form of behavior becomes out-of-date only when something else takes its place, and in order to invent forms of behavior which will make war obsolete, it is a first requirement to believe that an invention is possible.

DISCUSSION QUESTIONS

1. Mead uses a common organizational strategy—refuting the opposing view. (See an extended discussion of this on page 332.) In this essay she refutes several theories about the origin of warfare. Summarize these theories. Where does she state her own thesis?

2. Mead supports her argument with examples and analogies. Are they all equally convincing? How can a reader assess the strengths and weaknesses of her examples?

3. In the last part of her essay Mead acknowledges that war is a "usable invention" (para. 12). How does she answer this apparent weakness in her argument?

4. What solution to the problem of warfare does Mead propose? Do you find any flaws in her proposal? Explain your agreement or disagreement with the plausibility of her solution.

WRITING SUGGESTIONS

5. In an article entitled "Where Have All the Young Men Gone? The Perfect Substitute for War," the author marvels at the significance of a gathering

in 1998 of more than a million people to celebrate France's victory in the World Cup, a soccer game. "The vast majority of Europeans," he writes, "have found a way to hate one another without hacking one another to pieces."[1] (In a tragic irony, this article appeared in 1999 during the brutal "ethnic cleansing" of ethnic Albanians in Kosovo and the bombing of Serbia by NATO forces.)

Argue that sporting events do or do not represent a substitute for war. Develop two or three issues—similarities or differences—that support your claim.

6. Pacifism is defined by *Webster's New International Dictionary* as "opposition to war or the use of military force for any purpose." If you consider yourself to be a pacifist, write a defense of your belief, using examples and analogies to make your position clear. But if you believe with Bertrand Russell, the British mathematician and philosopher, that "Absolute pacifism, as a method of gaining your ends, is subject to very severe limitations,"[2] defend your point of view, again using examples, as Mead does.

---

[1] Paul Auster, *New York Times Magazine*, April 4, 1999, p. 144.
[2] *Dictionary of the Mind* (New York: Philosophical Library, 1952), p. 162.

Politics and the English Language

GEORGE ORWELL

M ost people who bother with the matter at all would admit that the English language is in a bad way, but it is generally assumed that we cannot by conscious action do anything about it. Our civilization is decadent and our language—so the argument runs—must inevitably share in the general collapse. It follows that any struggle against the abuse of language is a sentimental archaism, like preferring candles to electric light or hansom cabs to aeroplanes. Underneath this lies the half-conscious belief that language is a natural growth and not an instrument which we shape for our own purposes.

Now, it is clear that the decline of a language must ultimately have political and economic causes: It is not due simply to the bad influence of this or that individual writer. But an effect can become a cause, reinforcing the original cause and producing the same effect in an intensified form, and so on indefinitely. A man may take to drink because he feels himself to be a failure, and then fail all the more completely because he drinks. It is rather the same thing that is happening to the English language. It becomes ugly and inaccurate because our thoughts are foolish, but the slovenliness of our language makes it easier for us to have foolish thoughts. The point is that the process is reversible. Modern English, especially written English, is full of bad habits which spread by imitation and which can be avoided if one is willing to take the necessary trouble. If one gets rid of these habits one can think more clearly, and to think clearly is a necessary first step towards political regeneration: So that the fight against bad English is not frivolous and is not the exclusive concern of professional writers. I will come back to this presently, and I hope that by that time the meaning of what I have said here will have become clearer. Meanwhile, here are five specimens of the English language as it is now habitually written.

These five passages have not been picked out because they are especially bad—I could have quoted far worse if I had chosen—but because they illustrate various of the mental vices from which we now suffer. They are a little below the average, but are fairly representative samples. I number them so that I can refer back to them when necessary:

(1) I am not, indeed, sure whether it is not true to say that the Milton who once seemed not unlike a seventeenth-century Shelley had not

---

This essay, written shortly after World War II, develops George Orwell's claim that careless and dishonest use of language contributes to careless and dishonest thought and political corruption. Political language, he argues, is "largely the defense of the indefensible." But Orwell, novelist, critic, and political satirist—best known for his books *Animal Farm* and *Nineteen Eighty-Four*—believes that bad language habits can be reversed, and he lists rules for getting rid of some of the most offensive. This essay first appeared in *Horizon* in April 1946.

become out of an experience ever more bitter in each year, more alien
[sic] to the founder of that Jesuit sect which nothing could induce him
to tolerate.

Professor Harold Laski (Essay in Freedom of Expression)

(2) Above all, we cannot play ducks and drakes with a native battery
of idioms which prescribes such egregious collocations of vocables as
the Basic *put up with* for *tolerate* or *put at a loss* for *bewilder.*

Professor Lancelot Hogben (Interglossa)

(3) On the one side we have the free personality: By definition it is
not neurotic, for it has neither conflict nor dream. Its desires, such as
they are, are transparent, for they are just what institutional approval
keeps in the forefront of consciousness; another institutional pattern
would alter their number and intensity; there is little in them that is
natural, irreducible, or culturally dangerous. But *on the other side,* the
social bond itself is nothing but the mutual reflection of these self-
secure integrities. Recall the definition of love. Is not this the very
picture of a small academic? Where is there a place in this hall of mirrors for either personality or fraternity?

Essay on psychology in Politics (New York)

(4) All the "best people" from the gentlemen's clubs, and all the frantic fascist captains, united in common hatred of Socialism and bestial
horror of the rising tide of the mass revolutionary movement, have
turned to acts of provocation, to foul incendiarism, to medieval legends
of poisoned wells, to legalize their own destruction of proletarian organizations, and rouse the agitated petty-bourgeoisie to chauvinistic
fervor on behalf of the fight against the revolutionary way out of the
crisis.

Communist pamphlet

(5) If a new spirit *is* to be infused into this old country, there is one
thorny and contentious reform which must be tackled, and that is the
humanization and galvanization of the BBC. Timidity here will bespeak
cancer and atrophy of the soul. The heart of Britain may be sound and
of strong beat, for instance, but the British lion's roar at present is like
that of Bottom in Shakespeare's *Midsummer Night's Dream*—as gentle as
any sucking dove. A virile new Britain cannot continue indefinitely to
be traduced in the eyes or rather ears, of the world by the effete lan-
guors of Langham Place, brazenly masquerading as "standard English."
When the Voice of Britain is heard at nine o'clock, better far and infinitely less ludicrous to hear aitches honestly dropped than the present
priggish, inflated, inhibited, school-ma'amish arch braying of blameless
bashful mewing maidens!

Letter in Tribune

Each of these passages has faults of its own, but, quite apart from
avoidable ugliness, two qualities are common to all of them. The first is
staleness of imagery: The other is lack of precision. The writer either has
a meaning and cannot express it, or he inadvertently says something
else, or he is almost indifferent as to whether his words mean anything
or not. The mixture of vagueness and sheer incompetence is the most

marked characteristic of modern English prose, and especially of any kind of political writing. As soon as certain topics are raised, the concrete melts into the abstract and no one seems to think of turns of speech that are not hackneyed: Prose consists less and less of *words* chosen for the sake of their meaning, and more and more of *phrases* tacked together like the sections of a prefabricated hen-house. I list below, with notes and examples, various of the tricks by means of which the work of prose-construction is habitually dodged:

Dying metaphors.   A newly invented metaphor assists thought by 5 evoking a visual image, while on the other hand a metaphor which is technically "dead" (e.g., *iron resolution*) has in effect reverted to being an ordinary word and can generally be used without loss of vividness. But in between these two classes there is a huge dump of worn-out metaphors which have lost all evocative power and are merely used because they save people the trouble of inventing phrases for themselves. Examples are: *ring the changes on, take up the cudgels for, toe the line, ride roughshod over, stand shoulder to shoulder with, play into the hands of, no axe to grind, grist to the mill, fishing in troubled waters, rift within the lute, on the order of the day, Achilles' heel, swan song, hotbed.* Many of these are used without knowledge of their meaning (what is a "rift," for instance?), and incompatible metaphors are frequently mixed, a sure sign that the writer is not interested in what he is saying. Some metaphors now current have been twisted out of their original meaning without those who use them even being aware of the fact. For example, *toe the line* is sometimes written *tow the line.* Another example is *the hammer and the anvil,* now always used with the implication that the anvil gets the worst of it. In real life it is always the anvil that breaks the hammer, never the other way about: A writer who stopped to think what he was saying would be aware of this, and would avoid perverting the original phrase.

Operators or verbal false limbs.   These save the trouble of picking out appropriate verbs and nouns, and at the same time pad each sentence with extra syllables which give it an appearance of symmetry. Characteristic phrases are: *render inoperative, militate against, make contact with, be subjected to, give rise to, give grounds for, have the effect of, play a leading part (role) in, make itself felt, take effect, exhibit a tendency to, serve the purpose of,* etc., etc. The keynote is the elimination of simple verbs. Instead of being a single word, such as *break, stop, spoil, mend, kill,* a verb becomes a *phrase,* made up of a noun or adjective tacked on to some general-purpose verb such as *prove, serve, form, play, render.* In addition, the passive voice is wherever possible used in preference to the active, and noun constructions are used instead of gerunds (*by examination of* instead of *by examining*). The range of verbs is further cut down by means of the *-ize* and *de-* formation, and the banal statements are given an appearance of profundity by means of the *not un-* formation. Simple conjunctions and prepositions are replaced by such phrases as *with respect to, having regard to, the fact that, by dint of, in view of, in the interests of, on the hypothesis that;* and the ends of sentences are saved from anticlimax by such resounding commonplaces as *greatly to be desired, cannot be left out of account, a development to be expected in the near future, deserving of serious consideration, brought to a satisfactory conclusion,* and so on and so forth.

Pretentious diction.   Words like *phenomenon, element, individual* (as noun), *objective, categorical, effective, virtual, basic, primary, promote, constitute, exhibit, exploit, utilize, eliminate, liquidate,* are used to dress up simple statements and give an air of scientific impartiality to biased judgments. Adjectives like *epoch-making, epic, historic, unforgettable, triumphant, age-old, inevitable, inexorable, veritable,* are used to dignify the sordid processes of international politics, while writing that aims at glorifying war usually takes on an archaic color, its characteristic words being: *realm, throne, chariot, mailed fist, trident, sword, shield, buckler, banner, jackboot, clarion.* Foreign words and expressions such as *cul de sac, ancien régime, deus ex machina, mutatis mutandis, status quo, gleichshaltung, weltanschauung,* are used to give an air of culture and elegance. Except for the useful abbreviations *i.e., e.g.,* and *etc.,* there is no real need for any of the hundreds of foreign phrases now current in English. Bad writers, and especially scientific, political, and sociological writers, are nearly always haunted by the notion that Latin or Greek words are grander than Saxon ones, and unnecessary words like *expedite, ameliorate, predict, extraneous, deracinated, clandestine, subaqueous,* and hundreds of others constantly gain ground from their Anglo-Saxon opposite numbers.[1] The jargon peculiar to Marxist writing (*hyena, hangman, cannibal, petty bourgeois, these gentry, lackey, flunkey, mad dog, White Guard,* etc.) consists largely of words and phrases translated from Russian, German, or French; but the normal way of coining a new word is to use a Latin or Greek root with the appropriate affix and, where necessary, the *-ize* formation. It is often easier to make up words of this kind (*deregionalize, impermissible, extramarital, nonfragmentatory,* and so forth) than to think up the English words that will cover one's meaning. The result, in general, is an increase in slovenliness and vagueness.

Meaningless words.   In certain kinds of writing, particularly in art criticism and literary criticism, it is normal to come across long passages

---

[1] An interesting illustration of this is the way in which the English flower names which were in use till very recently are being ousted by Greek ones, *snapdragon* becoming *antirrhinum, forget-me-not* becoming *myosotis,* etc. It is hard to see any practical reason for this change of fashion: It is probably due to an instinctive turning-away from the more homely word and a vague feeling that the Greek word is scientific. [All notes are Orwell's.]

which are almost completely lacking in meaning.[2] Words like *romantic, plastic, values, human, dead, sentimental, natural, vitality,* as used in art criticism, are strictly meaningless in the sense that they not only do not point to any discoverable object, but are hardly ever expected to do so by the reader. When one critic writes, "The outstanding feature of Mr. X's work is its living quality," while another writes, "The immediately striking thing about Mr. X's work is its peculiar deadness," the reader accepts this as a simple difference of opinion. If words like *black* and *white* were involved, instead of the jargon words *dead* and *living,* he would see at once that language was being used in an improper way. Many political words are similarly abused. The word *fascism* has now no meaning except insofar as it signifies "something not desirable." The words *democracy, socialism, freedom, patriotic, realistic, justice,* have each of them several different meanings which cannot be reconciled with one another. In the case of a word like *democracy,* not only is there no agreed definition, but the attempt to make one is resisted from all sides. It is almost universally felt that when we call a country democratic we are praising it: Consequently the defenders of every kind of regime claim that it is a democracy, and fear that they might have to stop using the word if it were tied down to any one meaning. Words of this kind are often used in a consciously dishonest way. That is, the person who uses them has his own private definition, but allows his hearer to think he means something quite different. Statements like *Marshal Pétain was a true patriot, The Soviet Press is the freest in the world, The Catholic Church is opposed to persecution,* are almost always made with intent to deceive. Other words used in variable meanings, in most cases more or less dishonestly, are: *class, totalitarian, science, progressive, reactionary, bourgeois, equality.*

Now that I have made this catalog of swindles and perversions, let me give another example of the kind of writing that they lead to. This time it must of its nature be an imaginary one. I am going to translate a passage of good English into modern English of the worst sort. Here is a well-known verse from Ecclesiastes:

> I returned and saw under the sun, that the race is not to the swift, nor the battle to the strong, neither yet bread to the wise, nor yet riches to men of understanding, nor yet favor to men of skill; but time and chance happeneth to them all.

---

[2] Example: "Comfort's catholicity of perception and image, strangely Whitmanesque in range, almost the exact opposite in aesthetic compulsion, continues to evoke that trembling atmospheric accumulative hinting at a cruel, an inexorably serene timelessness. . . . Wrey Gardiner scores by aiming at simple bull's-eyes with precision. Only they are not so simple, and through this contended sadness runs more than the surface bittersweet of resignation" (*Poetry Quarterly*).

Here it is in modern English:

> Objective consideration of contemporary phenomena compels the
> conclusion that success or failure in competitive activities exhibits no
> tendency to be commensurate with innate capacity, but that a con-
> siderable element of the unpredictable must invariably be taken into
> account.

This is a parody, but not a very gross one. Exhibit (3), above, for in- 10
stance, contains several patches of the same kind of English. It will be
seen that I have not made a full translation. The beginning and ending
of the sentence follow the original meaning fairly closely, but in the
middle the concrete illustrations—race, battle, bread—dissolve into the
vague phrase "success or failure in competitive activities." This had to be
so, because no modern writer of the kind I am discussing—no one capable of using phrases like "objective consideration of contemporary
phenomena"—would ever tabulate his thoughts in that precise and detailed way. The whole tendency of modern prose is away from concrete-
ness. Now analyze these two sentences a little more closely. The first
contains forty-nine words but only sixty syllables, and all its words are
those of everyday life. The second contains thirty-eight words of ninety
syllables: Eighteen of its words are from Latin roots, and one from Greek.
The first sentence contains six vivid images, and only one phrase ("time
and chance") that could be called vague. The second contains not a
single fresh, arresting phrase, and in spite of its ninety syllables it gives
only a shortened version of the meaning contained in the first. Yet without a doubt it is the second kind of sentence that is gaining ground in
modern English. I do not want to exaggerate. This kind of writing is not
yet universal, and outcrops of simplicity will occur here and there in the
worst-written page. Still, if you or I were told to write a few lines on the
uncertainty of human fortunes, we should probably come much nearer
to my imaginary sentence than to the one from Ecclesiastes.

As I have tried to show, modern writing at its worst does not consist
in picking out words for the sake of their meaning and inventing images
in order to make the meaning clearer. It consists in gumming together
long strips of words which have already been set in order by someone
else, and making the results presentable by sheer humbug. The attraction
of this way of writing is that it is easy. It is easier—even quicker once
you have the habit—to say *In my opinion it is a not unjustifiable assumption that* than to say *I think.* If you use ready-made phrases, you not only
don't have to hunt about for words; you also don't have to bother with
the rhythms of your sentences, since these phrases are generally so
arranged as to be more or less euphonious. When you are composing in a
hurry—when you are dictating to a stenographer, for instance, or making a public speech—it is natural to fall into a pretentious, Latinized
style. Tags like *a consideration which we should do well to bear in mind* or *a*

conclusion to which all of us would readily assent will save many a sentence from coming down with a bump. By using stale metaphors, similes, and idioms, you save much mental effort, at the cost of leaving your meaning vague, not only for your reader but for yourself. This is the significance of mixed metaphors. The sole aim of a metaphor is to call up a visual image. When these images clash—as in *The Fascist octopus has sung its swan song, the jackboot is thrown into the melting pot*—it can be taken as certain that the writer is not seeing a mental image of the objects he is naming; in other words he is not really thinking. Look again at the examples I gave at the beginning of this essay. Professor Laski (1) uses five negatives in fifty-three words. One of these is superfluous, making nonsense of the whole passage, and in addition there is the slip *alien* for akin, making further nonsense, and several avoidable pieces of clumsiness which increase the general vagueness. Professor Hogben (2) plays ducks and drakes with a battery which is able to write prescriptions, and, while disapproving of the everyday phrase *put up with,* is unwilling to look *egregious* up in the dictionary and see what it means. (3), if one takes an uncharitable attitude towards it, is simply meaningless: Probably one could work out its intended meaning by reading the whole of the article in which it occurs. In (4), the writer knows more or less what he wants to say, but an accumulation of stale phrases chokes him like tea leaves blocking a sink. In (5), words and meaning have almost parted company. People who write in this manner usually have a general emotional meaning—they dislike one thing and want to express solidarity with another—but they are not interested in the detail of what they are saying. A scrupulous writer, in every sentence that he writes, will ask himself at least four questions, thus: What am I trying to say? What words will express it? What image or idiom will make it clearer? Is this image fresh enough to have an effect? And he will probably ask himself two more: Could I put it more shortly? Have I said anything that is avoidably ugly? But you are not obliged to go to all this trouble. You can shirk it by simply throwing your mind open and letting the ready-made phrases come crowding in. They will construct your sentences for you—even think your thoughts for you, to a certain extent—and at need they will perform the important service of partially concealing your meaning even from yourself. It is at this point that the special connection between politics and the debasement of language becomes clear.

In our time it is broadly true that political writing is bad writing. Where it is not true, it will generally be found that the writer is some kind of rebel, expressing his private opinions and not a "party line." Orthodoxy, of whatever color, seems to demand a lifeless, imitative style. The political dialects to be found in pamphlets, leading articles, manifestos, White Papers, and the speeches of undersecretaries do, of course, vary from party to party, but they are all alike in that one almost never finds in them a fresh, vivid, home-made turn of speech. When one watches some tired hack on the platform mechanically repeating the familiar phrases—*bestial atrocities, iron heel, bloodstained tyranny, free peoples of the world, stand shoulder to shoulder*—one often has a curious feeling that one is not watching a live human being but some kind of dummy; a feeling which suddenly becomes stronger at moments when the light catches the speaker's spectacles and turns them into blank discs which seem to have no eyes behind them. And this is not altogether fanciful. A speaker who uses that kind of phraseology has gone some distance towards turning himself into a machine. The appropriate noises are coming out of his larynx, but his brain is not involved as it would be if he were choosing his words for himself. If the speech he is making is one that he is accustomed to make over and over again, he may be almost unconscious of what he is saying, as one is when one utters the responses in church. And this reduced state of consciousness, if not indispensable, is at any rate favorable to political conformity.

In our time, political speech and writing are largely the defense of the indefensible. Things like the continuance of British rule in India, the Russian purges and deportations, the dropping of the atom bombs on Japan, can indeed be defended, but only by arguments which are too brutal for most people to face, and which do not square with the professed aims of political parties. Thus political language has to consist largely of euphemism, question-begging, and sheer cloudy vagueness. Defenseless villages are bombarded from the air, the inhabitants driven out into the countryside, the cattle machine-gunned, the huts set on fire with incendiary bullets: This is called *pacification*. Millions of peasants are robbed of their farms and sent trudging along the roads with no more than they can carry; this is called *transfer of population* or *rectification of frontiers*. People are imprisoned for years without trial, or shot in the back of the neck, or sent to die of scurvy in Arctic lumber camps: This is called *elimination of unreliable elements*. Such phraseology is needed if one wants to name things without calling up mental pictures of them. Consider for instance some comfortable English professor defending Russian totalitarianism. He cannot say outright, "I believe in killing off your opponents when you can get good results by doing so." Probably, therefore, he will say something like this:

> While freely conceding that the Soviet régime exhibits certain features which the humanitarian may be inclined to deplore, we must, I think, agree that a certain curtailment of the right to political opposition is an unavoidable concomitant of transitional periods, and that the rigors which the Russian people have been called upon to undergo have been amply justified in the sphere of concrete achievement.

The inflated style is itself a kind of euphemism. A mass of Latin words fall upon the facts like soft snow, blurring the outlines and covering up all the details. The great enemy of clear language is insincerity. When there is a gap between one's real and one's declared aims, one turns as it were instinctively to long words and exhausted idioms, like a cuttlefish squirting out ink. In our age there is no such thing as "keeping out of politics." All issues are political issues, and politics itself is a mass of lies, evasions, folly, hatred, and schizophrenia. When the general atmosphere is bad, language must suffer. I should expect to find—this is a guess which I have not sufficient knowledge to verify—that the German, Russian, and Italian languages have all deteriorated in the last ten or fifteen years, as a result of dictatorship.

But if thought corrupts language, language can also corrupt thought. A 15 bad usage can spread by tradition and imitation, even among people who should and do know better. The debased language that I have been discussing is in some ways very convenient. Phrases like *a not unjustifiable assumption, leaves much to be desired, would serve no good purpose, a consideration which we should do well to bear in mind,* are a continuous temptation, a packet of aspirins always at one's elbow. Look back through this essay, and for certain you will find that I have again and again committed the very faults I am protesting against. By this morning's post I have received a pamphlet dealing with conditions in Germany. The author tells me that he "felt impelled" to write it. I open it at random, and here is almost the first sentence that I see: "(The Allies) have an opportunity not only of achieving a radical transformation of Germany's social and political structure in such a way as to avoid a nationalistic reaction in Germany itself, but at the same time of laying the foundations of a cooperative and unified Europe." You see, he "feels impelled" to write—feels, presumably, that he has something new to say—and yet his words, like cavalry horses answering the bugle, group themselves automatically into the familiar dreary pattern. This invasion of one's mind by ready-made phrases *(lay the foundations, achieve a radical transformation)* can only be prevented if one is constantly on guard against them, and every such phrase anesthetizes a portion of one's brain.

I said earlier that the decadence of our language is probably curable. Those who deny this would argue, if they produced an argument at all, that language merely reflects existing social conditions, and that we cannot influence its development by any direct tinkering with words and constructions. So far as the general tone or spirit of a language goes, this may be true, but it is not true in detail. Silly words and expressions have often disappeared, not through any evolutionary process but owing to the conscious action of a minority. Two recent examples were *explore every avenue* and *leave no stone unturned,* which were killed by the jeers of a few journalists. There is a long list of flyblown metaphors which could similarly be got rid of if enough people would interest themselves in the job; and it should also be possible to laugh the *not un-* formation out of existence,[3] to reduce the amount of Latin and Greek in the average sentence, to drive out foreign phrases and strayed scientific words, and, in general, to make pretentiousness unfashionable. But all these are minor

---

[3]One can cure oneself of the *not un-* formation by memorizing this sentence: *A not unblack dog was chasing a not unsmall rabbit across a not ungreen field.*

points. The defense of the English language implies more than this, and perhaps it is best to start by saying what it does *not* imply.

To begin with it has nothing to do with archaism, with the salvaging of obsolete words and turns of speech, or with the setting up of a "standard English" which must never be departed from. On the contrary, it is especially concerned with the scrapping of every word or idiom which has outworn its usefulness. It has nothing to do with correct grammar and syntax, which are of no importance so long as one makes one's meaning clear, or with the avoidance of Americanisms, or with having what is called a "good prose style." On the other hand it is not concerned with fake simplicity and the attempt to make written English colloquial. Nor does it even imply in every case preferring the Saxon word to the Latin one, though it does imply using the fewest and shortest words that will cover one's meaning. What is above all needed is to let the meaning choose the word, and not the other way about. In prose, the worst thing one can do with words is to surrender to them. When you think of a concrete object, you think wordlessly, and then, if you want to describe the thing you have been visualizing you probably hunt about till you find the exact words that seem to fit. When you think of something abstract you are more inclined to use words from the start, and unless you make a conscious effort to prevent it, the existing dialect will come rushing in and do the job for you, at the expense of blurring or even changing your meaning. Probably it is better to put off using words as long as possible and get one's meaning as clear as one can through pictures or sensations. Afterwards one can choose—not simply *accept*— the phrases that will best cover the meaning, and then switch round and decide what impression one's words are likely to make on another person. This last effort of the mind cuts out all stale or mixed images, all prefabricated phrases, needless repetitions, and humbug and vagueness generally. But one can often be in doubt about the effect of a word or a phrase, and one needs rules that one can rely on when instinct fails. I think the following rules will cover most cases:

(i) Never use a metaphor, simile, or other figure of speech which you are used to seeing in print.

(ii) Never use a long word where a short one will do.

(iii) If it is possible to cut a word out, always cut it out.

(iv) Never use the passive where you can use the active.

(v) Never use a foreign phrase, a scientific word, or a jargon word if you can think of an everyday English equivalent.

(vi) Break any of these rules sooner than say anything outright barbarous.

These rules sound elementary, and so they are, but they demand a deep change in attitude in anyone who has grown used to writing in the style now fashionable. One could keep all of them and still write bad English, but one could not write the kind of stuff that I quoted in those five specimens at the beginning of this article.

I have not here been considering the literary use of language, but merely language as an instrument for expressing and not for concealing or preventing thought. Stuart Chase and others have come near to claiming that all abstract words are meaningless, and have used this as a pretext for advocating a kind of political quietism. Since you don't know what Fascism is, how can you struggle against Fascism? One need not swallow such absurdities as this, but one ought to recognize that the present political chaos is connected with the decay of language, and that one can probably bring about some improvement by starting at the verbal end. If you simplify your English, you are freed from the worst follies of orthodoxy. You cannot speak any of the necessary dialects, and when you make a stupid remark its stupidity will be obvious, even to yourself. Political language — and with variations this is true of all political parties, from Conservatives to Anarchists — is designed to make lies sound truthful and murder respectable, and to give an appearance of solidity to pure wind. One cannot change this all in a moment, but one can at least change one's own habits, and from time to time one can even, if one jeers loudly enough, send some worn-out and useless phrase — some *jackboot, Achilles' heel, hotbed, melting pot, acid test, veritable inferno,* or other lump of verbal refuse — into the dustbin where it belongs.

DISCUSSION QUESTIONS

1. Orwell disagrees with a common assumption about language. What is it? Where in the essay does he attack this assumption directly?

2. What faults do his five samples of bad language have in common? Select examples of these faults in each passage.

3. What "tricks" (para. 4) for avoiding good prose does Orwell list? Do you think that some are more dangerous or misleading than others? Explain the reasons for your answer.

4. What different reasons does Orwell suggest for the slovenliness of much political writing and speaking? What examples does he give to support these reasons? Are they persuasive?

5. How does Orwell propose that we get rid of our bad language habits? Do you think his recommendations are realistic? Can the teaching of writing in school assist in the remedy?

6. Why does Orwell urge the reader to "look back through this essay" to find "the very faults I am protesting against" (para. 15)? Can you, in fact, find any?

WRITING SUGGESTIONS

7. Choose a speech or an editorial whose meaning seems to be obscured by pretentious diction, meaningless words, euphemism, or "sheer cloudy

vagueness." Point out the real meaning of the piece. If you think that its purpose is deceptive, expose the unpleasant truth that the author is concealing. Use Orwell's device, giving concrete meaning to any abstractions. (One source of speeches is a publication called *Vital Speeches of the Day.* Another is the *New York Times,* which often prints in full, or excerpts major portions of, speeches by leading figures in public life.)

8. Orwell's essay appeared before the widespread use of television. Do you think that TV makes it harder for politicians to be dishonest? Choose a particular public event—a war, a street riot, a terrorist activity, a campaign stop—and argue either for or against the claim that televised coverage makes it harder for a politician to engage in "sheer cloudy vagueness." Or does it make no difference at all? Be specific in your use of evidence.

Letter from Birmingham Jail

MARTIN LUTHER KING JR.

My dear Fellow Clergymen,

While confined here in the Birmingham city jail, I came across your recent statement calling our present activities "unwise and untimely." Seldom, if ever, do I pause to answer criticism of my work and ideas. If I sought to answer all of the criticisms that cross my desk, my secretaries would be engaged in little else in the course of the day, and I would have no time for constructive work. But since I feel that you are men of genuine good will and your criticisms are sincerely set forth, I would like to answer your statement in what I hope will be patient and reasonable terms.

I think I should give the reason for my being in Birmingham, since you have been influenced by the argument of "outsiders coming in." I have the honor of serving as president of the Southern Christian Leadership Conference, an organization operating in every southern state, with headquarters in Atlanta, Georgia. We have some eighty-five affiliate organizations all across the South—one being the Alabama Christian Movement for Human Rights. Whenever necessary and possible we share staff, educational, and financial resources with our affiliates. Several months ago our local affiliate here in Birmingham invited us to be on call to engage in a nonviolent direct-action program if such were deemed necessary. We readily consented and when the hour came we lived up to our promises. So I am here, along with several members of my staff, because we were invited here. I am here because I have basic organizational ties here.

Beyond this, I am in Birmingham because injustice is here. Just as the eighth-century prophets left their little villages and carried their "thus saith the Lord" far beyond the boundaries of their hometowns; and just as the Apostle Paul left his little village of Tarsus and carried the gospel of Jesus Christ to practically every hamlet and city of the Graeco-Roman world, I too am compelled to carry the gospel of freedom beyond my particular hometown. Like Paul, I must constantly respond to the Macedonian call for aid.

Martin Luther King Jr. (1929–1968) was a clergyman, author, distinguished civil rights leader, and winner of the Nobel Prize for peace in 1964 for his contributions to racial harmony and his advocacy of nonviolent response to aggression. He was assassinated in 1968. In the following selections we meet King in two of his various roles. In "Letter from Birmingham Jail," he appears as historian and philosopher. He wrote the letter from a jail cell on April 16, 1963, after his arrest for participation in a demonstration for civil rights for African Americans. The letter was a reply to eight Alabama clergymen who, in a public statement, had condemned demonstrations in the streets. From *A Testament of Hope* (1986).

Moreover, I am cognizant of the interrelatedness of all communities and states. I cannot sit idly by in Atlanta and not be concerned about what happens in Birmingham. Injustice anywhere is a threat to justice everywhere. We are caught in an inescapable network of mutuality, tied in a single garment of destiny. Whatever affects one directly affects all indirectly. Never again can we afford to live with the narrow, provincial "outside agitator" idea. Anyone who lives in the United States can never be considered an outsider anywhere in this country.

You deplore the demonstrations that are presently taking place in 5 Birmingham. But I am sorry that your statement did not express a similar concern for the conditions that brought the demonstrations into being. I am sure that each of you would want to go beyond the superficial social analyst who looks merely at effects, and does not grapple with underlying causes. I would not hesitate to say that it is unfortunate that so-called demonstrations are taking place in Birmingham at this time, but I would say in more emphatic terms that it is even more unfortunate that the white power structure of this city left the Negro community with no other alternative.

In any nonviolent campaign there are four basic steps: (1) collection of the facts to determine whether injustices are alive, (2) negotiation, (3) self-purification, and (4) direct action. We have gone through all of these steps in Birmingham. There can be no gainsaying of the fact that racial injustice engulfs this community.

Birmingham is probably the most thoroughly segregated city in the United States. Its ugly record of police brutality is known in every section of this country. Its unjust treatment of Negroes in the courts is a notorious reality. There have been more unsolved bombings of Negro homes and churches in Birmingham than any city in this nation. These are the hard, brutal, and unbelievable facts. On the basis of these conditions Negro leaders sought to negotiate with the city fathers. But the political leaders consistently refused to engage in good faith negotiation.

Then came the opportunity last September to talk with some of the leaders of the economic community. In these negotiating sessions certain promises were made by the merchants—such as the promise to remove the humiliating racial signs from the stores. On the basis of these promises Reverend Shuttlesworth and the leaders of the Alabama Christian Movement for Human Rights agreed to call a moratorium on any type of demonstrations. As the weeks and months unfolded we realized that we were the victims of a broken promise. The signs remained. Like so many experiences of the past we were confronted with blasted hopes, and the dark shadow of a deep disappointment settled upon us. So we had no alternative except that of preparing for direct action, whereby we would present our very bodies as a means of laying our case before the conscience of the local and national community. We were not unmindful of the difficulties involved. So we decided to go through a process of self-purification. We started having workshops on nonviolence and repeatedly asking ourselves the questions, "Are you able to accept blows without retaliating?" "Are you able to endure the ordeals of jail?" We decided to set our direct-action program around the Easter season, realizing that with the exception of Christmas, this was the largest shopping period of the year. Knowing that a strong economic withdrawal program would be the by-product of direct action, we felt that this was the best time to bring pressure on the merchants for the needed changes. Then it occurred to us that the March election was ahead and so we speedily decided to postpone action until after election day. When we discovered that Mr. Connor was in the run-off, we decided again to postpone action so that the demonstrations could not be used to cloud the issues. At this time we agreed to begin our nonviolent witness the day after the run-off.

This reveals that we did not move irresponsibly into direct actions. We too wanted to see Mr. Connor defeated; so we went through postponement after postponement to aid in this community need. After this we felt that direct action could be delayed no longer.

You may well ask, "Why direct action? Why sit-ins, marches, etc.? 10 Isn't negotiation a better path?" You are exactly right in your call for negotiation. Indeed, this is the purpose of direct action. Nonviolent direct action seeks to create such a crisis and establish such creative tension that a community that has constantly refused to negotiate is forced to confront the issue. It seeks so to dramatize the issue that it can no longer be ignored. I just referred to the creation of tension as a part of the work of the nonviolent resister. This may sound rather shocking. But I must confess that I am not afraid of the word tension. I have earnestly worked and preached against violent tension, but there is a type of constructive nonviolent tension that is necessary for growth. Just as Socrates felt that it was necessary to create a tension in the mind so that individuals could rise from the bondage of myths and half-truths to the unfettered realm of creative analysis and objective appraisal, we must see the need of having nonviolent gadflies to create the kind of tension in society that will help men to rise from the dark depths of prejudice and racism to the majestic heights of understanding and brotherhood. So the purpose of the direct action is to create a situation so crisis-packed that it will inevitably open the door to negotiation. We, therefore, concur with you in your call for negotiation. Too long has our beloved Southland been bogged down in the tragic attempt to live in monologue rather than dialogue.

One of the basic points in your statement is that our acts are untimely. Some have asked, "Why didn't you give the new administration time to act?" The only answer that I can give to this inquiry is that the new administration must be prodded about as much as the outgoing one before it acts. We will be sadly mistaken if we feel that the election of Mr. Boutwell will bring the millennium to Birmingham. While Mr. Boutwell is much more articulate and gentle than Mr. Connor, they are both segregationists, dedicated to the task of maintaining the status quo. The hope I see in Mr. Boutwell is that he will be reasonable enough to see the futility of massive resistance to desegregation. But he will not see this without pressure from the devotees of civil rights. My friends, I must say to you that we have not made a single gain in civil rights without determined legal and nonviolent pressure. History is the long and tragic story of the fact that privileged groups seldom give up their privileges voluntarily. Individuals may see the moral light and voluntarily give up their unjust posture; but as Reinhold Niebuhr has reminded us, groups are more immoral than individuals.

We know through painful experience that freedom is never voluntarily given by the oppressor; it must be demanded by the oppressed. Frankly, I have never yet engaged in a direct-action movement that was "well-timed," according to the timetable of those who have not suffered unduly from the disease of segregation. For years now I have heard the words "Wait!" It rings in the ear of every Negro with a piercing familiarity. This "Wait" has almost always meant "Never." It has been a tranquilizing thalidomide, relieving the emotional stress for a moment, only to give birth to an ill-formed infant of frustration. We must come to see with the distinguished jurist of yesterday that "justice too long delayed is justice denied." We have waited for more than 340 years for our constitutional and God-given rights. The nations of Asia and Africa are moving with jetlike speed toward the goal of political independence, and we still creep at horse and buggy pace toward the gaining of a cup of coffee at a lunch counter. I guess it is easy for those who have never felt the stinging darts of segregation to say, "Wait." But when you have seen vicious mobs lynch your mothers and fathers at will and drown your sisters and brothers at whim; when you see hate-filled policemen curse, kick, brutalize, and even kill your black brothers and sisters with impunity; when you see the vast majority of your 20 million Negro brothers smothering in an airtight cage of poverty in the midst of an affluent society; when you suddenly find your tongue twisted and your speech stammering as you seek to explain to your six-year-old daughter why she can't go to the public amusement park that has just been advertised on television, and see tears welling up in her little eyes when she is told that Funtown is closed to colored children, and see the depressing clouds of inferiority begin to form in her little mental sky, and see her begin to distort her little personality by unconsciously developing a bitterness toward white people; when you have to concoct an answer for a five-year-old son asking in agonizing pathos: "Daddy, why do white people treat colored people so mean?"; when you take a cross-country drive and find it necessary to sleep night after night in the uncomfortable corners of your automobile because no motel will accept you; when you are humiliated day in and day out by nagging signs reading "white" and "colored"; when your first name becomes "nigger" and your middle name becomes "boy" (however old you are) and your last name becomes "John," and when your wife and mother are never given the respected title "Mrs."; when you are harried by day and haunted by night by the fact that you are a

Negro, living constantly at tiptoe stance never quite knowing what to expect next, and plagued with inner fears and outer resentments; when you are forever fighting a degenerating sense of "nobodiness"; then you will understand why we find it difficult to wait. There comes a time when the cup of endurance runs over, and men are no longer willing to be plunged into an abyss of injustice where they experience the blackness of corroding despair. I hope, sirs, you can understand our legitimate and unavoidable impatience.

You express a great deal of anxiety over our willingness to break laws. This is certainly a legitimate concern. Since we so diligently urge people to obey the Supreme Court's decision of 1954 outlawing segregation in the public schools, it is rather strange and paradoxical to find us consciously breaking laws. One may well ask, "How can you advocate breaking some laws and obeying others?" The answer is found in the fact that there are two types of laws: There are *just* and there are *unjust* laws. I would agree with Saint Augustine that "An unjust law is no law at all."

Now what is the difference between the two? How does one determine when a law is just or unjust? A just law is a man-made code that squares with the moral law or the law of God. An unjust law is a code that is out of harmony with the moral law. To put it in the terms of Saint Thomas Aquinas, an unjust law is a human law that is not rooted in eternal and natural law. Any law that uplifts human personality is just. Any law that degrades human personality is unjust. All segregation statutes are unjust because segregation distorts the soul and damages the personality. It gives the segregator a false sense of superiority, and the segregated a false sense of inferiority. To use the words of Martin Buber, the great Jewish philosopher, segregation substitutes an "I-it" relationship for the "I-thou" relationship, and ends up relegating persons to the status of things. So segregation is not only politically, economically, and sociologically unsound, but it is morally wrong and sinful. Paul Tillich has said that sin is separation. Isn't segregation an existential expression of man's tragic separation, an expression of his awful estrangement, his terrible sinfulness? So I can urge men to disobey segregation ordinances because they are morally wrong.

Let us turn to a more concrete example of just and unjust laws. An 15 unjust law is a code that a majority inflicts on a minority that is not binding on itself. This is difference made legal. On the other hand, a just law is a code that a majority compels a minority to follow that it is willing to follow itself. This is sameness made legal.

Let me give another explanation. An unjust law is a code inflicted upon a minority which that minority had no part in enacting or creating because they did not have the unhampered right to vote. Who can say that the legislature of Alabama which set up the segregation laws was democratically elected? Throughout the state of Alabama all types of conniving methods are used to prevent Negroes from becoming registered voters, and there are some counties without a single Negro registered to vote despite the fact that the Negro constitutes a majority of the population. Can any law set up in such a state be considered democratically structured?

These are just a few examples of unjust and just laws. There are some instances when a law is just on its face and unjust in its application. For instance, I was arrested Friday on a charge of parading without a permit. Now there is nothing wrong with an ordinance which requires a permit for a parade, but when the ordinance is used to preserve segregation and to deny citizens the First Amendment privilege of peaceful assembly and peaceful protest, then it becomes unjust.

I hope you can see the distinction I am trying to point out. In no sense do I advocate evading or defying the law as the rabid segregationist would do. This would lead to anarchy. One who breaks an unjust law must do it *openly, lovingly* (not hatefully as the white mothers did in New Orleans when they were seen on television screaming, "nigger, nigger, nigger"), and with a willingness to accept the penalty. I submit that an individual who breaks a law that conscience tells him is unjust, and willingly accepts the penalty by staying in jail to arouse the conscience of the community over its injustice, is in reality expressing the very highest respect for law.

Of course, there is nothing new about this kind of civil disobedience. It was seen sublimely in the refusal of Shadrach, Meshach, and Abednego to obey the laws of Nebuchadnezzar because a higher moral law was involved. It was practiced superbly by the early Christians who were willing to face hungry lions and the excruciating pain of chopping blocks, before submitting to certain unjust laws of the Roman Empire. To a degree academic freedom is a reality today because Socrates practiced civil disobedience.

We can never forget that everything Hitler did in Germany was 20 "legal" and everything the Hungarian freedom fighters did in Hungary was "illegal." It was "illegal" to aid and comfort a Jew in Hitler's Germany. But I am sure that if I had lived in Germany during that time I would have aided and comforted my Jewish brothers even though it was illegal. If I lived in a Communist country today where certain principles dear to the Christian faith are suppressed, I believe I would openly advocate disobeying these antireligious laws. I must make two honest confessions to you, my Christian and Jewish brothers. First, I must confess that over the last few years I have been gravely disappointed with the white moderate. I have almost reached the regrettable conclusion that the Negro's great stumbling block in the stride toward freedom is not the White Citizen's Councilor or the Ku Klux Klanner, but the white moderate who is more devoted to "order" than to justice; who prefers a negative peace which is the absence of tension to a positive peace which is the presence of justice; who constantly says, "I agree with you in the goal you seek, but I can't agree with your methods of direct action"; who paternalistically feels that he can set the timetable for another man's freedom; who lives by the myth of time and who constantly advises the Negro to wait until a "more convenient season." Shallow understanding from people of good will is more frustrating than absolute misunderstanding from people of ill will. Lukewarm acceptance is much more bewildering than outright rejection.

I had hoped that the white moderate would understand that law and order exist for the purpose of establishing justice, and that when they fail to do this they become dangerously structured dams that block the flow of social progress. I had hoped that the white moderate would understand that the present tension of the South is merely a necessary phase of the transition from an obnoxious negative peace, where the Negro passively accepted his unjust plight, to a substance-filled positive peace, where all men will respect the dignity and worth of human personality. Actually, we who engage in nonviolent direct action are not the creators of tension. We merely bring to the surface the hidden tension that is already alive. We bring it out in the open where it can be seen and dealt with. Like a boil that can never be cured as long as it is covered up but must be opened with all its pus-flowing ugliness to the natural medicines of air and light, injustice must likewise be exposed, with all of the tension its exposing creates, to the light of human conscience and the air of national opinion before it can be cured.

In your statement you asserted that our actions, even though peaceful, must be condemned because they precipitate violence. But can this assertion be logically made? Isn't this like condemning the robbed man because his possession of money precipitated the evil act of robbery? Isn't this like condemning Socrates because his unswerving commitment to truth and his philosophical delvings precipitated the misguided popular mind to make him drink the hemlock? Isn't this like condemning Jesus because His unique God-consciousness and never-ceasing devotion to His will precipitated the evil act of crucifixion? We must come to see, as federal courts have consistently affirmed, that it is immoral to urge an individual to withdraw his efforts to gain his basic constitutional rights because the quest precipitates violence. Society must protect the robbed and punish the robber.

I had also hoped that the white moderate would reject the myth of time. I received a letter this morning from a white brother in Texas which said: "All Christians know that the colored people will receive equal rights eventually, but it is possible that you are in too great of a religious hurry. It has taken Christianity almost two thousand years to accomplish what it has. The teachings of Christ take time to come to earth." All that is said here grows out of a tragic misconception of time. It is the strangely irrational notion that there is something in the very flow of time that will inevitably cure all ills. Actually time is neutral. It can be used either destructively or constructively. I am coming to feel that the people of ill will have used time much more effectively than the people of good will. We will have to repent in this generation not merely for the vitriolic words and actions of the bad people, but for the appalling silence of the good people. We must come to see that human progress never rolls in on wheels of inevitability. It comes through the tireless efforts and persistent work of men willing to be co-workers with God, and without this hard work time itself becomes an ally of the forces of social stagnation. We must use time creatively, and forever realize that the time is always ripe to do right. Now is the time to make real the promise of democracy, and transform our pending national elegy into a creative psalm of brotherhood. Now is the time to lift our national policy from the quicksand of racial injustice to the solid rock of human dignity.

You spoke of our activity in Birmingham as extreme. At first I was rather disappointed that fellow clergymen would see my nonviolent efforts as those of the extremist. I started thinking about the fact that I stand in the middle of two opposing forces in the Negro community. One is a force of complacency made up of Negroes who, as a result of long years of oppression, have been so completely drained of self-respect and a sense of "somebodiness" that they have adjusted to segregation, and of a few Negroes in the middle class who, because of a degree of academic and economic security, and because at points they profit by segregation, have unconsciously become insensitive to the problems of the masses. The other force is one of bitterness and hatred, and comes perilously close to advocating violence. It is expressed in the various black nationalist groups that are springing up over the nation, the largest and best known being Elijah Muhammad's Muslim movement. This movement is nourished by the contemporary frustration over the continued existence of racial discrimination. It is made up of people who have lost faith in America, who have absolutely repudiated Christianity, and who have concluded that the white man is an incurable "devil." I have tried to stand between these two forces, saying that we need not follow the "do-nothingism" of the complacent or the hatred and despair of the black nationalist. There is the more excellent way of love and nonviolent protest. I'm grateful to God that, through the Negro church, the dimension of nonviolence entered our struggle. If this philosophy had not emerged, I am convinced that by now many streets of the South would be flowing with floods of blood. And I am further convinced that if our white brothers dismiss us as "rabble-rousers" and "outside agitators" those of us who are working through the channels of nonviolent direct action and refuse to support our nonviolent efforts, millions of Negroes, out of frustration and despair, will seek solace and security in black nationalist ideologies, a development that will lead inevitably to a frightening racial nightmare.

Oppressed people cannot remain oppressed forever. The urge for 25 freedom will eventually come. This is what happened to the American Negro. Something within has reminded him of his birthright of freedom; something without has reminded him that he can gain it. Consciously and unconsciously, he has been swept in by what the Germans call the

Zeitgeist, and with his black brothers of Africa, and his brown and yellow brothers of Asia, South America, and the Caribbean, he is moving with a sense of cosmic urgency toward the promised land of racial justice. Recognizing this vital urge that has engulfed the Negro community, one should readily understand public demonstrations. The Negro has many pent-up resentments and latent frustrations. He has to get them out. So let him march sometime; let him have his prayer pilgrimages to the city hall; understand why he must have sit-ins and freedom rides. If his repressed emotions do not come out in these nonviolent ways, they will come out in ominous expressions of violence. This is not a threat; it is a fact of history. So I have not said to my people "get rid of your discontent." But I have tried to say that this normal and healthy discontent can be channelized through the creative outlet of nonviolent direct action. Now this approach is being dismissed as extremist. I must admit that I was initially disappointed in being so categorized.

But as I continued to think about the matter I gradually gained a bit of satisfaction from being considered an extremist. Was not Jesus an extremist in love—"Love your enemies, bless them that curse you, pray for them that despitefully use you." Was not Amos an extremist for justice—"Let justice roll down like waters and righteousness like a mighty stream." Was not Paul an extremist for the gospel of Jesus Christ—"I bear in my body the marks of the Lord Jesus." Was not Martin Luther an extremist—"Here I stand; I can do none other so help me God." Was not John Bunyan an extremist—"I will stay in jail to the end of my days before I make a butchery of my conscience." Was not Abraham Lincoln an extremist—"This nation cannot survive half slave and half free." Was not Thomas Jefferson an extremist—"We hold these truths to be self-evident, that all men are created equal." So the question is not whether we will be extremist but what kind of extremist will we be. Will we be extremists for hate or will we be extremists for love? Will we be extremists for the preservation of injustice—or will we be extremists for the cause of justice? In that dramatic scene on Calvary's hill, three men were crucified. We must not forget that all three were crucified for the same crime—the crime of extremism. Two were extremists for immorality, and thusly fell below their environment. The other, Jesus Christ, was an extremist for love, truth, and goodness, and thereby rose above his environment. So, after all, maybe the South, the nation, and the world are in dire need of creative extremists.

I had hoped that the white moderate would see this. Maybe I was too optimistic. Maybe I expected too much. I guess I should have realized that few members of a race that has oppressed another race can understand or appreciate the deep groans and passionate yearnings of those that have been oppressed and still fewer have the vision to see that injustice must be rooted out by strong, persistent, and determined action. I am thankful, however, that some of our white brothers have grasped the meaning of this social revolution and committed themselves to it. They are still all too small in quantity, but they are big in quality. Some like Ralph McGill, Lillian Smith, Harry Golden, and James Dabbs have written about our struggle in eloquent, prophetic, and understanding terms. Others have marched with us down nameless streets of the South. They have languished in filthy roach-infested jails, suffering the abuse and brutality of angry policemen who see them as "dirty nigger-lovers." They, unlike so many of their moderate brothers and sisters, have recognized the urgency of the moment and sensed the need for powerful "action" antidotes to combat the disease of segregation.

Let me rush on to mention my other disappointment. I have been so greatly disappointed with the white church and its leadership. Of course, there are some notable exceptions. I am not unmindful of the fact that each of you has taken some significant stands on this issue. I commend you, Reverend Stallings, for your Christian stance on this past Sunday, in welcoming Negroes to your worship service on a nonsegregated basis. I commend the Catholic leaders of this state for integrating Springhill College several years ago.

But despite these notable exceptions I must honestly reiterate that I have been disappointed with the church. I do not say that as one of the negative critics who can always find something wrong with the church. I say it as a minister of the gospel, who loves the church; who was nurtured in its bosom; who has been sustained by its spiritual blessings, and who will remain true to it as long as the cord of life shall lengthen.

I had the strange feeling when I was suddenly catapulted into the 30 leadership of the bus protest in Montgomery several years ago that we would have the support of the white church. I felt that the white ministers, priests, and rabbis of the South would be some of our strongest allies. Instead, some have been outright opponents, refusing to understand the freedom movement and misrepresenting its leaders; all too many others have been more cautious than courageous and have remained silent behind the anesthetizing security of the stained-glass windows.

In spite of my shattered dreams of the past, I came to Birmingham with the hope that the white religious leadership of this community would see the justice of our cause, and with deep moral concern, serve as the channel through which our just grievances would get to the power structure. I had hoped that each of you would understand. But again I have been disappointed. I have heard numerous religious leaders of the South call upon their worshipers to comply with a desegregation decision because it is the *law,* but I have longed to hear white ministers say, "Follow this decree because integration is morally *right* and the Negro is your brother." In the midst of blatant injustices inflicted upon the Negro, I have watched white churches stand on the sideline and merely mouth pious irrelevancies and sanctimonious trivialities. In the midst of a mighty struggle to rid our nation of racial and economic injustice, I have heard so many ministers say, "Those are social issues with which the gospel has no real concern," and I have watched so many churches commit themselves to a completely otherworldly religion which made a strange distinction between body and soul, the sacred and the secular.

So here we are moving toward the exit of the twentieth century with a religious community largely adjusted to the status quo, standing as a taillight behind other community agencies rather than a headlight leading men to higher levels of justice.

I have traveled the length and breadth of Alabama, Mississippi, and all the other southern states. On sweltering summer days and crisp autumn mornings I have looked at her beautiful churches with their lofty spires pointing heavenward. I have beheld the impressive outlay of her massive religious education buildings. Over and over again I have found myself asking: "What kind of people worship here? Who is their God? Where were their voices when the lips of Governor Barnett dripped with words of interposition and nullification? Where were they when Governor Wallace gave the clarion call for defiance and hatred? Where were their voices of support when tired, bruised, and weary Negro men and women decided to rise from the dark dungeons of complacency to the bright hills of creative protest?"

Yes, these questions are still in my mind. In deep disappointment, I have wept over the laxity of the church. But be assured that my tears have been tears of love. There can be no deep disappointment where there is not deep love. Yes, I love the church; I love her sacred walls. How could I do otherwise? I am in the rather unique position of being the son, the grandson, and the great-grandson of preachers. Yes, I see the church as the body of Christ. But, oh! How we have blemished and scarred that body through social neglect and fear of being nonconformists.

There was a time when the church was very powerful. It was during 35 that period when the early Christians rejoiced when they were deemed worthy to suffer for what they believed. In those days the church was not merely a thermometer that recorded the ideas and principles of popular opinion; it was a thermostat that transformed the mores of society. Wherever the early Christians entered a town the power structure got disturbed and immediately sought to convict them for being "disturbers of the peace" and "outside agitators." But they went on with the conviction that they were "a colony of heaven," and had to obey God rather than man. They were small in number but big in commitment. They were too God-intoxicated to be "astronomically intimidated." They brought an end to such ancient evils as infanticide and gladiatorial contest.

Things are different now. The contemporary church is often a weak, ineffectual voice with an uncertain sound. It is so often the archsupporter of the status quo. Far from being disturbed by the presence of the church, the power structure of the average community is consoled by the church's silent and often vocal sanction of things as they are.

But the judgment of God is upon the church as never before. If the church of today does not recapture the sacrificial spirit of the early church, it will lose its authentic ring, forfeit the loyalty of millions, and be dismissed as an irrelevant social club with no meaning for the twentieth century. I am meeting young people every day whose disappointment with the church has risen to outright disgust.

Maybe again, I have been too optimistic. Is organized religion too inextricably bound to the status quo to save our nation and the world? Maybe I must turn my faith to the inner spiritual church, the church within the church, as the true *ecclesia* and the hope of the world. But again I am thankful to God that some noble souls from the ranks of organized religion have broken loose from the paralyzing chains of conformity and joined us as active partners in the struggle for freedom. They have left their secure congregations and walked the streets of Albany, Georgia, with us. They have gone through the highways of the South on tortuous rides for freedom. Yes, they have gone to jail with us. Some have been kicked out of their churches, and lost support of their bishops and fellow ministers. But they have gone with the faith that right defeated is stronger than evil triumphant. These men have been the leaven in the lump of the race. Their witness has been the spiritual salt that has preserved the true meaning of the gospel in these troubled times. They have carved a tunnel of hope through the dark mountain of disappointment.

I hope the church as a whole will meet the challenge of this decisive hour. But even if the church does not come to the aid of justice, I have no despair about the future. I have no fear about the outcome of our struggle in Birmingham, even if our motives are presently misunderstood. We will reach the goal of freedom in Birmingham and all over the nation, because the goal of America is freedom. Abused and scorned though we may be, our destiny is tied up with the destiny of America. Before the Pilgrims landed at Plymouth we were here. Before the pen of Jefferson etched across the pages of history the majestic words of the Declaration of Independence, we were here. For more than two centuries our foreparents labored in this country without wages; they made cotton king; and they built the homes of their masters in the midst of brutal injustice and shameful humiliation—and yet out of a bottomless vitality they continued to thrive and develop. If the inexpressible cruelties of slavery could not stop us, the opposition we now face will surely fail. We will win our freedom because the sacred heritage of our nation and the eternal will of God are embodied in our echoing demands.

I must close now. But before closing I am impelled to mention one 40 other point in your statement that troubled me profoundly. You warmly commended the Birmingham police force for keeping "order" and "preventing violence." I don't believe you would have so warmly commended the police force if you had seen its angry violent dogs literally biting six unarmed, nonviolent Negroes. I don't believe you would so quickly commend the policemen if you would observe their ugly and inhuman treatment of Negroes here in the city jail; if you would watch them push and curse old Negro women and young Negro girls; if you would see them slap and kick old Negro men and young boys; if you will observe them, as they did on two occasions, refuse to give us food because we wanted to sing our grace together. I'm sorry that I can't join you in your praise for the police department.

It is true that they have been rather disciplined in their public handling of the demonstrators. In this sense they have been rather publicly "nonviolent." But for what purpose? To preserve the evil system of segregation. Over the last few years I have consistently preached that nonviolence demands that the means we use must be as pure as the ends we seek. So I have tried to make it clear that it is wrong to use immoral means to attain moral ends. But now I must affirm that it is just as wrong, or even more so, to use moral means to preserve immoral ends. Maybe Mr. Connor and his policemen have been rather publicly nonviolent, as Chief Pritchett was in Albany, Georgia, but they have used the moral means of nonviolence to maintain the immoral end of flagrant racial injustice. T. S. Eliot has said that there is no greater treason than to do the right deed for the wrong reason.

I wish you had commended the Negro sit-inners and demonstrators of Birmingham for their sublime courage, their willingness to suffer, and their amazing discipline in the midst of the most inhuman provocation. One day the South will recognize its real heroes. They will be the James Merediths, courageously and with a majestic sense of purpose facing jeering and hostile mobs and the agonizing loneliness that characterizes the life of the pioneer. They will be old, oppressed, battered Negro women, symbolized in a seventy-two-year-old woman of Montgomery, Alabama, who rose up with a sense of dignity and with her people decided not to ride the segregated buses, and responded to one who inquired about her tiredness with ungrammatical profundity: "My feet is tired, but my soul is rested." They will be the young high school and college students, young ministers of the gospel, and a host of their elders courageously and nonviolently sitting-in at lunch counters and willingly going to jail for conscience's sake. One day the South will know that when these disinherited children of God sat down at lunch counters they were in reality standing up for the best in the American dream and the most sacred values in our Judeo-Christian heritage, and thusly, carrying our whole nation back to those great wells of democracy which were dug deep by the Founding Fathers in the formulation of the Constitution and the Declaration of Independence.

Never before have I written a letter this long (or should I say a book?). I'm afraid that it is much too long to take your precious time. I can assure you that it would have been much shorter if I had been writing from a comfortable desk, but what else is there to do when you are alone for days in the dull monotony of a narrow jail cell other than write long letters, think strange thoughts, and pray long prayers?

If I have said anything in this letter that is an overstatement of the truth and is indicative of an unreasonable impatience, I beg you to forgive me. If I have said anything in this letter that is an understatement of the truth and is indicative of my having a patience that makes me patient with anything less than brotherhood, I beg God to forgive me.

I hope this letter finds you strong in the faith. I also hope that circumstances will soon make it possible for me to meet each of you, not as an integrationist or a civil rights leader, but as a fellow clergyman and a Christian brother. Let us all hope that the dark clouds of racial prejudice will soon pass away and the deep fog of misunderstanding will be lifted from our fear-drenched communities and in some not too distant tomorrow the radiant stars of love and brotherhood will shine over our great nation with all of their scintillating beauty.

Yours for the cause of Peace and Brotherhood,
Martin Luther King Jr.

DISCUSSION QUESTIONS

1. As in "I Have a Dream" (p. 706), King uses figurative language in his letter. Find some particularly vivid passages, and evaluate their effect in the context of this letter.

2. Explain King's distinction between just and unjust laws. Are there dangers in attempting to make such a distinction?

3. What characteristics of mind and behavior does King exhibit in the letter? Select the specific passages that provide proof.

4. Why does King say that "the white moderate" (para. 20) is a greater threat to African American progress than the outspoken racist? Is his explanation convincing?

5. How does King justify his philosophy of nonviolence in the face of continued aggression against Americans who are of African descent?

WRITING SUGGESTIONS

6. Can you think of a law against which defiance would be justified? Explain why the law is unjust and why refusal to obey is morally defensible.

7. In paragraph 12 King lists the grievances of African Americans in this country. King's catalog is similar to the lists in the Declaration of Independence. Can you think of any other group that might compile a list of grievances? If so, choose a group, and draw up such a list making sure that your list is as clear and specific as those you have read.

I Have a Dream

MARTIN LUTHER KING JR.

Five score years ago, a great American, in whose symbolic shadow we stand, signed the Emancipation Proclamation. This momentous decree came as a great beacon light of hope to millions of Negro slaves who had been seared in the flames of withering injustice. It came as a joyous daybreak to end the long night of captivity.

But one hundred years later, we must face the tragic fact that the Negro is still not free. One hundred years later, the life of the Negro is still sadly crippled by the manacles of segregation and the chains of discrimination. One hundred years later, the Negro lives on a lonely island of poverty in the midst of a vast ocean of material prosperity. One hundred years later, the Negro is still languishing in the corners of American society and finds himself an exile in his own land. So we have come here today to dramatize an appalling condition.

In a sense we have come to our nation's capital to cash a check. When the architects of our republic wrote the magnificent words of the Constitution and the Declaration of Independence, they were signing a promissory note to which every American was to fall heir. This note was a promise that all men would be guaranteed the unalienable rights of life, liberty, and the pursuit of happiness.

It is obvious today that America has defaulted on this promissory note insofar as her citizens of color are concerned. Instead of honoring this sacred obligation, America has given the Negro people a bad check; a check which has come back marked "insufficient funds." But we refuse to believe that the bank of justice is bankrupt. We refuse to believe that there are insufficient funds in the great vaults of opportunity of this nation. So we have come to cash this check—a check that will give us upon demand the riches of freedom and the security of justice. We have also come to this hallowed spot to remind America of the fierce urgency of *now*. This is no time to engage in the luxury of cooling off or to take the tranquilizing drugs of gradualism. *Now* is the time to make real the promises of Democracy. *Now* is the time to rise from the dark and desolate valley of segregation to the sunlit path of racial justice. *Now* is the time to open the doors of opportunity to all of God's children. *Now* is the time to lift our nation from the quicksands of racial injustice to the solid rock of brotherhood.

It would be fatal for the nation to overlook the urgency of the moment and to underestimate the determination of the Negro. This swelter- 5

In the widely reprinted "I Have a Dream" speech, Martin Luther King Jr. appears as the charismatic leader of the civil rights movement. This inspirational address was delivered on August 28, 1963, in Washington, D.C., at a demonstration by two hundred thousand people for civil rights for African Americans. From *A Testament of Hope* (1986).

ing summer of the Negro's legitimate discontent will not pass until there is an invigorating autumn of freedom and equality. Nineteen sixty-three is not an end, but a beginning. Those who hope that the Negro needed to blow off steam and will now be content will have a rude awakening if the nation returns to business as usual. There will be neither rest nor tranquillity in America until the Negro is granted his citizenship rights. The whirlwinds of revolt will continue to shake the foundations of our nation until the bright day of justice emerges.

But there is something that I must say to my people who stand on the warm threshold which leads into the palace of justice. In the process of gaining our rightful place we must not be guilty of wrongful deeds. Let us not seek to satisfy our thirst for freedom by drinking from the cup of bitterness and hatred. We must forever conduct our struggle on the high plane of dignity and discipline. We must not allow our creative protest to degenerate into physical violence. Again and again we must rise to the majestic heights of meeting physical force with soul force. The marvelous new militancy which has engulfed the Negro community must not lead us to a distrust of all white people, for many of our white brothers, as evidenced by their presence here today, have come to realize that their destiny is tied up with our destiny and their freedom is inextricably bound to our freedom. We cannot walk alone.

And as we walk, we must make the pledge that we shall march ahead. We cannot turn back. There are those who are asking the devotees of civil rights, "When will you be satisfied?" We can never be satisfied as long as the Negro is the victim of the unspeakable horrors of police brutality. We can never be satisfied as long as our bodies, heavy with the fatigue of travel, cannot gain lodging in the motels of the highways and the hotels of the cities. We cannot be satisfied as long as the Negro's basic mobility is from a smaller ghetto to a larger one. We can never be satisfied as long as a Negro in Mississippi cannot vote and a Negro in New York believes he has nothing for which to vote. No, no, we are not satisfied, and we will not be satisfied until justice rolls down like waters and righteousness like a mighty stream.

I am not unmindful that some of you have come here out of great trials and tribulations. Some of you have come fresh from narrow jail cells. Some of you have come from areas where your quest for freedom left you battered by the storms of persecution and staggered by the winds of police brutality. You have been the veterans of creative suffering. Continue to work with the faith that unearned suffering is redemptive.

Go back to Mississippi, go back to Alabama, go back to South Carolina, go back to Georgia, go back to Louisiana, go back to the slums and ghettos of our northern cities, knowing that somehow this situation can and will be changed. Let us not wallow in the valley of despair.

I say to you today, my friends, that in spite of the difficulties and 10 frustrations of the moment I still have a dream. It is a dream deeply rooted in the American dream.

I have a dream that one day this nation will rise up and live out the true meaning of its creed: "We hold these truths to be self-evident; that all men are created equal."

I have a dream that one day on the red hills of Georgia the sons of former slaves and the sons of former slaveowners will be able to sit down together at the table of brotherhood.

I have a dream that one day even the state of Mississippi, a desert state sweltering with the heat of injustice and oppression, will be transformed into an oasis of freedom and justice.

I have a dream that my four little children will one day live in a nation where they will not be judged by the color of their skin but by the content of their character.

I have a dream today.   15

I have a dream that one day the state of Alabama, whose governor's lips are presently dripping with the words of interposition and nullification, will be transformed into a situation where little black boys and black girls will be able to join hands with little white boys and white girls and walk together as sisters and brothers.

I have a dream today.

I have a dream that one day every valley shall be exalted, every hill and mountain shall be made low, the rough places will be made plain, and the crooked places will be made straight, and the glory of the Lord shall be revealed, and all flesh shall see it together.

This is our hope. This is the faith with which I return to the South. With this faith we will be able to hew out of the mountain of despair a stone of hope. With this faith we will be able to transform the jangling discords of our nation into a beautiful symphony of brotherhood. With this faith we will be able to work together, to pray together, to struggle together, to go to jail together, to stand up for freedom together, knowing that we will be free one day.

This will be the day when all of God's children will be able to sing 20 with new meaning

> My country, 'tis of thee,
> Sweet land of liberty,
> Of thee I sing:
> Land where my fathers died,
> Land of the pilgrims' pride,
> From every mountain-side
> Let freedom ring.

And if America is to be a great nation this must become true. So let freedom ring from the prodigious hilltops of New Hampshire. Let freedom ring from the mighty mountains of New York. Let freedom ring from the heightening Alleghenies of Pennsylvania!

Let freedom ring from the snowcapped Rockies of Colorado!

Let freedom ring from the curvaceous peaks of California!

But not only that; let freedom ring from Stone Mountain of Georgia!

Let freedom ring from Lookout Mountain of Tennessee! 25

Let freedom ring from every hill and molehill of Mississippi. From every mountainside, let freedom ring.

When we let freedom ring, when we let it ring from every village and every hamlet, from every state and every city, we will be able to speed up that day when all of God's children, black men and white men, Jews and Gentiles, Protestants and Catholics, will be able to join hands and sing in the words of the old Negro spiritual, "Free at last! free at last! thank God almighty, we are free at last!"

DISCUSSION QUESTIONS

1. King's style alternates between the abstract and the concrete, between the grandiloquent and the simple, with abundant use of metaphors. Find examples of these qualities. Are all the stylistic strategies equally effective? Explain your answer.

2. What specific injustices suffered by African Americans does King mention? Why does he interrupt his series of "Let freedom ring" imperatives at the end with the statement, "But not only that" (para. 24)?

3. What values does the speech stress? Would these values be equally appealing to both blacks and whites? Why or why not?

4. Forty years later, how much of King's indictment of conditions remains true? Mention specific changes or lack of changes. If conditions have improved, does that make his speech less meaningful today?

WRITING SUGGESTIONS

5. Using the same material as the original, rewrite this speech for an audience that is not impressed with the inspirational style. Think carefully about the changes in language you would make to convince this audience that, despite your dispassionate treatment, injustices exist and should be rectified.

6. Choose another highly emotional subject—for example, women's rights, child pornography, nuclear power—and write an inspirational speech or advertisement urging your audience to change their views. Be passionate, but try to avoid sentimentality or corniness. (You may want to look at other examples of the inspirational or hortatory style in a collection of speeches, among them speeches made in favor of the abolition of slavery and women's suffrage, declarations of war, and inaugural addresses.)

APPENDIX

Arguing about Literature

Writing a paper about a work of literature—a novel, a short story, a poem, or a play—is not so different from writing about matters of public policy. In both cases you make a claim about something you have read and demonstrate the validity of that claim by providing support. In papers about literature, support consists primarily of evidence from examples and details in the work itself and your own interpretation of the language, the events, and the characters. In addition, you can introduce expert scholarly opinion and history and biography where they are relevant.

First, a note about the differences between imaginative literature and argumentative essays. Although the strategies for writing papers about them may be similar, strategies for reading and understanding the works under review will be different. Suppose you read an essay by a psychologist who wants to prove that lying to children, even with the best intentions, can have tragic consequences. The claim of the essay will be directly stated, perhaps even in the first sentence. But if an author writes a short story or a play about the same subject, he or she will probably not state the central idea directly but will *show* rather than *tell*. The theme will emerge through a narrative of dramatic events, expressions of thoughts and feelings by the characters, a depiction of relationships, descriptions of a specific setting, and other elements of fiction. In other words, you will derive the idea or the theme indirectly. This is one reason that a work of fiction can lend itself to multiple interpretations. But it is also the reason that literature, with its evocation of the mysteries of real life, exerts a perpetual fascination.

Different kinds of literary works emphasize different elements. In the following discussion the elements of fiction, poetry, and drama are briefly summarized. The discussion will suggest ways of reading imaginative literature for both pleasure and critical analysis.

THE ELEMENTS OF FICTION

The basic elements of imaginative prose—a short story, a novel, or a play—are *theme, conflict,* and *character.* Other elements such as language, plot, point of view, and setting also influence the effectiveness of any work, but without a central idea, a struggle between opposing forces, and interesting people, it's unlikely that the work will hold our attention. (On the other hand, literature is full of exceptions, and you will certainly find examples that defy the rules.)

The theme is the central idea. It answers the question, What is the point of this story or play? Does the author give us some insight into a personal dilemma? Does he or she show how social conditions shape human behavior? Do we learn how certain traits of character can influence a human life? The answers to these questions apply not only to the specific situation and invented characters in a particular story. In the most memorable works the theme—the lesson to be drawn, the truth to be learned—embodies an idea that is much larger than the form the story assumes. For example, in "The Use of Force," the short story by William Carlos Williams in this appendix (p. 720), the title refers to the *subject* but not the theme. The author wanted to say something *about* the use of force. His theme is a complicated and unwelcome insight into human nature, with implications for all of us, not just the doctor who is the principal actor in the story.

Conflict is present in some form in almost all imaginative writing. It creates suspense and introduces moral dilemmas. External conflicts occur between individuals and between individuals and natural forces. Internal conflicts take place in the minds and hearts of the characters who must make difficult choices between competing goals and values—between right and wrong, pleasure and duty, freedom and responsibility. These two kinds of conflict are not exclusive of each other. A story of war, for example, may include suspenseful physical encounters between opposing forces, but the characters may also be compelled to make painful choices about their actions. In the best works, conflicts are important, not trivial. They may reveal uncommon virtues or shortcomings in the characters, alter their relationships with other people, and even change the course of their lives.

Conflicts exist only because characters—human beings, or in some satires, animals—engage in them. In contests with forces of nature, as in Hemingway's *The Old Man and the Sea,* it is the courage and persistence of a human being that gives meaning to the story. Memorable fictional characters are not easy to create. As readers we demand that characters be interesting, plausible, consistent, and active, physically and mentally. We must care about them, which is not the same as liking them. To care about characters means retaining enough curiosity about them to keep reading and to regret their departure when the story has come to an end. However different and unfamiliar their activities, we should feel that the characters are real. Even in science fiction we insist that the creatures exhibit human characteristics that we can recognize and identify with. But fictional characters should also be distinguishable from one another. Stereotypes are tiresome and unconvincing.

We learn about characters primarily from their speech and their actions but also from what the author and other characters reveal about them. Remembering that characters often withhold information or conceal their motives, even from themselves, we must often depend on our own knowledge and experience to interpret their behavior and judge their plausibility.

THE ELEMENTS OF DRAMA

Drama shares with fiction the elements we have discussed earlier— theme, conflict, and character. But because a play is meant to be performed, it differs from a written story in significant ways. These differences impose limits on the drama, as opposed to the novel, which can do almost anything.

First, stage action is restricted. Violent action—a war scene, for example—must usually take place offstage, and certain situations—such as the hunt for Moby Dick in Melville's novel—would be hard to reproduce in a theater. This means that a play emphasizes internal rather than external conflict.

Second, the author of a play, unlike the author of a short story or a novel, cannot comment on the action, the characters, or the significance of the setting. (It is true that a narrator sometimes appears on stage as a kind of Greek chorus to offer observation on the action, but this is uncommon.) A much greater burden must therefore rest on what the characters say. They must reveal background, explain offstage events, interpret themselves and others, and move the plot forward largely through speech. If the author of a novel lacks skill in reproducing plausible speech, he can find ways to avoid dialogue, but the playwright has no such privilege. She must have an ear for the rhythms and idioms of language that identify particular characters.

Another element which assumes more importance in a play than in a novel is plot. The dramatist must confine an often complicated and event-filled story to two or three hours on the stage. And, as in any listening experience, the audience must be able to follow the plot without the luxury of going back to review.

As you read a long play, you may find it helpful to keep in mind a simple diagram that explains the development of the plot, whether comedy or tragedy. The Freytag pyramid, created in 1863 by a German critic, shows that almost every three- or five-act play begins in a problem or conflict which sets in motion a series of events, called *the rising action.* At some point there is a *climax,* or turning point, followed by *the falling action,* which reverses the fortunes of the main characters and leads to a conclusion that may be happy or unhappy.

Shakespeare's *Macbeth* is an almost perfect example of the pyramid. The rising action in this tragedy is one of continued success for the main characters. The climax is a crisis on the battlefield, after which the fortunes of Macbeth and Lady Macbeth decline, ending in failure and death. In a comedy, the developments are reversed. The rising action is a series of stumbles and mishaps; then in the climax the hero finds the money or rescues the heroine, and the falling action ushers in a number of welcome surprises that culminate in a happy ending. (Think of a Jim Carrey comedy.) Typically the rising action in any play takes longer and thus creates suspense.

Reading a play is not the same as seeing one on stage. Many playwrights, like novelists, describe their settings and their characters in elaborate detail. In *Long Day's Journey into Night,* Eugene O'Neill's autobiographical play, descriptions of the living-room in which the action occurs and of the mother and father, who appear in the first act, cover more than three pages in small print. When you read, you fill the imaginary stage with your own interpretations of the playwright's descriptions, derived perhaps from places or persons in your own experience. You may forget that the playwright is dependent on directors, set designers, and actors, with other philosophies and approaches to stagecraft, to interpret his or her work. It can come as a surprise to see the stage version of the play you have read and interpreted very differently.

All playwrights want their plays to be performed. Still, the best plays are read far more frequently than they are produced on stage. Fortunately, reading them is a literary experience with its own rewards.

THE ELEMENTS OF POETRY

There are several kinds of poetry, among them epic, dramatic, and lyric. Epic poetry celebrates the heroic adventures of a human or superhuman character in a long, event-filled narrative. Milton's *Paradise Lost* is the preeminent example in English, but you may also be familiar with *The*

Iliad, The Odyssey, and *The Aeneid,* the epics of ancient Greece and Rome. Dramatic poetry also tells a story, sometimes through monologue, as in Robert Browning's "My Last Duchess," where the Duke recounts the reasons why he murdered his wife; sometimes through dialogue, as in Robert Frost's "The Death of the Hired Man." These stories are often told in blank verse, unrhymed five-beat lines. Playwrights of the past, Shakespeare among others, adopted this poetic form.

Modern poems are much more likely to be lyrics — poetry derived from song. (The term *lyric* comes from the word for an ancient musical instrument, the lyre.) The lyric is most frequently an expression of the poet's feeling rather than an account of events. The characteristics that make poetry harder to read than prose are the very characteristics that define it: compression and metaphor. A lyric poem is highly concentrated. It focuses on what is essential in an experience, the details that illuminate it vividly against the background of our ordinary lives. Metaphor is a form of figurative language, a way of saying one thing to mean something else. It is a simile which omits the "like" or "as": for example, "A mighty fortress is our God." The poet chooses metaphoric images that appeal to our senses in order to reinforce the literal meaning. In a famous poem Thomas Campion compared the beauty of his sweetheart's face to that of a garden.

> There is a garden in her face
> Where roses and white lilies grow,
> A heavenly paradise is that place,
> Wherein all pleasant fruits do flow.

A poem, like an essay, tries to prove something. Like a short story, its message is indirect, expressed in the language of metaphor. It seldom urges a practical course of action. What it tries to prove is that a feeling or a perception — a response to love or death, or the sight of a snowy field on a dark night — is true and real.

The lyric poet's subjects are common ones — love, joy, sorrow, nature, death — but he or she makes uncommon use of words, imagery, and rhythm. These are the elements you examine as evidence of the poet's theme and depth of feeling.

Precisely because the poem will condense her experience, the poet must choose words with immediate impact. For example, in a poem about an encounter with a snake, Emily Dickinson writes,

> But never met this Fellow
> Attended, or alone
> Without a tighter breathing
> And Zero at the bone —

Although we have never seen this use of "zero" before, it strikes us at once as the perfect choice to suggest a kind of chilling fear.

In the best poems images transform the most commonplace experiences. Here is the first quatrain of Shakespeare's sonnet number 73, about loving deeply what will not live forever.

> That time of year thou mayest in me behold
> When yellow leaves or none or few do hang
> Upon those boughs which shake against the cold
> Bare ruined choirs where late the sweet birds sang.

Nowhere does Shakespeare mention that he is growing old. Instead, here and in subsequent stanzas he creates images of dead or dying things — autumn trees, the coming of night, dying fires — that convey feelings of cold and desolation. The final couplet expresses the theme directly:

> Thus thou perceivs't, which makes thy love more strong,
> To love that well which thou must leave ere long.

It is the imagery, however, that brings the theme to life and enables us to understand and share the poet's feeling.

Rhythm, defined as measured and balanced movement, is almost as important as language. As children, even before we fully understand all the words, we derive pleasure from the sounds of Mother Goose and the Dr. Seuss rhymes. Their sound patterns reflect the musical origin of poetry and the fact that poetry was meant to be chanted rather than read. Listen to the rhythm of these opening lines from Andrew Marvell's "To His Coy Mistress" — "Had we but world enough and time, / This coyness, lady, were no crime" — and hear the lilting four-beat meter that suggests song. If you look through an anthology of poetry written before the twentieth century, you will see even from the appearance of the poems on the page that the cadence or rhythm of most poems creates an orderly pattern. Edgar Allan Poe's "The Raven" is a familiar example of poems in which rhyme and rhythm come together to produce a harmonious design.

Measured movement in poetry is less common today. Free verse breaks with this ancient convention. (The very regularity of "The Raven" is now a subject for parody.) The poet of free verse invents his own rhythms, governed by meaning, free association, and a belief in poetry as a democratic art, one capable of reaching all people. In "Song of Myself," Walt Whitman (1819–1892), one of America's most influential poets, writes in a new voice that resembles the sound of spoken language:

> A child said *What is the grass?* fetching it to me with full hands,
> How could I answer the child? I do not know what it is any more
>   than he.
> I guess it must be the flag of my disposition, out of hopeful green stuff
>   woven.

Notice, however, that the phrase "out of hopeful green stuff woven" is the language of poetry, not prose.

Much twentieth-century poetry dispenses altogether with both rhyme and formal rhythms, but the lyric remains unmistakably alive. Perhaps you have read poems by William Carlos Williams or e. e. cummings, who have used new rhythms to create their own distinctive versions of the lyric.

THE CULTURAL CONTEXT

Even those works that are presumed to be immortal and universal are products of a particular time in history and a particular social and political context. These works may therefore represent points of view with which we are unsympathetic. Today, for example, some women are uncomfortable with Shakespeare's *The Taming of the Shrew*, which finds comic possibilities in the subjugation of a woman to her husband's will. Jews may be offended by the characterization of Shylock in *The Merchant of Venice* as a Jewish money-lender who shows little mercy to his debtor. Some African Americans have resented the portrayal of Jim, the slave in *Huckleberry Finn*. Even *Peter Pan* has provoked criticism for its depiction of American Indians. In your own reading you may find fault with an author's attitude toward his subject; defending your own point of view against that of the author can be a satisfying literary exercise. To bring fresh, perhaps controversial, interpretations into an analysis may, indeed, enliven discussion and even revive interest in older works that no longer move us. But remember that the evidence will be largely external, based on social and political views that will themselves need explanation.

There is, after all, a danger in allowing our ideas about social and political correctness to take over and in imposing our values on those of another time, place, or culture. Literature, like great historical writing, enables us to enter worlds very different from our own. The worlds we read about in novels and plays may be governed by different moral codes, different social conventions, different religious values, many of which we reject or don't understand. Characters in these stories, even those cast as heroes and heroines, sometimes behave in ways we consider ignorant or self-serving. (Russell Baker, the humorist, observed that it was unfortunate that the writers of the past were not so enlightened as we are.) But reading has always offered an experience otherwise unavailable, a ready escape from our own lives into the lives of others, whose ways, however strange, we try to understand, whether or not we approve.

CHOOSING WHAT TO WRITE ABOUT

Your paper can take one of several different approaches. It is worth emphasizing that comedy and tragedy generally share the same literary elements. A tragedy, of course, ends in misfortune or death. A comedy typically ends with a happy resolution of all problems.

1. You may analyze or explain the meaning or theme of a work that is subject to different interpretations. For example, a famous interpretation of *Hamlet* in 1910[1] suggested that Hamlet was unable to avenge his

---

[1] Ernest Jones, *Hamlet and Oedipus* (New York: Norton, 1949).

father's murder because of guilt over his own Oedipal love for his mother. Or, having seen a distorted movie version of a familiar book (unfortunately, there are plenty of examples) you can explain what you think is the real theme of the book and how the movie departs from it.

Some stories and plays, although based in reality, seem largely symbolic. "The Lottery," a widely read short story by Shirley Jackson, describes a ritual that hints at other meanings than those usually attributed to lotteries. *Waiting for Godot,* a play by Samuel Beckett, is a work that has inspired a dozen interpretations; the name *Godot,* with the embedded word *God,* suggests several. But exercise caution in writing about symbols. Saul Bellow, the Nobel Prize–winning novelist, has written an essay, "Deep Readers of the World, Beware!" that explains the dangers. He reminds us that "a true symbol is substantial, not accidental. You cannot avoid it, you cannot remove it."

2. You may analyze the conflicts in a story or play. The conflicts that make interesting papers are those that not only challenge our understanding (as with Iago's villainy in *Othello*) but encourage us to reflect on profound moral issues. For example, how does Mark Twain develop the struggle in Huckleberry Finn between his southern prejudices and his respect for Jim's humanity? How does John Proctor, the hero of Arthur Miller's *The Crucible,* resolve the moral dilemmas that lead him to choose death rather than a freedom secured by lies?

3. You may choose to write about an especially vivid or contradictory character, describing his traits in such a way as to make clear why he is worth a detailed examination. The protagonist of *The Stranger* by Albert Camus, for example, is a murderer who, although he tells us little or nothing about himself and is therefore difficult to understand, eventually earns our sympathy.

4. You may concentrate on the setting if it has special significance for the lives of the characters and what they do, as in Joseph Conrad's *Heart of Darkness* and Tennessee Williams's *A Streetcar Named Desire.* Setting may include time or historical period as well as place. Ask if the story or play would have taken shape in quite the same way in another time and place.

5. You may examine the language or style. No analysis of a poem would be complete without attention to the language, but the style of a prose work can also contribute to the impact on the reader. Hemingway's clean, economical style has often been studied, as has Faulkner's dense, complicated prose, equally powerful but very different. But you should probably not attempt an analysis of style unless you are sure you can discuss the uses of diction, grammar, syntax, and rhythm.

GUIDELINES FOR WRITING THE PAPER

1. Decide on a limited topic as the subject for your paper. The most interesting topics, of course, are those that are not so obvious: original interpretations, for example, that arise from a genuine personal response.

Don't be afraid to disagree with a conventional reading of the literary work, but be sure you can find sufficient evidence for your point of view.

2. Before you begin to write, make a brief outline of the points that will support your thesis. You may find that you don't have enough evidence to make a good case to a skeptical reader. Or you may find that you have too much for a short paper and that your thesis, therefore, is too broad.

3. The evidence that you provide can be both internal and external. Internal evidence is found in the work itself: an action that reveals motives and consequences, statements by the characters about themselves and others, comments by the author about her characters, and interpretation of the language. External evidence comes from outside the work: a comment by a literary critic, information about the historical period or the geographical location of the work, or data about the author's life and other works he has written.

If possible, use more than one kind of evidence. The most important proof, however, will come from a careful selection of material from the work itself.

4. One temptation to avoid is using quotations from the work or from a critic so abundantly that your paper consists of a string of quotations and little else. Remember that the importance of your paper rests on *your* interpretations of the evidence. Your *own* analysis should constitute the major part of the paper. The quotations should be introduced only to support important points.

5. Organize your essay according to the guidelines you have followed for an argumentative essay on a public issue (see Chapter 9, pp. 325–45). Two of the organizational plans that work best are defending the main idea and refuting the opposing view—that is, a literary interpretation with which you disagree. In both cases the simplest method is to state your claim—the thesis you are going to defend—in the first paragraph and then line up evidence point by point in order of importance. If you feel comfortable beginning your paper in a different way, you may start with a paragraph of background: the reasons that you have chosen to explore a particular topic or a description of your personal response to the work—for example, where you first saw a play performed, how a story or poem affected you. (H. L. Mencken, the great American social critic, said discovering *Huckleberry Finn* was "the most stupendous event of my whole life!" What a beginning for an essay!)

It is always useful to look at book or movie reviews in good newspapers and magazines for models of organization and development that suggest a wide range of choices for your own paper.

SAMPLE STORY AND ANALYSIS

Read the following short story, and reflect on it for a few moments. Then turn back to the following questions. Were you surprised at the actions of the doctor? What is the author saying about the use of force? Do you agree? What kinds of conflicts has he dramatized? Are some more important than others? How do the characterizations of the people in the story contribute to the theme?

Thinking about the answers to these questions will give you a clearer perspective on the essay written by a student that follows the story. After reading the essay, you may see other elements of fiction that might have been analyzed in a critical paper.

The Use of Force

WILLIAM CARLOS WILLIAMS

They were new patients to me, all I had was the name, Olson. Please come down as soon as you can, my daughter is very sick.

When I arrived I was met by the mother, a big startled looking woman, very clean and apologetic who merely said, Is this the doctor? and let me in. In the back, she added, You must excuse us, doctor, we have her in the kitchen where it is warm. It is very damp here sometimes.

The child was fully dressed and sitting on her father's lap near the kitchen table. He tried to get up, but I motioned for him not to bother, took off my overcoat and started to look things over. I could see that they were all very nervous, eyeing me up and down distrustfully. As often, in such cases, they weren't telling me more than they had to, it was up to me to tell them; that's why they were spending three dollars on me.

The child was fairly eating me up with her cold, steady eyes, and no expression to her face whatever. She did not move and seemed, inwardly, quiet; an unusually attractive little thing, and as strong as a heifer in appearance. But her face was flushed, she was breathing rapidly, and I realized that she had a high fever. She had magnificent blonde hair, in profusion. One of those picture children often reproduced in advertising leaflets and the photogravure sections of the Sunday papers.

William Carlos Williams (1883–1963) wrote poems, novels, plays, and short stories. A pediatrician in the industrial city of Rutherford, New Jersey, much of his work, including "The Use of Force" (*The Farmers' Daughters*, 1938), depicts the daily hardships of his impoverished patients.

She's had a fever for three days, began the father and we don't know   5
what it comes from. My wife has given her things, you know, like people
do, but it don't do no good. And there's been a lot of sickness around. So
we tho't you'd better look her over and tell us what is the matter.

As doctors often do I took a trial shot at it as a point of departure.
Has she had a sore throat?

Both parents answered me together, No . . . No, she says her throat
don't hurt her.

Does your throat hurt you? added the mother to the child. But the
little girl's expression didn't change nor did she move her eyes from my
face.

Have you looked?

I tried to, said the mother, but I couldn't see.   10

As it happens we had been having a number of cases of diphtheria in
the school to which this child went during that month and we were all,
quite apparently, thinking of that, though no one had as yet spoken of
the thing.

Well, I said, suppose we take a look at the throat first. I smiled in my
best professional manner and asking for the child's first name I said,
come on, Mathilda, open your mouth and let's take a look at your throat.

Nothing doing.

Aw, come on, I coaxed, just open your mouth wide and let me take a
look. Look, I said opening both hands wide. I haven't anything in my
hands. Just open up and let me see.

Such a nice man, put in the mother. Look how kind he is to you.   15
Come on, do what he tells you to. He won't hurt you.

At that I ground my teeth in disgust. If only they wouldn't use the
word "hurt" I might be able to get somewhere. But I did not allow myself
to be hurried or disturbed but speaking quietly and slowly I approached
the child again.

As I moved my chair a little nearer suddenly with one cat-like movement both her hands clawed instinctively for my eyes and she almost
reached them too. In fact she knocked my glasses flying and they fell,
though unbroken, several feet away from me on the kitchen floor.

Both the mother and father almost turned themselves inside out in
embarrassment and apology. You bad girl, said the mother, taking her
and shaking her by one arm. Look what you've done. The nice man . . .

For heaven's sake, I broke in. Don't call me a nice man to her. I'm
here to look at her throat on the chance that she might have diphtheria
and possibly die of it. But that's nothing to her. Look here, I said to the
child, we're going to look at your throat. You're old enough to understand what I'm saying. Will you open it now by yourself or shall we have
to open it for you?

Not a move. Even her expression hadn't changed. Her breaths how-   20
ever were coming faster and faster. Then the battle began. I had to do it. I

had to have a throat culture for her own protection. But first I told the parents that it was entirely up to them. I explained the danger but said that I would not insist on a throat examination so long as they would take the responsibility.

If you don't do what the doctor says you'll have to go to the hospital, the mother admonished her severely.

Oh yeah? I had to smile to myself. After all, I had already fallen in love with the savage brat, the parents were contemptible to me. In the ensuing struggle they grew more and more abject, crushed, exhausted while she surely rose to magnificent heights of insane fury of effort bred of her terror of me.

The father tried his best, and he was a big man but the fact that she was his daughter, his shame at her behavior and his dread of hurting her made him release her just at the critical moment several times when I had almost achieved success, till I wanted to kill him. But his dread also that she might have diphtheria made him tell me to go on, go on though he himself was almost fainting, while the mother moved back and forth behind us raising and lowering her hands in an agony of apprehension.

Put her in front of you on your lap, I ordered, and hold both her wrists.

But as soon as he did the child let out a scream. Don't, you're hurt- 25 ing me. Let go of my hands. Let them go I tell you. Then she shrieked terrifyingly, hysterically. Stop it! Stop it! You're killing me!

Do you think she can stand it, doctor! said the mother.

You get out, said the husband to his wife. Do you want her to die of diphtheria?

Come on now, hold her, I said.

Then I grasped the child's head with my left hand and tried to get the wooden tongue depressor between her teeth. She fought, with clenched teeth, desperately! But now I also had grown furious—at a child. I tried to hold myself down but I couldn't. I know how to expose a throat for inspection. And I did my best. When finally I got the wooden spatula behind the last teeth and just the point of it into the mouth cavity, she opened up for an instant, but before I could see anything she came down again and gripping the wooden blade between her molars she reduced it to splinters before I could get it out again.

Aren't you ashamed, the mother yelled at her. Aren't you ashamed to 30 act like that in front of the doctor?

Get me a smooth-handled spoon of some sort, I told the mother. We're going through with this. The child's mouth was already bleeding. Her tongue was cut and she was screaming in wild hysterical shrieks. Perhaps I should have desisted and come back in an hour or more. No doubt it would have been better. But I have seen at least two children lying dead in bed of neglect in such cases, and feeling that I must get a diagnosis now or never I went at it again. But the worst of it was that I too had got beyond reason. I could have torn the child apart in my own fury and enjoyed it. It was a pleasure to attack her. My face was burning with it.

The damned little brat must be protected against her own idiocy, one says to one's self at such times. Others must be protected against her. It is social necessity. And all these things are true. But a blind fury, a feeling of adult shame, bred of a longing for muscular release are the operatives. One goes on to the end.

In a final unreasoning assault I overpowered the child's neck and jaws. I forced the heavy silver spoon back of her teeth and down her throat till she gagged. And there it was—both tonsils covered with membrane. She had fought valiantly to keep me from knowing her secret. She had been hiding that sore throat for three days at least and lying to her parents in order to escape just such an outcome as this.

Now truly she *was* furious. She had been on the defensive before but now she attacked. Tried to get off her father's lap and fly at me while tears of defeat blinded her eyes.

Rampolla   1

Jennifer Rampolla
Professor Harrington
English 102-C
May 2, 20--

*Title indicates
subject*

Conflicts in "The Use of Force"

Introduction

"The Use of Force" tells us something about human nature that probably comes as no surprise: The impulse to use

The theme

violence against a helpless but defiant opponent can be
thrilling and irresistible. But the conflict which produces this

*Theme emerges
through con-
flicts*

insight is not a shoot-out between cops and robbers, not a
fight for survival against a dangerous enemy, but a struggle
between a grown man and a sick child.

*Naming the
major conflicts
(external and
internal)*

In this story two major conflicts are dramatized, one external or physical, the other internal or psychological. The
conflicts seem obvious. Even the blunt, unadorned language
means to persuade us that nothing is concealed. But below

*A concealed
conflict (to be
explained
later)*

the surface, some motives remain unacknowledged, and we
guess at them only because we know how easily people deceive themselves.

Body

The external conflict is vividly depicted, a physical

*External con-
flict developed*

struggle between doctor and child, complete with weapon -- a
metal spoon. The outcome is hardly in doubt; the doctor will
win. One critic calls this story primarily "an accomplishment

*Evidence: com-
ment from a
critic*

(external conflict) story" (Madden 16). But the internal conflict that accompanies a difficult choice is the real heart of
the story. The doctor must decide between waiting for a more

*Internal con-
flict developed*

opportune time to examine the child or exercising brute force
to subdue her now. When he decides on brute force, he seems
aware of his motives.

*Evidence:
Quotation*

But the worst of it was that I too had got beyond reason.
I could have torn the child apart in my own fury and enjoyed it. It was a pleasure to attack her.

*Concealed con-
flict, based on
the characters
and their rela-
tionship*

This shocking revelation is not, however, the whole story.
Why has he got beyond reason? Why does he take pleasure in
attacking a child? The answer lies not only in what we know
about the antagonists but in what we can assume about their
relationship to each other.

Rampolla   2

The child is brilliantly portrayed in a few grim encounters with the doctor. She is strong, stubborn, secretive, and violent. Despite her size and age, she is a match for the doctor, a challenge that at first excites him.

> I had to smile to myself. After all, I had already fallen in love with the savage brat. . . . In the ensuing struggle . . . she surely rose to magnificent heights of insane fury. . . .

The picture of the doctor is somewhat harder to read. Sixty years ago (when this story was written) the doctor in a working-class community occupied a position of unusual power and authority. He would not be accustomed to challenges at any level. Clearly the differences in social and economic status between the doctor and his clients are another source of conflict that influences his use of force. Like many people in positions of power, the doctor is torn by contradictory emotions toward those below him. On the one hand, he despises those who are deferential to him, in this case the child's parents. On the other hand, it is unthinkable that a child should dare to oppose him, not only in refusing to obey his instructions but in trying, like a desperate small animal, to attack him. It is even more unthinkable that she should prevail in any contest. He confesses to "a feeling of adult shame." If we look for it, there is also a hint of sexual conflict. The child is blond and beautiful; the doctor says he is in love with her. (Would this story have worked in quite the same way if the child had been a boy?) The doctor attempts to rationalize his use of force, but he knows that it is not the child's welfare that finally compels him to overcome her resistance. In the end, reason gives way to pride and vanity.

Most of us respond to this story with a mixture of feelings -- anger at the pleasure the doctor takes in his use of force, confusion and even fear at the realization that doctors may not always behave like gentle and loving helpers, and pity for the little girl with whom it is easy to identify. The author doesn't spell out the moral implications of the doctor's internal conflict. But perhaps it is significant that the author

Description of the child

Evidence: Quotation

Description of the doctor

Unexpressed social conflict

Evidence: External, from history

Evidence: Quotation

Perhaps another concealed conflict?

The doctor's real motivation

Conclusion

The reader's mixed reaction

Rampolla   3

Sympathy for the child

Reaction to the theme

gives the last words to the little girl: "Tears of defeat blinded her eyes." I think he has chosen this ending in order to direct our sympathy to the victim, an unhappy child who struggled hopelessly to protect herself. Although we know that the doctor has performed a necessary and merciful act, we are left to wonder if it matters that he has done it for the wrong reason.

Rampolla   4

Work Cited

Madden, David. Studies in the Short Story. New York: Holt, 1980.

Trifles

SUSAN GLASPELL

CHARACTERS

GEORGE HENDERSON, county attorney
HENRY PETERS, sheriff
LEWIS HALE, a neighboring farmer
MRS. PETERS
MRS. HALE

SCENE: *The kitchen in the now abandoned farmhouse of John Wright, a gloomy kitchen, and left without having been put in order—the walls covered with a faded wall paper. Down right is a door leading to the parlor. On the right wall above this door is a built-in kitchen cupboard with shelves in the upper portion and drawers below. In the rear wall at right, up two steps is a door opening onto stairs leading to the second floor. In the rear wall at left is a door to the shed and from there to the outside. Between these two doors is an old-fashioned black iron stove. Running along the left wall from the shed door is an old iron sink and sink shelf, in which is set a hand pump. Downstage of the sink is an uncurtained window. Near the window is an old wooden rocker. Center stage is an unpainted wooden kitchen table with straight chairs on either side. There is a small chair down right. Unwashed pans under the sink, a loaf of bread outside the breadbox, a dish towel on the table—other signs of incompleted work. At the rear the shed door opens and the Sheriff comes in followed by the County Attorney and Hale. The Sheriff and Hale are men in middle life, the County Attorney is a young man; all are much bundled up and go at once to the stove. They are followed by the two women—the Sheriff's wife, Mrs. Peters, first; she is a slight wiry woman, a thin nervous face. Mrs. Hale is larger and would ordinarily be called more comfortable looking, but she is disturbed now and looks fearfully about as she enters. The women have come in slowly, and stand close together near the door.*

COUNTY ATTORNEY (*at stove rubbing his hands*): This feels good. Come up to the fire, ladies.

MRS. PETERS (*after taking a step forward*): I'm not—cold.

Susan Glaspell (1876–1948) was an American playwright and novelist. In 1916 she wrote *Trifles* for the Provincetown Players, a Provincetown, Massachusetts, theater troupe founded by Glaspell and her husband. Based on her recollection of a real murder case that she covered as a journalist in Iowa, *Trifles* was so successful that Glaspell decided to rewrite it as a short story, "A Jury of Her Peers."

SHERIFF (*unbuttoning his overcoat and stepping away from the stove to right of table as if to mark the beginning of official business*): Now, Mr. Hale, before we move things about, you explain to Mr. Henderson just what you saw when you came here yesterday morning.

COUNTY ATTORNEY (*crossing down to left of the table*): By the way, has anything been moved? Are things just as you left them yesterday?

SHERIFF (*looking about*): It's just about the same. When it dropped below zero last night I thought I'd better send Frank out this morning to make a fire for us—(*sits right of center table*) no use getting pneumonia with a big case on, but I told him not to touch anything except the stove—and you know Frank.

COUNTY ATTORNEY: Somebody should have been left here yesterday.

SHERIFF: Oh—yesterday. When I had to send Frank to Morris Center for that man who went crazy—I want you to know I had my hands full yesterday. I knew you could get back from Omaha by today and as long as I went over everything here myself——

COUNTY ATTORNEY: Well, Mr. Hale, tell just what happened when you came here yesterday morning.

HALE (*crossing down to above table*): Harry and I had started to town with a load of potatoes. We came along the road from my place and as I got here I said, "I'm going to see if I can't get John Wright to go in with me on a party telephone." I spoke to Wright about it once before and he put me off, saying folks talked too much anyway, and all he asked was peace and quiet—I guess you know about how much he talked himself; but I thought maybe if I went to the house and talked about it before his wife, though I said to Harry that I didn't know as what his wife wanted made much difference to John——

COUNTY ATTORNEY: Let's talk about that later, Mr. Hale. I do want to talk about that, but tell now just what happened when you got to the house.

HALE: I didn't hear or see anything; I knocked at the door, and still it was all quiet inside. I knew they must be up, it was past eight o'clock. So I knocked again, and I thought I heard somebody say, "Come in." I wasn't sure, I'm not sure yet, but I opened the door—this door (*indicating the door by which the two women are still standing*) and there in that rocker—(*pointing to it*) sat Mrs. Wright. (*They all look at the rocker down left.*)

COUNTY ATTORNEY: What—was she doing?

HALE: She was rockin' back and forth. She had her apron in her hand and was kind of—pleating it.

COUNTY ATTORNEY: And how did she—look?

HALE: Well, she looked queer.

COUNTY ATTORNEY: How do you mean—queer?

HALE: Well, as if she didn't know what she was going to do next. And kind of done up.

COUNTY ATTORNEY (*takes out notebook and pencil and sits left of center table*): How did she seem to feel about your coming?

HALE: Why, I don't think she minded—one way or other. She didn't pay much attention. I said, "How do, Mrs. Wright, it's cold, ain't it?" And she said, "Is it?"—and went on kind of pleating at her apron. Well, I was surprised; she didn't ask me to come up to the stove, or to set down, but just sat there, not even looking at me, so I said, "I want to see John." And then she—laughed. I guess you would call it a laugh. I thought of Harry and the team outside, so I said a little sharp: "Can't I see John?" "No," she says, kind o' dull like. "Ain't he home?" says I. "Yes," says she, "he's home." "Then why can't I see him?" I asked her, out of patience. "'Cause he's dead," says she. "*Dead*?" says I. She just nodded her head, not getting a bit excited, but rockin' back and forth. "Why—where is he?" says I, not knowing what to say. She just pointed upstairs—like that. (*Himself pointing to the room above.*) I started for the stairs, with the idea of going up there. I walked from there to here—then I says, "Why, what did he die of?" "He died of a rope round his neck," says she, and just went on pleatin' at her apron. Well, I went out and called Harry. I thought I might—need help. We went upstairs and there he was lyin'——

COUNTY ATTORNEY: I think I'd rather have you go into that upstairs, where you can point it all out. Just go on now with the rest of the story.

HALE: Well, my first thought was to get that rope off. It looked . . . (*stops; his face twitches*) . . . but Harry, he went up to him, and he said, "No, he's dead all right, and we'd better not touch anything." So we went back downstairs. She was still sitting that same way. "Has anybody been notified?" I asked. "No," says she, unconcerned. "Who did this, Mrs. Wright?" said Harry. He said it businesslike—and she stopped pleatin' of her apron. "I don't know," she says. "You don't *know*?" says Harry. "No," says she. "Weren't you sleepin' in the bed with him?" says Harry. "Yes," says she, "but I was on the inside." "Somebody slipped a rope round his neck and strangled him and you didn't wake up?" says Harry. "I didn't wake up," she said after him. We must 'a' looked as if we didn't see how that could be, for after a minute she said, "I sleep sound." Harry was going to ask her more questions but I said maybe we ought to let her tell her story first to the coroner, or the sheriff, so Harry went fast as he could to Rivers' place, where there's a telephone.

COUNTY ATTORNEY: And what did Mrs. Wright do when she knew that you had gone for the coroner?

HALE: She moved from the rocker to that chair over there (*pointing to a small chair in the down right corner*) and just sat there with her hands held together and looking down. I got a feeling that I ought to make some conversation, so I said I had come in to see if John wanted to put in a telephone, and at that she started to laugh, and then she stopped and looked at me—scared. (*The County Attorney, who has had his notebook out, makes a note.*) I dunno, maybe it wasn't scared. I wouldn't like to say it was. Soon Harry got back, and then Dr. Lloyd came and you, Mr. Peters, and so I guess that's all I know that you don't.

COUNTY ATTORNEY (*rising and looking around*): I guess we'll go upstairs first—and then out to the barn and around there. (*To the Sheriff.*) You're convinced that there was nothing important here—nothing that would point to any motive?

SHERIFF: Nothing here but kitchen things. (*The County Attorney, after again looking around the kitchen, opens the door of a cupboard closet in right wall. He brings a small chair from right—gets on it and looks on a shelf. Pulls his hand away, sticky.*)

COUNTY ATTORNEY: Here's a nice mess. (*The women draw nearer up center.*)

MRS. PETERS (*to the other woman*): Oh, her fruit; it did freeze. (*To the Lawyer.*) She worried about that when it turned so cold. She said the fire'd go out and her jars would break.

SHERIFF: (*rises*): Well, can you beat the woman! Held for murder and worryin' about her preserves.

COUNTY ATTORNEY (*getting down from chair*): I guess before we're through she may have something more serious than preserves to worry about. (*Crosses down right center.*)

HALE: Well, women are used to worrying over trifles. (*The two women move a little closer together.*)

COUNTY ATTORNEY (*with the gallantry of a young politician*): And yet, for all their worries, what would we do without the ladies? (*The women do not unbend. He goes below the center table to the sink, takes a dipperful of water from the pail, and pouring it into a basin, washes his hands. While he is doing this the Sheriff and Hale cross to cupboard, which they inspect. The County Attorney starts to wipe his hands on the roller towel, turns it for a cleaner place.*) Dirty towels! (*Kicks his foot against the pans under the sink.*) Not much of a housekeeper, would you say, ladies?

MRS. HALE (*stiffly*): There's a great deal of work to be done on a farm.

COUNTY ATTORNEY: To be sure. And yet (*with a little bow to her*) I know there are some Dickson County farmhouses which do not have such roller towels. (*He gives it a pull to expose its full-length again.*)

MRS. HALE: Those towels get dirty awful quick. Men's hands aren't always as clean as they might be.

COUNTY ATTORNEY: Ah, loyal to your sex, I see. But you and Mrs. Wright were neighbors. I suppose you were friends, too.

MRS. HALE (*shaking her head*): I've not seen much of her of late years. I've not been in this house—it's more than a year.

COUNTY ATTORNEY (*crossing to women up center*): And why was that? You didn't like her?

MRS. HALE: I liked her all well enough. Farmers' wives have their hands full, Mr. Henderson. And then————

COUNTY ATTORNEY: Yes————?

MRS. HALE (*looking about*): It never seemed a very cheerful place.

COUNTY ATTORNEY: No—it's not cheerful. I shouldn't say she had the homemaking instinct.

MRS. HALE: Well, I don't know as Wright had, either.

COUNTY ATTORNEY: You mean that they didn't get on very well?

MRS. HALE: No, I don't mean anything. But I don't think a place'd be any cheerfuller for John Wright's being in it.

COUNTY ATTORNEY: I'd like to talk more of that a little later. I want to get the lay of things upstairs now. (*He goes past the women to up right where steps lead to a stair door.*)

SHERIFF: I suppose anything Mrs. Peters does'll be all right. She was to take in some clothes for her, you know, and a few little things. We left in such a hurry yesterday.

COUNTY ATTORNEY: Yes, but I would like to see what you take, Mrs. Peters, and keep an eye out for anything that might be of use to us.

MRS. PETERS: Yes, Mr. Henderson. (*The men leave by up right door to stairs. The women listen to the men's steps on the stairs, then look about the kitchen.*)

MRS. HALE (*crossing left to sink*): I'd hate to have men coming into my kitchen, snooping around and criticizing. (*She arranges the pans under sink which the lawyer had shoved out of place.*)

MRS. PETERS: Of course it's no more than their duty. (*Crosses to cupboard up right.*)

MRS. HALE: Duty's all right, but I guess that deputy sheriff that came out to make the fire might have got a little of this on. (*Gives the roller towel a pull.*) Wish I'd thought of that sooner. Seems mean to talk about her for not having things slicked up when she had to come away in such a hurry. (*Crosses right to Mrs. Peters at cupboard.*)

MRS. PETERS (*who has been looking through cupboard, lifts one end of towel that covers a pan*): She had bread set. (*Stands still.*)

MRS. HALE (*eyes fixed on a loaf of bread beside the breadbox, which is on a low shelf of the cupboard*): She was going to put this in there. (*Picks up loaf, abruptly drops it. In a manner of returning to familiar things.*) It's a shame about her fruit. I wonder if it's all gone. (*Gets up on the chair and looks.*) I think there's some here that's all right, Mrs. Peters. Yes—here; (*holding it toward the window*) this is cherries, too. (*Looking again.*) I declare I believe that's the only one. (*Gets down, jar in her hand. Goes to the sink and wipes it off on the outside.*) She'll feel awful bad after all her hard work in the hot weather. I remember the afternoon I put up my cherries last summer. (*She puts the jar on the big kitchen table, center of the room. With a sigh, is about to sit down in the rocking chair. Before she is seated realizes what chair it is; with a slow look at it, steps back. The chair which she has touched rocks back and forth. Mrs. Peters moves to center table and they both watch the chair rock for a moment or two.*)

MRS. PETERS (*shaking off the mood which the empty rocking chair has evoked. Now in a businesslike manner she speaks*): Well I must get those things from the front room closet. (*She goes to the door at the right but, after looking into the other room, steps back.*) You coming with me, Mrs. Hale? You could help me carry them. (*They go in the other room; reappear, Mrs. Peters carrying a dress, petticoat, and skirt, Mrs. Hale following with a pair of shoes.*) My, it's cold in there. (*She puts the clothes on the big table and hurries to the stove.*)

MRS. HALE (*right of center table examining the skirt*): Wright was close. I think maybe that's why she kept so much to herself. She didn't even belong to the Ladies' Aid. I suppose she felt she couldn't do her part, and then you don't enjoy things when you feel shabby. I heard she used to wear pretty clothes and be lively, when she was Minnie Foster, one of the town girls singing in the choir. But that—oh, that was thirty years ago. This all you want to take in?

MRS. PETERS: She said she wanted an apron. Funny thing to want, for there isn't much to get you dirty in jail, goodness knows. But I suppose just to make her feel more natural. (*Crosses to cupboard*). She said they was in the top drawer in this cupboard. Yes, here. And then her little shawl that always hung behind the door. (*Opens stair door and looks.*) Yes, here it is. (*Quickly shuts door leading upstairs.*)

MRS. HALE (*abruptly moving toward her*): Mrs. Peters?

MRS. PETERS: Yes, Mrs. Hale? (*At up right door.*)

MRS. HALE: Do you think she did it?

MRS. PETERS (*in a frightened voice*): Oh, I don't know.

MRS. HALE: Well, I don't think she did. Asking for an apron and her little shawl. Worrying about her fruit.

MRS. PETERS (*starts to speak, glances up, where footsteps are heard in the room above. In a low voice*): Mr. Peters says it looks bad for her. Mr. Henderson is awful sarcastic in a speech and he'll make fun of her sayin' she didn't wake up.

MRS. HALE: Well, I guess John Wright didn't wake when they was slipping that rope under his neck.

MRS. PETERS (*crossing slowly to table and placing shawl and apron on table with other clothing*): No, it's strange. It must have been done awful crafty and still. They say it was such a—funny way to kill a man, rigging it all up like that.

MRS. HALE (*crossing to left of Mrs. Peters at table*): That's just what Mr. Hale said. There was a gun in the house. He says that's what he can't understand.

MRS. PETERS: Mr. Henderson said coming out that what was needed for the case was a motive; something to show anger, or—sudden feeling.

MRS. HALE (*who is standing by the table*): Well, I don't see any signs of anger around here. (*She puts her hand on the dish towel, which lies on the table, stands looking down at table, one-half of which is clean, the other half messy.*) It's wiped to here. (*Makes a move as if to finish work, then turns and looks at loaf of bread outside the breadbox. Drops towel. In that voice of coming back to familiar things.*) Wonder how they are finding things upstairs. (*Crossing below table to down right.*) I hope she had it a little more red-up up there. You know, it seems kind of *sneaking*. Locking her up in town and then coming out here and trying to get her own house to turn against her!

MRS. PETERS: But, Mrs. Hale, the law is the law.

MRS. HALE: I s'pose 'tis. (*Unbuttoning her coat.*) Better loosen up your things, Mrs. Peters. You won't feel them when you go out. (*Mrs. Peters takes off her fur tippet, goes to hang it on chair back left of table, stands looking at the work basket on floor near down left window.*)

MRS. PETERS: She was piecing a quilt. (*She brings the large sewing basket to the center table and they look at the bright pieces, Mrs. Hale above the table and Mrs. Peters left of it.*)

MRS. HALE: It's a log cabin pattern. Pretty, isn't it? I wonder if she was goin' to quilt it or just knot it? (*Footsteps have been heard coming down the stairs. The Sheriff enters followed by Hale and the County Attorney.*)

SHERIFF: They wonder if she was going to quilt it or just knot it! (*The men laugh, the women look abashed.*)

COUNTY ATTORNEY (*rubbing his hands over the stove*): Frank's fire didn't do much up there, did it? Well, let's go out to the barn and get that cleared up. (*The men go outside by up left door.*)

MRS. HALE (*resentfully*): I don't know as there's anything so strange, our takin' up our time with little things while we're waiting for them to get the evidence. (*She sits in chair right of table smoothing out a block with decision.*) I don't see as it's anything to laugh about.

MRS. PETERS (*apologetically*): Of course they've got awful important things on their minds. (*Pulls up a chair and joins Mrs. Hale at the left of the table.*)

MRS. HALE (*examining another block*): Mrs. Peters, look at this one. Here, this is the one she was working on, and look at the sewing! All the rest of it has been so nice and even. And look at this! It's all over the place! Why, it looks as if she didn't know what she was about! (*After she has said this they look at each other, then start to glance back at the door. After an instant Mrs. Hale has pulled at a knot and ripped the sewing.*)

MRS. PETERS: Oh, what are you doing, Mrs. Hale?

MRS. HALE (*mildly*): Just pulling out a stitch or two that's not sewed very good. (*Threading a needle.*) Bad sewing always made me fidgety.

MRS. PETERS (*with a glance at door, nervously*): I don't think we ought to touch things.

MRS. HALE: I'll just finish up this end. (*Suddenly stopping and leaning forward.*) Mrs. Peters?

MRS. PETERS: Yes, Mrs. Hale?

MRS. HALE: What do you suppose she was so nervous about?

MRS. PETERS: Oh—I don't know. I don't know as she was nervous. I sometimes sew awful queer when I'm just tired. (*Mrs. Hale starts to say something, looks at Mrs. Peters, then goes on sewing.*) Well, I must get these things wrapped up. They may be through sooner than we think. (*Putting apron and other things together.*) I wonder where I can find a piece of paper, and string. (*Rises.*)

MRS. HALE: In that cupboard, maybe.

MRS. PETERS (*crosses right looking in cupboard*): Why, here's a bird-cage. (*Holds it up.*) Did she have a bird, Mrs. Hale?

MRS. HALE: Why, I don't know whether she did or not—I've not been here for so long. There was a man around last year selling canaries cheap, but I don't know as she took one; maybe she did. She used to sing real pretty herself.

MRS. PETERS (*glancing around*): Seems funny to think of a bird here. But she must have had one, or why would she have a cage? I wonder what happened to it?

MRS. HALE: I s'pose maybe the cat got it.

MRS. PETERS: No, she didn't have a cat. She's got that feeling some people have about cats—being afraid of them. My cat got in her room and she was real upset and asked me to take it out.

MRS. HALE: My sister Bessie was like that. Queer, ain't it?

MRS. PETERS (*examining the cage*): Why, look at this door. It's broke. One hinge is pulled apart. (*Takes a step down to Mrs. Hale's right.*)

MRS. HALE (*looking too*): Looks as if someone must have been rough with it.

MRS. PETERS: Why, yes. (*She brings the cage forward and puts it on the table.*)

MRS. HALE (*glancing toward up left door*): I wish if they're going to find any evidence they'd be about it. I don't like this place.

MRS. PETERS: But I'm awful glad you came with me, Mrs. Hale. It would be lonesome for me sitting here alone.

MRS. HALE: It would, wouldn't it? (*Dropping her sewing.*) But I tell you what I do wish, Mrs. Peters. I wish I had come over sometimes when *she* was here. I—(*looking around the room*)—wish I had.

MRS. PETERS: But of course you were awful busy, Mrs. Hale—your house and your children.

MRS. HALE (*rises and crosses left*): I could've come. I stayed away because it weren't cheerful—and that's why I ought to have come. I—(*looking out left window*)—I've never liked this place. Maybe because it's down in a hollow and you don't see the road. I dunno what it is, but it's a lonesome place and always was. I wish I had come over to see Minnie Foster sometimes. I can see now—(*Shakes her head.*)

MRS. PETERS (*left of table and above it*): Well, you mustn't reproach yourself, Mrs. Hale. Somehow we just don't see how it is with other folks until—something turns up.

MRS. HALE: Not having children makes less work—but it makes a quiet house, and Wright out to work all day, and no company when he did come in. (*Turning from window.*) Did you know John Wright, Mrs. Peters?

MRS. PETERS: Not to know him; I've seen him in town. They say he was a good man.

MRS. HALE: Yes—good; he didn't drink, and kept his word as well as most, I guess, and paid his debts. But he was a hard man, Mrs. Peters. Just to pass the time of day with him—(*Shivers.*) Like a raw wind that gets to the bone. (*Pauses, her eye falling on the cage.*) I should think she would 'a' wanted a bird. But what do you suppose went with it?

MRS. PETERS: I don't know, unless it got sick and died. (*She reaches over and swings the broken door, swings it again, both women watch it.*)

MRS. HALE: You weren't raised round here, were you? (*Mrs. Peters shakes her head.*) You didn't know—her?

MRS. PETERS: Not till they brought her yesterday.

MRS. HALE: She—come to think of it, she was kind of like a bird herself—real sweet and pretty, but kind of timid and—fluttery. How—she—did—change. (*Silence: then as if struck by a happy thought and relieved to get back to everyday things. Crosses right above Mrs. Peters to cupboard, replaces small chair used to stand on to its original place down right.*) Tell you what, Mrs. Peters, why don't you take the quilt in with you? It might take up her mind.

MRS. PETERS: Why, I think that's a real nice idea, Mrs. Hale. There couldn't possibly be any objection to it could there? Now, just what would I take? I wonder if her patches are in here—and her things. (*They look in the sewing basket.*)

MRS. HALE (*crosses to right of table*): Here's some red. I expect this has got sewing things in it. (*Brings out a fancy box.*) What a pretty box. Looks like something somebody would give you. Maybe her scissors are in here. (*Opens box. Suddenly puts her hand to her nose.*) Why——(*Mrs. Peters bends nearer, then turns her face away.*) There's something wrapped up in this piece of silk.

MRS. PETERS: Why, this isn't her scissors.

MRS. HALE (*lifting the silk*): Oh, Mrs. Peters—it's——(*Mrs. Peters bends closer.*)

MRS. PETERS: It's the bird.

MRS. HALE: But, Mrs. Peters—look at it! Its neck! Look at its neck! It's all—other side *to*.

MRS. PETERS: Somebody—wrung—its—neck. (*Their eyes meet. A look of growing comprehension, of horror. Steps are heard outside. Mrs. Hale slips box under quilt pieces, and sinks into her chair. Enter Sheriff and County Attorney. Mrs. Peters steps down left and stands looking out of window.*)

COUNTY ATTORNEY (*as one turning from serious things to little pleasantries*): Well, ladies, have you decided whether she was going to quilt it or knot it? (*Crosses to center above table.*)

MRS. PETERS: We think she was going to—knot it. (*Sheriff crosses to right of stove, lifts stove lid, and glances at fire, then stands warming hands at stove.*)

COUNTY ATTORNEY: Well, that's interesting, I'm sure. (*Seeing the bird-cage.*) Has the bird flown?

MRS. HALE (*putting more quilt pieces over the box*): We think the—cat got it.

COUNTY ATTORNEY (*preoccupied*): Is there a cat? (*Mrs. Hale glances in a quick covert way at Mrs. Peters.*)

MRS. PETERS (*turning from window takes a step in*): Well, not *now*. They're superstitious, you know. They leave.

COUNTY ATTORNEY (*to Sheriff Peters, continuing an interrupted conversation*): No sign at all of anyone having come from the outside. Their own rope. Now let's go up again and go over it piece by piece. (*They start upstairs.*) It would have to have been someone who knew just the——(*Mrs. Peters sits down left of table. The two women sit there not looking at one another, but as if peering into something and at the same time holding back. When they talk now it is in the manner of feeling their way over strange ground, as if afraid of what they are saying, but as if they cannot help saying it.*)

MRS. HALE (*hesitatively and in hushed voice*): She liked the bird. She was going to bury it in that pretty box.

MRS. PETERS (*in a whisper*): When I was a girl—my kitten—there was a boy took a hatchet, and before my eyes—and before I could get there——(*Covers her face an instant.*) If they hadn't held me back I would have—(*catches herself, looks upstairs where steps are heard, falters weakly*)—hurt him.

MRS. HALE (*with a slow look around her*): I wonder how it would seem never to have had any children around. (*Pause.*) No, Wright wouldn't like the bird—a thing that sang. She used to sing. He killed that, too.

MRS. PETERS (*moving uneasily*): We don't know who killed the bird.

MRS. HALE: I knew John Wright.

MRS. PETERS: It was an awful thing was done in this house that night, Mrs. Hale. Killing a man while he slept, slipping a rope around his neck that choked the life out of him.

MRS. HALE: His neck. Choked the life out of him. (*Her hand goes out and rests on the bird-cage.*)

MRS. PETERS (*with rising voice*): We don't know who killed him. We don't *know*.

MRS. HALE (*her own feeling not interrupted*): If there'd been years and years of nothing, then a bird to sing to you, it would be awful—still, after the bird was still.

MRS. PETERS (*something within her speaking*): I know what stillness is. When we homesteaded in Dakota, and my first baby died—after he was two years old, and me with no other then———

MRS. HALE (*moving*): How soon do you suppose they'll be through looking for the evidence?

MRS. PETERS: I know what stillness is. (*Pulling herself back.*) The law has got to punish crime, Mrs. Hale.

MRS. HALE (*not as if answering that*): I wish you'd seen Minnie Foster when she wore a white dress with blue ribbons and stood up there in the choir and sang. (*A look around the room.*) Oh, I *wish* I'd come over here once in a while! That was a crime! That was a crime! Who's going to punish that?

MRS. PETERS (*looking upstairs*): We mustn't—take on.

MRS. HALE: I might have known she needed help! I know how things can be —for women. I tell you, it's queer, Mrs. Peters. We live close together and we live far apart. We all go through the same things—it's all just a different kind of the same thing. (*Brushes her eyes, noticing the jar of fruit, reaches out for it.*) If I was you I wouldn't tell her her fruit was gone. Tell her it *ain't*. Tell her it's all right. Take this in to prove it to her. She—she may never know whether it was broke or not.

MRS. PETERS (*takes the jar, looks about for something to wrap it in; takes petticoat from the clothes brought from the other room, very nervously begins winding this around the jar. In a false voice*): My, it's a good thing the men couldn't hear us. Wouldn't they just laugh! Getting all stirred up over a little thing like a—dead canary. As if that could have anything to do with—with—wouldn't they *laugh!* (*The men are heard coming downstairs.*)

MRS. HALE (*under her breath*): Maybe they would—maybe they wouldn't.

COUNTY ATTORNEY: No, Peters, it's all perfectly clear except a reason for doing it. But you know juries when it comes to women. If there was some definite thing. (*Crosses slowly to above table. Sheriff crosses down right. Mrs. Hale and Mrs. Peters remain seated at either side of table.*) Something to show—something to make a story about—a thing that would connect up with this strange way of doing it———(*The women's eyes meet for an instant. Enter Hale from outer door.*)

HALE (*remaining by door*): Well, I've got the team around. Pretty cold out there.

COUNTY ATTORNEY: I'm going to stay awhile by myself. (*To the Sheriff.*) You can send Frank out for me, can't you? I want to go over everything. I'm not satisfied that we can't do better.

SHERIFF: Do you want to see what Mrs. Peters is going to take in? (*The Lawyer picks up the apron, laughs.*)

COUNTY ATTORNEY: Oh, I guess they're not very dangerous things the ladies have picked out. (*Moves a few things about, disturbing the quilt pieces which cover the box. Steps back.*) No, Mrs. Peters doesn't need supervising. For that matter a sheriff's wife is married to the law. Ever think of it that way, Mrs. Peters?

MRS. PETERS: Not—just that way.

SHERIFF (*chuckling*): Married to the law. (*Moves to down right door to the other room.*) I just want you to come in here a minute, George. We ought to take a look at these windows.

COUNTY ATTORNEY (*scoffingly*): Oh, windows!

SHERIFF: We'll be right out, Mr. Hale. (*Hale goes outside. The Sheriff follows the County Attorney into the room. Then Mrs. Hale rises, hands tight together, looking intensely at Mrs. Peters, whose eyes make a slow turn, finally meeting Mrs. Hale's. A moment Mrs. Hale holds her, then her own eyes point the way to where the box is concealed. Suddenly Mrs. Peters throws back quilt pieces and tries to put the box in the bag she is carrying. It is too big. She opens box, starts to take bird out, cannot touch it, goes to pieces, stands there helpless. Sound of a knob turning in the other room. Mrs. Hale snatches the box and puts it in the pocket of her big coat. Enter County Attorney and Sheriff, who remains down right.*)

COUNTY ATTORNEY (*crosses to up left door facetiously*): Well, Henry, at least we found out that she was not going to quilt it. She was going to— what is it you call it, ladies?

MRS. HALE (*standing center below table facing front, her hand against her pocket*): We call it—knot it, Mr. Henderson.

CURTAIN.

To His Coy Mistress

ANDREW MARVELL

Had we but world enough, and time,
This coyness, lady, were no crime.
We would sit down, and think which way
To walk, and pass our long love's day.
Thou by the Indian Ganges' side   5
Should'st rubies find; I by the tide
Of Humber[1] would complain. I would
Love you ten years before the Flood;
And you should, if you please, refuse
Till the conversion of the Jews.   10
My vegetable love should grow
Vaster than empires, and more slow.
An hundred years should go to praise
Thine eyes, and on thy forehead gaze;
Two hundred to adore each breast;   15
But thirty thousand to the rest:
An age at least to every part,
And the last age should show your heart.
For, lady, you deserve this state,
Nor would I love at lower rate.   20
　　But at my back I always hear
Time's wingèd chariot hurrying near;
And yonder all before us lie
Deserts of vast eternity.
Thy beauty shall no more be found,   25
Nor in thy marble vault shall sound
My echoing song; then worms shall try
That long-preserved virginity;
And your quaint honor turn to dust,
And into ashes all my lust.   30
The grave's a fine and private place,

[1] An estuary in England. All notes are the editor's.

Andrew Marvell (1621–1678) was a longtime member of the British Parliament and a writer of political satires. Today, however, he is remembered for two splendid poems, "The Garden" and the one that appears here. "To His Coy Mistress" is a noteworthy expression of an idea familiar in the love poems of many languages—*carpe diem,* Latin for "seize the day," the idea that life is fleeting and love and other pleasures should be enjoyed while the lovers are still young and beautiful.

But none, I think, do there embrace.
   Now, therefore, while thy youthful hue
Sits on thy skin like morning dew,
And while thy willing soul transpires 35
At every pore with instant fires,
Now let us sport us while we may;
And now, like amorous birds of prey,
Rather at once our time devour,
Than languish in his slow-chapped[2] power. 40
Let us roll all our strength and all
Our sweetness up into one ball;
And tear our pleasures with rough strife
Thorough[3] the iron gates of life.
Thus, though we cannot make our sun 45
Stand still, yet we will make him run.

[2] Slow-jawed. — ED.
[3] Through. — ED.

Acknowledgments (continued from page iv)

Isaac Asimov. "God Is Not the Creator." Originally titled, "Do Scientists Believe in God?" from *Gallery*, June 1979. Copyright © 1979 by Montcalm Publishing Corp.

Ronald Bailey and Dinesh D'Souza. "Genetic Enhancement Allows for Even Greater Freedom" and "We Should Not Tamper with What Makes Us Human." Originally titled "Our Biotech Future," an exchange between Ronald Bailey and Dinesh D'Souza from *National Review*, March 5, 2001, pp. 45–46. © 2001 by National Review, Inc. Reprinted by permission.

Avraham Balaban. "Remote Control." Originally published in the *New York Times*, March 22, 1999. Copyright © 1999 by The New York Times Company. Reprinted by permission.

Malcolm W. Browne. "Left the Light on but Nobody Came." From the *New York Times*, January 1, 2000. Copyright © 2000 by The New York Times Company. Reprinted by permission.

Warren Burger. "The Right to Bear Arms." Originally published in *Parade*, January 14, 1990. Reprinted with permission from *Parade* and the author.

Peggy Carlson. "Why We Don't Need Animal Experimentation." Reprinted with permission by the Physicians Committee for Responsible Medicine (PCRM), 5100 Wisconsin Ave., Suite 400, Washington, DC 20016; <www.pcrm.org>.

Rachel Carson. "The Obligation to Endure." From *Silent Spring* by Rachel Carson. Copyright © 1962 by Rachel L. Carson. Renewed 1990 by Roger Christie. Reprinted by permission of Houghton Mifflin Company. All rights reserved.

Stewart Dalzell. "Free Speech on the Internet: Opinion on the Constitutionality of the Communications Decency Act." From the *New York Times*, June 13, 1996. Copyright © 1996 by The New York Times Company. Reprinted by permission.

Christie Davies. "Trial by Jury Should Be Abolished." From *National Review*, May 24, 1993, pp. 46–48. © 1993 by National Review, Inc. Reprinted by permission.

Alan Dershowitz. "Unsung Heroes—Juries Offer True Justice." Excerpt from *Contrary to Popular Opinion* by Alan Dershowitz. Copyright © 1992 by Alan Dershowitz. Reprinted by permission of the author.

Whitfield Diffie and Susan Landau. "Privacy: Protections and Threats." From *Privacy on the Line: The Politics of Wiretapping and Encryption* by Whitfield Diffie and Susan Landau. Copyright © 1998 by Whitfield Diffie and Susan Landau. Reprinted by permission of MIT Press.

John Patrick Diggins. "The Pursuit of Whining: Affirmative Action circa 1776." Originally published in the *New York Times*, September 25, 1995. Copyright © 1995 by The New York Times Company. Reprinted by permission.

Jeff Durstewitz. "'Cultural Vandals' Hide Behind Free Speech." Originally published in "Letters to the Editor" column in the *Wall Street Journal*, June 29, 1998. Reprinted by permission.

Barbara Ehrenreich. "Ice-T: The Issue Is Creative Freedom." From *Time*, July 20, 1992. Copyright © 1992 Time, Inc. Reprinted by permission.

Jean Bethke Elshtain. "The Hard Questions: Beyond Consent." From *The New Republic*, May 6, 1998. Copyright © 1998 The New Republic, Inc. Reprinted by permission.

Amitai Etzioni. "High-Tech Parenting." Reprinted by permission of the author.

Sandra Feldman. "The Childswap Society." From the January 1998 "Where We Stand" monthly column of the American Federation of Teachers. Reprinted with permission.

Milton Friedman. "Social Responsibility of Business and Labor." From *Capitalism and Freedom: With a New Preface* by Milton Friedman. Copyright © 1962 by Milton Friedman. Reprinted by permission of the author and the University of Chicago Press.

Evan Gahr. "Gore for Sale." Originally published in the *Wall Street Journal*, April 30, 1999. Reprinted by permission.

Henry Louis Gates Jr. "The Future of Slavery's Past." Originally published in the *New York Times*, July 29, 2001. Copyright © 2001 by The New York Times Company. Reprinted by permission.

David Gelernter. "Computers and the Pursuit of Happiness." Reprinted by permission.

Susan Glaspell. *Trifles*. Copyright © 1916 by Susan Glaspell. Reprinted with the permission of the Estate of Susan Glaspell.

Paul Goodman. "A Proposal to Abolish Grading." From *Compulsory Miseducation* by Paul Goodman. Copyright © 1964 by Horizon Press, New York. Reprinted by permission.

Elisha Dov Hack. "College Life versus My Moral Code." Originally published in the *New York Times*, September 9, 1997. Copyright © 1997 by The New York Times Company. Reprinted by permission.

Bob Herbert. "What Privacy Rights?" Originally published in the *New York Times*, September 27, 1998. Copyright © 1998 by The

New York Times Company. Reprinted by permission.

Adolph Hitler. "On Nation and Race." From *Mein Kampf* by Adolf Hitler, translated by Ralph Manheim. Copyright © 1943 and renewed 1971 by Houghton Mifflin Company. Reprinted by permission of Houghton Mifflin Company. All rights reserved. Canadian rights granted by Pimlico, an imprint of The Random House Group Ltd.

David Horowitz. "Ten Reasons Why Reparations for Slavery Is a Bad Idea—and Racist, Too." Featured in the Brown University *Daily Herald*. David Horowitz is President, Center for Study of Popular Culture. Reprinted by permission.

William S. Hubbartt. "Privacy Rights: The New Employee Relations Battlefield." Excerpt from *The New Battle Over Workplace Privacy* by William S. Hubbartt. Copyright © 1998 William S. Hubbart. Reprinted by permission of AMACOM, a division of American Management Association International, via Copyright Clearance Center, Inc. All rights reserved.

Evan Imber-Black. "Talk Show Telling versus Authentic Telling: The Effects of the Popular Media on Secrecy and Openness." From *The Secret Life of Families* by Evan Imber-Black. Copyright © 1998 by Evan Imber-Black. Used by permission of Bantam Books, a division of Random House, Inc.

Sarah Edith Jacobson. "Nike's Power Game." Originally published in the *New York Times*, May 16, 2000. Copyright © 2000 by The New York Times Company. Reprinted by permission.

Jeff Jacoby. "The 'MCAS' Teens Give Each Other." From the *Boston Globe*, December 4, 2000, p. A15. "A Desensitized Society Drenched in Sleaze." From the *Boston Globe*, June 8, 1995. Reprinted by permission.

Robert Jastrow. "God May Be the Creator." From *God and the Astronomers* by Robert Jastrow (W. W. Norton & Company, Inc., 1978). Reprinted by permission.

Holman W. Jenkins Jr. "Violence Never Solved Anything, but It's Entertaining." From the *Wall Street Journal*, October 28, 1998. Republished by permission of Dow Jones, Inc., via Copyright Clearance Center, Inc. © 1998 Dow Jones and Company, Inc. All Rights Reserved Worldwide.

Denis Johnson. "War at Home." Originally titled "September 11, 2001." From *The New Yorker* "Talk of the Town" column, September 24, 2001, pp. 29–31. Copyright © 2001 Condé Nast Publications, Inc. Reprinted by permission. All rights reserved.

Steffen N. Johnson. "A Case the Scouts Had to Win." Originally published in *The New York Times*, June 30, 2000. Copyright © 2000 by The New York Times Company. Reprinted by permission.

Burton S. Katz. "Juries on the Rampage." From *Justice Overruled* by Judge Burton S. Katz. Copyright © 1997 by Burton Katz. Reprinted by permission of Warner Books, Inc.

Martin Luther King Jr. "Letter from Birmingham Jail" and "I Have a Dream." Copyright © 1963 by Martin Luther King Jr. Renewed 1991 by Coretta Scott King. Reprinted by arrangement with the Heirs to the Estate of Martin Luther King Jr., c/o Writer's House, Inc., as agent for the proprietor.

Douglas W. Kmiec. "Military Tribunals Are Necessary in Times of War." From the *Wall Street Journal*, November 15, 2001. Republished by permission of Dow Jones, Inc., via Copyright Clearance Center, Inc. © 2001 Dow Jones and Company, Inc. All Rights Reserved Worldwide.

Alfie Kohn. "No-Win Situations." Originally published in *Women's Sports and Fitness*, August 1990. Reprinted by permission.

William Severini Kowinski. "Kids in the Mall: Growing Up Controlled." From *The Malling of America* by William Severini Kowinski (Morrow, 1985). Copyright © 1985 by William Severini Kowinski. Reprinted by permission of the author.

Peter D. Kramer. "Divorce and Our National Values." Originally published in the *New York Times*, August 29, 1997. Copyright © 1997 by The New York Times Company. Reprinted by permission.

Irving Kristol. "Sex, Violence, and Videotape." From the *Wall Street Journal*, May 31, 1994. Republished by permission of Dow Jones, Inc., via Copyright Clearance Center, Inc. © 1994 Dow Jones and Company, Inc. All Rights Reserved Worldwide.

Robert Kuttner. "Poking Holes in the Constitution." From the *Boston Globe*, November 26, 2001.

Charles R. Lawrence III. "On Racist Speech." Published in *The Chronicle of Higher Education*, October 25, 1989. Adapted from a speech delivered at a conference of the ACLU. Reprinted by permission of the author.

Thomas Lee. "Too Much Privacy Is a Health Hazard." From *Newsweek*, August 16, 1999, pp. 70–71. © 1999 by Newsweek, Inc. All rights reserved. Reprinted by permission.

John Leo. "Scotch the Ads? Absolut-ly!" From *U.S. News & World Report*, December 9, 1996, p. 20. Copyright © 1996 U.S. News & World Report, L.P. Reprinted with permission.

Richard Rothstein. "True or False: Schools Fail Immigrants." From the *New York Times,* July 4, 2001. Copyright © 2001 by The New York Times Company. Reprinted by permission.

Harold J. Rothwax. "A Jury of Our Fears." Excerpts from *Guilty: The Collapse of Criminal Justice* by Harold J. Rothwax. Copyright © 1996 by Harold J. Rothwax. Used by permission of Random House, Inc.

Heloisa Sabin. "Animal Research Saves Human Lives." From the *Wall Street Journal,* October 18, 1995, A20. Reprinted by permission of the author.

Hazem Saghiyeh. "It's Not All America's Fault." From *Time,* October 15, 2001. © 2001 Time, Inc. Reprinted by permission.

Candy Schulman. "E-mail: The Future of the Family Feud." From *Newsweek,* December 18, 2000. © Newsweek, Inc. All rights reserved. Reprinted by permission.

Carol Shields. "Family Is One of the Few Certainties We Will Take with Us Far into the Future." From the *Wall Street Journal,* January 1, 2000. Republished by permission of Dow Jones, Inc. via Copyright Clearance Center, Inc. © 2000 Dow Jones and Company, Inc. All Rights Reserved Worldwide.

Lee M. Silver. "Cloning Misperceptions." From *Remaking Eden: Cloning and Beyond in a Brave New World* by Lee Silver. Copyright © 1997 by Lee M. Silver. Reprinted by permission.

Robert Sirico. "An Unjust Sacrifice." Originally published in the *New York Times,* September 30, 2000. Copyright © 2000 by The New York Times Company. Reprinted by permission.

Jane Smiley. "Why Do We Marry?" Copyright © 2000 by *Harper's* magazine. Reproduced from the June issue by special permission. All rights reserved.

Wesley J. Smith. "Dependency or Death? Oregonians Make a Chilling Choice." From the *Wall Street Journal,* April 25, 1999, p. A18. Republished by permission of Dow Jones, Inc. via Copyright Clearance Center, Inc. © 1999 Dow Jones and Company, Inc. All Rights Reserved Worldwide.

Jaime Sneider. "Good Propaganda, Bad Economics." From the *New York Times,* May 16, 2000. Copyright © 2000 by The New York Times Company. Reprinted by permission.

A. C. Soud Jr., with Tom Kuntz. "Tightening the Nuts and Bolts of Death by Electric Chair." Originally published in the *New York Times,* August 3, 1997. Copyright © 1997 by The New York Times Company. Reprinted by permission.

Shelby Steele. ". . . Or a Childish Illusion of Justice?" From *Newsweek,* August 27, 2001, p. 23. © 2001 Newsweek, Inc. All rights reserved. Reprinted by permission.

C. Renzi Stone. "Live Longer and Healthier: Stop Eating Meat!" Reprinted by permission of the author.

Jacob Sullum. "Victims of Everything." From the *New York Times,* March 1, 1987. Copyright © 1987 by the New York Times Company. Reprinted by permission.

"Terror on Trial: An American Test." Letters to the Editor of the *New York Times,* Saturday, December 1, 2001.

Claudius E. Watts III. "Single-Sex Education Benefits Men Too." From the *Wall Street Journal,* May 3, 1995. Reprinted by permission of the author.

Michael M. Weinstein. "A Reassuring Scorecard for Affirmative Action." From the *New York Times,* October 17, 2000. Copyright © 2000 by The New York Times Company. Reprinted by permission.

John F. Welch Jr. and Sister Patricia Daly. "God versus G.E." Copyright © 1998 by *Harper's* magazine. All rights reserved. Reprinted from the August issue by special permission.

Robert Westley. "Legal Arguments in Support of Reparations." Excerpt from "Many Billions Gone: Is It Time to Reconsider the Case for Black Reparations?" Published in *Boston College Law Review,* December 1998, Volume XL, Number 1. Reprinted by permission.

Jack E. White. "Don't Waste Your Breath." From *Time,* April 2, 2001, pp. 48–49. Copyright © 2001 Time, Inc. Reprinted by permission.

John Noble Wilford. "Get Set to Say Hi to the Neighbors." From the *New York Times,* January 1, 2000. Copyright © 2000 by The New York Times Company. Reprinted by permission.

William Carlos Williams. "The Use of Force." From *The Collected Stories of William Carlos Williams.* Copyright © 1938 by William Carlos Williams. Reprinted by permission of New Directions Publishing Corp.

Robert Anton Wilson. "Jury Nullification: Freedom's Last Chance." © 1994 by Robert Anton Wilson. Reprinted by permission.

Lorraine Woellert. "National IDs Won't Work." Reprinted from the November 5, 2001 issue of *BusinessWeek* by special permission. Copyright © 2001 by The McGraw-Hill Companies, Inc.

David Yankelovich. "Moral Tactics." From *Mother Jones,* July/August 1997. Copyright © 1997 Foundation for National Progress. Reprinted by permission.

Glossary and Index of Terms

Abstract language: language expressing a quality apart from a specific object or event; opposite of *concrete language*

Ad hominem: "against the man"; attacking the arguer rather than the *argument* or issue

Ad populum: "to the people"; playing on the prejudices of the *audience*

Appeal to tradition: a proposal that something should continue because it has traditionally existed or been done that way

Argument: a process of reasoning and advancing proof about issues on which conflicting views may be held; also, a statement or statements providing *support* for a *claim*

Audience: those who will hear an *argument;* more generally, those to whom a communication is addressed

Authoritative warrant: a *warrant* based on the credibility or trustworthiness of the source

Backing: the assurances on which a *warrant* or assumption is based

Begging the question: making a statement that assumes that the issue being argued has already been decided

Claim: the conclusion of an argument; what the arguer is trying to prove

Claim of fact: a *claim* that asserts something exists, has existed, or will exist, based on data that the *audience* will accept as objectively verifiable

Claim of policy: a *claim* asserting that specific courses of action should be instituted as solutions to problems

Claim of value: a *claim* that asserts some things are more or less desirable than others

Cliché: a worn-out expression or idea, no longer capable of producing a visual image or provoking thought about a subject

Concrete language: language that describes specific, generally observable, persons, places, or things; in contrast to *abstract language*

Connotation: the overtones that adhere to a word through long usage

Credibility: the audience's belief in the arguer's trustworthiness; see also *ethos*

Data: facts or figures from which a conclusion may be inferred; see *evidence*

Deduction: reasoning by which we establish that a conclusion must be true because the statements on which it is based are true; see also *syllogism*

Definition: an explanation of the meaning of a term, concept, or experience; may be used for clarification, especially of a *claim,* or as a means of developing an *argument*

Definition by negation: defining a thing by saying what it is not

Enthymeme: a *syllogism* in which one of the premises is implicit

Ethos: the qualities of character, intelligence, and goodwill in an arguer that contribute to an *audience's* acceptance of the *claim*

Euphemism: a pleasant or flattering expression used in place of one that is less agreeable but possibly more accurate

Evidence: *facts* or opinions that support an issue or *claim;* may consist of *statistics,* reports of personal experience, or views of experts

Extended definition: a *definition* that uses several different methods of development

Fact: something that is believed to have objective reality; a piece of information regarded as verifiable

Factual evidence: *support* consisting of *data* that are considered objectively verifiable by the audience

Fallacy: an error of reasoning based on faulty use of *evidence* or incorrect *inference*

False analogy: assuming without sufficient proof that if objects or processes are similar in some ways, then they are similar in other ways as well

False dilemma: simplifying a complex problem into an either/or dichotomy

Faulty emotional appeals: basing an argument on feelings, especially pity or fear—often to draw attention away from the real issues or conceal another purpose

Faulty use of authority: failing to acknowledge disagreement among experts or otherwise misrepresenting the trustworthiness of sources

Hasty generalization: drawing conclusions from insufficient evidence

Induction: reasoning by which a general statement is reached on the basis of particular examples

Inference: an interpretation of the *facts*

Major premise: see *syllogism*

Minor premise: see *syllogism*

Motivational appeal: an attempt to reach an *audience* by recognizing their *needs* and *values* and how these contribute to their decision making

Motivational warrant: a type of *warrant* based on the *needs* and *values* of an *audience*

Need: in the hierarchy of Abraham Maslow, whatever is required, whether psychological, or physiological, for the survival and welfare of a human being

Non sequitur: "it does not follow"; using irrelevant proof to buttress a *claim*

Picturesque language: words that produce images in the minds of the *audience*

Policy: a course of action recommended or taken to solve a problem or guide decisions

Post hoc: mistakenly inferring that because one event follows another they have a causal relation; from *post hoc ergo propter hoc* ("after this, therefore because of this"); also called "doubtful cause"

Proposition: see *claim*

Qualifier: a restriction placed on the *claim* may not always be true as stated

Refutation: an attack on an opposing view to weaken it, invalidate it, or make it less credible

Reservation: a restriction placed on the *warrant* to indicate that unless certain conditions are met, the warrant may not establish a connection between the *support* and the *claim*

Slanting: selecting *facts* or words with *connotations* that favor the arguer's bias and discredit alternatives

Slippery slope: predicting without justification that one step in a process will lead unavoidably to a second, generally undesirable step

Slogan: an attention-getting expression used largely in politics or advertising to promote support of a cause or product

Statistics: information expressed in numerical form

Stipulative definition: a *definition* that makes clear that it will explore a particular area of meaning of a term or issue

Straw man: disputing a view similar to, but not the same as, that of the arguer's opponent

Style: choices in words and sentence structure that make a writer's language distinctive

Substantive warrant: a *warrant* based on beliefs about the reliability of *factual evidence*

Support: any material that serves to prove an issue or *claim;* in addition to *evidence,* it includes appeals to the *needs* and *values* of the *audience*

Syllogism: a formula of deductive *argument* consisting of three propositions: a major premise, a minor premise, and a conclusion

Thesis: the main idea of an essay

Toulmin model: a conceptual system of argument devised by the philosopher Stephen Toulmin; the terms *claim, support, warrant, backing, qualifier,* and *reservation* are adapted from this system

Two wrongs make a right: diverting attention from the issue by introducing a new point, e.g., by responding to an accusation with a counter-accusation that makes no attempt to refute the first accusation

Values: conceptions or ideas that act as standards for judging what is right or wrong, worthwhile or worthless, beautiful or ugly, good or bad

Warrant: a general principle or assumption that establishes a connection between the *support* and the *claim*

Index of Authors and Titles